Golden Gate Seminary Library

The Theology of Post-Reformation Lutheranism

The Theology of Post-LUTHER

A Study of Theological Prolegomena

Robert D. Preus

Reformation
ANISM

CONCORDIA PUBLISHING HOUSE / Saint Louis London

GOLDEN GATE SEMINARY LIBRARY.

Concordia Publishing House, St. Louis, Missouri
Concordia Publishing House Ltd., London, E. C. 1
Copyright © 1970 by Concordia Publishing House
Library of Congress Catalog Card No. 70-121877

MANUFACTURED IN THE UNITED STATES OF AMERICA

CONTENTS

Preface	15
Chapter One: Lutheran Orthodoxy and Its Champions	26
The Nature and Genius of Lutheran Orthodoxy	27
1. *A Conservative Attempt to Preserve the Evangelical Legacy of Luther's Reformation*	27
2. *An Ardent Zeal for the Purity of the* Doctrina Evangelii	29
3. *A Definite Confession and Doctrinal Position*	30
Important Characteristics	31
1. *Doctrinal Unity*	31
2. *Polemics*	33
3. *Catholicity and Confessionalism*	35
4. *Luther and Lutheran Orthodoxy*	40
5. *Exegesis and Dogmatics*	42
The Champions of Lutheran Orthodoxy	44
1. *Chronology*	44
a. FIRST PERIOD: "THE GOLDEN AGE OF ORTHODOXY"	45
b. SECOND PERIOD: "HIGH ORTHODOXY"	45
c. THIRD PERIOD: "THE SILVER AGE OF ORTHODOXY"	45
2. *Noteworthy Theologians*	47
a. JACOB HEERBRAND	47

b. MARTIN CHEMNITZ	47
c. NIKOLAUS SELNECKER	49
d. GILES HUNNIUS	50
e. MATTHIAS HAFENREFFER	51
f. LEONARD HUTTER	51
g. BALTHASAR MENTZER	52
h. JOHN GERHARD	52
i. HANS POULSEN RESEN	53
j. CORT ASLAKSSEN	54
k. JESPER RASMUS BROCHMAND	54
l. BALTHASAR MEISNER	55
m. NICHOLAS HUNNIUS	56
n. JOHN GEORGE DORSCH	56
o. JOHN HUELSEMANN	57
p. JOHN CONRAD DANNHAUER	57
q. JEROME KROMAYER	59
r. ABRAHAM CALOV	59
s. SEBASTIAN SCHMIDT	61
t. JOHN ANDREW QUENSTEDT	62
u. JOHN FRIEDRICH KOENIG	63
v. FRIEDEMANN BECHMANN	63
w. JOHN ADAM SCHERTZER	64
x. JOHN WILLIAM BAIER	64
y. DAVID HOLLAZ	65
3. *The Seats of Lutheran Orthodoxy*	65
Chapter Two: The Origin and Progress of Prolegomena in Orthodox Lutheran Dogmatics	72
Early Development	75
1. *Erasmus*	75
2. *Melanchthon*	77
The Contribution of Andrew Hyperius	82
1. *The Approach to Theology (Book I)*	82
2. *Reading and Interpreting Scripture (Book II)*	86
3. *Criteria for Dogmatics (Book III)*	86

The Contribution of Martin Chemnitz	88
1. *Preliminary Development of Wigand and Judex*	88
2. *Dedicatory Letter by Polycarp Leyser*	90
3. *The* Loci Theologici	92
a. THE CHURCH FATHERS	92
b. THE EARLY THEOLOGICAL *Loci*	93
c. THE TAINT OF PHILOSOPHY	94
d. THE RETURN TO SCRIPTURE	95
e. THE CHEMNITZ METHOD	96
The Theological Prolegomena of David Chytraeus	98
1. *Source for Theology*	99
2. *Darkness of Heathen Religions*	100
3. *Certainty of Doctrine*	100
4. *The Task of the Interpreter*	103
5. *Ten Rules for Study of Theology*	104
John Gerhard and the Changes in Dogmatics and Prolegomena	107
1. *Theology as Doctrine*	110
2. *Theology as an Aptitude*	112
3. *Archetypal and Ectypal Theology*	112
4. *Theology Viewed According to Its Causal Factors*	114
a. DIVINE REVELATION AND SCRIPTURE	115
b. THE GOAL OF THEOLOGY	117
c. DEFINITION OF THEOLOGY	117
d. PHILOSOPHY AND THEOLOGY	118
5. *Gerhard's* Methodus Studii Theologici	120
a. MARKS OF A THEOLOGIAN	121
b. PROPAEDEUTICS: PHILOSOPHY	122
6. *The Relation of Philosophy to Theology*	128
a. EARLY CONFLICT	129
b. GERHARD'S SYNTHESIS	130
c. CALOV'S ARGUMENTS	131
d. HOLLAZ ON THEOLOGY AND REASON	134
7. *Gerhard's* Methodus: *The Course of Study*	140

8. *Gerhard's Contribution to Dogmatics and its Prolegomena*	142
Nicholas Hunnius and the Classification of the Articles of Faith	143
1. *Hunnius' Fundamental Articles*	144
2. *Later Dogmaticians on Articles of Faith*	145
3. *Fundamental and Nonfundamental Articles*	147
a. PRIMARY FUNDAMENTAL ARTICLES	148
b. SECONDARY FUNDAMENTAL ARTICLES	149
c. NONFUNDAMENTAL ARTICLES	149
4. *Pure and Mixed Articles*	152
The Influence of George Calixt	154
Abraham Calov and the Silver Age of Lutheran Orthodoxy	157
1. *Theological Method, Its Meaning and Importance*	160
2. *The Meaning and Usage of the Term* Theology	162
3. *Original and Derived Theology and the Christological Implications*	167
4. *The Theology of Paradise and the Theology of the Church*	173
5. *Natural Theology*	173
6. *Revealed Theology*	180
a. IS THERE A REVEALED THEOLOGY?	181
b. SOURCE OF THEOLOGY: REVELATION	182
c. SUBJECT OF REVELATION	183
d. OBJECT OF REVELATION	185
e. AUTHOR OF REVELATION	186
f. PURPOSE OF REVELATION	187
g. CONTENT OF REVELATION, AND INERRANCY	188
7. *The Goal of Revealed Theology*	191
a. THE GLORY OF GOD	191
b. THE SALVATION OF MAN	191
8. *The Nature of Theology*	194
a. THEOLOGY IS A *Habitus*	195

b. THEOLOGY IS PRACTICAL	196
(1) *Proofs for Its Practical Nature*	197
(2) *Not* mixtus	198
(3) *Not "Wisdom"*	201
(4) *Not "Science"*	202
(5) *Application to Life*	204
(6) *Lack of Biblical Basis in Calov*	205
c. THEOLOGY IS GOD-GIVEN	206
9. *The Object, or Subject Matter, of Theology*	207
10. *Religion*	207
a. DEFINITION	208
b. FALSE RELIGION	209
c. THE MARKS OF TRUE RELIGION	209
d. SALVATION WITHOUT CHRIST?	211
e. THE PLACE OF THE OLD TESTAMENT	212
f. LUTHERANISM AND CHRISTENDOM	214
11. *Christ, the Master Theologian*	215
12. *The Theologian: His Training and His Posture*	216
a. THE PREKNOWLEDGE NEEDED BY AN ASPIRING THEOLOGIAN	216
(1) *The Nature and Goal of the Work*	216
(2) *Qualifications and Aptitudes*	217
(3) *The Purpose of the Theologian's Work*	218
b. REQUISITES FOR BECOMING A THEOLOGIAN	219
(1) *Prayer*	219
(2) *Study*	221
(3) *Affliction*	221
c. SCHOLARLY PREREQUISITES	222
d. BIBLICAL STUDY	222
(1) *Continual Reading*	222
(2) *Exegesis*	223
(3) *Didactic Theology*	224
e. STUDY OF HISTORY	225
13. *Calov's Impact and Importance*	226
Orthodoxy in Decline: 18th-Century Thought on Theology and Dogmatic Prolegomena	228
1. *Neumann and the Pietists*	228
2. *Loescher and the Philosophers*	233

Chapter Three: The Doctrine of Scripture	254
Scripture, the Source of Theology *(Sola Scriptura)*	256
1. *Its Normative Authority*	257
2. *The Abuse of Tradition*	258
3. *The Abuse of Reason*	261
Scripture as the Word of God	263
1. *Divine Origin*	263
2. *God's Voice Today*	265
3. *The* Materia *and* Forma *of Scripture*	267
4. *The Unity of the Word (Scripture as the Word)*	268
5. *The Necessity for Scripture*	272
The Inspiration of Scripture	273
1. *Inspiration Generally Defined*	275
2. *The Divine Command to Write Scripture*	277
3. *The Plenary Inspiration of Scripture*	278
4. *The Doctrine of Verbal Inspiration*	281
a. THE TEACHING OF SCRIPTURE	282
b. WORDS AND CONTENT	284
c. ANSWERS TO OBJECTIONS	284
d. UNRELATED TO PSYCHOLOGICAL THEORY	286
5. *The Relation of the Holy Spirit to the Authors of Scripture*	286
a. GOD THE AUTHOR	287
b. THE SPIRIT AND THE WRITERS	287
c. THE PARADOX OF INSPIRATION	290
d. ATTACKS ON INSPIRATION	291
6. *Inspiration and Revelation*	292
The Authority of Scripture	296
1. *The Nature and Extent of Scripture's Authority*	296
2. *External and Internal Criteria of Scripture*	300
3. *The Inner Witness of the Holy Spirit*	302
4. *Scripture as the Norm of Doctrine*	303

5. *The Canonicity of Scripture*	304
6. *The Authenticity of the Hebrew and Greek Texts of Scripture*	306
7. *The Authenticity of the Hebrew Vowel Points*	307
The Sufficiency of Scripture	309
The Clarity of Scripture	311
The Interpretation of Scripture	315
1. *General Alertness of the Day*	317
2. *The Necessity of the Spirit's Guidance for the Interpretation of Scripture*	319
3. *The Fundamental Hermeneutical Rule: Establishing the Literal Meaning of the Text*	321
4. *"Sensus literalis unus est"*	325
5. *"Scriptura est suipsius interpres"*	329
6. *The Unity of Scripture*	331
7. *New Testament Interpretation of the Old Testament Scriptures*	333
8. *The Legitimacy of Consequences Drawn from Scripture*	335
The Truthfulness of Scripture	339
1. *The Lutheran Position Stated*	340
2. *The Basis of Inerrancy*	341
3. *The Nature and Meaning of Biblical Inerrancy*	343
4. *Full Inerrancy*	346
5. *The Background for the New Stress on Scripture's Infallibility*	347
a. APPARENT CONTRADICTIONS	349
b. APPARENT ERRORS OF FACT	354
6. *Adjuncts to the Doctrine of Scripture's Inerrancy: Inerrancy and Hermeneutics*	358
7. *The Concerns Behind the Lutheran Doctrine of Inerrancy*	361
The Efficacy of Scripture	362
1. *The Power and Work of the Gospel*	363
2. *The Inherent Power of the Word*	367

3. *The Origin and Basis of the Word's Power*	371
a. GOD THE AUTHOR	371
b. CHRIST THE CONTENT	373
c. THE HOLY SPIRIT UNITED WITH THE WORD	374
(1) *Antithesis to the Calvinistic Position*	376
(2) *Antithesis to Enthusiasm*	377
Chapter Four: Summary Conclusion	404
"Soli Deo Gloria"	406
Certainty of Divine Origin	408
Correlation of Material and Formal Principles of Theology	410
Appendix: Preface to Melanchthon's *Loci Praecipui Theologici* of 1559	414
Bibliographies	421
Primary Sources	421
Secondary Sources	427
Index	437

KEY TO ABBREVIATIONS IN NOTES

CR *Corpus Reformatorum,* ed. Carl Gottlieb Bretschneider et al. (Halle: C. A. Schwetschke and Sons, 1834—).

CTM *Concordia Theological Monthly* (St. Louis: Concordia Publishing House).

Er. Lat. Martin Luther, *Opera Latina* (Frankfort and Erlangen: Heyder and Simmer, 1865—73).

Erl. Aus. Martin Luther, *Sämmtliche Werke* (Erlangen: Carl Heyder, 1826 to 1857).

LuW *Lehre und Wehre* (St. Louis: Concordia Publishing House).

PL *Patrologia Cursus Completus . . . Series Latina,* ed. J.-P. Migne (Paris: Garnier, 1878—90).

RE *Realencyklopädie für protestantische Theologie und Kirche,* begründet von J. J. Herzog, in dritter verbesserter und vermehrter Auflage unter Mitwirkung vieler Theologen und anderer Gelehrten herausgegeben von Albert Hauck, 3d ed. (Leipzig: J. C. Hinrichs'sche Buchhandlung, 1896—1913).

RGG *Die Religion in Geschichte und Gegenwart* (Tübingen: Verlag von J. C. B. Mohr, 1928).

WA *D. Martin Luthers Werke,* Kritische Gesamtausgabe (Weimar: H. Böhlau, 1883).

W^2 Martin Luther, *Sämmtliche Schriften,* herausgegeben von Dr. Joh. Georg Walch, 2. Auflage (St. Louis: Concordia Publishing House, 1881—1930).

Notes to Preface: pages 24—25.

PREFACE

The purpose of this work is to present clearly and sympathetically to the student and general reader the theology of a long and productive era in the history of Lutheranism, an era commonly called *classical Lutheran orthodoxy* and extending roughly from the time of the Formula of Concord to the first quarter of the 18th century. There is a pressing need for an investigation of this nature. No period in the history of Lutheran theology is so little known by direct acquaintance. The immense theological contribution of the era lies hidden for the most part in tomes that are inaccessible to the general public because so many of them are found only in rare-books sections of libraries and they are in an unfamiliar language. And yet, ironically, orthodoxy has exerted a tremendous influence on the theology of Lutheranism down to our present day. To a great extent Lutheran dogmatics even today, if it seeks to be confessional, still follows the doctrine, the methodology, and even the terminology of classical Lutheran orthodoxy. It should go without saying that everyone who aspires to be a theologian or pastor will wish to understand and appreciate his own theological heritage. The present study, therefore, seeks to offer the reader a large fund of facts and information about the theological leaders of that era and their contributions.

My purpose is not to trace all the theological strands and emphases of that day, much less sketch the novel opinions, however valuable, of one theologian or another, but to present a consensus of the period and trace the whole body of doctrine accepted by the orthodox Lutherans.

And a consensus is not difficult to find. To accomplish this aim the present study will be replete with citations. This is the surest and best method of acquainting the reader with the heart and mind of the old orthodox theology. Without apology I must add that these citations — some very lengthy in order to present an argument in its entire framework, others very brief or parenthetical, calculated to offer the reader only a theologian's turn of mind or impression — are chosen to exhibit orthodoxy's best side. One could easily bore the reader with tedious selections of outmoded casuistry, scholastic argumentation, or obsolete polemics, but that would have little value. If our study is to profit the reader we must select the best of what the orthodox theologians have to offer. We must, of course, criticize them when their theology is bad or when they ignore Biblical data in presenting articles of faith. But our chief purpose is to make Chemnitz, Gerhard, Calov, and the other great theologians of this epoch relevant for our day — or rather to recognize the relevance that is theirs.

It will not, however, be the aim of this work simply to present the doctrinal position of the old Lutheran dogmaticians. That task would be comparatively easy, simply gathering together the main theses on the various articles of faith. This is essentially what Heinrich Schmid has done in his *Doctrinal Theology of the Evangelical Lutheran Church*,[1] and this has been done also by the dogmaticians themselves, e. g., Hutter and Koenig. My interest is to show also how these Lutherans of a former day arrived at their theological position, the basis for their assertions, the way they thought and reasoned. A bald doctrinal statement may seem naïve and untenable until one examines its basis. In some cases a tremendous amount of thought and labor underlies what might appear in these old theologians to be mere dogmatic clichés or truisms. For this reason I will attempt in many cases (1) to clarify precisely what their doctrine is and (2) to trace the argumentation that leads to it. This procedure will, I am convinced, show the old dogmaticians in a better light than was formerly done and will be more rewarding to the reader. Even where the reader cannot agree with the exegesis or reasoning behind the dogmaticians' doctrine, he will at least know that the old Lutheran teachers did not pull their theology out of thin air. And he will discover that the orthodox Lutherans, unlike theologians of a later day, never descended to the level of voicing mere assertions and declamations to be accepted on the authority of the one making them.

To carry out such a program, I will, whenever advisable and possible, trace the exegesis of these theologians, paraphrasing it for the most part, to its conclusions in clear and concise doctrinal formulations. This was not done in the anthologies of Walther or Schmid or in the dogmatics of Hoenecke, Philippi, or Pieper, who very often cited the orthodox Lutheran theologians favorably. But this new approach in studying the orthodox dogmaticians is, I believe, quite justifiable. Their theology is no better than its Biblical basis. On exegesis they stand or fall. And this approach has the added advantage of taking these theologians on their own terms. For they would be the last to defend any statement of doctrine not grounded in Scripture.

A word must be said at this point about Scripture citations. The passages cited in this book will always be those cited by the dogmaticians themselves. These passages should be checked out. They are of fundamental importance to the argument and to the continuity of the entire theological presentation. It is not without good reason that the old Lutherans often supply long lists of Scripture passages relative to their discussions. They expected their readers to turn to these citations and find their relevance. Our present study, too, cannot present the dogmaticians' complete line of thought without interspersing the Biblical framework in which it all takes place. Therefore, if my discussion at times sounds something like a modern Biblical theology, it is because the discussions of the orthodox Lutherans often sounded just that way. In all my translations and discussions I have taken the liberty of correcting erroneous references to Bible verses. There is such a multitude of these mistakes that it would be sheer pedantry to point them all out and would serve no useful purpose.

I mentioned earlier that my study would be both factual and sympathetic. There are two reasons for this. First, I have always felt drawn to these men, to their spirit and to their theology. Behind all their activities was the earnest desire to remain faithful to Scripture and the Lutheran Confessions. And surely every Lutheran today ought to feel akin to such a spirit. There is, after all, an ecumenicity that runs vertically, deep into the past periods of the church's history, as well as the modern ecumenicity that appears to be chiefly horizontal and geographical in scope. One may rightly feel as close to a Luther or Chemnitz or Gerhard as to a contemporary brother in the faith. Second, a sympathetic study of a subject is more likely to effect a true account of things as they are; and where

theology is concerned there is no such thing as impartial objectivity. How difficult it is for modern dialectical theology, for instance, even to understand, much less assess correctly, the theology of Lutheran orthodoxy will be brought out in the course of these investigations. It is in accord with such a sympathetic motive, then, that I propose to portray, without being untrue to any facts, that which is most relevant and edifying in the theology of Lutheran orthodoxy.

The greatest problem encountered in preparing a work of this nature that is necessarily somewhat restricted is the question of selecting material. When one scans the scores of books by the representatives of classical Lutheranism, some of them immense in size as well as erudition, where does one begin in gleaning what is really valuable and pertinent? It is impossible to consult all the hundreds of dogmatic works written during this productive period — to say nothing of the works in exegesis that must also be studied. The best we can do is select our material critically, basing our conclusions on the theology of the most significant figures of the day and those who represent the best in evangelical orthodoxy. One of the remarkable features of C. F. W. Walther's enlarged edition of Baier's *Compendium Theologiae Positivae* is clearly the huge amount of reading that must have preceded the editor's work. Walther drew not only from the recognized dogmatic texts of the 16th and 17th centuries but delved into many of the rarer and less read volumes for numerous valuable and edifying citations. To an extent this has also been my aim, for one often finds real theological gems among the more obscure authors and writings of the orthodox period. But I must confess that I have returned again and again to the standard works of the day, the great texts of Chemnitz, Gerhard, Hutter, Quenstedt, and Calov, for these authors too have ransacked the lesser known works of their time and have often epitomized — if one may use such a word in reference to their enormous tomes — the best of what was being said. For instance, it is remarkable how well and with what brevity Quenstedt has summed up — albeit without his mentor's flair and homiletic tone — the results of the extensive research in Chemnitz's *De Duabus Naturis*.

In selecting representatives of Lutheran orthodoxy I have limited my attention to those theologians who were loyal to the Lutheran Confessions and were impeccably orthodox according to the confessional standards of that day. Hence I shall not consider, except in passing, the theology of

the Lutheran Syncretists or of the later Crypto-Calvinists unless it has direct bearing and influence on the development of genuine Lutheranism. Interesting as it might be to trace the theological conversations between these quasi-Lutherans and their orthodox contemporaries, pursuing these often bitter exchanges would add little of value to the present study.

This study is divided into two parts. The first volume presents background material to the period of Lutheran orthodoxy and a historical survey of the origin and development of theological prolegomena and dogmatics in Lutheran theology. It contains also a discussion of orthodoxy's doctrine of Scripture as the formal source of theology. Such preliminary investigations, which will be very thorough, are necessary before we can be in a position to appreciate and assess the theology of Lutheran orthodoxy.

The second volume will treat the actual position of the old Lutheran teachers on the chief articles of faith. The outline will bear a strong resemblance to the works of Pieper, Hoenecke, Hove, and even such modern and novel dogmaticians as Karl Barth and Emil Brunner — and the outline goes back to Melanchthon and Calvin. The reason for this similarity is that all these more recent dogmaticians follow, sometimes rather closely, the arrangement of the old classical dogmaticians. This should make the present work more relevant and handier to use in connection with other works in dogmatics.

Something must also be said about the literature pertaining to the period of orthodoxy. This secondary literature, which is quite scant, presents a bewildering picture. For instance, if one should take in hand two recent histories that deal in passing with this era, reading first the critical account of Lutheran orthodoxy in G. R. Cragg's *The Church and the Age of Reason*[2] and then turning to the accurate and sympathetic treatment in Bengt Hägglund's *Theologins Historia*,[3] one might well wonder if the two historians are writing about the same epoch. And unfortunately the busy reader would hardly be in a position to know that Hägglund has read the primary sources thoroughly and Cragg has not. These two modern studies are quite typical of an extreme diversity of opinion among scholars in their evaluation of Lutheran orthodoxy.

Of the 19th-century historians who dealt with the era of orthodoxy, most were highly censorious. Tholuck,[4] who in the mid-19th century did

more than any other historian to revive interest in the era, was too opinionated and partisan. He loved Gerhard, despised Calov; he admired the spirit in Wittenberg in the first half of the 17th century, deplored the spirit during the second half. Unfortunately Tholuck's judgments became normative for many historians who followed. Gass, Dorner, and Planck [5] were all too unsympathetic to be able to present a fair account of the spirit and theology of the era. Only with the more recent studies of Otto Ritschl [6] and Werner Elert [7] do we gain a reliable picture of the theology of Lutheran orthodoxy.

Some incredible judgments were made against Lutheran orthodoxy by these older historians. Tholuck in his *Vorgeschichte des Rationalismus* and his *Geschichte des Rationalismus* virtually makes orthodoxy the cause of the Enlightenment and of rationalism. Dorner does not hesitate to say that Lutheran orthodoxy made the material principle of theology the result of the formal principle and was thus unfaithful to the Reformation and to Luther. When one hears such charges from fellow Lutherans, one is amazed. Is there something sinister and evil in orthodoxy? Was there something un-Lutheran or un-Christian or unevangelical about Chemnitz or Gerhard or Quenstedt? But even more disappointing is the discovery that in our modern and more cautious day these sweeping and severe generalizations still seem to be fixed in scholars' minds as the accepted and irrefutable judgment of history concerning orthodoxy. Thus we find this long era of dynamic theology and concern for the Gospel brushed aside as a "nominalistic-intellectualistic" distortion of Luther's theology or as a period of "arid controversy" that "poisoned every phase of life."

There are two reasons for this negative judgment of the old Lutheran theology on the part of some historians.

First, these historians — even the knowledgeable Tholuck — have based some of their most damning conclusions on insufficient evidence. It would be surprising if this were not so. The literature of that era is astonishingly vast, and the temptation of busy historians to generalize on the basis of what one or a few theologians thought or did concerning a certain issue is a tendency easy to follow. Furthermore, it is difficult for even the most thorough reader to get through all the writings of these old dogmaticians, and the inclination to browse through the theses in large print and ignore the lengthy and often vital arguments that support

these theses is very great. I shall have occasion later to produce examples of this fault.

Second, the old Lutherans were so outspoken on issues of fundamental concern that it is extremely difficult for a historian with any opinions of his own not to take sides, and sometimes rather sharply. Luther with his carefree way of speaking and his common use of the overstatement can often be twisted to say things surprisingly congenial to some of our modern *Zeitgeist*. This is not the case with the following generations of Lutherans, who in their discussions with the Reformed, the Roman Catholics, and particularly the rationalistic Socinians become increasingly careful and unequivocal in their language. When they say things not congenial to our *Zeitgeist,* there is no reinterpreting their words. And right here is the great danger for the modern historian or theologian — that he reads the Lutherans of the late-16th and 17th centuries too exclusively in the light of modern issues and not on their own terms in the light of their concerns and their theological situation. Like Luther, these orthodox theologians have much to say also to our day, but we must allow them to say it from and in their own context.

Where this principle of procedure is overlooked, the most ludicrous caricatures of the theology of Lutheran orthodoxy often result. For instance, orthodoxy has more than once been lumped together with Fundamentalism.[8] Thus, the queer hermeneutics and obscurantism associated with the worst of modern Fundamentalism are linked with a theological posture that was the sanest and stablest and often the most open and unhampered of its day. Would one prefer Romanism of the 1600s or Socianism or Arminianism or the extreme rationalism that emanated from the British Isles? It is strange how often modern scholars forget that Lutheran orthodoxy flourished 300 and more years ago. We cannot expect these theologians to speak to many of our modern concerns. They knew nothing of historiography, sociology, psychology, or linguistics according to our modern understanding. We do them a grave injustice if we do not judge them in the light of their own day. We would have more reason to condemn a Galileo, who in his old age rejected Kepler's discovery that the planets move in eliptical paths. It is an ironic twist when one who would be a confessional Lutheran becomes hypercritical of Lutheran orthodoxy. Without the hundred years in which Lutheran orthodoxy upheld and defended the doctrine of Scripture and the Lutheran Symbols, it is difficult to see how a Lutheran Church could exist today.

Among more recent dogmaticians there has been far greater appreciation and understanding of the old Lutheran theology and this, in part, because dogmaticians have spent less time reading about the old Lutheran teachers and more time reading their actual writings. Not a few of these 19th- and 20th-century dogmaticians have leaned very heavily on the theology of Lutheran orthodoxy.

I might refer first of all to the four informative anthologies of C. F. W. Walther, Heinrich Schmid, Carl Ratschow, and Emanuel Hirsch.[9] Schmid's collection of citations went through many editions in Germany, and the translation was popular enough in our country to be reprinted in 1961. Walther's greatly enlarged edition of Baier's compendium contains many lengthy citations from all the great Lutheran theologians of the 16th and 17th centuries, including Luther. In this work, which was for many years the dogmatics text at Concordia Seminary, St. Louis, and also at Luther Seminary of the old Norwegian Synod in St. Paul, Walther shows that he was no haphazard citation theologian. He had immersed himself in the writings of Luther and the old dogmaticians, and consistently he found pertinent and edifying sections from a vast and largely unexplored literature.

Of dogmaticians whose works were greatly influenced, if not dominated, by the theology of orthodoxy, we might mention Philippi, Hoenecke, and Pieper, and to a lesser extent Gisle Johnson and Elling Hove.[10] Pieper and Hoenecke are two of the best secondary sources obtainable for the theology of Lutheran orthodoxy. Both lean heavily on Chemnitz and Gerhard; and among the later representatives of orthodoxy Pieper favors Quenstedt, Hoenecke prefers Calov. A better commentary on the Christology of 16th- and 17th-century Lutheranism could not be found than Pieper's discussion in the second volume of his dogmatics. It is worth noting that all these theologians who loved the old orthodox Lutherans were staunchly confessional Lutherans who drew heavily also from the theology of Luther. Only two contemporary theologians of note have read thoroughly in the old Lutheran theology, and in their dogmatic writings drew to some extent from this literature: Werner Elert, who is usually appreciative, and Karl Barth, who is less so. Both Elert and Barth evince a profound perception of the issues and the theology of that former day.[11]

Whether there will be in the future any revival of interest in the the-

ology of Lutheran orthodoxy is difficult to say at this time, although some excellent translations of works by Chytraeus, Chemnitz, and Gerhard and a few valuable monographs on the subject indicate some encouragement for the future.[12] One thing is certain: any responsible and appreciative renewal of study in the great literature of that former age will be all to the good. It has always struck me as noteworthy and gratifying that Roman Catholic and also Protestant scholars who have occupied themselves in the study of patrology and scholastic theology have been praised and encouraged in their endeavors by almost all. Their investigations have generally been marked by a growing respect toward and humility in the presence of the great theologians of the past. The days of disgust and overweening superiority toward the church fathers and even the scholastics seem to be at an end among systematic theologians and historians. We may disagree with an Augustine or a Thomas, and very intensely so, but we no longer belittle these men.

Such a fair and charitable disposition is, however, still lacking toward the old Protestant theology. Cruel and uncritical epithets are still hurled out at random, and orthodoxy is still the whipping boy for many a theologian who is cutting his teeth on a new thesis of his own. In the ensuing delineation I shall try to present the true image of Lutheran orthodoxy; to show from the sources themselves that these pillars of orthodoxy and of evangelical Lutheranism, with all their obvious faults, are nobody's whipping boy; and to illustrate from their own great theological output that in men like Chemnitz or Gerhard we have theologians of a stature as great as the Scholastics or the church fathers and much more evangelical.

By way of conclusion to these introductory remarks I would like to express my deep gratitude to a number of friends and scholars who have helped me offer this volume on the theology of post-Reformation Lutheranism. To my brother, Dr. J. A. O. Preus, to Dr. Fred Kramer of Concordia Theological Seminary, Springfield, Ill., to Dr. John W. Montgomery of Trinity Evangelical Divinity School, Deerfield, Ill., and to Dr. Elmer E. Foelber and the able editorial staff of Concordia Publishing House I am deeply indebted for carefully reading my manuscript, correcting errors, and offering valuable suggestions. To Concordia Publishing House, St. Louis, and to the Lutheran Brotherhood Insurance Company of Minneapolis I am indebted for generous grants, which made a year's

research in American and European libraries possible. To the members of the Commission on Church Literature of the Missouri Synod, particularly to my colleagues Dr. Lorenz Wunderlich and Dr. Herbert J. A. Bouman of Concordia Seminary, St. Louis, and to Rev. Arthur E. Bohlmann of Springfield, Mo., I wish to express my gratitude for encouragement and good counsel as I did my research. To Mr. H. M. Fiskaa, head of the reading room of the Universitetsbibliotek in Oslo, and to his staff I am very grateful for so much kindness and helpfulness shown me as I pursued my work with them during a writing leave. And finally I thank my many graduate students of the last eight years, whose active and fertile minds were a constant source of stimulation to me and who have contributed toward whatever relevance this study has to many modern concerns.

NOTES TO PREFACE

1. Heinrich Schmid, *The Doctrinal Theology of the Evangelical Lutheran Church,* trans. Charles A. Hay and Henry E. Jacobs (Philadelphia: United Lutheran Publication House, 1899; reissued 1961, Augsburg Publishing House, Minneapolis). A recent but scarcely better attempt at the same thing has been done by Carl Heinz Ratschow, *Lutherische Dogmatik zwischen Reformation und Aufklärung,* 2 vols. (Gütersloh: Gütersloher Verlagshaus Gerd Mohn, 1964). Unlike Schmid, Ratschow deals somewhat with the development of theology during the era. He also cites a larger number of theologians than Schmid; but it is doubtful if the choices he makes portray a clearer picture of the prevailing theology of the era.
2. Gerald R. Cragg, *The Church and the Age of Reason* (Baltimore: Penguin Books, 1960), pp. 93—106.
3. Bengt Hägglund, *Theologins Historia* (Lund: CWK Gleerups Förlag, 1963), pp. 274—302. A recent English translation, admirably done by Gene J. Lund, is entitled *History of Theology* (St. Louis: Concordia Publishing House, 1968); see pp. 299—324.
4. August Tholuck, *Der Geist der lutherischen Theologen Wittenbergs im Verlaufe des 17. Jahrhunderts* (Hamburg and Gotha: Friedrich und Andreas Parther, 1852); *Lebenszeugen der lutherischen Kirche aus allen Ständen vor und während der Zeit des dreissigjährigen Krieges* (Berlin: Wiegandt und Grieben, 1859); *Vorgeschichte des Rationalismus* (Berlin: Wiegandt und Grieben, 1861); *Geschichte des Rationalismus:* Erste Abtheilung, *Geschichte des Pietismus und des ersten Stadiums der Aufklärung* (Berlin: Wiegandt und Grieben, 1865).
5. Wilhelm Gass, *Geschichte der protestantischen Dogmatik,* 4 vols. (Berlin: Georg Reimer, 1854—67); Isaac A. Dorner, *History of Protestant Theology,* trans. George Robson and Sophia Taylor, 2 vols. (Edinburgh: T. & T. Clark, 1871); Gottlieb J. Planck, *Geschichte der protestantischen Theologie von der Konkordienformel an bis in die Mitte des achtzehnten Jahrhunderts,* 6 vols. (Göttingen: Vandenhoeck & Ruprecht, 1831).

6. Otto Ritschl, *Dogmengeschichte des Protestantismus,* 4 vols. (Leipzig: J. C. Hinrichs'sche Buchhandlung; and Göttingen: Vandenhoeck & Ruprecht, 1908—1927).
7. Werner Elert, *The Structure of Lutheranism,* trans. Walter A. Hansen (Saint Louis: Concordia Publishing House, 1962), Vol. I.
8. See, e. g., Regin Prenter, *Skabelse og Genlösning* (Copenhagen: G. E. C. Gads Forlag, 1951), p. 446; Alan Richardson and Wolfgang Schweitzer, eds., *Biblical Authority Today* (Philadelphia: Westminster Press, 1951), p. 110.
9. Schmid; Ratschow; John W. Baier, *Compendium Theologiae Positivae,* ed. C. F. W. Walther (St. Louis, 1879); Emanuel Hirsch, *Hilfsbuch zum Studium der Dogmatik* (Berlin: Walter de Gruyter, 1937).
10. Friedrich A. Philippi, *Kirchliche Glaubenslehre,* 5 vols. (Stuttgart: Verlag von Samuel Gottlieb Liesching, 1854); Adolph Hoenecke, *Evangelisch-Lutherische Dogmatik,* 4 vols. (Milwaukee: Northwestern Publishing House, 1909); Franz Pieper, *Christian Dogmatics,* trans. Theodore Engelder, John T. Mueller, and Walter W. F. Albrecht, 3 vols. (St. Louis: Concordia Publishing House, 1951); Elling Hove, *Christian Doctrine* (Minneapolis: Augsburg Publishing House, 1931); Gisle Johnson, *Den Systematiske Teologi* (Oslo: Dybwad, 1897). Positive theologians of the 19th century also made frequent use of the old Lutherans, although they can hardly be said to have sympathized with them. Cf. Karl Hase, *Hutterus Redivivus* (Leipzig: Breitkopf und Härtel, 1845); Christoph Ernst Luthardt, *Compendium der Dogmatik* (Leipzig: Dörffling und Franke, 1865).
11. Karl Barth, *Church Dogmatics,* trans. G. T. Thomson et al., 4 vols. (Edinburgh: T. & T. Clark, 1936—69); Werner Elert, *Der Christliche Glaube,* 3d ed. (Hamburg: Furche Verlag, 1956).
12. Three translations recently issued are John Warwick Montgomery, ed. and trans., *Chytraeus on Sacrifice* (St. Louis: Concordia Publishing House, 1962); Herman A. Preus and Edmund Smits, eds., *The Doctrine of Man in Classical Lutheran Theology* (Minneapolis: Augsburg Publishing House, 1962); and J. A. O. Preus, trans., Martin Chemnitz, *De Duabus Naturis* (St. Louis: Concordia Publishing House, 1970). Of recent monographs three of real merit are Jörg Baur, *Die Vernunft zwischen Ontologie und Evangelium: Eine Untersuchung zur Theologie Johann Andreas Quenstedts* (Gütersloh: Verlagshaus Gerd Mohn, 1962); Bengt Hägglund, *Die Heilige Schrift und ihre Deutung in der Theologie Johann Gerhards* (Lund: CWK Gleerups Förlag, 1951); Johannes Wallmann, *Der Theologiebegriff bei Johann Gerhard und Georg Calixt* (Tübingen: J. C. B. Mohr, 1961).

Lutheran Orthodoxy and Its Champions

THE NATURE AND GENIUS OF LUTHERAN ORTHODOXY
IMPORTANT CHARACTERISTICS
THE CHAMPIONS OF LUTHERAN ORTHODOXY

Notes to Chapter One: pages 66—71.

CHAPTER ONE

What do we mean by orthodoxy? When we speak of orthodoxy in connection with Lutheran theology and life, we do not mean merely a phenomenon of rigid conservatism, which has appeared in most Christian communions (Roman Catholic, Reformed, and Lutheran) and even in political parties from time to time. We refer rather to the concrete historical development that we see persisting in Lutheranism from the time of the Formula of Concord, and even before, to the first quarter of the 18th century — 150 years of a *theology and spirit* that has been called either *in malam partem* or *in bonam partem* "orthodoxy" by almost all historians and theologians.

THE NATURE AND GENIUS OF LUTHERAN ORTHODOXY

Why has the theology and spirit of that particular era been given such a title? What is Lutheran orthodoxy's unique nature or genius or rationale? It consists of three essential aspects.

1. *A Conservative Attempt to Preserve the Evangelical Legacy of Luther's Reformation*

A crisis faced the third, fourth, and fifth generations of Lutherans after the Reformation. They were no longer directly in contact with the deep religious experience and original theological insight of the Reformation. Although the issues underlying the Reformation still obtained, the

climate of thought had changed in the late-16th and 17th centuries, and scores of new issues had risen to challenge evangelical theology. How were the theologians of this era effectively to perpetuate the great work of the Reformation, its evangelical impact? How were they to interpret it all for their day? Those who have received the precious legacy of the Reformation must now stand back and assess what has happened, consolidate their forces, and continue Luther's work — this is clearly what Lutheran orthodoxy sees its task to be. It is fundamentally a theological task, a theological calling that claims each one of the great theologians of the day.

Edmund Smits has put it this way: "Martin Luther opened new horizons of the ancient church which had become obscured through the ages. However, to give aid to the lesser guide of the solitary traveler, the single shepherd of the local flock, there was needed a road map and a compass. At one point Luther compared himself to a pioneer and woodcutter chopping down the trees of the forest and clearing the way. After him subtler scholars would be needed, highly skilled agriculturists and gardeners, who would cultivate the soil and raise the growth with loving care."[1]

The work of Luther's successors will therefore be both constructive and conservative. There will be a healthy respect for tradition, the church fathers, Luther, and the Lutheran Confessions; and there will be a greater reluctance to break with the past than we find even in Luther. This outlook carries with it a distrust of new doctrines, an attitude aptly expressed in Selnecker's well-known stanzas:

> And ever is there something new
> Devised to change Thy doctrines true;
> Lord Jesus! as Thou still dost reign,
> These vain, presumptuous minds restrain;
>
> And as the cause and glory, Lord,
> Are Thine, not ours, do Thou afford
> Us help and strength and constancy,
> And keep us ever true to Thee.

But accompanying such a conservative viewpoint was a willingness and eagerness, born of necessity, to face new issues effectively and to find new approaches to the study and advancement of true theology.

2. *An Ardent Zeal for the Purity of the* Doctrina Evangelii

With what dauntless power, exact discipline, gigantic scholarship, and burning and stubborn devotion to a single end (evangelical orthodoxy) those old Lutheran theologians wrote and worked and fought the battles of their church has been brought out by even the most unsympathetic historians. That their zeal for the truth might have appeared at times to be inflexible and extreme, at least to our calm and cautious age of theologians, that their intense loyalty to Christ and His Word might result in forgetfulness of even the closest human ties are hardly faults to be despised. And this intensity of spirit and singleness of purpose were not the private possession of Lutherans during those two centuries following the Reformation but were common characteristics of Calvinists and Romanists as well. Even science and the arts, so long associated with heterodoxy and infidelity, were for the Lutherans, as well as the Jesuits, called into the service of orthodoxy.[2]

The Lutheran theologians of those days were generally well-rounded men who took in the whole range of theological study; they were not as specialized as today. This was the age of powerful chorales, deep and moving devotional literature, and even much philosophical reflection among theologians. The period of orthodoxy produced such evangelical hymn and devotional writers as Nikolaus Selnecker, John Heermann, Paul Gerhardt, George Neumark, Christian Scriver, Thomas Kingo, Hans Brorson, John Olearius, and a host of others. In Philipp Nicolai, John Gerhard, and John George Dorsch we see orthodox theologians and dogmaticians who were capable of writing the most stirring hymns, the most touching devotional literature, and the most moving sermons. Cundisius found time to edit a hymnbook, Dannhauer and others to produce fruitful studies in catechetics. There is nothing in evangelical orthodoxy that is withdrawn from practical church life or inimical to piety, nothing in the theology of the day that ignores the importance of the Christian life. However, to understand this age we must realize that Lutheran theology did not urge piety in isolation from the Gospel, for there was no piety in isolation from the Gospel. Christian piety was to be formed and incited by theology, by the *doctrina evangelii.*

Yet for some reason this spirit of orthodoxy is uncongenial and unpalatable to many today. Why? Certainly we cannot charge this move-

ment with hypocrisy. There is none of the spirit of dilettantism, inordinate pomp, or self-aggrandizement here, but rather an exertion toward spiritual growth, faithfulness, and fellowship with Christ. It is no doubt the spirit itself, the uncompromising and unbending zeal for purity of doctrine, the hatred of all syncretism and doctrinal indifference, that has estranged many. For this is a very significant feature of Lutheran orthodoxy: it is an attitude, a spirit, a posture; and it is difficult for one who is not vitally concerned about purity of doctrine to appreciate this. Tholuck has pointed out that "purity of doctrine" was an antiquated notion even in 1740 when Valentin Loescher was valiantly striving to keep orthodoxy alive.[3] But for the old Lutheran theologians pure doctrine was never an end in itself but always served the Gospel. The goal of all theology is evangelical and practical. This is seen particularly in their works in dogmatics where the *usus practicus* of every article of faith is carefully set forth. John Gerhard, for instance, in disputing against purgatory is careful to illustrate in every argument how this doctrine conflicts with the Gospel. The same may be said concerning the Lutheran polemic against the Roman Catholic *monstrum incertitudinis* and the doctrine of work righteousness. That pure doctrine is to serve the Gospel is seen also in Calov's and the later Lutherans' insistence that theology is a *habitus practicus,* a practical aptitude, practical always because of its aim: to foster living faith and bring salvation.

3. *A Definite Confession and Doctrinal Position*

Orthodoxy is more than a mere attitude or spirit. The concrete feature of Lutheran orthodoxy is its doctrinal platform, a definite and permanent doctrinal position based on Scripture as interpreted by the Lutheran Confessions and (in harmony with the Confessions) by the ancient creeds, the church fathers, and Luther. Since theology is based solely on God's written Word, its content does not change; Law and Gospel and the articles of faith remain the same, being the summation of God's unchangeable Word to man. This confessional and doctrinal constant is to the old dogmaticians more than a mere statement of belief and platform for action; it is an expression of the very Gospel, a power that controls and changes lives and ideas and movements in history. Lutheran orthodoxy is utterly convinced of this.

Theological formulations, however, will change, often swiftly and

radically, as the life and work and fears of the church shift direction. In this matter the orthodox Lutheran theologians were pliable and progressive, altering their terminology and sometimes their entire approach to a subject, whether for better or worse, and doing so thoroughly. We might mention that the *approach* made by the old Lutherans to the theological problems of their day was not nearly as monolithic as is commonly thought. While all held to the absolute authority of Scripture as the source of Christian doctrine and subscribed wholeheartedly to the Lutheran Confessions, there are great differences among the theologians of this period, differences in outlook and stress and treatment of issues. One need merely peruse the works of two contemporaries during the later period of orthodoxy, John Andrew Quenstedt of Wittenberg and John Conrad Dannhauer of Strasbourg, to learn how totally differently dogmatics can be presented by like-minded men.

Important Characteristics

We must now amplify our description of Lutheran orthodoxy by pointing out a number of important characteristics of this movement as it progressed and took shape.

1. *Doctrinal Unity*

A remarkable doctrinal unity prevails throughout the period of orthodoxy, a unity achieved by a very conscious and deliberate Biblical and confessional faithfulness. This unity is further bolstered by a thorough familiarity with Luther's writings and a firm loyalty to his theology. One will search long and possibly in vain to find any criticism of Luther's teaching among the orthodox Lutherans. Even his untenable utterances on canonicity were palliated or "explained," usually as outbursts that could not be taken as expressing his mature views. It was observed, for instance, that his editions of the Bible never omitted the antilegomena.[4] Even the controversies leading to the formation of the Formula of Concord did not contribute greatly to divide Lutherans after 1580 except in cases where political considerations prevailed, as in Sweden and parts of Germany. The Syncretistic Controversy among Lutherans in the 17th century served more to rally and unify confessional Lutherans than to divide them.

What is most surprising but also indicative of the feeling of unity

that prevailed after the Formula of Concord is the loyalty among orthodox Lutherans to Melanchthon's theological contributions. It is no doubt correct that the later orthodoxy in Denmark (after ca. 1600 when the Crypto-Calvinistic influence of Niels Hemmingsen, professor at Copenhagen, was finally subsiding) manifested a more Melanchthonian influence than the German orthodoxy of the day.[5] But German theology, too, recognized its debt to Melanchthon, followed his theology where possible, particularly his method, and was most reluctant to criticize him. Chemnitz patterns his *Loci Theologici* after Melanchthon's *Loci Communes.* So do Hafenreffer and others. Hutter, whose undeniable adherence to the Formula of Concord is evinced in more than one lengthy apology, writes his massive *Loci Communes Theologici* in conscious imitation of Melanchthon's work and with acknowledgements of his debt to "our Melanchthon" and "our blessed author" on almost every page. The works of Chemnitz and Hutter in turn become archetypes for later dogmaticians. Chemnitz is cited so often by the later Lutherans that by the time of Quenstedt, who is usually scrupulous in identifying his references, long quotations are not even acknowledged. Hutter's *Compendium Theologicum,* like Melanchthon's *Loci Communes* and Thomas' *Summa Theologica* in Roman Catholic circles, becomes the basis for large and important commentaries. The commentary of Cundisius is extremely useful, and that of Friedemann Bechmann is the best book Bechmann wrote. Thus it is the Biblical and confessional emphasis of the orthodox Lutherans and their profound respect for those great leaders who went before them (Heb. 13:7) that serves to unify them and their theology.

This unity of doctrine is not broken even by an occasional and bitter controversy among the orthodox Lutherans themselves. For instance, the Kenotic Controversy (1619—27) between the faculties of Giessen and Tübingen, although an offense and tragic waste of effort, served to reveal in a remarkable manner the unity of orthodox Lutheran Christology. Even the personal bitterness and extravagant charges of the two parties made it plain that there was only one Lutheran Christology.

The doctrinal unity common to Lutheran orthodoxy extended far beyond the borders of Germany into Sweden,[6] where Calov for a time exercised a particularly strong influence, and also into Denmark and Norway.[7] One will not fail to see the same spirit in Brochmand or Aslakssen as in the orthodox Lutherans of Germany.

2. Polemics

A characteristic of Lutheran orthodoxy, and in harmony with its deep concern for purity of doctrine and hatred of all heresy, was a polemical tone that pervaded much of the systematic and exegetical theology of the day. This fact must not lead us to conclude that there is some inevitable connection between orthodoxy and bitter invective and plain belligerence. Polemics was the order of the day, as it had been during the time of the Reformation. The greatest Roman Catholic theologian of the late-16th century, Robert Bellarmine, occupied the chair of controversial theology in Rome; and his *opus magnum* was entitled the *Controversies*. Today we have difficulty comprehending and abiding the polemics of the 16th and 17th centuries, which was so often carried on with bad purpose and unnecessary rancor. It is not impossible that polemics played a part in hastening the eclipse of orthodoxy in the Lutheran Church. Theologians sometimes purposely misunderstood the position of their adversaries. Particularly annoying to us today was the general practice among theologians of pressing the arguments of their adversaries to their logical but absurd conclusions. Thus we find the Lutherans explaining hundreds of times that they did not teach a Capernaitic, cannibalistic eating and drinking of Christ's body and blood in the Lord's Supper. And just as often the Calvinists are compelled patiently and firmly to protest that they believe in a real incarnation and personal union. Why should such endless expense of time and labor have been necessary? It was as if neither party really listened to the other side.

And yet the excesses of that day must not blind us to the fact that not all polemics is bad and there is a positive need of it at times. Can a disciple of Christ stand by silently when what to him is most precious in all the world is attacked, namely the Gospel? Polemics often springs from the highest Christian motives and concerns, from the strong desire to help a brother. "How often does the divine Spirit admonish us to employ ourselves earnestly and diligently in bringing an erring brother back on the right way. God definitely wills that we return the stray ox or ass of an enemy (Ex. 23:4). How much more are we bound to work for an erring brother and restore him to the right track (Matt. 18:25)." [8] A church no longer engaging in polemics may have lost the spirit of testimony.

Polemics should not be made light of, as though what is produced

in the midst of controversy is not very important or reliable. Justification by faith as taught by Paul in his letter to the Galatians is not a peripheral teaching but is so important that it occasions Paul's letter. However it may affect the church's theology or formulation, polemics does not make a doctrinal position less binding, even though the immediate cause of the doctrinal formulation may be long forgotten. The Lutheran teaching of justification, the communication of attributes, and the verbal inspiration of Scripture will always be important even though the heresy or heresies that occasioned the significant formulations of these teachings may not always be apparent. The real issues must be sifted from any polemical situation; then principles that are timely will often be found, even though these principles emerge from controversies that seem barren and futile. The church is strengthened in controversy and forced in times of tension to confess her faith boldly and articulately, as can be seen in the case of the Lutheran Confessions.

But if polemics is not to be minimized in the life of the church, neither is it to be exaggerated. Heresy and controversy must not be made, in Hegelian fashion, an inexorable force underlying and giving rise to the church's doctrine. Polemical circumstances may cause the doctrine of Scripture to be unfolded in a certain direction and with a certain terminology, but they will not contribute to the content of the church's doctrine. For this reason it may be wiser to study the old Lutherans dogmatically rather than historically.

The nature of polemics in the old Lutheran theology needs comment. Contrary to the opinion of some historians, Lutheran theology did not become more controversial as the 17th century wore on. Giles (Aegidius) Hunnius is more polemical than Calov, and Gerhard more than Dannhauer or Bechmann. What does happen during the last half of the 17th century is that polemics becomes more ordered, controlled, and even stereotyped. There is less of the broadside and sarcastic blast that was typical of Luther. A carefully worked out polemic theology develops — a calm, careful analysis of every influence that threatens Lutheran doctrine on each *locus,* and an elaborate, Biblically based defense of the Lutheran position. Dogmatics becomes *theologia didactico-polemica,* the didactic side consisting of a systematic, thetical arrangement of the Biblical material pertaining to each *locus,* and the polemic side dealing with the problems of terminology, Biblical interpretation, and historical development

as these factors impinge on each dogmatic *locus.* The first to produce such a *systema,* as it was called, was Abraham Calov. He was followed by John Quenstedt, whose work was the very quintessence of thoroughness, clarity, and command of the issues. Each *locus* is divided into a didactic and polemic section; and it is interesting that the second section, designed primarily to bolster the first, is often less polemic in tone than the didactic section. Polemics to Quenstedt involved tracing the many antitheses to every article of faith, clearing up misunderstandings and difficulties connected with the Lutheran position, and particularly providing exegesis for the pertinent *sedes doctrinae.* In all this almost none of the invective so common to Luther or, in a much later day, to Kierkegaard is found. If anything, Quenstedt bores the modern reader with his dispassionate approach to things. However, some of his contemporaries make up for Quenstedt's lack of fire.

3. *Catholicity and Confessionalism*

It would be a grave mistake for any serious theologian to consign the theology of Lutheran orthodoxy to the limbo of irrelevant and outdated matters that concern only the antiquarian. For orthodoxy not only works under the Scriptures as the only source of theology, but it also is eminently catholic and confessional in its approach to theology.

The orthodox theologians, therefore, will always be relevant and must be taken seriously. They were conservative theologians. They did not, as we shall see, whimsically jump on theological bandwagons, overwork precarious theological and philosophical motifs, or impose alien philosophical schemata on theology; but — even if we recognize that their exegesis was "dogmatic" at times — they were eminently catholic in all their work. A tremendous amount of labor was plied by the orthodox Lutherans in presenting the contributions of the church fathers on every point of theology. For they claimed the church fathers as their own. They also expended much time in refuting the numerous ancient heresies, which had a way of recurring at the time of the Reformation and later. Chemnitz in his *De Duabus Naturis* and Gerhard in his *Loci Theologici,* before they present their own theological positions, offer lengthy and accurate accounts of the Christological struggles of the 4th and 5th centuries. They stay primarily with the ancient creeds and the accepted church fathers, such as Damascenus, Augustine, Hilary, Gregory, Cyril,

and others.⁹ It may be recalled that the first patrology ever written was by Gerhard, who also coined the term. Gerhard's huge *Confessio Catholica,* which was written to support the Lutheran doctrine with citations from the fathers, more than demonstrates his great respect for the church fathers and his thorough acquaintance with them. Of the later dogmaticians Calov in particular makes extensive use of the fathers. It is worthy of note that at least the leading patristic students through the orthodox period (Chemnitz, Gerhard, and Calov) approach the fathers independently, each introducing his own catenae of citations. The Lutherans were convinced that the church fathers were worthy of being read directly, although critically, "dividing the straw from the gold." ¹⁰

There was also a certain amount of dependence among the orthodox Lutherans on the medieval scholastics, notably Thomas Aquinas. Chemnitz and his contemporaries, although well acquainted with the scholastic theology, had no time for it at all. With Gerhard a change takes place, and he often quotes Thomas to clarify or illustrate a point. His treatment of theology proper, for instance, is handled according to the scholastic arrangement. In 1656 John Dorsch wrote a book entitled *Th. Aquinas Confessor Veritatis* (Frankfort) in which he tried to show that Thomas Aquinas could be made to support Lutheran doctrine more than Roman Catholic. This was no mere tongue-in-cheek jest — one would hardly write 800 pages for such a flippant purpose — but a serious attempt to illustrate that Lutheranism was fully aware of the continuity of doctrine in the church and had no intention of leaving the mainstream of catholic dogma, which had been so vital for the church throughout her history. Something like this and Gerhard's *Confessio Catholica* had earlier been done by Matthias Flacius (Illyricus) in his *Catalogus Testium Veritatis* (1556), wherein were mentioned 700 witnesses through every century of the Christian era, even during the height of papal power, who had not "bowed the knee to Baal" and could be called forerunners of Protestantism. Flacius' list included even Catherine of Siena and Thomas Aquinas. The purpose of such books was to show that the Lutheran Church was no new sect but the continuation of the apostolic church.

The strict confessionalism of Lutheran orthodoxy is a well-known fact, which need not be demonstrated here.¹¹ This confessional loyalty ties high Lutheran orthodoxy theologically to the preceding era but not in such a way that the theology of orthodoxy becomes a mere redundant echo.

Important Characteristics 37

It is true that the orthodox Lutherans read the Scriptures with certain presuppositions and in the light of the Lutheran Confessions. This is also what C. F. W. Walther did in our country. And this is what it means to be Lutheran, that one recognizes the claim of the Confessions that they are the church's normative exposition of Scripture.[12]

At least one of the Lutheran dogmaticians, Leonard Hutter, constructed a *Compendium Locorum Theologicorum,* or small dogmatics book, that was really an epitome of the Lutheran Symbols. Hutter cited primarily the Augsburg Confession and the Formula of Concord. This work, first published in 1610 and going through many editions, was popular for generations as a textbook. But for the most part the Lutheran dogmatics was worked out without any subordination to the Confessions. Although the terminology is often the same, the Confessions are rarely cited in most of the works in systematic theology, not nearly as often as Luther and the church fathers. It is only when the Confessions have been misunderstood or misinterpreted that they are discussed to any extent, e. g., in the sections on man's freedom of will and the real presence of Christ's body and blood in the Sacrament of the Altar. In other words, there is a deliberate attempt, while never departing from the spirit or theology of the Lutheran Symbols, to work independently of them in producing dogmatics.

It is therefore quite without foundation and rather startling that scholars and theologians have described the orthodox Lutheran teachers as placing the Confessions above Scripture and no longer feeling any need of investigating their theological position on the basis of Scripture.[13] Such a charge ignores one of the chief purposes of dogmatic theology in those days: establishing Lutheran theology as solidly grounded on the Scriptures. During the period of orthodoxy, dogmatics, especially the larger polemical works, was a mode of conversation or dialog between Lutherans, Calvinists, Romanists, Socinians, and others. Lutheran dogmatics was written to be read by Lutherans and by a circle of readers outside the Lutheran Church. And obviously Romanists, Calvinists, and Socinians would not be impressed by citations from the Lutheran Confessions. This explains also the frequent appeals to the fathers, particularly Augustine, in Lutheran, Roman, and Calvinist dogmatic literature.

The idea that the Lutheran dogmaticians were traditionalists and enslaved by their Confessions is surprising also because of the polemical

situation of the day. Ever since the Reformation, Roman and Lutheran theologians had carried on a continuous debate over the Roman doctrine that unwritten tradition was the Word of God along with Scripture. Against the Roman doctrine the *sola Scriptura* principle was articulated with ever-increasing clarity and precision. And the orthodox Lutherans were fully aware that this principle was the principle of the Lutheran Symbols themselves. To place the Confessions above Scripture was a repudiation of the Confessions. Time and again the Lutherans maintained that Scripture was the source of all tradition and of all confession. Scripture is the *norma normans* of theology, tradition and the Symbols a *norma normata*.[14] In controversy the appeal must be made from the Symbols to the higher authority of Scripture.[15]

Among fellow Lutherans, particularly against the Syncretists, the Lutheran Confessions very often entered into discussion and were frequently quoted at great length.[16] In such cases the Symbols were never placed above the Scriptures but were used as a touchstone for genuine Lutheranism. In fact the Syncretists, like the Roman Catholics, compelled orthodox Lutherans to rethink the whole question of the relation between Scripture and the Symbols of the church and to reiterate unequivocally the Lutheran position. The Lutheran Syncretists George Calixt, John Latermann, Christian Dreier, and Conrad Horneius taught that the *consensus doctrinae* of the first five centuries could be considered apostolic and a secondary source of doctrine; they believed that because of the confusion caused by heretics a person could not always be convinced by Scripture alone but required the testimony of the church.[17] Such a view was roundly condemned by the orthodox Lutherans as Romanistic.

What, then, was the authority of the Lutheran Symbols to Lutheran orthodoxy? In an oft-cited statement, Leonard Hutter, an intensely confessional Lutheran, asserts that the Holy Spirit was the author of the Lutheran Confessions and that these writings were divinely inspired. By this he means that the doctrine of the Lutheran Confessions is divine doctrine because it agrees with the Scriptures.[18] There are three fundamental distinctions to be made between the Confessions and Scripture, according to Hutter. First, Scripture is the infallible rule of faith, and all confessions must be based on and judged by Scripture. Second, Scripture is the judge in all controversy in the church; the Confessions are only a witness to this judge. Third, Scripture is self-authenticating

(αὐτόπιστος and ἀναπόδεικτος) and in need of no outside source for its authority; symbolic and ecclesiastical writings are to be believed only insofar as they agree with Scripture *(quatenus nimirum cum scripturis consentiunt).*

Calov says much the same concerning the relation of Scripture to the Confessions.[19] The one essential requisite for a church symbol is that it agrees with Scripture and that it contains nothing contrary to Scripture, even by implication. The differences between Scripture and the Confessions are as follows: First, the Scriptures come to us immediately from God by virtue of their inspiration; the Confessions come from God mediately, based as they are on Scripture. Second, formally the Scriptures represent the thought and mind of God; the Confessions are the consensus of the church. For this reason, only Scripture is self-authenticating, above all criticism (ἀνυπεύθυνος), and of necessity true. Third, materially Scripture is the source of divine truth; symbols contain conclusions that are based on Scripture. Hence the authority of Scripture is primary and intrinsic (κατ' αὐτό); the authority of the ecclesiastical Symbols secondary and extrinsic (κατ' ἄλλο). The conclusions of the Confessions can therefore only be accepted on the basis of their source, Scripture. Fourth, Scripture is the rule and norm of faith; the Confessions are a witness of the faith of the church. Without flinching, Calov declares that the Lutheran Confessions are infallible; but this is only because they are based on the authoritative Word of Scripture, not because of the sufferance of the church or because of any special character they may possess.

Here we have a clear enunciation of the position of orthodox Lutheranism toward the Confessions of the Lutheran Church. If these theologians have subscribed to the Lutheran Symbols *quia,* it is only because they have first approached the Confessions to learn whether and to what extent *(quatenus)* these writings agree with Scripture. Although such a convinced and emphatic acceptance of the Confessions will serve to unite all orthodox Lutherans, there is no indication that the Confessions were used as a club. Even in the controversies with Calixt and the Syncretists we find that the Symbols could not be appealed to as often as the orthodox party might have liked, and this because the Confessions did not touch on many of the issues under debate (e. g., the inspiration of Scripture; the doctrine of the Trinity in the Old Testament) except in passing.

4. *Luther and Lutheran Orthodoxy*

Were the orthodox Lutherans of the late-16th and 17th centuries true followers of the spirit and theology of Luther? Or was genuine Lutheranism somehow truncated shortly before or after the time of the Formula of Concord, as has been implied even by such a sympathetic historian as Werner Elert? [20] A partial and tentative answer ought to be given to this question at this early point, just for the sake of orientation. A more complete answer will emerge only as one acquaints oneself with the whole theology of the orthodox era.

It is perhaps inevitable that the second and third and fourth generations of Lutherans would lose some of the intense spirit and original dynamic of Luther in teaching and declaring evangelical truth. Luther's lively and unrestrained proclamation of the Good News, which had seized him and changed his life, his fresh and exciting approach to theology, which discovered something new every day, gives way too often to a self-conscious and stereotyped theologizing, inhibited by the formidable array of Roman, Calvinist, and Socinian controversialists who lay in wait to pounce on the slightest misstatement. This new spirit of caution affects the presentation of doctrine. Almost any of Luther's writings are engrossing and fascinating. Not so with the later dogmaticians. It is sometimes hard work reading them, and often one must dip deep before drawing water. In the age of orthodoxy theology and the Gospel are just as vital as they were for Luther, but the pulsating joy of discovery is no longer dominant. We must bear in mind, of course, that the studied, ponderous style of writing dogmatics books that became so common in the period of orthodoxy did much to make the reading of theology less interesting, and it can hardly be expected to compete with the spontaneous, running style of Luther. However, even in the heaviest of these volumes men like Gerhard and Calov can become quite moving and almost lyrical at times. We might add that whatever intolerance or dogmatism we note in this later period will be found to just as pronounced a degree in Luther. Luther's zeal for purity of doctrine is reflected in all the orthodox theologians, and it is this very deep concern that prompts them to labor so assiduously in dogmatics.

But does the loss of some of Luther's inimitable and vital spirit imply a different theology from that of Luther? It can be said at once that Lutheran orthodoxy made every effort to retain at all costs Luther's Gospel

and his theology and, to my knowledge, never questioned the doctrine of its great teacher. A great many of the dogmaticians wrote books, sometimes very large books, on the Lutheran Confessions that were thought to represent Luther's theology. And they all knew Luther and his writings well, as we may perceive from their copious quotations from his writings, especially in their exegetical works. The stamp of Luther is unmistakably imprinted on their theology. They do not merely study him enthusiastically as a great figure and saint, as a modern historian might do; they do not merely draw from him eclectically as they do from the church fathers. They identify themselves with him, with his Gospel, his cause, his theology; and they follow him and defend him. In their own fashion and for their own day they reproduce Luther's theology and spirit as best they can.

It has been suggested that the old dogmaticians' methodology and emphasis on the use of philosophy separate them from Luther's theological legacy with its passionate dislike of philosophy and reason.[21] This matter will be discussed in detail in its proper place in the chapter on the origin and development of prolegomena. Suffice it to say at this point that there is some substance in this allegation. One has the distinct feeling that Luther would have been as repelled and disappointed by the excessive scholasticism of later dogmaticians like Baier and John Adam Osiander as we are today. But the fact is that among the theologians in the era of orthodoxy there was a very consistent and strong distrust of the use of reason and philosophy in judging God's revelation. Not even the regenerate reason could judge in matters of revelation. Until the 18th century Lutheranism's doctrine of the bondage of the human will and of original sin was virtually an exact repristination of Luther's doctrine. Such a doctrine of man left no place for an exaltation of unregenerate philosophies and the powers of human reason. And it is difficult to see how Luther could have faulted the later theologians for their views concerning the *usus ministerialis* of reason in the activity of the theologian. When Luther spoke of killing and butchering reason, he never meant that God wanted us to be stupid or to think and talk nonsense; he was speaking of the abuse of reason in judging God's revelation. Luther was quite happy to bring philosophy to the aid of revelation if philosophy was confined to the realms of rhetoric and dialectics.[22]

In fine, after all the differences in emphasis and methodology between

Luther and his orthodox successors have been noted, two persistent facts remain. First, we find that the orthodox teachers possess a religious and cultural make-up and temperament similar to Luther's. Second, we find that these theologians very consciously tried to emulate the theology and spirit of Luther. As we shall see, there is every reason to believe that they succeeded. There is no theological cleavage between the period of the Reformation and the period of Lutheran orthodoxy.

5. *Exegesis and Dogmatics*

Although we shall speak later about the interpretation of Scripture in orthodox Lutheran theology, a few general remarks about how exegesis was employed will be apropos at this time. The old Lutherans were possessed of a naïve and winsome confidence in the clarity of Scripture and in the power of the *nuda scriptura* to convince. This is why their works often teem with Scripture references but offer little positive exposition of Scripture. In this respect their writings resemble the Lutheran Confessions, particularly the Formula of Concord. We also find their theological works replete with Biblical imagery and allusions to Scripture, reminiscent of Luther's writings. The orthodox Lutherans speak out of the center of Scripture, so to speak, and from a comprehensive grasp of the essential content of all of Scripture, understood in the context of Law and Gospel.

Concerning the Lutheran Confessions Schlink [23] has told us that the authors often select their proof passages haphazardly, sometimes choosing verses that elucidate a secondary idea in the article, sometimes choosing verses of minor importance, sometimes offering no exegetical proof at all; and this because they offer a summary of the whole of Scripture. This is much less the case in the dogmatics writings of that era and of the years following. Although the dogmaticians (and this would include those who had a hand in writing the Formula of Concord) also speak from the very heart and center of Scripture and do not feel compelled to nail down every issue with Scripture proof, it would appear that a real and careful attempt is usually made to offer the most pertinent Biblical evidence for every article of faith. As we might expect, the orthodox Lutherans stuck rather consistently to fundamentals also in exegesis. They may weary us by the thoroughness with which they deal with various points, but they seldom consider irrelevant issues. In their exegesis they do not quibble

or bother over grammatical or lexical difficulties unless something of practical importance is at stake. For this reason they will sometimes miss some significant nuance of a passage or point of syntax. In their exegesis they are understandably much stronger in concordance study than in syntax or lexicography, which were not such highly developed pursuits in those days. Their etymologies, for instance, will often be naïve and fanciful.

One of the inherent weaknesses in dogmatics is that a theologian must be selective in gathering the Biblical data pertaining to the several articles of faith. There is simply no way in which this selectivity can be avoided. Neither Chemnitz nor Gerhard, in their massive *Loci Theologici,* nor Barth, the most prodigious dogmatician of our day, can give an exhaustive account of all the Biblical data. But we must give these old theologians, like Barth today, an *A* for effort.

Because of this weakness in dogmatics we will notice gaps in the work of the Lutheran dogmaticians. Sometimes they omit extremely significant Biblical material in their discussions. Sometimes they fail to discuss important Biblical motifs at length. This failing is due also to the fact that the theologians of that day were often preoccupied with disputed points of doctrine or with issues of interest in that day (e. g., *de magistratu politico,* or certain aspects of marriage such as the forbidden degrees). The burning issues of the day, which centered in Christology, soteriology, sacramentology, and the question of authority in the church, absorbed so much of their attention that the doctrines of eschatology and even certain phases of ecclesiology were given only perfunctory attention.

But in the nature of the case, lack of balance is a risk every theologian must take who would venture to write a systematic theology. Understandably the later dogmaticians enjoyed a certain advantage: they were able to recognize the more glaring gaps in the works of their theological forebears and fill in what was lacking. Thus we see the doctrine of the mystical union, which was almost totally neglected by Chemnitz, given thorough treatment by the later dogmaticians; the same is true, to some extent, of the doctrines of Scripture and of the church and of eschatology. With all its very definite weaknesses (which we shall mention later) this was probably the one advantage of the analytic method in dogmatics, introduced by Calixt and Calov, over the older *loci* method: it covered more completely the whole range of Biblical theology.

It has been said of dogmaticians past and present that they often operate with a limited scope of Biblical evidence for their doctrine; they belabor a few basic *sedes doctrinae* to the exclusion of vast and important Biblical data. The result of such a selective procedure may be a theology that lacks balance and becomes distorted. Again we can only say that every dogmatician, like every modern writer of New or Old Testament theology, will need to be selective in presenting evidence for his conclusions. There is, however, no evidence that the old Lutheran theologians erred in this regard any more than many of our more modern scientific theologians. The reason for this may be that many of these former theologians were also pastors and preachers who used the Scriptures continually in their practical day-to-day work. Moreover, most of the dogmaticians (John Gerhard, Calov, Chemnitz, Dannhauer, Dorsch, Sebastian Schmidt, Giles Hunnius, Brochmand) did extensive work also in exegesis. Thus, as we see from their dogmatic works, they had a knowledge of the whole Bible, and they drew from this. We might add that the same pericopes are not used by all the dogmaticians in presenting the chief articles of faith; and it is surprising sometimes how widely they differ in their selection of Biblical evidence.

THE CHAMPIONS OF LUTHERAN ORTHODOXY

1. *Chronology*

Chronologically the period of Lutheran orthodoxy extends from the time of the writing of the Formula of Concord, when the confessional position of the Lutheran Church was settled, to the time of David Hollaz in the early 18th century. There were, to be sure, orthodox theologians after that time. Most notable among these was Valentin Loescher (1673 to 1749), who labored tirelessly to keep confessional Lutheranism alive in the face of the encroachments of Pietism (with which the later Lutherans unfortunately could never come to terms) and the Enlightenment. Loescher understood only too well the spirit of the day with its emphasis on the autonomy of man's reason even in matters of faith, its stress on natural religion with morality as its chief element, and its new approach to Scripture without presuppositions, an approach that was already apparent in Spinoza's *Tractatus Historico-Politicus* and that led to the gradual loss of confidence in the divine origin of Scripture. But his acute analyses

of Locke, Spinoza, Cartesianism, and the Cambridge theology were like a small voice muffled in a great storm. Lutheran orthodoxy was already on the decline in the days of Hollaz, although Hollaz was still able to exert a great influence. His *Examen Theologicum Acroamaticum,* first published in 1707, may rightly be called the last important orthodox Lutheran dogmatics.

The age of Lutheran orthodoxy may be divided roughly into three periods.

a. "THE GOLDEN AGE OF ORTHODOXY." The first period extends from the time of the writing of the Formula of Concord to the second decade of the 17th century. It was a time of theological formation and may be called the golden age of orthodoxy. Many of the representatives of this period were either framers or signers of the Formula of Concord. The period is marked by a confident, aggressive spirit and a creative approach to theological issues. Dogmatics — if one can speak of dogmatics at this early date — was constructed according to the pattern of Melanchthon's *Loci Communes* and was in only a rudimentary phase of development. Dogmatics was not yet a discipline in its own right but was considered an essential part of exegesis; its purpose was to gather and summarize the most important Biblical testimony for the chief topics of Christian doctrine. This was done in a synthetic fashion, proceeding from cause to effect and treating the articles of faith according to such an order: God, Creation, Man, Sin, Christology, etc.

b. "HIGH ORTHODOXY." The second period, which may be called the period of high orthodoxy, takes us through the Thirty Years' War. The period is less productive and lacks some of the vigor of the former age. The *loci* method of dogmatics still prevails, and no significant development in method is observed. Polemics is more dispassionate and ordered and possibly more effective. The Lutheran doctrinal position is increasingly clarified relative to Romanism, Calvinism, and other antitheses, and a more noticeable unity of doctrine is apparent. We now find philosophy influencing the presentation of theology to a rather marked degree and Aristotelian terminology making its way into Lutheran dogmatics. The practical application of Christian doctrine is given great stress.

c. "THE SILVER AGE OF ORTHODOXY." The third period might be called the silver age of orthodoxy. It covers the time from the close of the Thirty

Years' War to the final decline of orthodoxy. The period is not wanting in originality or energy and is marked by an immense amount of theological activity in every area of theology, much of which is very positive. The most noteworthy advance in dogmatics is the introduction of the so-called analytic method, which seeks to treat theology inductively, proceeding from effect to cause, viewing theology in the light of its ultimate goal, man's blessedness and salvation. The analytic method was an attempt to present all theology as a unit. The actual arrangement of the theological themes did not vary much from the former *loci theologici;* and except for connecting articles of faith a little more closely to one another, it is doubtful if the new method achieved any good results. The excessive repetition common to the former synthetic method was cut down appreciably; but this was hardly an advantage, because the old *loci theologici* were not usually calculated to be read in one sitting. If one were to read, for instance, a *locus* in Chemnitz or Gerhard, he might be pleased to find the whole council of God brought to bear on the one article treated. In the so-called *Systema* of the later period, with their lack of repetition, the reader is forced to do a great deal of cross-reference. In the silver age of orthodoxy dogmatics becomes more chopped up, more rigidly arranged than formerly. An unparalleled clarity of expression is achieved but at a cost: the later "systems" often make more demanding reading. It is only when these works become very large, as in the case of Quenstedt, and deal fully with the exegesis of *sedes doctrinae,* that a modern reader will take them up with great enthusiasm.

Many of the shorter dogmatic works of the day were only meant to be textbooks and were not intended to be read with any other purpose in mind. As systematic and well-outlined texts they were very useful. Only a few of the works of the day were excessively scholastic in tone. Although the theologians of the silver age of Lutheran orthodoxy manifested a breadth and depth of learning that was unexcelled in those days, there is little pedantry or ostentation in their writings. They were determined to keep theology practical. Nor were they unappreciative of the contributions of heterodox Christians. Calvinists and Roman theologians are often cited favorably and followed when they have something that can be used. The deep Christian devotion of the former period is still clearly noticeable, and in their activity and writings the later orthodox theologians seek to inculcate Christian life and piety. Quenstedt instructed

his students in the works of John Arndt, Luetkemann, and H. Juller. Calov found much in Spener's *Pia Desideria* that he placed on the hearts of the people. And some of his most technical writings are sprinkled with pasasges that have a truly devotional ring to them.

2. Noteworthy Theologians

During this long epoch in which strict Biblical and confessional orthodoxy dominated the life and theology of the Lutheran Church, we observe a rather large number of theologians who stand out as important representatives of the age. So that the reader may come upon these theologians with some familiarity, brief summaries of the life and theological contribution of the more noteworthy of them follow.

a. JACOB HEERBRAND [24] (1521—1600) was born in Giengen in Swabia. He studied theology at Wittenberg and for 5 years had Luther and Melanchthon as his teachers. Most of his active life in the church he spent as professor at Tübingen. The reason for his reputation for both orthodoxy and moderation is evident in all his books, many of which were written against the Jesuits. His most important and enduring work was his *Compendium Theologiae,* first published in Tübingen in 1575. During the negotiations of the Tübingen theologians with the patriarch of Constantinople, this work was translated into Greek and published in a bilingual edition (1582). The compendium is in the form of questions and brief answers. It is clear and closely oriented to the Scriptures and commends itself as a textbook.

b. MARTIN CHEMNITZ [25] (1522—1586) was born at Treuenbritzen in Brandenburg. At the age of 14 he was sent to the Trivialschule in Wittenberg, where he had brief opportunity to hear Luther preach. After studying at Magdeburg and Frankfort, he returned to Wittenberg. He was then occupied for a time as librarian in Königsberg, where he was able to read widely in theology; but he returned again to Wittenberg, where he then became a student of theology under Melanchthon and substituted for him in some of his classes. In 1554 he was ordained in Wittenberg by Bugenhagen. While attending some of the unpleasant conferences between the Philippists and the Gnesio-Lutherans, Chemnitz came to recognize the importance of Lutheran unity especially against the threat of the Counter Reformation; and he determined to do his utmost to unite the

Lutherans doctrinally. In this he was eminently successful. He strengthened the theology of Jacob Andreae and was perhaps responsible for rescuing Selnecker from the compromising spirit of Melanchthonianism. He was the leading spirit in the writing of the Formula of Concord, which settled the many disputes that had plagued Lutheranism after the death of the Reformer.

Much of Chemnitz' profound theological impact was achieved through the written word. His first work of major importance is his *Examen Concilii Tridentini,* which appeared in four volumes between 1565 and 1573. This book was a critical study of the canons and decrees of the Council of Trent in the light of Biblical theology and of history. The interpretations of such commentators of Trent as Hosius and Andradius were also subjected to Chemnitz' penetrating judgment. In this definitive analysis Chemnitz was never bombastic or polemical in a vicious or unkind way. Herein Chemnitz reveals his skill in Biblical exegesis, his thorough familiarity with ancient and medieval philosophy, and his knowledge of church history. The book made a tremendous impact, and for generations Roman Catholic controversialists made it their business to refute Chemnitz' charges and conclusions that the theology of Trent was a rupture from the theology of the apostolic church and the church catholic.

Second in importance is Chemnitz' *Loci Theologici,* first published after his death by Polycarp Leyser in 1591. Although patterned after Melanchthon's *Loci Communes,* this work represents something quite new in Lutheran theology, an attempt at a definitive presentation of the Biblical material relative to the chief articles of the Christian faith. The book incorporates many Biblical themes under certain *loci* and presents fewer *loci* (18 in all) than any other similar work. It was never finished. The work resembles a Biblical theology as much as a dogmatics; it contains many lengthy and pertinent word studies of significant Biblical themes such as faith, grace, and justification, and it offers several very thorough exegeses of pericopes relevant to Baptism, the Lord's Supper, the Trinity, and the like. There are also allusions to history and to the development of dogmas in the church, and there are some rather long discussions of ecclesiastical terms, although Chemnitz expresses his desire to keep such discussion to a minimum. But essentially we have in this enormous book a systematic presentation of Biblical theology. It differs from modern

Biblical theology in one essential feature: Old Testament and New Testament are not divided, nor are the books of the New Testament considered separately. To Chemnitz the Bible is one book, presenting one theology, God's theology, which He has made known to the church; not the theology of Paul or John or the prophets.[26] Large as it is, the *Loci Theologici* makes enjoyable reading. It is not encumbered with scholastic or involved terminology or chopped up into an intricate outline like many later works in dogmatics.

Chemnitz *De Duabus Naturis*[27] is the greatest dogmatic work ever written on the person of Christ. Moderate and cautious in tone, this large and lucid study (about 200 folio pages) is noteworthy for three reasons. First, fully a fourth of the entire work is devoted to profuse citations from all the church fathers and possibly makes too much of a good thing. Chemnitz overwhelmingly establishes the fact that Lutheran Christology is in accord with the doctrine of the ancient creeds and the church fathers. Second, the book offers a number of comprehensive and classic studies of pertinent *sedes doctrinae* such as Colossians 1 and Philippians 2. Third, we find in this work a systematic and convincing presentation of the entire doctrine of Christology, a presentation that has never been surpassed and has become normative for all subsequent treatment of Christology. After reading Chemnitz one is persuaded not only that the old doctrine of a communion of natures and a communication of attributes with its threefold classification (*genus idiomaticum, genus majestaticum,* and *genus apotelesmaticum*) is in accord with Scripture but that this is still the most effective and successful way to present Christology.

A fourth opus Chemnitz never finished; it was completed after his death by Leyser and John Gerhard and was entitled *Harmonia Quatuor Evangelistarum*. This was a strictly exegetical work that spent less time trying to harmonize than to interpret meaningfully the message of the four gospels. It is particularly strong in concordance study, and it contributed much toward setting a pattern for later exegesis. It was very popular in the 17th century and, along with Calov's *Biblia Illustrata*, is the outstanding exegetical contribution of the orthodox period.

His fruitful literary output and his beneficial activity in the church make Chemnitz, after Luther, the most important theologian in the history of the Lutheran Church.

C. NIKOLAUS SELNECKER [28] (1530—92) came early under the influ-

ence of Melanchthon in Wittenberg, and although he emerged from the strife leading to the Formula of Concord untainted and orthodox, he never lost the irenic disposition of his mentor. He first located in Dresden after entering the ministry, left for Jena in 1564, and was expelled the following year. In 1568 the Elector Augustus appointed him professor at the University of Leipzig and pastor of Thomaskirche. After a brief stay in Wolfenbüttel as court chaplain, ecclesiastical councillor, and superintendent-general, he returned to Leipzig. During his second period at Leipzig he assisted in the promotion of the Formula of Concord. In 1586 he became involved in the second Crypto-Calvinistic Controversy and was finally suspended from office; but on the death of Christian I he was recalled.

Selnecker was a voluminous writer who produced books in every area of theology. His most important dogmatic contributions were his *Institutiones Christianae Religionis,* first published at Frankfort in 1573; his *Paedagogia Christiana,* Frankfort, 1577; and several works on Christology, which, although strictly Lutheran, shied away from such terms as *ubiquity,* which were most offensive to the Calvinists. These works all show Selnecker's keen interest in exegesis. Selnecker distinguished himself particularly as a writer of hymns and devotional literature.

d. GILES (AEGIDIUS) HUNNIUS[29] (1550—1603) was born near Stuttgart, attended preparatory schools at Württemberg, and studied theology for many years under Heerbrand at Tübingen. Called as professor to the University at Marburg, he fought hard to establish Lutheranism there. He was not successful; and largely through the controversy caused by his adherence to the strictest Lutheran Christology the state church of Hesse was split into upper and lower Hesse. In 1592 Hunnius was called to Wittenberg, where Duke Frederick William was intent on restoring Lutheran orthodoxy, which had long been in jeopardy through the machinations of Christian I. Now began that long and glorious reign of orthodoxy at that famous university. More orthodox Swabians and others were soon to join Hunnius, and for a century Wittenberg was a bulwark of orthodoxy, a highly respected institution that drew students from the farthest reaches of the Lutheran Church and whose theological contributions and opinions were eagerly sought after.

Hunnius, although producing no complete dogmatic work, wrote on most of the articles of faith. His writings are marked by their simplicity

of style, by their close conformity to the language of Scripture — sometimes Hunnius' presentation is a mere paraphrase of Biblical passages, although he rarely offers extensive exegesis — and by frequent polemical outbursts. Hunnius' polemics is not the drawn-out, tiresome kind that we observe in some of the works of Mentzer or Calov but, more in the style of Luther, consists of an occasional, juicy, vituperative blast, after which the author settles down again to positive theologizing. Hunnius also wrote compendious commentaries on all the gospels and most of the epistles of the New Testament. He was highly respected by his successors. His influence is apparent in the many quotations from his works in the later Lutheran writings. His interesting and original way of putting things makes him highly quotable.

e. MATTHIAS HAFENREFFER [30] (1561—1619) was court preacher at Stuttgart and later until his death professor of theology at Tübingen. He was a man of broad knowledge and peaceable temperament. He was not a prolific writer, but his best known work, his *Compendium Doctrinae Coelestis* of 1600, became very popular. The book resembles Heerbrand's compendium, consisting of questions and pithy answers. Its clarity, undisputed orthodoxy, and convenient size commended it as a textbook. It was used extensively in Sweden.

f. LEONARD HUTTER [31] (1563—1616) was born at Hellingen, Württemberg, and studied at Strasbourg, Leipzig, Heidelberg, and finally in Jena, where he received his doctorate in theology. After the final overthrow of the Philippists he was called to Wittenberg as professor of theology. Together with Giles Hunnius he was most effective in establishing confessional Lutheran orthodoxy. His activity centered primarily in dogmatics and symbolics. His most important work in symbolics was his *Concordia Concors,* written in 1614, in which he defended the Formula of Concord in reply to the Calvinist Rudolf Hospinian. An important contribution in dogmatics was his little *Compendium Locorum Theologicorum ex Scriptura Sacra et Libro Concordiae Collectum.* This work was ordered by Elector Christian II to be a textbook in strict conformity with the Formula of Concord. The book became popular in all quarters of the church and was used for generations in Germany. It was edited several times in the 19th century, and a new edition by W. Trillhaas was published in Berlin in 1961. Hutter's *Loci Communes Theologici* (1619)

was an enlargement of his compendium and was used as a textbook in seminaries. Although not particularly original, Hutter offers a clear and exceptionally well-outlined series of discussions.

g. BALTHASAR MENTZER [32] (1565—1627) spent his productive years as professor at the University of Marburg and later at the new University of Giessen (1607—1625), which was founded because of Reformed domination in Hessen Cassel. He later returned as rector at Marburg after the friction between the Reformed and Lutherans subsided. Mentzer was a keen and original thinker who was never afraid to go against the stream, and although his writings are often unsystematic and disjointed, he enjoyed a high degree of respect among the other Lutherans of his day and is quoted very often by later dogmaticians such as Calov, Quenstedt, and Hollaz. His writings were many, but with the exception of his commentaries on the Augsburg Confession, they deal primarily with interests that are confined closely to Mentzer's own day. For this reason his works were seldom reissued, although a splendid edition of his *Opera Latina* was published at Frankfort in 1669. Like Hutter, his contemporary in Wittenberg, Mentzer was very consciously intent on being faithful to the Lutheran Confessions. Mentzer has been unfairly described by E. Preuschen [33] as engaging almost exclusively in the field of polemics. This seems true if one glances only at the title of his works; but much of his writing is no more polemical than the "noncontroversial" works of his contemporaries, and his polemics were carried on in a spirit of kindness and from an evangelical concern. But they are of little value to us today. Polemics that are directed against specific individuals or parties have a way of losing their timeliness and importance rather quickly.

h. JOHN GERHARD [34] (1582—1637) is generally considered to be the third preeminent Lutheran theologian after Luther and Chemnitz. He came from Quedlinburg and in his younger days had John Arndt as his pastor. Arndt exerted a deep and lasting influence on him. Gerhard studied first at Wittenberg and then at Jena, concentrating on the church fathers and Hebrew. After receiving his master's degree he accepted a call to teach at Marburg, where he became closely associated with Balthasar Mentzer. When Landgrave Moritz of Hessen Cassel introduced Reformed theology into the territory, both men left the university, Gerhard returning to Jena. There he resumed his teaching and was also

made superintendent of the consistory at Heldberg, a position of great distinction for a young man in his 24th year. His piety, industry, and helpfulness brought Gerhard more and more responsibilities, visitations, lectures, and preaching, until poor health finally compelled him to seek release from administrative duties and return to Jena as professor in 1616. At Jena he became even more famous and beloved. His learning, ability to teach, and kindness endeared him to all his students. During his time at Jena he received no fewer than 22 calls to other positions, and people came from far and near seeking his advice just as they had come to Luther a century before.

Gerhard authored many books in almost every theological field: exegesis, dogmatic theology, devotional literature, history, and polemics. A large number of his sermons were published and avidly read. In his celebrated *Loci Theologici,* which in spite of its magnitude (23 large quarto volumes) is still his best known work, Gerhard manifests a deep evangelical piety, a strong systematic and philosophical bent (which is not apparent in his exegetical works), and a trenchancy and aptness of expression that make him very quotable at times. Treated in a relatively rigid fashion according to Aristotelian factors *(causa efficiens, causa formalis, causa materialis,* and *causa finalis)* Gerhard's *loci* are models of clarity, and his conclusions are easily retained by the reader. But his discourse loses much of the liveliness and readable character of Chemnitz. To Gerhard belongs the dubious distinction of bringing Aristotelian terminology and distinctions to the aid of Lutheran dogmatics. If this tendency toward systematization had progressed no further than it went in his great work, perhaps even today we would not object strenuously to it.

i. HANS POULSEN RESEN [35] (1561—1638) was born in Skodborg, Denmark, and studied at Copenhagen, Rostock, Wittenberg, Padua, and Geneva. Returning to Copenhagen he became attached to the university first as professor of dialectics and later (1597) as professor of theology, a chair he held until his death. In the wake of the Crypto-Calvinism that had held sway in Denmark under the influence of Niels Hemmingsen, Resen worked assiduously to uphold strict Lutheran orthodoxy according to the Formula of Concord. He accomplished much in changing the tone of theology in Denmark and Norway, and was adamant enough in his zeal to be instrumental in the banishment of one of his colleagues, Ivar Stub, who was tainted with Calvinism. Resen's most lasting accomplish-

ment was his translation of the Bible into Danish in 1607. He also wrote a number of monographs of a dogmatic nature, the most valuable of which was his *De Sancta Fide* (1614). Although Resen himself was not always an easy man to get along with, this work, which owes much to Luther, is a most winning and evangelical treatment of the main themes of Christology.

j. CORT ASLAKSSEN [36] (1564—1624) was the only Norwegian of note among the orthodox dogmaticians. He was born in Bergen and studied at Copenhagen as well as at the Reformed universities in Heidelberg, Basel, and Geneva. In 1600 he returned to Copenhagen, where he remained as professor at the university until his death. Although at first tinged with Calvinism, he later defended the Formula of Concord and orthodox theology. He was a man of broad interests that included science, philosophy, and philology in addition to theology. His temperament was far less belligerent than that of his colleague Resen. His most valuable theological contribution, entitled *De Immanuele Nostro D. Jesu Christo* (1620), treated Christology in a very evangelical manner. In his own day his most celebrated work was his *Physica et Ethica Mosaica* (1613), which was an attempt at synthesizing the astronomical finds of Tycho Brahe with the cosmology of the first three chapters of Genesis.

k. JESPER RASMUS BROCHMAND [37] (1585—1652) was the giant among the Scandinavian theologians during the period of Lutheran orthodoxy, the only Scandinavian to exert any real impact outside his own northern confines. After a brief sojourn in Germany he spent all his working days in Copenhagen, where he was professor of theology at the university and, upon the death of Resen, bishop of Seeland. In many ways he reminds one of Gerhard, who must have exerted some influence on him. His *Universae Theologiae Systema* (1633), his most celebrated work, was very like Gerhard's *Loci Theologici* in arrangement, content, and tone. Its unique feature was the inclusion of lengthy discussions of casuistry and the practical application of the articles of faith; this was a new development that greatly enhanced the value of the book. The book also resembles Gerhard's dogmatics in size, in erudition, and in its pious, exemplary tone. It contains much less of the philosophical jargon of Gerhard but also less of the solid exegesis.

Brochmand, however, was no mean exegete; his commentary on the

Book of James (1640) is one of the finest commentaries written during the period of orthodoxy. Brochmand's work demonstrates eloquently that the Epistle of James is deeply appreciated by the Lutheran Church; in addition to sound, scholarly exegesis, the author stresses under every pericope and in a moving manner the importance of a practical Christianity. Brochmand also wrote an excellent commentary on the Epistle to the Hebrews. He was a firm supporter of the Formula of Concord in Denmark, and a convinced Lutheran against Roman, Reformed, and Socinian theology; he had come to his convictions only after deep and heart-searching experience in his earlier years. Like Gerhard, Brochmand was capable of strong and effective polemics. In particular his *De Pontifice Romano* of 1628 is one of the most searching analyses of the Roman papacy ever made; e. g., 230 pages are devoted to the subject of Antichrist alone. Brochmand was also a powerful and well-known preacher, and his sermons were published often and read eagerly.

l. BALTHASAR MEISNER [38] (1587—1626) was born in Dresden, where his father was minister. At the age of 15 he began his studies at the University of Wittenberg under Giles Hunnius and the celebrated exegete Balduin, both of whom became very attached to him. He early distinguished himself as a man of penetrating intellect who felt a deep interest in philosophy and logic as well as theology. After continuing his studies at Giessen, Basel, Strasbourg, and Tübingen, he received his doctor's degree at Wittenberg, where he remained as teacher. The previous year, when only 24 years of age, he had finished his famous *Philosophia Sobria,* in which he attempted to illustrate with many examples just how philosophy could be employed in theological controversies and tried to correct the rationalistic abuse of philosophy and logic that he discerned in some Reformed theologians and in the Helmstedt Aristotelians (e. g., Cornelius Martini). While he wrote no complete dogmatics, Meisner's *Christologia Sacra* and his *Anthropologia Sacra* embrace most of the articles of faith and show him to be a dogmatician of high rank. His *Colloquium Adiaphoristicum,* written to explain the evangelical doctrine of Christian liberty and adiaphora, is a masterful presentation of the Lutheran position. Together with other leaders like Gerhard and Mentzer, Meisner contributed much in a practical way toward the revitalization of church life during the difficult times of war and theological controversy. He was especially appreciated for his devotional writings. In his day he was

called "the Joshua of the evangelical church." Tholuck calls him a "model of piety." [39]

m. NICHOLAS HUNNIUS [40] (1585—1643) was born in Marburg and studied in Wittenberg. After a brief superintendency at Eilenburg he succeeded Leonard Hutter as professor at Wittenberg. He was later pastor and superintendent at Lübeck, where he was a very effective and aggressive worker. He inherited the contentious temperament as well as the ability of his father, Giles Hunnius, and devoted himself primarily to writing against Reformed and Roman Catholic theology. He is known principally for two theological works. First is his Διάσκεψις *Theologica de Fundamentali Dissensu Doctrinae Evangelicae-Lutheranae & Calvinianae seu Reformatae* (1628), in which he classifies the Christian doctrine according to an elaborate system of fundamental and nonfundamental articles and shows that there is fundamental disagreement between Lutherans and Calvinists. His distinctions concerning the articles of faith were followed more or less by most of his successors. His second theological work of importance is his *Epitome Credendorum* (1625), which became very popular, also among the laity, as a brief and readable summary of the Christian faith. It was written in German and translated into English in 1844. The most original feature of this work was the author's dealing with soteriology according to an *ordo salutis* (call, repentance, justification, conversion, renewal, regeneration, and union with Christ), a feature that became a common procedure among the later dogmaticians.

n. JOHN GEORGE DORSCH [41] (1597—1659) was educated at Tübingen and Strasbourg, where he gained such high respect among the townspeople that he was given funds for a 3-year educational tour that took him to Leipzig, Jena, Wittenberg, and Marburg and into personal acquaintance with many of the prominent Lutheran leaders of the day. Soon thereafter he was called as professor to Strasbourg, where he worked tirelessly for the next 27 years. Together with his colleague, Dannhauer, he did much to build up the new university during and after the trying years of the Thirty Years' War. Dorsch was a man of irreproachable character; he was pious, kind, and always fair. He defended John Arndt against the attacks of Lukas Osiander and other Lutherans, and insisted on interpreting him in an orthodox Lutheran sense. He wrote many volumes of devotional literature, which along with his sermons was highly

treasured in his day. He was prolific in his writing, composing a number of commentaries and studies on individual pericopes. His many polemical writings, which were directed chiefly against Roman theology and the Lutheran Syncretists, were dominated by a real Gospel spirit. In all, his books number more than 50 titles. His best known dogmatic work was his *Synopsis Theologiae Zacharianae,* which was highly considered by his contemporaries and was quoted often by later Lutheran teachers, particularly Quenstedt.

O. JOHN HUELSEMANN [42] (1602—61) was born in Ostfriesland and educated by his father until he entered the gymnasium. After 2 years at Rostock he entered the University of Wittenberg, studying under such renowned theologians as Balduin, Meisner, and Jacob Martini. After the death of Balduin he transferred to Leipzig, where he studied with Hoepfner, under whom he received his master's degree. Soon thereafter he was called as professor to Wittenberg, where he taught exegetical and dogmatico-polemical theology, along with a little homiletics. Huelsemann was not the most talented of the orthodox Lutherans; he was of a practical bent, rather easygoing, a warm person who was well liked in his day. But his writings seldom indicate this. They are for the most part polemic or overly systematic, and they lack originality. He was always fair in these controversial writings, or at least tried to be, but was not very effective. His best known work, *Breviarium Theologicum,* does not come up to the quality of other shorter dogmatics of the day. His most useful work is his short *Manuale Confessionis Augustanae,* used in many schools as a textbook. During the last years of his life Huelsemann was a professor at Leipzig. He became a very popular preacher among all ages of hearers. It is very likely that Calov exerted a strong influence on Huelsemann at Wittenberg.

P. JOHN CONRAD DANNHAUER [43] (1603—66) is a most eminent representative of later Lutheran orthodoxy. The son of a pastor in Köndrigen in Baden, he was enrolled in the gymnasium at Strasbourg when he was only 7 years old and entered the seminary in the Reformation's jubilee year, 1617. After gaining a complete grasp of the humanities and receiving his master's degree in theology, he continued his studies at Marburg under Mentzer, Feuerborn, and Winkelmann. He also studied under Koenig at Altdorf and under Gerhard at Jena. In 1628 he received a call

to Strasbourg as director of the seminary. There he remained for 25 years, lecturing mainly in dogmatics and ethics. He was later elected cathedral pastor at Strasbourg, and soon after that appointed president of the *Kirchenconvent*.

Dannhauer's influence was far-reaching in every direction. Although ostentatious at times, his sermons were both textual and popular and were greatly appreciated throughout all of Alsace. His administrative ability was also remarkable. He inaugurated an effective system of visitations in all the parishes, improved catechetical instruction and the Christian training of the young, and over the years labored with zeal and success to maintain a pious and faithful clergy in his district. He was not blind to the faults within the church and to the limitations of his own efforts, and when Spener sought to revive the church and correct her failings, Dannhauer did not hesitate to support him. Dannhauer's greatest contribution was in the classroom, where he exercised a profound influence on the students. He was Spener's teacher.

Dannhauer was a man of peaceful disposition and reluctant to engage in controversy. But he despised false peace in the church; therefore, like Calov, he felt compelled to write a great number of polemical works against Roman Catholics, Calvinists, and the Lutheran Syncretists. His *Hodomoria Spiritus Calviniani* (1654) is a model of polemics. Lacking the sarcasm and vituperation that were common to the day, the work shows the real issues that divided Lutheranism and Calvinism and that had often been confused and covered up by some Calvinists and Lutherans for the sake of union. Dannhauer seeks to show just what is involved in the doctrinal controversies that prevailed on such vital matters as predestination and the means of grace, and the seriousness of these differences; and he stressed the importance of honesty and frankness in solving these differences. Against the Syncretists, both Reformed (John Dury) and Lutheran (Calixt), Dannhauer also wrote polemics, second in importance only to the numerous salvoes of Calov. Dannhauer was wary of the union efforts between Lutheran and Reformed theologians. The Reformed professed allegiance to Luther, often using Lutheran modes of expressing their theology; but at the same time they often tried to smuggle in their doctrines and invade Lutheran territory under the protection of Reformed princes. The history of the Thirty Years' War and of the house of Brandenburg had made the Lutherans suspicious of Reformed

efforts for church union. Dannhauer's *Mysterium Syncretismi Detecti, Proscripti, et Symphonismo Compensati* of 1648 is probably the most penetrating book written on the subject of syncretism and church union from the Lutheran point of view; in this work Dannhauer expresses his conviction that doctrinal unity based on the Word of God forms the only legitimate basis for the reunion of Christendom.

Dannhauer's greatest theological composition is unquestionably his compendium in dogmatics, entitled *Hodosophia Christiana sive Theologia Positiva* (1649). He portrays in a most original fashion, by means of 12 phenomena and using Scriptural imagery, how man ascends the way to heaven: the light upon the way (Scripture), the pilgrim (man), the candlestick (the church), the goal (God), the hindrances along the way (sin, temptation), etc. In all, Dannhauer produced over 50 books on the whole range of theology. His writings sometimes make fascinating reading, for he has an inimitable way of putting things. But they are also exceedingly difficult to read; his Latin style is compact, almost like Tertullian's, and loaded down with hundreds of allusions to ancient mythology and classical Latin and Greek authors.

In Dannhauer we see an orthodox theologian who was pious, industrious, practical, and evangelical, truly a great figure in the history of the Lutheran Church.

q. JEROME KROMAYER [44] (1610—70) studied at Leipzig, Wittenberg, and Jena. He taught philosophy and history at Leipzig and in 1643 was made professor of theology. The university at Leipzig was known for its staunch Lutheranism and its mild tone. Kromayer along with Huelsemann represented a strong voice against the Calixtine theology and syncretism. Kromayer was an astute and learned theologian, but his writings, although clear and forceful, do not achieve the standard of other works of the day. Because of its handy size and its usefulness as a textbook his *Theologia Positivo-Polemica* remained popular for two generations.

r. ABRAHAM CALOV [45] (1612—86) was the most brilliant and influential theologian of the silver age of Lutheran orthodoxy, a veritable pillar of orthodox Lutheranism. His childhood was not easy. Born in East Prussia, he was twice forced to move because of the plague. He was afflicted with an impediment in his speech that he was able to overcome only with great perseverance. He studied at home with his father until

he was 14, when he entered the University of Königsberg. There he studied under John Behm and the notorious Myslenta, a fire-eating controversialist. He studied next at Rostock, where he lived with the famous professor Quistorp. Because of the Thirty Years' War his hope for further study at Wittenberg or at Jena with Gerhard was never fulfilled. After his studies he returned to Königsberg, where he became professor and pastor and in 1641 superintendent of schools and churches. Two years later he was called to Danzig as rector of the *gymnasium* and pastor of Holy Trinity Church. In 1649 he was called as professor to the University of Wittenberg. Later he became superintendent of the Saxon churches and *professor primarius*.

Calov was an amazing man in many ways. His learning was prodigious. His memory was remarkable. He was versed in every area of knowledge. He was a man of indefatigable industry, and his administrative ability was highly efficient. His orthodoxy was inflexible, and his zeal for the purity of the Gospel and the glory of God dominated his life and all his activity. He was truly a *strenuus Christi athleta,* as he called himself. But his was a winning and contagious zeal that made an impression on his colleagues and especially on his students. He was a strikingly effective teacher, and his reputation drew so many students to the university that the Elector of Brandenburg finally prohibited young men from that territory from attending the university. Calov's lectures, which were mainly exegetical, drew as many as 500 students. All these unremitting duties of teaching, preaching, and administration, coupled with an unbroken literary output, indicate Calov's tremendous capacity.

Most remarkable of all was perhaps his literary activity. He wrote more than most people read in a lifetime, dozens of volumes in every area of theology and in philosophy — 28 works dealing with the Syncretistic Controversy alone. Some of his writings were immense, numbering thousands of pages. Most important of his theological works was without question his *Biblia Illustrata* (1672—76), a gigantic commentary on the whole Bible, which came to be very highly thought of even down to the 19th century. A great deal of independent thought went into this commentary, which treated both the individual verses and the larger pericopes of Scripture. Second in importance was Calov's *Systema Locorum Theologicorum* (1655—77) in 12 volumes. This work was not so carefully done as the former, and one gets the impression that Calov was in a great

hurry in the last volumes. There is also much wearying quotation throughout the work. The first volume, however, contains the finest discussions of prolegomena, revelation, and Scripture to be found among the orthodox dogmaticians. Calov's subsequent treatment of the Trinity, although less original, is also unparalleled in its depth and thoroughness. A much smaller but highly useful dogmatics was the *Apodixis Articulorum Fidei,* which presents a valuable summary of the theology of late orthodoxy. It is arranged according to doctrinal headings, each beginning with a short thesis and followed by rather extensive exegesis of the more weighty Biblical evidence for each article of faith. It is free of casuistry and polemics and contains no scholastic outline of terms, features that make it rather enjoyable reading to the modern reader. Calov's *Isagoges ad SS. Theologiam,* which first appeared in 1652, along with the works of Hyperius, Chytraeus, and Gerhard, is a very important contribution in the development of dogmatic prolegomena. Calov enjoys the distinction of having produced some of the most provocative and moving and some of the dullest and most repetitious writings of his day. His *Systema* belongs in both categories.

None of the orthodox Lutheran theologians have provoked such diverse reactions as Calov. In his day he was extolled by his friends and colleagues and vilified and degraded by his adversaries. Later theologians have expressed just as varied judgments. Tholuck,[46] on the basis of Calov's domestic life (Calov survived five wives and thirteen children) and judgments of Calov's adversaries, sees nothing good in him but depicts him as an arrogant and unfeeling person who treated human beings like numbers. Walther and Hoenecke, both of whom read extensively in Calov's works, speak very well of him, describe him as a great theologian, and hold him in highest respect.[47] Kunze[48] offers a less partisan opinion. He recognizes Calov's superb abilities. He feels that Calov's continuous involvement in controversy has left a misleading impression of him. Calov was first a theologian, Kunze points out, and only then a controversialist. Many of his concerns were precisely those of Spener. One thing about this controversial figure: whoever comes into contact with him is compelled to take sides.

S. SEBASTIAN SCHMIDT[49] (1617—96) was born in Lampertheim, a small village in Alsace. He studied at Marburg, Wittenberg, Königsberg, and Basel. His interests centered mainly in the humanities and the Oriental

languages. He also occupied himself with Talmudic and Rabbinic writings. Finding the way to Strasbourg, he was received graciously by Dorsch and encouraged in his studies. He became a pastor in nearby Ensheim and later the rector of the *gymnasium* at Lindau. On Dorsch's death he was elected professor of theology at the University of Strasbourg. There he became very famous as an exegete and received calls from as far away as Sweden. His literary activity was voluminous. He wrote massive and learned commentaries on most of the Bible, as well as short monographs on many of the chief Biblical themes. His *Compendium Theologiae* (1697), which was his best known dogmatic work, reflects his exegetical depth but is also marked by the scholastic tendency of the day.

t. JOHN ANDREW QUENSTEDT[50] (1617—88) spent his entire active ministry as professor at the University of Wittenberg. His life was not filled with the turmoil that Calov and other theologians of the day faced. He was a man of mild and humble disposition and, for his day, tolerant. His rather uneventful life culminated in his one great literary work, *Theologia Didactico-Polemica sive Systema Theologiae,* which was printed just 3 years before his death.

There is no question that after the *Loci Theologici* of Chemnitz and Gerhard (who was his uncle) the *Systema* of Quenstedt ranks as the greatest dogmatics book ever written by a Lutheran. Although this enormous volume would have cost a pastor many weeks' salary, it went through five editions between 1685 and 1715. One might say that Quenstedt's *Systema* killed systematic theology in the period of Lutheran orthodoxy as Michaelangelo killed Renaissance art by the unexcelled quality of his work. Quenstedt's lifework is so big, so complete, so concise and systematic, and so excellent that no later Lutheran ever came close to equalling it. Several factors make this a monumental work in Lutheran theology:

— Although very long and too scholastic in form for our liking today, it is a model of dogmatic systematization; and in spite of its bulk the reader may find his way around in this book with ease. Every possible point of doctrine that was discussed or at issue in those days is broached and treated with a lucidity that defies misunderstanding. Never before or since was systematization carried out with such skill and brilliance by a Lutheran.

— The book is highly informative. With the deftness of one who has complete command of his sources Quenstedt draws from the best that his

fathers and precursors said. He quotes church fathers, Luther, the Symbols, predecessors, colleagues, even scholastics and contemporary Catholic and Reformed theologians with remarkable selectivity and economy. Quenstedt never forces us to plunge into boring chains of citations. In a sense this dogmatics is a summary of over a hundred years of the best in Christian theology. Quenstedt's antitheses alone offer us an insight into the theological climate of the day that we could hardly gain from any other source. In all this the author is irenic and objective, and he rarely uses an unkind word.

— Because of its size the book is able to offer extensive exegesis (about one third of the book) in presenting the various articles of faith. This exegesis may strike one as too dogmatic in form; but it is no more so than most of the exegetical commentaries of the day. Quenstedt is probably more independent in his exegesis than in any other portion of his book. In Quenstedt we perceive that sound exegesis and a firm grasp of history (past and present) are the ingredients of good dogmatics.

U. JOHN FRIEDRICH KOENIG [51] (1619—64) entered late in life into the Christian ministry, but he was able to devote many years of service to the church. He studied at Wittenberg under Jacob Martini, Huelsemann, and William Lyser and became *professor extraordinarius* at Greifswald and later at Rostock. He wrote a great number of works, but only one has any lasting significance. This was his *Theologia Positiva Acroamatica* (1664), a brief skeletal outline of doctrinal theology, systematized according to an Aristotelian framework. The work commended itself as an outline for classroom use and went through at least 13 editions, some of them enlarged with copious citations from Scripture. Quenstedt followed the scheme of the book in writing his *Systema*. Apart from its function as a classroom syllabus, it is difficult to see any value in this book.

V. FRIEDEMANN BECHMANN [52] (1628—1703) studied at Jena and was soon called back to his alma mater, where he occupied a chair as professor of philosophy. After the death of J. E. Gerhard (son of John Gerhard), he became professor in theology. Bechmann penned a number of notable books, the best of which is his *Annotationes Uberiores in Compendium Theologicum Leonhardi Hutteri* (1690). This is the most readable, evangelical, and useful presentation of Christian doctrine one will find in the latter days of Lutheran orthodoxy. In another work, his

Theologia Conscientiaria (1700), Bechmann offers one of the most sympathetic and evangelical treatments of casuistic problems ever written by a Lutheran. His dogmatics manual, *Theologia Polemica,* does not maintain the high quality of the previous works but is still one of the best texts of the day. Bechmann is less known than the other orthodox theologians of the silver age, scarcely ever mentioned by historians. But he was a theologian of great ability and of indubitable orthodoxy. The reason for his lack of recognition may lie in the fact that he was overshadowed by his colleague John Musaeus, but neither the latter's synergistic tendencies nor his mediating position toward syncretism are to be found in Bechmann.

W. JOHN ADAM SCHERZER [53] (1628—83) spent his early years in France, taken there by his father, a Protestant lawyer who had to flee. He later returned to Germany to study at Altdorf, Jena, and Leipzig. He was a student of Cundisius and Musaeus at Jena, and of Huelsemann and Carpzov at Leipzig. Scherzer was an enormously learned man, having a vast knowledge of philosophy, natural science, and medicine as well as of Hebrew and Rabbinic studies. Most of his ministry was spent as professor at Leipzig University. Like Calov he was married several times and suffered the loss of many who were close and dear to him. His stormy polemics, apparent in many of his writings, brought him the nickname "the Leipzig Calov." He wrote mainly against the papists, Socinians, and Syncretists. His best known work, *Systema Theologiae* (1680), displays great learning and has no objectionable features, but it lacks color and originality and does not compare with similar works by Dannhauer, Calov, and Bechmann.

X. JOHN WILLIAM BAIER [54] (1647—95) studied at Jena, where he came under the influence of John Musaeus, who later became his father-in-law. He was called as professor at the University of Jena and later at Halle, where he did not always get along very peaceably with the pietists. However, like many of the later orthodox Lutherans, he was somewhat affected by Pietism. Baier is known primarily for one book, his *Compendium Theologiae Positivae* (1685). While demonstrating that the Jena theology was not syncretistic but orthodox, this work, which on every page leans on Musaeus, is not wholly free from the latter's synergism. Baier's presentation and formulations are very scholastic and indicate a

decline in the forcefulness of orthodox Lutheran dogmatics. His theological shorthand, although precise, becomes so abbreviated at times as to be quite bewildering to one who has not read in other theologians of that day. Nevertheless, because of its clarity and convenient size the book was used in many schools and was re-edited in Germany and America in the 19th century.

y. DAVID HOLLAZ [55] (1648—1713) was born in Pomerania and studied in Wittenberg under Calov and Quenstedt. He was somewhat influenced by Pietism, and we observe in Hollaz the tendency toward synergism, so common to Pietism, and the preoccupation with psychology in working out an *ordo salutis*. Hollaz was one of the few of the leading orthodox Lutherans who never taught but remained a pastor all his life. His only literary work of note was his *Examen Theologicum Acroamaticum,* which often reflects his pastoral concern. This is the last great orthodox dogmatics. It is a relatively large work (about 1,500 quarto pages) and a veritable masterpiece of arrangement and precise formulation. It is arranged according to questions, answers in the form of pithy theses, antitheses, proofs comprising one or more brief exegeses, and observations. Borrowing from the framework of Quenstedt's *Systema,* Hollaz sometimes includes in some of his more involved sections such headings as ἔκθεσις (subthesis), βεβαίωσις (added evidence or proof), and διάλυσις (solution of problems). A valuable feature of the work is the goodly amount of exegesis dispersed throughout. But although more usable, it lacks the sweep and completeness of Quenstedt's classic work. Its proliferation of scholastic distinctions, while adding to its clarity, actually detracts from the force of many of Hollaz' ideas. It was a highly respected book in its day, going through eight editions between 1707 and 1763. No later dogmatics ever rivaled it in popularity.

3. The Seats of Lutheran Orthodoxy

During the period of Lutheran orthodoxy the theological leadership in Germany was centered mainly in five prominent universities. In Wittenberg, Tübingen, and Strasbourg the strictest confessionalism and orthodoxy prevailed. In Leipzig and Jena a slightly milder tone was maintained, but the dominant theology was unquestionably orthodox. Giessen might also be included while Justus Feuerborn and B. Mentzer were there, but it was later dominated by the liberal spirit of Gottfried Arnold and

J. E. Gerhard. The following is a list of the leading theologians who occupied these seats of orthodoxy.

WITTENBERG

Leyser	Hutter	Meisner
G. Hunnius	Huelsemann	Weller
Balduin	Calov	Deutschmann
Franz	Quenstedt	

TUEBINGEN

Heerbrand	Osiander
Andreae	Thumm
Hafenreffer	

STRASBOURG

J. Schmid	Dannhauer
Dorsch	S. Schmidt

LEIPZIG

Huelsemann	Scherzer
Hoepfner	Kromayer
Carpzov	

JENA

J. Gerhard	Bechmann
Musaeus	J. E. Gerhard
Baier	Buddeus

NOTES TO CHAPTER ONE

1. *The Doctrine of Man in Classical Lutheran Theology* (Minneapolis: Augsburg Publishing House, 1962), p. xi. See *D. Martin Luthers Werke,* Kritische Gesamtausgabe (Weimar: H. Böhlau, 1883), 30 II 68; hereafter cited as WA. This is the judgment also of Otto Ritschl, who claims that the Gnesio-Lutherans of the 16th and the orthodox Lutherans of the 17th centuries were the truest followers of Luther. See *Dogmengeschichte des Protestantismus* (Leipzig: J. C. Hinrichs'sche Buchhandlung, 1908), I, 11.
2. An example of the interest in science may be seen in the case of Cort Aslakssen, who for a time worked under Tycho Brahe. Aslakssen wrote two works, *De Natura Caeli Triplicis* (Sigena of Nassau, 1597), part of which was translated into English in 1623, and *De Mundo* (Copenhagen, 1605 to 1607), in which he sought to synthesize the prevailing theories on the astronomy of the day with the Biblical world picture.

3. August Tholuck, *Geschichte des Rationalismus:* Erste Abteilung, *Geschichte des Pietismus und des ersten Stadiums der Aufklärung* (Berlin: Wiegandt und Grieben, 1865), p. 4.
4. See Friedrich Balduin, *Commentarius in Omnes Epistolas Beati Apostoli Pauli,* editio altera priore longe emaculatior (Frankfort on the Main, 1710), prolegomena. See also George Dedekenn, *Thesauri Consiliorum et Decisionum* (Jena, 1671), appendix nova, p. 58.
5. See Ludwig N. Helwig, *Den danske Kirkes Historie efter Reformationen* (Copenhagen: G. E. C. Gads Forlag, 1851), 6R 2, pp. 75 ff.
6. Sven Göransson, *Orthodoxi och Synkretism i Sverige 1647—1660* (Uppsala: Almqvist & Wiksells Boktryckeri, 1950), pp. 133 ff.
7. Oskar Garstein, *Cort Aslakssen* (Oslo: Lutherstiftelsen, 1953); Björn S. Kornerup, *Biskop Hans Poulsen Resen 1561—1615* (Copenhagen: G. E. C. Gads Forlag, 1928).
8. Jesper Rasmus Brochmand, *In Canonicam et Catholicam Jacobi Epistolam Commentarius* (Copenhagen, 1706), p. 242.
9. See Martin Chemnitz, *De Duabus Naturis* (Frankfort and Wittenberg, 1653), pp. 38—39, where the author treats the history of heresies connected with the personal union. See also Chemnitz' discussion of the ancients' use of terms in describing the personal union (pp. 41—52) and his investigation of the patristic material supporting the first genus of the communication of attributes (pp. 66—73). (For English translation, see Martin Chemnitz, *The Two Natures in Christ,* trans. J. A. O. Preus [St. Louis: Concordia Publishing House, 1970].)
10. Giles Hunnius, *Opera Latina* (Frankfort on the Main, 1608), II, 226. Hunnius, like Flacius, because of his antipathy to the Melanchthonian traditionalism, is more wary of the church fathers than the Lutherans who follow him. He often warns that the fathers have erred, and he does not make use of them to any extent.
11. A goodly number of the theologians wrote books either defending or commenting on the Lutheran Symbols, usually the Augsburg Confession or the Formula of Concord. The most important of these are Nikolaus Selnecker, *Erinnerung vom Concordienbuche* (Leipzig, 1581); Nikolaus Selnecker, *Erklärung etlicher streitiger Artikel aus der Concordienformel* (Leipzig, 1582); David Chytraeus, *Historia der Augsburgischen Confession* (Rostock, 1577); Giles Hunnius, *Theses de Augustana Confessione, Ecclesiarum Evangelicarum Symbolo Augustissimo* (Rostock, 1622); Leonard Hutter, *Augustanae Confessionis Analysis Methodica* (Wittenberg, 1602); Leonard Hutter, *Libri Christianae Concordiae: Symboli Ecclesiarum, Novissimo hoc Tempore, Longe Augustissimi; Explicatio Plana & Perspicua* (Wittenberg, 1609); Leonard Hutter, *Concordia Concors, de Origine et Progressu Formulae Concordiae Ecclesiarum Confessionis Augustanae* (Wittenberg, 1614); Abraham Calov, *Criticus Sacer vel Commentarii Apodictico-Elenchtici super Augustanam Confessionem* (Leipzig, 1646); Balthasar Mentzer, *Exegesis Augustanae Confessionis* in *Opera Latina* (Frankfort, 1669), I, 1—306; Balthasar Mentzer, *Collatio Augustanae Confessionis* in *Opera Latina* (Frankfort, 1669), I, 306—356; John Huelsemann, *Manuale Confessionis Augustanae* (Wittenberg, 1624); Jerome Kromayer, *Commentarius Didactico-Elenchticus in Augustanam Confessionem* (Frankfort and Leipzig, 1723); John Benedict Carpzov, *Isagoge in Libros Ecclesiarum Lutheranarum Symbolicos* (Leipzig, 1665); Sebastian Schmidt, *Articulorum Formulae Concordiae Repetitio* (Strasbourg, 1696).

12. Edmund Schlink, *Theology of the Lutheran Confessions,* trans. Paul F. Koehneke and Herbert J. A. Bouman (Philadelphia: Muhlenberg Press, 1961), p. xvii.
13. Ibid., pp. xxi—xxii; Friedrich A. Nitzsch, *Lehrbuch der evangelischen Dogmatik,* 3d ed. (Tübingen: J. C. B. Mohr, 1912), p. 26; Ernst Ludwig Th. Henke, *Georg Calixtus und seine Zeit* (Halle: Buchhandlung des Waisenhauses, 1853), II, II, 182. Jörg Baur in *Die Vernunft zwischen Ontologie und Evangelium: Eine Untersuchung zur Theologie Johann Andreas Quenstedts* (Gütersloh: Verlagshaus Gerd Mohn, 1962), p. 176, comes to quite the opposite conclusion, namely that the orthodoxy of the 17th century broke with the so-called Melanchthonian traditionalism and is in clear contrast to the later traditionalism of Calixt. He also implies that the later dogmaticians lost some of Chemnitz' feeling of oneness with the church fathers (as manifested in the Catalog of Testimonies of the *Formula of Concord*). This, I believe, cannot be proved, certainly not in the cases of Gerhard and Calov, who consistently showed the greatest respect toward the church fathers. However, it is true that there was less antipathy toward scholasticism among the Lutherans after Gerhard.
14. Abraham Calov, *Syncretismus Calixtinus* (Wittenberg, 1653), pp. 318 ff.
15. John Conrad Dannhauer, *Mysterium Syncretismi Detecti, Proscripti, et Symphonismo Compensati* (Strasbourg, 1648), p. 49.
16. See, e. g., the accounts of the discussions with the Syncretists in Abraham Calov, *Historia Syncretistica, d. i. Kirchlich Bedenken über den Kirchen-Frieden* (Wittenberg, 1685).
17. See Christian Dreier, *Gründliche Erörterung etlicher schwerer theologischer Fragen* (Königsberg, 1651), pp. 14, 25; George Calixt, *Catholicae Ecclesiae et Oecumenicorum Conciliorum Symbola et Confessiones* (Helmstedt, 1651); George Calixt, *Desiderium et Studium Concordiae Ecclesiasticae* (Helmstedt, 1651); Abraham Calov, *Systema Locorum Theologicorum* (Wittenberg, 1655), IX, 1 ff.; Abraham Calov, *Consensus Repetitus Fidei Vere Lutheranae* (Wittenberg, 1666).
18. Leonard Hutter, *Libri Christianae Concordiae,* prolegomena, pp. 1, 5. See also Dannhauer, *Mysterium Syncretismi Detecti,* p. 157; Leonard Hutter, *Irenicum vere Christianum* (Wittenberg, 1641), p. 126. For a fuller discussion of Hutter's odd phraseology at this point, see Robert Preus, *The Inspiration of Scripture* (Edinburgh: Oliver and Boyd, 1955), pp. 131 ff. Hutter's statement that the Lutheran Confessions are inspired merely meant that the Scriptures are the basis for the Lutheran Confessions and that the latter are inspired in their content for that reason. However, this rather misleading way of speaking was generally abandoned by the confessional Lutherans, and later we have Carpzov saying that, although the Lutheran Confessions contain divine doctrine, they are not inspired as are the Scriptures. See *Isagoge in Libros Ecclesiarum Lutheranarum Symbolicos* (Leipzig, 1665), p. 3.
19. *Exegema Augustanae Confessionis,* editio altera (Wittenberg, 1665), p. B1r.
20. *The Structure of Lutheranism,* trans. Walter A. Hansen (St. Louis: Concordia Publishing House, 1962), Vol. I.
21. In investigating the impact of Luther and Melanchthon on orthodoxy, the great cleavage between Luther and Melanchthon has frequently been emphasized (see Kjell Barnekow, *Niels Hemmingsens teologiska Aaskaadning* [Lund: C. W. K. Gleerups Förlag, 1940], p. 296; Ragnar Bring, *Förhaallandet mellan tro och gärningar inom Luthers teologi* [Abo: Abo Akademi, F. Tilgmanus Boktrykeri, 1934], pp. 233, 253 ff.). However, this split is too often repre-

sented as being due not to Melanchthon's synergism and other doctrinal aberrations but to his semischolastic methodology and preoccupation with philosophy. Then because Melanchthon's methodology rather than Luther's lack of method is followed by all the orthodox theologians, the conclusion is drawn that Luther's break with the Middle Ages and its scholastic theology was more or less repaired by all the later Lutherans. Repeatedly scholars have forgotten that Luther's intense dislike of scholasticism centered in its theology more than its method, and have paid more attention to methodological differences between Luther and Melanchthon than to the theological differences that really divided them. In this way a cleavage is driven between Luther and almost every Lutheran who followed him. But a comparison between Luther and Lutheran orthodoxy must be made on the basis of theology. We shall have occasion to return to this subject.

22. See Brian A. Gerrish, *Grace and Reason* (Oxford: Oxford University Press, 1962); Bengt Hägglund, *Theologie und Philosophie bei Luther und in der Occamistischen Tradition* (Lund: C. W. K. Gleerups Förlag, 1955); Bernhard Lohse, *Ratio und Fides: Eine Untersuchung über die Ratio in der Theologie Luthers* (Göttingen: Vandenhoeck & Ruprecht, 1958); Robert H. Fisher, "A Reasonable Luther," in *Reformation Studies: Essays in Honor of Roland H. Bainton,* ed. Franklin H. Littell (Richmond, Va.: John Knox Press, 1962).

23. Schlink, p. 15.

24. For further reference see C. G. Joecher, *Allgemeines Gelehrten Lexikon* (Leipzig: Johann Friedrich Gleditschen, 1750), II, 1433—44; Melchior Adam, *Vita Germanorum Theologorum* (Heidelberg: John George Geyder, 1720), pp. 668—80; Christian E. Weismann, *Introductio in Memorabilia Ecclesiastica Historiae Sacrae Novi Testamenti ad Juvandam Notitiam Regni Dei et Satanae Cordisque Humanae Salutem* (Halle: Magdeburg, 1745), I, 1456. An excellent biographical source for almost all the Lutheran theologians of the 16th and 17th centuries is *Allgemeine Deutsche Biographie* (Leipzig: Verlag von Duncker und Humboldt, 1875—1912). Less valuable is *Nouvelle Biographie Génerale,* ed. M. le Dr Hoefer (Paris: Firmin Didot Frères, 1862 to 1966).

25. For further reference see Edward Preuss, "Vita Chemnicii," Appendix to Martin Chemnitz, *Examen Concilii Tridentini,* ed. Edward Preuss (Berlin: Gust. Schlawitz, 1861), pp. 921—58; E. Kriewaldt, "The Life and Work of Martin Chemnitz," in *Australasian Theological Review,* VII (April 1936), 33—48; Arthur C. Piepkorn, "Martin Chemnitz' Views on Trent: The Genesis and the Genius of the *Examen Concilii Tridentini,*" in *Concordia Theological Monthly,* XXXVII (January 1966), 5—37; for Chemnitz' own autobiography see Philipp Julius Rehtmeyer, *Kirchenhistorie der Stadt Braunschweig* (Braunschweig: Christoph Fr. Zilliger, 1707—20), III, 277 ff., and for other information on Chemnitz in this work see I, 365—88, II, 519—36 *et passim;* John Theodore Mueller, "Der 'ander Martin' und seine hohe Bedeutung," in *Concordia Theological Monthly,* VII (September 1936), 661—70; Friedrich Bente, *Historical Introduction to the Book of Concord* (St. Louis: Concordia Publishing House, 1965).

26. Cp. John Wigand and Matthew Judex, *Syntagma seu Corpus Doctrinae Veri & Omnipotentis Dei* (Basel, 1560). This is even more similar to a Biblical theology than the *Loci Theologici* of Chemnitz. It too is structured according to Biblical themes, but it contains none of the reference to historical matters and ecclesiastical terms that we find in Chemnitz' work.

27. Martin Chemnitz, *De Duabis Naturis,* has recently been translated into English

by J. A. O. Preus under the title *The Two Natures in Christ* (St. Louis: Concordia Publishing House, 1970).

28. For further reference see Bente; Heinrich Heppe, *Dogmatik des deutschen Protestantismus* (Gotha: Verlag von Friedrich Andreas Perthes, 1857); Melchior Adam, p. 663; Weismann, I, 1,454—55.
29. For further reference see Joecher, II, 1775—77; Melchior Adam, pp. 723—30; Weismann, II, 919—21; Heinrich Heppe, *Geschichte der hessischen Generalsynoden von 1568—1582* (Kassel: Th. Fischer, 1847), 2 vols.
30. For further reference see John Warwick Montgomery, ed. and trans., *Chytraeus on Sacrifice* (St. Louis: Concordia Publishing House, 1962); John Warwick Montgomery, "Cross and Crucible," unpubl. diss. (Strasbourg, 1964).
31. For further reference see *Die Religion in Geschichte und Gegenwart* (Tübingen: Verlag von J. C. B. Mohr, 1928), II, cols. 2,059—60, hereafter cited as *RGG;* Johann Heinrich Zedler, *Grosses vollständiges Universal-Lexikon* (Graz: Akademische Druck — U. Verlagsanstalt, 1961), XIII, 1323—24; Gustav Frank, *Geschichte der protestantischen Theologie* (Leipzig: Breitkopf und Härtel, 1862), I, 330 ff.; Weismann, II, 923—24.
32. For further reference see *RGG,* 3d ed., IV, col. 832; Meno Hanneken, *Oratio Parentalis in Honorem Magni Illius Theologi Dr. Balthasaris Mentzeri,* in Balthasar Mentzer, *Opera Latina* (Frankfort, 1669), I, 1—32; Weismann, II, 927.
33. *Realencyklopädie für protestantische Theologie und Kirche,* begründet von J. J. Herzog, in dritter verbesserter und vermehrter Auflage unter Mitwirkung vieler Theologen und anderer Gelehrten herausgegeben von Albert Hauck, 3d ed. (Leipzig: J. C. Hinrichs'sche Buchhandlung, 1896—1913), XII, 634, hereafter cited as *RE.*
34. For further reference see Friedrich Schenke, *Der Kirchengedanke J. Gerhards und seiner Zeit* (Gütersloh, 1931); August Tholuck, *Lebenszeugen der lutherischen Kirche aus allen ständen vor und während der Zeit des dreissigjährigen Krieges* (Berlin: Wiegandt und Grieben, 1859), pp. 177—97; Carl J. Böttcher, *Das Leben Dr. Joh. Gerhards* (Leipzig and Dresden: Justus Naumann, 1858); Erdmann R. Fischer, *Vita Johannis Gerhardi* (Leipzig, 1723); Karl Heussi, *Geschichte der theologischen Fakultät zu Jena* (Weimar: Hermann Böhlau, 1954), pp. 114 ff.; Johann Friedrich Cotta, *Praefatio de Vita, Fatis et Scriptis Io. Gerhardi,* found in John Gerhard, *Loci Theologici,* ed. Johann F. Cotta (Tübingen: Io. Georg Cotta, 1763), I, viii—lii.
35. For further reference see Helwig; Kornerup.
36. For further reference see Helwig; Garstein.
37. For further reference see Helwig.
38. For further reference see Max Wundt, *Die deutsche Schulmetaphysik des 17. Jahrhunderts* (Tübingen: J. C. B. Mohr, 1939), p. 110; August Tholuck, *Der Geist der lutherischen Theologen Wittenbergs im Verlaufe des 17. Jahrhunderts* (Hamburg and Gotha: Friedrich und Andreas Parther, 1852), pp. 14 ff.; Hans Leube, *Die Reformideen in der deutschen lutherischen Kirche zur Zeit der Orthodoxie* (Leipzig: Verlag von Dörffling und Franke, 1924); Weismann, II, 926; Tholuck, *Lebenszeugen,* pp. 202—209.
39. Tholuck, *Der Geist,* p. 26.
40. For further reference see Otto Ritschl, *Dogmengeschichte des Protestantismus,* 4 vols. (Leipzig: J. C. Hinrichs'sche Buchhandlung; and Göttingen: Vandenhoeck & Ruprecht, 1908—27), IV, 290—341; Joecher, II, 1777—78; Zedler, XIII, 1248—50; Leube.

Notes to Chapter One

41. For further reference see Joecher, II, 198—200; Zedler, VII, 1334—35; Weismann, II, 939; Wilhelm Hornig, *Dr. Johann Pappus von Lindau 1549 bis zu 1610* (Strasbourg: Druck und Verlag von J. H. Ed. Heitz, 1891).
42. For further reference see Tholuck, *Der Geist,* pp. 164 ff.; Joecher, II, 1752 to 54; Weismann, II, 939.
43. For further reference see *RGG,* 3d ed., II, 32; *RE,* 3d ed., IV, 460—64; Leube; John Adam, *Evangelische Kirchengeschichte der Stadt Strassburg bis zur französischen Revolution* (Strasbourg: Druck und Verlag von J. H. Ed. Heitz, 1922), pp. 386 ff.
44. For further reference see Joecher, II, 2171.
45. For further reference see Wundt, p. 117; Jörg Baur; Christoph Hartknoch, *Preussische Kirchen-Historia* (Frankfort on the Main and Leipzig: Beckenstein, 1684); Tholuck, *Der Geist,* pp. 185 ff.; Leube; Weismann, II, 950; J. B. Neveux, *Vie Spirituelle et vie Sociale entre Rhin et Baltique en XVIIe Siècle* (Paris: Libraire C. Klincksieck, 1967), pp. 110—113 *et passim,* also pp. 635—38.
46. Tholuck, *Der Geist,* p. 207.
47. See C. F. W. Walther, "Was ist Theologie?" in *Lehre und Wehre,* XIV (1868), pp. 4 ff.; Adolph Hoenecke, *Evangelisch-Lutherische Dogmatik,* 4 vols. (Milwaukee: Northwestern Publishing House, 1909).
48. *RE,* 3d ed., III, 653.
49. For further reference see Joecher, IV, 301—303; Zedler, XXXV, 421—27; Weismann, II, 961; John Adam, pp. 462 ff.
50. For further reference see Baur; Tholuck, *Der Geist,* p. 214.
51. For further reference see Joecher, II, 2137; Zedler, XV, 1238—39; Ritschl, IV, 216 ff.; Hans Emil Weber, *Der Einfluss der protestantischen Schulphilosophie auf die orthodox-lutherische Dogmatik* (Leipzig, 1908), pp. 35 ff.
52. For further reference see Joecher, I, 891.
53. For further reference see Joecher, IV, 256—57; Weismann, II, 945.
54. For further reference see Heussi, pp. 142 ff.; Weismann, II, 959; John W. Baier, *Compendium Theologiae Positivae,* ed. Carl F. W. Walther (St. Louis: Concordia Publishing House, 1879), I, iii—ix.
55. For further reference see Joecher, II, 1675; Zedler, XII, 635; *RGG,* 2d ed., col. 1, 996.

The Origin and Progress of Prolegomena in Orthodox Lutheran Dogmatics

EARLY DEVELOPMENT
THE CONTRIBUTION OF ANDREW HYPERIUS
THE CONTRIBUTION OF MARTIN CHEMNITZ
THE THEOLOGICAL PROLEGOMENA OF DAVID CHYTRAEUS
JOHN GERHARD AND THE CHANGES IN DOGMATICS
   AND PROLEGOMENA
NICHOLAS HUNNIUS AND THE CLASSIFICATION
   OF THE ARTICLES OF FAITH
THE INFLUENCE OF GEORGE CALIXT
ABRAHAM CALOV AND THE SILVER AGE
   OF LUTHERAN ORTHODOXY
ORTHODOXY IN DECLINE: 18TH-CENTURY THOUGHT
   ON THEOLOGY AND DOGMATIC PROLEGOMENA

Notes to Chapter Two: pages 235—252.

CHAPTER TWO

Protestant dogmatics, as it developed in the 16th and 17th centuries, was something new and singularly significant in the history of Christian doctrine. It was neither an imitation of scholastic theology nor a continuation of Luther's *ad hoc* approach to theological issues. It has an origin and rationale of its own that can be correctly traced and fully grasped only after we have investigated thoroughly the principles and assumptions that underlie it. To understand and evaluate Lutheran dogmatics — or any teaching, for that matter — we must know (1) the presuppositions on which it stands and (2) the attitudes and posture that the dogmatician has felt he must assume for the assignment he has set for himself. In short, we must know a good deal about what is generally called *prolegomena*, and we must know something about the background to these prolegomena.

In prolegomena the theologian looks at himself and his work. Prolegomena seek to set the stage for the theological task. They do not merely outline what the theologian intends to do; but they set the tone for all that will follow, and above all, they lay the ground rules for the theologian in constructing a Christian dogmatics. Prolegomena are the attempt to establish a substructure and starting point for the work of presenting Christian doctrine in the church.

But just as other human disciplines or pursuits are often put into practice before their underlying axioms and assumptions are clearly conceived and spelled out, so it has been in theology. Only after they have been

involved in the work of theologizing — after they have grappled with great problems, encountered serious and pernicious aberrations, and arrived at momentous decisions and conclusions — do theologians look back, retrace their steps, assess what they have done in the light of the sometimes unexpressed principles they have followed, and finally articulate these principles and attitudes that have been so fundamental to their task all along the way. Often belatedly, and necessarily so, the theologians begin to ask the elementary questions of dogmatic prolegomena: What is theology? What is the theologian? What is the source of theology? What is theology's relation to reason and philosophy? What is religion? Significantly, theologians find that they have been implicitly asking these questions continually and answering them piecemeal and unsystematically. They also discover that now in answering the questions explicitly they must bring to bear the conclusions of all their previous theological endeavors. Thus we find that in the more thorough prolegomena of Calov and Quenstedt and Musaeus an entire systematic theology is present in embryo; every major article of faith is considered at least in passing. And we learn as well that theological prolegomena are an ongoing business, for the theologian's assumptions and principles and work must continually be considered anew.

Like philosophy, theology and its concerns and prolegomena will move with the times. But this movement is something like the waxing and waning of the moon: it is usually more or less within a prescribed orbit. The basic, elementary matters have a way of persisting through the years — Is theology (language about God) possible? What is its object? its nature? its goal? Is there a divine revelation? What is the heart of theology (the Gospel)? and so on. In other words, the interests and the subject matter of dogmatics and its prolegomena are perennial. And so Melanchthon or Gerhard or Calov, theologians very influential in their own day, will often say much that is relevant to our age too. Our world view and other scientific, social, and cultural factors conditioning our approach to these perennial concerns of theology have, of course, changed with the times, but the same old concerns remain. In fact, it is surprising how little change there has been in the basic prolegomena of Protestant dogmatics since they were first gradually worked out after the Reformation.

EARLY DEVELOPMENT

The development of prolegomena in Lutheran dogmatics has been long and gradual, becoming with each generation increasingly comprehensive and complex. In the first flush of theological literature by Lutherans after the Reformation there were no formal prolegomena to dogmatic works, and prolegomenous matter can be culled only from the practice of these presuppositions and principles in the body of the dogmatic writings. By the close of the 17th century very large books were written that pertained solely to the introduction to theology. We shall now trace the origin and development of prolegomena in Lutheran theology, a long development covering roughly the period of Lutheran orthodoxy.

The subject and consideration of prolegomena are not new with the theologians of the Reformation. Among the scholastic theologians during the late Middle Ages, subjects such as the nature and purpose of theology, revelation, Scripture, and principles of theological knowledge were considered as prolegomena to the actual working out of any theological system or summa. Thomas' treatment of such prolegomena is brief but most useful. Scotus is far more lengthy. Thus it is not surprising to find Luther expressing himself on the subject of what makes a theologian,[1] on the opposition of theology to philosophy and reason,[2] on the source of theology, and on other matters that could be called prolegomena — but as we might expect with Luther, only in passing. The first edition of the first Protestant dogmatics, Melanchthon's *Loci Communes,* has no prolegomena, and whatever presuppositions Melanchthon had must be garnered from the various *loci.* Melanchthon no doubt thought that such subjects as revelation, Scripture as the source of theology, and theology in relation to philosophy were not necessary to consider in a brief work such as this.

1. *Erasmus*

It is a small book by Erasmus, appearing a year before the first edition of Melanchthon's dogmatics, that first dealt with the study of theology. It therefore merits our attention as the first new contribution to theological prolegomena by one who had broken with the old scholastic tradition. The book, entitled *Ratio seu Methodus Compendio Perueniendi ad Ueram Theologiam,* was printed in Basel in 1520, just 4 years after

Erasmus' edition of the New Testament, and was designed as a help in the study of theology, specifically of the New Testament. It no doubt served somewhat as a justification for his great interest in the Greek New Testament.

Herein Erasmus points out that the narratives of the New Testament are more than mere philosophy; they are prophecy, which is a gift of the Holy Spirit. Therefore the believer ought to prepare his heart for the study of this Word that he might merit being called θεοδίδακτος. The eye of faith must be focused on heavenly things, for theology requires a thirsting soul that thirsts for nothing but the water of life. The theologian seeks nothing for himself. He works with a simple, adoring faith and does not become involved with vain curiosity. The function *(scopus)* of theology, then, is passive; it is to be moved, to be transformed, to be seized by the subject that is studied. In all his advice here Erasmus is quite sane and sound, and some of his pious thoughts are carried over into later introductions by Protestants. He naturally advises a simple, undogmatic approach that avoids contention but retains modesty, peacefulness, and open-mindedness.

The importance of the study of languages for the theologian, especially Latin, Greek, and Hebrew, is dwelt on at great length, a theme also emphasized by most of the later theologians. Translations of the Bible are not sufficient, for Jerome and others have erred, and newer and better manuscripts are being discovered. Besides the languages other subjects ought to be studied — dialectics, geography, history. Erasmus goes on to illustrate at great length the importance of these areas of study for the understanding and interpreting of Scripture. His program for dogmatics is quite simple: "My feeling in this matter is that our young beginner should be offered teachings *{dogmata}* which have been brought together into a summa or compendium, and that this compendium be drawn primarily from the Gospel fountains and secondly from the letters of the apostles, so that the beginner might have definite objectives *{scopos}* to which he correlates those things which he reads." Such a program is significant because, with the exception of the author's partiality toward the gospels over the epistles, it was followed and carried out by Melanchthon, Chemnitz, and the later Lutheran teachers.

The great bulk of Erasmus' book dwells on the type of person a Christian is and on the fundamental (to Erasmus) teachings of Chris-

Early Development

tianity. The Christian is simple, untouched by the world, humble, modest, loving, yet also in his own way wise, rich, noble, and powerful. Here, then, we have the objectives of theology; "these are the new teachings of our author [Jesus Christ]," says Erasmus, "teachings which no family of philosophers ever propounded." There is little solid doctrine in Erasmus' summa or compendium; it is rather in values, in ethics, that Christianity differs primarily from all human wisdom; that is, we have better and more lasting precepts than Aristotle or Plato or Epicurus.

2. Melanchthon

Discussions such as this by Erasmus started theologians thinking in terms of prolegomena. Melanchthon too, with his interest in philosophy, would naturally study and think along such lines, for dialectics and rhetoric, which were a part of philosophy, would be of great use in theology. It was also incumbent on the Lutherans at the very outset of the Reformation to express themselves on the relation of philosophy (not dialectics) to theology and the Gospel, and Melanchthon would be the natural one to undertake this task in a systematic way. Melanchthon's chief contribution in philosophy, *Erotemata Dialectica,* was composed as early as 1520.[3] We must examine some of his contributions in this book, for it had an effect on his *Loci Communes* of the following year — not on the doctrinal content but on the method and arrangement he employed in presenting Christian doctrine.

To the question, What is dialectics? Melanchthon answers: "Dialectics is the art or method of teaching correctly, in an orderly way, and with clarity. This is carried out by rightly explaining, arranging, and connecting the valid evidence, and by unravelling and refuting badly connected and false arguments." Such a definition makes dialectics most useful for dogmatics, and we see Melanchthon taking this fact for granted in the introduction to the 1559 edition of his *Loci Praecipui Theologici.* Chemnitz and the later Lutherans also apply such dialectics in working out their *methodus* of presenting theology in *loci theologici.* To the next question, on the purpose of dialectics, Melanchthon has this to say:

> The purpose of dialectics is to teach correctly, in an orderly manner, and with clarity. Let us then consider the great usefulness and value of this activity. Inasmuch as man has been fashioned in such a way that he might know God, that he might understand the functions of virtues, and that he might explore nature, it is obvious that the work

of teaching man concerning such important matters is of special distinction. The parts of this activity or office are four: to define, to distinguish *(dividere)*, to connect the arguments properly, and finally to refute poorly and falsely connected arguments, and, by making the reason for such error plain, to lead the student away from error to the standards of certainty that we call criteria.

Does all this apply to theology? Melanchthon would reply that dialectics deals with all questions wherein the learning operation takes place, not merely in arithmetic but also in theology. For here too distinctions must be made lest everything be confused and confounded. "One must know that God is one thing, His creatures something else; substances are one thing, accidents something else; God is one thing, the devil who is God's enemy is something else again." And so here too dialectics is the *ars artium,* not because of what it is in itself but because it serves all the arts and sciences.

Melanchthon then goes into the techniques of definition, division, etc., and into the many philosophical distinctions such as universals, species, indivisible entities, genus, difference, attribute, accident, quality, number, etc. In most of this he merely follows Aristotle or sometimes Plato, and he treats the subject as purely analytic. But theological interests are never forgotten by Melanchthon. Thus in speaking on the subject of certain knowledge, he mentions *scientia, ars, prudentia,* and *fides,* such faith being a *noticia* of certain propositions that are embraced with a firm assent because of the statement of a truthful and credible witness. Hence we believe that Alexander was king of Macedon because this information was transmitted by reliable witnesses. Here Melanchthon is treating faith as a *habitus intellectus.* However, faith may also be considered a *habitus voluntatis,* which we would identify with the Christian idea of faith. This is his definition of the latter kind of faith: "Faith is that knowledge by which we embrace with a firm assent all the doctrine which God has vouchsafed to His church, and in this doctrine faith embraces also the promise of reconciliation. As we apprehend this promise with trust in the Son of God we receive the remission of sins; and as with this trust we find our rest in the Son of God, we approach unto God and pray to Him, convinced that we are received and heard."

It is significant that Melanchthon speaks of these two kinds of faith also in his *Loci Communes* of 1539. First there is what the sophists call

assensus, "assent to those things that are set forth in Scripture," [4] what Melanchthon calls "an inactive quality of the mind." This corresponds to the *habitus intellectus* above. But then there is the faith that is nothing else than *fiducia misericoridae,* "trust in the mercy promised in Christ," which puts the heart at peace and causes one to give thanks to God for such mercy and to obey the Law joyfully and willingly.[5] And this corresponds to the *habitus voluntatis* outlined above. A parallel to the above illustration is found also in the *Loci Communes* of 1521 where Melanchthon discusses man. Here he states that man has two capacities: first, understanding *(vis cognoscendi),* by which he thinks and understands, reasons things, compares them, and draws conclusions; second, will *(voluntas),* which contains the passions and affections.[6] From such an anthropology we see how Melanchthon could envision a faith as a *habitus intellectus* and a faith as a *habitus voluntatis.* The point is that the distinctions made in philosophy and the philosophic description of faith as a *habitus* have been brought into dogmatics. Melanchthon is quite hard on both Aristotle and Plato in his writings, especially his *Loci Communes,* and he complains that the church of late had preferred Aristotle to Christ. Yet here, as in many other cases, he is quite in agreement with Aristotle regarding the two parts of the soul.[7] We would expect Melanchthon to say that the intellect serves the will, and he does. Melanchthon will follow Aristotle, often uncritically, wherever he can; but he intends to break with Aristotle the moment the latter conflicts with divine revelation.

In the second book of the *Erotemata* Melanchthon speaks about language *(propositiones)* in which people must speak to be understood and in terms of which people think. Scripture too observes the rules of language. Melanchthon maintains that a proposition is an indicative statement that is one and open in meaning, a statement signifying either truth or falsehood without ambiguity of words, as, e. g., *The sun moves.*

> This is the way we are accustomed to speak and write so that we do not pour forth ambiguities to others in our speech and writing; but we guide our speech along the lines of certain definite propositions and clear statements. From such a viewpoint we also read not only the profane writers but also the writings of the apostles and prophets and we do this with the intention of investigating the statements in these writings just as we might investigate the decisions of judges; we consider what they actually say, and we do not attach diverse interpretations to the single verses, as many have done with the psalms and with Paul.

Melanchthon next analyzes propositions, taking his examples from Scripture. Actually he is here simply working out rules of good grammar.

From the foregoing we see that Melanchthon is not inclined to impose any philosophy or foreign system on dogmatics, but merely to make use of dialectics wherever they can be of help. It is of great significance that Luther has only favorable comments to make on the work of Melanchthon's that we have been considering. Melanchthon has done something here that no one can surpass, Luther contends, and Luther himself proceeds to repeat verbatim the rules and observations of his colleague.[8]

All through his life Melanchthon conscientiously tried to keep his theology free of all philosophical presuppositions and doctrines.[9] Thus in his *Disputatio de Discrimine Evangelii et Philosophiae,* written after Luther's death,[10] he insists that philosophy deals only with the art of speaking, with science, and with civil ethics. As such it is God's gift and is a necessary concern of our bodily and social life, just as food, drink, and public laws. But philosophy teaches only those things that are subject to reason and knows nothing of the Gospel. Hence the Gospel is not a philosophy and must not be turned into a philosophy. It is higher than all philosophy. "The Gospel is not a philosophy or a law, but *it is* the remission of sins and the promise of reconciliation and eternal life for Christ's sake. Human reason in itself is able to grasp nothing concerning such things. Therefore inasmuch as the Gospel teaches God's will concerning us whereas philosophy teaches things that are subject to reason and does not affirm anything regarding the will of God, it is sufficiently clear that the Gospel is not a philosophy." This disputation of Melanchthon's is important. Written after the death of Luther, who might have been a restraining influence on him, it shows that Melanchthon never really changed his views on the relation between theology and philosophy. It reveals also that Melanchthon did not progress beyond what he said in his earlier works that Luther fully endorsed. We must bear in mind that a disputation such as this was ordinarily a carefully organized and well-planned set of theses, which was used again and again at a university. It would not represent immature and undeveloped opinions.

At about the same time as this disputation the final edition of Melanchthon's dogmatics appeared (1559). In this edition he offers a preface to show what he is attempting to do with his dogmatics. Previous to the preface he had written a short letter to the reader in which he said: "It

is beneficial to have clear declarations *{testimonia}* set forth as on a tablet concerning each of the articles of Christian doctrine arranged in good order, in order that, when we consider these things and tie them together, certain definite thoughts come to our view by which troubled people may be instructed, elevated, strengthened, and comforted." Here we have a brief, clear statement: the purpose of dogmatics is to set forth the teachings of Scripture in an orderly way for the edification of the church. Naturally dialectics will be employed to serve this purpose, because dialectics can serve any method of presentation. But as Melanchthon points out in his preface, the method in theology is entirely different from the method in philosophy. Philosophy begins with sense experience or prime notions, which are called principles. Theology does not operate with such demonstration but simply sets forth in proper arrangement those things God has revealed in His Word. The things of God are outside the normal judgment of the human mind, and we become convinced of them only through faith. And it is most necessary that the church teach with such a method (which is actually implied in Scripture itself, e. g., in the Epistle to the Romans) lest the church fall into all kinds of error and blasphemy. Consecrating our wills to this simple task, we will find that the Spirit of God will rule us and keep us from the trickeries of the devil.[11]

Melanchthon's *Loci Praecipui Theologici* of 1559 has many faults and aberrations in doctrine, notably its synergism, but contrary to much popular opinion, there is no indication that philosophizing is the cause of these faults. The preface, which might be called the first prolegomenon to Lutheran dogmatics, spells out the purpose of the book and the method to be used in a concise and highly creditable fashion. The limitations and different method of philosophy are clearly defined. Therefore we cannot blame the aberrations in the body of the book to the presuppositions Melanchthon states or to the method he sets up for himself in this preface. The same presuppositions and method were accepted by later Lutherans who strenuously rejected Melanchthon's doctrinal errors. This is true even of Flacius, whose views on philosophy were as negative as Luther's; like Melanchthon, Flacius is willing to praise Aristotelian ethics as useful for promoting human virtues and happiness in this life, as long as one understands that such ethics do not produce true piety (before God), which is engendered only by the Gospel.[12] A better explanation for Melanchthon's doctrinal errors would be that the devastating nature of humanism, which

Melanchthon never became free of, even after being influenced by Luther for years, finally asserted itself; and we have the full-blown result of this in his synergism expressed in his later writings.[13] Aristotelianism is not the reason for his synergism; rather synergism and humanism are possibly the reason he does not abandon much of his Aristotelian anthropology.

THE CONTRIBUTION OF ANDREW HYPERIUS

After Melanchthon the most important contribution to the advancement of Lutheran dogmatics and prolegomena was a highly significant book by Andrew Hyperius, *De Theologo, seu de Ratione Studii Theologici Libri IIII,* printed in Basel in 1556. The book, by far the most thorough work on the subject to this time, contains four parts. Book I deals with the material to be considered by one who first approaches the subject of theology, that is, the material from other disciplines that must be used also in this study. Book II deals with rules and notations for reading and interpreting Scripture. Book III treats the criteria for dogmatics, or *loci communes,* and deals with the purpose for such a dogmatics. Book IV speaks of the practical application of doctrine within the church; patrology and church history are considered. We must now summarize in some detail the contents of the first three sections.

1. *The Approach to Theology (Book I)*

In Book I Hyperius begins with the proper emphasis on theology as something that can be pursued only with the guidance of the Holy Spirit and at His impulse.[14] No one will work in theology who is not completely dedicated to the Lord: "You will find that no one will seriously make his way into the sacred writings unless God first of all sets his heart ablaze with the earnest desire of knowing Christian teachings"; the arrogant cannot theologize; to be a theologian is a calling. To be discerned here is an emphasis not unlike the stress of Erasmus that was noted above. And it is to be observed that theologizing is identified with working in the Holy Scriptures.

What are the requirements for preparing the mind for teaching the contents of Scripture — for to be regenerate and to be called are only the first requisites? First of all, Hyperius remarks, all vain thoughts must be discarded when we read Scripture, and a holy fear of God must be estab-

lished; this is the beginning of all wisdom. This means total involvement in our task. Simple knowledge in theology is not enough. *Scientia inflat, charitas aedificat.* When knowledge is measured by the norm of love, then true understanding and love increase as one studies in theology. Finally, prayer is required, continuous prayer to God for light and for His Spirit, who would cleanse us and inflame us for theological study.

How may one be assured of advancing steadily in the study of theology? To this question Hyperius replies that it is most important that the student continually keep in mind the priceless value of the subject he is studying. Nothing can be compared to it. For these are heavenly things he is turning his mind to, and God is his Teacher (2 Peter 1:19). He is dealing with the wisdom of very God in a mystery. Moreover, here is something true and certain, since God is the author of theology and God is very Truth, who is unchangeable and cannot deceive or be deceived. And surely God who has told us to read His Word will give us the aptitude to understand it. God has told us that all the Sacred Scriptures and these Scriptures alone *(& solae inquam)* are able to make us wise unto salvation through faith in Christ Jesus. And to this promise He adds that the inspired Scripture is useful for doctrine, etc., that the man of God might be perfectly prepared for all good works. This the apostle tells us that we might know where to find the true and useful doctrine. "Now since you have easily accessible in the Sacred Scriptures that which pertains to your learning, to your actions and to your comfort, what more could you desire? Will you forfeit any part of such a discipline from which all these things are drawn at once, and drawn so munificently and with such certainty?" Philosophers inquire in many roundabout ways concerning what is the highest good, what is the end of man, some saying that this is true, some saying that something else is true; and so it happens that they send out disciples more confused than when they received them. And all the while the Holy Scriptures are able to do away with these controversies, make an end to errors and contention, and demonstrate in a most beautiful manner that the highest good consists in the knowledge of the one true God. Such knowledge Scripture lays bare for all to have.

There is a devotional and hortatory tenor prevailing through these observations of Hyperius'. To him theology is work in the Scriptures toward which he holds the highest reverence and regard. This means that for Hyperius, as for Luther and Melanchthon, theology's conclusions are

certain, momentous, and comforting. Prolegomena will then consist merely in learning what we bring with us in our approach to the Scriptures and in the method and manner in which we deal and work with them. There is a spirit of optimism pervading his writing, a serene confidence that when we place ourselves under the Scriptures they will do their work in us and that in all our study of these writings the Spirit of God will make theologians of us.

What prerequisites in other areas of knowledge are necessary for the future theologian? Hyperius now turns to the subjects of philosophy, dialectics, and language and their bearing on theology. He urges his readers not to listen to those who snarl that there is no reason for such study. Like Melanchthon he insists that God has ordained that these tools be learned as instruments. And he who will not learn them is like a man who refuses to work in order to eat. It is true that God teaches us our theology, but meanwhile it is by no means unnecessary for us to learn the languages, the liberal arts, and the other tools necessary for the theological discipline. God has endowed man with reason, in contrast to beasts; hence speech and reasoning must be cultivated by man in order that he might portray divine things — for God has fashioned all of us that we might contemplate these divine things — portray them in such plain fashion that they can be grasped by faith. The philosophy Hyperius speaks of here is merely the dialectics of language. This is of greatest importance to him, for it is by means of language that God makes Himself known to man and communicates with him.

> For what is the purpose of words? Experience shows that in these matters that commonly come up for discussion among writers the basic principles of the subject matter, the progression, the conclusions, the accompanying circumstances, and whatever other important factors enter in are all considered with much more acuteness by those who are steeped in the fine arts than by those who have never tasted them. Similarly will one who is directed to theological study, as long as he lives and whenever he has occasion, turn the force of his natural talents to the liberal arts, and he will enter on those studies with the best efforts of a diligent disciple. By listening, by repeating, by reading, by composing he will occupy himself in a very justifiable manner, and by persistent work he will try to conquer all difficulties.

The conclusion is that such human philosophy is a gift of God if used properly. And so we ought to learn it, not to test Scripture by its laws,

much less use it as a judge in theological matters, but to clarify Scripture and understand it better. Thus philosophy is admitted as a maidservant or handmaid, as Hagar was once joined to Abraham; but never must we abrogate the right of the wife, Sarah, namely theology.

Following Melanchthon Hyperius designates the three parts of philosophy as (a) dialectics, which deals with language; (b) physics, which pertains to the things of nature; and (c) ethics, which deals with customs and the ways of life.

(a) In regard to dialectics we do not insist on holding to everything known as Aristotelian logic, but we simply speak in terms of definitions, distinctions, arguments, etc., which may aid us in teaching true doctrine.

(b) Physics crosses into the area of theology now and again as when it deals with heavens and earth, fire and water, astronomy, and other natural phenomena such as man, animals, plants, etc. The study of such things, says Hyperius, leads us to the knowledge of the invisible things of God (Rom. 1); and he pursues the matter no further than that. He apparently is not concerned with difficulties that arise sometimes between the reports of Scripture and natural phenomena. Regarding discussions concerning principia, motion, infinity, nothingness, etc., which offer probable and not necessary answers, Hyperius warns that the theologian had best leave such matters alone. Above all the student should avoid the metaphysics of Aristotle and stick with the "true and absolute metaphysics set forth in the Sacred Scriptures." It is clear from the foregoing that Hyperius, like all the theologians of the 16th and 17th centuries, believed that the statements Scripture makes concerning the realm of nature are true and completely binding. Such a belief did not imply that scientific investigation is no longer necessary in those cases where Scripture has spoken concerning various data of nature. In fact the belief implied the very opposite, that scientific finds and a knowledge of nature will sometimes aid us in interpreting Scripture (e. g., the parable of the lost sheep, the parable of the sower).[15] The belief was predicated on the conviction (based on hermeneutics) that many statements in Scripture pertaining to nature were meant to be informative (even though they might be figurative statements) not merely as information concerning nature but as information adjunctive to the articles of faith. To question this belief would be docetic and would threaten such articles of faith as Creation,

the natural knowledge of God, and the Incarnation as well as the facticity of the miracle stories.

(c) As far as heathen ethics and politics are concerned, Hyperius feels that these have little value for the Christian. Christianity knows no especial politics. On this point he departs from Melanchthon's emphasis.

2. *Reading and Interpreting Scripture (Book II)*

The second section of Hyperius' book deals with guides and helps for Scripture reading. His hermeneutical observations are strikingly advanced for that day; but for our purposes it is enough to mention the rules he lays out for reading Scripture. (a) The mind should be free from all vain and earthly thoughts and concerns. (b) We should attempt to draw out the simple and necessary meaning of the words. Whoever looks for hidden or second meanings will never arrive at the truth. (c) We should read the Scriptures always with the concern that practical fruits might come from our reading. And such fruits are manifold. (d) We must pray for the gift of the Holy Spirit, who alone makes us theologians (1 Cor. 2:11). (e) We should explore the Scriptures continually; then what is unclear may often be explained in time. It is the old rule of *Lectio lecta placet, decies repetita placebit.* (f) We must employ patience in our study. When it takes so long sometimes for us to perceive things pertaining to human philosophy and earthly matters, we must realize that we will never fully understand the things that are of God. (g) We ought to employ δοξολογία and humbly thank God for those things we have learned in His Word. After these suggestions for the interpreter's approach to Scripture Hyperius discusses at length specific difficulties and peculiarities in reading Scripture. This discussion of hermeneutics is very instructive.

3. *Criteria for Dogmatics (Book III)*

In Book III Hyperius treats the problem of reading and constructing dogmatics. He points out that the *loci communes* method is simply a thematic treatment of a subject, whether in law, natural science, or theology. Typical *loci* that could be considered in theology are Scripture, God, Trinity, Creation, angels, man, the church, the Fall, etc. We notice that Scripture is suggested as the first *locus* already at this early date. Such *loci* Hyperius calls the rudiments and general principles of theology

(elementa, & communia quaedam principia theologiae), and unless these are placed and handled in their proper order, "you will never gain certainty concerning the questions proposed in theology." At this point Hyperius is taking his lead from the medieval scholastics who taught that sacred theology is a science proceeding from *principia* established by God, namely, the articles of faith.[16] Hyperius next mentions in summary the work that had been done in the past in systematic theology, tracing also the deterioration that, beginning with John of Damascus, reached its culmination in Peter Lombard and his many intricate and vain questions.

As hints and rules for the reader of systematic theology Hyperius has the following suggestions to make: Know the background, the method, and the presuppositions of the writer. Do not be bound to him in all that he says, for he may be speaking only to his day; a theological work will always breathe the spirit of its own day. Read an author completely. Know the Scriptures and the commentaries, for therein we have help in judging any author. There are also certain common dangers to be avoided in studying theology: (a) the fact that certain systematicians agree does not mean that they have always exhausted the subject of discussion. (b) Beware of making judgments based on the evidence of only one theologian. (c) Be careful to judge every theologian by the Scriptures, for even the best theologians have sometimes brought an admixture of philosophy into theology.

In the last part of Book III Hyperius expends no fewer than 40 pages projecting an outline for sound Lutheran dogmatics.

Hyperius' discussions that we have considered are most important in the history of the development of prolegomena and of dogmatics in the Lutheran Church. Nothing even approaching its vast scope had ever appeared before. His studies illustrate that the compartmentalization of the various theological disciplines had not been envisaged nearly so rigidly then as we have carried out the program today. It is noteworthy that hardly anyone in the 16th century worked merely in dogmatic theology, and the dogmatics books were filled with exegetical elaborations and discussions. It is also worthy of note that the first Lutheran dogmatics, the *Loci Communes* of Melanchthon, was merely a methodical arrangement of the theology of Romans, sprang from a classroom exposition of that book, and was designed only as an aid to those who undertook the study of Scripture.[17] Thus as late as Hyperius we find no clear-cut distinction

88 CHAPTER TWO *Origin and Progress of Prolegomena*

between what we today call exegetical theology and systematic theology. And we find that Hyperius' suggestions and prolegomena are as much directed to exegesis as to dogmatics.

THE CONTRIBUTION OF MARTIN CHEMNITZ

Before turning to the contribution of Martin Chemnitz in the development of dogmatics and its prolegomena, we must briefly consider the *Syntagma* of Wigand and Judex, which on a few points advances beyond the position of Hyperius.

1. Preliminary Development of Wigand and Judex

This remarkable book by Wigand and Judex resembles more closely what we today would call a Biblical theology than a work in dogmatics.[18] The introduction to the book reminds the reader of the various gifts of God, which include both the things of nature and revealed theology. In respect to the things of nature we must speak according to certain categories *(metae),* such as origin, simplicity and diversity, form, matter, purpose, properties, etc. In like manner we must speak of theological things, since theology too is a gift of God.[19]

Having offered this brief explanation of what they will be doing in the lengthy study to follow, Wigand and Judex proceed to insist against certain ignorant and rude men that theology cannot be mixed with philosophy. Here they emphasize what Melanchthon and Hyperius have already taught on the relation of philosophy and theology, but one will note a more negative note toward philosophy. "Philosophy does not give rise to things theological, and we should not seek theology from philosophy. We learn sacred theology and draw articles of faith from the fountains of Israel, the authentic Biblical texts. He who does otherwise and confuses philosophical principles with the articles of faith commits an awful crime." For philosophy in the nature of the case has its own categories and limitations.

On the other hand, theology does not spurn human aids *(adiumenta);* it does not do away with language and the art of speaking. God is not a God of disorder, but the Holy Spirit is the author of the Sacred Scriptures and of all good pursuits. Hence no one will object to a sound framework of doctrine *(corpus integrum doctrinae)* drawn from Scripture, un-

less he is more stupid than stupidity itself. The Scriptures themselves contain such a framework in that they set forth a historical narrative.[20] Therein the deeds of God are portrayed and related according to the unique inspiration and goodness of God, and for this goodness we should be eternally grateful. However, to employ these sacred writings usefully and thus to teach sacred doctrine consists not merely in drawing out certain notable passages but in marking out the entire structure of doctrine, the harmony and context into which everything ties together, and in distinguishing between those things that ought to be kept apart. For an unwise and dissonant fusing of articles of faith will give rise to serious errors. It is difficult to retain between readings the entire framework of theology offered in the Scriptures. Therefore this corpus can well be set forth with clear notations in order that it may be recognized and known. For the sake of orderly arrangement categories may be observed. Then a single and solid doctrine, clearly drawn from Scripture, can be recited in an orderly way and explained to the understanding of all. Such an orderly arrangement of the parts of doctrine always makes for clarity and for ease in teaching. To reject such a method is to make theology an unnecessarily difficult task.

What is the purpose of a body of doctrine of this sort? It is useful in confirming definitely the chief parts of doctrine and for discerning true doctrine from false in times of controversy. Precisely this is what Paul admonishes when he says, "Prove all things" (1 Thess. 5:21). We prove and hold fast that which is good by means of the Word of God. When one does not observe the above practice, one will be driven by every wind of doctrine. It is this practice of producing a *corpus doctrinae* that the authors wish to present in their *Syntagma;* they wish to gather the thoughts and doctrine of God into one unified structure, one corpus.

There is perhaps nothing so very new or remarkable in all that Wigand and Judex have said here except the increased emphasis on the fact that the *loci* method and the method of setting forth a *corpus doctrinae* is the method of Scripture itself. Not that Wigand and Judex are merely quoting or repeating Scripture, but they are using a method implicit in Scripture and employing it for their own day. It is important that we recognize that neither Melanchthon nor Wigand and Judex nor Chemnitz (as we shall see) were aware of imposing anything upon the Scriptures in operating as they did with the *loci* method in theology. There is no assumption

here of any higher synthesis than that which may be drawn from Scripture itself, the synthesis of Law and Gospel. It ought to be mentioned that the *Syntagma* is not a work in what we would call systematic theology. Thus we discern that to the theologians of the 16th century the structuring of *loci theologici* and of a *corpus doctrinae* belong as much to the exegete as to the dogmatician. In fact there was at that time no clear demarcation between dogmatics and exegesis.

2. *Dedicatory Letter by Polycarp Leyser*

We must now turn to the most important contribution to dogmatic theology in the Lutheran Church in the 16th century, the *Loci Theologici* of Martin Chemnitz. This large work, patterned after the *Loci Communes* of Melanchthon, was first published in 1591, five years after Chemnitz' death. It was brought out and dedicated by Polycarp Leyser. Neither Leyser in his dedication nor Chemnitz is concerned about the relation of philosophy to theology, and there is still no formal prolegomenon. There are, however, a number of interesting points we must note, first in Leyser's dedication and then in Chemnitz' introductory statements on the *loci* method and in his later statements on theology.

Leyser begins his remarks with a strong defense of the *loci* method of presenting theology. He comments that the church of God from the very beginning has had special articles of doctrine *(praecipui loci)*, compressed and set forth in summary fashion according to certain order and method. All other doctrine was in turn examined and tested by the norm of these *praecipui loci*. Leyser insists that such a practice is no modern innovation but is a mode of operation derived from Scripture itself, where we find severe prohibitions from God against departing from sound doctrine by following our own opinions (Eph. 4:14). The very decay of the church is marked by this, that every man did what was right in his own eyes (Judg. 17:6; 21:25). Leyser says that according to the evidence of Scripture God has always desired a brief and definite summation *(summa)* of His doctrine to prevail in the church and that this be set forth without ambiguity. Such a summa — not to be confused with the medieval idea of a summa — or summation, serves as a norm and rule *(canon & certa regula)* according to which simple people may examine the doctrine that is taught; and if the public doctrine does not agree with this canon it may safely be rejected. Leyser no doubt has in mind those many passages of

the New Testament that speak of holding fast sound doctrine and tradition, e. g., 2 Thess. 2:15; 3:6; 2 Tim. 3:10; 1 Tim. 4:6, 13, 16; 6:1-2; Titus 1:9; 2:1, 10; Rom. 6:17; 16:17; 2 John 9; 2 Tim. 1:13. Such a method of summing up doctrine Leyser traces back to the first promise given our first parents after the Fall. That brief saying *(sententia)* came to serve as a source of all later prophetic preachments.

> Hence it is the sum of the entire Christian doctrine and of all the articles of our faith. For although our first parents and the other patriarchs after them spoke in the church and in their public meetings with many words about creation, about their bitter fall and the sin and corruption of their entire nature, about the wickedness, cleverness, and power of the devil, about the Redeemer Christ and faith in Him the Mediator, about the exercise of that faith and of repentance, about cross-bearing, death, resurrection, and other matters, still that brief saying remained always their canon and rule of faith.

At the time of Moses too the same procedure was carried out, and the law of Moses served as a touchstone even for those later prophets whose testimony was confirmed by miracles and who were preserved by God. Indeed we hear the very last of the prophets urging, "Remember the law of Moses" (Mal. 4:4). "Whence it is clear that in the whole ancient church faithful teachers arranged with correct and clear words the body of doctrine into short summations; and all their explanations and public preaching from then on were brought into harmony with these summations. As a result they confined themselves in their teaching within these definite limitations, and thus their hearers were able to grasp mentally these summations of doctrine." Where this practice was not observed in the church, philosophical opinions inevitably became mixed with the true doctrine of the Scriptures and the articles of heavenly doctrine made to conform to human reason.

From the foregoing, Leyser concludes, it is clear that theology, as it was carried out in former days under the Spirit's inspiration and guidance and as it is pursued today with the Spirit's guidance, is a necessary activity of the church. And so the church must engage in this sort of dogmatics; this is the teaching ministry of the church. It was this activity that was carried on by John the Baptist and also by the Son of Man Himself, who repeatedly corrected the teachings of scribes and Pharisees not by a new *corpus doctrinae* but by calling forth the testimony of Moses, the psalms, and the prophets. Time and again He summarized their teachings, and He urged

His disciples to continue in this when He commanded, Go and teach all the nations; teach them to observe all things; preach repentance and remission of sins in My name. This command was observed not only by the immediate apostles but also by Luther in his Small Catechism, which brings together the pure apostolic and prophetic doctrine into one fine corpus. Melanchthon did the same with his *Loci Communes;* and now Chemnitz elaborates on Melanchthon's work to show how the various articles of faith cohere and what the limits are to which one can proceed. Chemnitz also includes the struggles of the ancient church and the controversies of the present in his work, for theology must always be relevant and timely.

In this dedicatory letter of Leyser's there is a more definite and clearer idea of the purpose and nature of a dogmatic work than has been seen heretofore. The strong emphasis on summa is new, and it is important to appreciate that to Leyser this is the practice of Scripture. We must understand, therefore, that what he is advocating is not just an arbitrary, orderly structuring of theology but a God-given duty incumbent on the confessing church. We notice also a stronger symbolic emphasis in that this ecclesiastical summa becomes or is called a *norma, canon, regula, archetypus.* Systematic theology — if the term is appropriate even at this time in the Lutheran Church — works to establish a norm in the church that will delimit and also unify theology. As we shall see, these emphases of Leyser's are drawn from Chemnitz' *Loci Theologici.*

3. *The* Loci Theologici

a. THE CHURCH FATHERS. Chemnitz begins his great dogmatic work with a section on the importance of reading the church fathers. As a librarian he had acquired a great interest in patrology. In his answer to the Council of Trent he had also dug deeply into the theology of the church fathers. As was noted, Melanchthon too had stressed the importance of reading the church fathers, and so had Hyperius; but in Chemnitz we have a specific introductory section on the subject. He feels that the fathers have contributed much to the church. Often they have put things well and clearly. By studying the controversies in which they were engaged, we may be helped to settle similar controversies of our own day. Moreover, we learn from such reading the form of doctrine that was present in the church of all ages. Most of this section contains a summary of the activity and an estimate of the value of the leading church fathers.

The attention given by Chemnitz to the fathers is carried on by John Gerhard and Abraham Calov in their dogmatic works, and to a lesser degree by all the later Lutherans. But never again in a dogmatics was there a special section like this one on the importance of reading the church fathers. This innovation of Chemnitz' is not insignificant: Chemnitz is the first to bring the systematic study of church history and the history of doctrine into a book dealing specifically with Christian doctrine.

b. THE EARLY THEOLOGICAL *Loci.* Another new feature of Chemnitz' work is an introductory section "on the use and benefit of theological *loci.*" This section, like the preface to Melanchthon's *Loci Praecipui Theologici,* might be considered an attempt at a sort of prolegomenon. As in Leyser's dedication, Chemnitz explains that a *summa doctrinae coelestis* was contained in the promise first given Adam and Eve after the Fall. He then traces the development of this method through the history of the church. He suggests that this summa was perhaps expanded at the time of Enoch, who began to call on the name of the Lord: no doubt there was at that time conversation about sin, the devil, the coming Redeemer, and faith in Him. Moses does not record all this because the one simple promise could serve as a sufficient *canon* and *regula,* as a *fons totius illius doctrinae.* Moses offers only a brief summa of the promises and revelations of God. During Moses' time God showed that He was a very excellent artificer of orderly teaching *(optimus methodi artifex)* when He gave the doctrine of the law written on two tablets of stone. And the prophets based all their doctrine of the law and their amplifications of it on Moses (Mal. 4:4). The prophets too used the same method, arranging their discourses according to chief doctrines of theology *(praecipua doctrinae capita),* that the doctrine might be remembered and be clear to all who heard and read. Time and again the prophets were commanded to write the visions they saw and to explain them (Hab. 2:2; Deut. 1:5; Is. 8:1; etc.). "Thus Isaiah is commanded to write such a summation in a human style, that is to say, to write such a summation in words that are correct and clear and in common use, in such a way that the summation be neither ambiguous nor unclear, neither difficult nor involved, but that all might be able to understand it."

The same practice is carried on by John the Baptist, the apostles, and Christ Himself (see above, p. 91). Such a method is found particularly in Paul's letters, where he touches and explains all the articles of faith.

We find him presenting doctrine in a brief manner without elaborate proof and confutation (Ephesians); and we find him teaching and explaining each of the articles of doctrine in an orderly fashion (Romans). This is done to suit the exigencies of the time and of future generations.

After the canonical Scriptures were written, the church soon felt the need to sum up the doctrine these books embrace. Hence the Apostolic Creed arose, which was called by Tertullian, Irenaeus, and the older fathers the *regula et canon fidei,* for it summed up in a few heads the apostolic doctrine. Because of wolves this was called also a symbol (as in military parlance) that would serve as a standard around which the church could rally and by which it could judge who preached Christ according to the apostolic norm. Thus Irenaeus remarks that the barbarians of his day had the apostolic tradition and were actually able to judge doctrine, although they had no writings. As time went on, more controversies gave rise to more creeds. For teaching purposes summae were written. Practically all the fathers wrote something according to such a method — e. g., Hermas, Clement of Alexandria, Theophilus *(Tres Libri Institutionum),* Origen *(Peri Archon),* Cyprian *(Expositiones Symboli),* Augustine *(Enchiridion).* No fewer than 10 titles have been given these orderly summae over the years: *Symbolum, Canon Fidei* (Irenaeus), *Regula Fidei* (Tertullian), εἰσαγωγή, *Elementa,* Κατήγησις, ὑποτύπωσις, *Institutiones, Principia, Dogmata Ecclesiastica,* and *Enchiridion,* which we call *Loci Communes.* All this was to preserve the truth of doctrine against all adversaries and to preserve and propagate sound doctrine in the church.

c. THE TAINT OF PHILOSOPHY. Chemnitz points out that by the time of John of Damascus the form of sound doctrine that had obtained in the earlier church began to degenerate: human opinions and curious questions that did not make for edification were incorporated in the teaching; Scripture lost its centrality, and books on extraneous and fanciful questions replaced the testimony of Scripture; the Scriptural mode of speaking was gradually abandoned, and a new and more involved mode of speaking was introduced, which brought a change of doctrine. This tendency, beginning with John of Damascus, became more pronounced as time went on until it was full-blown in medieval scholastic theology. "These theologians did not construct their doctrine *{corpus doctrinae}* from Scripture or from the fathers but from the common and chronic errors and abuses of their own times and from the writings of philosophers. The result was that the

form of doctrine and the terminology of the church were utterly transformed; and faith was taken captive in obedience to reason, as their writings show."

Here we see the same ardent dislike for scholastic theology that was so evident in Luther. Although he followed the method of Melanchthon, Chemnitz was untainted with Aristotelianism. Not only specific statements but his entire treatment of theology is a quiet polemic against the superfluous use of philosophic and scholastic concepts and jargon. Chemnitz points out that it was not until Luther that the church was finally liberated from the deadly tendency that had taken hold already with John of Damascus. Luther brought theology back to the fountains of Scripture and to the rule of the prophetic and apostolic faith.

d. THE RETURN TO SCRIPTURE. Chemnitz stresses what he considers extremely urgent advice for every theologian. He is intensely concerned that theology remain plain and simple, unencumbered with scholastic and philosophical terminology, which not only confuses but perverts clear teaching in the church. "There ought to be a limit to subtleties in distinctions," he says later in his dogmatics, "and they should be applied only for the sake of enlightenment and instruction. Otherwise all points, even those that have been most fittingly transmitted, can be disturbed by sophistries."[21] We must return to the terminology and wording of Scripture. In presenting doctrine Chemnitz is determined that "the language of the Holy Spirit and the modes of speaking used in the ancient church be imitated, and that except in cases of necessity we abstain from new phrases."[22] Not only the Biblical phraseology but the very Biblical order of presentation ought to be observed whenever possible. In speaking of the arrangement of the *locus* on justification, Chemnitz believes that a definite Pauline order should be maintained; the theologian should consider (1) what the Gospel is in contrast to the Law; (2) the meaning of the words *justify, righteousness,* and *righteous* as they are used in the Gospel, (3) the meaning of such words as *grace* and *freely,* (4) what justifying faith is and what it clings to, and (5) the place of good works, since these are expressly removed from the article of justification.[23] To retain the Scriptural arrangement of doctrine and the Scriptural terminology is the first rule to be observed in dogmatics. Chemnitz continues:

> We must not fancy that the explanation of words is a trivial or childish pursuit. Just as the subject matter in this article occupies a place

far above and beyond the range of reason, so also in this doctrine of justification the Holy Spirit has certain words of His own that diverge from common usage. Thus the church ought to be philological *(Grammatica)*, that is, it should not fashion new things or give rise to new dogmas, but the church ought to teach those things that have been handed down by the Holy Spirit and teach from the genuine meaning of the words that Scripture uses in presenting the divine doctrine. We will show later that the neglect of true philology has been the fountain and spring of all errors in this article.

Chemnitz' earnest insistence on a return to the categories and terminology of Scripture in writing dogmatics was an invaluable contribution to Lutheran theology, and it is only to be regretted that later Lutherans often failed to follow his wise counsel.[24] Chemnitz' convictions in this matter do not grow out of scholarly interests only, but also from a pious and practical concern that theology be kept plain and clear. This is also the reason for his advocating the construction of a clear and simple *corpus doctrinae*. It is just this practical concern that prompts Chemnitz to extol Melanchthon's Augsburg Confession, "which brings together a very fine *corpus doctrinae* from the various writings of Luther and contains a summation of all the articles of faith, explained in a correct and clear manner." Chemnitz also praises Melanchthon's *Loci Communes* for its simple and excellent method of presenting and explaining the articles of faith. His conclusion is that "it is by all means necessary to have a summation of doctrine presented in a definite systematic arrangement and in proper words."

This is precisely what Chemnitz aims to accomplish in his great *Loci Theologici,* which, although bulky and repititious, is very easy reading and quite free of intricate terminology. On a much grander scale Chemnitz is carrying out the same purpose as Melanchthon — gathering all the Scripture evidence pertaining to the various *loci* that he considers, examining this evidence, and then presenting the doctrine of Scripture on each *locus*. The only things arbitrary are the choice and arrangement of *loci,* and of course his selection of Biblical data. The only element in this work that makes it differ from the *Syntagma* of Wigand and Judex is the historical perspective and reference.

e. THE CHEMNITZ METHOD. The method of *loci theologici* as proposed and carried out by Chemnitz has some definite advantages to commend it. Unhampered by any higher synthesis that would hold the *loci* together, each

locus is a unit in itself. Hence there is an extreme flexibility in the method. We find the theologians of the 16th and early 17th century varying widely in their arrangement of the various *loci* and in the subject matter they consider under specific *loci*. For instance, Heerbrand, who wrote before Chemnitz, begins with a *locus* on Scripture. Chemnitz offers no such *locus*. Hafenreffer begins with the *locus* on God and then proceeds to Scripture as his fourth *locus*. Concerning the subject matter to be considered under individual *loci*, the possibilities were limitless. Hafenreffer and Brochmand present the work of Christ and justification as separate *loci*. Gerhard discusses the work of Christ under one *locus* and then proceeds to present much of the same material in his *locus* on justification. His treatment of Christ's active obedience under the Law within the *locus* on justification makes good sense and relates justification to Christology in a manner that the later analytic method was not capable of doing. Chemnitz, who presents fewer *loci* than the other dogmaticians, brings a great many Biblical themes under his treatment of justification. He begins with a long discussion of Law and Gospel. He also treats the Gospel (promises) in the Old Testament as it relates to the doctrine of justification. Universal grace and many other themes are also dealt with. Thus the necessary connection between the articles of faith is maintained by the *loci* method of writing dogmatics.

It might be asked whether the method Chemnitz advocates does not lead to too much freedom in presenting Christian doctrine, so that a certain amount of confusion results. Chemnitz would probably answer that as long as pure doctrine is taught, freedom in arranging the articles of faith is no disadvantage. But Chemnitz would also insist that there is an inner unity in Christian theology, a harmony between the articles of faith. This harmony will guide the dogmatician in his work; the dogmatician must merely observe the analogy of faith. Chemnitz says: "Paul in Rom. 12:6 rightly warns that every prophecy, that is, all doctrine and interpretation of Scripture in the church, must be referred to and guided according to the analogy of faith; that is, that all doctrine and interpretation must be in agreement with the fundamental or primary points of the faith that have express, clear, sure, and firm witness in the Scripture, and there must be no conflict with these primary and fundamental points." [25] And how will the theologian be sure that he is observing the analogy of faith in all his activity? By relating all to Law and Gospel. "For these two are the

foremost *loci* and the foremost heads of Scripture, to which all parts are to be related." [26] Chemnitz is persuaded that when the theologian properly divides Law and Gospel, any approach may be made in presenting the articles of faith and will be successful; for the source of all error lies in the confusion of Law and Gospel. "The desire to reconcile the doctrine of the Law and of philosophy with the Gospel is the source and origin of all corruptions." [27]

One more remark must be made before we leave our study of Chemnitz. Chemnitz is the first Lutheran to write an expansive dogmatics in the modern sense, that is, with a view toward the history of Christian doctrine. Chemnitz' interest in history is an important advance in the development of systematic theology. To him dogmatics is the combination of two specific disciplines: history (church history and the history of dogma) and Biblical study (exegesis). All his discussions may be classified as either historical or Biblical. For instance, in his treatment of the doctrine of justification he feels constrained to deal with the historical development of the article. This procedure, he feels, "shapes the judgment in the present controversies; it sharpens the earnestness in preserving the purity of sound doctrine and in avoiding all corruptions of whatever kind." [28] It is interesting that Chemnitz' rather thorough investigations of the heresies that have arisen concerning this *locus* begin with the account of our first parents immediately after the Fall and continue through the Old and New Testaments and through the entire history of the church.

THE THEOLOGICAL PROLEGOMENA OF DAVID CHYTRAEUS

It has been evident that dogmatics, whether it takes the form of *loci theologici* or of a compendium, works in Lutheran theology to serve exegesis, that is, to present a summation of Biblical testimony on the articles of faith.[29] This being the case, it will not be surprising to find that similar methodology will be employed within exegetical works and what we might envisage as belonging to dogmatic prolegomena will be found within many commentaries. It is true that the Lutheran theologians of the 16th century did not identify the method of exegesis with the *loci* method, but they did regard the purpose and task of exegesis and of *loci theologici* as quite the same. This fact becomes apparent when one peruses

some of the commentaries of the 16th century. The commentary of David Chytraeus on the five books of Moses [30] will now be examined to learn what similarities are to be found between what he says by way of prolegomena and what has already been said by the dogmatic theologians we have studied. We find that Chytraeus considers also many new matters that were later to become important interests for dogmatic prolegomena.

1. *Source for Theology*

In the introduction to this commentary Chytraeus begins with an interesting section on the self-disclosure of God and on the authority and certainty of the divine Word and doctrine revealed to the church in the books of Moses and the other inspired writings. He says:

> The foundation of all theology and of the Christian religion, the criterion and norm of the certainty and the truth of all doctrine and all theological convictions, dogmas, and worship in the church is the divine authority and revelation, which is one and immovable, i. e., the Word of God. This Word is the clear authority of God Himself and of His Son the Logos, who speaks and announces the divine majesty to the human race and who is our Lord and Redeemer Jesus Christ. This Word was revealed directly by voice and then handed down to the church by the fathers (Moses, the prophets, and the apostles), who were incited by the inspiration and afflatus of the Holy Spirit. It was confirmed by the sure and clear testimonies of miracles, such as the exodus from Egypt, the giving of the Law on Mount Sinai, many resurrections from the dead, and similar signs.

Because of the corruption of human nature it was not possible for man to know God without God *(sine Deo Deum cognoscere)*. God must become his teacher. And God teaches man what he must believe and do in this one way, "by revealing Himself to man in His Word." In no other way will man know God's nature and will. In no other way will he learn to worship God, praise Him, or believe in Him. In no other way will he even discover how to govern his own actions. Chytraeus then shows that this principle that God must inform us of God and of faith in Him and that He does this in His Word, the prophetic and apostolic Scriptures, is precisely the principle that Christ and the apostles used. (Luke 16:31; Is. 8:20; John 5:39; 1 Cor. 1:21; 3:11; Eph. 2:20; Is. 51:16; Rom. 10; Matt. 15:9)

2. Darkness of Heathen Religions

Having considered the source for all theology, Chytraeus next turns to a consideration of heathen religion, a subject that was to become important in later dogmatic prolegomena. The heathen (Plato) taught that there was a God who was eternal and who established and preserves all things, that He is just and punishes evil, etc. But heathen religion does not know of the promised Seed who would reconcile the sinful world to God. Moreover, heathen religion foolishly worshiped many gods and introduced gruesome rites and orgies into its worship. Plato said we ought to worship God with a pure heart, and not created things. Aristotle too saw the error of such idolatry. But even the most enlightened heathen had nothing positive to offer. Against such darkness, Chytraeus says: "The true Christian religion means to know *{agnoscere}* rightly the one true God, Maker of heaven and earth, who is the eternal Father, the Logos His Son, our Lord Jesus Christ, and the Holy Spirit, to call upon Him, to worship Him with true faith and obedience, as He has revealed Himself in the Law and the Gospel, which has been brought forth from the hidden counsel of divinity through Christ." It is Law and Gospel that makes Christianity unique and distinguishes it from false religions. This is the simple distinction according to Chytraeus: "Christians have the Law, the complete Law, and they have it incorrupt. But in particular they know rightly the Son of God, our Lord Jesus Christ (according to the Gospel), who suffered and rose for us; and for the sake of this Son Christians say that they obtain forgiveness of sins and eternal life. And with trust in the Mediator they call upon God, and they praise Him with a grateful mind and with works of obedience."

3. Certainty of Doctrine

But how may we become certain of the Christian doctrine? And God desires us to have a strong certainty *(certa & immota sententia)* in such matters. God's revelation, says Chytraeus, has been transmitted in His Word, which reveals God and is accompanied by certain and infallible witnesses *(testimonia)*. In all other teaching there are three sources *(fontes, normae)* of certitude: general experience; principia, or innate ideas; and logical conclusions *(intellectus consequentiae)*. Under innate ideas Chytraeus included (like Melanchthon) not only mathematics (which is self-evident) but also natural law. The Gospel, however, which deals with

the grace of Christ and His work on our behalf, is not learned from sense experience or through natural knowledge but is known and embraced because of divine authority and revelation, an effective authority that authenticates itself.

But in spite of God's workings in history with clear words and unmistakable testimonies, there are many who reject God and fancy His revelation and Word to be just so many fables. And others feel that all religions are of equal validity. In giving answer to this problem Chytraeus embarks on a new course that will be pursued by many stystematic theologians of the following century and that unfortunately is far from convincing in many places. There are many arguments, he maintains, that should help the Christian distinguish between Christianity and all pagan religions. Chytraeus is clearly engaging in apologetics as he presents his arguments, and he seems to sense the inherent weakness of such an approach — he points out that it must be said by way of introduction that these arguments are not in themselves convincing; only God can confirm and seal in our hearts full assurance. But apparently these arguments carry some weight for the believer, for Chytraeus dwells on them at some length.

(a) One argument is miracles, which accompany the proclamation of the doctrine of the Gospel. This may be observed throughout the Bible history.

(b) The general experience of all pious people is "a weighty and important criterion" of certainty. Here the author is speaking of the experience of being delivered from the wrath of God, the experience of forgiveness and a peaceful conscience, experiences common to children of God. Just as experience verifies and certifies in philosophy, it offers certainty in theology. But there is a vast difference between philosophic and Christian experience, just as there is a difference between the principia of both. In philosophy experience precedes assent: I first observe the heavens moving in a certain pattern; then I assent to the proposition that the heavens move in a circular path. In matters of faith and Christianity assent precedes experience: David first believes Nathan's absolution; then he feels comfort and peace of conscience. Scripture testifies to this by word and example very often, as in 2 Chron. 20:20, "Believe in the Lord your God, so shall ye be established; believe the prophets, so shall ye prosper"; and in Is. 7:9, "If ye will not believe, surely ye shall not be established"; and in Rom. 5:1, "Being justified by faith, we have peace with God."

Cicero, Brutus, Cato, and all the others can join in extolling philosophy as sustaining them in trouble and in death, but David can boast of an experience of God's help (Ps. 18) that no philosopher has ever known. Clearly no one will occupy himself long in the study of theology unless in his daily prayers and tribulations he experiences the force and power of the Gospel. Thus the Christian experience and certainty come through the deep experience of sin and grace.

(c) Another argument for the truth of Christianity is its antiquity. Chytraeus favors Tertullian, who taught that innovations in teaching were *eo ipso* false. Since God has fashioned the human race to worship Him, it follows that He would at the very beginning instruct man about the correct doctrine and worship. Chytraeus observes that Christ points to Moses and the prophets. The first compendium of theology was already included in the first four chapters of Moses, and all the later prophets went on from there and drew from that first theology. The doctrine of Moses that came to be handed down is the most ancient doctrine.

(d) Prophecy and fulfillment is an argument for the truth of the Christian faith. Only in Christianity has such predictive prophecy obtained. Chytraeus offers four reasons for such prophecy taking place. First, God thereby demonstrates Himself to be the true God as He has revealed through the prophets. Second, His doctrine is certified as divine. Third, fulfillment was a constant source of comfort to God's faithful people, especially in times of trouble and persecution. Fourth, the church was guided in her present actions by a knowledge of what was to transpire. There are many examples of the comfort predictive prophecy has inspired.

(e) The Christian doctrine authenticates itself. It is above all philosophy and all that our reason can grasp or imagine. No human wisdom could have spun out such teachings as the Incarnation, the Passion of the Son of God, the Resurrection, the cause of sin and death, forgiveness, immortality, and the future judgment.

Thus far, one might not perhaps be inclined to criticize Chytraeus. Many of his observations in these arguments are Biblical and convincing. But as he goes on, his arguments become completely extraneous to the message of Scripture and the Gospel, and hence unconvincing. He betrays a certain lack of conviction himself in making these latter arguments very brief. (f) Only Christianity has brought fully correct morality into the world, e. g., monotheism against polytheism, the outlawing of human sac-

rifices, gladiatorial games, and many other awful customs. (g) True chastity is taught only in Christianity. (h) Christianity offers the best explanation of the origin and history and chronology of the world. (i) There has been a continuity of teaching in the Christian church from the beginning. (j) Christianity has remained through all ages. (k) In spite of persecution the teachings of Christianity have held up. (l) The devil hates Christianity. (m) The great deeds of God serve as testimonies to the truth of Christianity, e. g., the giving of the Law and the resurrection of Christ. (n) The witness of the martyrs continues from Abel to the present. (o) Punishments have descended on blaspheming heretics, e. g., Jeroboam, Ahab, Sennacherib, Herod, Julian, Nero, Arius. (p) The power of the divine Word works in our lives (1 Thess. 2:12), for the Word is effectual both for judgment and for salvation. (2 Peter 1:19)

Such observations are for the most part well taken, but with the exception of the last one it does not follow from them that Christianity is proved to us to be the true religion. It is rather because we hold that Christianity is the true religion that we profess many of the above arguments. These arguments, some of which were taken over from Melanchthon,[31] were never before so elaborately presented by a Lutheran to show the divine origin of Christianity. The same arguments were used by the later Lutherans, beginning with Giles Hunnius,[32] to demonstrate for the believer the divine origin of Scripture. It is difficult to see why Chytraeus saw any need of these evidences, especially the external ones, for the truth of Christianity. He had already made it clear that in themselves the arguments were not convincing and that only God can vouchsafe to a person divine certainty. It is the strong emphasis on these external proofs that is most disturbing, and the formal presentation of them. This emphasis is what is new in Chytraeus. Even Luther had made use of observation (o) when he derived a definite lesson from the way in which the heretic Arius had died, but for Luther this was merely a passing statement and an illustration. It was not until the time of Calov that Lutherans began to see the rationalistic tendency behind this approach to the divine origin of Christianity and Scripture.

4. *The Task of the Interpreter*

As Chytraeus passes over to a discussion of the task of the interpreter, the systematic ring to his comments is still observable. The exegete, he

says, must show the summation, the scope and order of the books he interprets. It is most useful that he tie up and coordinate the individual sections of Scripture into general *loci theologici,* or articles of faith; and that, as Paul admonishes, for the edification of the church, for the strengthening of faith and piety. In other words, the interpreter will determine and take account of those passages that deal with, let us say, the knowledge of God, prayer, Law and Gospel; he will distinguish those passages and relate them with other passages that deal with the same subjects. In so doing he will have a simple summary of the most important parts of Christian theology and will, in a sense, set bounds for himself so that he does not stray beyond the doctrine of the church. In view of the foregoing it is little wonder that Loesche would brand his commentaries as dogmatizing.[33] What Chytraeus has outlined above is not primarily the function of the exegete but of the dogmatician — not that the exegete will reject what he says or will not sometimes practice his suggestions, but this is certainly not the first task of the exegete. Chytraeus goes on to say that the interpreter must next seek to explain the grammatical meaning of the text, the meaning of words, phrases, figures of speech, in order to offer a summary of what is presented therein. There is only one simple and primary meaning of a text. Grammatical exegesis must be maintained.

It is clear that to Chytraeus the function and method of exegesis and of what was being attempted in *Loci Theologici* were really quite similar. We would consider much of what he has said as belonging properly within the purview of dogmatics. But like all the 16th-century writers, Chytraeus, who reveals a definite dogmatic leaning, envisions the construction of summae and the occupation with *loci theologici* (which we would consider dogmatics) as a part of Biblical interpretation and exegesis, as something that serves exegesis and results from it.[34] It is interesting that in this commentary he has included much prolegomenous material not found in his other writings that are of a more systematic nature.

5. *Ten Rules for Study of Theology*

For purposes of comparison we shall review an earlier work by Chytraeus, *De Studio Theologiae,*[35] which belongs within the scope of systematic theology. This book, Chytraeus says, was written by one who sat at the feet of Luther and Melanchthon and who does not presume to go beyond what he heard firsthand from his masters and read from

their writings. The book offers beginners in theology ten basic rules for their study, rules that serve the study of dogmatics quite adequately.

First: *Prayer.* It must always be borne in mind that without God nothing can be learned in theology. When we consider that heathen have never progressed in theology and when we consider that our own congenital weakness prevents us from understanding spiritual things, we must surely commend all our studies to God. For we are not working with a philosophy but with something far greater and deeper, the hidden and divine wisdom, which even the angels cannot comprehend. We must note also the pitfalls into which even the greatest minds have fallen and recognize that we could not retain our faith, to say nothing of working in theology, if the Spirit of God did not enlighten our hearts and impress on our minds the true meaning of Scripture and Christian doctrine. And we who so often become apathetic and lazy must not assume that such sincere prayer is easy.

Second: *Assiduous and Attentive Familiarization with the Scriptures.* God's nature and will and the Gospel are known from no other source than Scripture. Hence we must not read Scripture as a mere history, but we must search out the chief articles of faith, for by the knowledge of these teachings our personal faith, our prayer life, and all virtues are stimulated, nourished, and strengthened. All this is what Melanchthon was driving at when he said that a theologian must be first of all *textualis.* Chytraeus offers a few simple suggestions for reading Scripture, with special emphasis on this, that we must often stop in our reading and take in all the significance of a single word. He mentions how Luther on one occasion spent the better part of an hour bringing out all the implications of the "unto us" of Is. 9:6.

Third: *The Practice of Summa.* Years ago Polybius had already urged that we synthesize (σωματοποιεῖν) in reading history. This method of σωματοειδής is also to be observed in theology. Paul calls this ὑποτύπωσις, i. e., a *formation* and *summation* of theology, which ought to be transmitted to students. Having constructed a summa from Scripture, we may then relate the parts of Scripture to it. And thus we have a norm in times of controversies. This is the function played by creeds and symbols and by *loci theologici.*

Fourth and Fifth: *Dialectics and Rhetoric.* These disciplines are important in teaching and arranging *loci.* In presenting theology, method

must be observed, and definitions, divisions, and distinctions must be made. Paul urges this in 1 Tim. 1, 2 Tim. 1, and Titus 1, and when he speaks of being apt to teach (2 Tim. 2:24). Dialectics, then, are an important gift of God. For in proclaiming the Word it is not enough simply to talk and consume time or even speak with eloquent words, but the message must increase piety and must therefore be coherent. Dialectics are particularly important in controversy, that the real issues may be made plain and objections refuted. The very life of the church is involved in propagating and defending the doctrine of God. It is therefore not difficult to perceive the importance of correct and clear language.

Sixth: *Language Study.* In studying the Scriptures versions are very helpful, but we must always be sure we know when and where these versions agree with the original text. Word studies on the basis of the original text will often reveal how certain adversaries have misunderstood such basic terms as *grace, faith, Gospel,* etc.

Seventh: *Commentaries and Works of the Fathers.* The books of Luther, Lyra, Jerome, Augustine, and many others are recommended.

Eighth: *History.* Such study often aids the church in assessing the difficulties of present times.

Ninth: *Philosophy.* At this point Chytraeus discusses the relevance of ethics and politics and physics to theology. Ethics and politics are useful as a tributary of the divine law, which was written in the human heart. For this reason what theology says on such matters will often be acceptable to pagans. However, we must not lose sight of the fact that philosophy knows nothing of the Gospel, as Melanchthon insisted. Herein was a wisdom unknown to any philosopher. A certain acquaintance with physics and mathematics is often useful to the theologian and may aid him in understanding difficult Scripture passages. We find Christ often alluding to natural phenomena, e. g., to chickens, to seeds, to trees, to vines, etc.

Tenth: *The Cross and Affliction.* At this point Chytraeus refers to Luther's *tentatio* as an important requirement in the making of a theologian. All other skills will never make one a theologian unless God adds the *crux* (the cross) by which He works in us appreciation and understanding of Christ and His promises and by which He works in us hope, patience, humility, and other virtues. "For inasmuch as theology consists not only in knowledge and understanding but especially in the employment and practice of true piety, it is not enough for the mind to be

instructed with excellent learning and to be fluent as an instrument of language, unless there are present in the will and heart the activities of piety, penitence, faith, comfort, patience, prayer, and love of God and neighbor. Nor can we ever understand the nature of such activities without serious afflictions, difficulties, and temptations." Crosses are as necessary for the life of the theologian as food and air for his bodily sustenance. The Gospel is consolation only to the heart that has been crushed by the sense of sin and misery. Hence God makes and fashions the theologian throughout; it is He who works in us both to will and to do. Here we observe the fundamental difference between philosophy and theology. For man makes himself a philosopher.

Again Chytraeus points out that in philosophy experience precedes faith and assent, but in theology the order is reversed. This emphasis on involvement that we noticed in Hyperius is very strong also in Chytraeus, and rightly so. It is only natural that he will allude to his concluding words to Luther's *oratio, meditatio,* and *tentatio* and to Melanchthon's advice that two things are necessary in the making of a theologian: reading Scripture daily, and arranging the theology of Scripture into clear summae.

There is nothing particularly original in Chytraeus' *De Studio Theologiae.* It displays neither the scope nor the insight of Hyperius' earlier work. The author merely intends to offer the best that Luther, Melanchthon, and others have said on the stubject of studying theology. As such a summary it is significant in the development of Lutheran prolegomena to theology and dogmatics.

JOHN GERHARD AND THE CHANGES IN DOGMATICS AND PROLEGOMENA

In the 16th century no lengthy or definite formal prolegomenon to dogmatics appeared, although the subject matter that later came to constitute prolegomena was discussed in both exegetical and dogmatic works. Exegesis and dogmatics were still very closely associated, the method of *loci theologici* being thought of as the activity of exegesis. Theology had not yet become clearly compartmentalized, and it was only later that various disciplines of theology appeared. There was little talk about theology itself and much more interest in what helps a Christian to be a good theologian and in the work of the theologian.

But with the turn of the 17th century, there is a step forward in the development of prolegomena, the *Loci Theologici* of Matthias Hafenreffer, first published in 1600. In this comparatively small dogmatics Hafenreffer, like Heerbrand, writes his own preface in which he presents an overview of the entire plan of his dogmatics. But he also offers a formal discussion of dogmatic prolegomena. He arranges his prolegomena according to the outline of Luther's *oratio, meditatio,* and *tentatio,* expanding on what Luther had said and urging the reading of Scripture in the original text, the structuring of *loci theologici,* and much other advice repetitious of previous works mentioned. From this we conclude that although there is still no discussion of theology as such, theology is thought of as essentially a practice. As one reads through the prolegomena, one concludes that this section is calculated to lead naturally into the early *locus* on Scripture. To Hafenreffer "Scripture is a sea the depths of which we can never sufficiently search out and the abundance of whose contents we can never fully exhaust." He urges the reading of the church fathers and the study of history, but he warns that the early fathers should be distinguished from the later Scholastics, who commingled philosophy with theology and from the two (each perfect in its own realm) brought forth an obscure and imperfect mixture that wrought only darkness. Hafenreffer is most insistent that every father and teacher be judged closely by the norm of Scripture, which alone is θεόπνευστος and αὐτόπιστος. "For whatever is contrary to the Sacred Scriptures is against the truth, even if the whole world or an angel from heaven should teach it." It is clear that Hafenreffer's prolegomena are mainly a discussion of the theologian's attitude toward Scripture and of the place of the Scriptures in the activity of the theologian. In his final treatment of *tentatio* he quotes long portions from Luther and breathes much of the spirit of Chytraeus, again indicating that to him theology is a practical pursuit and a gift of God. Hafenreffer is very concise and accurate throughout his dogmatics, a fact that also indicates a certain advance over his precursors, an advance that became more obvious in Gerhard.

But dogmatic prolegomenon at this time is still only in an incipient and rudimentary state. It has acquired no definite place in Lutheran dogmatics and fulfills only the function of allowing the author to make a few introductory statements. No definite subject matter is yet envisaged as constituting prolegomena. This is clearly indicated by the fact that neither

of the important dogmatic works of Leonard Hutter offers any prolegomena at all. The great impetus of constructing a formal prolegomenon that would contain definite subjects for consideration is found in John Gerhard's *Loci Theologici,* written from 1610 to 1622. In Gerhard we have what Hoenecke calls *"das Muster der Prolegomena,"* [36] for in Gerhard's short prolegomena are contained the elements of practically everything that was to be considered under prolegomena for the next hundred years. We will therefore consider his remarks closely, for a great deal of what he says is new in Lutheran theology.[37]

Gerhard was the first Lutheran to address himself specifically to the subject of the nature of theology. As was his custom, Gerhard introduces his discussion by considering the meaning of the term *theology.* Against the Calvinist, George Sohn,[38] and others he maintains that theology ought to be considered discourse concerning God and divine things, and not the language of God Himself. The term is of course old, going back to Plato (*De Republica,* bk. 1) and Aristotle (*Metaphysics,* X, 6) and in both cases meaning the treatment of the natural knowledge of God with no consideration of faith or divine revelation. Although the term is not Scriptural, Gerhard shows that there are many synonyms found in Scripture. There is, for instance, the term חָכְמָה used in Job 28:28 and later used by the rabbis and called by the Greek Fathers θεοσοφία or simply σοφία. We find Paul using the word θεοσέβεια, which would point to the correct worship of God, whereas the θεοσοφία denotes the correct understanding of God *(verum Dei sensum).* Other synonyms are γνῶσις σωτηρίας in Luke 1:77, σοφία ἐν μυστηρίῳ in 1 Cor. 2:7, λόγος σοφίας in 1 Cor. 12:8, γνῶσις τῆς δόξης τοῦ θεοῦ ἐν προσώπῳ Ἰησοῦ Χριστοῦ in 2 Cor. 4:6, ἐπίγνωσις τοῦ θελήματος τοῦ θεοῦ ἐν πάσῃ σοφίᾳ καὶ συνέσει πνευματικῇ in Col. 1:9, ἐπίγνωσις τοῦ θεοῦ in Col. 1:10, εὐσέβεια in 1 Tim. 3:16, ἐπίγνωσις ἀληθείας τῆς κατ' εὐσέβειαν in Titus 1:1. This last phrase is the most beautiful and complete paraphrase of theology. Some of the church fathers also employed interesting similes in speaking of theology. Chrysostom compares it to a magnificent palace in which are high towers, chambers, gardens, etc. Augustine likens it to heaven; John of Damascus to paradise and the tree of life.

But is there such a thing as theology? This question, which seems now to be first asked by Gerhard, is answered in a very simple way. The answer was enlarged greatly by the later dogmaticians.[39] Gerhard

says that the reply must be yes for the following five reasons: (a) We know that there is a divine revelation, and this is the source or *causa efficiens* of theology. (b) The very nature of God makes revelation a necessity; He who is the highest Good will surely communicate and spread abroad His fame, for He would communicate to rational creatures a knowledge that leads to salvation. (c) The very purpose of creation argues that there must be a theology. God has created rational creatures in such a way that they might acknowledge Him and celebrate Him with praise; and that both in this life and in the life to come. (d) That there is a theology is indicated by the conviction in the mind of men that there is a God and that He ought to be worshiped. (e) The consensus of the heathen indicates that there is a theology; for although such people are outside the church and err from true theology, still they know that there is a theology, and they often direct their attention to its study. It is likely that Gerhard had certain mystics or enthusiasts in mind as he offers these arguments, for they seem almost too simple and obvious. What he is contending for might be quite pertinent today when many deny that God reveals Himself in words or deny that revelation and the Word of God are dianoetic in nature and purpose. Such a denial could easily lead to a denial of theology, certainly in the sense Gerhard meant, namely, true language about God. There is good reason why Gerhard would entertain this question, although it is extremely doubtful if any mystic or enthusiast of his day would be impressed with his arguments, for such a one would naturally have a totally different conception of revelation from Gerhard's.

1. *Theology as Doctrine*

Gerhard next tries to classify theology, if possible. He rejects Thomas Aquinas' classification of theology as a science.[40] To believe and to know, says Gerhard, are disparates; for certainty of knowledge *(scientia)* depends on inherent and coherent principles, whereas the certainty of faith depends on external things, namely, the authority of revelation. Augustine put it well when he said: "What we believe we owe to authority; what we understand *{intelligimus}* we owe to reason." [41] Theology, says Gerhard, is not knowledge but *doctrina fidei*.

It must be understood that Gerhard is here speaking of knowledge only in the Thomistic sense of *scientia*. He would not hesitate to call theology knowledge in the sense of *notitia*, for he has already identified it

with the ἐπίγνωσις of Col. 1:9, although he would not limit theology to this. But *notitia* or *cognitio* is involved in the theological aptitude just as it is involved in faith. For faith, says Gerhard, is the knowledge of salvation; and theology too is the knowledge of salvation (cf. Luke 1:77 and above). Gerhard says:

> Knowledge *{cognitio}* pertains either to the question, Whether a thing is, or to the question, What a thing is and its purpose. In the first case it is the existence of the thing that is known; in the second case it is the essence, the cause and fashion of the thing, that is known. The former is called a certain knowledge *{notitia certitudinis}* because a thing is known with certainty to exist; the latter is called evident knowledge *{notitia evidentiae}* because in addition to its quiddity a thing is known through perception or through demonstration *{per rationem apodicticam}*. We are speaking only of the first kind of knowledge when we say that we know the mysteries of God through faith. And here we must distinguish between γνῶσις and ἐπιστήμη. The former denotes the knowledge of a thing in general, whatever it may be; the latter denotes a more specific knowledge of the necessity of things through demonstration. Faith is not ἐπιστήμη, but γνῶσις.[42]

This statement indicates just how Gerhard considers theology to be knowledge; and it is clear why to him it cannot be considered *scientia*.

This fact is significant, for it opens the way to later discussions by Lutherans on the impossibility of an unregenerate theology. If theology were *scientia*, if it were speculative, then one could approach it in an impersonal and detached way, for its proofs would then be self-evident. But if theology involves a γνῶσις σωτηρίας, then faith is necessary for theology. Thus we find Gerhard reminding us that the subject of theology is Christ, whom we cannot know in any scientific manner *(scientifico modo)*, but it is only by divine revelation that we know Him and take refuge in Him (Matt. 16:17; 1 Cor. 2:7). Gerhard points out that the source of science *(scientiae principium)* is understanding *(intellectus)*, which takes place when conclusions are drawn from definite principles.[43] In theology, on the other hand, understanding is not the source or beginning but the end. Hence Augustine says: "We believe in order to understand; we do not understand in order to believe."[44] And this is in agreement with Is. 7:9: "If ye will not believe, surely ye shall not be established."[45] Finally Gerhard contends that theology, if it were science, would be subject to error, for inasmuch as discursive reasoning is subject

to error, the conclusions of science are subject to error.[46] But faith that is based on the revelation of God is not subject to error.[47]

2. *Theology as an Aptitude*

Other Scholastics have called theology wisdom, in agreement with Aristotle, who said that this was the highest and most precise wisdom of all (*Ethics* VI, 7, and *Metaphysics* VI, 2). Gerhard grants that theology may be called a wisdom in the sense that it excels all other knowledge; but speaking very accurately it must be regarded as a God-given aptitude (*habitus* θεόσδοτος) rather than as belonging merely to the class of intellectual aptitudes, for Jesus has said that theologians are taught of God (διδακτοὶ θεοῦ, John 6:45).

But theology is more than merely an aptitude given by God. If we consider the end of theology, that it is not merely γνῶσις but also πρᾶξις in that everything considered in theology leads to application in life, we must say that theology is above all a practical aptitude — if not immediately and directly, at least mediately and indirectly. Gerhard brings many Scripture passages to bear on this point (Matt. 7:21; John 13:17; 1 Cor. 4:20; 1 Tim. 1:5). He also quotes many of the church fathers; e. g., Chrysostom, "The finest syllogism in theology is the syllogism of works," and Augustine, "All theology is ordered to the end that we might enjoy God."

Gerhard warns that there is also a false theology, i. e., untrue discourse concerning God, for as Luther commented somewhere, "Not only God's people know and talk about God, but the devil's people as well." However, we must note that false theology is called theology only according to an equivocation. There are two kinds of false theology, according to Gerhard, common or vulgar and that which can be called philosophical. The former he seems to identify with what we might call natural theology; the philosophical he seems to identify with what we call rational theology. Concerning the latter he says that it leads people into error through false reasoning (Rom. 1:21). He does not suggest that one has any advantage over the other.

3. *Archetypal and Ectypal Theology*

True theology must be considered either in an absolute sense *(in se, in subjecto)* or in a relative sense. Here we have to do with the distinction

between archetypal theology and ectypal theology, a distinction that would be brought out by all the later Lutheran dogmaticians. Gerhard's discussion is worth quoting:

> Archetypal or original theology is in God the Creator. It is the theology according to which God knows Himself in Himself and also knows everything that is outside Him by an indivisible and immutable act of knowing. This theology in the Creator is ἄκτιστος καὶ οὐσιώδης, uncreated and essential, infinite and original, and differs entirely from ectypal theology, which is συμβεβηκῆα καὶ κτιστή, accidental and finite, and is a sort of outflow and efflux [ἀπορροὴ καὶ ἀπαύγασμα] of the former. Ectypal theology is expressions and utterances derived from the former through a gracious communication, and by reason of its subject is either in Christ the Head or in His members. In the man Christ this ectypal theology is an inherent wisdom embracing an absolutely perfect knowledge of God and of divine things. This is called the *theologia unionis.* It differs entirely from the theology of rational creatures in that the human spirit of Christ, having taken to itself the hypostasis of the Logos, is raised far above the eminence of all angels and men, and thus is clearly unique.

This simple position of Gerhard's was followed by all the later Lutherans and expanded at great length. As we shall see in the case of Calov, the later dogmaticians went a step beyond Gerhard in teaching that Christ, by virtue of the hypostatic union, possessed also the original or archetypal theology. This caused a prolonged controversy with the Calvinists.

Gerhard speaks of two kinds of ectypal theology. The first is the *theologia beatorum,* which is a clear and intuitive knowledge of God that angels and men possess only in heaven when they see Him face to face (1 Cor. 13:12; 1 John 3:2). This is in distinction to the *theologia viatorum,* which consists in the knowledge of divine things that God by means of His revelation has extended to us in this life. Such theology is given us in nature *(theologia naturalis)* but especially by the light of grace in the revealed Word *(theologia supernaturalis, arcana sive gratiosa).* Natural theology is both *innate,* in that certain common notions (κοιναὶ ἔννοιαι) are inborn in man (e. g., that there is a God, that He is good and should be worshiped), and *acquired,* by contemplating God's creatures and works in nature (Rom. 1:20). "*Supernatural theology* which has come to us from the light of grace is acquired either in a unique manner through the immediate illumination and inspiration of God, as we see in the case of the apostles and prophets, or in the usual manner through prayer, meditation, and affliction."

The many distinctions Gerhard made concerning theology were something new in the thinking of Lutheran dogmaticians. However, these and other distinctions were not the invention of Gerhard but were already in use in Reformed circles and had their origin in scholastic theology. The development of dogmatic prolegomena and dogmatics in Lutheran and Reformed circles was closely parallel in the late 16th and early 17th centuries, with the Reformed usually being in advance of the Lutherans. All the distinctions thus far mentioned by Gerhard were already discussed by Amandus Polanus and John Alsted in the early 17th century and even as early as 1594 by Francis Junius.[48] There is little or no difference between Lutheran and Reformed theology on any of these points, except on the matter of the *theologia unionis,* mentioned earlier. In fact Gerhard followed the very order of Francis Junius, who became normative for many Reformed theologians in their discussions of theology and dogmatic prolegomena. The one noticeable difference lies in the fact that the Reformed theologians, following Thomas and Scotus, taught that theology was in part practical and in part theoretical, although there was no difference on the nature of theology as a God-given *habitus.*

About the time of Gerhard, however, the close parallel development of prolegomena among the Reformed and Lutheran theologians began to cease. This was because the Reformed treatment after the time of Alsted and Keckermann became too philosophical in form to suit the Lutherans, although this was not the tendency of all the Reformed. Dorner correctly says that compared with the Reformed the Lutheran Church was the subject of a slower but also a more united and consecutive development in dogmatics and dogmatic prolegomena.[49] As a rule the Lutherans followed the lead of their own theologians but at the same time cautiously followed the lead and advances of Calvinists when this was possible. Although the Lutheran theologians often differed in their approach to theological questions, the basic doctrinal position remained unified, whereas for the Calvinists (possibly because they had no totally accepted confessions like the Lutherans) doctrinal differences became sometimes rather pronounced.

4. *Theology Viewed According to Its Causal Factors*

The reader has no doubt noticed by now that Gerhard brings Aristotelian terminology and thought patterns to bear upon theology — not that

he would dream of imposing metaphysics and philosophical categories upon theology, but he sees nothing harmful in arranging his discussions according to Aristotle's causal factors and in retaining Aristotle's terms and definitions when this seems helpful. This is a far-reaching innovation, and in the later dogmaticians this causal terminology, which was introduced by Gerhard for the sake of clarity, becomes needlessly involved at times and defeats its own purpose. One may well ask if the innovation was not an unfortunate one. To treat theology and every article of faith according to its efficient, final, formal, and material cause is artificial and makes theology dreadfully stereotyped.

We now examine how Gerhard views the various causes of theology.

a. DIVINE REVELATION AND SCRIPTURE. The efficient cause of supernatural theology is divine revelation, which has been set forth in the revealed Word of God. The principal efficient cause is of course God Himself, who is the One revealing (see Matt. 11:27; 16:17; 1 Cor. 2:10). The instrumental cause of theology is the Word as the means of revelation.

At this point Gerhard pauses to remind the reader that there is a twofold way of considering the word of men. There is, first, the inner word, which resides in the mind, which one might call the offspring of the mind, and which Gerhard calls the λόγος ἔσω. Second, there is the external word, the λόγος ἔξω, which represents the inner thoughts of the mind either by mouth or in writing. This insight Gerhard finds in "the philosopher."[50] Gerhard then proceeds to argue that there is also in God a twofold Word. There is the internal and eternal Word, which is begotten from eternity of His own substance. This is the hypostatic Word, which must be completely distinguished from any word of man. There is also the external Word by which God speaks to men in time, and this Word comes to man both immediately by divine inspiration and enlightenment (as in the case of the prophets and apostles) or mediately (as when a pastor preaches a message based on Scripture). The Word communicated directly by God to the prophets and apostles and the Word that He speaks mediately to us today does not differ essentially, however; it is one and the same Word.

From the foregoing we conclude, says Gerhard, that the adequate and proper source of supernatural theology is divine revelation, which does not obtain today except in the Sacred Scriptures. Scripture, then, is the one *principium cognoscendi* of theology. The *principium essendi,* the source

of the very existence of theology, is of course God. At this point Gerhard breaks with Thomas, who taught that the articles of faith were the sources (*principia*) of theology.[51] Gerhard states that articles of faith are *principiata*, truths based on the one principium of theology, namely Scripture.

Here again Gerhard traverses a new path. He brings within the scope of prolegomena the discussion of Scripture as the source of theology. Much the same arguments are employed again when he discusses the authority of Scripture later in his dogmatics, but properly the subject is a prolegomenon to dogmatics. Gerhard has already said that "the dogma of the canon, properly speaking, is not an article of faith, inasmuch as Moses, the prophets, evangelists, and apostles did not by their act of writing construct a new article of faith that was superadded *de novo* to preceding articles that they taught by word of mouth."[52] To Gerhard Scripture viewed as a canon, as a source of doctrine, is a presupposition of theology and dogmatics. The later dogmaticians all followed Gerhard in this by considering Scripture as a source of theology within their prolegomena, whereas the divine origin and attributes of Scripture were usually considered under the *locus* on Scripture.

There is another innovation in what Gerhard is doing here. Although he is obviously only attempting to maintain the Protestant *sola Scriptura* principle, he is operating with a new concept in speaking of Scripture as a principium. Whereas earlier theologians were content to state that Scripture was the only rule and norm by which doctrine is judged and that all doctrine was to be drawn from Scripture, Gerhard brings philosophy to his aid in calling Scripture a principium. A principium, according to Aristotle, if it is to be a principium of demonstrated knowledge, must be true, primary, and immediate, and it must be better known and prior to the conclusions drawn from it.[53] Gerhard adds more qualifying adjectives: ἀνυπεύθυνος, αὐτόπιστος, ἀναντίρρητος. We see here that Gerhard is using the common jargon of the Scholastics to nail down on their terms the sole authority of Scripture in theology. For if Scripture is a principium, there can be no other source of doctrine or theology if Scripture is not *eo ipso* to lose its quality and position as a principium.[54] At this particular point Gerhard is concerned that the principles of human reason do not become a judge or norm in theology but that all theology be drawn from the one source of God's Word. He is quite insistent, however, that he is not illicitly drawing in philosophical principles and imposing them on

theology. He says: "In the above manner the theologian borrows something from the philosopher, not as though he were unable without the principles of philosophy to know this from Scripture as the proper and suitable source of his knowledge, but because in the examination of the standard of his own principle he recognizes the truth of philosophy." Gerhard has shown from philosophy as well as theology that to operate in theology with any other source and norm than Scripture is to commit the mistake of the μετάβασις εἰς ἄλλο γένος.

Still operating with the Aristotelian framework of causes, Gerhard speaks also of the *materia* and *forma* of theology. The *materiae* are the theological conclusions that are drawn from the Word of God. The *forma* is the arrangement of these truths *(veritates)*. This *forma* can vary and has varied greatly among theologians.

b. THE GOAL OF THEOLOGY. The goal *(causa finalis)* of theology is the glorification of God, for God has revealed Himself to us that we might know Him in this life and in the life to come, that we might glorify Him, worship Him, and call upon Him. There is also an intermediate goal of theology that consists in informing man of the way of salvation and in man's following this way of life (Luke 1:77; John 5:39; 20:30-31; Rom. 15:4; 2 Tim. 3:16). Whatever does not lead to this goal either directly or indirectly is not theological knowledge at all but mere logomachy (1 Tim. 1:6). The desired effect of theology is that men might be made wise unto salvation, that they might be enriched in all utterance and in all knowledge (2 Tim. 3:15; 1 Cor. 1:5). The subject matter of theology will be the same as the goal: we learn how to glorify God and how man is saved. Or putting it a little differently, God and His creatures are the proper subject of theology. But we do not study about God in His absolute nature but only as He relates Himself to us; God must be sought, as Luther said, *"non in praedicamento substantiae, sed relationis."* "The correct subject of theology is man, who is guilty of sin and lost, and also God, who justifies and who is the Savior of sinful men."

c. DEFINITION OF THEOLOGY. Finally, Gerhard's concluding comprehensive definition of theology is this:

> Theology is an aptitude given by God, conferred upon man by the Holy Spirit through the Word. By this theology a person is prepared by his knowledge of divine mysteries through the illumination of his mind to apply those things that he understands to the disposition of

his heart and to the carrying out of good works. By theology a person is also given the skill and ability to inform others about these divine mysteries and the way of salvation and to defend the heavenly doctrine from the corruptions of those who oppose it, to the end that men, shining with true faith and good works, may be brought to the kingdom of heaven.

d. PHILOSOPHY AND THEOLOGY. Of the many new features Gerhard brought into the discussion of prolegomena in Lutheran circles, most significant were two innovations: (1) Prolegomena took on a fixed pattern, so that from Gerhard's time to our present day certain definite items have been considered as prolegomena to the study of theology and of dogmatics (e. g., Scripture as the source of theology, the nature of theology, the relation of theology to philosophy or reason). (2) Philosophical terminology, arrangement, and factors *(causae)* intruded on theological endeavor. Whether this intrusion was helpful or innocuous or cumbersome or harmful we must still judge. Whatever our judgment may be, there can be no doubt that the responsibility for bringing philosophical thought and terminology to bear on theology belongs to Gerhard fully as much as to Melanchthon.

But let us try to assess the effect of Gerhard's innovation. One thing is certain: Gerhard is not aware of imposing philosophy upon theology or of conditioning theology in any way by philosophical principles. He attacks any attempt of human reason to encroach on the province of theology. Reason has no power to judge in matters of doctrine.[55] This does not mean that regenerate reason contends against the articles of faith: insofar as man's reason rejects articles of faith, it is not regenerate; for regenerate reason always accepts the Word of God (1 John 3:9). For instance, if a person's reason insists that Christ's body and blood cannot possibly be present in the Lord's Supper, it is not regenerate reason that makes such a judgment, and a Christian must not follow its lead just as he should not follow the reason of a Unitarian who insists that God cannot be One and Three Persons at the same time. Right reason[56] *(ratio recta)* will confine itself to its own limitations and will not judge in matters of faith, but will allow itself to be led by the light of the Word and the Holy Spirit. Gerhard says: "We must distinguish between those things that are completely matters of revelation and solely matters of faith and those things that are subject to the discernment of reason. In the latter concerns some light of reason remains; the former things, which are above

our minds, above our description, above all comprehension, must not be vitiated by reason, but received by faith." It is *per accidens* that reason conflicts with Christian doctrine; *per se* reason does not conflict with Christian doctrine. In like manner we may say that the articles of faith are not *per se* contrary to reason but above reason. Before the Fall reason was not yet corrupt and depraved; however, after the Fall the articles of faith are found to be contrary to corrupt reason.

Gerhard says much the same thing about philosophy and theology. On the one hand philosophy must not encroach on the sphere of theology, for it is blind to the mysteries of faith. On the other hand theology is not *per se* contrary to philosophy, if philosophy is carried on properly. He says:

> There is no contrariety or contradiction *per se* between philosophy and theology, because philosophy wisely and seriously realizes that the things concerning the high mysteries of faith that theology presents from Scripture must not be attacked and assessed by the principles of reason, lest a μετάβασις εἰς ἄλλο γένος result and the distinct principles of the separate disciplines be confused. Thus when Scripture teaches that Mary gave birth and yet remained a virgin, philosophy wisely refrains from saying that this assertion conflicts with its own conclusions, which are that a virgin is not capable of giving birth; and that because philosophy knows that the former conclusion must be accepted in accordance with the limitation that a virgin cannot in a natural way give birth and remain a virgin. But theology does not assert the contrary of this, for theology says that in a supernatural manner and by divine order it happened that she remained a virgin. Now when some philosophizer wants to make his own axioms and utterances so all-embracing that he thinks the high mysteries of faith must be judged by these and thus invades foreign boundaries, then it happens *per accidens* that what is true in theology is said to be false to philosophy, not as touching the true use of correct philosophy but as touching the disgraceful abuse of the same.[57]

The above remarks indicate something of Gerhard's position on the relation of theology and philosophy. At a later point Gerhard's views on this matter will be treated and the origin of this position traced. His position was very carefully worked out and became normative for all Lutheran theologians during the later period of orthodoxy.

But first another book of Gerhard's must be considered in order to come to a full grasp of his thoughts on the use of philosophy by the theologian and on the relation between the two disciplines. Gerhard's

Methodus Studii Theologici, first published in 1620, offers us a comprehensive view of his ideas on the theologian, the study of theology, and in particular the use of philosophy by the theologian. To illustrate precisely what prolegomena were conceived to be by this great theologian, a brief overview of this short book is offered.[58] Here one will find that some of the misgivings concerning his judgments on the use and place of philosophy in the practice of theology may be allayed somewhat.

5. *Gerhard's* Methodus Studii Theologici

Theology, Gerhard contends, excels all other activity, first by reason of its principles. For its source is the Word of God, than which nothing in heaven or earth is more firm and certain. The principles of all other disciplines are λόγος καὶ πεῖρα, reason and experiment. The light of *nature and experience,* which are of a lower order, cannot offer the degree of certainty given by the light of *Scripture and grace.* Second, theology excels by reason of the superior nature of its object. Theology deals with the high mysteries of faith, things that are above all human comprehension. Theology deals with God's essence and will, with the way of salvation. Other activities consider only such things as the mind can prove or work out, such as politics and natural sciences, and then evolve doctrines for practical living. Third, theology excels by reason of the goal to which it proceeds and leads. All theology is directed to the salvation of our souls. All other activities lead only to ends within the course of this life. Hence all other disciplines are subordinate to theology. Theology judges all things but is itself judged by nothing.

We see here how insistent Gerhard is that theology must reign as queen and all else must be subordinated to it. We recall how he refused to grant that it was a science among other sciences, although he does call it a discipline among other disciplines, but by discipline he means merely an ordered activity, and he does not mean to subsume theology under the genus discipline. Gerhard concludes his praise of theology with a quotation from Gerson: "As grace is superior to nature, as a mistress is over her handmaid, as a teacher is above his disciple, as eternity is greater than time, as understanding is to be desired above mere thinking, as those things that are not seen are more excellent than the things that are visible, so theology reigns far above philosophy, although it does not reject philosophy, but holds it in obedience."[59] Gerhard maintains that the

principles of theology — not the archetypal theology but the theology in which we engage from day to day — are simple in contrast to all other endeavor and the principles of all other activity. These eulogies of theology are more than mere Gerhardian rhetoric; we must appreciate that Gerhard is truly overwhelmed by the thought of the depth and wonders of the subject with which the theologian is called to deal. It is for such theological study that he now wishes in his book to prescribe a certain order of progression, set definite limitations, and list certain aids.

Gerhard's study contains three parts: (1) general requirements of a theological student, (2) preliminary studies for the student of theology (προπαιδεία), and (3) the course of study itself.

a. MARKS OF A THEOLOGIAN. After a brief reference to Luther's *oratio, meditatio,* and *tentatio,* Gerhard points out three requisites or marks of the theologian. (1) The theologian labors only for the glory of God and the building up of God's church, never for his own prestige or glory or honor. Especially in theology the eye must be single (Matt. 6:22). The intentions and attitude of the theologian are most important. (2) Piety is required of every Christian but especially of one who studies theology and ministers to the church. By *piety,* a word we have already run across very often, is meant a dutiful, filial fear of God, a trustful obedience born of the Gospel. The term denotes a loving obedience in doctrine and in life. We must allow the Spirit of God to be *"internus ille Doctor"* who leads us into all truth (1 John 2:27). One who lives in sin cannot engage in theology (Eph. 5:14; John 14:17; 1 Tim. 1:18 ff.). Here Gerhard is saying what became such an important principle to the later orthodox Lutherans, that there is no such person as an unregenerate theologian. (3) Daily prayer is required for every theologian. We must pray for enlightenment, for there can be no salutary understanding of the truth without the enlightenment of the Spirit (Ps. 119). Thus far Gerhard has offered nothing original but is following the direction encouraged by earlier theologians, Luther, Hyperius, and Chytraeus. It is clear that he shares their concern that a theologian be involved personally in everything he undertakes as a theologian and their conviction that there is no such thing as a detached, standoffish — what we would call in modern jargon "scientific" — theologian. A theologian is committed to Christ and His Gospel.

b. PROPAEDEUTICS: PHILOSOPHY. The burden of Gerhard's concern in his book comes in part II, where we find the material significant for our present interest, namely, Gerhard's attitude toward and use of philosophy as a theologian. Here Gerhard deals with what he calls the propaedeutics of theological study. First, he submits a long argument for the importance of training in the Biblical languages, again following closely the suggestions of the earlier Lutheran theologians. Second, he discusses the importance of the theologian knowing philosophy; and at this point we will want carefully to delineate his discussion. Gerhard begins by reminding us that philosophy has different subject matter from theology. Philosophy knows nothing of Christ. However, philosophy can be used in the service of theology. Gerhard lists a threefold use of philosophy as it relates to theology: the *usus* ὀργανικός, the *usus* κατασκευαστικός, and the *usus* ἀνασκευαστικός.

The organic function *(usus organicus)* of philosophy is didactic also when it pertains to theology. Gerhard offers the following outline of the organic function of philosophy:

I. Instrumental parts
   A. Logic
   B. Rhetoric (including language study)
II. Real parts
   A. Theoretical
      1. Metaphysics
      2. Physics
      3. Mathematics
   B. Practical
      1. Ethics
      2. Politics
      3. Political Economy

All these parts or divisions of philosophy tend to sharpen men's minds also for the study of theology. The real parts in particular may serve the theologian in explaining certain terms. For theology uses not only Biblical terminology but also ecclesiastical terminology such as *ens,* the good, the true, the perfect, the finite, person, existence, essence, act, potency, etc., all of which are metaphysical terms. Theology also employs terms

from physics such as time, place, heaven, earth, sea, fire, etc. The theologian must also seek the meaning of such terms, which are found in both Scripture and the natural sciences. There are, however, certain terms in Scripture that philosophy can in no way help to explain — e. g., Christ, Holy Spirit, election, etc. Of course philosophy functions here only in an auxiliary manner. "Philosophy *serves* in explaining terms," says Gerhard, "and even in this function we allow it only a ministering, not a ruling, office." Thus the theologian will find himself constantly refining and baptizing philosophical terms, e. g., the term *principium* as it is applied to God the Father, or the term *generation* as applied to the Son. To take over uncritically the meanings these terms have in philosophy would be disastrous.

Logic too may serve theology, and that in presenting doctrine distinctly and in proper arrangement, in explaining questions and sometimes in refuting error. Rhetoric explains figures of speech, grammar, etc., and is therefore important for theology.

The *usus* κατασκευαστικός of philosophy consists in offering support to certain theological questions. There are two kinds of questions in theology. Some questions pertain to the mysteries of faith, which are above all human understanding — e. g., the Trinity, the Incarnation, the Resurrection, etc. Other questions are of such a nature that they can also be known by the human understanding through a natural act of thinking (*per* κοίνας ἐννοίας) or by discursive analysis of data — e. g., the existence of God, and the goodness and justice of God. The former questions Gerhard calls πιστά, the latter he calls ἀπιστητά. Here we notice the beginning of the later common distinction between *articuli puri* and *articuli mixti*, that is, between articles of faith known only from God's revelation and articles of faith known from the light of nature as well as from revelation. But Gerhard would differ somewhat from such a distinction inasmuch as he goes on immediately to say that the latter (ἀπιστητά) are not articles of faith, for articles of faith are not known by nature but only by divine revelation or valid conclusions drawn from it. The former questions philosophy is unable to prove or support, since philosophy knows nothing about such things. However, here too philosophy may give aid in explaining terms. To the latter questions philosophy can offer answers and arguments, not as though these answers were necessary — the answer of theology based on divine revelation is always sufficient — but

philosophy may serve to show that answers and arguments are clear from the light of nature as well as from the light of grace.

The third use of philosophy is polemic and apologetic (*usus* ἀνασκευαστικός or the *usus* ἐλεγκτικός). Philosophy may aid the theologian in refuting false doctrine from the Scriptures, and this is one effective means of refutation. Philosophy is able to show that false doctrine is often not only against the light of grace but against the light of reason as well. But, Gerhard warns, such apologetics is only "a secondary and minor kind of proof and without the former proof [from Scripture] is completely ineffective."

Just as there are many uses of philosophy there are many abuses, and there is an abuse corresponding to every use. Relative to the first use of philosophy, the *organic,* the danger is always present that one becomes so preoccupied with philosophy that one loses sight of the theological issues and forgets that the important concerns of theology cannot be investigated by philosophy. Another danger lies in the tendency to give philosophy too much influence in explaining terms. This abuse of philosophy is exemplified by the papists, who impose their false doctrine of infused righteousness upon the Scriptural doctrine of justification. Still another danger lies in the tendency of philosophy to abandon its ancillary function and judge theology by the principles of logic. This abuse was common among the old scholastic theologians.

The second, *catasceuastic,* function of philosophy may be misused in the following ways. (1) One may attempt to verify the mysteries of faith by philosophical reasoning rather than by the one source of theology. (2) One may postpone or overlook the testimony of Scripture and employ reason as proof for Christian doctrine, thus giving the impression that reason is more important and sure than Scripture. This abuse of philosophy was practiced constantly by the Scholastics with their emphasis on Aristotle. (3) One may try to fortify saving faith by reason as though reason were more certain than the articles of faith. (4) When dealing with mixed questions where one term is theological and the other philosophical, one may seek to conform the argument with philosophy. For instance, the question whether the body of Christ can be in more than one place is not and cannot be answered by philosophy. In such a case philosophy does not assist theology but must keep quiet and come completely under theology's rule.

The third, *anasceuastic,* use of philosophy is misused and misapplied in the following ways. (1) One may treat mysteries of faith as being subject to reason, whereas all mysteries of faith are above reason (Eph. 3:8-9; 1 Cor. 2:7, 14-16). It is true that some mysteries such as creation from nothing and the resurrection are recognized as possible by reason and do not imply a contradiction. Other articles, however, cannot be known by reason to be possible; reason is simply ignorant of them to the degree that it cannot even judge as to their possibility. An article of this nature would be the mystery of the Trinity. (2) Reason and the philosophic rule of reason cannot judge concerning the power of God, what He can or cannot do. Therefore philosophy cannot judge whether certain mysteries of faith are contradictory or not (Gen. 18:14; Luke 1:37). Regarding the omnipotence of God and the difficulty philosophy has had with this, Gerhard has some significant comments to make.

> We must distinguish between the ordinate and absolute power of God. The latter can perform things that seem contradictory to us. For God by virtue of His absolute power is not bound to the law of contradiction or to the law of reason. We must also distinguish between a contradiction of divine logic that far transcends our comprehension and a contradiction of human logic that does not transcend our comprehension. We must distinguish between things and utterances that are above the limitations of logic and our reason and those things that are subject to the limitations of our logic and that can be perceived by our reason. . . . The power of God is infinite without any limitations and above the grasp of our reason. It may seem to be our duty to want to limit this power and to want to say, God can do all possible things. But Scripture speaks in a different way and says, With God nothing is impossible.

It cannot be known with certainty just whom Gerhard has in mind here. But he is obviously arguing against the contention that God must work according to our ideas of contradiction. His warning would certainly be against what Thomas Aquinas had said on this matter when he maintained that God's power is in reference to possible things only.[60] Gerhard wishes only to insist that human reason must not be allowed to become the rule for divine power; human reason after the Fall is blind and must be taken captive. (2 Cor. 10:5)

Inasmuch as philosophy is fraught with all these dangers, why should Gerhard seek to retain its use in the church, especially after Luther with so much labor and sweat drove it out? Gerhard answers that it is necessary

to engage in philosophy because the adversaries have used philosophy in their polemics. For instance, philosophy is used by the Calvinists in opposing the Scriptural doctrine of the communication of attributes. By a restrained and limited use of philosophical terminology we are able to refute these errors, whereas if we were completely to discard all philosophical aids and terminology, the difficulty of the task would be greatly increased.

From the above summary of Gerhard's ideas on the use of philosophy by the theologian in his *Methodus Studii Theologici* we gain a slightly different impression from what we may have gotten from his *Loci Theologici,* where Gerhard is offering a positive prolegomenon to dogmatics and is following the adventitious instruction of philosophy where he feels it might offer him aid. We might wonder, for instance, whether he always observes his own rules and does not perhaps fall into some of the pitfalls he warns against in this smaller work of his.

For instance, Gerhard does not hesitate to consider whether the holy Trinity as a doctrine can be investigated by natural reason, and after considering the speculations of Scotus, Thomas, Augustine, and other church fathers, he concludes: "Indeed we do not condemn this pious endeavor of the ancients, although at the same time we warn that this philosophizing concerning such a lofty mystery must be carried out in a sober, cautious, and reverent manner." [61] However, Gerhard would deny that such pious activity would prove or in any way aid in proving the doctrine of the Trinity. Such activity merely shows *a posteriori* that the doctrine of the Trinity, which is drawn from Scripture and accepted by faith, is not necessarily contrary to reason. Gerhard says: "We must distinguish between on the one hand any kind of *a posteriori* declarations and approbations by which this mystery, revealed first in Scripture, is explained and shown to be not absurd, and on the other hand accurate *a priori* demonstrations by which we deny that that mystery can be investigated or acknowledged by us. In this *a posteriori* manner the Trinity is demonstrated by showing that after it has first been established from the Scriptures our arguments then agree with it." Actually such *a posteriori* reasoning does not bolster or confirm the doctrine but at most serves only to illustrate what has already been established and demonstrated from Scripture. "Our reasonings that are taken from the light of nature and applied to the mystery of the Trinity must not be thought of as occupying

the function of corroborating this mystery but only of illustrating it in various ways." This, Gerhard says, we must insist on because a mystery such as this is, in the nature of the case, above all comprehension of human reason; and human reason cannot, according to its own principles, come to any knowledge of it. Reason and philosophy, therefore, do not support the doctrine of the Trinity, but at the same time it can be shown that reason and philosophy do not oppose this mystery.

At this point Gerhard quotes Luther's *De Votis Monasticis:*

> The gross light of nature by itself does not extend to the light and works of God; hence, in affirmative statements [concerning divine matters] its judgment is false, although in negative statements its judgment is certain. And so, although it does not see what is right and good before God (which is of course faith), still it does know obviously that faithlessness and murder are evil, a fact that Christ draws from when He says, Every kingdom divided against itself shall fall, and Paul too when he says that it is against nature for a woman to prophecy with her head not covered. Now that which is clearly contrary to this reason is much more against God, for how can that which opposes earthly truth not also oppose heavenly truth? [62]

Gerhard says that some have interpreted Luther here to the effect that the great mysteries of faith can be considered by reason and, if shown to be contrary to reason, may be rejected. But here Luther is not speaking of all the mysteries of faith, he is not speaking of those things known only to revelation, but only of the things known to reason, as the first part of his statement indicates. Elsewhere Luther has made it abundantly clear that philosophy can in no way disprove theology. In his *Disputation on the Verse Verbum Caro Factum Est* Luther says: "The Sorbonne, the mother of all errors, defines in a most pernicious way that the same thing is true in philosophy and theology and then impiously condemns those who define the contrary." [63]

Gerhard's reason for quoting Luther is simply to confirm his own contention that the mystery of the Trinity cannot be opposed by reason because it cannot be considered and taken up by reason. He insists that this is in accordance with the rule of reason itself, and he goes on to offer nine arguments that reason itself should be able to understand. (a) A demonstration must not draw from concerns outside its sphere but from facts within its own sphere of knowledge. (b) Reason is imperfect. (c) Reason is corrupt (1 Cor. 2:14; 1:19; Rom. 1:21; Eph. 4:17). (d) Reason

judges in matters that are known (τὰ νοητά), not in matters that are believed (τὰ πιστά). (e) The axiom of philosophy that every person must denote a separate essence is true when we refer to finite essences but not when we refer to the infinite essence of God. (f) The very nature of a mystery is that it is not known by reason (Eph. 3:8; 1 Cor. 2:7; 1 Tim. 3:16). (g) The divine power of God is so great that reason cannot dictate what God can or cannot do (Eph. 3:20). (h) The apostle tells us that if reason conflicts with mysteries of faith we must take reason captive (2 Cor. 10:5; cf. also Prov. 3:5). (i) Gerhard lists many absurd consequences that would result if reason should be allowed to be given a hearing in matters of revealed doctrine: Ultimately our faith will depend not on what is drawn from the Scriptures but on the judgment of reason; the judgment of reason is considered to be greater than the judgment of the Spirit of God that is set forth and revealed in Scripture; the genera and principles of completely separate disciplines are utterly confused; human reason is given prerogative above the understanding of the very angels who desire to look into the things of God (1 Peter 1:12). All the mysteries of faith are vitiated in one stroke because reason, which cannot understand them, will indiscriminately cast them out.

6. *The Relation of Philosophy to Theology*

Our rather lengthy excursus on Gerhard's treatment of the place of reason and philosophy in assessing the doctrine of the Trinity illustrates clearly his attitude toward philosophy and reason. It is manifest that he considers himself to be quite agreed with Luther; although he would make assertions that might seem contradictory to Luther — e. g., that what is true in philosophy is true in theology — he sees no need even to explain this apparent discrepancy. Actually the apparent discrepancy can easily be explained by pointing out that Luther is speaking of philosophy in the concrete and Gerhard of philosophy in the abstract, or as it would be employed by a Christian. Luther is speaking of philosophy without regard to theology, Gerhard of philosophy as it serves theology. The difference between the two theologians would not appear, therefore, to be a fundamental one but rather to center in this, that Luther would take a much dimmer view of the usefulness of philosophy in the work of the theologian and would strive to rid theology of philosophical terms and categories (although he never succeeded), whereas Gerhard would actually

welcome new philosophical terms and helps under the conditions outlined above.

a. EARLY CONFLICT. But why this new approach and willingness to use philosophy that is so evident in Gerhard? Gerhard's thoughts on the relation of philosophy to theology were not conceived overnight nor are they particularly original, but they represent a careful distilling of the mature results of a great deal of deliberation by orthodox Lutherans on the subject at the turn of the 17th century. Luther and Melanchthon had bequeathed the Lutheran Church a somewhat conflicting legacy. Luther had railed against philosophy and seen it as an archenemy of God's revelation. Melanchthon had taught philosophy for years, and although recognizing its limitations he had urged that philosophy could with discrimination be used for the benefit of theology. The difference was a strong difference in attitude. Luther viewed philosophy as a representation of fleshly wisdom, which begets only pride and puffs itself up against the Gospel.[64] A Christian could only break with this wisdom and accept the foolishness of the Cross. Melanchthon, the humanist, as we have seen, criticized not so much the arrogance and sinfulness of concrete philosophies as their limitations. Philosophy was good as far as it went, at least some philosophy, but it had no knowledge of God's grace and the Gospel.

It was inevitable that this unresolved difference in emphasis and approach would sooner or later develop into open conflict in the Lutheran Church, especially inasmuch as Aristotelianism and humanism were being revived in many of the German universities. A bitter and confusing controversy finally broke out at the turn of the century, the chief antagonists being two Helmstedt professors, Daniel Hoffmann and Cornelius Martini,[65] Hoffmann breathing the spirit of Luther and Martini the spirit of Melanchthon. Martini was a leader in bringing metaphysics back into the university curriculum and was a humanist at heart. Hoffmann not only condemned the teaching of metaphysics but rejected all philosophy as ungodly, contentious, and obstinate. Quoting Luther's attack against the Sorbonne, he insisted that what is true in philosophy is false in theology. Human reason and God's Word are always opposed to each other. The controversy raged far beyond the confines of Helmstedt, and both of the chief participants were condemned for their extreme views. More than any other theologian of the day, Gerhard succeeded in settling the controversy to the satisfaction of practically all orthodox Lutheran theologians.

It is important to understand, as Bengt Hägglund has pointed out,[66] that the revival of Aristotelian philosophy in the universities and the great impetus toward strict Lutheran orthodoxy were two separate developments, and we must not seek to make one the cause of the other or assume that there was some necessity for the two movements occurring simultaneously. However, it was inevitable that Lutheran orthodoxy and the Neo-Aristotelianism would confront each other; and either a clash would ensue — and this is how Daniel Hoffmann viewed the confrontation — or there would be some attempt to direct and use what was of value in the new philosophy. It was Gerhard's role, along with Balthasar Meisner and others, to inaugurate in a manner acceptable to his orthodox coreligionists the use of the new philosophy as a help toward the defense and presentation of theology. Two aspects of Aristotelianism seemed to be quite acceptable to Gerhard and those who followed as they dealt with theology. First, Aristotle's empirical method of gaining knowledge was accepted along with all that it implied. Second, the causal factors *(causa efficiens, causa finalis, causa materialis, causa formalis)* were used extensively in the presentation of doctrine, and particularly the distinction between *materia* and *forma* was deemed helpful.

b. GERHARD'S SYNTHESIS. But with all the novelty of his approach, Gerhard does not differ from Luther on the relation of philosophy to theology. Nor can we lay to Gerhard's charge any mixing of the two activities or any responsibility for the Enlightenment or the scourge of rationalism, which were later so dominant in Germany. Like Luther, Gerhard held that within philosophy, which included all rational knowledge, there are several different disciplines or sciences. And these must be judged separately in their relation to theology. Metaphysics and much of Aristotelian physics are useless to theology; but logic and rhetoric may be of service.[67] Luther's most definite statement of his views on philosophy are presented in his disputation on John 1:14, which Gerhard quoted above. Herein Luther is most insistent against the theologians of the Sorbonne on a number of points.

First, he contends that philosophy and theology operate in two entirely separate spheres. "Philosophy deals with those things that are knowable *{cognoscibilia}* to our human reason. Theology deals with those things that are to be believed, that is, with things that are grasped by faith." This is precisely Gerhard's position, as we have seen. When Luther goes on to

say that this principle implies that what is true in philosophy is false in theology, Gerhard does not hesitate to quote him with approval; for Luther meant that all things cannot be true in different levels of discourse (*in diversis professionibus*). It is one thing to believe, another thing to understand. Thus, there is a world of difference between philosophy and theology. With all this Gerhard is in complete agreement. And he is also in accord with Luther when he calls philosophy and theology *contraria*, like black and white. This means that *God* and *man* mean something different in philosophy and in theology. The statement "God is man" is true in theology and false in philosophy.[68] Luther even goes so far as to say that in this respect "mathematics is entirely at enmity *(inimicissima)* with theology." Mathematics says that one cannot be three, as in the article of the Trinity. Mathematics cannot accept that in the Sacrament of the Altar bread is the body and wine the blood of Christ. In all this Luther is not rejecting philosophy, surely not mathematics, but merely insisting that philosophy and mathematics remain in their own sphere (*sphaera*), which is different from that of theology. "Although in nature a thing is not true, nevertheless in God it can be and is true."[69]

Second, Luther points out that faith cannot be subjected to the rules and categories of philosophy but is free of them *(Fides non est regulis seu verbis philosophiae adstricta aut subjecta, sed est inde libera)*, nor can God be subjected to the canons of reason and syllogisms. This means that God can become man even though God is infinite and man is finite. "Philosophy," says Luther, "does not say that God is a man and a man is God and the Son of God. But we say that a man is God, and we affirm this by the Word of God without any syllogism and philosophy. In our vocabulary philosophy amounts to nothing." Again Gerhard agrees completely with Luther and even follows him closely by showing with the same analogies that philosophy cannot judge theology.[70]

There are, therefore, two reasons for Gerhard's more positive judgment of philosophy and its usefulness in theological endeavor. First, living in the wake of the revival of Neo-Aristotelianism in both Lutheran and Reformed circles, Gerhard could not have simply rejected philosophy out of hand as Luther did, even if he had wanted to. Second, we find him viewing philosophy as it is carried on by the believer, a philosophy completely in the service of God's revelation. Luther never envisaged such a philosophy.

C. CALOV'S ARGUMENTS. That Gerhard and his generation made peace

with philosophy had some far-reaching results in Lutheran circles. First of all, a fresh interest results in philosophy in orthodox Lutheran circles; an eclectic semi-Aristotelianism is worked out that is entirely in the service of theology. Then it is argued rather elaborately that there can be no conflict between philosophy and theology. By the time of Calov a number of arguments are formally worked out to show that philosophy is not contrary to theology.[71] (1) The truth always agrees with itself and cannot contradict itself (Aristotle, *Ethica*, I, 8). This means that truth discovered from the light of nature is no less true than that revealed to us in Scripture. Scripture itself teaches the truth of natural knowledge (Rom. 1:19) and even calls it wisdom (1 Cor. 1:21). If truth is defined as the correspondence of our thought or belief with actuality *(conformitas intellectus cum re)*, then we cannot speak of a double truth, one carnal and the other spiritual. To Calov truth is nothing else than the agreement of the concepts of the mind with a state of affairs *(veritas nihil aliud est, quam adaequatio notionum mentis cum re ipsa)*, and a true statement merely says that this state of affairs obtains *(vera est oratio, quando ita pronunciat rem esse)*. On this definition a theory of double truth, one carnal and the other spiritual, is impossible, for this understanding of truth has no necessary moral implication. Truth merely obtains. To speak of carnal truth is to speak ineptly. Truth is not derived from the flesh. The absurdity of a double-truth theory is seen in Hoffmann's desperate distinction between false truth (philosophy) and true truth (theology). (2) Natural and philosophic knowledge has its origin from God, and what comes from God does not contradict itself. Philosophy is a gift of God and therefore does not conflict with theology. (3) God has revealed Himself in His creation and through the Law, which is written in man's heart (Rom. 1:19; 2:14), and this that man might be led to God (Acts 14:17; 17:27). Philosophy arises through the investigation of natural things, which reveal the glory of God (Ps. 19:1). How then can philosophy conflict with theology when it leads to it? (4) Philosophy is often praised in the Scriptures: natural science (Job 38; Ps. 19; Ps. 148), astronomy (Is. 40:26), music (2 Chron. 5:12-13; Ps. 150), arithmetic, geometry, architecture, etc. (5) Logic and synthetic and analytic studies are useful in presenting theology. (6) If philosophy opposes theology, then theology conflicts with right reason, which is a gift of God. It is clear that in all these arguments Calov is considering philosophy in the

broadest sense as embracing all knowledge and even the arts. There is nothing in these arguments of Calov's that is not already incipient in Gerhard. These arguments become the common stock of all the later Lutherans.

The second result of the rapprochement of philosophy and theology brought about by Gerhard, Meisner, and others was, as we have seen, the increase of scholastic terminology in theological discourse. This scholastic and philosophical terminology and structure became increasingly intricate as time went on. Such a time-bound feature of the old orthodox dogmatics is of course difficult for us to appreciate and impossible to imitate today when we are quite out of contact and out of sympathy with the outmoded Aristotelian terms and thought patterns of a past age. However, we must remember that scholastic formulation and categories were the bag and baggage of all theologians in the 17th century. Theologians could not have written to a wide and learned audience without employing the terms common in those days, or at least few thought they could do so. We must also bear in mind that Aristotelian terminology and thought forms were never considered essential by Lutherans for the presentation of Christian doctrine or for theological discourse. They would willingly have shed such terminology completely, if this could have been done for the advancement of true doctrine. We shall see that in only a very few cases did Aristotelian or philosophical concepts have any harmful effect on their theology as it was actually worked out. Lutheran theology consciously labored under the Scriptures alone. Its interest in philosophy, as Dorner correctly points out, was chiefly on dialectical grounds, for purposes of defense and attack.[72] Bengt Hägglund has aptly summed up the climate in the time of Gerhard as follows:

> The orthodox presentation of doctrine rests mainly on a Biblical manner of argumentation. An ongoing study of Scripture likewise forms the basis of the structure of theology. The connection with the scholastic philosophy does not imply fundamentally any mixing of the principles of faith and reason. The apparatus of philosophical concepts should in the end function as a means of aid in the defense of faith and in the doctrinally oriented explanation of theological questions. In regard to the content of the teaching every argument of reason must give way to the witness of Scripture. On this point Lutheran orthodoxy is distinguished from medieval scholasticism and from the contemporary Reformed orthodoxy, where to a certain extent the attempt was made to harmonize the content of revelation with rational

argumentation. Thus, for instance, Keckermann maintained that the doctrine of the Trinity can be proved philosophically, while the Lutherans deny this. The ideal of the latter is what Balthasar Meisner calls a *philosophia sobria,* that is to say, a limited philosophy that reverently subjects itself to the witness of revealed truth.[73]

Mention was made of the fact that the later Lutheran dogmaticians became even more scholastic than Gerhard in their formulations and in their treatment of doctrine. This was true of Quenstedt, Baier, and Hollaz, and especially of Koenig and John Adam Osiander, but not of Calov or Bechmann. There is no indication, however, that the Lutherans of the later orthodox period went beyond Gerhard on any fundamental point. To illustrate this, we will examine the position of Hollaz, the last of the great dogmaticians, on the relation between philosophy (and reason) and theology,[74] and this will conclude our discussion of this very important issue.

d. HOLLAZ ON THEOLOGY AND REASON. It must first be noted that when Hollaz and the Lutherans following Gerhard speak of an agreement between theology and philosophy, they are, like Gerhard, not speaking of any concrete philosophy but of what we might call perfect philosophy, philosophy as *scientia veritatis.* As such it cannot contradict theology, for truth cannot contradict truth. Another point to bear in mind is that philosophy, according to the dogmaticians, is the knowledge of the truth in the realm of finite objects, what is ordinarily observable in the realm of nature. Hence it correctly judges that there cannot be three persons in one essence *(quot sunt personae finitae, tot sunt essentiae),* but this judgment has nothing to do with the infinite Godhead. Philosophy concludes that a virgin in the ordinary course of nature does not give birth to a child, but this conclusion does not pertain to what occurs by the supernatural intervention of the Holy Spirit. It is clear that in this context the Lutherans are not speaking of philosophy as we generally understand the term. They are thinking of philosophy much in the sense of the empirical method of modern science, as the analysis of the conclusions drawn from the orderly accumulation of human experience. But with one qualification: this philosophy, this *scientia veritatis,* is the philosophy *secundum Christum.* It has no independent activity, although it has its own principles. Philosophy must be a Christian interpretation of all things. Aristotelianism, Platonism, Stoicism, etc., are all philosophies that Paul

has in mind when he warns against vain philosophies (Col. 2:8; Gal. 4:9). Thus, the Christian's understanding of every aspect of human knowledge will reflect his faith in Christ and will be dominated by Christian theology. Philosophy cannot conflict with theology, because it is absolutely subordinate to theology.

What about reason (and the area of logic in philosophy) as it relates to theology? At first it may seem that particularly the later representatives of Lutheran orthodoxy make too much of reason, especially to our age of theologians who are influenced by existentialism and unreason. Hollaz,[75] for instance, speaks of reason with a sort of affection that might well have repelled Luther. But this first impression, which one might receive if one merely glanced at the outer form and structure of the later dogmatics, is misleading. It is true that Hollaz says that the principles of reason are absolute and universally binding — they are rules for thought, and even Scripture cannot set them aside. For instance: it is impossible for a thing both to be and not to be at the same time; or, whatever is, when it is, has being; or, each person is an essence. Scripture teaches many articles of faith that excel these principles, but the mysteries of our faith never contradict or abrogate them. But this is no more than Gerhard had taught; it was an attempt to keep theology and philosophy each in its own sphere, maintain the validity and truth of each, but at the same time reject any double-truth theory. Hollaz is quite convinced that such a position makes no extravagant claim at all for reason and its prerogatives; and he would have been shocked if anyone had accused him of overly exalting reason. It is true, he says, that philosophers have proved the existence and attributes of God in metaphysics from the principles of reason. But this is equally true: "Reason left to itself knows nothing of the pure articles of faith but grows blind and dizzy at the mysteries of faith. (1 Cor. 2:14)"

In reference to the organic, or ministerial, use of reason Hollaz finds himself in agreement with Luther. Reason is a gift of God, even for the unregenerate man who constantly misuses it. The organic principles are indispensable tools in acquiring the theological aptitude, for without them no sense or meaning could be made out of theological statements. Hollaz is speaking of such principles as logic, grammar, and rhetoric. He is saying that, although we can and do misuse our reason, it is not therefore a virtue to be stupid or irrational; and although God wishes us

to take our reason captive in obedience to Christ, He never tells us to be unreasonable.

> Without the use of reason we cannot understand theological teachings, we cannot support them [Hollaz means with Scriptures], and we can not defend them against the artifices of the adversaries. In His Word God has revealed wisdom unto salvation, not to brutes certainly, but to men who use sound reason. And He enjoins them to read His Word, to listen to it and meditate on it (Deut. 6:6; John 5:39). Hence it is incumbent on the intellect as subject to receive all this and as instrument to apprehend it. Just as we see nothing without our eyes and hear nothing without our ears, we understand nothing without our reason. At the same time, however, human reason is not the fountain or fundamental element from which the proper and central principles of faith are derived.

Hollaz is saying here that — granted the paradoxical character of Christian doctrine, granted that the articles of faith are above all rational explanation, and granted that logical thinking is inadequate in matters of faith — still man's mind and intellect and powers of reason are involved in accepting these great mysteries and in proclaiming them. This is essentially Hollaz' point in all the kindly statements he makes concerning human reason. He is defending a theology that, although paradoxical, is intelligible. God's revelation can be proclaimed in meaningful statements. This emphasis is particularly important to Hollaz in his dispute with mystics (Weigel) and Quakers (Robert Barclay), who taught that faith and a saving knowledge of God could be engendered without the preaching of the Gospel.[76] Faith comes by preaching, the preaching of a cognitive, meaningful message. The mysteries of which the message speaks are beyond the search of reason, but the message itself is comprehensible, couched as it is in ordinary and intelligible language and syntax. We might just add at this point that for Lutheran theology Scripture, as far as it is clear, is clear to human reason and comprehension.

In his discussion of reason and theology Hollaz defends the use of deductions and syllogisms drawn from Scripture. And he is by no means reluctant to use the syllogism, as any reader of the *Examen* will discover, often to his dismay. However Hollaz sweetens his fare somewhat by saying: "It is not always and everywhere necessary to reduce theological demonstration to categorical and clearly expressed syllogisms. Syllogistic expression, where another way of putting things is quite evident and

John Gerhard and the Changes in Dogmatics and Prolegomena 137

easy to understand, becomes superfluous and even irksome." How many superfluous and even irksome syllogisms find their way into Hollaz' theologizing is anybody's guess, but they must run well into the hundreds. However, we must not suppose that there is any real difference between Hollaz at this point and Luther when he said that "a syllogism is not admitted in the mysteries of faith." [77] Luther too drew hundreds of syllogisms and conclusions from Scripture in his career and felt no compunction to justify such a procedure. Luther is protesting against a Procrustean syllogizing that in the interest of logic does violence to the articles of faith, and especially against the scholastic ideal that the mysteries of faith can be presented in syllogistic form. It is this concern that prompts him to condemn mathematics when it seeks to comprehend the divine mysteries. Hollaz, on the other hand, is speaking of something quite different in defending the use of deductions and syllogisms in theology. He has in mind the orderly presentation of theology and the conclusions that are rightly drawn from Biblical premises; for instance:

> Whoever has a human body and a human soul is a true man.
> Christ has a human body and a human soul.
> Therefore Christ is true man.

In defending the use of syllogisms in showing correct conclusions drawn from Scripture, Hollaz no doubt has in mind the position of orthodox Lutheranism that necessary and evident consequences drawn from Scripture are as true and binding as Scripture and may be considered substantially *(quoad rem & sensum)* the Word of God.[78] The practical importance of Hollaz' position regarding conclusions rightly drawn from Scripture is seen when the sinner by faith applies the universal promises of the Gospel to himself; such a sinner is drawing a theological conclusion.[79]

One final observation ought to be made concerning Hollaz' idea of the relation of reason and theology. Like Luther and Gerhard, he holds that reason and theology belong in two distinct realms. He says:

> Although the mysteries of faith are not contrary to the principles of reason, at the same time they must not be judged by these principles. Medicine and jurisprudence are not contrary to each other, and yet a physician in curing a fever does not employ a method that is used in the legal process, nor does a lawyer seek to settle a damage action in court by an appeal to anatomy. The arts of painting and of making

shoes do not conflict with each other, but let the shoemaker stick to his last. Right reason, as long as it confines itself within the limits of its own object, does not contradict the mysteries of faith. *Per accidens,* however, it may happen that corrupt reason transgresses the boundary of its own activity and opposes divine revelation violently and inconsistently.

It is Hollaz' opinion that reason, when it does not give heed to God's revelation, will according to its own canons resolutely oppose the mysteries of faith. To the mystery of the Trinity it will oppose the axiom of philosophy that for every person there must be an essence. To the doctrine of the incarnation reason will place in opposition the principle that every intelligent nature is in its essence complete and a person. Against the doctrine of the presence of Christ's body and blood in the Sacrament reason will counter that every natural body must occupy one determinate place. But these principles of reason, which hold true in the sphere of nature and finite objects, cannot be applied to matters of faith without a μετάβασις εἰς ἄλλο γένος. "Reason is not the lord of theology but the handmaid. Let the handmaid Hagar serve her mistress and not order her around." It will be noticed that Hollaz is offering the same examples of the impotence of reason outside its sphere as Luther did. We may conclude that there is in the later orthodoxy no weakening of the limitations of reason in grasping and assessing God's revelation, that is, no weakening in principle.

That the later dogmaticians become rationalistic in practice as they work out and try to answer certain theological problems will be mentioned later. On two essential points, however, they were quite consciously in agreement with Luther: First, they believed that there was an essential unity of all Christian doctrine; one article could not oppose another article and thus make some sort of chaotic nonsense out of Christian theology. Second, they believed that there were gaps *(lacunae)* between the articles of faith that could not be settled logically; there was a paradoxical element belonging to the articles of faith. On the first point we find Hollaz, for instance, saying the following: "There is a harmony belonging to the articles of faith that is beautiful; they are like a sweet symphony. Consequently it has been the custom to call faith one connected entity *{una copulativa},* and it has been compared with a chain connected by many links. Destroy one link, and you have rent the chain; remove one article of faith, and you have disturbed the inner harmony of faith. By virtue of

this inner harmony it cannot happen that one article of faith could be placed in contradiction to another." [80] Hollaz is not maintaining here that all the articles of faith conform to some logical system, much less does he fancy a theology unified on the basis of some foreign synthesis. His illustrations show that this is not what he has in mind. He is merely saying that Christian doctrine is one perfect whole, like a beautiful picture or symphony or like the human body. He is not thinking of a rational unity but of a structural or organic unity. This is why all Christian doctrine was so important to Hollaz and all the orthodox Lutherans: all Christian doctrine (the term is always used in the singular) is of one piece, and whatever affects a part affects the whole body of doctrine.

There was nothing new about this idea. It was derived from Luther. Luther had said: "In philosophy a very small error in the beginning is very serious in the end. So also in theology a little error overturns the whole doctrine. . . . Doctrine is like a mathematical point. It cannot be divided, that is, you cannot take away from it or add to it. . . . Therefore doctrine must be one continual, round golden ring in which there is no break; if even the least break occurs, the circle is no longer perfect *{integer}*." [81] Again, still commenting on Gal. 5:9, Luther says: "One article is all articles, and all articles are one; and if one is laid aside all are lost." When the dogmaticians follow Luther on this point, their interest is the same as his when he says, "We will not play with doctrine."

But if doctrine is one unified whole, there are still *lacunae* between the articles of faith, gaps that cannot and must not be resolved. This is the purpose of many of the distinctions found in the later Lutheran dogmatics, to bring out in sharp relief these gaps and the paradoxical nature of faith. Thus, the universality of grace and the sufficiency of grace are both taught with equal forcefulness, although there is no reconciling the two teachings without resorting to universalism. The antecedent and consequent will of God are both emphatically taught, although strictly speaking there is only one will in God, which however we cannot penetrate; and again the two ideas cannot be reconciled rationally. And we could multiply such examples. So, although faith is *una copulativa,* it is still above reason, and the articles of faith cannot be forced into any rational coherence.

We must mention one more point before leaving this discussion of the relation of philosophy and reason to theology. There is no necessary

connection between scholastic terminology or structure and rationalism. The most rationalistic theologians of the 16th and 17th centuries were the Socinians. They held that all theology could and should be subjected to reason, and nothing should be believed that could not be grasped by one's reason.[82] Yet for the most part their works are remarkably free of all scholastic form and terminology. Nor do strict orthodoxy and scholasticism necessarily go hand in hand, any more than in the theology of the medieval scholastics. During the period of Pietism an even more rigid scholasticism reigned among those who had departed from orthodoxy (Buddeus) or were even opposed to it (Breithaupt).

7. *Gerhard's Methodus: The Course of Study*

We now return briefly to Gerhard and consider the third section of his *Methodus Studii Theologici,* which deals with the actual course of studying theology. He divides his outline into parts or years of study, and we need only review summarily his suggestions, noting that he has the contributions of Hyperius and Chytraeus in mind as he offers the following outline.

The *first part* of studying theology consists in reading the Scriptures. This must be done with prayer and with the single desire of learning the sense of the Scriptures. In all such reading the mind must be submissive, ready to take every thought captive in obedience to Scripture, willing simply to let the Word speak. And this reading must be assiduous. Gerhard is aware that here too the rule applies: Repetition is the mother of learning. "Sacred Scripture," he says, as Hafenreffer has said before, "is a sea, the depths of which we cannot probe in this life, much less exhaust." Beware, he warns, of becoming surfeited, tired of reading Scripture, for when that happens no fruit will be forthcoming. Gerhard emphasizes forcefully the importance of cursory Bible reading, getting the broad sweep and outline of a book. But intensive reading must also be practiced whereby all the nuances of syntax and emphases and vocabulary are observed. He lists the following things to look for in reading Scripture. (a) The general theme or scope of the passage. (b) An outline of the partitions. (c) The meaning of individual words and phrases. (d) The different interpretations of the fathers and commentators. (e) The solution of difficulties, textual or doctrinal, that may present themselves. (f) Insights that may not appear on the first reading. (g) Sensitive re-

marks of commentators. These simple rules, if observed, will offer great reward, although we must remember that we cannot always observe them all as we might desire.

The *second part* in the study of theology consists in the attempt to reduce the contents of Scripture to *loci theologici*. Here Gerhard follows the direction given by Chemnitz, Chytraeus, and others, and offers suggestions on arrangement similar to those of Hyperius and Selnecker.[83] Like his predecessors he attempts to illustrate the usefulness of this practice. (a) This activity will encourage theologians to seek the truth. (b) It may serve to correct aberrations that have been taken over uncritically from heterodox teachers. (c) It may help sometimes to dispel doubt. (d) It aids further the future teachers in the church (Titus 1:9) and is useful not only *ad* διδασκαλίαν but also *ad* ἔλεγχον. (e) The method enables insights to be shared as they are discovered, thus bringing advance in theological perception. (f) It renders the theologian sharper in speaking and in judging doctrine. (g) It helps us discuss theology more clearly, and this is necessary for every Christian (1 Peter 3:15). (h) It forms good habits in the theologian and frees his mind from hazy thinking and slovenly practices. (i) It may often aid in explaining difficult passages. Possibly Gerhard has in mind at this point the analogy of Scripture, a principle that will be drawn from heavily in constructing *loci theologici*. Like the former theologians, Gerhard insists that this is the method of Scripture itself, of Christ and the apostles. He goes beyond the earlier theologians, however, in offering a great deal of guidance in carrying out the practice of and laying down the rules for theological disputations.

The *third part* of the study of theology continues intensive Bible reading and enters on the practice of disputation. The art of polemics is taken up, with Chemnitz' *Examen Concilii Tridentini* as suggested reading.

The *fourth part* (or year) continues the activities of the previous part and goes on to consider the controversies with the Calvinists. In this part Gerhard also suggests that homiletics be considered. His discussion of homiletics is very long and includes pointers on the purpose, method, etc., of homiletics.

The *fifth part* studies church history and the readings of Luther, the church fathers, and the scholastics. Here Gerhard is quite specific; the church fathers ought always to be read in such a way that they are com-

pared with Scripture. Regarding the Scholastics, it is true that Luther did away with such reading and brought theological students back to the pure fountains of Scripture, and he insisted that "scholastic theology is nothing else than ignorance of the truth and vain deceit" — and with all this Gerhard is in complete sympathy — but because of this very fact the scholastic theologians must be studied lest such an awful scourge again deceive unwary people. Gerhard proceeds to indulge in a lengthy and documented critique of scholastic theology. We might merely mention his conclusions. (a) By failing to observe the Scripture principle, scholastic theology has mixed philosophy with theology into one grand chaos. (b) Scholastic theology disputed endlessly about "idle, curious, irritating, useless, absurd, and superstitious matters," all of which was impious in the very nature of the case.

Gerhard concludes his *Methodus Studii Theologici* with a touching short section entitled *"Coronis de Tentatione,"* which is calculated to show the way the Holy Spirit molds and makes us theologians, namely by afflictions.

8. *Gerhard's Contribution to Dogmatics and Its Prolegomena*

In Gerhard we find a theologian who is both eclectic and creative in the best sense of the word. Whatever his predecessors have contributed to the prolegomena of the study of theology that is good and useful he eagerly incorporates into his own discussions of the subjects. Thus the method and purpose of dogmatics is the same as Melanchthon's *Loci Communes*. On one point after another Gerhard follows the direction taken by Selnecker, Chytraeus, Hyperius, and Chemnitz in his suggestions concerning theological study, his outlines for dogmatics, etc. At the same time Gerhard is original. He is the first to present a well-organized formal prolegomenon to a dogmatics. He is the first to consider the subject of theology in any extended fashion. He is the first to mark out precisely the relation of philosophy to theology as this pertains to the work of the theologian. And he is the first to bring philosophy, limited rigidly by theological principles and interests, to the aid of theology. In all this Gerhard's work became a pattern for future occupation in prolegomena. There were, of course, certain advances made by the later Lutheran dogmaticians and certain innovations as well (e. g., the dividing of theology into various disciplines, the discussion of religion, the classification of

the articles of faith). The only innovation of far-reaching significance was the introduction of the analytic method in dogmatics, first worked out by George Calixt and followed, sometimes with unfortunate results, by most of the orthodox Lutherans after that time. Even this method, however, which views theology in the light of its goal, may have had its seed in Gerhard as he brought Aristotelian factors to bear on his treatment of the articles of faith. If there is any truth in this, it is to Gerhard's credit that he never went beyond the simple synthetic method of considering one Scripture teaching after another in an orderly arrangement. In Gerhard, then, we have an impressive, simple, useful, full-fledged prolegomenon to dogmatics.[84]

As far as his actual working out of dogmatics is concerned, Gerhard continues in the exegetico-historical approach of Chemnitz and Flacius, an approach already discernible in Luther and Melanchthon. It was not enough for the dogmatician to know the Scriptures and the method of exegesis. He must know and interpret also the life and development of Christ's church through her history; he must know something of the historical background to the creeds and the doctrine of the church, and something of the history of Biblical interpretation. Church history is brought right into the study of dogmatics by Gerhard, interpreted soteriologically and applied practically. There is an ecumenicity in Gerhard's dogmatics (which again places him in the tradition of Melanchthon and Chemnitz) that is theological and doctrinal and places him in fellowship with the church of all ages. It is this feeling of unity with the church of the past and his strong confessional stand that lead to the exegetico-historical approach to dogmatics.

NICHOLAS HUNNIUS AND THE CLASSIFICATION OF THE ARTICLES OF FAITH

It was perhaps inevitable that a classification of the articles of faith would develop in Lutheran theology and an idea of fundamental articles would emerge. There was first of all a practical reason for this development. The laymen, plagued and confused by innumerable doctrinal controversies in those days, had an urgent practical concern to know what was necessary to believe to be saved. It also became increasingly necessary to illustrate to laymen that sects such as Socinianism had abandoned Christianity by rejecting articles of faith that were fundamental to it.

1. Hunnius' Fundamental Articles

To fill the first practical need of the Lutheran people Nicholas Hunnius composed a popular presentation of the essential elements of the Christian faith. The book, entitled *Epitome Credendorum* and published first in 1625, made the center of faith Christ's work and the forgiveness He brings. The book was designed to show with an abundance of Biblical citations and in an elementary manner what was fundamental to the Christian faith.[85] To fill the second practical need of warning against the unchristian character of Socinianism, Hunnius wrote another book, in which he showed that Jesus Christ is the foundation of our faith (1 Cor. 3:11).[86] The essential feature of our faith is that we know Christ, and any false doctrine concerning Him endangers our faith. Hunnius also distinguished between those teachings of Scripture that directly affect saving faith and those that do not.

Another influence that necessitated a careful classification of the fundamental articles of faith was the polemical situation of the day, particularly between the Lutheran and Reformed theologians. The irenic efforts of many Calvinists created the impression that there was really nothing of importance dividing the Lutherans and the Reformed. Francis Junius had taught that there existed a fundamental doctrinal unity between the two communions, and John Dury had contended that Christ was the foundation of faith and that faith in Him served as sufficient basis for ecclesiastical union. In the light of this situation the Lutheran theologians felt called upon to show that there was a basic difference between the two theological positions. Again it was Nicholas Hunnius who led the way toward the final articulation of what were the basic articles to the Christian faith. In his Διάσκεψις *Theologica de Fundamentali Dissensu Doctrinae Evangelicae-Lutheranae & Calvinianae seu Reformatae* (1626) Hunnius sets forth what he considers to be fundamental to the Christian faith and then classifies the articles of faith according to primary fundamental articles, secondary fundamental articles, and nonfundamental articles. He also shows that the Reformed theologians err on fundamental issues. There is nothing very new about Hunnius' classification except that everything is most clearly and concisely set forth. The medieval scholastic theologians had already mentioned most of his categories.[87] In Reformed circles Junius had long since (in 1593) attempted to isolate

what in the Christian doctrine was fundamental to believe for salvation. He concluded that God was the foundation of our salvation and the object of our faith; and the main part in the article concerning God is that He is gracious and forgives sins.[88] In Lutheran circles Leonard Hutter had operated with a classification of the articles of faith in his attack against the unionism of David Pareus.[89] But Hunnius' treatment is much more thorough and useful than anything his forerunners had produced, and his classification of the articles of faith soon became normative for all the following orthodox dogmaticians.[90]

2. *Later Dogmaticians on Articles of Faith*

We shall now examine carefully this arrangement of the articles of faith as it was presented by the Lutherans after Nicholas Hunnius. For here we have one of the more significant advances in the shape of dogmatics and prolegomena after the time of Gerhard.

"An article of faith," according to Hunnius, "is a portion of Christian doctrine through which we are led to eternal salvation."[91] This definition sounds quite wooden until we learn that in this definition faith is understood as subjective faith, my faith in Christ *(fides qua creditur)*, and doctrine is understood as the *doctrina evangelii.* Hunnius explains that it would be better to speak of articles of doctrine, inasmuch as faith arises out of doctrine. But he sticks with the accepted ecclesiastical usage. The term *article* is very carefully chosen. The term implies that it is a part of a whole body of doctrine; it implies a relation to the other articles of faith like the mutual relation of the members of the human body; and the term implies that each article is distinct and must not be confused with other articles. According to the later dogmaticians articles of faith possess definite characteristics. (a) They must be drawn from the Word of God. (b) They must have reference to man's salvation. An article of faith is taught in order to be believed. All the articles have a soteriological purpose. (c) There is a harmony among the articles of faith as sweet and pleasing as a symphony. All the articles are intimately connected with one another and cannot be made to oppose one another. (d) The articles of faith cannot be known or learned by any natural process, for they transcend the grasp of human reason. They are revealed by God, and we must cast down every imagination that would exalt itself against God

(2 Cor. 10:5; Rom. 4:18; Gen. 17:17), for the articles of faith appear inconsistent *(absona)* and ridiculous to reason (Rom. 8:5; 1 Cor. 1:17, 19-20; 2:14). The articles of faith are therefore truly πιστά, things to be believed. And what are these πιστά? Materially they are God Himself and divine things (the Gospel). Formally they are God's revelation, which has been given for man's salvation.

Before continuing this résumé, a few comments are in order. Thus far Hollaz, Quenstedt, and the later dogmaticians are on very safe ground as they follow Hunnius. They are employing the term *doctrine* (the term is always used in the singular) in the Biblical sense of Gospel teaching. Quenstedt says that the Biblical term for *articulus fidei* is *mystery*. Strictly speaking, the Law is not an article of faith, for the Law is to be obeyed, not believed. We might stress this point that doctrine — and this includes all the articles of faith — is soteriological in purpose, it serves to create and bolster faith, it is to be believed. This is not to say that the articles of faith take the place of Christ as the object of saving faith. The Lutherans are most careful to say that the articles of faith are believed by that faith which trusts in the merits of Christ. They do not think to separate God from what He has revealed about Himself, *Deus* from *res divinae*. Nor do they have any mind to separate Christ from what is said about Christ in the Gospel. To believe in Christ is to believe the doctrine about Christ. Hollaz says: "In essence one object of faith is meant, whether we speak of it as being Christ the Mediator, or the grace of God, or the promises of grace given for the sake of Christ the Mediator. It is merely a difference of conception and mode of speaking." [92] To believe in Christ does not exclude faith in God's grace and mercy and promises in the Gospel, but includes all this.[93] Thus to believe the articles of faith is to believe in Christ, for the articles of faith are no more than an orderly arrangement of the Gospel message. At this point we might recall what the Lutheran dogmaticians said about the unity of the articles of faith. They are all related to the Gospel, and no article could be rejected lest that golden chain of Christian doctrine be severed and the Gospel itself be corrupted. We have already noted how to the Lutherans the unity of the articles of faith was not according to a logical or rational structure. It was for practical, not theoretical, reasons that the interrelationship of the articles of faith was upheld so consistently: just as the Gospel is one message of salvation, the articles of faith are of one piece.

3. Fundamental and Nonfundamental Articles

Unfortunately the distinction between primary fundamental, secondary fundamental, and nonfundamental articles of faith — which was necessarily but also somewhat arbitrarily worked out — tended, regrettably and unintentionally, to obscure the unity of the articles of faith and to conjure up the specter of some sort of complex machine rather than a grand and inspiring symphony or choir.

Let us now explore this complicated and elaborate structure, which was so minutely worked out. As first devised by Nicholas Hunnius and followed by Huelsemann, Calov, Quenstedt, Dannhauer, Kromayer, and Baier, Christian doctrine was divided into fundamental articles of faith and salvation, secondary fundamental articles, and nonfundamental articles. Fundamental articles are those divisions *(partes)* of Christian doctrine that one must know and accept "if one is to retain the foundation of faith *{fundamentum fidei}*" (Hollaz); and to the extent that these articles are denied, the foundation of faith is overthrown. What is this so-called foundation of faith? It is that on which faith rests. But the dogmaticians feel the necessity of conceiving this foundation in different ways. Baier and Hollaz explain that the foundation is both the *object* or thing *(res illa)* upon which our faith and salvation are based, namely Christ, and the doctrine *(doctrina)*, which is the complex of divine teaching that leads us to faith in Christ (1 Cor. 3:11; Eph. 2:20). Quenstedt, following Hunnius, speaks of a threefold foundation — substantial, organic, and dogmatic. The substantial foundation is Christ, the real object of faith; the organic foundation is the Word of God, which is the source *(principium et medium)* of faith; the dogmatic foundation is that doctrine from which faith is conceived and sustained. It is obvious that the Gospel is meant in the last two cases. We must bear in mind that these are not two (or three) different foundations, but one, which is merely conceived in two (or three) different ways. Christ is the real foundation *(ex parte rei)* of our faith and spiritual life; the doctrine concerning Christ is the foundation in respect to our knowledge of Christ *(ex parte nostrae cognitionis)*. Hollaz makes this point clear by the following statement: "The doctrine concerning Christ is nothing else than Christ Himself as He is known by the intellect and presented in written or preached form so that He might be known by others." [94] This statement serves to explain the rationale underlying the idea of a twofold foundation of faith. You cannot abstract

Christ from His work and from the Gospel and all that is said about Him. To know and have Christ is to know and have the Gospel. Thus the fundamental articles of faith are the Gospel. And contrariwise, all heresy is against the Gospel. "Heresy," says Quenstedt, "is not just any error against the Word of God but an error that sets aside and overturns the very foundation of faith."[95]

What are the fundamental articles of faith? Here we can only close our eyes and plunge into the waves of distinctions that loom before us — and hope to come up alive. But we must make this effort, for there is good reason for every distinction that is made. Fundamental articles of faith are divided into primary and secondary fundamental articles.

a. PRIMARY FUNDAMENTAL ARTICLES. Baier defines these rather negatively as those articles that "we not only cannot deny if we are to retain our faith and salvation, but that we cannot be ignorant of." Following Hunnius, he then immediately subdivides these primary articles into (1) those that constitute the very foundation of faith (*fundamentum constituens:* Hunnius) or that "part of doctrine that is directly the cause of faith" (Hunnius), e. g., the article of Christ the God-man and His redemption; and (2) those that, although not the direct cause of faith, are nevertheless so intimately connected with it that unless they are explicitly known, the articles constituting the foundation of faith cannot produce and sustain faith. These articles Hunnius called the *pars doctrinas conservans fundamentum.* Examples of such articles are the Trinity, the gracious will of God to save all men, the articles of sin, justification, faith, and eternal life.

Hollaz subdivides the primary fundamental articles into three: constituent, antecedent, and consequent articles. (1) All articles of faith that directly enter into the definition of faith are considered constituent articles, e. g., the articles of God, sin, the Word, conversion, regeneration, God's justifying grace, Christ, saving faith, salvation. (2) Antecedent articles are those that are presupposed by the definition of faith, although they do not form a part of it. These correspond in order to the constituent articles listed just above. For instance, the existence of God is a presupposition for the doctrine of the Trinity. (3) Consequent articles follow justifying faith, strengthen it, serve it, and issue from it, e. g., the doctrine of the Word as a means of grace, Baptism, the Lord's Supper, church, ministry, etc. Granted that this elaborate scheme has the admirable purpose of

placing every facet of Christian doctrine in its proper light and of welding all Christian doctrine around the central article of Christ and forgiveness, it becomes artificial and very involved. It is further complicated by the fact that no two of the later dogmaticians offer the same scheme. For instance, Quenstedt, citing Huelsemann, includes under the consequent articles the justice of God, sanctification, and the communication of attributes in Christ; Hollaz lists the last of these under secondary fundamental articles.

b. SECONDARY FUNDAMENTAL ARTICLES. As defined by Hunnius, this is an article "that we can be unaware of without endangering our faith and salvation, but we cannot deny it." Examples of such articles, according to the later dogmaticians (Baier), are the communication of attributes in Christ, original sin, election, and justification by faith alone without works. The dogmaticians wish to stress the difference between ignorance or simplicity and disbelief. There may well be many simple people who speak the terminology of the trinitarian doctrine but do not grasp the difference between the concepts of person and essence or the distinction between the persons in the Trinity. Such simple ignorance does not damn. But an outright denial of the eternal generation of the Son or the procession of the Holy Spirit will overturn the fundamental article of the Trinity. In regard to justification Hollaz says:

> The justification of a converted sinner through faith in Christ is a constituent fundamental article of faith. Now it is possible for a sinner who recognizes and hates his sins to put all his confidence in Christ the Mediator and still not know about the exclusion of good works. Who would condemn such a person? But to deny that a sinner is justified by faith alone in Christ is to oppose the primary fundamental articles of God's grace and the merit of Christ.

It is perfectly clear what Hollaz is trying to get at here and what is the point of the whole concept of secondary articles. The dogmaticians are stressing the importance of all doctrine and the great danger of denying even a secondary article of faith. But at the same time our faith in Christ may be a very imperfect thing; it may be inarticulate and wanting in knowledge and not even reflective, and still be centered in Christ the Mediator. One may be ignorant of much that God has revealed and still know Jesus Christ as his Savior.

c. NONFUNDAMENTAL ARTICLES. These are the parts of Christian doctrine that one may be unaware of or even deny and still be saved. On this

definition of Hunnius' all the later Lutherans seem to be agreed. But which are the nonfundamental articles and why are they nonfundamental? Here there is great diversity among the Lutherans. For the most part they follow Hunnius in listing examples of nonfundamental articles. Such articles are, for instance, the article of traducianism as opposed to creationism, the immortality of man before the Fall, the sin against the Holy Spirit, the doctrine of the church visible and invisible, the marks of the church, Antichrist, etc. Such articles were considered to be clearly revealed in Scripture but were thought to be so far withdrawn from the foundation of faith that even a denial of them would not necessarily threaten faith.

The doctrine of Antichrist is perhaps the best example of what is implied when we call an article nonfundamental. Quenstedt points out [96] that the article is certainly not necessary to know for salvation; in former days there were countless Christians in the papacy who had no idea of it, for the church fathers had all sorts of discrepant opinions. However, the doctrine is not thereby unimportant. The many warnings in Scripture urge us to identify Antichrist just as we must identify the works of the devil. The people of Noah's day were not without guilt because they failed to see the signs of the times. In short, nonfundamental articles of faith are important. They are not merely exegetical or historical judgments, but articles of faith. It is sometimes by attacking the doctrine of Antichrist that an oblique assault is made against more serious matters. And so although the rejection of a nonfundamental article does not destroy one's faith, it is still a sin. Anything taught in God's Word, even those things that cannot be called articles of faith, such as the history of Samson or David or the divine institution of circumcision, is to be accepted. And if anything is deliberately rejected, our faith is in danger.[97] For to reject anything revealed in Scripture may result in one's sinning against one's conscience and ultimately affecting the foundation of faith.

By the turn of the 18th century the very notion of nonfundamental articles of faith had become suspect, and for several reasons. First, it would seem almost contradictory to call a teaching an article of faith when the rejection of it does not affect faith. Second, the tendency naturally developed to multiply nonfundamental articles ad infinitum. It is true that men like Quenstedt and Dannhauer had warned against this tendency. Quenstedt had clearly stated: "Although in a general way faith is concerned with all that is contained in the Word of God — his-

torical matters, ethical, and dogmatic — still specifically faith has to do with the dogmas of faith that are to be believed as such." [98] It was simply absurd when the Jesuit Adam Tanner asserted at the colloquy at Ratisbon that every statement in Scripture had the force of doctrine and could be considered an article of faith. Was it an article of faith that Judah committed incest and Tobias' dog wagged its tail? Such facts as the age of Methuselah or the building of the tower of Babel or the account of Balaam's ass are not by any stretch of the imagination articles of faith. Dannhauer too had maintained that not every assertion or statement in Scripture was an article of faith, and certainly not every gloss such as the time of the creation of the world or the year and day of Christ's birth.[99] Yet it is just such things that Hollaz lists as nonfundamental articles of faith. In view of this confusion it is little wonder that John Fecht says that nonfundamental articles are only in a remote and loose sense called articles of faith.[100] What the Lutherans from the time of Nicholas Hunnius had striven to do — to show by a discussion of the articles of faith that there was a fundamental difference between Calvinism and Lutheranism — had resulted by the time of Hollaz in a confusion with which later theologians like Fecht could only become impatient. And yet, in spite of problems created by classification of articles and by the disagreement among later Lutherans, it was a work that had to be done and as first outlined by Hunnius was a definite aid in clarifying Lutheran theology.

There was one side aspect of this complicated discussion that was not unimportant. Against the Socinians it was maintained that fundamental articles of faith are not necessarily taught in Scripture explicitly (αὐτολεξεί). Although many articles are presented in Scripture in so many words (ῥητῶς *sive disertis verbis*), certain articles are contained in Scripture only according to their sense (διανοητικῶς & *secundum rem*) and are reached by clear and firm consequences or inference. We have already mentioned this in our discussion of the usefulness of using syllogisms in drawing the correct conclusions from Scripture. Calov states the Lutheran position as follows:

> Although we recognize that those things necessary to believe for salvation ought to be taught and set forth in Scriptures so clearly that all can find them there, still we do not admit that these things are expressed in the sacred writings in just so many words, as though those things that are drawn from the Sacred Writings by inference, however

easy and leading and obvious this inference is, ought not to be considered articles of faith and necessary to believe.[101]

Calov goes on to point out that he is only defending the method of Christ and the apostles. Christ taught the resurrection as an article of faith, but He drew this article from the Old Testament by inference (Mark 12:26). That Christ was Messiah and Savior of the world is without question an article of faith, yet this article too Christ proved from the Old Testament Scriptures by inference (John 5:39). Again we can see the great practical importance of what Calov is maintaining. That I can apply the death and redemption of Christ to myself is an inference, Calov points out. Personal faith is predicated on an inference.[102]

4. *Pure and Mixed Articles*

Before leaving the subject of the articles of faith we must mention another classification of the articles that became common after the time of Gerhard — the division of the articles of faith into pure articles *(articuli puri)*, which are known only by revelation, and mixed articles *(articuli mixti)*, which are revealed but may also be known to some extent by the principles of reason. We have already noted that Gerhard has hinted at this distinction but made little of it. Hunnius had no need of such a classification. However, the distinction, which was bound to occur to Lutheran theologians, may be traced back to medieval times and was used by Lutherans prior to Gerhard or Hunnius. Cornelius Martini, for instance, had made much of the distinction, no doubt because of his interest in philosophy and the natural knowledge of God. He asserts that certain articles of faith pertain to faith per se, other articles only *per accidens*. Those that pertain to faith per se are articles that cannot be known or assessed by any inner light of man but can only be known by revelation — e. g., the Trinity, the Incarnation, justification by faith, the resurrection, the Last Judgment, etc. Those articles that pertain to faith *per accidens* are articles that can be demonstrated or deduced from nature or can be proved by principles of nature — e. g., that God is one, good, and immortal, that man has a rational soul, which is immortal. In themselves the latter do not pertain to faith *(in se & in sua natura)*, since they can be shown by reason, even though many people do not know or recognize these facts. Martini then goes on to say that it is foolish for one to try to prove the immortality of the soul from reason to anyone who recognizes the authority of Scripture.

One wonders, in the light of this statement made by one who was an avowed humanist, why so much effort was spent by Lutherans on the subject of natural theology and the natural knowledge of God, guarded as they were in all that they said.[103]

By the middle of the 17th century the classification of the articles of faith into pure and mixed articles was rather common among all Lutherans, although not a great deal of attention was given this distinction. Quenstedt offers perhaps the most complete definition:

> There are some dogmas in Scripture that are simply πιστά [matters of faith] and cannot be known from reason in any way but are far above it. But there are also certain dogmas that are πιστὰ κατά τι, things to be believed only in a certain sense. These dogmas, although they are revealed in Scripture and must be known, are nevertheless of such a nature that reason by its own principles is able to attain some sort of a knowledge of them. Thus this distinction between pure and mixed articles arises. The former are drawn from the Word of God alone and can only be believed, such as the article of the Trinity, the Incarnation, etc. The latter, although they can be known to some extent from the light of nature, are nevertheless only believed insofar as they are known from divine revelation. For instance, that God is, that He exercises care over all things, that He is powerful, wise, one, good, etc.— these things are *known* through clear demonstration; they are *believed* because of divine revelation. However, all those things that can be known in some way by the light of nature are not believed insofar as they are drawn from the light of nature but insofar as they are drawn from divine revelation.[104]

One can perceive from this statement of Quenstedt's that he feels a certain weakness in the distinction. If an article of faith is mixed, if it can be drawn from the light of reason, why should it be called an article of faith at all? Calov, who says much the same as Quenstedt, admits that the distinction is merely nominal and equivocal.[105] Hollaz tries to rescue the distinction from the obvious objection concerning *articuli mixti* by arguing that no article of faith, considered formally as an article of faith, can be mixed; however, when articles are considered materially in reference to their content, there are certain aspects of the mixed articles that can be known without divine revelation, although these aspects are not known with such clarity and benefit without divine revelation.[106] Hollaz' point is that something may be known, perhaps vaguely, that becomes an article of faith when it is revealed to be just that. Or a fact may be known the

meaning and significance of which is only apprehended by means of revelation. For instance, one may be aware without a divine revelation that God created the world, but only by revelation do we know that the creation was finished in six days and was accomplished at the Word of God (Heb. 11:3). Hollaz' defense of the *articuli mixti* may not satisfy us completely; to say that the mixed articles, considered materially, are known (although with limitations) by the light of nature seems to dissociate the content of the articles from their form as something revealed. But it would be difficult to find a better defense. And we must admit that some sort of idea of mixed articles is necessary if we are to be faithful to the witness of Scripture concerning God's revelation in nature. To deny that anything about the so-called mixed articles (as they are listed by the dogmaticians) can be known, to reject *articuli mixti* in this sense, would be to deny that God is actively working in nature and history.

The Influence of George Calixt

We must now interrupt our commentary on the origin and development of dogmatics and prolegomena in orthodox Lutheran theology and take a brief look at the influence of George Calixt (1586—1656).[107] Calixt was the student of the humanistic philosopher Cornelius Martini and for 42 years was professor at the University of Helmstedt, which was known for its Melanchthonian-humanistic character. Calixt was quite outside the orthodox Lutheran mold. He leaned strongly toward humanism. He was a syncretist who worked diligently for the reunion of Christendom on the basis of the doctrinal consensus of the first five centuries after Christ. He emphasized the role of tradition and reason in theology to a point that shocked his orthodox contemporaries. He was never able to accept the Formula of Concord. Yet he made an impact on orthodox Lutheran theology after Gerhard. Most of his impact was negative, and some orthodox Lutherans devoted tomes to refuting him and upholding the true Lutheran position. On a few points he was followed rather closely. At any rate we cannot consider the advances in prolegomena and dogmatics made by Calov and others without first saying a few words about Calixt's legacy.

Whereas Gerhard's ideas concerning theology and the theological method follow closely the direction taken by Luther and his Lutheran

predecessors and draw from the old scholastic theology for terminology and classifications, Calixt launches forth in a different direction. His humanistic predilections, imbibed from John Caselius and Cornelius Martini, prevented him from following Luther's ingenuous *oratio, meditatio, tentatio* approach to theology with its monergism and its depreciation of human reason. His humanism also made scholastic categories unpalatable to him, although he had a high respect for ancient philosophy.

As we examine Calixt's prolegomena,[108] we are at once struck with the marked contrast in content and form with all that we have considered before. The old scholastic divisions taken over by Gerhard and many of the Reformed theologians — e. g., *theologia viatorum, theologia beatorum, theologia visionis,* archetypal theology, natural and supernatural theology — are not found in Calixt. But more serious than these omissions was Calixt's basically synergistic approach to theology. This is not to say that he taught that the unregenerate could be theologians or that he made theology a science in the modern sense; faith was a presupposition for theological activity.[109] But just as Calixt did not think of faith primarily as a gift of God but as a *habitus* (a view rejected by the orthodox Lutherans), he did not consider theology primarily as a *habitus* θεόσδοτος but as "an aptitude acquired through study and hard work."[110] This "humanization of theology," as Wallmann has called it, tended to turn theology into a form of scientific scholarship that owes much to human powers.[111]

This is discernible in Calixt's double-source theory for theology.[112] In his view revelation is the source of theology, the divine *causa efficiens principalis* of theology. But logic may then be used to deal with those things that we believe, and it may deduce results in order to prove that we do not harbor mere human opinions but have an immovable Christian certainty. Calixt is most careful to stress that revelation is the *principium primum* of all our theological activity; but his very mention of a secondary principle is un-Lutheran and a threat against the *sola Scriptura* principle. Here he is going beyond Gerhard's straightforward *usus ministerialis* of reason. However, Calixt is wholly Lutheran in his insistence on the self-authenticating power of Scripture: Scripture is able to fix in a believer a firm confidence in its divine message. "Therefore we claim with every right that the assent Scripture works in a Christian man does not depend on any other source, far or near, besides Scripture itself. Scripture is

absolutely self-authenticating and self-demonstrative [αὐτόπιστος καὶ ἀναπόδεικτος]."[113] It is after the demonstration of Scripture that reason is given too much play by Calixt. It would be expected that Calixt with his emphasis on the powers and value of human reason would follow the Melanchthonian tradition in proving the divine origin of Christianity by various internal and external criteria,[114] and showing that Christianity has all the characteristics of true religion. This he does on the basis of a theory of natural religion. Thus, the superiority and truth of Christianity is shown to the non-Christian on the basis of the validity of natural religion and the moving of the Holy Spirit through revelation. By such a procedure, which would have been impossible for Gerhard, Calixt attempts to show that right reason is in harmony with revelation.

The one positive influence Calixt exerted on all the later orthodox Lutheran dogmaticians was his initiation of the so-called analytic method in dogmatics. It was Calixt who established the analytic method as the method of a practical *habitus* and the synthetic method as the method of a theoretical *habitus*. He offers no reasons why this must be so; he assumes that his position is valid in the nature of the case. And no doubt he is correct. But if one compares the concrete analytic method as put into practice by Calixt or Calov with the *loci* synthetic method of Gerhard, one cannot for the world see what is any more practical about the former. Calixt of course follows Gerhard, as does Calov, in contending that theology is a practical aptitude or activity, for it is never satisfied with mere knowledge of the truth but seeks to apply the truth to concrete living.[115]

The analytic method proceeds from effects to causes. This means that in theology the subject matter is taken up teleologically, beginning with man's final goal (eternal life), turning next to man as the subject, and finally to the means whereby man reaches his goal. Using this method, the outline for dogmatics would be as follows, according to Calixt:[116] (1) *De fine hominis*. This section would contain discussions on man's highest good, immortality, resurrection, and eternal life. (2) *De subjecto*. This section treats the articles of God, creation, man, and sin. (3) *De principiis et mediis*. In this section Calixt would discuss first the grace of God, then predestination, Christology. Then would follow a treatment of soteriology, the means of grace, the office of the ministry, absolution, repentance, and good works. The rationale underlying this outline was

followed by the orthodox Lutheran dogmaticians after Gerhard. The outline was taken over only in part. Eschatology was usually considered at the end of dogmatics. A great many variations of the outline appeared.

ABRAHAM CALOV AND THE SILVER AGE OF LUTHERAN ORTHODOXY

By the middle of the 17th century there are clearly discernible two different currents of theological thought within the Lutheran Church. The one, following Melanchthon, is humanistic, unionistic, synergistic, catholic, and philosophically inclinded. The other, in the footsteps of Luther and Chemnitz, is confessional and monergistic, but also catholic and not averse to the adventitious help of philosophy in presenting theology. The Calixtine thought contributed the analytic method to orthodox Lutheran dogmatics but apart from this accomplished only negative results within confessional Lutheran theology. Calixtine theology was absorbed into the syncretistic movement of the day and later into rationalism.[117] The impact of John Gerhard's theology and discussions in prolegomena was remarkable in magnitude upon both his contemporaries and the following generations of Lutheran theologians.

We observe a degree of influence already on Jesper Brochmand's *Universae Theologiae Systema* of 1633. This work, containing only brief prolegomena, does not advance beyond Gerhard in any significant particular, but it does distinctly reflect the burden of all Gerhard's discussions. Brochmand strongly stresses the fact that theology and philosophy operate in different spheres and, unlike Gerhard, speaks of theology as both a theoretical and practical aptitude.[118] He forcefully repeats Chemnitz' emphasis that a methodical and brief treatment of sacred doctrine is of divine origin. And he considers questions of conscience as a legitimate part of doctrinal theology.

As dogmatic works multiply in the succeeding decades, it becomes quite apparent that the prolegomena are modeled roughly after Gerhard's prototype and that they evince generally his concerns. It is neither necessary nor possible to explore all these works, which number in the dozens and which all bear in form a marked similarity. Our procedure will be to examine the contributions and new issues in prolegomena and the development of dogmatics introduced by the chief representative of the

silver age of Lutheran orthodoxy, Abraham Calov. Calov is typical and somewhat normative for the prolegomena and dogmatics of the late 17th century. We can see his influence on Huelsemann, Quendstedt, Scherzer, Kromayer, and others. Therefore, following Calov's outline, our survey will contain also the contributions of his contemporaries when this seems apropos.

In Calov we have the most penetrating, exact, and comprehensive studies of theological prolegomena and method yet to be undertaken. Later theologians, like Musaeus and Walch, wrote more on the subject, if we improperly broaden prolegomena to include general theological propaedeutics, but their efforts possessed neither the keenness nor the attractive savor of Calov's eminent productions.

Calov was endowed with an acute and logical mind, a tremendous capacity for work, and a truly evangelical regard for the edification of Christ's church. These qualities, together with an excellent knowledge and background in law, mathematics, philosophy, and philology, fitted him preeminently for the task of producing a genuine Lutheran contribution in dogmatics and prolegomena, and this at a time when the big guns of alien philosophies, empirical sciences, Romanism, and Socinianism all threatened to breach the walls of Lutheran doctrine. That Calov was definitely recognized in his day to be the qualified pioneer in this advancement is shown indisputably by the close dependence of his colleagues and many of his coreligionists on the conclusions of his theological work.[119] Therefore it is Calov and his writings that we must examine in our efforts to gain the best information of the presuppositions and prolegomena of dogmatics in the second half of the 17th century. Not until Hollaz do we find any original and significant advances beyond Calov's themes and argumentation, and then little of value.

As we apply ourselves to the study of Calov and the other Lutheran dogmaticians of this period, we become impressed with the timeliness of their utterances on questions of dogmatics and prolegomena. Practically all the problems that vex us today were present then, at least in a rudimentary state, and were pursued by these learned men. In fact, as in the case of philosophy, we would with difficulty find any present concern in dogmatic prolegomena that did not also obtain in the latter half of the 17th century.

As we laboriously wend our way through the writings of the Lutheran

dogmaticians after John Gerhard, we soon find ourselves turning frequently to Aristotle to detect the basis for many of their assumptions, arguments, and terms. The reader may feel estranged, for instance, by Calov's tedious and insistent discussion of the definition of theology, and he may well be tempted to discount this as only another example of the all but complete sway and rule of Aristotle over 17th-century philosophy and theology. Must Calov, even in this case where he disagrees with Aristotle, retain Aristotle's terminology and manner of definition? Is Calov's stubborn adherence to his particular definition of theology really anything more than a battle over terms? We must reply that there are some vitally important considerations involved in what Calov is doing. Roman Catholic theologians, following Thomas and Scotus, have at this time not really advanced beyond the categories and terminology of Aristotle in discussing the matters prolegomenous to dogmatics, nor did they feel any need or desire to do so. Their interests and thought forms remained in the pattern of medieval scholasticism. One would less expect to see, however, the abject dependence of the early 17th-century Calvinists, like Keckermann and Alsted, on Aristotle and the medieval scholastics. Among the Lutherans of this period, and particularly in Calov, we observe an attempt to break with Aristotle while at the same time using him. Not that they desired to cast him off entirely — this they never contemplated — but they wished to correct the many terms and concepts that had been understood and defined according to Aristotelian determinants rather than from Biblical data. This was an arduous task at the time, but a task the need of which Calov felt acutely. And this is surely all in his favor. Such a desire to return to the Biblical categories, which are living and dynamic and practical, is reminiscent of Chemnitz, who wished to strip away all unnecessary philosophical and ecclesiastical jargon in discoursing on theology. Calov's desire, then, is to rid the church of logomachy and especially to make theology a living and aggressive force in the church.

Many new and important issues in dogmatics and prolegomena arose during the silver age of Lutheran orthodoxy. These are considered by Calov in a number of writings [120] but particularly in a book specifically dealing with prolegomena. This work, entitled *Isagoges ad SS. Theologiam Libri Duo de Natura Theologiae et Methodo Studii Theologici* and first appearing in 1652, represents its author's first serious attempt to cover the field of prolegomena, and Calov never really goes beyond what he

says here. It will be our purpose now to describe and assess the contributions of Calov in this highly important work.

1. *Theological Method, Its Meaning and Importance*

Calov begins his study by reminding the reader that method is very necessary in every human activity. This fact is particularly evident in theology, which often becomes difficult and involved. Method for the theologian is like a compass for the seafarer: it leads him safely past the Charybdis of confusion and the Scylla of error to the port. Without method all other pursuits come to nothing.

What Calov is advocating in these introductory words was nothing new. Teachers were recommending and employing method long before Descartes and Bacon. Books on the idea of method and the various kinds of method were already common in the 15th and 16th centuries.[121] Just what was this method that was so necessary to the carrying out of theology? Method, according to Aristotle, was a manner and way (μετά + ὁδός) of pursuing inquiry in a given area, a special form of procedure in any branch of intellectual activity, whether for investigation or teaching purposes.[122] Method was the efficient logical approach to any problem, "the most direct manner of any explanation." [123] According to Melanchthon, method "is the direct way and order of investigating and explaining either simple questions or propositions. . . . It is the skill of constructing a way of doing things according to reason [ἕξις ὁδοποιητικὴ μετὰ λόγου]." Melanchthon calls method a *habitus,* but also a *scientia, seu ars.* It would appear that Calov, Gerhard, and the other dogmaticians follow Melanchthon closely. By the 17th century method was associated with the pedagogical procedure (not scientific experimentation and process) and hence came to denote the organization of the pertinent subject matter to be taught in any curriculum subject. Thus, a book on theological method (as we have seen in the case of Gerhard, Chytraeus, and now Calov) would consist in an orderly arrangement and discussion of the tools and steps in carrying out the study of theology, but not the actual theologizing or executing of the theological study. Method is, therefore, definitely in the scope of theological prolegomena.

According to Calixt, method was so important to the pursuance of theology that, along with other things, it was necessary to know it before a Christian could become a theologian. A student of theology must

not merely teach what ought to be believed, but he must know *"how* that which we are to believe ought to be explained and substantiated and defended."[124] To teach catechists is one thing; to teach students of theology is another. Therefore Calixt stressed that three tools were necessary to the theological method: a knowledge of the Biblical languages; philosophy, which includes not only logic but also metaphysics; and an acquaintance with the church fathers and Scholastics.

It was with Calixt's presentation of the second tool, what he calls the *usus primae philosophiae* (metaphysics), that Calov takes issue. Calixt emphasizes the importance of this *usus* more than anyone before him. The theologian cannot abstain from using such terms as *act, potency, cause, effect, necessary, contingent, part, whole, substance, accident*, etc.[125] It is important, he says, to know the difference between an efficient and an instrumental cause, for only then do we know, e. g., the role of faith in justification. It is important to know whether sin is of man's substance or only accidental. And when Jesus says, "It must needs be that offenses come" (Matt. 18:7; cf. John 12:39; 1 Cor. 11:18), it is important to know the distinction between absolute necessity and hypothetical necessity.

It is difficult to see just why Calov would take issue with what Calixt says at this point, at least with the examples he has chosen. The latter has not advanced beyond Gerhard's treatment of the so-called *usus metaphysices*,[126] although he had gone into more detail. And it is of interest that Calov does not dispute any specific allusion by Calixt. It is therefore the emphasis on the usefulness of metaphysics and physics that Calov dislikes. Such an emphasis presents the danger of making theology no longer a mere *doctrina vocum* but rather also a *doctrina rerum*. For in Calixt's view theology depends on a knowledge of science and metaphysics in the same sense that it depends on a knowledge of the languages; that is to say, it cannot do without such knowledge. Calov denies that such a broad technical training is necessary for theology. He says: "What is more necessary to the acquiring of theology than the study of the sacred writings? This must be the first, the middle, and the last in the entire curriculum of sacred things."

Calov is convinced that Calixt, with his concentration on other concerns, has abandoned the *sola Scriptura* principle. To Calov good theology depends on good grammatical exegesis; nothing can be allowed to violate this principle. He quotes with approval the words of Chemnitz:

"Just as the things that have been revealed in Scripture by divine utterance have been revealed by way of word, so also these things cannot be correctly understood except from the true and genuine meaning of the words that the Holy Spirit employed in handing down the divine doctrine. And this is a battle that centers not only in grammar, but it is a battle in fundamental articles of doctrine. If you allow error in words, you allow just as great error in the matters themselves." Calixt said that the Latin version was usually good enough for the theologian to use, and this was what had antagonized Calov. To him the languages are the golden key that opens the hidden treasures of the divine Word. It is interesting to note at this early stage Calov's fear of philosophy.

Calov grants that logic as an organ is required to arrive at the sense of Scripture, although there is no place for an artificial logic that sits in judgment over the words of Scripture. But metaphysics he rejects; this cannot give us the sense of Scripture. At this point again he cannot agree with the method of Calixt, which places other studies almost on a par with the study of Scripture.

2. *The Meaning and Usage of the Term* Theology

By Calov's time the term *theology* was used in a great many ways by different theologians, and there was much argument and confusion over what the term really meant and how it should be used. Calov tries to bring some order out of this chaos without rejecting any legitimate past usages of the term.

Theology, he says, which deals with God and divine things, may be considered as both an internal and external word. The internal word is called by Calov a *verbum* ἐνδιάθετον *vel mentale* (λόγος κατ' ἔσω) (cf. Matt. 3:9; 9:21). The external word (*verbum externum*, κατ' ἔξω), which is the sign of the internal word, is either spoken or written (in Scripture). In both cases it is the sign of the mental concept. This external word is rightly called theology. At the same time, the aptitude (*habitus*) that embraces this doctrine in the mind is also called theology. And when we speak of theology, we usually have the theological *habitus* in mind rather than the actual doctrine or language about God *(verbum externum* or *internum)*. It is well to make a point of this last distinction at the very outset of our study in Calov, for it is important always to know what he understands by the term *theology*.

Calov next traces the term as it was used in antiquity (Plato, *Polit.* II; and Aristotle, *Metaphysica,* V, 1; X, 6). The first Christian to take over the term seems to have been Lactantius,[127] although the inscription in the Book of Revelation uses the term θεόλογος in describing John, the author. Because John stressed the deity of Christ, the term took on a narrow connotation of discourse concerning Christ's deity. Later the term generally embraced all Christian doctrine.

In the Scriptures of the Old and New Testaments there are many terms used that are paraphrases and synonyms. The Hebrews called theology חָכְמַת אֱמוּנָה, *sapientia fidei,* or simply אֱמוּנָה, faith or doctrine. Synonyms occur often in Ps. 119: דַּרְכֵי יְהוָֹה and again עֵדוֹתָיו, i. e., the way of the Lord, or His testimonies. On still other occasions the phrases דֶּרֶךְ אֱמוּנָה (the way of truth or faith) and אִמְרַת יְהוָֹה (word of God) are used. In the New Testament still more paraphrases are employed: θεοδιδασκαλία (1 Thess. 4:9); εὐσέβεια (1 Tim. 3:16); θεοσέβεια (1 Tim. 2:10); λόγος σοφίας (1 Cor. 12:8); σοφία θεοῦ ἐν μυστηρίῳ (1 Cor. 2:7); σοφία πολυποίκιλος (Eph. 3:10); ἡ σοφία ἄνωθεν κατερχομένη (James 3:15); ἐπίγνωσις τοῦ θεοῦ (Col. 1:10); γνῶσις τῆς σωτηρίας (Luke 1:77); ἐπίγνωσις τῆς ἀληθείας κατ' εὐσέβειαν (Titus 1:1); ἐπίγνωσις τοῦ θελήματος τοῦ πατρός ἐν πάσῃ σοφίᾳ καὶ συνέσει πνευματικῇ (Col. 1:9); γνῶσις τῆς δόξης τοῦ θεοῦ ἐν προσώπῳ τοῦ Ἰησοῦ Χριστοῦ (2 Cor. 4:6); μυστήριον τῆς πίστεως (1 Tim. 3:9; Gal. 1:23); φρόνημα τοῦ πνεύματος (Rom. 8:6); ὑποτύπωσις τῶν ὑγιαινόντων λόγων (2 Tim. 1:13); ὁδὸς κυρίου or κατήχησις ἡ διδασκαλία περὶ τοῦ κυρίου ὁδοῦ. (Acts 18:25)

Calov proceeds to note many extra-Scriptural terms that were coined through the years, such as θεοσοφία, θεογνωσία, θεοφροσύνη. He is especially impressed by two terms chosen by William Ames,[128] the English Calvinist: θεοζοΐα and θεουργία. It is well to pause at this point and examine Ames's precise meaning as he uses the terms and his purpose in creating them; for we will later note that Calov and the Lutherans closely follow Ames.

Ames prefers to call theology *doctrina,* inasmuch as it differs from every other wisdom, science, and art in that it is not acquired naturally or from human ingenuity but by divine revelation and instruction. He then discusses the theological life, which to him, it would appear, is the basic consideration prefatory to the study of theology. The theological life is the most perfect life; it is the life that approaches the living and life-

giving God and lives unto Him according to His will and to His glory (Gal. 2:19-20; 1 Cor. 2:10; Phil. 1:20). Since the theological life and aptitude and will is above all our other activity *(praxis)*, it differs from all other disciplines in being practical above them all. Nothing that cannot be applied either directly or indirectly to the final goal of man (his relation to God) is theological. Furthermore, theological *praxis* must pervade all other activity, such as administering the house, ethics, politics, law, etc. To be viewed properly, such activities must be viewed theologically. According to Ames theology has two parts: faith (2 Tim. 1:13; 1 Tim. 1:19; Acts 24:14-15) and observation (Matt. 28:20; Titus 3:8). Faith he calls the source, the *actus primus*, of the spiritual life. The *actus secundus* (the result), observation, emanates from this source. Nothing else is required for theology. These two parts, although distinguished, are always together. Ames's whole book is arranged according to faith and observance, believing and doing. There is good reason why Calov would like this manner of talking of theology: he is always interested in keeping theology practical.

Calov next remarks that we may speak either of God's theology or of man's theology. "Theology has its name either from the wisdom of divine things in God or from the knowledge of these same things in intelligent creatures such as angels and men." In God theology is an *actus purus*, an absolute and perfect knowledge. In creatures theology is a reflection, or representation, as it were (*quoddam* ἀπεικόνισμα), an *actus imperfectius*. We human beings study, we grow, we test theology. We desire to look into the mysteries of God. This distinction, which will develop into the distinction between archetypal and ectypal theology, is very important to Calov. The reason for speaking of something apparently so remote as theology in God, or archetypal theology, is to trace all theology back to God. The theology, properly speaking, that we engage in is not the result of guesswork or a search for self-understanding but has its origin in God. As the other dogmaticians put it: We formulate articles of faith, which are drawn from Scripture; but God is the source, the *principium essendi*, of these articles.[129] This is why the articles of faith and theology are so vitally important.

Our theology *(hominum theologia)* we possess either by nature or by revelation. The theology we have by nature is what we call the natural knowledge of God, although persons with such knowledge are said not

to know God because they are unaware of the saving knowledge revealed in God's Word. Paul calls such persons ἄθεοι (Eph. 2:12) not because they have no knowledge of God but because they have no saving knowledge. The revealed theology of men refers to the knowledge commonly held by all believers. At times it refers to the more accurate understanding of the faith that obtains only in the case of advanced theologians. Sometimes this revealed theology is understood as the aptitude for reaching salvation oneself, sometimes as the aptitude for leading others to salvation. For it is one thing to know what we ought to believe, another thing to teach others.[130] Calov goes no further for the present in delineating natural and revealed theology. He is merely discussing the use of the term *theology*.

Next Calov distinguishes between theology in the special or narrow sense (μερικῶς), which deals with God and Christ, and theology in a more general sense (ὁλικῶς), which deals with everything pertaining to our faith. The Greek fathers distinguished between θεολογία and οἰκονομία, the former having to do with God's nature, the latter with His saving acts.[131] It is interesting to note that Athanasius and others are cited approvingly for applying certain Scripture statements *secundum* οἰκονομίαν and others *secundum* θεολογίαν. For instance, John 14:28, "My Father is greater than I," must be understood *secundum* οἰκονομίαν.

Still another distinction is mentioned by Calov in his discussion of the term *theology*. The term is sometimes used for an inner word and sometimes for an outer word. As the former, theology is a *habitus* of the mind; as the latter, it is the doctrine concerning God and divine things. Put differently, theology may be either the knowledge *(notitia)* one possesses or the doctrine one learns and teaches. The former is theology in its essential and fundamental sense *(consideratio essentialis)*, the latter a secondary or accidental meaning. For essentially theology is a *habitus*, not a doctrine or system that is transmitted by voice or comprehended in writings.

Calov offers one final distinction before closing his introductory presentation of the meaning and usage of the term *theology:* true theology and false theology. Strictly speaking, only true theology is deserving of the name. True theology is marked by its conformity with divine revelation, which is the source and norm of theology.[132] False theology does not conform to revelation; that is to say, it either conflicts with God's

revelation or at least has no support from it. True theology is one, inasmuch as there can never be more than one truth. False theology is manifold, inasmuch as error has many forms. What does Calov mean when he says that true theology is one? He uses the adjective *"unica,"* which means singular or one of a kind, and clearly he has in mind the basis of true theology, which is God's revelation, or God Himself. On the other hand, false theology is manifold because it can spring from any number of false sources. Calov is very likely reflecting the common view among the orthodox Lutheran theologians of his day. Balthasar Meisner, for instance, had said:

> The standard of truth is nothing else than the divine intellect. Whatever conforms to it is deemed to be true; whatever does not agree with it is considered false. For since the standard itself is one, unbroken, unchanging, and consistent with itself, it is not possible that the truth that is measured by it be anything else but one and always the same. On the other hand, since falsehood in defending itself makes use of many different norms, which are fabricated by either the wantonness or the spite of men, it therefore turns out to be changeable, and it works its way out in many forms. Meanwhile the features and appearance of truth do not change in the slightest.[133]

On this point Calov takes issue with the views of the Reformed theologian Francis Junius. Junius called false theology commonplace *(vulgaris)* in that it was drawn from the imperfect principles of our nature and could not rise above human understanding and reasoning. Again he called false theology philosophical because it came to false conclusions through error in reasoning. These are the head and body of false theology, he affirmed.[134] Calov cannot agree that false theology is vulgar in the sense meant by Junius. Basic principles *(principia)* and common ideas *(notiones communes),* even though they may offer only imperfect knowledge and may yield error by virtue of our faulty reasoning, nevertheless are not in themselves false but are actually implanted in us by God (Rom. 1:18). Furthermore, the root of all error in theology is not these common principles; rather false theology arises from the misuse of these principles. Finally, philosophy does not yield a false knowledge of God, but error obtains only when philosophy is misused. It is clear what Calov's interests are in this issue. He is concerned to maintain that natural theology is true as far as it goes. He is anxious to uphold the point that there is no contradiction between philosophy in the abstract and theology. The

cause of bad theology is not innate principles that are at fault but man's own sin and error. In this discourse we see Calov reflecting the interests of Gerhard.

3. *Original and Derived Theology and the Christological Implications*

Calov's first prolonged discussion centers in his reflections on archetypal and ectypal theology. The reader will recall how terse and pithy Gerhard's treatment of this subject was. Gerhard simply stated his position and remarked that the ectypal theology in Christ was, by virtue of the personal union, a perfect knowledge of God and of divine things. Certain Calvinists would no doubt object to this allegation, and debate would surely follow. Calov goes further than Gerhard; he asserts that also the original, archetypal theology is in Christ, and that according also to His human nature, again because of the personal union. There is no reason to assume that Gerhard would not have drawn the same inference if he had felt the necessity to do so. As we now follow Calov in his lengthy discourse on this matter, we become aware of the complexity controversy adds to the prolegomenous matters that would otherwise be quite elementary and straightforward. All the results of Lutheran Christology now come under the compass of prolegomena, and we see that theology proper and prolegomena are thoroughly entwined. Prolegomena may set the stage for theologizing, but it is not worked out in a vacuum before dogmatic conclusions have been reached. Rather, although it articulates the presuppositions and approaches to theology and dogmatics, it is dependent on exegesis and dogmatics. Logically it precedes dogmatics; as it is worked out, it follows dogmatics.

The usual distinction between archetypal and ectypal theology is retained by Calov. The former is uncreated, infinite, and essential; the latter representative, acquired, and accidental. The former is in God; the latter in creatures. Calov says:

> The theology in God must, according to its entire genus, be distinguished from that which is outside God, not because they are inconsistent with each other or of a different nature, for both are true and hence agree with each other. But the two differ in essence and quiddity, inasmuch as wisdom in God is infinite but is only finite in intelligent creatures, wisdom in God is essential but in His creatures only accidental. The origin, pattern, and cause of wisdom is in God; in creatures there is only an ἀπόρροια, a sort of emanation or likeness

of that wisdom which is in God. The former is an utterly perfect and absolute knowledge, a truly divine and complete wisdom, an absolutely pure act. The latter is not perfect but partial, communicated to creatures according to their capacities; it is something that is put forth for study, something dispositional.

Francis Junius had insisted that the archetypal theology as such was incommunicable; it could not be shared by any creature. Only an image of this ineffable wisdom could be communicated to men. Meanwhile the original exemplar remains in God.[135] Calov agrees, but with one important reservation: the human nature of Christ, which subsisted in the person of the Son of God (see Col. 2:3, 9). The infinite wisdom of God (and this applies also to archetypal theology) was, by virtue of the communication of the natures of Christ, the possession also of Christ according to His human nature. Calvinists granted that the wisdom communicated to Christ's human nature was infinite only in a restricted sense *(secundum quid)*, in respect to us, not in respect to God. The Calvinistic position is set forth in four concise arguments by Junius. (a) For the divine nature it is the same to know as to be. Just as the essence *(esse)* of the divine nature is not communicable, the knowledge it possesses is not communicable. (b) The human nature is no more capable of divine knowledge than of divine being. (c) The personal union must not be construed as a confusion or commingling of the two natures. (d) Christ was like us in all things, also in matters of knowledge. It is not difficult to discern the Christological implications in all four of these arguments and the basically divergent Christologies separating Calvinist and Lutheran on this issue.

It was the Lutheran position that all personal propositions made regarding the person of Christ could be predicated of either the divine or the human nature; this is merely to take seriously the statements in Scripture concerning the person of Christ. Since the personal union is real and true, all predications concerning the communication of attributes are to be taken as real and true.[136] An example of the Lutheran line of reasoning may be found in one of Calov's comments on Col. 2:3: "According to Christ's human nature, by virtue of the personal union, all these treasures [of wisdom and knowledge] have been hidden in Him. Hence Christ according to His human nature, in virtue of the personal union, is omniscient with a complete and truly divine omniscience."[137]

In replying to the arguments of Junius in our present context, Calov is most meticulous. False hypotheses and the lack of a carefully worked out Christology lie behind Junius' reasonings. The communication of attributes of the two natures of Christ is not to be understood as producing something new (κατ' ἀλλοποίησιν) or as though a complete transition has taken place (κατ' μετάβασιν) or in the sense of an effusion or osmosis (κατ' ἔκχυσιν). But this communication is a unique communication, or impartation (μετάδοσις), as the fathers liked to call it, whereby the human nature shared the divine majesty and wisdom; not in the sense that this wisdom somehow passed into the human nature or was transfused into it but in the sense that the human nature possessed this wisdom by virtue of the fact that it possessed all the fullness of the Godhead.[138] Junius in his first argument is virtually denying the communication of the divine nature with the human, according to Calov. In his second argument he is confusing an active capacity with a passive capacity (the latter belonging to the human nature in virtue of the personal union), a subjective permanent inherence *(inhaesio)* with a personal communication. His third argument is a case of irrelevant thesis. Against Junius' fourth argument Calov contends that Christ was indeed like us in all things that are essential to the human nature. This does not extend to His entire person, however, or to what may be communicated to the human nature through the personal union.

The allegations of Junius were not the only occasion for Calov's dwelling at length on archetypal and ectypal theology. Anthony Walaeus [139] reasoned in much the same vein, asking how divine knowledge could be revealed to the humanity of Christ. He accused the "Ubiquitarians" (his name for the Lutherans), with their doctrine of a real communication of attributes, of confusing the natures of Christ in a Eutychian fashion. Calov responds to this "inept" man by remarking that the question is not concerning revelation but communication, and that he detests any idea of communication by transfusion as intensely as Walaeus. And once more he patiently rehearses the Lutheran position on the communication of attributes. Furthermore, he says, there is no intimation in Scripture that knowledge was revealed to Christ's human nature (cf. John 3:32; 5:20; Rev. 1:1).

It was prevalently held among Roman Catholics of the 17th century that a beatific vision into divine things was granted the human nature of

Christ, and in such a sense one could speak of revelation taking place. Certain Calvinists also approached this idea.[140] Calov readily concedes that in a sense we must agree with this. There can be no doubt that Christ possessed both habitual and acquired knowledge, for Scripture says He increased in wisdom (Luke 2:52). It was, however, ectypal theology, theology considered as an acquired *habitus,* that thus increased in Jesus and was added to. "But," says Calov, "this must be clearly distinguished from the divine wisdom that was communicated to Christ according to His human nature by means of the personal union. The former ectypal theology was only finite, the latter infinite; the former, properly speaking, was not the result of the personal union, the latter was a consequence and result of the same."

We might expect Calov somewhere in the present discussion to dig up the old scholastic threefold division of knowledge in Christ, and he does not fail us. He cites Peter Lombard,[141] who maintained that the human nature of Christ was given *(datam)* wisdom *in Verbo Dei* by virtue of the incarnation, wisdom according to which it knew everything that God knew; but the human nature did not know everything God could know, and hence its wisdom was not equal to that of God. Actually it was Thomas Aquinas and not Peter who taught the threefold distinction of knowledge in Christ.[142] Both Lutherans and Calvinists made use of this distinction. Thomas taught the following: (a) The soul of Christ had a beatific knowledge of God that consisted in the vision of God. But this beatific knowledge did not imply that Christ in His human soul comprehended the divine essence ". . . quod infinitum non comprehenditur a finito." [143] But according to this knowledge Christ knew all things *"in Verbo."* (b) Christ's soul possessed an infused knowledge *(scientia indita vel infusa)* that was perfect. This is the knowledge whereby He knew things in their own nature "by means of intelligible species proportioned to the human mind." This is in agreement with the fact that the human nature assumed by the Word should not be imperfect. (c) The soul of Christ possessed acquired knowledge and empiric knowledge. In Christ there was not only a passive but also an active intellect (the power to abstract). Such human, acquired knowledge was perfect in Christ.

In using this distinction the Lutherans spoke of Christ's *scientia visionis* as the infinite knowledge of the Logos communicated to the human nature of Christ,[144] whereas the Calvinists (e. g., Junius, Zanchi) and Scholastics

(generally) distinguished this beatific knowledge from the infinite wisdom of the Logos. And so, although both sides go to the same source for their terminology, the debate persists; and it is a Christological debate. Here we see how involved dogmatic prolegomena have become just 30 years after Gerhard; we observe how prolegomena have now become a catchall for all sorts of problems and disputes. Some consideration of practically every article of faith is now, for this or that reason, brought within the purview of prolegomena. Here we learn that prolegomena not only precede dogmatics but often presuppose much of what will follow. Just as the rules of basketball will not all be laid down until a good deal of basketball has been played, prolegomena, the ground rules of theology, arise out of definite and concrete theological positions.

But having begun with Calov, let us doggedly follow his discussion to the end. He must settle the Christological question before leaving the subject of ectypal theology and going further. The question is simply this: Does Christ by the knowledge that is proper to His human soul know all things? John Berg, who is Calov's adversary at this point, maintained that such passages as Is. 11:2, John 16:30 (cf. vv. 17-27), John 2:25, and Col. 2:3 taught that Christ's knowledge was infinite only by reason of the objects of knowledge, "while in itself it is only a finite act, not comparable to divine knowledge, whether viewed as a way of knowing or according to the quantity of things known." Calov points out that the Scholastics themselves were not agreed on this point — Albert and Durandus claiming that the *scientia visionis* of Christ extended to all things absolutely, Thomas affirming that it pertained to all possible things, and Bonaventure asserting that it comprised all things that are matters of habitual knowledge but not of actual knowledge. But none would call such knowledge finite, as Berg does. Calov asks, How could Berg, who insists that Christ's knowledge was only finite, prove the deity of Christ against Arius? To know all things, to search the hearts — these are actions of infinite, not finite, knowledge. Calov argues that the so-called *visionis scientia* exists not only among saints in heaven and angels, but is something that God Himself possesses inasmuch as He knows all things; and it is this absolute knowledge of God that is communicated to the human nature of Christ through the personal union. Calov concedes that formally and *in se* the mind of Christ was not omniscient but only multiscient; but subjectively and personally *(personaliter)* — and this is the way in which the mind of

Christ must be considered — it is omniscient because the infinite wisdom of the Logos has been communicated to it.[145] Calov concludes by reminding the reader that derived, ectypal theology inheres in Christ formally, whereas Christ possessed the original theology personally. The entire issue in this long controversy is really quite clear: the Reformed and Scholastics are too much inclined to think of the human nature and to treat the soul of Christ in the abstract, while the Lutherans correctly refrain from doing so.

It might appear from this excursus that dogmatic prolegomena have now certainly gone too far afield. But actually Calov would maintain that such problems rightly belong within the discussion of prolegomena. By prolegomena one first of all attempts to make one's theological position clear, to nail down his presuppositions and principles for everything he intends to do theologically. At times this will properly involve Christological utterances and affirmations. And Christological presuppositions are by no means irrelevant to the discussion of theology at this particular point. Reformed Christology, in Calov's opinion, will likely result in the false conception of a theology that has definite limitations, is finite and not grounded sufficiently in God's self-manifestation. The church's theology can be no better than Christ's theology. But if Christ is a prophet and teacher come from God, the very Son of the Father, if the doctrine of this Man is divine doctrine, then the church can be safe and certain with the theology she has learned from Christ, because it agrees with God's own original theology.

We must bear in mind that to the Lutherans, ectypal theology, although it is finite and "created," nevertheless conforms to the original archetype. It is an "emanation and reflection, or image" of the wisdom and theology that is in God (1 Cor. 2:13), as Quenstedt puts it.[146] The deep concern of the Lutherans, therefore, in the whole discussion of original and derived theology is to show that the church possesses and teaches a *doctrina divina*. This emphasis on the divine origin and certainty of the church's theology is perhaps stressed even more forcefully by Quenstedt when he says that the archetypal theology is not only in God but is God Himself. For the being and knowing and wisdom of God are all one and the same. In reference to original theology, Quenstedt says: "God is the subject who knows, the object that is known, and the knowledge itself; or in other words, the *res Theologica,* the *Theologus,* and the *Theologia."*

And this theology that is God Himself and that only God knows has been revealed to us by the Son and the Spirit. (Matt. 11:27; 1 Cor. 2:10-11)

4. The Theology of Paradise and the Theology of the Church

Another distinction common in Calov's era and going back to medieval times was between paradisical and Christian theology. The distinction is quite simple. The paradisical obtained prior to the Fall while man was still in a state of integrity. It can be called absolute. The latter was revealed to the church and was called modified or dispensational. There is also a different source for the paradisical and the Christian theology. The source of the former is the concreated primeval wisdom of our first parents, who were created in God's image; the source of the latter is divine revelation. But there was also a revealed theology in Paradise, for much that Adam and Eve knew was from the external Word of God, e. g., concerning the tree of knowledge, their association as man and wife, their dominion over the earth, the Sabbath, etc. The orthodox Lutherans, like the Reformed and Catholics, even list a number of *loci theologiae paradisiacae,* many of which are quite farfetched. These *loci* include the nature and attributes of God, creation, the image of God, the Law, divine providence, revelation, sin, marriage, eternal life; but also a doctrine of the church, the ministry, and political magistrates. But there was no article on sacrifices or the Messiah, as the Roman Catholics maintained. And when certain Calvinists taught that the theology in Paradise included an article on Christ, not as Mediator and Savior from sin but as the One who would preserve our first parents from sin,[147] Calov replies that such an opinion represents only unbiblical, curious speculation. Apparently such speculation was quite common even in the 17th century.

5. Natural Theology

There is nothing particularly original or new in the way Calov and the later Lutherans deal with the subject of natural and revealed theology, except that Calov goes much deeper into the subject than anyone prior to his time. Perhaps one should qualify this statement. There are three points in a dogmatics where natural (and revealed) theology can be treated; it can be considered within prolegomena as Calov does, it can be discussed under the heading of the natural (and revealed) knowledge

of God (Gerhard, Hollaz, Quenstedt), or it can be treated under the article *de lege*. The third possibility was carried out by Melanchthon, particularly in his *Loci Praecipui Theologici* of 1559; and to a certain extent he was followed by all the later Lutherans in this. What happens, then, is that more or less the same subject matter is discussed at two, possibly three, points in a dogmatics. It is typical of Calov's tendency to pack everything into prolegomena that he now dwells on the subject at great length. But there is very good reason for his discussing the subject at this early point. Unless God can be known, there is no point in even starting any work in theology; it would be a contradiction in terms. We shall be compelled to discuss the subject of the natural knowledge of God both now under prolegomena and later under the article on God. The source of both natural and revealed theology (supernatural theology) is God. The means of attaining natural theology is the natural light of man. The purpose and end of natural theology is to prepare men to accept supernatural grace. By nature it is a *habitus* by which one knows God and divine things as fully as this can be done by nature. We may consider natural theology after the Fall as it obtains in either the unregenerate or the regenerate man. The sources of this natural theology remain but are now obscure and imperfect. Thus, not all things that are advanced by heathen on matters of theology can be classified as natural theology, for unregenerate men have not always followed the correct principles and right use of reason in reaching their conclusions.

What is the scope of natural theology after the Fall? What does it include? The answer to this question is very explicit in Lutheran theology. Although natural theology is sufficient to render all men without excuse for their unbelief, it is not sufficient to lead anyone to salvation. The extent of this theology may be summed up in five points. (a) Natural theology is able to discuss God, His nature and attributes. It knows nothing, however, of the three persons of the Deity, of God's evangelical will and works of grace. (b) Natural theology knows the law of God, as heathen philosophy and religion abundantly demonstrate. (c) It knows that sin is the transgression of the Law. (d) It is aware of the guilt incurred by sin, for the conscience testifies to this. (e) Natural theology knows of the immortality of the soul and of life after death. At this point Calov cites evidence from Zoroaster, Plato, and many others. Calov here is not going beyond what Luther spoke of as *"Erkenntnis des Gesetzes"* in contrast to evangelical knowledge.[148]

By the time of Calov natural theology had been neatly divided into that which was inborn *(indita, insita)* and that which was acquired *(acquisita)*. The former had to do with innate ideas (κοιναὶ ἔννοιαι), which were written by nature in the minds of all men; the latter was drawn from these innate ideas and was known by reason to be based on certain principles. The former dealt with principles, the latter with conclusions and inferences. Both existed without a knowledge of the divine Word. The distinction can be traced clearly back to Melanchthon, who combined Stoic and Pauline ideas in working out a position on natural theology.[149] Melanchthon held that there were certain notions *(notiones)* innate in the human mind just as the eye has the congenital power to see. These innate conceptions or mental pictures (προλήψεις) are both speculative, having to do with number, order, logic, etc., and practical, dealing with the difference between right and wrong and with our duty toward God. The speculative conceptions are certain. Who would doubt that twice four is eight? The practical conceptions are less certain only because our assent is hesitant and our hearts hard. But Paul speaks of such notions clearly in Rom. 1:25, where he says that the heathen changed the truth of God into a lie. This would indicate that the knowledge they had of God, a knowledge indelibly fixed *(impressa)* in them, was true knowledge. "Nor is this natural knowledge concerning God ever utterly destroyed." And what specifically are these notions we have of God? "The first law of nature," says Melanchthon, "is to know that there is one God, an eternal mind, wise, righteous, good, the Maker of all things, who rewards the just and punishes the unjust, by whose agency there has been born in us a distinction between things honorable and base; and it is to know that He is to be obeyed according to this inbred distinction, that we are to pray to this God and expect good things from Him."[150]

It would appear from these last statements of Melanchthon that he is denying the possibility of theoretical atheism. This inference may also be drawn from the arguments of the Lutherans in Gerhard's and Calov's day in their discussions of natural theology. They state that natural theology tells us that there is a God (τὸ ὅτι) but not who God is (τὸ τί ἐστιν). Natural theology cannot tell us that God is triune (against Keckermann, Gerson, Richard of St. Victor), that He is a gracious God and the Father of our Lord Jesus Christ. But although the heathen are ignorant of who God is, their ignorance is not a complete negation of knowledge (cf.

1 Thess. 4:5 and the ἄθεοι in Eph. 2:12). Therefore Quenstedt says: "Even though there are those who deny that God is, still they are not ignorant that God is."[151] This would mean that the fool who says there is no God does so against his conscience and against better knowledge. Quenstedt puts it very plainly: "Hence the heathen and ungodly people deny not so much the essence and existence of God as they do His providence. And they deny Him out of spite, not by nature; they deny Him by their desires, not with their intellect; by their life, not out of knowledge." Atheism therefore is not due to any evidence from observation *(ex animi sensu)*, it is not due to nature nor to an inability to find God. This would all follow from Melanchthon's position outlined above. The fault is with man, with his willful rebellion against God.

It was stated that Lutheranism on the whole followed Melanchthon in working out its position on natural theology. One significant exception to this consensus is Matthias Flacius, with whom all the later Lutherans felt constrained to differ. Flacius admitted that the Second Table of the Law was written in man's heart but denied that this was true of the First Table. This position was tantamount to denying that natural theology was true theology. Flacius' anthropology might well have led him in this direction. He reasons on the basis of Ps. 14:3, 1 Cor. 2:14, and Gal. 5:20 that the idea of the unity of God is not innate at all.[152] By nature man will reverence many gods or will make a caricature of God. Through its own wisdom the world does not know God (1 Cor. 1:21). If there were innate ideas, or *principia prima,* of God, then the world would know and recognize God. Furthermore, we are said to *believe* that there is a God, not to *know* this. We *know* things according to innate ideas. "Wherefore there are no principia for the essence of God; this knowledge is sustained by faith alone." If such innate ideas existed, then philosophy and reason would be our teacher in theology just as in mathematics, logic, and other areas of knowledge. "For this reason Luther also insisted that man by nature knows no more about God than does the brute, for he possesses no principles concerning God." If someone quotes Plato against him, Flacius quotes Aristotle in rebuttal. Flacius points out that practically every argument for natural theology is taken from Scripture. But Scripture (Acts 14:15; 17:24; Rom. 1:18-19) when it argues from nature for God's power and unity points always to God's works and creation, never to innate principles and ideas.[153]

It is clear that Flacius, like Luther, feels that natural theology must be considered as it actually exists in concrete life, in all its sinfulness and stupidity. Calov is concerned to maintain a different emphasis of Luther's "knowledge of the left hand," whereby man from his knowledge of the Law knows something also about God, the Lawgiver. Against Flacius' position Calov says that the "natural inclination toward error should not be placed in opposition to the natural knowledge of God, which we acknowledge is associated with imperfections and great corruption after the Fall. Such things are not in real opposition. For the apostle Paul teaches that the knowledge of God (γνῶσις τοῦ θεοῦ) can coexist with vanity of judgment and knowledge (ματαιότης τῶν διαλογισμῶν); and that in one and the same heart, inasmuch as it recognizes God but does not know Him." Naturally this is not a true (sic!) knowledge of God, but something piecemeal, inactive, and shifting. Therefore Calov distinguishes between the knowledge *(notitia)* of the mind and the inclination, disposition, and perversity of the heart. The former pertains to the natural realm and is a little residual door *(portiuncula),* as it were, of man's original wisdom; the latter pertains to man after the Fall. We must further distinguish, Calov says, between a knowledge that is feeble and insufficient and confused and a knowledge of God that is certain and sufficient and distinct; between a certain limited knowledge of God and a knowledge of the Gospel, the high mysteries of God. Finally we should distinguish between τὸ *scire vel nosse* and τὸ *credere:* we know by means of rational demonstration that there is a God (and Flacius admits this); but we believe that there is a God only through the illumination of the Spirit of God. Hence it is consistent to know something by innate knowledge and to believe it by means of revealed knowledge.

It is interesting how closely Flacius' views concerning innate ideas resemble the ideas of the Socinians and of John Locke. His arguments in many cases are quite similar to those of Locke, particularly when he reasons that innate ideas would have to be common to all and that this is disproved by experience. The reason for Flacius' conjectures, however, lies in his doctrine of man, whereas the Socinians and Locke arrived at their conclusions by reason of their empiricism. It is not, however, any affinity of Flacius with Locke and the Socinians that prompts all the Lutheran theologians to differ with Flacius.

The Socinians went further than Flacius or even Locke. They denied not

only an innate knowledge of God but also any rational or acquired knowledge. It was their conviction that God cannot be known on the basis of the data given us in the world *(e mundi machina)*. Calov answers with an appeal to Rom. 1:19-20; Acts 17:21 ff.; and Acts 14:15. The fact of a Creator God to whom we are responsible seems to Calov to be the point of contact that Paul used in preaching the Gospel to unbelievers. Furthermore, Ps. 19:2 ff. argues a posteriori from nature to show God's power and majesty. God's works in nature bless and celebrate Him, not effectively, of course, but objectively in that they show intelligent creatures the reason for praising Him (Ps. 103:22; cf. Job 12:7). It is interesting that Calov brings all his arguments for a natural knowledge from Scripture and refrains from alluding to any extra-Biblical evidence.

There was complete agreement among all the Lutherans that natural theology is never sufficient for salvation. Against the Arminians, Zwingli, and certain papists, Calov offers the following stock arguments, which are typical of the Lutheran position: (a) The way of salvation is always and everywhere the same (John 3:16; Acts 15:11; Rom. 3:9 ff.). By nature all men are lost sinners, and there is no release from sin except through Christ, who alone is the propitiation for sin (1 John 2:2). (b) By means of natural theology alone no one can come to a knowledge of the Gospel and of salvation. For in the realm of nature only the Law is known, and this cannot save (Gal. 3:21; Rom. 8:3). Faith in Christ is necessary (Rom. 3:24; John 3:18; Heb. 11:6; John 17:3; Acts 4:12; Jer. 23:6); and natural theology cannot teach us this. (c) True saving faith is worked only through the Gospel, whether Baptism or the preached Word. (Eph. 5:26)

> The Gospel sets forth those things that are sufficient to believe for salvation. The Gospel and faith are related and belong together. In the Gospel the proper object of faith is revealed, and there can be no knowledge of this object and thus no faith that applies this knowledge [*quae infert* γνῶσιν] apart from the Gospel. Only the Gospel brings {*exhibet*} Christ to us, the Christ in whom we are to believe and in whom alone we have life eternal (1 John 5:11-12). Apart from the revelation of the Gospel there is no knowledge of Christ (Matt. 11:27; 16:17; Rom. 16:25; 1 Cor. 2:7; Col. 1:26). Because the Gospel is the means that has been divinely ordained to incite faith, it is called the power of God unto salvation to everyone who believes (Rom. 1:16). Through the Word of the Gospel faith is born. (Rom. 10:17)

(d) The Gentiles simply do not have any revelation of this Word. Here it is not a question of what God could do but of what He wills to do, namely, to bring people to salvation through the Gospel Word. Calov does not wish to deny that God may reach certain persons in an extraordinary manner; but only through the Word and sacraments do we have assurance that people will be brought into the kingdom of God. Special grace is never promised to those who do not have the Word (Rom. 10:14). Finally, Calov notes that the knowledge of heathens is always only a vague, awkward, and piecemeal thing.

In Calov we have seen a typical Lutheran treatment of natural theology — moderate, cautious, learned, critical, and exhaustive. The excesses of both Melanchthon and Flacius have been avoided, and a presentation is offered that in Calov's conviction is totally Biblical. In his discussion he seeks to steer a middle course between the view of the Socinians, which denied natural theology altogether, and the position of certain Remonstrants who fancied that natural knowledge of God rightly used prompted God to give His grace.[154] When we ask why the orthodox Lutherans spent so much time on the subject of natural knowledge when it was utterly useless toward bringing man or helping to bring man to a saving knowledge or relationship with God, it is no doubt these antitheses that provide the chief answer.

Is there any value for the Christian in this natural knowledge of God? Does he not have all things when he has the Gospel? To the natural man, of course, this knowledge is only a Law preachment, telling him that he stands before God guilty and without excuse. But this function hardly applies to the Christian. Calov appears to be a little hard pressed, but in his *Systema* he does offer a brief *usus practicus* for the doctrine. He says:

> The practical usefulness of this doctrine is that we may know whether, what, and how much we can understand {*cognoscere*} about God through nature, and this, lest we either deny these things that are disclosed in nature or make too much out of them. Rather we are to acknowledge this manifestation with a grateful mind and improve our natural knowledge by a daily perusal of the book of nature. We are not to conceal or misuse this knowledge, but in the proper way we are to add the book of Scripture to the book of nature. Finally, we are to be strengthened and encouraged by the doctrine and example of those who are learned and who study the truth.[155]

It is important that we understand the meaning of this statement. In the last sentence Calov is referring to learned philosophers and scholars who study only the book of nature and do not have the book of Scripture. We can learn from these people, and can sometimes be confirmed in the truth by their studies, for they can teach nothing against the truth. It is important to note what Calov says about adding the book of Scripture to the book of nature. He does not mean to say that the theology of Scripture adds what is lacking to natural theology, like putting a roof on an edifice or a final stroke on a painting. We must remember that he is speaking of the usefulness of natural knowledge to the Christian, and what he is saying is that the piecemeal and vague knowledge of God and His Law that can be derived from nature can be understood and interpreted through the Gospel. For the Christian every pursuit in the book of nature comes under the scrutiny of the Gospel and takes on new meaning. The Christian, for instance, sees in God's handiwork something far different and more magnificent than does the unbeliever.

6. Revealed Theology

We now pass over to the subject of supernatural theology. Supernatural theology is, first, that which is directly mediated by the Spirit of God to man and, second, that which is learned from the revealed Word of God. The former obtains in the case of the prophets, evangelists, and apostles, who were moved to speak by the Spirit of God and whose inspired word was reduced to writing. The latter is drawn from those inspired writings. The former may be called infused theology; the latter acquired theology. The source of infused theology is the Word of God that was revealed to inspired men (Heb. 1:1). Calov mentions the various forms of revelation, pointing out that the Word came sometimes externally through images and the senses, sometimes internally through infusion and inner spiritual illumination *(irradiatio)*, but in either case immediately. As Calov uses the terms, the Word of God as the basis of theology is used interchangeably with revelation, for revelation is always a word, a dianoetic disclosure or communication. This is perfectly in keeping with Calov's strong emphasis that revelation is action.[156] Calov is very thorough in reviewing the various forms of revelation, which is the basis of all revealed and supernatural theology. His position can be summed up in the following quotation:

> To a certain few God has revealed Himself immediately either according to an internal disclosure or by an external word or even through

the exhortation of angels. This He has done that He might instruct the rest of the world by means of these few. This occurs sometimes when they set forth what has been revealed to them directly by word of mouth, sometimes when they inform the church by reducing to writing what has been revealed by divine inspiration. . . . Ordinarily the church is informed not by direct but by the mediate instruction of men who have been divinely chosen and called to this task, men chosen either directly or mediately.

After the formation of the canon God no longer teaches His church by immediate revelation, dreams, apparitions, angelic visions, etc., as the enthusiasts claim. Such passages as Jer. 31:31 ff., Joel 2:28, and John 14: 25 all refer to the mediate instruction through the revealed Word.

a. IS THERE A REVEALED THEOLOGY? Having spoken concerning natural and supernatural theology, Calov feels that he must now backtrack. The discussion has led him to the subject of revelation. So he asks the question that to us seems quite superfluous at this point: Is there a revealed theology? There are actually two questions involved here. First, is there a revelation of supernatural theology that will yield knowledge of God and divine things? Second, is revealed theology a distinct discipline, having its own object? In answer to the first question Calov replies that God has so fashioned man that he might know and embrace revealed theology, which is another way of saying that man might enjoy God and eternal salvation.[157] There can be no knowledge of salvation without theology (John 17:3; 1 Cor. 2:9). To Calov the very fact of revelation demonstrates the existence of revealed theology. Many things are known concerning God — such as the Trinity, Christology, predestination, and justification — things that could not be known except by revelation. Finally Calov argues that the existence of the theologian shows that there is a revealed theology. It is hard to see just why he should argue at this juncture for a point (revealed theology) he has tacitly accepted all along, unless it is merely to tie things up. His arguments are unnecessary for the believer and unconvincing, even circular, for the unbeliever.

The second question is more valid, for the question of theology's place beside all other disciplines can and must be answered. The term *discipline* was used rather generally in those days, sometimes equated with *ars, scientia, methodus,* or *doctrina*. It denoted usually a definite area of research or curriculum. It is, says Calov, a way of storing up what is known

or what is knowable and of transmitting such knowledge accurately. Disciplines must be separated from one another in order that each discipline may be distinctly known and transmitted. It can be readily discerned that reavealed theology is totally diverse from all other faculties of discipline. Why? First it deals with a specific object, God and divine things. No other discipline is competent for this. In all other disciplines human reason operates and judges, but not in theology. All other disciplines are confined to a consideration of the things of this world. Second, revealed theology differs from other practical disciplines in its purpose and aim: its purpose is spiritual, a healing of the soul *(animae medicatio)*, a blessing, salvation and fellowship with God. And so, although theology is a discipline in the sense of being an activity, it is not a discipline among other disciplines but is *sui generis* and independent.

It is most important to maintain the unity of the theological discipline. Although revealed theology deals with many objects, there is really only one purpose of this discipline, to lead poor sinners to salvation.[158] Calov's concern at this point may have been quite valid in his day, and perhaps it is even more valid today. He is apparently fearful of a cleavage of theology into compartments (catechetical, homiletical, casuistic, etc.), which in our present day of experts presents an even greater threat to good, well-balanced theologians. Calov, like his Lutheran forebears, is concerned to see theological generalists in the church. His insistence on theology being a discipline *par excellence* and not to be judged by the categories of any other discipline was another emphasis that is needed today, an emphasis that dominates Calov's entire approach to the subject.

b. SOURCE OF THEOLOGY: REVELATION. Calov's actual discussion of the sources of theology is quite perfunctory. However, it is of some value inasmuch as it leads into a lengthy and important treatment of the doctrine of revelation as the source of theology. Following Gerhard and the earlier Lutheran teachers, Calov makes the source of theology the triune God who in Paradise set forth theology αὐτοφώνως and later ἀμέσως by means of inspired men. Today theology is brought to us through the written Word and by instruction in the church. It is His infinite goodness and inexhaustible mercy that prompt God to communicate His wisdom to men and reveal Himself from the hidden seat of His majesty to the human race. And outside of God it is our ignorance of divine

things since the Fall, our insurmountable misery on account of which, but for God's mercy, we deserve damnation — it is this that prompts God to lead us to a knowledge of Himself and reveal to us His precious doctrine (Eph. 2:1-2). Calov makes much of the congenital blindness of all men in spiritual affairs. There is nothing abstract or detached in his discussion: God who is the Source of all good things and the Giver of all good things and the Fountain of all wisdom (James 1:17) — God alone brings to us a knowledge of theology.[159] And so God as revealer is not only the source of all language about Himself, but He is the one who in every case makes an individual a theologian. This is why theology is a unique discipline and such a marvelous treasure and why we dare not play or dabble in it.

The organic source of revealed theology is God's Word, either as it is disclosed to men or as it is embraced by men. The Augsburg Confession (Art. V) calls the Word the means through which the Holy Spirit works faith. This is precisely what Calov has in mind at this point. "For we can know nothing of revealed theology except through divine revelation. And this revelation is the very Word of God. This Word is the first and foremost source for our knowing theology; from this Word all theological conclusions are drawn. This then is the appropriate and immediate source {causa} of theology, this is that incorruptible seed by which the church is born, by which theology is brought into being (1 Peter 1:23, 25)."[160] We notice how Calov links together the so-called normative and causative authority of Scripture in this discussion. For when he speaks of revelation in this context he has in mind the revealed Word of Scripture. This revealed Word is normatively authoritative as the source of all doctrine in the church; it is causatively authoritative in authenticating itself as God's Word of revelation and working faith in Christ. And so the Word of God not only makes us Christians, it makes us theologians (2 Tim. 3:15 to 17); but we are made theologians by a Word that is understood and used by us for our edification.[161]

As we would expect, Calov makes the ministering source of theology those who bring and teach the Word of God.

c. SUBJECT OF REVELATION. Having spoken of revealed theology and of revelation as the source of theology, Calov has arrived at the point where he must devote his attention to the subject of revelation.[162] His

treatment of the subject of divine revelation is most significant for a number of reasons. First, no other Lutheran theologian of that day or prior to that day dealt with the subject to any extent. But Calov both in his *Systema* and his *Isagoges* considers the topic in depth. Just why he treats revelation as a special subject is hard to say; perhaps he felt that it was not right to subsume the idea of revelation under the *locus* on Scripture (and the *locus* on God) as the earlier dogmaticians had done. At any rate he gives the doctrine of revelation a prominence not given before in Lutheran theology. There is nothing in his discussion, however, that would appear surprising to a Gerhard or a Chemnitz. Second, Calov displays remarkable balance and insight in his study of revelation. He does not exhaust the subject by any means; he considers revelation primarily as it pertains to theology and dogmatic prolegomena. But he does make several observations that are pertinent also today. Third, in the light of modern interest in the idea of revelation Calov's handling of the subject shows that historic Lutheranism definitely did not make revelation a mere matter of "communicating a body of knowledge," as has been sometimes attributed to all of 17th-century theology indiscriminately.[163]

According to Calov, "Revelation is an action of God *{actus Dei externus}* whereby He disclosed Himself *{sese patefecit}* to our human race through His Word *{per verbum suum}*, thereby bringing us to a saving knowledge of Him *{ad salutarem ejusdem informationem}*." Such a definition makes revelation at once dynamic, involving always a personal self-disclosure and confrontation of God with man, and dianoetic, involving always saving information. Thus, the Word of God as the means of revelation is the source of theology, and consequently theology is divinely revealed. We notice also that God's revelation, strictly speaking, is evangelical and soteriological *(ad salutarem Dei informationem)*. This revelation as God's self-manifestation is, of course, to be distinguished from God's revelation in nature. Supernatural revelation embraces either the immediate, direct inspiration and disclosure that obtained in the case of the prophets or the revelation that takes place by means of God's Word *(mediante Dei verbo)*, whether that Word is announced orally or is in the written form in Scripture. Revelation must be associated with those actions of God that pertain to the illuminating and informing of God's people; however, this does not imply that revelation is something essentially speculative, as Calov makes clear later when he insists on the

practical nature and purpose of revealed theology.[164] At the same time Calov maintains that God's revelatory self-disclosures are *dona ministrantia*, not *dona sanctificantia*, inasmuch as they were communicated to such as Balaam, Saul, and others who prophesied even though they were reprobate. Revelation is never *mere* enlightenment to Lutheran theology. In former times revelation came to men through an inner word *(verbum internum)*, an inner inspiration or afflatus. At present revelation occurs ordinarily through the external Word *(verbum externum)* drawn from Scripture, either preached or taught or read. In this latter case it so happens that by the mediation and intervention of this Word (which is never separated from God Himself and His power) our mind is informed, and as a result an inner word arises in our minds. In such a case we have a mediate self-disclosure of God according to which our mind is instructed concerning the sense of the divine Word revealed in Scripture, and through the ordinary means of interpreting our minds gain certainty. The inner testimony of the Holy Spirit brings us this divine certainty *(infallibilis certitudo)*.

The "subject," or content *(objectum)*, of revelation is God. God reveals Himself. We may say the same thing by asserting that God reveals His essence and will. When the dogmaticians speak of "divine things" or "revealed things" or "the things of God," they have in mind either things that can be said about God or things that God has done or God Himself, and sometimes they mean all three. But strictly speaking, God does not reveal things, He reveals Himself. But He reveals Himself by telling us things about Himself or things that He has done. "Revealed things *{revelata ea}* are what God wishes us to know about Himself and His will. Consequently all revealed things bring us to a knowledge of God's will, to a knowledge on the one hand of what He wills us to believe and do, and on the other hand of what He has willed and now wills to do in regard to us." This statement indicates that when Calov emphasizes that God reveals Himself he is not thinking of God in terms of His essence only but also in terms of His will,[165] and His will is made known in a cognitive message that is summed up in Law and Gospel. That God reveals Himself through a cognitive message of Law and Gospel was a conviction expressed in Lutheran theology long before Calov, but here we have a new emphasis on the personal nature of this revelation.

d. OBJECT OF REVELATION. The object *(subjectum)* of revelation, those

to whom revelation is given, is all men; God intends and desires that all should receive His revelation. However, God's self-disclosure actually *(actu)* touches only certain individuals. Such revelation is delivered to men in this life, in our time and history. Calov is not referring to the direct vision disclosed to angels and departed saints, what the Scholastics called *speculum essentiae divinae* (1 Cor. 13:12; 2 Cor. 5:7). Even after receiving God's revelation we see only through a glass, as it were, and not directly *(per intuitum)* and face to face. The revelation that has been granted us is only piecemeal, or imperfect.

e. AUTHOR OF REVELATION. The author of all revelation is God, and this in the very nature of the case, whether it is immediate and direct, whether it takes place through means, or whether it is given through the prophets in the Old Testament and apostles in the New. God is the author of revelation, but not merely because He is the *prima veritas,* and all truth and goodness have their origin ultimately in Him. No, He is directly the author of revelation, He is the one who delivers revelation. A deep spiritual insight or a profound interpretation of an action of God in history is not revelation unless God directly grants the insight or the interpretation. No man through the usual process of history could ever know or experience what God's revelation discloses. Revelation is a special act of God. It is His revelation. We might call this a monergistic view of revelation.

But how may we know that a revelation that another professes to have received is from God? Calov lists three criteria for judging the validity of a revelation; these may seem rather superficial and unconvincing on the surface because of their simplicity, but actually they are quite fundamental. (1) There are usually definite circumstances and settings in which a revelation is given. The majesty of a divine revelation and the miracles that often accompany such a disclosure are often sufficient to convince God's creatures that He has spoken. (2) The content of divine revelation has always been true and useful and salutary (Deut. 18:22). This is a highly significant point. Calov views revelation according to the rubrics of Law and Gospel. The Gospel will determine the authenticity of any revelation. (3) The purpose of all revelation is always the same, says Calov; "divine revelation always has as its aim the salvation of men" *(Divina revelatio semper intendit salutem hominum)*. The emphatic word here is *"intendit."* All revelation is therefore evangelical and

soteriological in purpose. In fact, there can be no revelation without this soteriological purpose. For instance, when a spirit of divination possessed a maiden and she prophesied that Paul and Barnabas were servants of the most high God, Calov contends that her words, strictly speaking, were not revelation; and Paul rightly cast out such a spirit (Acts 16:16-18). Thus, what the Lutheran Confessions make the basis for understanding all Scripture — the Gospel, or the doctrine of justification (Apology of the Augsburg Confession, IV, 2. German text) — Calov makes the criterion for assessing and grasping all revelation. Calov's insight at this point is uniquely Lutheran and much to be appreciated.

f. PURPOSE OF REVELATION. The next point for discussion is just this subject we have already broached, the purpose of revelation. The purpose of God's revelation is twofold: to inform man and tell him what God would have Him know; and to bring sinful man to salvation. And so revelation pertains either directly or indirectly to man's salvation, and it always *intends* this.

Commenting on the first, or intermediate, aim of revelation, Calov has the following to say:

> As touching the intermediate purpose of revelation, namely, to inform, revelation either brings about a divine and supernatural knowledge that could not be acquired apart from divine revelation, or it leads one to a fullness and certainty of natural human wisdom, inasmuch as there are some things having to do with our natural knowledge that, having been divinely revealed by God, we apprehend with a more complete and certain knowledge. It is the former things that God intends primarily to make known through His revelation. The latter things He intends to reveal only with a secondary and subordinate purpose insofar as He might recall us to those former things in such a way. For that very natural knowledge can lead us back to God's wisdom, and that both dianoetically in that we may recognize God's wisdom, goodness, power, and providence, and also practically in that we are incited and moved more and more to worship and praise God.

This is a passage of palmary significance, indicating as it does that the one and only purpose of the dianoetic nature of revelation is practical, and also indicating that revelation from nature may actually facilitate, although only obliquely, bringing a person to a knowledge of that which is above and outside the realm of nature and to a practice of divine worship and adoration.

The ultimate purpose of every divine revelation is the eternal salvation of man. This is *directly* so in the case of those things that pertain to faith and are necessary to know to be saved. But it is also *indirectly* the case with those things that have been revealed relative to temporal concerns, our external condition, and the things of nature *(res naturales)*. Again Calov emphasizes that without this saving purpose a fact is not revelation. This means that there are many facts of various kinds known to men; but these facts become revelation when they are presented and seen in the context of God's soteriological counsel and economy.

g. CONTENT OF REVELATION, AND INERRANCY. Keeping in mind the soteriological purpose of revelation, Calov comments next on the content of revelation. Like all Lutherans of the day, he thinks of the content of revelation in terms of facts, doctrine, precepts. He takes for granted that revelation has a cognitive content in contrast to any idea of revelation as merely a mystical and ineffable confrontation or theophany. Following Gerhard he offers a distinction between those things that are completely matters of faith, that can only be known by means of a divine disclosure, and those things he calls *mixtae,* which are known by revelation but are also known in some other manner. Among the former he lists the articles of faith, divine precepts and institutions, prophecies concerning future events, and also events *(historiae)* of the past and present. Among the latter things that are known also aside from divine revelation, Calov includes matters pertaining to nature and morality. Why does he speak of these so-called *mixtae* if, strictly speaking, they are not articles of faith and do not require a supernatural revelation to be known? Calov's reason is that Scripture deals with many of these *mixtae,* which can be known apart from divine revelation — and yet these things pertain to our salvation somehow and can be used for the same ultimate purpose as the pure articles of faith. Calov here is quite consciously refusing to make a distinction between theological matters in Scripture or in God's revelation and matters that are only historical or geographical, etc. All is theological (2 Tim. 3:16-17); all has a theological purpose (Rom. 15:4). And God has revealed things that pertain to the realm of history and of nature; or putting it slightly differently, His revelation to us by His own condescension is bound within the framework of history and nature. This implies that nothing of God's revelation in Scripture can be unimportant or irrelevant to theology, even though it may appear to

be so to us. All of God's revelation, every aspect of it, is binding, however remotely or indirectly it may appear to touch on the ultimate soteriological purpose of Scripture. It is, in fact, the soteriological purpose of revelation and of Scripture that demands that every aspect of God's revelation be taken seriously. Such are the implications of the Lutheran position that Scripture is *vere et proprie* God's Word and a form of God's revelation.

There were some in his day — Calov is no doubt alluding primarily to the Socinians — who maintained that whenever Scripture deals with matters pertaining to the physical world (and here revelation has invaded an area of philosophical concern), we are offered something that is never apodictic and certain but only probable. This theory — and perhaps we are surprised at how old it is — was predicated on the assumption that divine revelations in themselves do not intend to offer knowledge of the things of nature but only information to salvation. We discern in the Socinian position here something very like Lessing's use of Leibniz' distinction between eternal and contingent truths. But whereas Leibniz' distinction was logical and ontological, Lessing applied it to religion. But even prior to the advent of Lessing the Socinians had assumed the same position. They could have agreed completely with his dictum: "Accidental truths of history can never become proof of necessary truths of reason."[166] Just as Kierkegaard struggled with a reply to Lessing, Calov was forced to give answer to the skepticism inherent in the Socinian distinction. The whole position leads to Pyrrhonic doubt, he insists, by making every allusion in Scripture to history or the external world merely academic. And this makes everything in God's revelation doubtful, since, if theological statements are not per se historic statements, they are made under the conditions of history. Hence, the position is both absurd and wicked, since all Scripture is revelation and God is the author of all. The position makes God the author of something doubtful. Furthermore, Calov maintains that such a conjecture makes all revealed things doubtful, even though such things pertain directly to faith and salvation.

> For if the source of theology (divine revelation) is not always infallible, incapable of being doubted and wholly beyond human criticism, but in some matter or other is only probable and of limited authority, then there can be no theological conclusions that are infallible and not subject to doubt. For a conclusion cannot be more certain than its genuine, adequate and single source. Now if the proposition

"Whatever God has spoken is infallibly true and must be believed with utmost certainty" is not true in all cases but is made to be binding only in certain cases and thus doubtful, then it follows that some things have been spoken and advanced by God that are only probable. . . . Thus, the entire issue concerns the certainty and authority of the Word of God. For if certain things have entered in [to God's revelation] that are not certain and are not of divine authority, how can there be any certainty or infallible authority in other matters? As Augustine says in his eighty-second letter, "If you grant any untruth to obtain in such a crowning height of authority (and this is done by doubting Scripture or not holding it to be absolutely sure), then not the smallest portion of these books will remain that cannot be called into question."[167] Now it so happens that the aforementioned axiom regarding the primary and supreme source of theology does not depend on an intention of God's whereby He reveals something for man's eternal salvation merely in such a way that those infallible things that are directly, legitimately, and in themselves pertinent to that purpose are to be believed. No, the axiom depends on the very unchangeable and infallible truthfulness of God, according to which He cannot lie (Heb. 6:18) but is absolutely reliable and entirely infallible in those things He reveals. Consequently, every word of God, no matter what it deals with, is certain and infallible. In the end we never seem able to get rid of this difficult question of certain skeptics, a question born of Socinian unbelief: it is said that "Christ and the apostles were influenced by the opinions of men, and in certain matters they are able to adapt and accommodate themselves to those opinions that flourished at that time. As a result, some of the divine writers upheld the truth better than others do, and sometimes in a minor way a writer has been mistaken about those things that only slightly deal with what we are to believe or do" (see Socinus, *De Auctoritate Scripturae*).[168]

This statement of Calov's is significant. It is the inerrancy and infallibility not of Scripture or of revelation as such that he is concerned to maintain, but the reliability of God, who has revealed Himself. We notice that Calov is not willing to grant that Scripture or revelation is merely unerring in purpose (which the Socinians readily admitted), but rather it is wholly and infallibly true by virtue of its divine origin, of its Author, who is God. Calov will not be sidetracked from the nature of God's revelation to its purpose. The nature and purpose of divine revelation belong together, but they cannot be confused.

We observe from the foregoing that the germs of modern critical

historicism were already present in the 17th century, and the problems connected with such an approach to God's revealed Word were present already for Calov. Whereas Kierkegaard in his day solved the problem by appealing to God's "moment" whereby He made God's past historical revelation contemporary for the present individual, Calov solves the problem by identifying Scripture with God's revelation, which is ἀνυπεύθυνος, i. e., self-authenticating. Scripture is today a powerful revelation of God, a means of grace, which brings God to man and brings to man and bestows upon him God's redemption wrought by Christ in history.

The form of revelation (as the source of theology) is divine inspiration (θεοπνευστία). Inspiration (Calov is not thinking primarily of the inspiration of Scripture at this point) makes revelation what it is. In a sense, inspiration, God's act of inspiring, is the source of revelation. But ordinarily inspiration is considered the form of the divine Word; inspiration is the *esse* of the Word, what makes it different from every other word. The authority, the majesty, and the power of God's Word are derived from the fact of θεοπνευστία. And as Calov later says, "Form gives being to a thing and constitutes the nature and essence of the thing."[169] With this Calov concludes his lengthy discussion of divine revelation. In his *Isagoges* and in the prolegomenon to his *Systema* he has presented the fullest treatment of this subject ever offered by a Lutheran theologian. He has still not offered anything like an exhaustive treatment of the subject but has discussed revelation only as something prolegomenous to the subject and study of theology. However, his doctrine of revelation is sane and balanced, and offers much of what is essential to the subject.

7. *The Goal of Revealed Theology*

The purpose of theology is a subject dear to the heart of the old Lutheran theologians. For here they get down to practical issues.

a. THE GLORY OF GOD. On God's side the goal is His glory. And nothing will promote God's glory among men more than theology, language about God. "The more God is known the more He is worshiped and glorified. And whence will one gain a greater understanding of God than through theology?"

b. THE SALVATION OF MAN. On our side the goal or purpose of all theology is eternal salvation. Here again the *Heilsegoismus,* so typical

of Lutheran theology, becomes apparent. Theology is a practical pursuit (as Calov will demonstrate later), and its purpose is eminently practical, just as is the purpose of God's revelation. The practical, soteriological purpose of all theological activity is illustrated in a number of ways.

(1) The purpose and goal of Scripture is practical (John 20:31; 2 Tim. 3:15), and "whatever is the goal of Scripture is also the goal of theology. For both deal with the same subject: Scripture presents the articles of faith in a sporadic fashion, theology arranges these articles in a systematic, methodical, and orderly way. Scripture supplies the content, theology provides the outer form, as it were, and presents everything according to the rules of method. Scripture becomes the source of theology; theology proposes the conclusions that are drawn from this source. Hence, Scripture and theology have one and the same purpose."

(2) The practical purpose of theology is seen from theology's general object, which is religion and everything pertaining to it. Religion, according to the later orthodox Lutherans, is really nothing else than a way *(ratio)* of life, a way of worshiping God according to His Word, a way dominated by faith and leading to eternal fellowship with God. "By this *ratio* man, who is an enemy of God, is restored to Him to have fellowship with Him forever." Hence, many of those theological considerations that appear to be quite theoretical and merely contemplative are actually eminently practical, for they lead to action and our deeper appreciation of God and our gaining everlasting life and blessedness.

(3) The goal of theology is the same as the goal of faith, which is salvation.

(4) The practical goal of the theologian also shows us the goal of theology. "Theologians have as their aim not mere knowledge, but also practical application *(praxis)* and perseverance unto salvation. Teachers and ministers in the church carry on their activity, or at least they ought to do so, in order to bring men to everlasting salvation. Thus, their work centers in saving men, and for this reason they are called saviors in the sense that they are ministers of salvation (Acts 11:14; 1 Cor. 9:22; 1 Tim. 4:16)." Not everyone who believes and perseveres to the end is to be called a theologian (e. g., children), but only those who lead others to salvation or are able to lead others into theological activity. Therefore theology has to do not with attaining salvation but with leading others to salvation. Theology acts not as a medicine *(habitus patientis)* but as

a physician. "Hence theology is not the art or activity of being saved and healed spiritually, except *per accidens;* but it is the business of the theologian and teacher to bring spiritual healing to others. It is sufficient for the theologian that he have the aptitude to lead a poor sinner to salvation, and that either by being occupied with the salvation of others or indirectly by having a sure knowledge of his own salvation."

(5) The healing nature and purpose of theology is emphasized again and again by Calov and the Lutheran theologians. In the dedicatory letter to Volume VIII of his *Systema* he waxes eloquent on the analogy between theology and medicine:

> The analogy between medicine and theology is an appropriate one and thoroughly apt; it delineates the nature of both in a very beautiful fashion. Medicine is not a theoretical discipline but a practical one. It is not content with mere speculation but in all things directs itself to practice. So it is also with theology, which indeed surveys God and divine things as its object but never in order to stop with mere cognition. Rather, it directs whatever it considers to the highest of all goals, the glory of the triune God and our blessed fellowship with Him. Medicine deals with the body of man, theology with the soul. Medicine seeks to cure the body, theology the soul. Medicine does not treat a body that in itself is perfectly healthy, a body of such a sort that it has suffered no weakness after the Fall; it treats sick bodies or bodies prone to sickness — and this is the kind of bodies we all have. Thus all its activities are preventative; they are to prevent the loss of health. Just as the Prince of Life, Jesus Christ, by His death brought back life out of death, likewise theology undertakes the cure of the soul, which is not only full of sorrow but crushed, not only spiritually feeble but spiritually dead. Now the source of this comparison is clearly in the sacred writings. The Son of God Himself calls Himself the Physician of Israel (Ex. 15:26). He declares that He came into the world that, like a physician, He might restore those who are spiritually diseased (Matt. 9:12). He professes that He was anointed for the very purpose of binding up the brokenhearted (Is. 61:1), healing hearts that are crushed, giving sight to the blind, and announcing healing to those who have been broken. (Luke 4:18) [170]

(6) But why belabor the point? Calov asks. If Scripture always assigns to theology such a practical purpose, the issue is closed. Therefore Thomas Aquinas and all the others are wrong who say that the goal of theology is more speculative than practical because it deals principally with divine actions and not human actions. Thomas argued that since theology

deals with divine things, it is in a certain sense *(secundum quid)* primarily theoretical.[171] Calov counters that indeed divine acts are more worthy of consideration than human acts. However, theology does not deal principally with divine acts as such. Rather theology informs a person that he might follow the way of eternal life. Nor can theology be partly theoretical and partly practical in purpose, for the two are in opposition to each other. One says that knowledge *(cognitio)* is the ultimate aim; the other says that knowledge is not the ultimate aim, but knowledge ought to be put into practice. Calov's emphasis on the practical aim of theology, an emphasis that antedates the works of the pietists and goes back to Luther and Gerhard, is most important. He is following the old adage that what is not practical is simply not theological. He is linking inseparably doctrine and life. All theology is for concrete living. The older position of Bonaventure was not so objectionable to Calov. Bonaventure made theology a blending of speculative and practical activity: Theology begins in knowledge and is brought to completion in an ability or aptitude *(affectio)*. Calov feels that this amounts to the same thing as making theology practical in purpose.

8. *The Nature of Theology*

The longest, the most controversial, and by far the most involved of all Calov's discussions in prolegomena is his treatment of the nature of theology. And so it is with most of the later orthodox Lutherans. But in spite of the complexity of his discussions and his scholastic approach, Calov is attempting to say something to his day that is of abiding importance; and his conclusions, which are the same as Gerhard's are taken over by all the Lutherans who come after him. Speaking against the scholastic theology of both Roman and Reformed theologians, Calov seeks to maintain the practical nature of all theological activity — and this is a worthy effort indeed. If he seems to become lost at times in technicalities and apparent logomachy, this is due only to his intense desire to present his point of view in the face of all aberrations and misunderstanding. He who appreciates the importance of what Calov is getting at will not fault him unduly for his prolixity and an occasional intricate digression. For to maintain the practical character of theology against all forms of theological dilettantism, speculation, scientism, and dead orthodoxy is the perennial task of evangelical theology. All true evangelical

Lutherans have seen the importance of this responsibility.[173] Chemnitz expressed the Lutheran concern very well when he said:

> We must at all times bear in mind that the Son of God did not proceed from the hidden seat of the eternal Father and reveal the heavenly doctrine in order to sow hotbeds for all sorts of disputations that a person plays at to show off his talents, but in order that men might be taught about the true knowledge of God and about all those things it is necessary to follow for eternal life. Therefore we must pay special care to each *locus* of doctrine; we must pay special attention to how and in what manner the doctrine that has been handed down to us may be put to use in the serious exercise of repentance, faith, obedience, and prayer. In this way our minds make progress in both doctrine and piety. For it has truly been said that theology consists more in a disposition *{affectu}* than in mere knowledge.[174]

Calov discusses the nature *(forma, genus)* of theology step by step, as it were. He considers the nature of theology according to its broadest classification *(genus remotius)*, its nature according to the more specific classification *(genus propinquum)*, and its nature according to its immediate genus *(genus proximum)*.[175] Viewed in this classification, theology is (a) a *habitus,* (b) *practicus,* and (c) θεόσδοτος.

a. THEOLOGY IS A *Habitus.* In reference to its *genus remotius* theology is a *habitus,* according to all the Lutheran theologians. The Latin word *"habitus"* is hard to render precisely into English. The term may be traced back to one of the categories of Aristotle (ἔχειν) and pertains basically to one's having or possessing something. This was ordinarily the meaning of the medieval scholastics when they used the term. *Habitus* meant a property or attribute, and then capacity or ability. Thomas would speak of *habitus* as *qualitates inclinantes,* the term denoting persistence and complete inherence.[176] The Lutheran theologians appear to be using the term more as Aristotle did on occasion, as an aptitude or skill.[177] The theological *habitus,* then, is both a posture and attitude, and an aptitude and ability; it is not passive or dormant but active (Heb. 5:14). Thus, for Calov and all the Lutheran theologians theology resides, strictly speaking according to its genus, not in a book but in the mind of the theologian.

In contrast to this position many had taught that theology in its nature was doctrine.[178] Calov would say, however, that doctrine is not the essence of theology but rather follows from it and in that sense is related to it.

"The genus," he says, "is the essence of the thing defined." True, the theologian teaches *(docere)*, but this has to do with the aim of theology, which is not a part of its essence. Meanwhile the theologian, even if he is not engaged in the act of teaching, is still a theologian, because he has been instructed and has acquired the aptitude *(habitus)* of teaching. Some have said the Word of God itself is doctrine. But strictly speaking, the Word of God is to be considered the source of doctrine and theology, and therefore cannot at the same time constitute the nature and essence of theology. Calov is following Aristotle at this point,[179] and we have here a good example of his dependence on Aristotle in a case where it does not really matter. After all, those who called theology doctrine are merely using the term in a loose and general sense, as is their prerogative. In our day, Francis Pieper has done the same thing in speaking at one time of theology as aptitude and at another time of theology as doctrine.[180]

What about those who, like the philosopher and theologian Jacob Martini, called theology a discipline? Calov grants that this is permissible, if by discipline is simply meant *habitus*. But a discipline is not usually defined as a genus of anything. Theology may or may not be carried on according to the procedure of a discipline; therefore it is only *per accidens* that it is a discipline. Again, conjuring up Aristotle, he says that a genus of something cannot exist unless its species are able to exist.[181]

May revelation be considered the nature of theology? Again no, for revelation is the source of theology. Moreover, revelation is an act, but theology, properly speaking, is not. Would it be proper to identify the nature of theology as the knowledge of the truth? It is true that Scripture often describes theology as a knowledge of the truth, but in such cases no definition of theology's proper genus is meant. Scripture, on the other hand, does seem to define theology according to its genus (Heb. 5:14) when it speaks of those who through aptitude (habit, διὰ τὴν ἕξιν) have their senses exercised to discern between good and evil.

b. THEOLOGY IS PRACTICAL. The *genus propinquum*, that is to say, the nature of theology according to its more specific classification, is *habitus practicus*. To establish the practical nature of theology Calov devotes the bulk of his discussion. We will recall that Gerhard gave this matter only passing attention. Our first reaction to Calov's long and involved argumentation may be quite negative. Does the subject really deserve such lengthy and detailed treatment? What practical difference

does it make if Calov's position is maintained? Calov's discussions are indeed tedious, and to thread one's way through his veritable labyrinth of subtleties is wearying, to say the least. But Calov has some eminently legitimate and vital concerns to uphold, and we venture to offer an exposition of his point of view.

Calov offers a number of proofs for the practical nature of theology. Although all the other Lutherans of his day agree with him on this point, they expend little labor in supporting their position. Apparently they feel that the point has been sufficiently established.[182] Calov submits the following arguments on behalf of his thesis that theology is a practical aptitude.

(1) *Proofs for Its Practical Nature.* (a) The practical nature of theology may be demonstrated from its purpose, which is practical, namely, to bring men to conversion and salvation and the enjoyment of God.[183] (b) The object with which theology deals reveals its practical nature:

> If a discipline deals with a certain object not in order to demonstrate anything but to accomplish something, then that discipline is a practical and not a speculative one. Now theology deals with its object not to demonstrate anything to it but to work something in it. Its object is man; not man as that concerning which something is to be proved, but man as an object who is to be blessed and saved forever.

Again we notice how important for Calov the soteriological purpose of theology is; such a purpose makes all theology ultimately doxological and thus eminently practical. (c) Calov continues:

> [The practical nature of theology may be shown] from the means [by which it proposes to accomplish its work]. Every discipline that sets forth certain means by which the one engaging in it may reach a certain goal is by all means practical. Now theology proposes certain means that accomplish such a goal. The subject engaging in theology, namely sinful man, gains the enjoyment of God. These means on God's part are the Word and sacraments, on man's part, his faith.

(d) [The practical nature of theology may be shown] from its general object. Whatever is considered by theology is either purely practical, or else it is considered primarily and properly for no other reason than that it has to do with action [πρᾶξις]. Hence all that is an object of theological attention is either practical in itself *{actu}* or by virtue of its being directed toward action, as we mentioned when speaking of the purpose of theology and showed inductively. (e) [The practical nature of theology is seen] from its usual function or activity. Since all the activities *{functiones}* of theologians, inso-

far as these activities are theological at all, are by their very nature practical, the theology from which they get their name has to be practical. And this is certainly the case with all the activities of theologians as theologians, whether they are teaching or exhorting or warning or consoling, whether they absolve penitent sinners or administer the sacraments, whether they initiate examinations or exercise church discipline — all these activities are in the nature of the case practical. (f) [That theology is practical may be shown] from the source of theology, which is divine revelation, and specifically those revelations that are contained in the Holy Scriptures. You see, if the purpose of revelation, which is the source of theology, is practical, then assuredly theology itself must be regarded as practical. Now our premise is true, since all things contained in Scripture, either by their very nature or certainly by their intention and divine ordination, are directed and relegated to action [*ad* πράξιν] (John 20:31; Rom. 15:4; 2 Tim. 2:15-17). And therefore our conclusion is also true.

(g) Calov next argues from the way in which theology proceeds. Theology's activity is analytical in procedure. Synthetic procedure attempts to show certain aspects of a subject from its causes. This is the direction in which theoretical disciplines wish to move. The analytic method attempts to indicate the purpose or goal of that which is under consideration, and from this terminus to trace the means that achieve this purpose. Since this analytic method is our method in theologizing, Calov avers, it is clear that theology is practical. Calov's argument at this point is questionable and circular. He has not demonstrated that the method of theology *is* analytic. The earlier Lutherans would have disagreed with him on this matter or at least left the matter open.[184] (h) Calov finally contends that the requisites for studying theology illustrate its practical nature, for these are practical requisites, namely *oratio, meditatio,* and *tentatio.*

(2) *Not mixtus.* But is not theology a mixture of the theoretical and the practical, since faith deals with both theoretical and practical matters? Calov answers no, "for theology must not concern itself so much with whether the object of faith is susceptible of speculation or of activity. Rather, theology has to do with faith itself, which is the goal of theology, and this faith certainly brings about activity [πράξειν]." Continuing, Calov says: "The activity *{actus}* of faith is involved with many different sorts of objects, but never merely that these objects might be known or assented to (as the papists would have it). No, faith is concerned to

apply and grasp such objects, and this is something practical." Again, Calov says: "The concern or interest of saving faith and its proper activity is not an incidental concern of either speculation or practice, but this concern or interest consists rather in the practice [of faith] itself." Finally, Calov argues that although things that have been divinely revealed are oftentimes materially diverse, still there is a certain formal unity in all of them in that they all lead to eternal salvation. It is his contention that a discipline is named according to its form, or nature, not from the content of objects it considers.

One reason for Calov belaboring his discussion on the practical nature of theology was that, for the most part, Roman Catholic and Reformed theologians of the day claimed that theology was both theoretical and practical. John Berg and John Alsted [185] among the Reformed agreed with the Scholastics in this matter, because, they said, in theological discussions some things are set forth simply to be recognized as true (e.g., creation), other things for practice. The Lutheran dogmaticians are most adamant in their reply.[186] But again Calov goes into much greater detail than any of his contemporaries, and what he says is pertinent also today, when theology is often considered a science. He points out that the first objects of theological discussion, "although by nature they may seem theoretical, are nevertheless directed toward action [*ad* πρᾶξιν] and are to be revealed for the sake of action." Thus, for instance, by knowing God's creation, we learn to adore and worship Him as our Creator. The theologian is never satisfied with bare knowledge *(nuda cognitio)* of creation or anything else, but he directs all knowledge to its purpose in his own life of faith.

But is not theology a mixed aptitude, inasmuch as it projects something to be believed and other things to be done? Not at all, replies Calov. "For faith is never satisfied with knowledge alone, but faith involves action; and therefore the things that are to be believed also involve practical activity." Calov has no dispute with the contention that theology seeks primarily to set forth the mysteries of our faith. But he holds that a discipline is described ordinarily according to its ultimate goal, which in the present case is practical.

> Theology propounds the mysteries of our faith not that we might acquiesce to them with a bare cognition but that we should embrace them with a true and living faith. . . . The intention of theologians, and therefore of theology, is not the mere acquaintance with our faith,

but it is to turn men to faith and salvation. To this end all theology is directed. And therefore theology is truly practical and in no wise theoretical or mixed.

And it is irrelevant to argue that theology is a mixed discipline because theologians are to teach as well as to lead. Of course theologians teach, but all their doctrine is directed toward a practical end.

> The theologian ought not to maintain and direct his knowledge simply for its own sake, but in order that the truth that is known might be embraced by a trusting heart. Now the true and living Christian activity is the practice of faith from which flows and follows the practice of piety, or the fruits of true faith. The knowledge of the truth (γνῶσις ἀληθείας) in theology is not something theoretical merely, but something singularly practical; for this knowledge works and perfects not theoretical but practical understanding, and that not intensively but extensively. And such knowledge brings about, or certainly ought to aim at, faith.[187] Furthermore, there is a double activity in theology: there is not only the obvious practice of piety, but also the practice of faith, which in a certain sense is a work (John 6[:29]). All religion operates with this twofold activity. And so theology in its entirety is purely practical and not mixed. This fact can be shown from the example of ethics, medicine, and other practical disciplines that yield knowledge, true enough, but a knowledge that is directed toward practice. And hence this knowledge is not theoretical but practical. He who has learned to distinguish between knowledge and theory [γνῶσις and θεωρία] will not adroitly claim that something theoretical enters into practical disciplines, although it is undeniable that knowledge has a place in these matters.

Throughout his discussion Calov wishes to preserve theology as one formal discipline. In philosophy theory and practice are concurrent, and thus philosophy is not one formal discipline. Rather it is a complex or aggregate aptitude *(habitus aggregatus)* consisting of many disciplines, some theoretical and some practical. Calov seems to have two vital interests at stake in all that he says. (a) He wishes to stress the value of theology for every phase of the Christian life. Theology is always relevant and applicable for life. (b) He stresses that there is nothing speculative or theoretical about theology. And yet at the same time theology qualifies as γνῶσις. As γνῶσις it is sure, certain, and true, and only then can it be practical. Such basic concerns are wholly commendable; they are both Biblical and evangelical. Quenstedt eloquently summarizes Calov's concerns:

Knowledge of God is directed toward the service of God (θεοσέβεια) and the practice of faith through which we aspire to gain eternal life (John 20:31). "These things are written that you might believe etc.," namely, that we might with our will worship, love, praise, and embrace with genuine trust God our Creator and Christ our Redeemer, who are known by the intellect. The purpose of this is that we might seize hold of God's grace and Christ's merit with true faith and apply these treasures to ourselves, and through this faith attain eternal life and enjoy God eternally.[188]

There is a certain advance in Calov's emphasis on the practical nature of theology, an urgency and insistence that is new. Former Lutherans had called theology a mixed *habitus* but apparently felt uneasy in doing so. Balthasar Meisner, for instance, called theology a mixed *habitus* because theology deals with both dogma and morals.[189] He contended that insofar as a discipline seeks to inform the intellect it is theoretical. He reasons in the following way:

> Now because the goal of theology is not only to shape man's actions but also to reveal the mysteries of faith and perfect man's knowledge, theology cannot be merely a practical aptitude. In the light of this, may we not call it a mixed aptitude? Yes, that would seem reasonably to follow. For we cannot deny that theology has a twofold duty and function: first, to teach the knowledge of the truth that is of faith by setting forth the true dogmas and by refuting the false; and second, to set forth the practice of worship by correcting bad morals and inculcating good morals.

Does this then destroy the unity of theology by making it a *habitus mixtus?* Not at all; no more than the unity of faith is destroyed when it is made something intellectual *(notitia, assensus)* and practical *(fiducia).* Is there any difference between the positions of Meisner and Calov? In spite of what would appear to be strong disagreement, there is no real difference. Calov, out of concern to maintain the practical nature of theology, merely "extends the meaning of a *habitus practicus* beyond philosophical precision and takes it in a somewhat wider manner." [190] By Calov's day his position was established among Lutherans.

(3) *Not "Wisdom."* May theology rightly be called wisdom? The term *wisdom* was used by Scotus and other Scholastics [191] in defining theology and was taken over by some of the leading Lutheran and Reformed theologians,[192] some of whom wished to make theology a mixed *habitus.* The majority of Lutherans disliked the definition of theology as wisdom,

because it appeared to threaten the practical nature of theology. Moreover, wisdom is a term too tied up with philosophical determinants (προσκείμενα).[193] Furthermore wisdom, which pertains to all things, is too broad a classification. Calov says: "According to the Philosopher [Aristotle], it is the task of wisdom to be concerned with all things according to their general classification and insofar as they are in common with each other. But God, even though He is the source of all things, is in no sense in common with these things but is totally above them." It is clear that Calov is fearful of bringing theology down to the level of a skill or capacity based on human powers of ingenuity. He is viewing wisdom as Aristotle did, as proceeding from the first principles of every field of knowledge and being highly skilled in teaching (διδασκαλικοτέρα).[194] Theology does not fit into such a paradigm. For theology proceeds only from authority and operates more a posteriori than a priori. It is very doubtful that those who called theology wisdom thought of wisdom in this Aristotelian sense. It is true, Calov points out, that theology is frequently described in Scripture by such terms as *understanding* (Ps. 119:27; Prov. 1:2; Eph. 3:4. νόησις), *knowledge* (Ps. 119:66; Is. 5:13; James 3:13. ἐπιστήμη), and *wisdom* (Ps. 119:125, 130; Prov. 1:2; 9:10. σοφία). But these terms are not always those by which theology is designated as a *habitus*. And they are not used in Scripture as they are in philosophy. Theology is even called foolishness on occasion. Not every predicate is generic. Theology is not only called σύνεσις and ἐπίγνωσις and σοφία but also the way of the Lord, doctrine, etc. Certainly these cannot all be of the same genus.

(4) *Not "Science."* Nor is the nature of theology a science, according to Calov. Here he holds forth against a vast array of notable theologians, both Roman and Reformed. Calov is thinking of science in the philosophic sense, as ἐπιστήμη, as the demonstration of things that are necessary (ἕξις ἀποδεικτικὴ ἐξ ἀναγκαίων).[195] It is exceedingly important that theology be not confused with science of this sort, for then theology is no longer a matter of revelation and faith but becomes a series of rational demonstrations, without the aim or the power to change men's lives or viewpoints. In his antipathy against making theology a science, Calov stands squarely in the tradition of Luther and Gerhard, and he realizes how much is at stake at this point. Theology has to do with faith; science has nothing to do with faith. Calov says:

> Theology is not a skill or posture (ἕξις) of the kind that demonstrates something from necessary starting points, or principles. Theology has its own kinds and methods of demonstrations [*causae,* ἀποδείξεις], which are not epistemological but pneumatological (1 Cor. 2:4). Scientific methods of demonstration make it necessary for our conclusions concerning necessary and a priori subjects to be based on their own reasons, or arguments. Theology does not act as a basis of demonstrating something but has as its object to work something in people. It does not consist of conclusions to be demonstrated rationally; but it has the role of bringing the means of salvation to people. It proves its points chiefly in an a posteriori, not in an a priori, manner. It definitely does not use reason, but employs divine authority. Properly speaking, it is such authority that is its effectual proof, not rational demonstration. Nor does theology beget scientific knowledge, if we are to speak properly, but rather it enjoins faith.

Moreover, theology operates entirely differently from science. Theology does not start from demonstrable principles (like science)[196] and thus yield necessary and universal conclusions, but all theological conclusions are drawn from revelation, from the authority of God alone. Scientific knowledge and theological knowledge are entirely different in character. Scientific knowledge is evident knowledge;[197] theology is by no means evident in the same sense, for it deals not with things to be known but things to be believed (τὰ πιστά). Therefore theology insists that reason that seeks to know theological matters be taken captive. Finally, the aims of science and theology are entirely different. The goal of science is theory, θεωρία in the sense of something to be considered and observed, dispassionately and without any necessary involvement; it is thus speculative. In contrast, the aim of theology is *praxis,* that is, action, achievement, operation.[198]

We need not follow Calov's intricate discussions further, but we can pause for a brief comment. To him speculative theology, theology as science, is a disaster; for Aristotle would limit such a science to a knowledge of necessary or eternal truth, and for a Christian to follow this would be docetic and would separate faith (if it is science) from life. Calov maintains the inseparable connection between faith and life. "This is our position: we are simply claiming that we must not merely rest in that knowledge of God but must direct it toward concrete living."[199] Calov goes on to say that faith is both knowledge of the mind and trust of the heart and indivisibly so; both are primary and cannot be divided. Hence

things that are to be done cannot be opposed to things to be believed, as though they were of a different order, for faith leads to action and is required for action. The sacraments, for instance, are not merely to be taught and understood; they are to be used. Faith, then, is a sort of practice *(Quia fides ipsa praxis quaedam est)*. The things to be believed do not exist as some sort of *theoria mentis* but must be apprehended trustfully — and this is very definitely a *praxis cordis*. "For whoever wishes to be saved ought not merely to know God and, with a mental acquaintance, accept the fact that He has revealed Himself, but he should believe in God with a true heartfelt confidence."

By his insistence that theology is not science, Calov is really carrying on an oblique polemic against the Roman Catholic doctrine of dogmatic faith and unformed faith, i. e., faith as the acceptance of doctrine and faith as insufficient for justification until formed by love *(fides formata)*. He is emphasizing, first, Luther's doctrine of *fides specialis,* a faith that not merely knows facts but trusts personally in God. And he is, second, against the Roman idea of *fides informis,* insisting that faith is always *fides activa,* involved in action. This dynamic concept of faith is vitiated if theology is made into a science.

(5) *Application to Life.* We miss in Calov's presentation of the practical nature of theology two very important things: a sound Biblical basis for his position and clear examples of how his position works — i. e., how are certain articles of faith practical, when they seem to bear no relation to concrete living?

In regard to the second matter Calov is not so remiss as might appear at first. In his *Isagoges* he has already said that the Biblical doctrine of angels, which to many in these days seemed rather withdrawn from everyday life, was propounded to bear upon life. "The knowledge of angels has not been disclosed merely for the sake of pure speculation so that we stop with this knowledge, but that we might devote ourselves to gaining and enjoying their companionship and becoming like them." [200] But it is chiefly in his *Systema* where we see the application of all theology in those sections called *usus practicus,* which regularly follow the discussion of every article of faith. As in the case of Gerhard and Brochmand, the most enlightening and edifying portions of Calov's dogmatics are just those sections where he applies the articles of faith to the life of the Christian. And this desire to bring out the practical application of Chris-

tian doctrine is really only another legacy of Chemnitz and Luther. Chemnitz is always a little embarrassed when forced to enter any sort of technical discussion that might becloud the practical aim of his theology. For instance, after one very long discourse on the terminology relative to the personal union, he says: "We must not dispute with clever and curious subtlety about that hidden and wonderful communion by which the divine and human natures have been joined in the person of Christ; rather we must see with our partial understanding, on the basis of knowledge from God's Word, how this entire doctrine can be put to serious use in the true exercise of faith." [201] Chemnitz would contend that only when theology becomes practical can it be really known and understood at all. After listing all the comfort he can find in the personal union, he says: "If we consider these matters in a reverent and pious way, then the whole doctrine of the hypostatic union becomes sweet to us. And if it is put to this use, then it will be easier and plainer to us." [202] To use doctrine is to Chemnitz "the most advantageous and safest method of all." [203]

(6) *Lack of Biblical Basis in Calov.* Concerning Calov's failure to lay a solid Biblical basis for the practical nature of theology it is difficult to offer an explanation. All the later Lutherans were remiss in this respect. Perhaps it was because Scripture does not speak specifically to the point under discussion. In one of his shorter books, however, Calov does offer some Biblical evidence for his position.[204] His main argument is from the example of Christ Himself. Jesus preaches the Gospel to the poor not merely that they might understand it intellectually but that they might embrace it with faith. The comfort He offers poor sinners is a practical comfort that sustains us in every exigency of life. He gives beauty for ashes and oil of joy for mourning. Surely when theology accomplishes all this, it must be considered to be something practical. Furthermore, both Law and Gospel have practical aims as they are employed by Christ and every theologian. According to Paul the theologian is to be ἄρτιος . . . πρὸς πᾶν ἔργον ἀγαθόν (2 Tim. 3:17). The good works Paul refers to here are not virtues in the ordinary sense but activities befitting a pastor or man of God.[205] Finally, Calov supports the practical nature of theology from 1 Cor. 2:2, where the apostle calls theology wisdom, not a wisdom of this world, not a philosophical wisdom, but a *sapientia mystica* the object of which is Christ crucified. The theologian propounds nothing

but this doctrine of Christ, which is practical in the highest sense. For to know Jesus Christ means to rest in His merits *(Cur enim agnoscimus Christum Jesum, nisi ut ejus merito nitamur?)*. Theology is set forth that our faith might not stand on human wisdom but in the power of God. And all this is practical.

c. THEOLOGY IS GOD-GIVEN. Calov gives only perfunctory attention to the so-called proximate genus of theology, theology classified as a gift of God. Unfortunately he is again too wrapped up in the polemics of the day. In presenting his view Calov makes Bartholomew Keckermann, the celebrated Reformed theologian from Danzig, his foil. Keckermann followed Aristotle quite rigidly in all matters of theological methodology and prolegomena. He placed theology in the class of prudence,[206] which is a practical skill or art that God infuses in His elect. Calov feels that this is going too far with Aristotle, who made prudence an "art" that is not revealed but emerges from the human heart and can be acquired by human capacities. In spite of Keckermann's monergistic affirmations, his making of theology mere prudence puts it in an utterly wrong genus and tends to obscure the fact that it is given by God. "For," says Calov, "theology is not acquired by human ingenuity, nor is it undergirded by principles known to nature; it has an aim and object of a completely different nature from prudence as defined by Aristotle."

Keckermann had brought 1 Cor. 10:15 in to support his Aristotelian position ("I speak as to wise men [φρονίμοις]; judge ye what I say"). But this, says Calov, speaks of something entirely different from what Aristotle was getting at. Theology — and now Calov defines his own position — does not represent conclusions drawn from human deliberation or motivation (*effectus* τῆς προαιρέσεως), but it is an activity brought about by divine operation. It is God who makes a person a theologian. And this is not the same as making a man a Christian. Only some Christians may be called theologians. Calov asserts that not all theologians are elect, and not all the elect are theologians. As a gift of God, theology is among the *dona ministrantia,* not the *dona sanctificantia.* It is not a gift of God bestowed along with faith and hope and love, but a gift drawn from divine revelation. It is an acquired gift, acquired in a most extraordinary manner by the apostles and prophets, and today acquired through means such as *oratio, meditatio,* and *tentatio.*[207]

9. The Object, or Subject Matter, of Theology

As in the case with revelation, the object, or content, of all theology is God. This means the living, acting God, *Deus pro me*. In theology we are concerned with God as Savior, "just as in medicine we are concerned first of all with those things that can restore a person to health or keep him in health." Thus in theology we do not consider the Deity in the abstract *(ipsa Deitas praecise vel in sese)* but as He comes to us and as we are able to know Him, respond to Him, and have fellowship with Him. Again, we are not concerned about God as He can be grasped by the intellect, but we are concerned to deal with the knowledge of God as it bears on our salvation.[208] In like manner, theology does not consider man as merely something possessing a certain quiddity, but eschatologically in relation to God's plan for him. Both God and man, His creatures, then, are considered by theology not as objects for contemplation but as they are active in relation to each other. True, theology considers such great themes as the Fall, sin, regeneration, justification, the sacraments, and eternal life — themes that, strictly speaking, are neither God nor His creatures — but these themes lead us to an understanding of God and of man, lead us to true piety, and nourish us in our faith. The object of theology is therefore all that leads us to true blessedness.

All theology is theology of God. This pleonasm expresses quite well a very basic concern and conviction of Lutheran orthodoxy. As a theologian I am not dealing with external truths — how often has Calov emphasized this point! — or "my understanding of my own existence," or "being itself," or some referent "beyond finitude," or mere facts; I am dealing with the living, acting, speaking God. God is not only the author of all theology, but the content and center of all theology. Gerhard has put it all very well: "As Sacred Scripture is the one source of knowledge in theology, God, who is of boundless goodness and power, is the one and supreme source of the existence not only of the Sacred Scripture itself (in which God's Word and revelation is contained) but also of the divine deeds of which theology treats. The center of the entire Scripture, the kernel of all theology, the goal of all our knowledge and desire are one and the same [namely, God]." [209]

10. Religion

In the silver age of Lutheran orthodoxy the subject of religion is often considered in great detail. This development takes place not because the

Lutherans have found some common feature in all religions — their interest in religion has nothing to do with their ideas on natural theology — but because of an increasing necessity to declare the unique character of Christianity as opposed to Judaism, Mohammedanism, Socinianism, and other religions and to distinguish Lutheranism from Romanism, Calvinism, Arminianism, and other sects. In the 17th century there was a growing number of theologians and philosophers who felt that there was some good in non-Christian religions, possibly even salvation. Furthermore, the Socinians and some of the Arminians and Anabaptists had clearly overthrown the foundation of the Christian faith. What about these people? Were they to be classified with Mohammedans and Jews? How were they to be dealt with? Could one force the Christian religion on them? It was such questions, together with the problems confronting Lutheranism as a worshiping church that was often threatened by Roman and Reformed theology, that prompted lengthy discussion on the subject of religion. One thing was very definite, according to the studies of all the orthodox Lutherans: any speculation about salvation outside the Christian religion could only lead to skepticism, libertinism, and atheism. Christianity was the true religion; strictly speaking, Christianity alone could be called religion.

a. DEFINITION. Religion was defined in orthodox Lutheranism according to its root, *religo,* which meant to fasten, or bind. Thus, we are bound to God as with a chain, and being bound to Him we are brought to salvation. But because such a meaning is so broad, the term *religion* has been abused often and equated at times with mere superstition or with obedience to the rules of the Roman Church.[210] But such "evangelical counsels" are papistic fictions. Christ and the apostles must be our examples in religion, and they know nothing of monkery and human merits.

In a somewhat restricted sense *religion* is a term for our worship of God or for piety, which concerns the worship of God according to the first table of the Law (θρησκεία, worship, invocation according to James 1:27; Gal. 5:6; and Matt. 9:13). Sometimes this can be mere outward show (Matt. 23:13). The full meaning of the term includes both piety toward God and love toward our neighbor; it includes all things considered in theology, whether they pertain to what is to be done or what is to be believed by Christians — in other words, an entire way of life (Acts 26:5). Insofar as religion is practiced, religion may be described as

a way *(ratio)* prescribed by God according to which a man, alienated from God, is brought back to Him and directed to eternal life. This way has been shown in God's Word of revelation; it is not a way of human wisdom or invention. (Matt. 11:27; 1 Cor. 2:11)

b. FALSE RELIGION. Although false religion can only be called religion by equivocation, the distinction between true and false religion is a very necessary and important one, for it serves to set forth in sharp relief the unique character of the Gospel and the Christian religion. False religions are called religions that oppose Christianity. They are usually divided into those that are outside the church, such as pagan worship and philosophies, Mohammedanism, and Judaism, and the false religion that is found within the sphere of the church's activity *(intra Ecclesiam),* such as heresy, superstition, and every sort of error that opposes the Gospel. Quenstedt lists a third category, which he calls Epicureanism, that is, "formal irreligiosity according to which a person despises all religion. Thus, after denying God's providence and emancipating himself from His justice, a person does with impunity and security whatever he pleases." [211] Quenstedt is speaking here of what we call practical atheism, and both he and Calov agree that this would belong within the classification of false religion that is *intra Ecclesiam.* Calov lists two kinds of atheism: incipient atheism *(atheismus inchoatus)* and complete atheism *(atheismus consummatus).* To him incipient atheism is the mixing and confusing of religions and worship that springs from fleshly motives and in the interest of outward peace. This is nothing but a collusion in dishonesty, however attractive its outer facade (Titus 1:12). It is interesting that for Calov syncretism and religious indifferentism are the beginning of practical atheism, which is basically indifference to God. Consummate atheism is the final nadir of syncretism, which holds that every man can be saved in his own religion, or it may be pure libertinism or Epicureanism. Calov is clearly operating with the Biblical idea of atheism and syncretism. He supports his remarks with allusions to the syncretism in the Old and New Testaments. (2 Kings 17:32-33; Acts 15:1, 5; Gal. 4:9-10; 5:4)

c. THE MARKS OF TRUE RELIGION. Such a discussion of false religion will lead to two questions: What are the marks of Christianity as the one authentic religion in the world? Is there salvation for those who do not know the Christian Gospel?

At the time of Calov the attributes of religion were usually seven in number. (1) *Necessity.* That religion is necessary is shown from the fact that God has revealed Himself to man (Matt. 11:21; 16:17; 1 Cor. 2:11-16); hence trust in Him and worship are according to His will. (2) *Antiquity.* True religion has been enjoined upon man from the very beginning of history. Immediately after the Fall there was a revelation (Gen. 3:15), and God continued to manifest Himself in every epoch of His people's history. From the beginning of time His name has been preached, He has been worshiped, and sacrifices have been made to Him. (3) *Unity.* Although there are many false religions and kinds of idolatry, there is only one God of whom are all things, and we in Him (1 Cor. 8:6); only one way to God through the one Mediator, Christ Jesus (John 14:6; 1 Tim. 2:6; Heb. 5); and only one way of receiving forgiveness of sins and justification before God (Ps. 32:1; Acts 10:43; Rom. 4:6; Eph. 1:7; Col. 1:14; Is. 45:24; 53:11; Jer. 23:6; Rom. 3:21-26; 4:3-8; 1 Cor. 1:30; Gal. 2:16; John 3:15-16; etc.). (4) *Truth.* Christianity is true because it agrees with God's revelation, His Word given us in Scripture. More precisely, there are three marks of Christianity that distinguish it as the true religion. First, it directs us and our worship to the true God. Second, it teaches a worship that has been revealed by God and never abrogated. Third, it makes known a way of reconciliation between God and man that satisfies God's justice and brings eternal salvation to man. It is obvious that these three marks of the truth of Christianity have to be accepted on faith. We find here a far less elaborate defense of the truth of Christianity than those worked out by Melanchthon and Chytraeus, and a defense not based on any extra-Biblical criteria. However, later in his polemical section, Calov again speaks of the truth of Christianity, this time according to measures *(modi)* and indications *(indicia)* that were "customarily" used; and this time he borrows most of Chytraeus' criteria. It would be a mistake to put too much weight on this apparent concession to rationalism of Calov's. His treatment of the truth of Christianity in this second section in which he takes up specific questions relative to religion is unoriginal and perfunctory. He does not even say that he personally stands behind the criteria he offers, but he merely lists them. The other dogmaticians of the era do not offer such lists of criteria at all. (5) *Holiness.* The Christian religion is holy because God is holy, because the mysteries He has revealed and His precepts are holy, and because He has

prepared eternal holiness for those who worship Him. (6) *Power and efficacy*. Christianity offers consolation in trials, peace of conscience against sin, and joy and confidence even in tribulations. (7) *Invincibility*. Christ has promised that His church shall prevail until the end of the world (Matt. 16:18, 28). The church of Christ may be in subjection in times of persecution, she may suffer disfigurement, her light may seem eclipsed and even extinguished, but she emerges again reformed, and by divine grace she triumphs.

d. SALVATION WITHOUT CHRIST? The second question, which stems from the first, is taken up by all the dogmaticians: Can one be saved who does not know Christ and the Gospel? With one voice Lutheran orthodoxy answers in the negative.[212] Without a knowledge of Christ and faith in Him no one can be saved. There is only one way of salvation (John 3:3, 5, 16; 14:6; Acts 4:12; Is. 28:16; 1 Peter 2:6; 1 John 5:10 to 12). John 14:6 proclaims a universal negative, Calov says; therefore apart from Christ there is no truth, no way, no life. "And Christ is not the way unless He is known. We walk this way by faith alone, for Christ has said, Believe in the Father, believe also in Me." It is therefore the implication of the Gospel itself that demands this negative and terrifying conclusion, not a dogmatism or sadistic cruelty of the Lutheran dogmaticians. Where other ways of salvation are conjectured, the Gospel itself is vitiated. Christ, the Savior of the world, is the foundation of the Christian religion; if that foundation is taken away, the entire structure of Christianity falls to the ground. Calov says "The source from which all genuine religion is drawn, if you are considering faith in Christ, is the Word of the Gospel, and this Gospel is one. St. Paul expressly says: 'Though we or an angel from heaven preach any other gospel unto you than that which we have preached unto you, let him be accursed' (Gal. 1:8). There is no gospel besides that which Paul and his brother apostles preached. Faith comes from the hearing of this Gospel." Just as there is one foundation of the Christian religion and one Gospel, there is only one faith (Eph. 4:5; John 14:6; Gal. 3:26-27), and there is only one love, which springs from faith and pervades one's life (Gal. 5:6; Acts 4:32). The absolute claims of Christ proclaim Christianity as the absolute religion; and the warnings in Scripture against error and heresy and false teachers (Matt. 7:15; Rom. 16:17; 2 John 10; 2 Tim. 2:17; 1 Tim. 4:1-3;

1:19) are unjustified if salvation can be attained by those who are not Christians.

e. THE PLACE OF THE OLD TESTAMENT. But what of the Old Testament? If there is only one Gospel and only one religion, what can we say of those who preceded Christ? The answer given in great detail by all the orthodox Lutherans is that the religion of the Old Testament and that of the New Testament are the same. This was not just the naïve claim of a precritical era of Biblical interpretation. It was commonly held in the 17th century among the Socinians and Arminians and even some Roman Catholic theologians that the theology of the Old Testament was different from that of the New in fundamental matters, and this was held on alleged Biblical grounds.[213] The orthodox Lutherans were compelled to show exegetically from both the Old and New Testaments that "in substance the religion of the Old Testament is no different than that of the New," as Calov put it.

It is not possible even to summarize the vast amount of exegesis produced to support the Lutheran position, but we can mention the basic ideas that make up the Lutheran doctrine. Lutheran theology, like the early church fathers, considers the Old Testament the possession of the church: the Old Testament Scriptures are Christ's Scriptures, they are Christian. The New Testament, in turn, offers us not a new or different theology from the Old, but it is a message reciting the fulfillment of the Old Testament Scriptures. It is an interpretation, an inspired theology, of the Old Testament in the light of fulfillment. The theology of the New Testament is Christ's theology, taught through the writings of His apostles. As they relate a history, the New Testament Scriptures offer something new; as they teach theology, they offer nothing new, for both Christ and His apostles presume to teach nothing that is not based on the Scriptures of the Old Testament. Thus, the Lutheran teachers read the Old Testament Scriptures through the light of the New, not because they are uncritically following the custom of Luther or some ancient hermeneutical rubric, but consciously and deliberately because they believe that faithfulness to their Lord Jesus Christ demands such a course of action.

This is not to say that there are no differences between the religion of the Old Testament and that of the New Testament, but they are differences of circumstances, not in matters of substance. Quenstedt lists three such differences: (1) In the Old Testament Christ the Mediator was

prefigured in types and shadows; in the New Testament the man Christ was present. (2) In the Old Testament was the time of expectation; in the New the awaited Savior has come. (3) There is a fullness of clarity in the New Testament that was not possible in the Old, when the revelation was covered by a cloud of types and temporal things.[214] But nevertheless there is no new religion in the New Testament. "When Simeon took Jesus in his arms (Luke 2:28) he did not change his religion; certain circumstances surrounding his faith were changed, but the faith itself and the religion itself remained the same." With great insistence Lutheran theology teaches that the same Gospel that is proclaimed in the church today was preached in the Old Testament. A typical statement, followed almost verbatim by the later dogmaticians, is that of Gerhard:

> From the time when the first Gospel promise was made known by the Son of God in Paradise, the voice of the Gospel has continually sounded forth in the church, repeated and declared by the patriarchs and the prophets. Hence it is one and the same Gospel that not only was produced and declared in the New Testament but was proclaimed to our human race from the very earliest times. By this Gospel, God's grace, the forgiveness of sins and salvation, one and the same, were announced and offered to all the saints.[215]

Gerhard then goes on to maintain that the sum of the Gospel consists in the preachment concerning the person, office, suffering, resurrection, and other works of Christ and in all the benefits He brings to the world.

Very specifically, it was unanimously taught that the doctrine of the Trinity was adumbrated in the Old Testament and that the two natures of Christ and His redemptive work were proclaimed with sufficient clarity that these articles can be shown from the Old Testament. For this, after all, was precisely what Jesus did: He proved His Messiahship and His divine claims from the Old Testament Scriptures.[216] Neither He nor His disciples presume to teach a new religion but insistently preach and demonstrate that they are teaching the religion of Moses and the prophets (Matt. 5:17; John 5:39). Commenting on John 5:39, Calov says: "Although He had the testimony of John and His own miracles and even of His Father from heaven, Christ appealed to Scripture, that He might proclaim the identical [doctrine]." It is the persistent apostolic claim, too, that all their doctrine is taken from the Old Testament Scriptures (Acts 24:14-16; 26:22-26; 2 Tim. 3:15, 17; Acts 10:43; Jude 14). Quenstedt maintains that there are specific statements in Scripture that affirm that the

way of salvation is the same for those in the Old Testament as for those in the New (Acts 15:11) and that one faith and one religion is proclaimed in both (Eph. 4:5; Rom. 4:23-24; Gal. 3:8; Heb. 11:26). But is this evidence not all taken from the New Testament Scriptures and therefore invalid? Ingenuously Calov replies to the effect that one ought to believe the testimony of the apostles that there is only one religion. He is fully convinced that an inductive examination of the Old Testament will bring out the same fact.

f. LUTHERANISM AND CHRISTENDOM. One final problem was considered by the later orthodox teachers under treatment of religion. This problem, which was discussed at greater length under the *locus* on the church, had to do with the relation of Lutheranism to the rest of Christendom. Lutheranism, along with Romanism and Calvinism and Socinianism, was called a religion. And it was asserted that the evangelical religion Luther brought to light through the divine Word was true. According to Calov, the true saving Christian religion is expounded in the Augsburg Confession and not among the Socinians, papists, and Calvinists. In his *Systema* he discusses the errors of Calvinism, Romanism, and Socinianism under the heading of false religion. Only in the case of Socinianism does he deny that the religious system is Christian. But there is much that is against true religion taught within the papacy and in the Reformed churches. In the case of the Calvinists, for instance, by denying the universal grace of God, they are in effect preaching "another Gospel" than that of the apostles. Their doctrine of an absolute decree of predestination definitely opposes the Gospel, which in brief proclaims that he who believes shall be saved. Calvinism impugns the truth of God when it teaches that His revealed will to save all men is not sincere; it impugns the power of God when it insists that Christ's body cannot be present in many places at once; it impugns the righteousness of God by teaching an absolute decree of predestination and the goodness of God by its false doctrine of grace. In each case the Gospel is being threatened. Calov is obviously not judging the personal faith of Calvinists; he is judging the theology of Calvinism. The fact that Calvinists have faith in Christ is irrelevant to the point he is making; for Calvinism attacks faith when it impugns God's truth and power and justice and goodness, and to that extent inculcates false religion.[217] In view of what Calov has just said, it follows that the Calvinists, as long as they persistently teach heresies that threaten

the foundation of faith, cannot be considered spiritual brethren.[218] And he who would offer them the hand of fellowship would be guilty of syncretism.

11. *Christ, the Master Theologian*

The one example and pattern for every theologian is Jesus Christ, the Master Theologian. Here we have in mind Christ according to His prophetic office. It was already foretold by Moses (Deut. 18:15, 18-19) that Christ would be the theologian κατ' ἐξοχήν. In fact, Christ was already a teacher *(doctor)* when He came to the patriarchs as the Angel of the Lord. In Is. 63:9 this same prophet or angel is called by His proper names, יֵשׁוּעַ and גֹּאֵל, Jesus and Redeemer, who saves His people according to righteousness (cf. Gen. 48:16). It is this Messiah and Redeemer who speaks through David in the Old Testament (Ps. 45:1). Solomon calls Him wisdom and a shepherd, and all are urged to listen to Him (Prov. 8:33-34; Eccl. 12:10). Zechariah says the same (Zech. 1:13). Calov offers an exhaustive list of Old and New Testament evidence for the prophetic office of Christ. But Christ is the Master Theologian not only because He is the teacher of all theology but because all theology centers in Him. He is the core *(nucleus)* of all the Scriptures. And since He is the center of the entire Scripture, the "marrow of Christ" must be clearly present in all sermons and teaching in the church. This was quite obviously Christ's own practice and the practice of the evangelists. Calov is trying to say that we draw all our theology from this one teacher, Christ, who has been a perfect and clear teacher. This involves patterning not only our style but also our polemics, practical applications, homiletics — our whole approach — after His discourses. He must be our teacher as He was for His own disciples and as He also was in the Old Testament in visions, confrontations, etc.

Calov is most emphatic that Christ be not only the one whom we emulate as theologians but also the theme *(scopus)* of all our theological discourse. Specifically, the sufferings and death of Christ, which brings salvation, is the theme of all theology. Calov likes the old adage that says that Scripture must be read as though it were written in the blood of Christ. The theme sung by the apostles is nothing else but Christ crucified (1 Cor. 2:2). And this is the theme also of the Spirit of Christ, who inspired the Old Testament (1 Peter 1:10). As one harmonious

and mellifluous melody sounds throughout all Scripture, that same Christ-centered theme should be the burden of all preaching and theology in the church today.[219]

12. The Theologian: His Training and His Posture

In the lengthy delineation of Calov's prolegomena, there has been a great deal about theology and little about the theologian. This is because Calov devotes the entire second volume of his *Isagoges Theologicae* to the subject of the theologian and how he is equipped for his labors. At the risk of some repetition, there follows a brief summary of his thinking on the subject, for his remarks and suggestions are not only the most comprehensive up to his time but are strikingly practical and evangelical.

a. THE PREKNOWLEDGE NEEDED BY AN ASPIRING THEOLOGIAN. Calov's volume on theological training *(Paedia Theologica)*[220] is designed to be a practical help for the theologian, young or old, in the study of theology. We would, of course, find much wanting in such a volume, and yet our age of theologians has produced nothing quite like Calov's contribution. Here he is speaking of the endowments, the disposition, the attitude, and the tools the theologian brings to his task. And he is particularly interested in illustrating how God trains the theologian in His school. For the theologian must know what he is, what his task is, and how he is to prosecute it before he can effectively engage in theology. Hence there is a necessity for theological training (παιδεία), for a platform *(judicium)* for what we are to do as theologians. Theological *paedia* seeks to establish the necessary preknowledge for fruitful theological labor, the guidelines that lead us along as we theologize.

(1) *The Nature and Goal of the Work.* The first things we must know in advance of our actual labors *(praecognita)* are the nature and goal of our work as theologians. We must know and appreciate the necessity for theological study (John 5:39; 17:3; 2 Tim. 3:15). Even if all cannot be theologians, still all must know the way of salvation, and all are called on to test the spirits (1 John 4:1; Matt. 7:15; Rom. 16:17). Theology touches every aspect of life. Politicians and physicians particularly ought to study theology, because they are involved in so many ethical and theological issues. We must know and appreciate that theology is the highest of all studies and the most rewarding. Here we are

dealing with the sublime mysteries of God, and the goal of our study is eternal life. At this point Calov speaks eloquently and with conviction:

> Theology proceeds from God, teaches us about God, and leads us to God. Only theology is the light of our mind, the healing remedy of our will, the antidote against sin, and the most effective stimulant for true piety. Only theology unites us with God and God with us. It is the stairway from earth to heaven. By it we ascend to heaven, and God descends to us and overwhelms us with heavenly gifts of every description. And so earth becomes to us a heaven, and heaven and earth are the same to us, and God becomes our portion. In theology we who are on earth teach those things the knowledge of which continues even in heaven. By means of theology the blind see, the deaf hear, the lame walk, the dumb speak, the dead are given life; men are made partakers of the divine nature (2 Peter 1:4). Such is the high value we place on the study of theology. Ps. 119:130: "The declaration of Thy words giveth light and giveth understanding to little ones."

The study of theology is a sacred study. It is prompted by the Holy Spirit, it gains knowledge through the Holy Scriptures, it deals with the sacred things of God, and its goal is our sanctification (John 17:17). Therefore it should be undertaken with utmost consecration. The study of theology is the most extensive of all studies. It prepares a person for every aspect of life *(tota vita)*. It embraces exegesis, history, ethics, teaching, preaching, and ministering and thus perfectly prepares us for the life hidden with Christ in God. Hence it is never a burden but is the *negotiorum negotium,* to be taken up with enthusiasm and love and humility. Although theology is so vast that even a Methuselah could never master it all, yet it can be distilled so that a little child can know all that is necessary. Meanwhile we aspire to graduate from the school of this trivial life and enter the heavenly academy, where we shall hear directly the testimony of the holy Trinity and behold Him face to face. Finally the study of theology is difficult because of the vastness and depth and fullness of the things God has revealed. But by God's grace we surmount every obstacle through our work and prayers; and the impossible becomes possible, and the difficult becomes easy. (Mark 9:23)

(2) *Qualifications and Aptitudes.* The second kind of antecedent knowledge necessary for the theological aspirant has to do with the theologian himself. Here Calov is speaking of the qualifications and aptitudes necessary for becoming a theologian. Just as wood does not have

the capacity to become mercury or some other metal, some Christians do not have the qualities *(indoles)* requisite for a theologian. What are the ingredients of this theological disposition *(indoles)?* They are the capacity to judge spiritual things (1 Cor. 2:13); a good memory to retain a knowledge of language, Scripture, history, etc.; sincerity; and a love for theological study. But not only is a disposition of the mind required for such study; the theologian's will, too, must be formed, purged of carnal affections, and denied to take up the cross (Matt. 16:24). A contentious frame of mind and will can have no place in the study of theology (1 Tim. 6:4-5; 2 Tim. 2:24; James 3:5). Rather there must be purity of heart (1 Tim. 4:7; Ex. 40:31-32), obedience (John 7:17), patience in controversy, gentleness, modesty, temperance, chastity, concern for the truth, adorned with the doctrine of God (Titus 2:10). At this point Calov is no longer speaking of natural endowments but is asserting that the theologian ought to possess those gifts that Scripture makes requisite for pastors and ministers of the Word.

(3) *The Purpose of the Theologian's Work.* The third kind of antecedent knowledge necessary for the student of theology is an understanding of the purpose of theology. The theologian must be possessed of a holy purpose *(sacra intentio),* his eyes fixed always on the soteriological goal of all theology (Matt. 6:22-23). The glory of God must be his highest aim (1 Cor. 10:31; Col. 3:17). And why not? All theology and only theology informs us concerning the true glory of God. The student of theology earnestly strives for the edification of the church, and all his efforts are directed toward this aim (1 Peter 5:2). The church is edified "in truth and orthodoxy, or in sincere faith, and in piety and holiness." Truth and orthodoxy are concomitant with faith in the subjective sense, as far as Calov is concerned. He is very earnest that no one theologizes for any other purpose than edification. "Those who seek merely after new ideas, who delight in useless subtleties, who are enamored in a lot of empty talk, who are accorded praise for their capacities so that they appear to excel above others, such people do not strive for the building up of the church. They are more correctly to be considered students of empty words than of true theology; their wont is to harm rather than aid the church." But theology must be directed to my own personal edification as well as that of the church (1 Tim. 4:16). "We are to study, therefore, to advance in the knowledge of those things that are

necessary for salvation, to be strengthened in our faith, to remove every scruple of doubt, to arrive at full certainty concerning all things; and all this that with a happy and untroubled conscience we might be able to teach others, admonish them, and console them. For he who teaches others to believe things concerning which he himself is embarrassed and has doubts, such a one easily wounds tender consciences."

b. REQUISITES FOR BECOMING A THEOLOGIAN. Calov, having outlined the preknowledge that every aspiring theologian ought to have, now settles down for a thorough discussion of the general requisites for becoming a theologian, requisites that are distinct but are always together: *oratio, meditatio,* and *tentatio.* Prayer, meditation, and affliction remain with the theologian and fashion him throughout his activity (Phil. 4:6; James 1:5; Ps. 85; Is. 28:19; 1 Peter 1:7). We must consider briefly what Calov says on each of these essential requirements, for although he is only repeating the old theme developed by Luther and a long line of Lutheran theologians, his treatment of the subject is most convincing and uplifting and sets the tone for all that follows.

(1) *Prayer.* Prayer for the theologian "is nothing else than the humble and faithful request for divine enlightenment and a beneficial progress in theological study." Whether it is done vocally through formal petitions or psalms or hymns, or is merely the raising of the heart to God, it is all the same. Prayer is a matter of the heart, not of the lips, as Bernhard said. Our congenital spiritual blindness, our proclivity for error, as well as God's command and the example of the saints, should induce us to frequent prayer. But for the theologian it is particularly the depth and breadth of what confronts him that incites him to pray. In our study we come face to face with the mysteries of very God, which exceed our powers of comprehension. Through these mysteries we gain not just a knowledge of words and facts, but a spiritual and saving knowledge of God (Matt. 16:17; 1 Cor. 2:14). And this knowledge is power; it produces action in our lives (John 13:17); we become strengthened in God's might. Should we not ask in prayer when such blessings are available to us? "The streams of divine grace do not descend on us except through the channels of prayer." Furthermore, we require the illumination of the Spirit for all theological study; otherwise we can never know the mysteries of divine revelation (Matt. 11:25; 1 Cor. 2:11), nor will we progress in true faith and piety (2 Tim. 2:7; Eph. 3:16). "Just as no one can see

the sun without the sun, no one can know God without God, without divine illumination. . . . The Scriptures are not understood in a beneficial way except through the Spirit, by whom they were brought about (2 Peter 1:20-21); we must daily implore His grace and enlightenment by our prayers (Eph. 1:17; 3:16)." [221] Not only are there general commands to pray at all times and under all conditions, but specific admonitions in Scripture to pray for the gift of the Spirit (Luke 11:13), for wisdom and knowledge (Eph. 1:17; James 1:5), and for the free course of the Word (2 Thess. 3:1). The danger of falling into error must always incite the theologian to pray. Prayer is therefore of inestimable value for the theologian in every way.

> Prayer is the military rear guard for the one who prays, his sacrifice to God, his scourge of the devil. Prayer showers on us the treasures our faith beholds lying hidden in the Gospel. Just as Moses after entering the tabernacle returned with a divine response, the students of theology approach God with their prayers so that they might understand His utterances. Through prayers wisdom from heaven is imparted to us and flourishes (Prov. 2:3; James 1:5), and we lay hold of the true goal of this wisdom and whatever we could in any way desire (John 16:24).

But Calov is not intent merely to emphasize in general the prayer life of the theologian. Prayer is a very specific help for the theologian, a veritable *sine qua non* to him in his labors. "He who prays diligently has by his praying completed half of his studies" *(Qui diligenter orat, orando dimidium studiorum absolvit).* And Calov proceeds to show all the concrete practical blessings that prayer opens up to the theologian. But this prayer must be devout and genuine, for God does not hear us unless we hear Him (Ps. 5:2-3). In his prayers the theologian offers his heart to God; he is humble, always penitent, seeking only God's glory. And above all he is faithful; his prayer is rooted in the merits of Christ. He begins and ends his task in prayer; his mind is continually turned to God in prayer (1 Thess. 5:17; Luke 18:1) that he may turn from error and idle controversy and work only for the edification of Christ's church. This means setting aside definite hours for prayer; but more than this, the theologian must be a *jaculator* of prayer, repeatedly flinging his prayers and sighs to God. His every breath is a petition for God's guidance and grace. But there is no need to pursue Calov's discussion any further or to list any of the beautiful prayers he suggests for the theologian's use. We have

seen that Lutheran orthodoxy recognizes only a praying theologian, and it speaks with utmost conviction and sincerity on the matter.

(2) *Study.* The second general requisite for the theologian is study *(meditatio).* This involves the use of the Scriptures; it means reading them attentively and rereading them, often aloud. And it means listening, writing, discussing theology eagerly, lecturing, repeating, reasoning — and all such activities are centered in the Scriptures (John 5:39; 1 Tim. 4:13; Ps. 1:2; Prov. 2:4). The object of this study is only one: the Word of God committed to writing in the Scriptures and everything that can be drawn from this Word and said about it. All the languages and every other discipline are to be directed to this single study, that we might know and keep and propagate the Word of God. Our aim in such study is to gain and store up by attentive consideration sacred doctrine, and then to apply it; to gain spiritual understanding (σύνεσις πνευματική) and the capacity to teach (δύναμις ἑρμηνευτική), what Jesus calls "a mouth and wisdom" (Luke 21:15) and what Paul calls aptness to teach (1 Tim. 3:2; 2 Tim. 2:2). It is by listening and working that this goal is attained.

It is most important that such meditation maintain the proper balance. There are certain things the theologian cannot do without; he must read and know the Scriptures, he must have a knowledge of the articles of faith *(loci theologici),* he must understand the theological climate and the controversies of his own day, and then he must put all this knowledge to use. He must avoid vain and futile pursuits no less than scandalous pursuits. He must avoid fanaticism and enthusiasm and remain with the testimony of the apostles and prophets. His meditation should be day and night (Ps. 1:1), but ordinarily he works by day, because that is what God did and that is God's order. Meditation should be well ordered; definite times and order ought to be established for study. The theologian should listen (learn) before he goes to work and practices his theological study *(Acroases praecedere oportet* γυμνάσματα). By "listening" Calov has in mind giving ear to those who teach the Word directly and through writings. There is necessity for schools of the prophets, Calov thinks. For theological study often involves discussion, argumentation, collation, reasoning, and other related activities.

(3) *Affliction.* The third requisite for the theologian is *tentatio,* affliction. To Calov this is the practical testing of our theological proficiency and growth. We are tested by the weakness of our own flesh,

by crosses of God's sending, and by the siftings of Satan. And so affliction is of three kinds: human, divine, and Satanic. All such afflictions under God's providence tend to inform the mind (Is. 28:19) and to equip and make perfect the will of the Christian theologian (2 Cor. 12:7; 1 Peter 1:7). In all such affliction the theologian learns to arm himself only with spiritual weapons (Eph. 6:11-18). But really God is the one who tests us, and hence affliction is the practical experience of the one who listens to God's speaking. In the school of the cross and of persecution one learns to lift his eyes to God's Word of light and comfort; cf. 2 Cor. 4:17.

c. SCHOLARLY PREREQUISITES. We can safely pass over Calov's long treatment of the scholarly prerequisites for the theologian — the languages, philosophy, "neology" (epistemology and logic), natural science, mathematics, history, etc. — he offers little that was not said by Hyperius and Gerhard and Chytraeus.

d. BIBLICAL STUDY. A summary of just what he considers Biblical study to be is important, for theological study is essentially Biblical study, and this, says Calov, is the *caput rei* of the theologian's labors. We find that Calov is still in the tradition of Luther and Chemnitz in conceiving Biblical study as something very broad in scope. It includes (1) a continual and extensive cursory reading of Scripture, (2) exegesis, or the more intensive and careful investigation into the meaning of the text, and (3) didactic theology *(studium didacticum)*, which is the systematic arrangement of the articles of faith that are drawn from Scripture. This is a rather broader concept of Biblical study than we usually meet today. Calov would even include polemics, practical theology (application), and homiletics under Biblical study, but not history, which does not always involve the direct approach to Scripture. What is important to note is that for Calov dogmatics is a part of exegesis. One is engaged in the Scriptures just as much when he writes a *systema* as when he writes a commentary. Or to state his ideas in a slightly different way, sound Biblical exegesis (in our narrow sense) invariably and necessarily leads to dogmatics. This means that Calov's exegesis, like Luther's, will indicate a conscious dogmatic bent and a certain amount of application. We now consider these three functions of Biblical study in more detail.

(1) *Continual Reading.* The continual, reverent reading of Scrip-

ture is the first and most important part of Biblical study, "the bow and stern," so to speak. Everything must begin with this. How often are we urged and encouraged to engage in the frequent reading of Scripture, not only by commands (Deut. 6:6; Josh. 1:8; John 5:39; 1 Tim. 4:13; Col. 3:16) but by the value and usefulness of what we read (John 20:31; Rom. 15:4; 2 Tim. 3:16), by the depths of what is there set forth (John 5:39; 1 Cor. 2:6), by the worthiness of the activity itself (Ps. 119:72; Prov. 3:14), by the blessings that accrue to us thereby (Ps. 119:2, 103), and finally by the example of the most worthy saints, such as David (Ps. 119) and the Beroeans (Acts 17:11), Timothy (1 Tim. 4:14-15), and others. Calov is here thinking of the devotional and reverent reading of Scripture. Every student of the Bible must first stand under the Scriptures and read them for his own personal edification and comfort. The student "must read Scripture reverently, with humility and ardor." Why? "Because in Scripture God speaks with him." To Calov Scripture can only be read devotionally "with a humble spirit, submitting to God, who teaches us therein." For the result of such reading is that "we take our reason captive in obedience to faith; we accord faith to those things that ought to be believed and obedience to those things that ought to be done." Reading Scripture must result in faith and action. Only such reading is worthy of the Bible student. Calov commends many suggestions on how we might improve our devotional reading of Scripture, such as using various versions, noting the main theme of each chapter and book, recalling chronology and setting, reading longer units at a sitting, etc.

(2) *Exegesis.* Exegetical study concerns itself with drawing out the meaning of the Scriptures. Here is required a careful and accurate reading of the Scriptures that scrupulously examines the terms and phrases, establishes the context in terms of what precedes and follows, makes notes of similar passages and contexts, and compares all with the analogy of faith. Only after such work has been finished do we consult the explanations of other interpreters.

The Spirit of God is the one infallible interpreter of Scripture. It is therefore of prime importance that we study the language He employs to achieve His intent and aim *(mens, intentio, scopos).* Particularly the unbroken meaning and sense of the Holy Spirit *(perpetua Spiritus S. sententia),* "which in dogmatics we call the analogy of faith," must always be borne in mind by the student of Scripture. The entire Scripture be-

comes clear in the light of this unity, this single message, this *Spiritus Sancti sententia*. It is clear that Calov at this point is speaking not of one among many hermeneutical rules but of a presupposition for all exegesis, a presupposition that was originally gained inductively from the Christian student's devotional reading of Scripture but now is a basic assumption for anyone who does thorough and intensive exegesis. To apply this principle and see its bearing on all Scripture involves five things that must be looked for or observed in our study of Scripture: (a) signification, which is to establish the precise meaning of a section or text; (b) intention, which is to establish what the Holy Spirit intends to say in a pericope or verse; (c) sequence of the context (*contextus* συνεχεία); the analogy of faith throughout Scripture; and (e) the overall harmony of Scripture (παναρμονία *Scripturae*). Precisely what is entailed in each of these five basic norms is not entirely clear, but Calov's interest is very clear: to let the Holy Spirit interpret His own Word to us. Calov does not omit mention of the usual necessary helps the student of Scripture must have. He lists (a) concordances and lexica; (b) critical studies on the nuances and thought patterns of Scripture; (c) analytical studies of various sections of Scripture (of which there were very many in those days); (d) harmonies of Scripture, which attempt to reconcile difficulties and tie together apparently disjointed sections of Scripture; (e) versions and paraphrases; (f) commentaries and even works in dogmatic theology; and (g) works in textual criticism.

(3) *Didactic Theology.* Didactic theology is the thematic presentation of the theology of Scripture. Didactic theology draws from Scripture the chief articles of faith and sets them forth in some sort of order. The product of such study may be as brief as a catechism or as vast as a syntagma. It is clear that such a procedure is a form of Biblical study to Calov and requires all the training and background necessary for exegetical theology, for it is the result of exegesis. The value of this method is that judgment is made concerning the relative importance of the articles of faith and concerning their relation to each other and to Law and Gospel. Therefore to Calov "the study of didactic theology is necessary in the highest degree for the student of theology." Why is this so? Because every Christian must have a knowledge of the articles of faith and of their bearing on Law and Gospel. How else can he give a reason for the hope that is in him (1 Peter 3:15)? To present a system of faith and doctrine

is incumbent on anyone who would hold fast the sure Word or give instruction in sound doctrine to others. The exegete who is concerned about his understanding of the Gospel and about proclaiming it inevitably becomes a dogmatician.[222] It must be borne in mind at this point that Calov is not speaking of dogmatics in the modern sense but of didactic theology. The purpose of approaching Scripture systematically is that we might understand and teach. By definition, then, didactic theology is necessary for every theologian. The finest example of such a method is, according to Calov, the small catechism or compendium that offers the kernel of the theology of Scripture with sufficient Biblical evidence added. Thus the message of Scripture is easily apprehended even by children.

e. STUDY OF HISTORY. It was mentioned earlier that Calov placed the study of church history outside the sphere of Biblical study because it does not always involve a direct approach to the Scriptures. This does not imply, however, that he has no interest in history, either Biblical or church history, and has nothing to say on the subject. A few of his thoughts on the subject follow.

The ideas of orthodox Lutheranism on history are not, for the most part, deep or original. History did not occupy the same interest for theologians then as in our day. True, sacred histories and church histories were written. In the case of Flacius and Seckendorf we see the serious attempt to write a church history as the progress of the Gospel under the providential governance of God. But in general the Lutherans possessed neither the facilities nor the concern, except for the sake of polemics, to study deeply and thoroughly the history of the church or to venture any philosophy of history beyond a modified Augustinianism. In the various introductions of theology that were written, the reader was often urged to study Bible history and church history seriously and note certain things in his readings and study. Selnecker, for instance, says that in studying sacred history one should note the origin of doctrinal concepts and should note examples of God's ruling His church, crosses the church has borne, the development of doctrine, and the life, customs, faithfulness, etc., of God's people.[223] The reasons for the study of sacred history are to learn to defend and understand the contemporary church better, to strengthen God's people in their faith, and to promote prayer, fear of God, knowledge of salvation, etc. Every purpose of studying history, as we see, is theological, never humanistic. There is a great difference between sec-

ular and sacred history, according to Selnecker, although both have lessons to teach us. Secular history lies under the shadow of the Law. Sacred history sets forth the whole Law and Gospel as revealed by God, and in particular God's miracles among men (*miracula & testimonia doctrinae*). By miracles Selnecker means God's mighty acts in history.

Calov has some rather interesting notions regarding the study of history in connection with theology. Secular history (*historia exotica*) is important as well as sacred history as background to the study of theology. Calov accepts the usual division of history into divine, natural, and human history. Divine history is what is inspired in the Old and New Testaments. Natural history, whose goal is knowledge (*scientia*), deals with universals (*universalia*, i. e., general or common phenomena in contrast to individual actions) and therefore belongs within the domain of philosophy rather than history. Human history deals with human events that have actually taken place. Sacred history not only is necessary for theological study but also enables one to interpret secular history.

13. *Calov's Impact and Importance*

Abraham Calov enjoys the distinction of having produced the most thorough discussions on dogmatic prolegomena ever offered by a Lutheran during the period of orthodoxy. In a conservative fashion he continues and develops the work of his forebears, but, as we have seen, he also adds much that is new. However, in all his contributions he consciously and devotedly follows in the footsteps of Luther and Gerhard, especially in the way he delimits the province of philosophy and reason in theological activity, in his emphasis on the theologian's involvement in his work (*habitus practicus*), and in his insistence that God makes one a theologian (*oratio, meditatio, tentatio*). His contemporaries offer nothing in the area of prolegomena and dogmatic presentation that is not at least suggested by Calov, and many of them (Quenstedt, Huelsemann, Scherzer) depend very heavily on his prolegomena and theology. Calov easily ranks as the most original, challenging, and influential Lutheran theologian of the silver age of orthodoxy, and this is especially true in the area of prolegomena.

A deterioration and general loss of vigor and theological direction is clearly discernible in the prolegomena and theology of those who write dogmatics after Calov in the last part of the 17th century. This is not

always noticeable, certainly not in the works of Quenstedt or Bechmann, but it can be seen clearly in writings of such men as John Adam Osiander, Musaeus, Baier, and Hollaz. By the time of Osiander [224] a good number of the older issues in prolegomena had been solved, and new issues had arisen. For instance, there was no longer any need to debate at great length on the practical nature of theology, because most of the Calvinists were in agreement. Osiander and Hollaz had to debate, rather, with fanatics and Quakers that theology was a *habitus* at all, for many at that later time were making theology synonymous with visions, inspiration, and ecstasy. In general, however, Osiander follows Calov quite closely in his treatment of revelation, the articles of faith, the marks of true religion, the truth of Christianity, and heresy and schism. But there is an intellectualism and excessive scholasticism in Osiander's entire approach that is not found in Calov. The same is true of Musaeus and Baier,[225] both of whom were also unfortunately infected by synergism. In the case of Musaeus, excessive emphasis was placed on the importance of natural religion.

By the time of Hollaz theological prolegomena had taken another step backwards by becoming too involved in speculation regarding the psychological and cognitive processes of the theologian. Hollaz even tries to analyze the kind of knowledge the unregenerate man, imperfectly illumined by the Holy Spirit, has in respect to God and spiritual things.[226] The Schwenkfelders and Weigelians maintained that such knowledge was simply carnal. The Quakers held that no spiritual knowledge could come from meditating on the Holy Scriptures. Just why Hollaz felt compelled to answer these strange opinions as he did is not certain; possibly it was due to his inclination toward Pietism with its predisposition for dabbling in psychology. At any rate he comes up with a bewilderingly intricate solution to the problem. The unregenerate man who has been only incompletely and pedagogically illuminated by the Holy Spirit has a literal theological knowledge, that is to say, he gets the literal sense of Scripture. And this knowledge is supernatural; it is the result of divine persuasion. But it is not absolutely spiritual in the mind of one who is not yet regenerate. However, in a certain sense *(secundum quid et certo respectu)* it is spiritual because of its source (Scripture), because of the one who gives this knowledge (the Holy Spirit), because of its content (the deep things of God), and because of its goal (man's conversion).

In the light of the antitheses we can appreciate that Hollaz' motives are the best: the Gospel message of Scripture is a means of grace, and it is a cognitive and intelligible message that the Spirit of God uses in bringing a sinner to faith in Christ. This is surely what he wishes to stress in the present discussion. But by dwelling on the noetic functions of the unregenerate man, by classifying the unbeliever's knowledge of God and theology as spiritual, by speaking of a man being illuminated spiritually before he is converted, Hollaz not only goes beyond Scripture but fails to take seriously what Scripture says about the spiritual condition of the unregenerate man and opens the way to synergism. There is a great deal of original thinking and valuable insight in Hollaz' prolegomena, as we have had occasion to mention several times, but this one fault, which is so patent and infectious and pervasive, portends the further deterioration of Lutheran theology in the 18th century.

ORTHODOXY IN DECLINE: 18TH-CENTURY THOUGHT ON THEOLOGY AND DOGMATIC PROLEGOMENA

By the turn of the 18th century two very great influences were making themselves felt within the Lutheran Church, influences that were considered dangerous by orthodox Lutherans. They were the pietistic movement and the modern philosophy of the day (particularly the new interest in epistemology). How orthodox Lutheran theology tried to meet the impact of these two movements may be seen fairly clearly by reviewing the contributions in prolegomena of two leading Lutheran theologians of the day. In general the answer given to the extravagant emphases of Pietism was not so well taken as the analyses of the philosophical trends of the day.

1. *Neumann and the Pietists*

John George Neumann, a rigidly orthodox Lutheran, was for a time professor of philosophy at Wittenberg; his chief work, *Theologia Aphoristica*, published in Wittenberg in 1718, was directed primarily against the pietists.[227] Neumann's prolegomena are of interest to us principally in that the author insists against the pietists that there is a theology of the unregenerate. This was a thesis that Gerhard and those who followed him — Calov, Quenstedt, Huelsemann, Brochmand, Dannhauer, et al. — would

have roundly condemned. However, we have noticed a definite tendency in this direction in Hollaz when he taught that the *notitia literalis* of theology in the unregenerate man is not simply carnal but supernatural and that this involves an enlightenment of the Holy Spirit. But Hollaz would never arrive at Neumann's conclusion. We briefly review Neumann's arguments for his position.

Neumann is as insistent as any of his predecessors that theology be defined as a practical aptitude. To him theology is an aptitude of the intellect [228] that concerns itself with true religion and is acquired from the written Word of God. Here Heb. 5:14 is pertinent; the writer speaks of strong food, that is, a solid knowledge of divine things, as being an ἕξις, a *habitus*, as the philosophers call it. To Neumann theology is a τελαίωσις, or *quality,* rooted firmly in the mind of the theologian by which he is made apt to teach (2 Tim. 3:16-17). Theology is more than mere acceptance of divine things but in the nature of the case is active and brings and directs all the things of God into a living practice. Theology is a gift of God (1 Thess. 4:9; 2:13; 2 Cor. 3:5-6; Eph. 4:11), and all theological activity is carried on by God's grace (2 Tim. 2:7; 1 Sam. 2:21; Luke 1:80). And yet "theology is not only a divinely given aptitude but is in a definite sense something that is acquired and mastered *{acquisitus}*." It is this practical nature of theology that prompts Neumann to mention the importance of systematic theology "as a brief and connected summary of the articles of faith" set forth in such a way simply because of the advantage it has for teaching. It is this concern for upholding the practical nature of theology that convinces Neumann, like Calov, that the analytic method in dogmatics is to be desired. For the analytic method, looking always to the end, the *causa finalis,* makes theology eminently practical. It is important to recognize Neumann's insistence on theology as a *habitus practicus* θεόσδοτος lest we do him an injustice as we outline and comment on his arguments for a theology of the unregenerate.

Neumann feels that he must concede that there is an unregenerate theology in the case of the lapsed. For they have been instructed in Christianity, and in some cases it would appear that they are unregenerate *"non secundum intellectum, sed voluntatem,"* and therefore they fail not in doctrine but in life. If lapsed teachers in the church became simply ψυχικοί like Turks or heathens, they would perceive nothing in divine matters, but this is simply not the case. If, on the other hand, they were

to become completely blinded and rejected the counsel of God against themselves (Luke 7:30) or defected from the Christian truth like apostates or heretics (2 Thess. 2:3-4; 2 Peter 2:2, 15), then it would have to be said that the true knowledge of God that was in them was either obscured or entirely effaced. Neumann points out that the Pharisees who were unregenerate had a knowledge of theology, of the coming Messiah. Others recognized Christ's person and work although they remained unbelieving.

Neumann maintains that this unregenerate theology is not false theology, nor is the term *theology* used equivocally here. This is seen by the fact that this theological knowledge often corresponds to divine things that are revealed through nature or Scripture.

The theology of the unregenerate man is, of course, not the product of the treasures of his own heart but is of divine origin and may therefore be correctly called spiritual (1 Cor. 2:11). An impious minister who administers sacred things to his flock does so only by the strength of God (1 Peter 4:11). Whatever is drawn from the Word, even by the unregenerate, is spirit and life (John 6:63). Therefore, Neumann argues, "all the factors connected with this theology are spiritual and supernatural; thus its source is the Holy Spirit working through the Word (1 Thess. 2:13); its subject matter is τὰ τοῦ θεοῦ, or divine things (1 Cor. 2:11); the subject engaging in the activity is man, enlightened intellectually and thus getting the name theologian (Num. 24:15-16); the nature or way of coming to a knowledge of theology consists in the opening of the eyes and the enlightening of the mind (Acts 24:8; Eph. 1:17) and in spiritual discernment (1 Cor. 2:15); and the goal of theology is the pressing forward to salvation (Phil. 1:15, 19)." Gottfried Hoffmann says the same thing in a slightly more guarded fashion, when he declares: "The theology of the unregenerate is correctly said to be of the Spirit of God and is regarded as among His ministering gifts (1 Cor. 12:8), although such theology is not carried on with the Spirit and does not have simultaneously His indwelling grace which is the prerogative only of the theology of the regenerate."[229] Hoffmann adds that the theological *habitus* perishes in one who persists in mortal sin and falls from grace.

In respect to the foregoing we would ask: Is this not dissociating in an arbitrary manner the intellectual functions of man from his other

activities as he deals with theology? Is theology exclusively a matter of the intellect, as Neumann tends to make it? Just as a *fides humana* (the mere intellectual assent to an article of faith) or *fides historica* cannot be called faith, a mere *notitia* or *theologia irregenitorum* cannot be called theology. This is certainly the case if theology is viewed as an aptitude. Neumann's protests to the contrary notwithstanding, there is an equivocation here in his treatment of theology.

Neumann backs up to take another running start, so to speak, at his subject. *Theologia impiorum* must not be likened to a philosophy concerning divine things; it is not a "spectre of reason." "No, its strength and power is derived from the divine Word, and it is therefore living and effectual and salutary in itself." Neumann is attempting at this point to dissociate theology from the subject, the theologian. This becomes clear as he goes on to point out that the Pharisees led their hearers to the way of salvation although they themselves did not pursue it (Matt. 23: 2-3). "Therefore in itself their theology is saving theology." Neumann's position is made quite clear in the following statement: "The unbelieving theologian, insofar as he is enlightened by the Holy Spirit, is not σαρκόσοφος, that is, fleshly wise, as the pietists whine, nor is he ψευδόλογος; but he is actually θεόσοφος and θεοδίδακτος, inasmuch as he has learned his theology not from the principles of reason but from revelation through the assistance of the Holy Spirit." Examples of this, Neumann points out, are Balaam and Caiaphas and the false prophets of Matt. 7:22. He goes on to say: "According to the Scriptures the theological knowledge one possesses is either apprehensive and discursive, or subjective and pertaining to the emotions, that is, conjoined with faith and love. We do not attribute the latter but only the former to the unregenerate." Scripture supports this view, Neumann affirms, when it sometimes joins to the knowledge of divine things faith and love.

It is clear against whom much of Neumann's presentation is directed. The pietists made the mistake of equating theology with saving faith or with Christianity.[230] This tended to make every Christian a theologian and to minimize the importance of the Christian ministry. But Neumann's severest complaint is that it makes theology something very subjective and tends to tone down the importance of pure doctrine. The same is true of mysticism, which taught an immediate illumination and union with

God by apotheosis; of the ascetic theology of monks and hermits; and of the "comparative theology" of the Syncretists. In each case indifference to pure doctrine and true theology is fostered. Against the pietists Neumann contends that theology as an *aptitude* is acquired and is difficult to come by, faith is an *act* that can be lost, and Christianity is a *state* that is preserved by both theology and faith. Faith and Christianity are to be considered the end and fruit of theology and therefore cannot be considered the essence of theology. It is perfectly possible for one to be a Christian and a true believer and yet not be a good theologian in the sense of 2 Tim. 3:17. On the other hand a theologian may preach to others and himself become a castaway. (1 Cor. 9:27; 13:1-2)

It is clear from all that Neumann has said that he is attacking something that is both false and pernicious, but he goes too far in the other direction when he separates theology from the theologian, and he opens wide the door to the very danger the pietists were so rightly afraid of, the grave danger of a theologian not being involved in and caught up by his material. To Pietism an unregenerate theologian was a contradiction in terms. If Gerhard, Dannhauer, and Calov would not have said exactly this, they would at least have insisted that an unregenerate theologian is an impossibility according to 1 Cor. 2:14. These earlier theologians, as also the pietists, were deeply concerned over maintaining a pious clergy, and the notion of theology being practiced by unbelievers was unthinkable and scandalous to them.

There was no need for Neumann to have gone so far. Bechmann, a generation earlier, had answered the pietistic error without falling into the opposite extreme by merely showing the difference between theology and faith. So had Hollaz, even with all his weaknesses on this point.[231] Hollaz pointed out that in several respects theology and faith have much in common and are similar. They are both gifts of God. They are both drawn from God's revelation and steadfastly rely on that revelation. They both have to do with knowledge and an assent of the intellect. They both are directed toward eternal salvation. But theology and faith also differ from each other in several important respects. Theology is an intellectual *habitus;* faith in the sense of trust resides principally in the will. Theology is a totally practical aptitude that includes faith as its object and its goal. The number of the faithful is therefore far greater than the number of those who are theologians.

2. Loescher and the Philosophers

The second and no doubt most serious threat to orthodox Lutheranism in the early 18th century was the various philosophical systems being propounded. To analyze the views of Leibniz, Locke, Spinoza, and the Cartesians in the light of the Gospel was imperative for Lutheranism at that time, lest all theology be drawn into the web of speculative metaphysics or be undermined by the rationalism and inherent skepticism of Lockean epistemology. Valentin Loescher, a theologian of far greater stature than Neumann, attempts to discuss and point out the dangers of these philosophies and of many other false ideologies of his day in a book entitled *Praenotiones Theologicae*.[232] This work deals with the ideas of Hobbes, Locke, Spinoza, and many other philosophers, and a book quite like it had not appeared previously. Herein we find Loescher dealing with physics, metaphysics, epistemology, and other areas that we might prefer the theologian to stay clear of. But Loescher is convinced, and rightly so, that in certain matters all these areas of human wisdom touch on theological concerns; and therefore a critique in the light of evangelical theology is called for.

For instance, he sides with Leibniz against Hobbes in teaching that truth is both real or objective *(qua rem)* and notional and subjective *(qua nos)*. Hobbes had maintained that truth consisted only in the conjunction of words into propositions to which the mind either acquiesced or did not. That there was anything real corresponding to our ideas he could not affirm. Loescher rightly insists that it is a matter of life and death for theology to combat such an idea. Loescher also insists that there are fundamentals of truth, such as Scripture, experience, *communes notiones* (e. g., logical, analytical operations), and sufficient testimony. He attacks the then commonly held opinion that all knowledge comes through sensation and reflection. Locke was the chief proponent of this theory that "nothing is in the intellect that was not in the senses." Although this is generally true, it is particularly false in matters of religion and theology. For the mysteries of faith do not have their origin in our senses nor in what our mind may call to memory. Loescher's method throughout is simply to point out the difficulties and dangers of the opposition and then to assert his Christian answer. Thus, we find him rejecting Aristotle's doctrine of the mind as a *tabula rasa* and also Plato's doctrine of remembrance. He also contends that there are common notions that

are self-evident notions of reason. Against Locke he asserts that there are not only *notiones communes* that deal with the ways for men to think, but also knowledge of God that is inherent, such as knowledge of His existence, His justice, etc. (Rom. 2)

Against those who oppose dogmatics (C. Democritus had called systematic theology a *Talmud Lutheranorum*), Loescher contends that systematic Bible study is not to be identified with scholastic theology. It is true that the early church did without formal systematic theology, but in the earliest times there were applications and commentaries made on the Scriptures. Moreover, technical terms are often most helpful. These terms can both adequately represent divine doctrine and shed light after heresy has darkened a given issue.

Loescher's method makes it quite difficult to criticize him. He works on the principle that all doctrine and opinions of men must come under the scrutiny of the Gospel and, where they oppose sound doctrine, must be exposed and condemned. Loescher is not in the slightest interested in working out any theory of metaphysics or epistemology of his own but purposes merely to judge all existent systems and theories — where this is necessary, but only where this is necessary — in the light of divine revelation. One epistemology is as good as another to him unless some aspect of it conflicts with revealed theology. Throughout, Loescher is extremely cautious not to allow any philosophy to enter into his proofs for things — more so, one might feel, than Gerhard and the earlier dogmaticians — and this is understandable for one living in the 18th century. For instance, he is most insistent that theology has its own proofs *(Theologiam demonstrationes suas habere, credimus & propugnamus)* against all skeptics and indifferentists. But this is a matter of faith. True theology is not a science in the strict Aristotelian sense and therefore will not offer demonstrations that will satisfy the demands of science. Nevertheless theology is true knowledge *(notitia)*, built on a sure foundation; and it brings forth a *demonstratio Spiritus* that does the job of refuting *(elenctica)* and of convincing positively *(obsignante)*. Here we discern that Loescher has abandoned much of the elaborate apologetics of the later 17th-century theologians in their defense of the truth of Christianity, the divine origin of Scripture, etc., and confines himself to a simple statement in Pauline terms of what Christian knowledge is and how it is supported and maintained. There is much in the 18th-century dogmatics that represents

a degeneration from the earlier work of a Chemnitz or Gerhard, but in Loescher we have a sane and balanced approach and a real desire to meet effectively the issues of his day. And it must be remembered that the issues of his day were far different from those that pressed the church a century earlier.

In Loescher we have a refreshing instance of a Luther *redivivus*, wielding the sword of the Word against every false doctrine of man and refusing to become enmeshed in the endless intricacies of rationalistic apologetics, which was to fight the battle of faith with blunted weapons or even to turn these weapons against oneself.[233] But Loescher was unable to stem the tide. The seeds of the Enlightenment and of rationalism had already been sown. Wolff and Lessing were soon to arrive on the scene with their devastating doctrines. Confessional Lutheranism and orthodoxy was losing its hold in the universities and among the theologians. And in the wake of its first great impulse of evangelical fervor Pietism in many instances was degenerating into extremism. Loescher stands as the last great representative of a long and impressive line of orthodox Lutheran dogmaticians.

NOTES TO CHAPTER TWO

1. Martin Luther, *Sämmtliche Schriften*, herausgegeben von Dr. Joh. Georg Walch, 2. Auflage (St. Louis: Concordia Publishing House, 1881—1930), V, 456, hereafter cited as W^2. "The first concern of a theologian should be to be well versed in the text of Scripture, a *bonus textualis*, as they call it. He should adhere to this first principle: in sacred things there is no arguing or philosophizing; for if one were to work with rational or probable arguments in this sphere, then I could twist all the articles of faith as easily as Arius, the Sacramentarians, and the Anabaptists have done. No, in theology we must merely hear and believe and be convinced in our heart that God is truthful, no matter how absurd that which God says in his Word may seem to reason." See also *D. Martin Luthers Werke*, Kritische Gesamtausgabe (Weimar: H. Böhlau, 1883), 50, 654 ff., hereafter cited as WA.
2. WA, TR 5, 25, No. 5245: "Philosophy does not grasp sacred things, and I fear too much of it will be mixed with theology. I do not disapprove of its use, but let us use it as a phantom and a comedy of civic righteousness. But to want to let it be the substance of theology — that will never do." Luther rejected the theology of the Scholastics because it was saturated with philosophy. See W^2 XVIII, 840: "Let others decide for themselves what they have learned from scholastic theology. As far as I am concerned, I know and confess that I have learned nothing from it but ignorance of sin, righteousness, Baptism, and the whole Christian life. Nor did I learn what the power of God, the work of God, the righteousness of God, faith, and hope,

and love are. I not only learned nothing (which could be tolerated), but what I did learn I only had to unlearn again."

3. *Corpus Reformatorum,* ed. Carl Gottlieb Bretschneider et al. (Halle: C. A. Schwetschke and Sons, 1834—), 13, 509—752, hereafter cited as *CR.* This first Protestant textbook in philosophy became immensely popular. The *prima forma* (1520) was revised into a second form in 1528 and finally a third form in 1547. The first form went through nine editions, the second form nine editions, and the third form ten editions. The last edition of the final form was in 1580.

4. *CR* 21, 160.

5. *CR* 21, 163.

6. *CR* 21, 86 ff.

7. *De Anima,* 411a, 26—28. Peter Petersen, *Geschichte der Aristotelischen Philosophie im protestantischen Deutschland* (Leipzig: Felix Meiner, 1921). Petersen shows how Melanchthon follows a good deal of Aristotle's anthropology in his *Loci Communes* even though he is consciously polemizing against Aristotle. Aristotle's influence is shown in his discussions on the will and reason, freedom, and active and passive intellect. See *CR* 21, 93 f.

8. Luther wrote in 1540: "Plures hodie scribunt dialecticas, sed unus Philippus scripsit dialecticam, ex quo fonte reliqui omnes hauriunt sua, et nemo tamen assequitur Philippum, nedum ut superent eum" (WA, *TR* 4, 647, No. 5082b). Luther then repeats much of what Melanchthon has written in his *Erotemata.* See also Luther's *Dialectik oder der theologische Gebrauch der Logik, von ihm angezeigt,* which is a presentation of Luther's *usus logices theologicus* (containing somewhat more than is in the WA citation above) by Valentin E. Loescher from a MS of about 1540 (of doubtful authenticity) in Wolfgang Gotlob Roertschel's *Lexicon Luthers* (see W² XIV, 742 ff.). Luther's position concerning Aristotle was that his *Ethics, Metaphysics, Physics,* and *De Anima* should be discarded unceremoniously as false and pernicious, but his *Logica, Rhetorica,* and *Poetica* could be read and were of value to Christians (Martin Luther, *Sämmtliche Werke* [Erlangen: Carl Heyder, 1826—57], XXI, 344 ff., hereafter cited as Erl. Aus.). His opinion was cited repeatedly by later Lutherans. It is also the position Melanchthon seeks to maintain. He defends Luther against the charge that the latter rejected every branch of philosophy (e. g., mathematics and natural science, confined to their own sphere); it was Aristotle's speculative physics, metaphysics, and theology that were the object of Luther's attack. See *CR* 1, 290.

9. His strongest blasts against philosophy were, however, in his earlier years. (See Petersen, pp. 32 ff.)

10. *CR* 12, 689—91.

11. The preface to the *Loci Praecipui Theologici* (1559) is found in *CR* 21, 603—607. Cf. Appendix.

12. Matthias Flacius, *Clavis Scripturae Sacrae* (Copenhagen, 1695), pp. 914 ff.

13. Although Melanchthon's preoccupation (as a professor) with philosophy no doubt hindered him from throwing off his synergistic predilections, Otto Ritschl has gone too far when he makes Melanchthon's "return" to Aristotelian philosophy the "root" of his synergism. See Otto Ritschl, *Dogmengeschichte des Protestantismus,* 4 vols. (Leipzig: J. C. Hinrichs'sche Buchhandlung, and Göttingen: Vandenhoeck & Ruprecht, 1908—1927), II, 232.

14. Andrew Hyperius, *De Theologo, seu de Ratione Studii Theologici Libri IIII* (Basel, 1556), pp. 25 ff.

15. The Lutheran theologians of the day were particularly insistent that a knowledge of nature is an indispensable help in understanding the Scriptures with their allusions to natural phenomena in presenting the truths of theology. See Matthias Flacius, *Clavis Scripturae,* II, 577 ff. (Tractatus VI, Admonitio, de necessitate cognitionis variarum rerum potissimum in communi vita existentium).
16. See Thomas Aquinas, *Summa Theologica* (Rome: Marietti, 1948), L. I., Q. I., Art. 2.; John Gerhard, *Loci Theologici,* ed. Johann F. Cotta (Tübingen: Io. Georg Cotta, 1763), II, 8. Gerhard denies that articles of faith may be called principia. This would mean that articles of faith are derived from another source than Scripture. Thomas himself, however, did not fall into this error, for he speaks of Scripture being the highest science, having its own principles (L. I., Q. I., Art. 8), which are the articles of faith. It is obvious, however, where Thomas' idea could and would lead.
17. In his dedicatory letter to the *Loci Communes* he states his purpose as follows: "We are carrying out no other purpose than to give aid somehow to the studies of those who wish to occupy themselves in the Scriptures." (*CR* 21, 84)
18. John Wigand and Matthew Judex, *Syntagma seu Corpus Doctrinae Veri & Omnipotentis Dei* (Basel, 1560).
19. Cf. the similar approach of Melanchthon in his *Loci Communes, CR* 21, 84.
20. This is a direct allusion to what Melanchthon has said in his *Loci Praecipui Theologici, CR* 21, 605—606.
21. Martin Chemnitz, *Loci Theologici* (Frankfort and Wittenberg, 1653), II, 215.
22. Martin Chemnitz, *De Duabus Naturis* (Frankfort and Wittenberg, 1653), p. 98. (An English translation is available titled *The Two Natures in Christ,* trans. J. A. O. Preus [St. Louis: Concordia Publishing House, 1970].)
23. Chemnitz, *Loci Theologici,* II, 201.
24. Many of the later Lutherans spoke like Chemnitz with great conviction, although they did not always follow his example. E. g., see M. Foertsch, *Selectorum Theologicorum Breviarium, id est, Discussio Principalium Punctorum Theologicorum* (Jena, 1708). System without scholasticism is Foertsch's motto. He contends (p. 15) that the Augsburg Confession has order and arrangement; although it is not scholastic, it is systematic. In the scholastic theology many abuses arose, such as gathering together "many husks" that had no bearing on theology and leaving the real kernel. The Scholastics became involved in much vain squabbling over terminology and brought forth numerous demonstrations that were not from Scripture. However, Foertsch held that these abuses can be averted, and a scholastic, systematic method in theology can be used to advantage. In this he was much more optimistic than Chemnitz.
25. Chemnitz, *De Duabus Naturis,* p. 101.
26. Chemnitz, *Loci Theologici,* II, 211.
27. Ibid.
28. Chemnitz, *Loci Theologici,* II, 217.
29. Jacob Heerbrand's *Compendium Theologiae* (first published Wittenberg, 1573), which was written in the form of questions and answers, was composed according to the dedicatory letter for the same purpose as Chemnitz' dogmatics — to present a summa of Christian doctrine, in this case a summa designed to be used by students in the schools.

30. David Chytraeus, *Opera* (Leipzig, 1594), Vol. I.
31. *CR* 7, 1078.
32. Giles Hunnius, *Tractatus de SS. Majestate, Auctoritate, Fide ac Certitudine Scripturae.* See *Opera Latina* (Frankfort on the Main, 1608), I, 1 ff.
33. *Realencyclopädie für protestantische Theologie und Kirche,* begründet von J. J. Herzog, in dritter verbesserter und vermehrter Auflage unter Mitwirkung vieler Theologen und anderer Gelehrten herausgegeben von Albert Hauck, 3d ed. (Leipzig: J. C. Hinrichs'sche Buchhandlung, 1896—1913), 4, 115; hereafter cited as *RE.*
34. In his *In Genesin Enarratio* (Wittenberg, 1568) Chytraeus finds the following *loci* taught in the book of Genesis: (1) God and the Trinity, (2) Creation and Providence, (3) Sin and the Cause of Sin, (4) Law, (5) Gospel and Promise, (6) Good Works, (7) The Sacraments, (8) Repentance, (9) The Church, and (10) The Final Judgment and Resurrection. And the student will do well to bear in mind these 10 *membra doctrinae Christianae* as he interprets the book of Genesis.
35. David Chytraeus, *De Studio Theologiae* (Wittenberg, 1562).
36. Adolph Hoenecke, *Evangelisch-Lutherische Dogmatik,* 4 vols. (Milwaukee: Northwestern Publishing House, 1909), I, 6. Hoenecke devotes no fewer than 192 pages of his first volume to the development of prolegomena.
37. Most of the following material is taken from John Gerhard, *Loci Theologici,* ed. J. F. Cotta (Tübingen, 1762), II, 1 ff.
38. See George Sohn, *Opera* (Herborn, 1609), Vol. I.
39. See John Andrew Quenstedt, *Theologia Didactico-Polemica sive Systema Theologiae* (Leipzig, 1702), I, II, quaes. 1. (I, 13). Quenstedt elaborates at great length on the same five proofs. By the time of Hollaz the question has been omitted.
40. Thomas Aquinas, *Summa Theologica,* P. I, q. 1, art. 2.
41. Augustine, *De Ordine,* II, 5 (*Patrologia Cursus Completus . . .* Series Latina, ed. J.-P. Migne [Paris: Garnier, 1878—90], 32, 1002. Hereafter cited as *PL.*)
42. Gerhard, *Loci Theologici,* VII, 78.
43. This observation is probably taken from Aristotle, *Analytica Posteriora,* I, 9, 76a, 26—29 or I, 6, 74b, 6—8.
44. Augustine, *De Trinitate,* 15, 2 (*PL* 42, 1057).
45. Gerhard is aware that only his own rendering of the passage *(Nisi credideritis, non intellegitis)* supports Augustine's statement on this point.
46. He is probably drawing from Aristotle, who said that if one premise of an argument is problematic, the conclusion will be problematic. (*Analytica Priora,* I, 20—21, 39b, 8—10)
47. On this point Gerhard does not disagree with Thomas, who said that theology is higher than the other sciences because it derives its certainty from the light of divine knowledge. (*Summa Theologica,* P. I, q. 1, art. 5)
48. Amandus Polanus, *Systema Theologiae Christianae* (Geneva, 1612), pp. 4 ff.; John Henry Alsted, *Synopsis Theologiae* (Hanover, 1627), p. 9; John Henry Alsted, *Lexicon Theologicum* (Hanover, 1620), pp. 4—5; Francis Junius, *De Theologiae Verae; Ortu, Natura, Formis, Partibus, et Modo Illius* (Leyden, 1594), pp. 1 ff.
49. Isaac A. Dorner, *History of Protestant Theology,* trans. George Robson and Sophia Taylor, 2 vols. (Edinburgh: T. & T. Clark, 1871), II, 98.

50. Aristotle, *De Interpretatione*, I, 16a, 4—5.
51. *Summa Theologica*. P. 1, q. 1, art. 7. Roman theology held the same position in Gerhard's day. See Francis Sylvius, *Commentarius in Totam Primam Partem S. Tho. Aquinatis* (Douay, 1641), I, 3. There was a serious difficulty in the Roman position, and this was felt by Roman theologians (see Sylvius, *Commentarius*, I, 15). If the articles of faith are the principia of theology, how and by what right does theology prove the articles of faith? Sylvius argues that as in other sciences the principia of theology also can be shown by their accomplishments and results *(per effectus)*. "And yet the position of our author [Thomas] must be held, and we must state that theology does not argue to prove its own principles. The principles of every individual science are presupposed as recognized in themselves, and therefore not proved by the science. Theology too is a science; therefore in similar fashion it does not prove the articles of faith, which are its principia, but assumes them as already acknowledged. However, if someone should abandon some principle of theology or deny it, the theologian would be able to prove against him or to him that principle which he denies. For the superior science has the ability to dispute against those who deny its principia, and theology is the higher science."
52. Gerhard, *Loci Theologici*, I, 11.
53. Aristotle, *Analytica Posteriora*, I, 2, 72a, 19—36.
54. Quenstedt, *Systema*, I, III, sect. II, q. 1 (1715 ed. I, 49), argues for *sola Scriptura* from the properties of a principium, following both Thomas and Aristotle, but quoting for support also John 17:17; 2 Cor. 6:7; Eph. 1:13; James 1:18.
55. Gerhard, *Loci Theologici*, I, 78 ff. There was good reason for Gerhard to be most emphatic in maintaining such a position. Socinianism of his day presented theology as something that was only probable historically or rationally. Theology must be compatible with evidence and sound reason (see John Gerhard, *Catechesis Ecclesiarum Racoviae* [Cracow, 1609], praefatio). In all this Socinianism threatened Lutheran theology.
56. Gerhard, *Loci Theologici*, II, 372.
57. Ibid. See also I, 78.
58. My citations are from John Gerhard, *Methodus Studii Theologici* (Jena, 1654).
59. John Gerson, *De Consolatione Theologiae* (Cologne, 1469), Lib. 1, prosa 1.
60. Thomas Aquinas, *Summa Theologica*, P. 1, q. 25, art. 3. Thomas draws from Aristotle, *Metaphysica*, V, 17.
61. Gerhard, *Loci Theologici*, I, 208—210. Even Luther is cited as one who recognized analogies to the Trinity in nature: "D. Lutherus in coll. mensal. cap. 4, pag. 40. 'Herbae & flores habent formam, qua significatur Deus Pater: odorem seu saperem, quae est nota Filii ejusque sapientiae: vim, vires, seu effectus, qui sunt vestigia Spiritus S. ejusque bonitatis: ita licet in omnibus creaturis invenire Trinitatis vestigium impressum esse.'" ("Plants and flowers have a form that points to God the Father; they have an odor and taste that denote the Son and His wisdom; they have a power and strength and efficacy that are indications of the Holy Spirit and His goodness. Thus it is legitimate to find vestiges of the Trinity embossed in all creatures.")
62. See Martin Luther, *Opera Latina* (Frankfort and Erlangen: Heyder and Simmer, 1865—73), VI, 318—19. Hereafter cited as Er. Lat.
63. See *Die Disputation über Joh. 1.14* (1539). WA 39, II, 6.

64. WA 1, 352 ff. For Luther's views concerning philosophy, see Bengt Hägglund, *Theologie und Philosophie bei Luther und in der Occamistischen Tradition* (Lund: CWK Gleerups Förlag, 1955), pp. 15 ff.; also Brian Albert Gerrish, *Grace and Reason* (Oxford: Oxford University Press, 1962), pp. 28 ff.
65. For a concise account of the controversy, see Gottfried Thomasius, *De Controversia Hoffmanniana* (Erlangen, 1844); also Petersen, *Geschichte*, pp. 264 ff. See also the works by Daniel Hoffmann, *Disputatio pro Duplici Veritate Lutheri a Philosophis Impugnata et ad Pudendorum Locum Ablegata* (Magdeburg, 1600); and Cornelius Martini, *Compendium Theologiae et Epitome Theologiae Naturalis* (Wolfenbüttel, 1650), which most fully express the views of each. See also Ernst Schlee, *Der Streit des Daniel Hoffmann* (Marburg: Elwert, 1862).
66. *Theologins Historia* (Lund: CWK Gleerups Förlag, 1963), p. 277.
67. Hägglund, *Theologie und Philosophie*, pp. 9—10.
68. We see the same approach of Luther in *Die Disputation de Divinitate et Humanitate Christi* (1540), WA 39, II, 93 ff. Here Luther affirms that a signification in philosophy is not necessarily the same in theology. For instance, *homo* and *humanitas* signify the same thing in philosophy but not in theology.
69. WA 39, II, 22.
70. That Gerhard follows very closely in Luther's footsteps in his idea concerning theology, what it is and how it is to be carried on, is shown with abundant evidence by Johannes Wallmann, *Der Theologiebegriff bei Johann Gerhard und Georg Calixt* (Tübingen: J. C. B. Mohr, 1961). From Luther's entire discussion of this problem, and from Gerhard's as well, we must not conclude that for Luther, theology as cognitive discourse, or Scripture also for that matter, is contradictory or in conflict *(inimicissima)* with itself. This would result in an impossible condition that would render all theological activity (exegetical, confessional, etc.) an incoherent chaos. See above, p. 80 *passim*, on Luther's opinion of the place of dialectics in the theological enterprise. See also below, p. 349, for Gerhard's position that Scripture, and therefore also true theology, does not contradict itself. The marked similarity between Luther's and Gerhard's entire theological position is brought out in an interesting study probably by J. Christfried Sagittarius (in *Luthers Werke*, Altenburg, 1644. Haupt Register, pp. 1041—1204). The study, which is a simple comparison between the theologies of the two theologians, is given the lengthy title, "Des Haupt-Registers eilftes Capitul, in welches zusammen getragen die Theologischen Sachen, welche in denen neuen Tomis Herrn D. Martini Lutheri, nach denen Locis Theologicis des vornehmen und berühmten Theologi, Herrn D. Johannis Gerhardi eingerichtet." The attention given this fact in an edition of Luther's writings indicates the importance of Gerhard's theology in the 17th century and the firm conviction that he and Luther were one theologically. We might mention that on the relation between faith and reason (theology and philosophy) all the Lutherans after Gerhard were quite at one with Luther. This fact is brought out convincingly in Jörg Baur's study of Quenstedt's theology *(Die Vernunft zwischen Ontologie und Evangelium: Eine Untersuchung zur Theologie Johann Andreas Quenstedts* [Gütersloh: Verlagshaus Gerd Mohn, 1962], p. 186). Cf. also Bernhard Lohse, *Ratio und Fides: Eine Untersuchung über die Ratio in der Theologie Luthers* (Göttingen: Vandenhoeck & Ruprecht, 1958), pp. 55 ff. The same will be shown from our subsequent study of Hollaz on this point.

Notes to Chapter Two

71. Abraham Calov, *Systema Locorum Theologicorum* (Wittenberg, 1665), I, 69—75.
72. Dorner, *History of Protestant Theology,* II, 113.
73. Hägglund, *Theologins Historia,* p. 276.
74. David Hollaz, *Examen Theologicum Acroamaticum* (Rostock and Leipzig, 1718), Prol. I, Q. 27, pp. 31 ff.
75. The following discussion is based on Hollaz, *Examen Theologicum Acroamaticum,* Prol. III, Q. 4, I, 75 ff.
76. Hollaz, *Examen,* P. I, C. 1, q. 9. I, 220—31.
77. WA 39, II, 12.
78. See Quenstedt, *Systema,* C. IV, Sect. 2, q. 5. Ekthesis 5. (I, 78). Quenstedt is referring only to those consequences that are inherent in the Scripture *(consequentiae Scripturae innatae, sive quae virtualiter, materialiter & fundamentaliter in Scripturis continentur).*
79. Hollaz, *Examen,* P. III, S. 2, C. 7, q. 9. II, 656.
80. Hollaz, *Examen,* Prol. II, q. 14. I, 47. Hollaz is drawing from Calov, *Systema.* I, 773: "Like the parts in a human body, the dogmas of faith are closely and mutually connected with each other. For this reason we are wont to call faith one connected entity *{una copulativa}.* No article ought to be taken from the chain of faith; for if a single link of the faith is unfastened, the entire perfect chain will be broken. The harmony between the articles of faith ought to be strict and correct, lest one dogma of faith be made to oppose another, since all should be reliable and certain. Hence nothing should be allowed that could disturb this harmony." See also Quenstedt, *Systema.* P. I, C. 1, Sec. 1, Th. 2 Nota 5 (1702 ed. I, 243): "Hence we have that well-known axiom: Faith is *una copulativa:* this means that all fundamental articles of faith are so closely connected that he who denies one denies the others." See also Friedrich Balduin, *Commentarius in Omnes Epistolas Beati Apostoli Pauli,* editio altera priore longe emaculatior (Frankfort on the Main, 1710), p. 300.
81. WA 40, II, 46 ff. See Giles Hunnius, *Opera Latina,* II, 458, who also follows Luther on this matter; and Jerome Kromayer, *Theologia Positivo-Polemica* Frankfort and Leipzig, 1711), I, 1.
82. See *Catechesis Ecclesiarum Racoviae,* Praef. (Faustus) Socinus, *Opera Omnia* (Amsterdam, 1656), I, 275 ff.; Quenstedt, *Systema,* I, 40.
83. In his *Notatio de Studio Sacrae Theologiae, et de Ratione Discendi Doctrinam Coelestem* (Leipzig, 1579), pp. 66 ff., Selnecker, after discussing Scripture, offers a very complete outline of doctrinal theology.
84. At least one modern theologian, Barth, seems to feel that Gerhard has gone as far as ought to be gone; see Karl Barth, *Church Dogmatics* (Edinburgh, 1936), I, 2, 870.
85. The full title of the book was *Epitome Credendorum, oder Inhalt der ganzen Christlichen Lehr so viel einer davon in seinem Christenthum zu seiner Seelen Seeligkeit zu wissen und zu glauben bedürfftig* (Wittenberg, 1625).
86. Nicholas Hunnius, *Examen Errorum Photinianorum* (Wittenberg, 1618).
87. See Thomas Aquinas, *Summa Theologica,* P. II, q. 1, art. 6; q. 2, art. 5. Bonaventure, *Bonaventurae Opera Theologica Selecta* (Florence, 1934). Cf. Lib. 3 Sententiarum, Dist. 35, Art. 1, q. 1.
88. Francis Junius, *Eirenici Pars I et II* in *Opera Theologica* (Geneva, 1607), I, pp. 716 ff.

89. Leonard Hutter, *Irenicum vere Christianum* (Wittenberg, 1616); and *Quaestiones Duae de Fundamento Fidei Catholicae Apostolicae* (Wittenberg, 1616).
90. See Quenstedt, *Systema*, P. I, C. 5 (I, 241 ff.); Calov, *Systema*, I, 767—879; Hollaz, *Examen*, Prol. II, C. 2 (1718 ed., pp. 35—66); John W. Baier, *Compendium Theologiae Positivae*, ed. C. F. W. Walther (St. Louis, Concordia Publishing House, 1879), Prol. C. 1, par. 29—34. I, 49—68. For good treatments of the Lutheran classification of the articles of faith, see Hans Leube, *Kalvinismus und Luthertum im Zeitalter der Orthodoxie* (Leipzig: Dörffling und Franke, 1928), I, 138—63; Otto Ritschl, *Dogmengeschichte des Protestantismus*, IV, 231—362. Francis Pieper in his *Christian Dogmatics* (trans. Theodore Engelder, John T. Mueller, and Walter W. F. Albrecht, 3 vols. [St. Louis: Concordia Publishing House, 1951—53], I, 80—93) follows Hunnius essentially and defends such an arrangement of articles as in harmony with Scripture.
91. Nicholas Hunnius, *Diaskepsis Theologica* (Wittenberg, 1626), p. 35. My survey will follow Hunnius and the later dogmaticians, especially Hollaz. For a much more thorough survey and analysis, see Otto Ritschl, *Dogmengeschichte des Protestantismus*, IV, 306—363.
92. Hollaz, *Examen*, P. III, S. 2, C. 7, q. 7 (II, 650).
93. Quenstedt, *Systema*, P. IV, C. 8, S. 2, q. 4 (1702 ed., IV, 300). See also John Musaeus, *De Conversione Hominis Peccatoris ad Deum* (Jena, 1661), p. 179.
94. Hollaz, *Examen*, Prol. II, q. 19 (I, 51).
95. *Systema*, P. I, C. 5, S. 1, Th. 2 (I, 242).
96. *Systema*, P. IV, C. 16, S. 2 (IV, 528).
97. Nicholas Hunnius, *Diaskepsis Theologica*, p. 214.
98. *Systema*, P. I, C. 5, S. 1, Not. 6, Th. 1 (I, 241).
99. John Conrad Dannhauer, *Hodosophia Christiana sive Theologia Positiva* (Strasbourg, 1649), p. 662. See Gerhard, *Loci Theologici*, VII, 165; Quenstedt, loc. cit.
100. John Fecht, *Compendium Universam Theologiam Theticam et Polemicam Complexum* (Zerbst, 1740), p. 29.
101. *Systema*, I, 804. See also Hollaz, *Examen*, Prol. II, q. 22 (I, 57).
102. Calov is thinking of the syllogism of faith that was commonly expounded by Lutherans: God wishes to save all men and bring them to a knowledge of the truth; I am a man; therefore God wishes to save me. See Nicholas Hunnius, *Diaskepsis Theologica*, p. 40. Calov's entire discussion here is very similar to Hunnius', *Diaskepsis Theologica*, pp. 312—14.
103. The foregoing was based on Cornelius Martini, *Compendium Theologiae et Epitome Theologiae Naturalis* (Wolfenbüttel, 1650), pp. 27 ff.
104. *Systema*, P. I, C. 5, S. 1, Th. 1 Not. 9 (I, 242).
105. *Systema*, I, 773.
106. Hollaz, *Examen*, Prol. II, q. 17 (I, 48).
107. For further information see Ernst Ludwig Th. Henke, *Georg Calixtus und seine Zeit* (Halle: Buchhandlung des Waisenhauses, 1853); Hermann Schüssler, *Georg Calixtus: Theologie und Kirchenpolitik, eine Studie zur Oekumenizität des Lutherthums* (Wiesbaden: Franz Steiner Verlag, 1961); Heinrich Schmid, *Geschichte der synkretistischen Streitigkeiten in der Zeit Georg Calixts* (Erlangen: Carl Heyder, 1846); Otto Ritschl, *Dogmengeschichte des Protestantismus*, IV, 363—422.
108. See George Calixt, *Epitome Theologiae* (Braunschweig, 1634); *Apparatus*

Notes to Chapter Two 243

Theologici et Fragmenti Historiae Ecclesiae Occidentalis (Helmstedt, 1661); *Apparatus Theologicus* (Helmstedt, 1628).
109. *Epitome Theologiae,* Praefatio, VIII.
110. Ibid., V
111. Wallmann, *Der Theologiebegriff,* p. 113.
112. *Epitome Theologiae,* pp. 13—14.
113. Ibid., p. 31.
114. *CR* 7, 1078. See above, pp. 100 ff.
115. Calixt, *Epitome Theologiae,* pp. 3 ff. What Calixt is advocating as he introduces the analytic method is not new. Flacius (*Clavis Scripturae* [Leipzig, 1695], II, 54) had advocated the same method precisely, although he never actually used it in constructing a dogmatics. Flacius believed that the orderly manner *(series)* of presenting *(traditio)* the Scriptures ought to be threefold: through synthesis (composition), analysis (resolution), and definition (division). Scripture is already a synthesis. It devolves upon the Christian interpreter and the church (a) to analyze the Scriptures, that is, to apply them and put them to use, and (b) to divide the Scriptures so that they can be easily and quickly grasped. Calixt would see these two steps as just the business of dogmatics. Actually, the analytic method as envisioned by Calixt and those who followed was introduced primarily to present all Christian theology according to a single soteriological theme: How does man reach his highest goal, eternal bliss? This approach made all theology practical.
116. This outline is worked out in his *Epitome Theologiae* and in his *Disputationes de Praecipuis Christianae Religionis Capitibus* (Helmstedt, 1611).
117. Since the time of Troeltsch (*Vernunft und Offenbarung bei Johann Gerhard und Melanchthon* [Göttingen: Vandenhoeck & Ruprecht, 1891]) it has been an opinion quite widely held that Lutheranism in the 17th century was rather monolithic. Troeltsch saw no material difference between Gerhard's and Calixt's approach to theology, except that Calixt was possibly more irenic. This view was shared by Hans Emil Weber (*Der Einfluss der protestantischen Schulphilosophie auf die orthodox-lutherische Dogmatik* [Leipzig, 1908]), who felt that the schools of Calixt and Calov had much in common because they both used the analytic method and insisted that theology was a practical aptitude. Ritschl too (*Dogmengeschichte des Protestantismus,* IV, 372) seems to find no basic theological difference between Calixt and his contemporaries except in manner of presentation. In our day Hermann Schüssler *(Georg Calixtus: Theologie und Kirchenpolitik* [Wiesbaden: Franz Steiner Verlag, 1961]) follows this judgment and lumps together the theology of 17th-century Lutheranism, probably because of the similarity of method and dependence on philosophy. In a recent book *(Der Theologiebegriff bei Johann Gerhard und Georg Calixt)* Johannes Wallmann, agreeing more with the conclusions of Wundt (*Die deutsche Schulmetaphysik des 17. Jahrhunderts* [Tübingen: J. C. B. Mohr, 1939]), has taken issue with this common theory, which was based on such slender evidence. On the basis of massive evidence he has shown that a great theological cleavage existed between Gerhard (and later orthodoxy) and Calixt. He correctly traces two lines of approach to theology within Lutheranism. The first line goes from Luther (with his emphasis on the *theologia crucis*) through Gerhard (with his concept of theology as a *habitus* θεόσδοτος) to Spener with his demand for a *theologia regenitorum*). The second line goes from Melanchthon (and his concept of *doctrina ecclesiae*) through Calixt (with

his traditionalism, emphasis on reason, and tendency to separate faith and theology, a tendency brought to fruition at the time of rationalism) and culminating in Semler and rationalism. The first part of Wallmann's thesis was borne out in our study of Gerhard's approach to theology; it will be borne out again by our study of Calov.

118. Jesper Rasmus Brochmand, *Universae Theologiae Systema* (Ulm, 1658), pp. 2 ff.
119. See Jörg Baur, *Die Vernunft zwischen Ontologie und Evangelium*, p. 18.
120. Abraham Calov, *Apodixis Articulorum Fidei* (Lüneburg, 1684); *Dissertationes Theologiae Rostochienses* (Rostock, 1637); *Scripta Philosophica* (Lübeck, 1651); *Systema Locorum Theologicorum*, Vol. 1; *Theologia Positiva* (Wittenberg, 1652).
121. For a complete and excellent survey of the immense amount of discussion on the matter of method in the 15th and 16th centuries, see Walter J. Ong, *Ramus, Method, and the Decay of Dialogue* (Cambridge: Harvard University Press, 1958), pp. 225 ff.
122. *Analytica Posteriora*. I, 1 ff.
123. Melanchthon, *Erotemata Dialectica* (*CR* 13, 573 ff.). Melanchthon's concept of method and his stress on its importance were taken over by all his disciples and, in fact, all Lutherans after his time. Some of his followers, imitating him very closely, left his mark on theological studies and university training for generations to come. We might mention the Danish Melanchthonian, Crypto-Calvinist, and humanist, Niels Hemmingsen. Hemmingsen defines method as follows: "Methodus, est via docendi certa cum ratione, hoc est Methodus est ratio docendi, cuius admonitu, et ductu, singula in rerum explicatione aptis & accommodatis loci collocantur" (See *Opuscula Theologica, Quae Conquiri Potuerunt Omnia in Unum Volumen Collecta* [Geneva, 1586], pp. 9 ff.). He then divides method into two parts: (1) universal methodology, which is synthesis (proceeding from the parts of a subject to the whole), analysis (viewing the whole or goal of a subject and then progressing toward and finding its causes or its parts), and *diairesis* (which divides a subject into classifications of species); and (2) particular methodology, or the actual method at work, sometimes called dialectics in the broad sense. "Particular method," Hemmingsen says, "is the manner of showing the way to explain questions dealing with any subject at all." Hemmingsen follows not only Melanchthon but Aristotle and the medieval scholastics as well. He dominated the University of Copenhagen for almost two generations and left a definite scholastic stamp on Scandinavian theology, as Melanchthon did on German theology and method. As far as method was concerned, Lutheranism never broke with the pre-Reformation tradition or with Aristotle, although changes and innovations and improvements were constantly made. All the later dogmaticians of Scandinavia follow Hemmingsen in this matter without question, just as the German Lutherans did Melanchthon.
124. George Calixt, *Apparatus Theologici et Fragmenti Historiae Ecclesiae Occidentalis* (Helmstedt, 1661), pp. 12 ff.
125. Ibid., pp. 24 ff.
126. See above, p. 122.
127. *De Ira Dei*. I, 11 (*PL* 7, 111).
128. William Ames, *Medulla Theologiae* (Amsterdam, 1623). See *Opera* (Amsterdam, 1658), I, I, 13. pp. 3 ff.
129. Quenstedt, *Systema*, P. I, C. 5, S. 1, Th. 1. Not. 5 (I, 241).

Notes to Chapter Two 245

130. Calov quotes Augustine (*De Trinitate.* 14, 1, 3 [*PL* 42, 1037]): "It is one thing to know merely what a man ought to believe to gain that blessed life which is eternal; it is quite another thing to know how to assist pious people with this doctrine and to defend it against impious people."
131. Calov's words are: "Illa de DEO Triuno, haec de Christo biuno: Illa de natura Dei, haec de reparatione generis humani per Christum facta." (*Apodixis*, p. 18)
132. Calov, *Systema.* I, 268: "Principium SS. Theologiae est divina revelatio." Calov is identifying revelation in this instance with Scripture. He is unique in calling revelation the source of theology. The other Lutherans call Scripture the source of theology; but there is no real difference here, because they too identify revelation with Scripture when speaking of the source and norm of doctrine. See Gerhard, *Loci Theologici.* II, 18: "Scripture is nothing else than divine revelation put in sacred writings." See John W. Baier, *Compendium Theologiae Positivae*, C. F. W. Walther (St. Louis, 1879), I, 30.
133. Balthasar Meisner, *Philosophia Sobria* (Rinteln, 1626), pars secunda, p. 1.
134. Junius' position is found in his *De Theologiae Verae; Ortu, Natura, Formis, Partibus, et Modo Illius*, Cap. 1, p. 9.
135. Junius, *De Theologiae Verae*, Cap. 6, p. 46.
136. See Calov, *Systema*, VII, 242. See Quenstedt, *Systema*, P. III, C. 3, Memb. 1, S. 2, Q. 7 (III, 147 ff.).
137. *Systema*, VII, 359. See Quenstedt's comment on Col. 2:9 (*Systema.* P. II, C. 3, S. 1, Thesis 76, Nota 2 [1715 ed. II, 145]): "If the whole fullness of the Godhead dwells in Christ according to the flesh, then that same flesh must possess actually all the communicated divine attributes; for these attributes are not distinct from the Godhead, much less from the fullness of the Godhead. That this dwelling place of the fullness of the Godhead is not the divine but the human nature is obvious from the fact that the Godhead cannot with meaning be said to inhabit the Godhead and something cannot be its own home and its own host — and significantly the apostle adds the expression σωματικῶς, i. e., ἐν σαρκί." See ibid., II, 246 ff.
138. The Lutherans are most careful in explaining the meaning of the communication of divine attributes to the human nature of Christ. See Quenstedt, *Systema*, P. II, C. 3, S. 1, Thesis 78 (1715 ed. II, 147): "This communication of the divine majesty was not in word only but is actual and real. It is not according to any due of the human nature, it is not temporary, it is not according to any external condition, it is not a mere manifestation, it is not according to any outside assistance, it is not to be understood in a synecdochical sense, it is not according to any active participation of the human nature (μεθεκτικῶς), it is not in the sense of an operation *ad intra*, it is not to be taken in the sense of a gracious indwelling that can be lost, it is not by any confusion or mixing, not according to any conversion or change, it is not by making the human equal to the divine, it does not obtain in the sense of one thing being poured into another (ἐκχυτικῶς) or of one thing passing into another (μετεκβατικῶς), it is neither by effusion nor transfusion, nor finally is it by one thing being made into another or being multiplied." (See P. III, C. 3, Memb. 1, S. 1, Th. 78.) Chemnitz (*De Duabus Naturis*, Cap. 23) devotes a long chapter to clearing away all false conceptions regarding the communication of the divine majesty to the human nature of Christ.
139. Anthony Walaeus, *Loci Communes S. Theologiae* (Leyden, 1640), p. 5.

140. John Berg, *Analysis Controversiae de Persona Christi* (Frankfort, 1619), Th. 230.
141. *Sententiarum Libri Quatuor*, 3, 14 (PL 192, 783—84).
142. *Summa Theologica.* P. III, q. 9, a. 2.
143. Ibid., P. III, q. 10, a. 1.
144. Chemnitz, *De Duabus Naturis,* Cap. 24. p. 131.
145. See David Hollaz, *Examen Theologicum Acroamaticum,* P. III, S. 1, C. 3, p. 712: "Christ the man, if we view Him according to the attributes of His human nature, truly did not know certain things. In the state of exinanition He did not always and everywhere exercise His majesty of omniscience but did so only when and where He pleased."
146. *Systema,* P. I, C. 1, S. 1, Th. 3 & 4 (1702 ed. I, 4).
147. Amandus Polanus, *Syntagma Theologiae Christianae* (Geneva, 1612), I, 6, Cap. 27 (II, 269); William Bucan, *Institutiones Theologicae* (Geneva, 1609), Art. 10.
148. WA 46, 672 ff.
149. CR 21, 711.
150. CR 21, 713.
151. *Systema,* P. I, C. 6, S. 2, Q. 1 (1715 ed. I, 374).
152. Matthias Flacius, *Clavis Scripturae Sacrae* (Jena, 1674), cols. 574 ff.
153. Flacius' entire treatment of the subject draws heavily from Luther and quotes abundantly from him. See WA 42, 93 ff.
154. See Walaeus, *Loci Communes S. Theologiae,* p. 10: "No one can be saved by the law of nature alone, but if one makes right use of the gifts of nature, God will reveal the Gospel grace to him." This kind of Pelagianism was what the old Lutherans were so strongly set against when they insisted that a saving knowledge of God was only revealed through the Gospel of Christ. For the Socinian denial of natural knowledge of God, see Faustus Socinus, *Praelectiones Theologicae,* C. II (found in Faustus Socinus, *Opera Omnia* [Amsterdam, 1656], I, 537 f.).
155. *Systema,* II, 51.
156. See *Systema,* IX, 3; I, 26; Abraham Calov, *Commentarius in Genesin* (Wittenberg, 1671), pp. 148, 149, 161. Calov's characteristic definition of revelation goes as follows: "Revelation is an outgoing act of God. By this action He discloses Himself to us through His Word in order to bring us to a saving knowledge" (*Systema,* I, 270). Hollaz speaks in much the same way (*Examen,* Prol. III, q. 2 obs. 3. 1718 ed. I, 68). Of the dogmaticians after Calov, John Adam Osiander follows him in devoting a section to a thorough discussion of revelation (*Systema Theologicum* [Tübingen, 1679]). Quenstedt has no treatment of revelation at all.
157. Abraham Calov, *Isagoges Theologicae. Liber II. Paedia Theologica, de Methodo Studii Theologici* (Wittenberg, 1652), p. 110. Calov reflects Melanchthon here. See CR 21, 603 ff.
158. This was also the conviction of Thomas Aquinas. See *Summa Theologica,* P. I, Q. 1, a. 3.
159. Calov's outline of the causes of theology is similar to that of his contemporaries. See Quenstedt, *Systema,* Par. I, C. 1, S. 1. Th. 31—32. (1702 ed. I, 11—12); John Friedrich Koenig, *Nucleus Theologiae Positivae* (Leipzig, 1706), pp. 9—13.

160. Calov, *Isagoges,* 124.
161. Ibid., 125: "Through the Word of God alone we become theologians, but ... it is necessary to understand the Word of God and use it profitably for our edification." See Luther, WA 50, 658, whom Calov cites here.
162. All the other theologians except Hollaz speak of Scripture as the source of theology. Calov prefers to speak of revelation as the source of theology, perhaps because he wants to stress the revealedness of theology or because theology, as he considers it, has a broader source than Scripture; e. g., there was theology before there was Scripture.
163. John Baillie represents all of 17th-century theology as teaching such a distorted and one-sided theory of revelation. See *The Idea of Revelation in Recent Thought* (New York: Columbia University Press, 1956), pp. 4—18.
164. Calov's position bears only a superficial similarity to that of Aquinas. See Paul Synave and Pierre Benoit, *Prophecy and Inspiration,* trans. Avery R. Dulles and Thomas J. Sheridan (New York: Desclee Company, 1961), pp. 109 ff., for Thomas' position.
165. This is explicitly said by Calov in his *Systema,* I, 271: "The principal object of revelation is God. In a certain sense everything else can be reduced to this, especially when we view God not only in reference to His essence but also in reference to His will. For revealed things are whatever God wishes us to know about His essence and will. Hence all revealed things prompt us to acknowledge God's will, both what He wills us to believe and do and what He has willed and wills to do about us. The whole Scripture can be divided into Law and Gospel, and Scripture has brought to completion the legal and the evangelical will of God."
166. See G. E. Lessing, *Sämmtliche Schriften* (Stuttgart, 1827), V, 80. See also *Lessing's Theological Writings,* trans. Henry Chadwick (Stanford: Stanford University Press, 1957), p. 53.
167. For Augustine's statement quoted by Calov, see *PL* 33, 277.
168. The position of Socinus is found in *De Auctoritate S. Scripturae,* Cap. I (*Opera Omnia,* I, 266 f.). See Calov, *Isagoges,* p. 162, for the citation above.
169. See *Isagoges,* 198. Aristotle, *De Anima,* 412a8, says that form or essence is that by which a thing may be called a "this." This comes closest to what Calov is saying. See also *Metaphysica,* 1029a5 ff., and 1032b1 ff.: εἶδος δὲ λέγω τὸ τί ἦν εἶναι ἑκάστου καὶ τὴν πρώτην οὐσίαν.
170. *Systema,* VIII. Epistola Dedicatoria, a2v—a3r.
171. *Summa Theologica,* P. I, Q. 1, a. 4. This was the predominant position outside Lutheranism. See Cajetan (Thomas de Vio), *Commentarius super Summam Theologicam* (Lyre, 1892), P. I, Art. 2. p. 5. Also Gregory of Valencia, *Commentariorum Theologicorum Tomi Quatuor* (Ingolstadt, 1591), I, Disp. 1, Q. 1. Among the Reformed see John Berg, *Decas Disputationum Theologicorum* (Frankfort, 1621), Dis. 1, Th. 16. Also later, Francis Turrettin, *Institutio Theologiae Elencticae* (Geneva, 1688), I, 25. An exception among the Reformed was John Henry Heidegger, *Corpus Theologiae Christianae* (Zürich, 1700), I, 21. Heidegger's position is very Lutheran sounding. He says: "We have said that theology is directed only toward the glory of God and the salvation of the sinner. And so it follows, as seen from its final and intermediate aim, that theology is totally practical. Therefore no truth is taught in theology unless it leads either straight to activity *{praxin}* — glorifying, loving, and seeking after God and believing in Him — or at least has the implanted power to produce piety."

172. Bonaventure, *Bonaventurae Opera Theologica Selecta,* Lib. I Sententiarum, Dist. 1, A. 2. 2.1. pp. 27 ff.
173. In 1868 C. F. W. Walther wrote a long series of articles on the subject "Was ist Theologie?" (*Lehre und Wehre,* XIV [1868], pp. 4 ff.), in which he follows Calov very closely in setting forth the practical nature of theology and even translated extensively from him. He tries to bring the matter up to date but leans heavily on the major orthodox Lutherans.
174. *Loci Theologici,* I, 17.
175. Calov's treatment here (see also *Systema,* I, 26) conforms to the old scholastic classification of *genus generalissimum* (supreme genus), *genus subalternum* (intermediate genus), and *genus proximum* (immediate genus), derived from Aristotle, *Topica,* I, 5, 102a31-102b3. Also *Topica,* IV. Also *Metaphysica,* Δ, 28 (entire).
176. See Hans Meyer, *The Philosophy of St. Thomas Aquinas* (St. Louis: B. Herder, 1944), p. 112. Also Ludwig Schütz, *Thomas-Lexikon* (New York: F. Unger Publishing Company, 1947), pp. 350—55.
177. *Ethica Nicomachea,* 1098b33. Also *Problemata,* 955b1.
178. See Peter Ramus, *Commentarius de Religione Christiana* (Frankfort, 1577), p. 6; David Pareus, *Collegiorum Theologicorum Decuria* (Heidelberg, 1621), p. 5. Even some of the earlier Lutherans seemed satisfied to speak of the nature of theology loosely as doctrine, e. g., Chytraeus in his *Catechesis* (Wittenberg, 1555) and John Schroeder in his *Opusculum Theologicum de Principio Theologiae, et Naturali Notitia Dei* (Schweinfurt, 1605).
179. *Topica,* 120b15 ff. Often, one might say usually, Aristotle's definitions were useful, inasmuch as they were generally accepted and used in those days. One almost had to use them. But the later Lutherans, even Calov — who we shall see tended to be critical of Aristotle as often as not — lean too heavily on him.
180. Pieper, *Christian Dogmatics,* I, 46—75.
181. *Topica,* 111a27—30, 123a29 and particularly 127b6: "Genus is always predicated of its species synonymously."
182. See Quenstedt, *Systema,* C. I, S. 1, Th. 30 (I, 11); Gottfried Hoffmann, *Synopsis Theologiae Purioris Dogmaticae* (Tübingen, 1730), pp. 1 ff.; John Adam Osiander, *Theologicum Systema seu Theologia Positiva Acroamatica* (Tübingen, 1679), pp. 4 ff.
183. I can see no reason for Werner Elert (*The Structure of Lutheranism,* trans. Walter Hansen [St. Louis: Concordia Publishing House, 1962], p. 68) finding fault with the later Lutherans making the goal of theology the enjoyment of God. Because Luther does not use this expression does not make it suspect. The old dogmaticians merely took over an old well-established phrase and gave it their own meaning, as Luther did on many occasions. To them the enjoyment of God simply meant eternal fellowship with Him.
184. Until the time of Calixt the Lutheran theologians used the method of *loci theologici,* which was often called synthetic, not however because they denied or overlooked the practical nature of theology or because they had not envisaged an analytic method in presenting Christian doctrine. See above, p. 156.
185. John Berg, *Decas Disputationum Theologicorum;* John Henry Alsted, *Theologia Scholastica Didactica Exhibens Locos Communes Theologicos* (Hanover, 1618). Among the Romanists who made theology a mixed *habitus,* see John Capreolus, *In Libros Sententiarum Amplissimae Quaestiones* (Venice, 1589),

prol. Q. 2. p. 13. See Francis Sylvius, *Commentarius in Totam Primam Partem S. Tho. Aquinatis,* I, 12. The Roman doctrine, taken from Aquinas, was that theology was both speculative and practical, but more speculative.
186. See note 182 above. Also Hollaz, *Examen,* Prol. I, q. 12 (1718 ed., p. 9).
187. Quenstedt, *Systema,* P. I, C. 1, S. 2, q. 3. Ekthesis 13 (I, 16—17).
188. *Systema.* P. I, C. 1, S. 2, q. 3. Fontes Solutionum 14 (I, 19).
189. *Philosophia Sobria,* I, 246 ff. See also Brochmand, *Universae Theologiae Systema,* I, 2.
190. The citation is from Meisner (*Philosophia Sobria,* p. 247), who must have anticipated the development in Calov's time.
191. See John Duns Scotus, *Opera Omnia* (Vatican City: Typis Polyglotis Vaticanis, 1950—), I, 165. Scotus (Ordinatio Prol. p. 5, q. 2) taught that theology was a practical science because of its goal. Alexander of Hales (Tract. Intro. q. 1 C. 1; see Alexander of Hales, *Summa Theologica* [Florence, 1924], I, 2) also called theology a science but preferred to call it "properly and chiefly a wisdom." See Aquinas, *Summa Theologica.* P. I, q. 1, art. 7. This was still commonly taught in Calov's day; see Sylvius, *Commentarius,* I, 14.
192. There was much confusion among the Lutherans and Reformed on this point, and little clarity even on what kind of wisdom theology was. Friedemann Bechmann (*Theologia Polemica* [Jena, 1719]) and John Adam Scherzer (*Systema Theologiae* [Tübingen, 1679]), who write after Calov, call theology *scientia practica* and *sapientia* (according to its proximate genus), respectively. Quenstedt and John Adam Osiander are in agreement with Calov. Hollaz, who writes in 1707, defines theology in the following manner (*Examen,* Prol. I, Q. 12. I. 7): "Theology is wisdom, for it is the highest knowledge of God and of divine things, which are eminently worth knowing but are also very difficult to know. It is a high wisdom, for it is far above all human wisdom. It is a practical wisdom, for all its conclusions lead to practical activity, if not formally, then certainly by implication and ultimately." Thus, we see Hollaz embracing a definition quite similar to that of Scotus. It is difficult to see how this would be in essential variance with the position of Calov, although Calov will not define theology as wisdom. By the time of Gottfried Hoffmann *(Synopsis Theologiae)* the issue seemed to be no longer in question. It was not even broached.

Among the Reformed there was also no unanimity on this matter. Of the earlier theologians Zachariah Ursinus never considers theology as a *habitus* at all. All his prolegomena, which are uniquely original and evangelical, are structured around the concept of doctrine that he divides clearly into Law and Gospel (*Explicationum Catecheticarum D. Zachariae Ursini Silesii Absolutum Opus . . .* [Geneva, 1604], pp. 1—13). Following Keckermann and Alsted, Francis Turrettin (*Institutio Theologiae Elencticae,* I, 22 f.), like most of the Lutherans, speaks of theology as doctrine (speaking systematically and objectively) and as an intellectual *habitus* (speaking subjectively). But this *habitus* was not equated with intelligence or knowledge or wisdom or prudence or art. Theology was not a *habitus sciendi* but a *habitus credendi.* However, to Turrettin such a *habitus* was partly theoretical and partly practical. This last point, which was probably prompted primarily by a fear of Socinianism and Arminianism, would not be in opposition to the opinion of the earlier Lutherans like Meisner. Socinianism agreed with Calov that all theology was practical but disagreed that everything in Scripture was theological; hence Turrettin's apparent disagreement with Calov. By the time of Heidegger there was also little interest in this matter in the Reformed camp.

193. See Aristotle, *Metaphysica,* A, 2, 982a5—19.
194. *Metaphysica,* A, 2, 982a13.
195. See Aristotle, *Ethica Nicomachea,* IV, 3, 1139b18—36. Aristotle says that when a man believes in a certain way (πῶς) and the first principles (ἀρχαί) are known to him, then he has scientific knowledge (ἐπίσταται). To him scientific knowledge is an ἕξις ἀποδικτική and is necessary (ἐξ ἀνάγκης). Calov believes that theological demonstration is of a completely different order than what Aristotle has in mind. Calov is not so critical of Gabriel Vasquez, Gregory of Valencia et al., when, commenting on Aquinas (*Summa Theologica,* P. I, 2. 1, a. 2), they call theology a science in a rather loose sense as a *scientia ob sui perfectionem* (see 1 Cor. 12:8; 13:8).
196. Aristotle, *Analytica Posteriora,* I, 7, 75a39—43. Also I, 10, 76a12—16.
197. Ibid., I, 2 (entire).
198. Aristotle, *Metaphysica,* A. I, 993b19 ff. Aristotle says: "For the end of theoretical knowledge is truth, while that of practical knowledge is action. . . ." Theoretical knowledge, then, would deal with necessary truth, "eternal things." Actually Aristotle called theology a theoretical science, which was the highest of all sciences (see *Metaphysica,* K. 7, 1064b1 ff. and E. I, 1026a19).
199. *Isagoges,* 250. See ibid., 226; *Systema,* I, 61 ff.
200. *Isagoges,* 244. Other Lutheran theologians speak in very much the same way. See Meisner, *Philosophia Sobria,* P. III, S. 5, C. 2. p. 162; Calixt, *Epitome Theologiae,* p. 4.
201. *De Duabus Naturis,* p. 52.
202. Ibid., p. 53
203. Ibid., p. 56.
204. *Apodixis Articulorum Fidei,* pp. 1—4.
205. See *Isagoges,* p. 249, where Calov says that theology is practical not as a practice of good works (which cannot save us) but as a practice of faith, by which alone we strive for eternal life. Calixt (*Epitome Theologiae Moralis* [Helmstedt, 1634], p. 3) erred in making theology the practice of both faith and good works. He said that theology was the *"studium bonorum operum a quo pendeat finis ultimus salus aeterna."*
206. Bartholomew Keckermann, *Systema Theologicum* (Geneva, 1602), Lib. I, p. 3. Keckermann followed Aristotle in what the latter said about "practical wisdom" (φρόνησις), which is man's ability to deliberate well about what is good and expedient (συμφέροντα) for himself and in respect to the good life in general. (See *Ethica Nicomachea,* VI, 5, 1140a 24 ff.)
207. See Quenstedt, *Systema.* P. I, C. 1, S. 2, q. 3. Ekthesis 4 (I, 16). Calov is not teaching a theology of the unregenerate here, nor do any of the theologians of his day. See Quenstedt, ibid., Ekthesis 6—15 (I, 16—17); Bechmann, *Theologia Polemica,* p. 49; Meisner, *Philosophia Sobria,* 244; John Musaeus, *Introductio in Theologiam* (Jena, 1679), p. 126. This disastrous teaching came later as the orthodox Lutherans battled with Pietism.
208. *Systema,* I, 57: "Nec Deus hic proponitur in quantum intelligi potest a finito intellectu, sed qua ejus notitia fecit ad salutem." I am following Calov's *Systema* in the present discussion.
209. *Loci Theologici,* III, 1.
210. Robert Bellarmine, Lib. 4 *de Monachis,* C. 2 (see *Disputationes de Controversiis Christianae Fidei* [Milan, 1721] II, 310—311).

211. *Systema.* P. I, C. 2, S. 1, Th. 4, Nota 7 (I, 22). Quenstedt borrows heavily in his treatment of religion from the longer discussions of Calov, *Systema,* I, 91—267. See also Calov, *Apodixis,* 280—92.
212. See Calov, *Apodixis,* 5—11; and Hollaz, *Examen,* Prol. II, q. 7 (I, 38), whose remarks are particularly well taken.
213. See Socinus, *Tractatus de Ecclesia (Opera Omnia,* I, 352—53); see also Quenstedt, *Systema,* P. I, C. 2, S. 2, q. 1. Antithesis (I, 23), where he lists a large number of theologians who were opposed to the Lutheran view.
214. Quenstedt, *Systema,* P. 1, C. 2, S. 2, q. 1, Ekthesis (I, 23); Calov, *Systema,* I, 122; Dannhauer, *Hodosophia Christiana sive Theologia Positiva,* p. 484.
215. *Loci Theologici,* V, 122; see also Quenstedt, *Systema,* P. IV, C. 2, S. 2, q. 1. Thesis (IV, 61). Gerhard reflects the position of Luther and the Lutheran Symbols, which teach that the Gospel was preached throughout the Old Testament and patriarchs were saved through faith in the coming Savior who would make propitiation for their sins. See Apology of the Augsburg Confession, IV, 57—59; XII, 54—55, 72—73; Formula of Concord, SD, VI, 23.
216. Calov, *Apodixis,* p. 11.
217. Ibid., pp. 12 ff.
218. Calov, *Systema,* I, 215—29. Calov is reproducing in substance the arguments of Mentzer's *Exegesis Augustanae Confessionis (Opera Latina,* I, 1 ff.) and of Nicholas Hunnius in his *Diaskepsis,* pp. 440 ff.
219. For the foregoing, see Calov, *Isagoges,* pp. 317—45.
220. *Isagoges Theologicae. Liber II. Paedia Theologica, de Methodo Studii Theologici* (Wittenberg, 1652 [also 1665]).
221. *Paedia Theologica,* p. 44. Calov is drawing from Luther (WA 18, 609) where Luther speaks of a twofold clarity and obscurity in Scripture, the one external and the other internal. "If you speak of that internal clarity," Luther says, "no man will see one iota in the Scriptures unless he has the Spirit of God. The hearts of all men are so darkened that even if they were to speak and know how to cite all the things of Scripture, still they would know and really understand none of these things. They do not believe in God or that they are creatures of God, or anything else, according to the psalm [13], The fool has said in his heart, God is nothing. No, the Spirit is needed if we are to understand the whole Scripture or any part of it."
222. *Paedia Theologica,* p. 236. This is precisely the position of Elert *(The Structure of Lutheranism,* p. 201).
223. *Notatio de Studio Sacrae Theologiae, et de Ratione Discendi Doctrinam Coelestem,* pp. 63 ff.
224. *Systema Theologicum,* pp. 4 ff.
225. Musaeus, *Introductio in Theologiam;* Baier-Walther, I, 1 ff.
226. Hollaz, *Examen,* Prol. I, q. 21 (I, 16 ff.).
227. John George Neumann, *Theologia Aphoristica* (Wittenberg, 1718), pp. 1 ff. Other theologians of the day who were of somewhat the same mind were G. Wernsdorf, *Brevis et Nervosa de Indifferentismo Religionum Commentario* (Wittenberg, 1716); M. Foertsch, *Selectorum Theologicorum Breviarium, id est, Discussio Principalium Punctorum Theologicorum* (Jena, 1708); John Fecht, *Compendium Universam Theologiam Theticam et Polemicam Complexum* (Zerbst, 1740); John Fecht, *Dissertatio Theologica de Sensu Sacrarum Literarum Carnali* (Rostock, 1709); John Fecht, *Philocalia Sacra* (Rostock, 1708); J. P. Hebenstreit, *Systema Theologicum* (Frankfort and

Leipzig, 1718). Not all the theologians of the early 18th century were either pietists or antipietists. Francis Buddeus, for instance (*Institutiones Theologiae Dogmaticae* [Leipzig, 1724]), tried to steer a middle course in the spirit of Hollaz.

228. Here Neumann also follows Hollaz, who made theology primarily an intellectual skill (*Examen*, Prol. I, q. 20 [I, 15 ff.]). Hollaz would describe the regenerate theologian as one who has *notitia* and also faith.

229. Gottfried Hoffmann, *Synopsis Theologiae*, p. 2.

230. For the position of Pietism on this matter, see Martin Schian, *Orthodoxie und Pietismus im Kampf um die Predigt* (Giessen: Verlag von Alfred Töpelmann, 1912), pp. 86—97.

231. See Bechmann, *Theologia Polemica*, p. 49; Hollaz, *Examen*, Prol. I, q. 29 (I, 33—34).

232. The full title of this work was *Praenotiones Theologicae contra Naturalistarum et Fanaticorum Omne Genus Atheos, Deistas, Indifferentistas, Antiscripturarios, etc.* It was first published in Wittenberg in 1708 and appeared in at least five editions. It was well received and was very important in its day.

233. For an account of the lengths to which such apologetics went in the British Isles at this time, see John Stewart Lawton, *Miracles and Revelation* (New York: Association Press, 1960).

The Doctrine of Scripture

SCRIPTURE, THE SOURCE OF THEOLOGY *(Sola Scriptura)*
SCRIPTURE AS THE WORD OF GOD
THE INSPIRATION OF SCRIPTURE
THE AUTHORITY OF SCRIPTURE
THE SUFFICIENCY OF SCRIPTURE
THE CLARITY OF SCRIPTURE
THE INTERPRETATION OF SCRIPTURE
THE TRUTHFULNESS OF SCRIPTURE
THE EFFICACY OF SCRIPTURE

Notes to Chapter Three: pages 378—403.

CHAPTER THREE

The development of dogmatic prolegomena and the development of an article on Sacred Scripture go hand in hand. As Lutheran theology seeks to spell out its presuppositions and basic approach to the study of theology, it is compelled to deal with such themes as the authority, power, divine origin, and perfection of Scripture. Indeed a treatment of Scripture becomes the chief interest of theological prolegomena. Some prolegomena are really little more than an attempt to establish the place of Scripture in the life of the church and the theologian's approach to Scripture. This was true in the case of Hyperius and Chytraeus and is even more evident in the instance of Nikolaus Selnecker.[1] After praising theology as the fountain of all other knowledge, as the *prima philosophia,* which ought to permeate our whole life and all our activity, Selnecker structures his entire *Notatio de Studio Sacrae Theologiae* around Scripture as the source of theology, and the theologian's proper attitude toward Scripture and use of it. This book, which was designed to help the theologian in his study of theology, indicates the trend that was taking place, for it includes two sections that with increasing frequency find their way into Lutheran dogmatics: first, Scripture as the source of theology, and second, the divine origin of Scripture and its properties — authority, truthfulness, clarity, and power. Discussions on the authenticity of Scripture, the versions, and the interpretation of Scripture are also included.

We have chosen deliberately to review the article *de Scriptura* dogmatically, taking the orthodox Lutherans as belonging to one single theological stream or school. The reason for this is obvious; if the doctrine

of Selnecker or Chemnitz is not as articulate as that of Calov or Quenstedt, it is nevertheless the same doctrine (in a less developed form) on every major point, as will become evident in the course of the discussions. The Lutheran doctrine of Scripture is definitely not something that emerged, either suddenly or gradually, in the 17th century. It would be a mistake, therefore, to attempt to trace *historically* a development of the *doctrine* of Scripture, as a number of historians have tried to do, each arriving at a different conclusion. It is, however, possible to trace a definite development in *terminology* that was brought on by the swiftly changing theological climate of those days, and this we shall do.

Scripture, the Source of Theology ("sola scriptura")

The doctrine of Scripture is generally the first article to be considered in Lutheran dogmatics. The reason for this arrangement is a purely practical one; the orthodox Lutherans felt that they ought to establish the source of theology before they engaged in theology. In most of the earlier dogmatics the treatment of the article on Scripture centered in clarifying and bolstering the Lutheran position that Scripture alone was the source and norm of all Christian theology. As time went on, rather long discussions of the divine origin and the attributes of Scripture became common. This development took place not because of any new and advanced interest in the doctrine of inspiration per se but because it became increasingly apparent to Lutheran theologians that the authority of Scripture as the source of theology cannot be maintained in the church unless the divine origin of Sacred Scripture is confessed and upheld. Actually in their entire treatment of Scripture the orthodox Lutherans, like Luther himself, really have only two basic concerns. First, they desire to maintain the principle of *sola Scriptura:* only Sacred Scripture can establish articles of faith; all theology is to be drawn from the written Word of God alone. Second, they are intent on emphasizing the power and efficacy of Scripture as God's Word of Law and Gospel; Scripture possesses the power of very God, the power to judge and to save, to kill and to make alive. All the orthodox dogmaticians' concentration and insistence on the divine inspiration and inerrancy of Scripture, even their occupation with the sufficiency and clarity and interpretation of Scripture, are directed to support

these two principles, what we might call in the words of the dogmaticians themselves the *normative* and *causative* authority of the Scriptures.

1. Its Normative Authority

What then is this normative authority of Scripture? Precisely what is meant by the principle of *sola Scriptura?* The principle simply means "that the prophetic and apostolic writings of the Old and New Testaments are the only rule and norm according to which all doctrines and teachers alike must be appraised and judged," as the writers of the Formula of Concord say (Epitome I, 1); all other teachers and writers must be subordinated to the Holy Scriptures. Scripture is the one source *(principium cognoscendi)* of theology; that is to say, the only way we know God and His will and the only source and norm for our speaking about Him is His own revelation, which is contained in Scripture. "We can know nothing of the mysteries concerning God except through the divine revelation that is contained in the sacred writings."[2] This is a unique way of gaining knowledge, and no other way is open for knowing God and divine things. But it is a sure source of knowledge, more sure and certain than heaven and earth and all empirical evidence. Any other basis for teaching or preaching concerning Christ will only lead to error. "The norm and standard for portraying [Christ]," says Dannhauer, "is the divine Word. If one departs from this, he portrays not Christ but his own dreams."[3] To be sure, there is a natural theology whose source is not supernatural revelation but God's creation; but nature and reason can tell us nothing of the Gospel, and they offer only a fragmentary knowledge of God's existence and the Law. For a knowledge of the Gospel a special revelation was required. And for us today that revelation is the written Word of God, the Sacred Scriptures. In the Old Testament and at the time of Christ and the apostles the *viva voce* utterance of an inspired spokesman of God could establish articles of faith and was authoritative, but since the completion of the canon, God's evangelical revelation, that is, His revelation viewed objectively as that which has been revealed, is to be sought only in Scripture. Gerhard says: "We conclude that the correct and exclusive source of supernatural theology is divine revelation, which does not exist today except as found in the Holy Scriptures, that is, the books of the Old Testament prophets and New Testament apostles.

Therefore we say that the written Word of God, or in other words the Holy Scripture, is the one and only source of theology."[4]

Scripture is only an organic, or instrumental, source of our theology and faith. Theology has its origin in God as the One who reveals Himself; He is the cause, the so-called *principium essendi,* of all theology, all language about Himself. It is most important to distinguish between the One who reveals the truth, who is God, and the truth that is revealed, which is Scripture. The former, says Quenstedt,[5] is the *principium essendi,* the foundation of all theology, for theology has its being from God; the latter is the *principium cognoscendi,* for theology is known and understood from Scripture.[6] Therefore Scripture as the source of theology is a directive principle, nothing more than that by which we judge in doctrinal matters.[7]

Most of the Biblical support for the Lutheran principle of *sola Scriptura* is provided within the later discussion of the authority of Scripture as God's Word. Therefore little more is offered to prove the *sola Scriptura* principle early in Lutheran dogmatics than the allusion to the practice of Christ and the apostles, who drew all their theology and judged all doctrine from Scripture. On all points Christ teaches the doctrine of the Old Testament Scriptures. He neither alters the Law nor changes the doctrine of the Old Testament in the slightest but rather draws from the Scriptures for all His teaching, and He cites Scripture as authoritative.[8] And we as His disciples can do no better than to follow His example. Furthermore, since Scripture claims to contain all that is necessary to know for salvation, no other source of theology is necessary.

2. *The Abuse of Tradition*

It is against two extremely serious aberrations that the Scripture principle assumes such importance in Lutheran theology. First, the principle is turned against the Roman Catholic doctrine that unwritten tradition and the decrees of popes and church councils were revelation along with Scripture, and therefore a source of doctrine. Lutheran theology unanimously teaches that Scripture must stand alone as the source of theology.[9] To establish other sources of Christian doctrine beside Scripture vitiates *eo ipso* the Scripture principle entirely. Scripture as a principium of theology must stand alone and independent, or it ceases to be a principium. When the papists say that Scripture is imperfect and obscure, a waxen nose and a frequent cause of strife and controversy in the church, they

forsake the Scriptures as the norm of truth, and they do so in the interest of promoting the authority of the church. The same is true when they subject Scripture to the interpretation of the church and of the pope. In effect this places the church and the pope above Scripture, and it enhances the importance of unwritten traditions in the church.

What is the position of unwritten traditions in the church? Unwritten traditions as such are to be neither totally rejected nor totally accepted. There are, of course, many ways in which we can speak of tradition.[10] We may speak of the Old Testament as containing a tradition or of the apostolic teaching as a tradition. We can even speak of the books of Scripture themselves as a tradition. We can speak of the continuation of the apostolic message as a tradition. The rites that go back to apostolic times may be called traditions. The principle of *sola Scriptura*, however, conflicts with the so-called unwritten traditions of the Roman Church. These traditions pertain to cultus and life; they are alleged to be apostolic and are considered necessary for the church. Such traditions are the sacrifice of the mass, the invocation of the saints, consecrating the water of baptism, private confession including the enumeration of all mortal sins, satisfactions, and the like. They may include also many innocuous customs that in themselves are not wrong and need not be rejected. But bad or good, these traditions cannot be placed beside Scripture as a necessary part of worship or Christian faith. Christ Himself rejects traditions of such a kind as a source of theology and urges people to return to the clear fountain of Scripture (Luke 16:29; 24:27). Unwritten traditions are not infallible like Scripture. They are in fact often contradictory, and their origin is usually obscure. Therefore, even when they do not conflict with Scripture, they cannot be considered binding or authoritative in the church.

It follows that the decrees of popes and church councils cannot be considered sources of Christian doctrine. Calov points out that the Roman claim concerning the authority of the pope and of church councils also sets aside the Scripture principle.[11] For *de facto* this claim also places the authority of pope and church above Scripture. For the pope alone is said to be the infallible interpreter of Scripture; his pronouncements, definitions, and public utterances are said to be inerrant, and when he speaks ex cathedra he does so with the assistance of the Holy Spirit. Thus, Sacred Scripture becomes subject to the authority and whim of the pope

as its interpreter, and no one can appeal to Scripture against the pope. Calov argues that the pope must either make his pronouncements in accordance with Scripture or against Scripture. If he speaks against Scripture, he comes under God's curse. If he speaks in agreement with Scripture, he differs in no way from any other minister of God's Word. Actually the countless instances of popes who have fallen into pernicious error and heresy ought to show the absurdity of such extravagant claims. And what is said of unwritten traditions and the pope may be brought with equal force against the allegation that church councils may establish doctrine. Church councils are subject to the authority of Scripture; their testimony is only human, and no human testimony can be a source in matters of divine truth.

But is not the Lutheran Church with its subscription to symbols and its normative exegesis of *sedes doctrinae* guilty of traditionalism and a violation of the Scripture principle? This charge was often brought against Lutheran theology by Roman theologians. Quenstedt feels that there is no conflict in Lutheran theology at this point. When Lutheran teachers profess their adherence to the *sola Scriptura* principle, they do not view Scripture merely as a list of words in a certain order — one need not support every article of faith with an explicit statement from Scripture — but they have in mind also the content of Scripture and everything that can legitimately be elicited from Scripture. The sense of Scripture and everything that can be rightly drawn from Scripture are considered to be Scripture. Quenstedt states the Lutheran position as follows:

> When the Protestants say that our faith must be taken from Scripture alone, they never understand the sayings of Scripture in such a way that all judgment is limited to the reading of just the syllables, letters, and words and no more. Neither do the terms *alone* and *only* rule out valid inferences drawn from Scripture or interpretations of Scripture, rather they exclude foreign and outside sources and ways of knowing theology that are not drawn from Scripture but from some other sources. Sources of this kind are unwritten traditions, decrees of councils, definitions of popes, the authority of the fathers, judgments of reason, new revelations, and the like, all of which the heterodox join with Scripture as sources of theology.[12]

It is apparent from the foregoing that to Quenstedt the Scripture principle does not operate as a straitjacket on sound Biblical interpretation but rather supports a free and intelligent reading of Scripture and is the

greatest possible deterrent to either atomistic or fanciful exegesis. It is also clear that the principle can only be applied by one who has some grasp of the use of language and of elementary Biblical hermeneutics. That by adopting the Scripture principle, one rules out traditions, reason, and all extra-Biblical sources as norms for judging Christian doctrine does not immediately guarantee one's orthodoxy. One must also be able to distinguish between Law and Gospel, and apply the analogy of faith and other basic rules of interpretation — rules, however, that are not imposed on Scripture but drawn from it. Of all this we have heard before when the orthodox theologians spoke of the necessary prerequisites for the study of Scripture.

3. *The Abuse of Reason*

The second common aberration against which the Scripture principle was directed was the inordinate use of reason in judging matters of doctrine. As an instrument reason is necessary for understanding the Gospel and the message of Scripture. Theology is not presented to brutes but to rational human beings, who are expected to think and use their reason. As that which is employed with organic principles, such as logic and language, reason is necessary for the intelligent application of the Scripture principle. But a *ratio magisterialis* that presumes to sit in judgment over the doctrine of Scripture is to be condemned. Reason and faith belong to two entirely different spheres. Reason is therefore incompetent to assess or judge God's revelation, which can only be believed; and according to its own principles, reason must refrain from passing judgment in spiritual matters. Furthermore, the reason of the natural man is utterly corrupt. Corrupt reason regards the things of God as foolishness (1 Cor. 2:14), and nothing of God's revelation would remain if reason were to have her way. Ironically, reason acts most irrationally in opposing the things of God; and yet this must be: "The carnal mind is enmity against God" (Rom. 8:7), "unable not to oppose God in the most hostile fashion." [13] When reason *in concreto,* as we see it behaving in real life, only despises God and His wisdom and truth, how can it be considered a source of theology? No, if a Christian is to retain the Gospel and his own faith, he must not trust his reason, which as Luther says, is a liar; but like Abraham and Naaman, he must cling to God's Word of promise.

Even the reason of the regenerate man cannot bolster or serve as any

material aid to the Scripture principle. In fact, there would be no sense in making regenerate reason a source of Christian knowledge subordinate to Scripture, for regenerate reason in the nature of the case operates with the Scripture principle. But even the reason of a Christian is tainted with sin and inclined to reject the mysteries of God. Consequently the believer must constantly be wary of it and take it captive in obedience to Christ; for even though the Christian with his reason bows to the authority of Scripture, his reason is never fully enlightened and sanctified. Against those who would make the regenerate reason a source of theology subordinate to Scripture Dannhauer says: "This argument would be valid if man's reason had remained incorrupt and if a stream still polluted with sin had not flowed into it. But the water has been disturbed, like pure water that is suspected of being poisonous, since every imagination of the human heart is only evil continually. And was not Sarah born again? And yet she ridiculed and derided the promise of the Lord as something absurd."[14] To classical Lutheran orthodoxy Scripture stands alone as the one and only source of theology.

As we read through the careful, painstaking discussion of the orthodox Lutheran theologians as they uphold the Scripture principle against all encroachments of reason, we must realize that they are not only condemning the excessive and illicit use of reason as it operates deductively, but they also have in mind all inductive reasoning on the basis of human experience and observation that might conflict with anything said in Scripture. Thus it is not only the doctrine of the Trinity, which seems to be in opposition to the analytical principles of mathematics, that is above every criticism and judgment of reason. But any statement in Scripture concerning fact is to be believed simply on its own account and is not in any way subject to the conclusions or canons of inductive reason, that is, research and evidence in the realm of history or nature. Included here would be statements concerning God's active providence, the presence of Christ's body and blood in the Lord's Supper, the miraculous birth of Isaac or of Jesus, and any historical event, even though the statement might conflict with the usual evidence of research or testimony. Such is the absolute and unqualified commitment of Lutheran theology to the *sola Scriptura*. Later discussions concerning the inerrancy and authority (αὐτοπιστία) of Scripture only serve to uphold and clarify this understanding of the Scripture principle. As Christians we accept Scripture

and yield to all its utterances as though God Himself were speaking directly to us, for Scripture is the Word of God. No external evidence and nothing outside of Scripture prompts us to believe its message; we simply accept on faith everything Scripture says.[15]

SCRIPTURE AS THE WORD OF GOD

Unequivocally and without reservation the orthodox Lutheran theologians call Scripture the Word of God. They regularly call the Sacred Scriptures "the voice of God" and "the very Word of God," and they employ many similar expressions. A typical definition of Scripture as God's Word is given by Gerhard: "Holy Scripture is the Word of God, reduced to writing according to His will by the evangelists and apostles, revealing perfectly and clearly the teaching of God's nature and will, in order that man might be instructed from it to life everlasting."[16] Precisely what do the old Lutherans mean when they identify Scripture with God's Word? What are the implications of this doctrine? These questions can best be answered by investigating first their reasons for calling Scripture the Word of God. Their reasons are twofold: the divine origin and the divine nature of Scripture as God's voice today.

1. *Divine Origin*

Scripture is called the Word of God by virtue of its divine origin. Scripture is the Word of God because its author, strictly speaking, is not a number of men but God Himself. "The supreme author of Scripture is God."[17] The human writers are only His hands, so to speak, His penmen, His amanuenses, who wrote by His command, His impulse and afflatus, yet without being deprived of their individuality, their consciousness, or their natural endowments. The orthodox Lutherans consider the Scriptures to be "nothing else than epistles sent to us from our eternal fatherland, epistles in which our Lord instructs us abundantly and mercifully concerning His will toward us and our duty toward Him."[18] Giles Hunnius, commenting on Rom. 3:2, does not hesitate to say of the Old Testament: "And so we regard that volume of prophetic writing as having originated for our sake from the hand of God and from His heavenly mansions."[19] Again it is Gerhard who has perhaps stated the Lutheran position most definitely:

God is the highest author of Scripture.... It is God alone who has come forth from the hidden abode of His majesty and has revealed Himself, His essence and His will, not only in the work of His creation, but in express words also, words to our first parents before the Fall as well as to the patriarchs and prophets during the Old Testament. Thus it is that the prophets so often repeat the words נְאֻם־יְהֹוָה, "The Lord has spoken," "The Word of Jahve," "The Word of the Lord came *(factum est)*," "The mouth of the Lord has spoken," "Hear the Word of the Lord," etc. And in the New Testament God has spoken to us through His Son (Heb. 1:1). The Son of God in turn sent forth His apostles into all the world and said, "Who hears you hears Me" (Luke 10:16). Through these same apostles who were evangelists He willed to put into writing the necessary and most important elements of His divine revelation. Thus God is the author of Scripture, or to say the same thing, God is the author of the divine revelation that has been incorporated into the Sacred Scriptures.[20]

With one voice Lutheran theology teaches and confesses that Scripture is God's Word because it has its origin in God, because it is the product of His breath, it is θεόπνευστος (2 Tim. 3:16). As my words reveal my will and heart and innermost thought, Scripture is the revelation of God. This means that God's Word is not merely reflected in Scripture through the words of men, God's Word is not obliquely brought to us in Scripture. But the obviously human words of Sacred Scripture are in fact the utterances, the speaking, of God to man. Calov makes this point very clear:

> Sacred Scripture is the result of divine revelation and inspiration not only in respect to its principal parts or to the portions that it treats chiefly and per se but also in respect to the individual parts and to all things that are contained therein. It is the product of divine revelation and inspiration not only in respect to the thought and intention of the statements but also in respect to the very statements and words themselves. All this is understood in the sense that the individual words of the prophets and apostles, as they are contained in Scripture, have been determined by the Holy Spirit.[21]

This doctrine of the old Lutheran teachers that Scripture is the Word of God by virtue of its inspiration, its *terminus a quo,* is opposed to what might be called the pragmatic view of much of modern theology, which speaks of Scripture as the Word of God only by virtue of its *terminus ad quem,* its effects — or rather, the effects of God in making the Bible the Word of God in an event.[22] To Lutheran orthodoxy *Paulus dixit* and *Deus dixit* are not two different things, which become one only when

somehow the Word of God becomes an event, but *Paulus dixit* is *Deus dixit*. This, Lutheran theology is convinced, is the conviction of Paul himself. "In 1 Cor. 2:12-13 the apostle testifies that his doctrine was delivered to him by the revelation of the Holy Spirit. He teaches that his entire kerygma has proceeded from the Holy Spirit (v. 4). In 2 Cor. 3:5 he denies that he offers anything of himself. And in Gal. 1:12 he asserts that all things were delivered to him through the revelation of Christ." [23] Thus, Scripture is not God's Word merely in the sense that God providentially uses men's thoughts and words and makes them His own, Scripture is not God's Word merely in the sense that it successfully conveys a message of God to man, but Scripture is itself God's message to man.

Such a doctrine is bound to influence one's entire approach to Scripture and to theology and will materially affect specific dogmas. After all, it makes a great difference whether Paul's presentation, for instance, of justification represents his own insight on the matter (under the benevolent economy of God) or whether it represents God's own declaration concerning man's relationship to Him.

2. *God's Voice Today*

Thus far we have seen that Lutheran theology calls Scripture the Word of God because of a past action. But Scripture is also called the Word of God because of a present action, that God today and always works through Scripture. According to its very nature *(forma)* Scripture is the Word of God. "The Holy Spirit speaks to us in and through Scripture, and so we must look for the Word and will of the Spirit in these words of Scripture." [24] Notice the present tense in this statement from Gerhard. Scripture is not just the possibility of God speaking to me, not merely a vehicle through which God may speak today. Scripture IS *Deus loquens;* it is God speaking to me today. "Scripture is no less the Word of God," Calov affirms, "than that which passed from the mouth of God." [25] There is materially no real difference between Scripture and the Word of God.[26]

To emphasize that God speaks to me now in Scripture, Gerhard likes to compare Scripture to a letter that God has imparted to all men. Just as I read with avidity the letter of a dear and trusted friend and know that he speaks to me therein, I read the Sacred Scriptures with the

confidence that the living and present God always addresses me there. Gerhard says: "If you read the letter of a friend, you are persuaded that you are hearing there the voice and sentiment of that friend. If you hear the judgment of a ruler repeated from a document, you conclude that you are hearing the decision of that same ruler. Now the Word of God is set forth for us in the canonical Scriptures. Hence in those writings God speaks to us. Thus this Scripture is called the oracles of God, nay, it is the voice of God." [27] But if Scripture is a letter from God, it is like no other letter that was ever written. Scripture is an epistle that comes to me but never really leaves its divine Author; or rather, its Author accompanies this heavenly missive. I write a letter to a dear one because I cannot be present with him; God has given us Scripture in order to be present with His grace and salvation. This is the point Brochmand makes as he comments on Heb. 1:1. God's speaking "by the prophets" may be likened to a king who speaks through an ambassador or legate but with one very important difference, Brochmand says. The kings of this world employ the labors of ambassadors to carry out their business because they themselves cannot be present. God, however, is never absent, but very present, when He speaks by the prophets and announces His will through them and their writings.[28]

When Lutheran theology spoke of Scripture as *Deus loquens,* it was with a very practical motive in mind. As the Word of God, Scripture is God's power — for God speaks, and it is done — it is a life-giving Word, a divine impetus, a word that not merely says things but creates faith in men. For God is never separated or absent from His Word. God's speaking is always God's working and acting. His speaking is never mere words, but deeds *(res).*[29] It is highly significant that Calov, as he devotes a lengthy discussion in his *Systema* to show that Scripture is *vere et proprie* God's Word, directs his arguments not against those who denied the inspiration of Scripture but against those Romanists, Calvinists, and fanatics who denied the power of Scripture.[30] When Lutheran theology affirms unequivocally that Scripture is to be called *vere et proprie* the Word of God, it is fully as much to establish Scripture as God's dynamic Word of judgment and grace today as to confess that God has inspired Scripture. To call Scripture God's Word predicates both its divine origin and its divine nature. Scripture is never considered merely a divine book and set

of divine oracles but is formally God's Word and carries with it God's presence and power.

In order to bring out more precisely what Lutheran theology meant when it called Scripture the Word of God, we must understand something about the distinction between the so-called *materia* and *forma* of Scripture and about the Lutheran doctrine concerning the unity of God's Word.

3. *The* Materia *and* Forma *of Scripture*

According to Lutheran theology, the *materia* of Scripture is the letters, syllables, words, and phrases that together constitute Scripture. The teachings and precepts of Scripture, considered as mere concepts, are also sometimes called the *materia* of Scripture. In this sense Scripture differs in no way from any other book. The *forma* of Scripture is its inspired meaning, the thoughts of God concerning our salvation and divine mysteries, what the dogmaticians call the *sapientia Dei,* the *mens Dei,* the *consilium Dei,* the τὰ τοῦ θεοῦ of 1 Cor. 2,[31] thoughts that God revealed to us in time and communicated to us in Sacred Scripture. Considered according to its *materia,* Scripture is the Word of God only in a secondary and inappropriate sense (*improprie et* σημαντικῶς), inasmuch as it is only the vehicle that brings the thoughts of God to us. It is the *forma* of Scripture, the inspired meaning, that makes Scripture what it is — the Word of God — and distinguishes it from all other books. The dogmaticians, therefore, when they speak of Scripture as the Word of God, are thinking primarily of the divine intention and meaning, the inspired content, of Scripture. A statement of Gerhard's will help make this important point clear:

> By the term *Scripture* we have in mind not so much the outer form or sign, that is, the particular letters, the act of writing, and the words with which the divine revelation has been written down, as the matter itself and the thing signified, as that which is meant and designated by the writing, namely, the Word of God, which teaches us of His nature and will. Some have expressed it this way: the Word of God may be viewed essentially as the very thoughts God expresses, or nonessentially and accidentally as preaching and writing. In other words, as in every writing done by an intelligent and rational agent, so also in the prophetic and apostolic Scriptures two things should be borne in mind: first, the letters, syllables, and words that are written and are outer symbols indicating and expressing the ideas of the mind; and second, the thoughts themselves, which are the things signified, ex-

pressed with the symbols of letters, syllables, and words. Accordingly, in the term *Scripture* we include both of these, but especially the latter.[32]

The common distinction between the *forma* and *materia* is important to bear in mind if we are fully to appreciate the Lutheran doctrine of the Word. Whether we count the distinction to be well chosen or not, we must always understand whether the old Lutheran theologians are speaking of the *forma* or the *materia* of Scripture when they speak of its inspiration or its properties. The inspiration of Scripture pertains to both *forma* and *materia*. The so-called normative authority of Scripture (*sola Scriptura*) pertains primarily to the *materia* of Scripture; so also the clarity and the inerrancy of Scripture. The so-called causative authority of Scripture, its power, is due entirely to its *forma*. In other words, the Word of God, whether read from a book, preached from a pulpit, or treasured in our hearts, is always the power of God, whatever the outer form it may take. But in all these later discussions of the dogmaticians we must realize that the *forma* and *materia* of Scripture or the Word of God cannot be separated from each other.

4. *The Unity of the Word (Scripture as the Word)*

A full appreciation of the Lutheran doctrine of Scripture can be gained only after we understand what appears to be a unique Lutheran insight concerning the unity of the Word of God. In keeping with the idea that the *forma* of Scripture makes it the Word of God, Lutheran theology maintained that the Word of God was one regardless of the outward mode of communication that was attached to it. The external Word of God is always the same, whether delivered to men by God *viva voce* or through the mouths of angels or through the writings of men. Caesar is Caesar whether represented on a canvas or a coin, says Dannhauer, using a rather inapt analogy;[33] so also the Word of God, whether preached or written, remains the same, for the things that pertain to faith and life are not changed when spoken of and put into writing. Hence the difference between the written and spoken Word of God pertains only to the *materia* of the Word, a difference of outward mode of expression only. Quenstedt says: "The act of writing, just as the act of preaching, is incidental to the Word of God and is only an external feature [πάθος] of the Word, an auxiliary mode of proclaiming and communicating the Word, which does not alter the essence of the divine Word. For it is

Scripture as the Word of God

one and the same Word of God that the prophets and apostles, taught as they were by inspiration, preached with the living voice and put down and expressed in letters and writing." [34] The identity of the divine Word is indicated in certain passages of Scripture such as Phil. 3:1: "Finally, my brethren, rejoice in the Lord. To write the same things to you, to me indeed is not grievous, but for you it is safe." The αὐτά of this passage does not indicate a sameness in mode of communication but an identity of doctrine (cf. also Acts 15:27).

The unity of the Word also extends to the Word as it exists in the mind of God or as it is conceived in the mind of men. The so-called *verbum* ἐνδιάθετον, the Word as it exists in God, is not a different Word but the same Word that He reveals to us. "There is no real difference between the inner Word, which is in God, and the external Word, which is presented by the Holy Scriptures or made known by word of mouth, still less is that inner Word that is received in a man's mind and bears godly fruits any different. For there is only one Word of God." [35] The Word that is in God and the Word that He makes known to us are the same, although there are, of course, many things hidden in God that we shall never know. Thus, however we conceive of the Word of God — whether in God originally, or as it was held in the mind of a prophet or apostle before the act of writing, or as it is cherished in a believer's heart, whether we hear it or read it or meditate on it — this Word is one, its divine *forma* remains the same.[36]

The so-called prophetic Word (*verbum* προφορικόν) and the Word that is in God (*verbum* ἐνδιάθετον), which we have been speaking of thus far, are never to be dissociated or separated from the λόγος ὑποστατικός, the eternal Son, through whom God speaks and works. Although the prophetic Word (Scripture) must be distinguished from the personal Word (Christ), the two are always together. There can be no prophetic Word apart from the personal Word. How often do the Lutherans speak of Christ as the author of Scripture and of Scripture as Christ's Word! [37] God always works and speaks through the hypostatic Word, and without Him He will not speak or work.[38] This fact is brought out particularly in the account of creation. Commenting on the "God said" of Gen. 3:1, Calov says:

> The "God said" denotes not merely a word of command; but inasmuch as God does not command anything or do anything except through

His hypostatic Word "through whom all things were made" (John 1:3), the term "God said" must here, where the creation of all things is spoken of, be taken on the one hand as the Word by whom God the Father spoke, the hypostatic Word through whom the Father speaks and works and without whom He neither speaks nor works, and on the other hand as the Word that He spoke or uttered, the prophetic Word, the Word of command, as a divine impulse.

This means that there is an intimate relationship between the prophetic and the hypostatic Word of God. "God has not spoken apart from that Word without whom nothing was made." And the personal Word is not merely the Logos through whom God speaks His prophetic Word. He is the heart and content and meaning of the prophetic Word; He is the message and the purpose of all the Scriptures. "Inasmuch as Christ is the end of the Law (Rom. 10:4) and the center of the Gospel (John 20:31), therefore Christ Jesus is to be considered the length and depth and breadth and the focal point to which all things in the Scriptures are related (Ps. 40:7-8; John 5:39; Acts 3:19, 24; 10:43), nay, He is the epitome and the totality of the entire Scriptures." [39]

Lutheran theology is most emphatic in maintaining the Christocentricity of Scripture, and statements like that of Calov's which we just cited could be multiplied by the hundreds. Dannhauer, for instance, has a preference for likening the writers of Scripture to painters whose one and only theme is Christ crucified: "The apostles and their successors are painters. The object to be portrayed is not a lot of fabrications and dreams, not the gifts of ministers that are to incite the imagination and applause of their hearers, but Christ crucified, who is the head, the entire sweep, the center, the nucleus, the treasure, the pearl of all the Scriptures, and this in order that that image which was lost through the first Adam might be restored from the image of Christ, who is the express image of the divine person." [40] The Christocentricity of Scripture is not a principle to which Lutheran orthodoxy out of loyalty to Luther gave lip service and then tried to apply as best it could. The orthodox Lutherans actually found Christ throughout Scripture. And the Christocentricity of Scripture is more than merely a fact that is apparent to any believing reader of that Word. To Lutheran theology the Christocentricity of Scripture is evidence of the identity of the Word of God, evidence of the intimate relation and conjunction of the hypostatic Word of God (Christ) and the prophetic Word of God (Scripture), of the material principle of theology and the formal

principle of theology. This is a fact of paramount importance. Any interpretation of the Lutheran *sola Scriptura* principle and the orthodox doctrine of Scripture that ignores this insight results in a gross caricature of the Lutheran doctrine of the Word.

The Lutheran insistence on the identity of the Word of God is in conscious opposition to the views of Hermann Rathmann, a renegade Lutheran, and various enthusiasts of the day. Rathmann believed that there was an inner word of God (Christ) and an outer Word (Scripture), but he separated the two. Scripture was itself a dead letter, like a signpost, that pointed to Christ, the Word. On other occasions Rathmann said that the inner Word of God was the wisdom of God, which could not be put down in writing except by the Holy Ghost on the believer's heart. Strictly speaking, only this inner Word was the Word of God. It was against this confused opinion that the Lutherans of the early 17th century articulated their doctrine of the unity of the Word of God, that the Word was one no matter what outer form it might take. The Word was a genus, and Scripture one species of that genus; although there were different species of this genus, they did not oppose one another.[41]

The Lutheran insistence that Scripture be identified as the Word of God was also against Rathmann, Andrew Osiander, the Schwenkfelders, and other enthusiasts who held that Scripture, properly speaking, was not the Word of God, but only Christ was the Word of God. Lutheran orthodoxy maintained that on the basis of many passages that call Scripture the Word of God and the product of God's breath (Rom. 3:2; 1 Peter 1:23; 2 Tim. 3:16), Scripture must be called, not metonymically but truly and simply, the Word of God. Furthermore, the men who wrote Scripture were said to be φερόμενοι, God is said to speak to us through Scripture, and the apostolic preachment is called the Word of God (2 Peter 1:21; 2 Sam. 23:2; 1 Thess. 2:13). The term λόγος in Scripture denotes sometimes the λόγος ὑποστατικός, sometimes the *verbum* προφορικόν, not some confused concept between the two, as the fanatics imagine.[42]

One final word ought to be said about the Lutheran identification of Scripture as the Word of God. Lutheran theology never called Scripture the Word of God in the sense of a one-for-one equation. The Word of God is not restricted to the Sacred Scriptures. Nor is the *forma* of Scripture necessarily restricted to Scripture. If on occasion the Lutheran dog-

maticians state that the Word of God is to be found today only in Scripture, such statements must always be understood in the light of the Lutheran polemic against the Roman doctrine of unwritten tradition and in the context of the Lutheran defense of *sola Scriptura*.[43] It is the unremittent claim of all the orthodox Lutheran teachers that all preaching and teaching that in the church is drawn from Scripture is the Word of God.

5. *The Necessity for Scripture*

What was the necessity for a written Word of God? Why were the Scriptures written? The Lutheran theologians point out that the church of God could exist without the Scriptures. God cared for His church and preserved the saving doctrine for milleniums before the Scriptures were recorded. Therefore there was no absolute necessity for Scripture. However, it pleased God to reveal Himself not only through theophanies and acts in history but through a written Word, and He has not indicated that He wishes to make Himself known to us today through any other medium. (Luke 16:29; 2 Tim. 3:15-17; 2 Peter 1:19; Phil. 3:1)[44]

Selnecker lists four reasons for God putting His Word into writing,[45] and he is followed more or less by the later dogmaticians: (a) The pure doctrine will be less easily corrupted and adulterated if there is a permanent record of God's Word and revelation. (b) It is most important that the message of Law and Gospel flow forth continually in the church, and what better channel is there for this than by a permanent divine account of God's acts of judgment and mercy, of His Law and grace, through the generations of history? By means of Scripture one is able to review the many Gospel promises God gave throughout history through His agents, the patriarchs, prophets, and apostles. (c) In times of controversy a permanent *regula fidei* can keep the man of God secure against all the machinations, snares, and deceits of men, against the violence of tyrants, the subtleties and hypocrisy of false teachers, and his own doubts. In Scripture we have clear warnings of what the church can expect, so we should not be taken by surprise. (d) Scripture is necessary for the sake of evangelization. A permanent verbal revelation of God may now be translated into all languages, and the Gospel can be brought to all.

Actually the supreme usefulness of Scripture predicates its necessity. The value of Scripture to fallen mankind, which is so lackadaisical, so inclined to forget God's acts of grace and redemption, so prone toward

The Inspiration of Scripture

sin and heresy and unbelief, is inestimable. The Holy Scriptures stand as a monument to God's condescension and mercy toward His people and all mankind. Gerhard says:

> No Christian can deny that the Holy Scriptures are useful, since the apostle says so in no uncertain terms (2 Tim. 3:16). Now the Scriptures inform us of things that are unknown naturally, as is clear from the doctrine of the Gospel; they preserve purity of doctrine against error and corruption (Matt. 22:40); they keep us in assurance (Luke 1:3; 2 Peter 1:19); and, I might add, they are profitable for doctrine, for reproof, for correction, for instruction in righteousness, which is the reason we are invited to read them diligently and with devotion (John 5:39; 1 Tim. 4:13; 2 Tim. 3:15). This leads us to the question whether along with their usefulness there is not also connected a certain necessity according to which God wants the Scriptures in the church.[46]

This is merely a mild way of saying what Calov affirms more expressly, that whatever God in His wisdom and love has ordained to give His church is for that very reason necessary. The very purpose of Scripture, which is our faith and salvation, presupposes its necessity.

The Lutheran doctrine of the necessity of Scripture was directed against two antitheses: the view of Quakers, fanatics, and mystics, who held that God speaks to men and saves them apart from His written or spoken Word; and the rather common Roman Catholic opinion that the church of Christ could progress and pure doctrine could be maintained by means of tradition without the aid of Scripture.[47] Against the Roman position, which was by no means general, the Lutherans replied that they wished to maintain not an absolute necessity of the Scriptures as if God could not preserve His church in any other way, but only a hypothetical necessity. The Scriptures are necessary because God has seen fit to bless His church, preserve His church, and extend His church by giving the church a permanent, written Word.

THE INSPIRATION OF SCRIPTURE

The inspiration of Scripture — and the orthodox Lutherans are all concerned to stress the inspiration of Scripture more than the inspiration of the holy writers — is, as treated by these theologians, merely an adjunct to the doctrine that Scripture is the Word of God. Indeed Lutheran

theology means to say nothing more by its doctrine of inspiration than that Scripture is *vere et proprie* God's Word. As an adjunct to the doctrine of the divine origin of Scripture, the doctrine of inspiration tells us that the Bible did not drop from heaven as a finished product but that God's Word in Scripture comes to us in the human words of prophets and apostles and in the style and thought forms of real men, who wrote out of their own concrete situation and experience, but men whom He has claimed for Himself, called, enlightened, and moved to write not their own thoughts, fancies, or insights but His Word.

The reason for the inspiration of Scripture receiving so much attention among the later dogmaticians is not due to any innovation or development in the Lutheran doctrine of Scripture but to a change of theological climate. According to the judgment of John Huelsemann, Jesuit controversialists wished to render the doctrine of inspiration doubtful in order to enhance the necessity for unwritten tradition in formulating Christian doctrine.[48] There is no reason to doubt the correctness of Huelsemann's observation. At any rate, it was only at about the turn of the 17th century that special discussions in Lutheran dogmatics centered in the doctrine of inspiration. This was due not only to developments among the Jesuits but to the very weak position of Socinians, Arminians, and even certain Lutherans like Calixt on the divine origin of Scripture. Orthodox Lutheranism was compelled to articulate a very clear doctrine of inspiration in order to maintain an unequivocal doctrine of Scripture as the Word of God.

The inspiration of Scripture was considered to be not a theory but a doctrine of Scripture. Huelsemann points out that the Augsburg Confession, although it had no reason to treat the doctrine of inspiration, nevertheless presupposes that Scripture is divinely inspired. This is also the judgment of Hutter, who insists that the *sola Scriptura* principle cannot be upheld unless one assumes the inspiration of Scripture.[49] As a doctrine of Scripture, the inspiration of Scripture becomes a matter of confession, a divisive article of faith; to deny the inspiration of Scripture is un-Lutheran. Furthermore, a serious subscription to the Lutheran Confessions is impossible unless at least tacit recognition of the inspiration of Scripture is given, for the divine doctrine of the Lutheran Confessions is taken entirely from the Scriptures.[50] We must add, however, that for classical Lutheran theology the doctrine of the inspiration of Scripture

The Inspiration of Scripture

intends to say no more than what had always been confessed and taught in the Christian church, that Scripture was the speech and Word of God.

1. *Inspiration Generally Defined*

According to Lutheran orthodoxy inspiration is an act of the triune God whereby He communicates to men that which He wishes written for men's sake. Inspiration is not a general act of God like that by which He incites good works in all men. Neither is inspiration a more special and advanced action of God like that by which He is present in believers, guiding and approving their actions and giving them understanding (Job 32:8). Inspiration is more than a mere assistance or direction whereby men write an infallible human word. It is not mere divine guidance. The Scriptures are not merely the indirect result of God's guiding hand and providence. But Scriptures are directly the product of God's breath, the direct result of a divine action.

Inspiration, according to Quenstedt, is an "absolutely unique and extraordinary action" of God that pertains only to Scripture. It includes, first, a supernatural and absolutely exceptional enlightenment of the minds of the human writers, an enlightenment that is not necessarily a permanent *habitus* but a passing activity; and second, "a unique impulse, urge, inspiration, afflatus, incitement, and suggestion" for the particular writing of Scripture and nothing else. Explaining himself further, Quenstedt says on the basis of 2 Peter 1:21 that the writers of Scripture were moved by God to apply their minds to the writing of doctrine and to move their pens with their hands (Acts 17:16); they were inwardly enlightened by the Spirit with a supernatural light; and they were inwardly supplied by the Holy Spirit with all that was necessary for their writing, both with respect to the content and with respect to the very words.[51]

Dannhauer expresses the same doctrine with a little more originality. He says that the inspiration or God-breathed nature of Scripture (θεόπνευσις) is not the result merely of the Spirit's *aspiration,* or general command, such as the command to make disciples of all the nations. Neither is the God-breathed character of Scripture brought about merely by the Spirit's *postspiration,* which would resemble a teacher correcting and approving what his disciples had written. But it is the product also of His *inspiration* according to which the Spirit by His present concomitant grace reveals things that are above human understanding and

unerringly certifies things that have been seen and heard by the holy writers. And it results finally from the Spirit's *respiration:* "As a musical wind instrument, when played artistically, seems to revive people and actually to breathe and to sound forth with beauty, the Holy Spirit through His instrument breathes forth and utters divine words, as it were, and makes known thoughts necessary for salvation from the innermost recesses of the divine heart." [52]

This is about all that the old dogmaticians say about the act of inspiration. No attempt is made to analyze the inner processes and experiences of the human writers. Perhaps the writers themselves could not describe the *how* of what happened when they wrote as instruments of the Holy Spirit. The dogmaticians are interested in upholding the *that* of inspiration and the extent of inspiration, not the *how*. Specifically, they had three basic concerns to which we shall now address ourselves and try to understand fully their position: they wished to affirm that inspiration was completely under the control of God and that the human writers of Scripture wrote by a specific and definite command and impulse; that all the contents of Scripture are the product of God's breath; and that the very words of Scripture are inspired by God.

Before discussing these three points in order, one passing remark ought to be made. According to the presentation of Quenstedt and Dannhauer mentioned above, inspiration pertained only to the Scriptures. Although God enlightened the authors of Scripture spiritually and prepared them beforehand for their work of writing, although the writers of Scripture thought and prepared their material and sometimes preached before the act of writing, still θεόπνευσις pertains only to the Scriptures. Only Scripture is said to be θεόπνευστος, not all the activity that preceded the writing of Scripture. This does not imply that the preached word of the prophets (at least some of the time) and of the apostles was not inspired. The dogmaticians definitely affirmed the inspiration of the preached word of the prophets and apostles as chosen men of God. And we have learned that there is no difference between the preached and written Word except the outer mode of presentation. But the orthodox theologians would not have broadened inspiration to include the whole historical process that antedated the writing of the various Scriptures or the research the writers may have done or the traditions and sources Moses and other writers may have used.

The Inspiration of Scripture 277

2. *The Divine Command to Write Scripture*

The Lutheran dogmaticians teach that inspiration includes a divine impulse or command to write. The very act of inspiration involves an impulse to write the Scriptures, according to 2 Peter 1:21.[53] The command to write the Scriptures was not necessarily an external command, but the fact that the writers of Scripture were moved by the Spirit of God means that they did not write from their own initiative but in obedience to an inner *mandatum scribendi.* Thus the divine activation in the act of inspiration is, in fact, an internal, hidden command of God to write.[54] Not only the things to be written but the Scriptures themselves were written by the command of God.[55] Although there is no indication in many of the books of the New Testament of a specific command to write, such a command is implied in the commission to evangelize all nations; for such evangelization could not have been carried out by means of only a generation or two of apostolic preaching. The apostolic office to testify to Christ comprised writing as well as preaching (Acts 10:42). This is evident from the fact that the apostles regarded their writings as testimonies of things that God wanted made known (John 21:24). For future generations the apostles wrote the same message they preached to the people of their day (1 John 1:1).[56] The apostles would not have dared to speak without divine authority; much less would they have written without a command from God. Peter thought it wrong to announce the Gospel to the Gentiles without a divine command. (Acts 10:19, 26)

The Lutherans during the period of orthodoxy belabored the *mandatum scribendi* for one very good reason: Roman Catholic theologians of the day taught that Scripture was not written by a command of God, although it was written by God's will and inspiration. This they affirmed in order to safeguard their doctrine of unwritten tradition. Both Scripture and unwritten tradition were considered to be the Word of God, and both derived their authority from the church. According to this teaching the pope and the church were in the last analysis placed above Scripture. The church could exist without Scripture but not without the pope, who was divinely appointed by Christ. The Lutherans retorted that if Scripture was written by God's will it was written also according to His command. "For God's will is the same as a command."[57] But what about the fact that there were certain definite occasions that prompted the various books of Scripture to be written? Such external occasions, along with the

research and study of the writers, do not rule out a *mandatum scribendi* but confirm it, since the occasions for writing the various books of Scripture were brought about under God's providence.

3. *The Plenary Inspiration of Scripture*

Inspiration pertains to all the contents of Scripture; there is nothing in Scripture that was not God-breathed. This position was maintained in contrast to the views of the Jesuits, Bellarmine [58] and Bonfrère, and the Lutheran, George Calixt, who apparently confused inspiration and revelation and taught that whatever history and facts were known prior to the writing of Scripture were not inspired. Calixt also believed that insignificant matters and incidental details mentioned in Scripture (e. g., the mention of Paul's cloak being left in Troas, 2 Tim. 4:13) were not inspired. The orthodox Lutherans agreed that there was much in Scripture that the writers knew before they wrote, but as these matters were actually recorded in Scripture everything was communicated to the writers by the Holy Spirit.[59]

Quenstedt classifies all the contents of Scripture as follows: (a) those things that could have been known to the writers but were not because they happened in a remote time or place (e. g., the history of the Flood and the destruction of the Sodomites as described by Moses); (b) those things that cannot be known because of their exalted nature (e. g., the mysteries of our faith) or because they had not yet happened (e. g., future events) or because of their absence from our senses (e. g., the emotions of the heart); (c) those things that were knowable (e. g., the Exodus to Moses and the history of the judges to Samuel). Now all these things, whether knowable or not, were inspired and actually dictated to the amanuenses by the Spirit of God.[60] The writers of Scripture recorded much that they had learned from history and tradition and their parents and much that they had gained from their own experience, but the time, manner, and circumstances in which these things were to be recorded were given them by the Spirit of God, were revealed and dictated by God. In this sense, all in Scripture, even what was well known to the penmen before they wrote, was revealed. Hollaz says: "Although the sacred writers were informed concerning certain things of which they wrote before the act of writing, they did not know whether it was God's will that they

put these things into writing, or under what circumstances, in what arrangement, and with what words they were to write."

From the position outlined above it follows that also those things in Scripture that did not pertain directly to doctrine were given by inspiration. Again Hollaz says: "There are present in the holy Scriptures matters pertaining to history, chronology, genealogy, astronomy, physics, and politics that obviously it is not necessary to know for salvation; and yet they are divinely revealed because the knowledge of them contributes in no small degree to the interpretation of the Holy Scriptures, as well as to the elucidation of the doctrine of faith and the demands of the Law." Even commonplace matters in Scripture are inspired, no matter how unimportant they may seem to be. There is a great difference in the importance of the various matters in Scripture but no difference in respect to the inspiration of these things. Considered by themselves, a passing statement in Scripture and even relatively large sections may seem quite trivial and unworthy of the Spirit's attention and inspiration, but taken in the wider context and viewed in the light of the whole purpose of God, there is good reason for everything that is recorded in Scripture (Rom. 15:4). And so there are no real *levicula* (trivial matters) in Scripture, as Calixt had imagined. The very idea of Scripture containing *levicula* is an impious thought. Nothing that God has seen fit to record in His Word is unimportant or unworthy of the Holy Spirit. But what about the lying, the sinful orgies, the blasphemies recorded in Scripture? Surely all this is repugnant to the high majesty of the Spirit of God. Of course, reply the dogmaticians; but these incidents are recounted in Scripture as examples of what we are to avoid, not because they are condoned, and we need to be taught and warned by means of such examples of sin and blasphemy.

The dogmaticians are careful to point out that their doctrine of plenary inspiration does not rule out what was obvious to anyone who read the Scriptures, namely, that the writers of Scripture studied beforehand those things about which they wrote and that they gained knowledge from reliable witnesses (Luke 1:3). The study of human sources antedated the inspiration of Scripture, which was concomitant with the writing of Scripture; in the actual writing of Scripture the choice of things to be recorded and the very words were given by the Spirit of God, with the result that there was no possibility of error.

Plenary inspiration is the doctrine of Scripture itself. According to 2 Tim. 3:16 it is not enough to say that only the doctrinal portions of Scripture were inspired or that only certain sections were written by divine guidance. If the prophets and apostles were not inspired in everything they wrote, then all Scripture is not inspired. According to 2 Peter 1:21, the holy writers wrote nothing by their own private initiative or fancy but were moved and incited by the Spirit to write everything in Scripture. They were merely God's chosen instruments, His penmen, who would not have imposed their own thoughts on Scripture. Commenting on this passage, Quenstedt says:

> The λαλιά of the prophets and apostles does not pertain only to the great mysteries of our faith or those things that have to do with saving faith, as if the holy men of God spoke and wrote only such things by the inspiration and activation of the Holy Spirit while other things, such as historical, ethical, and scientific concerns, were added by their own free action and instigation after the urge of the Spirit had ceased. But the content and sweep of the λαλιά includes all things that are contained in Scripture. For the apostle speaks generally when he says, ὑπὸ πνεύματος ἁγίου φερόμενοι ἐλάλησαν. From the preceding verses it is clear that this indefinite statement denotes a collective concept. This is shown from the fact that the λαλιά of the holy men of God, v. 21, the λόγος προφητικός, v. 19, the προφητεία, v. 21, and the προφητεία γραφῆς, v. 20, mean the same thing; but to this concept the collective πᾶσα is added. Therefore no prophecy came at any time by human initiative, and thus no prophecy of Scripture is of private interpretation nor ought to be, but whatever the prophets and apostles spoke and wrote, they spoke and wrote by divine activation. And concerning this matter of activation there is neither hint nor trace of limitations or restrictions of any kind to only certain parts of Scripture.

Actually Christ promised that all the contents of the New Testament would be inspired when He said that the Holy Spirit would teach His apostles and bring to their remembrance all things that He had said to them (John 14:26). The fact that Christ said πάντα ἃ εἶπον ὑμῖν ἐγώ indicates that not some but all things the apostles wrote were given by the Spirit. Finally, Scripture knows no distinction between certain of its contents that were written by divine inspiration and revelation and other sections recorded by divine approval and assistance. All of Scripture is simply called indiscriminately τὰ λόγια τοῦ θεοῦ.

The theory of Calixt and certain Jesuits that only the important

matters in Scripture were given by inspiration was impossible to apply, according to the Lutheran theologians. So was the theory that only those things previously unknown to the writers were inspired. In each case the interpreter of Scripture is faced with the impossible task of trying to discern either what was of sufficient importance to warrant divine inspiration or what precisely was known to the writers in advance of their writing of Scripture. Both theories were arbitrary and unworkable. The theory that only the doctrinal portions of Scripture were inspired was built on a false assumption. For everything in Scripture pertains to Christian doctrine, perhaps not directly — and of course there is much in Scripture of which we may be ignorant and still be saved — but somehow all things in Scripture are related to Christian doctrine (2 Tim. 3:16).[61] The rejection of the inspiration of some things in Scripture will result only in the search for what is human and divine in Scripture, and will lead to uncertainty regarding everything.

4. *The Doctrine of Verbal Inspiration*

Not only the content *(res)* of Scripture but the very words as they appear together and separately *(verba omnia et singula)* were given by divine inspiration. This was the position of all the orthodox Lutheran teachers, but the doctrine was given special attention and spelled out in detail only in the 17th century after the time of Calixt. Calixt was unable to accept the inspiration of the very words of Scripture but preferred to speak of a divine guidance and direction whereby the writers were preserved from error. They wrote God's message but in the words they themselves chose. This seemed to be the opinion of Socinus at times and of certain Jesuits.[62]

The orthodox Lutheran doctrine is defined with characteristic precision by Quenstedt: "The Holy Spirit not only inspired in the prophets and apostles the content and the sense contained in Scripture, or the meaning of the words, so that they might of their own pleasure clothe and furnish these thoughts with their own style and their own words; but the Holy Spirit actually supplied, inspired, and dictated the very words and each and every term individually."[63] The Spirit suggested to the authors what they were to write and how they were to write. "Πᾶσα γραφὴ θεόπνευστος. There is no word of Scripture, not even a jot, that does not occur by divine inspiration."[64] It should be stated emphatically that this

doctrine of verbal inspiration, as confessed by Lutheran theology, never views the words of Scripture atomistically, as though they could possibly be viewed apart from their logical order and intended sense. The inspiration of the *verba* and the *res* of Scripture belong together as one action of God, just as the *materia* and *forma* of Scripture belong together.

a. THE TEACHING OF SCRIPTURE. The inspiration of Scripture is the doctrine of Scripture itself. And it is not begging the question when the Lutheran theologians appeal to Scripture for their doctrine; one proves God from God, the sun from the sun, color from color, and the divine origin of Scripture from itself.[65]

The *locus classicus* for the doctrine of inspiration is 2 Tim. 3:16. Calov comments on this passage as follows:

> The whole of Scripture is inspired, according to the apostle's testimony in 2 Tim. 3:16 — not merely the meaning of Scripture, but the very Scripture itself and whatever pertains to Scripture. Thus if only one word is found in Scripture that is not inspired, it cannot be said that πᾶσα γραφή, *all* Scripture, is θεόπνευστος. Not only the *forma,* or content, belongs to Scripture, but also the *materia,* the words, syllables, and symbols. In this passage Scripture is viewed in this complex sense in reference to both its formal and material aspect, inasmuch as the reading of Scripture is enjoined upon Timothy, who was obliged to observe both the meaning of Scripture and the individual words with careful scrutiny and with devotion to the Scripture, which he as a teacher was bound to explain to others in respect to its meaning and even the inferences of the words.[66]

This statement of Calov's indicates that he feels it would be nonsense to speak of the inspiration of Scripture unless we speak of the inspiration of the words, for Scripture consists of words. The exegetical support this Scripture passage gives to the doctrine of verbal inspiration is brought out more fully by Hollaz. There are three reasons, he contends, why this passage must be understood as supporting the verbal inspiration of Scripture:

> (1) The apostle does not merely say: every word of God is inspired. If that were the case, then one could understand the passage as referring to the divine Word in the formal sense, as the divine meaning. But he says: πᾶσα γραφή, all Scripture, which signifies not only the divine meaning but the written words. (2) The apostle does not say, πάντα γεγραμμένα θεόπνευστα, but πᾶσα γραφή θεόπνευστος, in

order to show that not only the content of the Sacred Scripture was divinely revealed but that even the very words were dictated to the penmen by the Holy Spirit. (3) In speaking of these Scriptures the apostle tells how Timothy as a boy read them and how, when he had been made bishop, he studied them diligently and expounded them to his hearers. Now he read and explained Holy Scripture not only in terms of its content but also in terms of its written words.[67]

Quenstedt remarks that the subject of the verse, γραφή, immediately calls to mind the external act of writing and therefore has to do with symbols and characters that are written with the hand. The apostle does not say πάντα ἐν γραφῇ are θεόπνευστα, but πᾶσα γραφὴ θεόπνευστος, in order to show that not only the things that were written but the writings themselves were inspired. And whatever is said of the Scriptures as writings is said of every part of Scripture, also the words.

The passage 2 Peter 1:21 also teaches the inspiration of the very words of Scripture, affirming that the sayings of Scripture do not have their origin in man's will but are the result of the Spirit's impulse. The λαλιά in this verse denotes words, not thoughts. And the φορά includes, among other things, a word-for-word dictation to the penmen. "The φορά," Calov says, "embraces both an inner enlightenment of the mind and communication of what was to be said and written, and an external urge of such a nature that the tongue and pen no less than the intellect and mind acted by that impulse. The result was that not only the *forma,* or content, was suggested, but the words also, which are placed in their mouth and dictated to their pen by the Holy Spirit, were communicated to the individual amanuenses, or men of God." [68]

Still other Scripture evidence is brought forth to support the verbal inspiration of Scripture. In Matt. 10:20 Jesus promises that the Spirit will speak in the apostles when they preach His Word; and surely such a promise will apply also to their writings in which they were to instruct all future generations. In 1 Cor. 2:12-13 the apostle Paul claims to be verbally communicating to the Corinthian congregation what was given him by God as mysteries of divine wisdom. In the Old Testament repeated commands were given the prophets to write the words of God. And the constant refrain "Thus saith the Lord" indicates that their speaking and writing was God's speaking and writing. The whole Scripture is called the words and oracles of God (Ps. 119; Rom. 3:2), and what is true of the whole of Scripture must also be true of the individual words.

When God promised that His Word would be in the mouth of His prophets (Ex. 4:15; Num. 23:12; 2 Sam. 23:2; Is. 51:16; Acts 2:4; Jer. 1:9; Mark 13:11; Luke 1:70; 21:15), the meaning is that God inspired the very words His spokesmen preached and wrote.

b. WORDS AND CONTENT. The content of Scripture cannot be separated from its words. The meaning of God's self-communication to us is inextricably bound to the words of Scripture.[69] The very purpose of words is to express thought or content. In the case of any writing the only way we can get at the meaning is through the words. Thus, we cannot possibly speak of the inspiration of Scripture without adhering to the inspiration of the words of Scripture. And we can never be certain of what the Spirit of God means in Scripture unless we can be certain that the words of Scripture were expressly given by Him.[70]

c. ANSWERS TO OBJECTIONS. By the time of Hollaz a number of objections to the doctrine of verbal inspiration were apparently in vogue. The Jesuits argued that the stylistic differences between the authors of Scripture were obvious; each author used a vocabulary and literary style that was his own. How then could these words be called God's speech? Hollaz replies that the Spirit of God in inspiring Scripture adapts Himself to the stylistic and other differences that obviously obtained between the various writers of Scripture.[71] He adds that in a certain sense the style of all Scripture is uniform, that is, in respect to its substance. The literary characteristics and expressions of the human authors of Scripture are only accidental to the Spirit's speech. The Spirit of God condescends and "stoops down," so to speak, to the abilities, the feelings, and the backgrounds of the inspired men (*ingenia, studia, nationesque virorum* θεοπνεύστων). The Spirit's inspiring of all the various books and genres of Scripture may be likened to the playing of a great organ on which one dominant theme and harmonious melody resounds; and all the time the artist accommodates himself to all the various pipes and stops of this vast and complex instrument.[72] But what was the need of inspiring words and also concepts that were already fully known to the writers of Scripture? To this objection Hollaz replies that words may be inspired whether they were previously known or not. The words of Scripture were not inspired *ad sciendum* but only *ad scribendum*. The writers of Scripture were not simply left to themselves to express various thoughts any way they pleased;

The Inspiration of Scripture

if such had been the case, even if God had kept them from error, their autographic writings would not differ from any good version of Scripture.

What about the apographal Scriptures that we possess today? May they be said to be inspired? Without going into the problems connected with the authenticity of the present texts of Scripture, problems that can only be solved by sound textual criticism, the dogmaticians reply generally in the affirmative. Huelsemann states that at least relatively we can say that our present texts of Scripture are inspired.[73] Baier affirms that the apographa are inspired, inasmuch as they possess the same *forma,* or content, as the autographic Scriptures. In spite of the many codices today with their many material variations, we still have the inspired meaning of the original texts.[74] Hollaz goes farther. He maintains that the very words as well as the content of the apographa are inspired. A good copy of an inspired writing is inspired like the original writing itself. Quenstedt explains this point of view more fully:

> Every Holy Scripture that existed at the time of Paul was θεόπνευστος (2 Tim. 3:16) and authentic. Not the autographic (for they had perished long before) but the apographal writings existed at the time of Paul. Therefore the apographal Scripture also is θεόπνευστος and authentic. God, not the hand of Moses, gave authenticity to the Pentateuch. For although inspiration and divine authority inhered originally in the autographs, these attributes belong to the apographal Scriptures by virtue of their derivation, since they were faithfully transcribed from them so that not only the sense but also the words were precisely the same.[75]

Whether Quenstedt and Hollaz would press their argument to apply with equal force to the apographa of their day is not clear. But they were convinced that God in His providence had preserved for His people a genuine and trustworthy text of Holy Scripture, and they were fully persuaded that sound textual criticism could establish that text. Hollaz says: "Variant readings cannot render the canonical authority of Scripture doubtful, because it is easy to trace and tie together the correct reading from the way the text itself hangs together." Such an optimistic statement may reveal a certain naïveté; but on the other hand the orthodox Lutherans were well aware of the science of textual criticism as it had developed to their day, and they (Calov in particular)[76] even make occasional use of the results of this method in their dogmatics.

There was really only one critical issue in connection with the doctrine

of inspiration and the apographal Scriptures, and the dogmaticians are all agreed and convinced on this one point: we do not need the autographic Scriptures today in order to have an authentic and inspired Word of God, no more than we would require the cup from which Christ drank in order to celebrate a valid Eucharist.[77]

d. UNRELATED TO PSYCHOLOGICAL THEORY. One more word must be said before we leave the doctrine of verbal inspiration. Verbal inspiration as confessed by Lutheran theology has nothing to do with a pyschological theory. The doctrine that the words of Scripture were God-breathed says and intends to say nothing about what transpired in the mind or heart of the writers of Scriptures as they were moved by the Spirit. The doctrine pertains only to the extent of inspiration, not to the how of inspiration, which remains an impenetrable mystery; it pertains to the Scriptures as the product of God's breath, not to the authors as spokesmen of God. Verbal and plenary inspiration are teachings that are merely correlative to the doctrine that Scripture is *vere et proprie* the Word of God; they are teachings that were emphasized only after it became apparent that some theologians (Calixt, Socinians, and certain Jesuits) equivocated in calling Scripture the Word of God. The idea that verbal inspiration leads somehow to a mantic theory of inspiration is the result of a total misunderstanding of the Lutheran doctrine.[78]

5. *The Relation of the Holy Spirit to the Authors of Scripture*

When the Lutheran theologians of the 16th and 17th centuries speak of the writers of Scripture as being the hands, penmen, secretaries, and scribes of the Holy Spirit and describe the writers as being led, moved, impelled, and activated by the Spirit, they have one and only one purpose in mind: to stress that the apostles and prophets in writing Sacred Scripture acted as instruments of the Holy Spirit. This is also the aim of the orthodox Lutherans when they describe the writers of Scripture as writing by the command, the afflatus, the suggestion, and the dictation of the Spirit.[79] These holy writers were the means through whom God put His Word into writing. To press the rather elaborate terminology used by the orthodox Lutherans beyond this one obvious point of comparison would result in a vicious caricature of their position and make nonsense of the Lutheran doctrine of inspiration.

The Inspiration of Scripture

a. GOD THE AUTHOR. Lutheran theology, we must repeat, is not interested in the psychology of inspiration but only in maintaining that God, strictly speaking, is the author of Scripture. And this is only another way of saying that Scripture is God's Word. The fact that God communicates to our fallen race through chosen vessels, that He employed men to speak and write His Word, indicates that these men of God were authors of Scripture only in a secondary sense *(autores secundarii)*. Quenstedt says:

> The Holy Spirit wrote and spoke with the prophets and apostles in one and the same action but in a different sense, He as the first cause and they as the instrumental cause.[80]

In stronger language Hutter expresses the same conviction:

> God Himself is the principal author of Scripture. Therefore even if God did not immediately write Scripture but deigned to employ the pen and service of the prophets and apostles, still nothing is thereby subtracted from the authority of Scripture. For it is God and God alone who inspired in the prophets and apostles both what they were to speak and what they were to write, and He used their mouths, their tongues, their hands and pens. In such a manner Scripture as such was written by God Himself; the prophets and apostles were merely His organs.[81]

These typical statements by Quenstedt and Hutter exemplify the attempt of Lutheran theology to express the Biblical theme that as God spoke through the mouths of the apostles and prophets He wrote through their hands and pens. And hence Scripture is not a human word, not a synergistic human-divine composite, but it is God's Word, which the holy penmen wrote. This, according to the Lutheran theologians, was the conviction of the writers of Scripture themselves.

b. THE SPIRIT AND THE WRITERS. The rigorous monergistic doctrine of inspiration that we have outlined in no way suggests that God violated the personalities of His penmen when they wrote His Word, that they wrote without thought or feeling or were reduced to mere automata. These men wrote consciously, from understanding, and out of deep experience and conviction.[82] Quenstedt says: "The writers are said to be φερόμενοι, activated, incited, borne, by the Holy Spirit, not as though they were unconscious, as the enthusiasts say of themselves and as the heathen imagine the ecstasy of their prophets. Neither is it to be understood as though the prophets did not understand their prophecies of the things that they

were to write."[83] Inspiration includes a divine illumination of the mind, as we have already learned, and also a gift of interpreting the highest of divine mysteries, a δύναμις ἑρμηνευτική, as Hollaz calls it.[84] This exceptional comprehension of spiritual matters pertained, of course, only to τὸ ὅτι, not to τὸ πῶς. A mantic, Montanist conception of the relation of the Holy Spirit to the writers of Scripture is foreign to the old Lutheran dogmaticians and consciously rejected by them.

Nor does the monergistic doctrine of inspiration imply a violation of the wills of the holy writers. In a gentle manner God prepared His chosen vessels, enlightened their mind and incited their will to write His Word.[85] He made them willing penmen. Considered in a contributory sense *(efficienter et originaliter)*, as it functions in the natural domain, man's will did not produce Scripture but was utterly passive. But subjectively and materially the will of the writers was active in the writing of Scripture. Thus, the will of the writers cannot be excluded from the act of inspiration, Quenstedt says, "as though the amanuenses had written without and against their will, without consciousness and unwillingly; for they wrote voluntarily, willingly, and knowingly."[86] In the above sense the wills of the holy writers were alive and active when they wrote Scripture, although they contributed nothing of their own will to Scripture. In everything they were ruled by the Spirit of God.

Finally, the monergistic doctrine of inspiration does not submerge or violate the linguistic and stylistic identity of the various writers. This was a fact obvious to even the most casual reader of Scripture and was always taken into account by the Lutherans in their exegesis of Scripture. And not only the distinctive terminology and stylistic peculiarities but the thought processes and predilections of the individual writers are apparent throughout Scripture. However, the various styles and other distinctive characteristics of the different books do not imply that the writers of Scripture wrote independent of the Holy Spirit. Just as God condescended to speak to man in a human language and by means of human thought forms, He accommodated Himself in His speaking to the comprehension *(captum)* and the natural endowments *(indoles)* and the manner of speaking *(genus loquendi)* that were already possessed by the writers of Scripture. Quenstedt maintains that this doctrine of accommodation is perfectly consistent with the fact that God determined the very words of Scripture. He says:

> We must distinguish between the *genus loquendi* and the phrases, words, and terms themselves. The holy writers employed the *genus loquendi* in daily use according to the everyday custom and meaning, and hence diversity of style arose, especially among the prophets. Now insofar as they were instructed in and accustomed to a lofty or ordinary style of speaking and writing, the Holy Spirit chose to adjust and accommodate Himself to the natural endowments of these men and to express the same things through some in an ornate manner, through others in an inferior manner. The Holy Spirit accommodated Himself to the understanding and natural endowments of the holy writers in order that He might record mysteries according to the usual mode of speaking.[87]

This doctrine of accommodation is either explicitly taught or at least inferred by all the Lutheran dogmaticians.[88] Calov differs from the others slightly by emphasizing a divine accommodation, or condescension (συγκατάβασις), to the readers of Scripture as well as to the writers and to the content as well as the style of the writing, but there is no essential difference.[89] It is important for us to realize that this accommodation doctrine is not a passing thought or a mere adjunct to the Lutheran doctrine of inspiration but an essential part of it.

In their treatment of Scripture the Lutheran dogmaticians say a few things that to one who reads them only superficially might imply that their doctrine of inspiration does not sufficiently take into account the personal involvement of the writers and the human side of Scripture. We must briefly comment on these.

(1) We find statements that at first seem to conflict with an accommodation doctrine. Quenstedt says, for instance, that the writers of Scripture "contribute nothing of their own beyond the external act of portrayal and of writing down the letters."[90] Calov, commenting on Is. 51:16, asserts that there is nothing human about the message of the prophet, except that his mouth was the organ used by the Lord in uttering the divine Word.[91] Such statements, however, do not intend to imply that the writers of Scripture were mere unthinking, unfeeling robots as they wrote or that they did not think and plan and study before the act of writing. The statements intend merely to say, but to say as emphatically as possible, that God inspired all the words of Scripture. We must not press such language, which is couched in the imagery of Scripture, beyond its point of comparison.

(2) Among the later Lutheran teachers it was held that there were

no barbarisms or solecisms in Scripture. Again such a position does not suggest that the Scriptures were written in a manner somehow contrary to established linguistic usage, or that the personalities and literary style of the sacred writers were violated, or that there is something artificial about the way the Scriptures were written. The very opposite is expressly stated by the Lutheran teachers.[92] They are voicing their disagreement with Erasmus and others who said that the language of Scripture was not only crude and faulty in construction but also confused.[93] When the Lutheran dogmaticians speak of barbarisms and solecisms, they have in mind not loan words or departures from ordinary syntax or linguistic usage, but inept and incongruous language.[94] And this, they maintain, is unworthy of the Holy Spirit, who would surely suggest to the prophets and apostles a mode of writing that was seemly and apt in conveying meaning.

(3) The term "dictate" *(dicto)* is used commonly by the Lutheran theologians in describing the influence of the Spirit on the prophets and apostles as they wrote Scripture. Could such terminology possibly be used by those who take the human side of Scripture seriously and really believe that the writers of Scripture were totally involved in all that they wrote? The answer is that the Lutheran teachers, like the Reformed and Catholic theologians of the day, mean no more by the term *"dicto"* than they mean by the terms *"suggero"* and *"inspiro."*[95] It is often a serious mistake to translate a Latin term by its modern English derivative. In the case of the term *"dicto"* such a mistake would result in a travesty of the Lutheran doctrine of inspiration. God did not dictate the Scriptures the way a modern business executive might dictate a letter to a stenographer, who could be utterly disinterested in the letter and whose mind could be a thousand miles away. According to Lutheran theology God's "dictation" employs the spiritual experiences, the study and preparation, the thought patterns, the *modus loquendi,* the witnessing, the total personality of the writers of Scriptures. Again the term *"dicto"* is only one of many expressing the divine monergism of inspiration.

c. THE PARADOX OF INSPIRATION. The Lutheran doctrine of inspiration presents a paradox. On the one hand it was taught that God is the *autor primarius* of Scripture, that He determined and provided the thoughts and actual words of Scripture and that no human cooperation concurred *efficienter* in producing Scripture. On the other hand it was maintained that the temperaments *(ingenia),* the research and feelings *(studia),* and

the differences in background *(nationes)* of the inspired writers are all clearly reflected in the Scriptures; that there is nothing docetic about Scripture; that God's spokesmen wrote willingly, consciously, spontaneously, and from the deepest personal spiritual conviction and experience; that psychologically and subjectively *(materialiter et subjective)* they were totally involved in the writing of Scripture.[96] These two salient features of the doctrine of inspiration must be held in tension. Both points are clearly inferred from the common Biblical refrain that God speaks through the prophets and apostles and puts His Word in their mouth. (Deut. 18:18; Is. 51:16; Jer. 1:9; Matt. 10:20; 1 Cor. 2:12-13)[97]

Now it may seem utterly inconsistent that the Spirit of God could in one and the same action provide the very words of Scripture and accommodate Himself to the linguistic peculiarities and total personality of the individual writer so that these men wrote freely and spontaneously. But this is precisely what took place according to the Biblical evidence and data. And if Scripture does not inform us how both of these facts can be true, we must not do violence to either or try to probe the mystery of inspiration beyond what has been revealed. The Lutheran teachers are well aware that there is a lacuna in their theology at this point (just as there is a lacuna in their doctrine of conversion, which is at once exclusively God's operation and also man's own change of heart and deep spiritual experience); and they are content to retain this logical gap and accept the paradox.

d. ATTACKS ON INSPIRATION. Although it is paradoxical, as we have shown, the Lutheran doctrine of inspiration is set forth with a clarity that defies misunderstanding. And yet the doctrine has been misunderstood and consequently misrepresented again and again. Indeed no other doctrine of classical Lutheran orthodoxy has been the object of such gross misrepresentation and violent attack as the monergistic doctrine of inspiration. As far as I have been able to ascertain, the criticism of the doctrine has been due either to a rejection of the doctrine of accommodation as nonsense or mere subterfuge,[98] or to a failure to acknowledge the importance of this doctrine and to recognize the paradoxical nature of inspiration. Thus Luthardt pictured the old Lutheran doctrine of inspiration as ignoring the mental activity of the Biblical writers.[99] Dorner accused the Lutheran doctrine of destroying the individuality of the Biblical writers and withdrawing them from living reality.[100] Cremer rep-

resents the Lutheran doctrine as a mechanical inspiration, lacking only ecstasy to be a renewal of the magic doctrine of Philo.[101] Self-preparation of the writers is no longer necessary, he said. And on such a theory there is no room for personal witness.

Unfortunately the distorted conclusions of these 19th-century theologians were uncritically accepted by most of the succeeding historians and theologians, who had neither time nor inclination to read the old Lutheran theologians. In a more recent day Elert[102] has continued this same line of criticism and, if anything, has gone further. In a discussion entitled "The Inadequacy of the Inspiration Doctrine," after conjecturing without any basis that the Lutheran doctrine was borrowed from Calvin and Trent (of all things), Elert contends that the monergistic doctrine is unable to explain Paul's forgetfulness in 1 Cor. 1:16, his distinction between his own command and the command of the Lord (1 Cor. 7:12), and his reference to his own personal judgment (1 Cor. 7:40). Nor is the old Lutheran doctrine compatible with the fact that Luke investigated sources before writing his Gospel (Luke 1:3). And why? Because Quenstedt and the other Lutherans taught a dictation theory of inspiration. Elert's polemic is climaxed by the inexplicable charge that Quenstedt's doctrine borders on blasphemy.

Thus we see a doctrine based on Scripture confused with a psychological theory and the old Lutheran theologians accused of an aberration that in their day they were the first to reject. In the final analysis it is no doubt the monergistic doctrine of inspiration, which sets Scripture above all human criticism, that has annoyed our modern theologians and precipitated so much criticism. I can only hope that the present study may help to explode the myth of mechanical inspiration that has been associated with orthodox Lutheran theology once and for all, and dissociate classical Lutheranism from the fictitious heterodoxy that has been attributed to it.

6. *Inspiration and Revelation*

The orthodox Lutherans do not confuse inspiration and revelation, as has been sometimes alleged,[103] but carefully distinguish between the two. Inspiration pertains only to the Holy Scriptures and to the writers of Scripture. Revelation is something far broader in its scope and can denote many things.[104] The term, taken materially *(materialiter)*, may signify

The Inspiration of Scripture

the things God has made known; or taken formally *(formaliter)*, it may denote God's act of revealing. Understood materially, it may be taken in the broad sense as everything God has revealed, even in the realm of nature (Rom. 1:19); or it can be taken as that which God has made known by a very special and supernatural activity, namely, the mystery of the Gospel. Often the term refers to the final appearing of Christ. Furthermore, God's revelation has taken place in a great variety of ways: by theophany and personal encounter, by dreams and visions, by the Urim and the Thummim in the breastplate of Aaron (Ex. 28:30), by external deeds, or by the mouth of a prophet. And finally God has revealed Himself hypostatically (αὐτοπροσώπως) in the person of the Son (John 1:18). Today God's revelation is found in Scripture, which is more than a mere account of revelation; Scripture is a revelation or, more accurately, God's revelation committed to writing.[105] Thus, God reveals Himself also today, but mediately through His Word in Scripture.[106] Today God's church should look for God's supernatural revelation only in Scripture, for apart from Scripture and the preached Word there is today only false enthusiasm.[107]

But if revelation and inspiration are two distinct and different concepts, they are nevertheless related to each other as they have to do with Scripture. We recall how Calov, in speaking of Scripture, spoke of inspiration as the form of revelation. In such contexts Calov is thinking of revelation as a communication from God and therefore as a word of communication — a word that in the nature of the case is God-breathed. According to a statement of Quenstedt's, it would appear that inspiration is at times considered to be one of the various modes of revelation:

> We must distinguish between divine revelation and inspiration. Formally and by virtue of its name, revelation is the disclosure of something unknown and hidden, and it can take place in many and various ways, through external speech or through dreams and visions (for "to reveal," ἀποκαλύπτειν in Greek, is to uncover something that was hidden). Inspiration is an act of the Holy Spirit whereby the actual knowledge of things is communicated supernaturally to the created intellect, or it is an inner suggestion or infusion of concepts, whether the concepts were known or unknown prior to the writing. The former (revelation) could antedate writing, the latter was concomitant with writing and was a part of the very writing itself. However, I do not deny that the same θεοπνευστία or divine inspiration can be called revelation according to this idea, that is, insofar as

it is a manifestation of certain circumstances as well as of the arrangement and method by which facts were written and set down, and also when revelation concurs and coincides with divine inspiration itself, namely, when divine mysteries are revealed by inspiration and inspired by revelation in the same writing.[108]

It must be borne in mind that for Lutheran theology revelation has always been an auxiliary concept. As we have mentioned, no full and formal treatment of revelation as a *locus* was ever offered. And we might ask whether the Lutherans did not purposely refrain from working out a *locus* on revelation in the light of the scant use of the term in Scripture and its wide range of meaning. But this does not mean that the idea of revelation was neglected. On the contrary, the terms *revelation* and *reveal* occur thousands of times in the writings of the orthodox Lutherans, and the subject of revelation touches on every aspect of their theology, especially in the sections on Scripture, on God as hidden and revealed and our knowledge of God, and in particular in the discussions revolving around Law and Gospel. In fact, all revelation may be summed up as revelation of Law and Gospel.

But just as Law and Gospel are vastly different, they are revealed in different ways. The orthodox Lutherans repeatedly stress that the Gospel is in no sense contained in a general revelation. However wide the range of general revelation, it is restricted to the Law. When the Lutheran theologians speak, as they often do, of God revealing His will, they usually have in mind a revelation of God and His will in terms of Law and Gospel.[109] But the revelation of the Gospel is infinitely higher than the revelation of the Law. It is God's revelation κατ' ἐξοχήν. In His Gospel Word, which centers in Christ and proclaims forgiveness and peace, God has revealed many things that could never be known in any other way:[110] His hidden wisdom (Eph. 3:10), the riches of His grace (Eph. 1:7), His righteousness from faith to faith (Rom. 1:17), His power (1 Cor. 1:24), and His truthfulness (Rom. 15:8). This final Word of His revelation God speaks ἐν τῷ υἱῷ, not merely in order that we might know a doctrine that is advanced by His Son, but that we might know the doctrine *of* His Son, who is in the bosom of the Father. Thus God reveals His gracious will that we might know Him. But strictly speaking, the Gospel alone is revelation, for the grace of God can only be known through the Gospel. Unlike the Law, the Gospel "is not a doctrine known naturally

by reason; but a mystery hidden for centuries, which the Son of God declared."[111] This is clearly the import of such passages as Rom. 1:17 and Gal. 1:12, according to Chemnitz. He says: "The doctrine of the Law is in some way known naturally to reason; but the Gospel is a mystery hidden for centuries and revealed only by the ministry of the Spirit."[112] Again he says: "There is one Law, and this is known by nature to all pagans and to all generations. And there is one Gospel, but this is not known by nature but is only divinely revealed. Therefore Paul calls it a mystery, which has been hid [Col. 1:26; Rom. 16:25], and John says that the Son who is in the bosom of the Father has declared it to us [John 1:18]."[113]

All that Chemnitz has said — and similar statements may be found in all the Lutheran theologians — is quite in keeping with the Lutheran insistence that the purpose of all revelation is doxological and soteriological. When the Lutherans say that the purpose of revelation is to inform man, they do not have in mind anything resembling a mere "rectification of false conceptions," as Elert suggests.[114] The purpose of revelation is precisely the same as the purpose of the Gospel: it is to glorify God's redemptive work in Christ and to bring us justification, reconciliation with God, and eternal salvation.[115]

It has been said that the Lutheran dogmaticians "by their strong and almost exclusive emphasis on the divine revelation as doctrine almost completely forgot what is fundamental, namely, the revelation by deed."[116] This is not true. In the first place, Lutheran theology almost never speaks of the revelation of doctrine except by implication in such stereotyped phrases as *"theologia revelata"* and in the references to the revelation of Law and Gospel. Rather the Lutheran theologians, as we have seen, prefer to speak of God as revealing Himself and His will. But actually the revelation of God and the revelation of the Gospel are the same revelation. In the second place, if it seems as if the orthodox Lutherans did not emphasize revelation as deed, it is only because they do not make a point of linking the term *revelation* with the deeds of God, but with the Gospel, which is the record of those deeds and their significance and, in a sense, a continuation of those deeds. Usually the old Lutherans call the mighty acts of God in history His miracles (e. g., the Exodus, the Resurrection), and these miracles and signs in turn are called "testimonies," "witnesses," of God's judgment and grace. They could just as well be called revelations of God's judgment and grace.

The Authority of Scripture

As a Word that is God-breathed, Scripture carries with it the authority, the truthfulness, and the power of God Himself. The divine properties of Scripture (authority, sufficiency, clarity, inerrancy, and power) result from its divine origin, and they stand or fall with the inspiration of Scripture. In offering evidence for these attributes of Scripture, the orthodox theologians appeal again and again to its divine origin. Indeed the primary purpose of orthodox Lutheranism in expending so much effort to show the inspiration of Scripture is to support these divine properties of Scripture, and especially the principle of *sola Scriptura*.

1. *The Nature and Extent of Scripture's Authority*

The lengthy discussions of the authority of Scripture that occupy a place in all Lutheran dogmatics during the period of orthodoxy are really amplifications of the implications of the *sola Scriptura* principle. In these discussions the Lutheran theologians attempt to determine and define the nature and the extent of Scripture's authority.

The authority of Scripture is that property by which it requires faith and obedience to all its declarations. This authority is not based on its antiquity or the reliability of the human authors or any external standard of judgment, but alone on the fact that it is God's Word. Scripture's authority is the authority of very God. "The authority of the Holy Scriptures and the authority of God are one and the same, although the one pertains to God and the other to Scripture. The authority of God is by Him and of Him. The authority of Scripture is due to a unique decree of God and to the fact that it was written by divine inspiration."[117] Thus, the authority of Scripture cannot be questioned, enhanced, or disparaged by the church, by human reason, or by any extra-Biblical evidence of any kind. Its divine authority is intrinsic, self-contained, and absolute. Scripture is, in the words of Dannhauer, "a light in itself, a principium that requires no proof, and a revelation in which the highest knowledge of all divine truth finds its attainment."[118]

In order to emphasize the infallible and absolute nature of Scripture, the orthodox Lutherans after the time of Gerhard were accustomed to speak of the αὐτοπιστία of Scripture. Calov explains precisely what the αὐτοπιστία of Scripture is:

Every Word of God is ἀξιόπιστος and αὐτόπιστος and must be be-

lieved per se simply because it is the Word of God, because God has declared it and said it, even though our reason may not understand or grasp it. This is demanded by the divine authority and unfailing truth of the divine Word. Because it is the Word of very God, it has a divine authority that is under no obligation to give an account of itself, and it is above every limitation and worthy of faith per se. It must be accepted by faith per se, not on account of something else, because God cannot receive authority from another. Because it is the infallible truth of God, our faith must be grounded in it unquestionably. Everything recorded in Scripture is the Word of God. If it says in Scripture that God became man, that Christ made atonement for us, that the Son of God made reconciliation, we must by all means accept that as the Word of God and put our faith in it because it is contained in Scripture.[119]

With fewer words Gerhard makes the same claim:

Now because the author of Scripture is God, by whose direct inspiration the prophets, evangelists, and apostles wrote, it also possesses divine authority. Because Scripture is θεόπνευστος, brought about and produced by divine inspiration, it is also αὐτόπιστος, τὸ πιστὸν ἀφ' ἑαυτῆς ἔξουσα.[120]

The implications of this rigid position are obvious. Every declaration of Scripture must be accepted a priori. Scientific, historical, or other rational enquiry cannot disprove the truthfulness or delimit the authority of Scripture. Not only the judgments of deductive reasoning but the judgments of inductive reasoning and all empirical investigation as well are incompetent to pass any critical opinion on the reliability of any Biblical utterance. It is clear that the Lutheran doctrine of the αὐτοπιστία of Scripture rules out much in the approach of our modern historico-critical method as it is applied to Scripture. And we must not suppose that the orthodox Lutherans were merely stubborn or naïve or children of their day in taking such a rigid stand. There was enough of the critical spirit in Socinianism and other heresies of their day, as we shall see, to make them well aware of the various antitheses to their position.

As was already mentioned, the authority of Scripture is predicated on the basis of Scripture's divine inspiration and nature. Thus every testimony of the divine origin of Scripture (2 Tim. 3:16; 1 Cor. 2:14; 1 Thess. 2:13; etc.) is evidence of its unqualified authority. A great deal of weight was also placed on the complete submission of Christ and the apostles to the authority of Scripture as God speaking (John 5:39; Acts 3:21, 24;

8:14; 17:11; 26:22; Eph. 2:20; etc.). However another very important consideration entered into the Lutheran doctrine of the authority of Scripture; it was that any and every attempt to reduce or condition the authority of Scripture constitutes the open resistance against God and defiance of His lordship of which all men are so terribly prone. There is no alternative to the authority of God speaking. As man stands before the speaking God, he must renounce all human authority and autonomy, he must renounce himself and his Old Adam, which is a *habitus destructivus,* destructive of all spiritual wisdom and understanding. The only possible response to God speaking is faith. And this response always involves casting down reasonings and every high thing that exalts itself against the knowledge of God; it always involves the painfully humiliating, mortifying *sacrificium intellectus,* so repugnant to all men. To bow to the authority of Scripture often means believing in what the natural reason of man considers impossible and absurd. It is Calov's conviction that "if our mind and intellect are to be taken captive in obedience to faith, then it is necessary for us to believe even if we cannot assent with our mind, nay, even if we are persuaded in our mind that what we believe is false." [121] The burden of such passages as Is. 7:9, 2 Cor. 10:4-5, and Rom. 8:7 that belong in a discussion of the authority of Scripture is that man's νοήματα contend against faith. Therefore it is absolutely necessary for us to take our mind and thoughts captive to the Scriptures. The slightest failure to do this undermines not only the authority of Scripture but the very nature of Christian faith as *fides divina.* "If faith were to be determined according to the judgment of reason, then the final appeal would rest in the judgment of reason, and faith would no longer be a divine certainty, but a human opinion." Thus man's slightest diminution of the authority of Scripture reflects a failure to grasp the Biblical testimony concerning man and sin and faith and grace.

The Lutheran insistence on the a priori acceptance of the αὐτοπιστία of Scripture was directed against two formidable adversaries, the Socinians and the Jesuits. The Socinians argued at great length for the authority of Scripture but not as a matter of principle derived from its divine inspiration.[122] Rather they demonstrated the authority of Scripture completely on the basis of what they considered to be valid a posteriori evidence, e. g., the antiquity of the Biblical books, the authenticity of these writings, and the reliability of the Biblical writers as witnesses. The

Socinian view, which was in advance of its day and closely approximates the approach of much Biblical theology today, assumed that the writers of Scripture were inspired children of their time and necessarily accommodated themselves to many commonly held errors in matters of science, chronology, geography, etc. But the Biblical message was essentially reliable and doctrinally sound. Scripture commanded the same measure of authority that one could attribute to the various authors themselves. It possessed a high and noble human authority.

The wide cleavage between this position and the Lutheran doctrine of authority is at once apparent. The attempt to verify the authority of Scripture by the scientific method proceeds from the assumption that the authority of Scripture is only probable and subjects the authority of Scripture to the results of human investigation. Hence all theological conclusions can be no more than probable. "If the source of theology is not at all times infallible, trustworthy, and entirely above human criticism, but in certain matters is only probable and of limited application, then there are no theological conclusions that are infallible and absolute, since it is impossible that a conclusion can be more certain than its own one legitimate source." [123] In addition to violating the αὐτοπιστία of Scripture, the Socinian position naïvely but inevitably leads one down the one-way road to skepticism.

In contrast to the Socinian position, the Roman Catholic theologians with whom the Lutherans carried on their conversations held to the divine authority of Scripture. However, this authority belonged to Scripture only per se and in an absolute sense. As far as we are concerned *(quoad nos)* the testimony of the church is needed to establish the authority of Scripture. This by no means implies that the authority of Scripture was somehow dependent on a merely human authority, for the authority of the church was divine and the church's testimony a divine revelation.[124] From the time of Chemnitz all the Lutheran theologians occupy themselves with refuting this fundamental Roman Catholic claim, and a great deal of polemics was devoted to this task. The *status controversiae* between Lutheran theology and Romanism, as Gerhard sees it,[125] lies not so much in the authority of Scripture as in the authority of the church and in the source of Scripture's authority. If the authority of Scripture depends on the testimony of the church, then Scripture's authority is no longer absolute, and it is vitiated.

Briefly the case for the Lutheran doctrine of the authority of Scripture against Roman claims rests on two very simple and basic arguments. First, the Lutheran theologians contend that Scripture derives its authority and majesty from God alone, who is the author of Scripture.[126] Scripture was written by inspired penmen before and apart from the judgment of the church.[127] For instance, Paul did not need the testimony of the church before his word was accepted as God's Word. The Thessalonians (1 Thess. 2:13) are praised because they accepted the apostle's word as having God's authority; and no mention of the church's imprimatur is introduced.[128] Paul's letter to the Romans was authentic and αὐτόπιστος in itself before the church added its testimony.[129] If Scripture did not require the authority of the church then to establish its claims, it does not need the church today.[130] The authority of any writing depends on its author, not on its readers or custodians; and God, not the church, is the author of Scripture.

The nature of the church as well as the nature of Scripture indicates that the authority of Scripture does not depend on the church. "The church," says Hollaz, "is not the lord but the servant of Scripture; not the mother but the daughter; not the author but the guardian, witness, and interpreter; not the judge but the one who testifies of and vindicates Scripture."[131] To be sure, the church has been called upon to judge doctrine and has the authority to do so. But the church must carry out this obligation on the basis of Scripture. Thus, it is not *propter ecclesiam* but *per ecclesiam* that we believe the testimony of Scripture and acknowledge its authority. The church cannot create faith in Christ or the Scriptures but can only urge such faith. Scripture, however, as the Word of God has the inherent power to enlighten our intellect and move our will (Ps. 19:7-8; John 6:63; Rom. 1:16; 1 Cor. 1:18; 2 Tim. 3:15); it is able not only to create faith but to create faith in itself.[132]

2. External and Internal Criteria of Scripture

How does one become convinced of the authority of Scripture? There are, according to Lutheran dogmatics, a number of criteria, both external and internal, that testify to the divine authority of Scripture. Such criteria are capable of convincing the unbeliever who does not harden himself that Scripture is a unique and divinely inspired Word; however these

criteria are able to effect only a human opinion or conviction *(fides humana)* concerning the authority of Scripture, not a genuine Christian faith *(fides divina)*.

Among the external criteria are the following: (a) the antiquity of Scripture, (b) the spiritual insight of the human authors and their concern for the truth, (c) the miracles of Christ and the apostles, which accompanied their preaching and authenticate their message, (d) the faithfulness of the church to the Biblical message over the centuries, (e) the constancy of countless martyrs and the perseverance of the church of Christ in times of persecution, (f) the swift propagation of the Christian faith throughout the world, (g) the personal experience of those who have experienced the impact of Scripture, repented, and prayed, (h) the tragic end of blasphemers, tyrants, and all enemies of Scripture. We notice that these criteria are similar to those employed by Chytraeus to support our certainty of the Christian religion.[133] These external criteria are able to break down some of the barriers that hinder the unbeliever from accepting Scripture, but they can accomplish no more. They can only pave the way for Scripture to testify concerning itself.

The internal criteria that may convince us of Scripture's divine authority are the following: (a) the depth of the mysteries revealed in Scripture, (b) the majesty of God speaking to us in Scripture, (c) the truthfulness of Scripture, (d) the sufficiency of the teachings and precepts of Scripture, (e) the profound and yet simple manner in which Scripture speaks to us, (f) the power of Scripture to bend the hearts of sinful men and give them hope, (g) the fact that Scripture has maintained its authority in the face of time and opposition, (h) the remarkable harmony between the Old and the New Testament. Again the Lutheran theologians for the most part maintain that these inner criteria can work only a human faith in Scripture's authority. However, later Lutherans such as Hollaz and John Osiander affirm that the internal criteria of Scripture are able to bring about a true faith and divine certainty in the divine origin and authority of Scripture, and this because these criteria are nothing more than the divine form of Scripture itself. Hence Hollaz and Osiander are affirming no more than the self-authenticating power, the αὐτοπιστία of Scripture itself, what Hollaz calls the causative authority of Scripture to create faith in its own divine message and authority.[134]

3. The Inner Witness of the Holy Spirit

But if we cannot become certain of Scripture's authority by its criteria, as was taught until the time of Osiander, how may we gain such certainty? The answer is that Scripture must convince us of its own authority. Or putting the reply somewhat differently, the Holy Spirit works through Scripture to convince us that Scripture is the Word of God and authoritative. Huelsemann sums up the Lutheran position as follows: "The ultimate reason why and on account of which we believe this Word with a Christian certainty and a divinely awakened faith, and believe that this Word in itself is true, is God who reveals and who authenticates His revelation. The reason is not the integrity of the ministering causes, it is not the conformity of Scripture with our intellect and common sense, nor is it the consensus of the well-known doctors of the church."[135] This *testimonium Spiritus Sancti internum* by which the Spirit moves and enlightens our hearts to believe the Scriptures and promises of God is never something immediate but always *per verbum*.[136] It is, like faith, the work of the Spirit in the believer's heart; and it is also the work of the Scripture itself.

Some theologians[137] have found a fundamental difference between the earlier Lutheran dogmaticians who emphasize the inner testimony of the Holy Spirit and later theologians such as Calov who stressed the self-authenticating property of Scripture itself as the cause of our believing in the divine authority of Scripture.[138] But there is really no difference on this point except in emphasis. All the Lutheran theologians faithfully teach that the Holy Spirit works through the Scriptures in bringing us to acknowledge their authority — not through every word and phrase of Scripture, to be sure, but through the inspired meaning, which is not lost in translation.[139] Furthermore, all the Lutheran theologians stress that the work of the Spirit and the work of the Word in this regard, as in the work of conversion itself, is not two operations but one work, one unity of operation.[140] There is for later Lutheran dogmatics, as for Luther, a perpetual unity between the Spirit and the Word of God. In all spiritual effects that are worked in men the Word of God operates organically and instrumentally, while God Himself is the principal agent.[141]

Another, more serious, complaint is brought against the Lutheran doctrine that the *testimonium Spiritus Sancti internum* certifies the authority of Scripture. It is alleged that this doctrine, which is taken from

Calvin,[142] ignores what is more important, namely, the testimony of the Holy Spirit in witnessing to the believer that he is a child of God.[143] This complaint is not altogether justified. When Lutheran orthodoxy offers Biblical support for the doctrine of the inner testimony of the Holy Spirit, such passages as 1 John 5:6, Rom. 1:16, John 6:63, 1 Thess. 1:5-6, and 1 Thess. 2:13 are cited. Such passages speak of general spiritual effects that are wrought in man by the witness of the Spirit, among which effects are faith itself, the conscious certainty of faith, and a confidence in the power and authority of the Scriptures. Hollaz sums up his definition of the *testimonium Spiritus Sancti internum* without any allusion to the Holy Scriptures, saying merely that the believer truly feels that the Word of God has been communicated to him by God Himself.[144] In other words, my belief in the authority of Scripture is only a part of the total effect of the Spirit's witness in me, a part that assumes importance at the present particular juncture in Lutheran dogmatics. We must in the case of some of the dogmaticians wait until the section on soteriology to gain a more complete picture of the Spirit's testimony in the life of the believer. As Hollaz makes very clear, however, confidence in the authority of Scripture can never be divorced from faith in the Gospel; certainty in Scripture's authority is a usual concomitant of the certainty of faith.

But if it is the Spirit of God alone who through the Scriptures convinces us of their authority, why the great emphasis on the criteria of Scripture that we find in the earlier dogmaticians? At best these criteria can produce only an intellectual assent *(fides humana)* to the divine origin and authority of Scripture. The emphasis no doubt springs from an attempt to make the authority of Scripture reasonable and knowable. Such a procedure is highly questionable, for it invariably tends to minimize the importance of the witness of the Holy Spirit and the αὐτοπιστία of Scripture, which alone can work a faith in Scripture's authority. Here we have one of the most unfortunate concessions to rationalism in the theology of Lutheran orthodoxy. For the power of Scripture and the witness of the Holy Spirit that is faith in my heart rule out any necessity or validity for observable criteria, although these criteria for the authority of Scripture might be mentioned as points of interest.

4. *Scripture as the Norm of Doctrine*

As a result of its divine character and authority Scripture is to be the only norm of doctrine in the church and the only judge in all controversy.

For this reason God obligates His church to settle all doctrinal controversy by Scripture alone. And this was actually the practice of Christ and the apostles (Matt. 4:4; 19:4; 22:29; Mark 9:12; Luke 10:26; 24:27; Acts 3:22; 7:2; 13:33; 26:22). The reforms of Josiah and Hezekiah were brought about by a return to the Word of God as the only norm of doctrine. The Bereans (Acts 17:11) are commended for examining all doctrine according to the rule of Scripture alone and for judging doctrine from no other point of view than from Scripture alone. In the church all is subordinate to Scripture; the judgment of Scripture is the judgment of God. It is true that "in a human legal process no one can act as plaintiff, witness, and judge at the same time, but in the divine judgment that is exercised through Scriptures all these roles are united." [145]

The intense Lutheran and Roman Catholic debate concerning the authority of Scripture resulted in three drawn-out but subordinate skirmishes that must now be mentioned briefly.

5. *The Canonicity of Scripture*

First, Roman theology in its polemic against the *sola Scriptura* principle and in the interest of ecclesiastical authority maintained that the canon of Scripture was determined by the church. The canon was an article of faith that was not to be found in Scripture but was established by the church. The Lutheran theologians replied that such a position was destructive of both the inspiration and divine authority of Scripture. Gerhard and those who follow maintain that the canon is not an article of faith. Moses and the prophets and apostles did not by their writing construct a new article of faith. It is true that all Christian doctrine is drawn from the canonical Scriptures. But the canon as such, viewed as a certain number of books, is not an article of faith but the source and norm of all articles of faith. Furthermore, the church does not determine the canon. God has established the canon: a book of Scripture is canonical by virtue of its inspiration. The church witnesses to this fact, and insofar as she does so can make a beginning toward convincing us that certain books are canonical; but ultimately the Scripture must testify of itself, and the Holy Spirit must convince us through the Scriptures. What long ago persuaded the hearers of the Word to believe the preaching of the prophets and apostles now persuades us to believe their writings. Gerhard sums up his position as follows:

> We therefore believe the canonical Scriptures because they are the canonical Scriptures, that is, because they have been brought about by God and written by the direct inspiration of the Holy Spirit. And we do not believe them because the church testifies concerning them. . . . The canonical books are the source of our faith. From this source the church itself and all its authority must be proved. One believes in a principium because of itself, not because of something else. True, a principium can be demonstrated a posteriori, but it cannot be proved by something intrinsically prior to it; otherwise it would not be a principium. We must choose one of two alternatives: either the church or Scripture is the source of our faith and religion. We believe the church insofar as it agrees with Scripture, which is the voice of God; we do not believe in Scripture because of the church, that is, the testimony of men, but because of itself, because it is the voice of God.[146]

In their insistence that God has created the canon, Gerhard, Hutter, Brochmand, and their followers are stressing a most important fact; but at the same time they tend to ignore history and the testimony of the early church as it led to the acceptance of the New Testament canon. Against the decisions of the Council of Trent Chemnitz had argued that history forces the church to leave the New Testament canon open and take the problem of the antilegomena seriously. This is the position of Heerbrand, Giles Hunnius, Hafenreffer, and the other Lutheran theologians until about the turn of the 17th century.[147] The later dogmaticians still retained a distinction between the antilegomena and homologoumena; but they never doubted the inspiration of the former, only the authorship. To them the antilegomena were on a much higher plain than the apocryphal books of the Old Testament, whereas Giles Hunnius and other earlier theologians had called the antilegomena apocryphal books of the New Testament. From the time of Gerhard there was no hesitancy in quoting from the antilegomena. For all practical purposes the antilegomena were canonical.[148] The reason for the uncritical change of position we find in the later dogmaticians is undoubtedly due to their fear of allowing a historical judgment concerning the authenticity of authorship of a book to affect saving faith. To them the canon must remain above all historical and ecclesiastical judgment. The testimony of history in respect to the authorship of an anonymous book such as Matthew cannot be made a matter of doctrine. Thus we observe that in its polemic against Rome, in its attempt to maintain that the canon was created by the Spirit of

God and not the church, Lutheran theology grossly oversimplifies the problem of the New Testament canon and fails to be faithful to the historical data.

We must not suppose, however, that because inspiration (attested by the Holy Spirit) is the crucial and decisive criterion of canonicity, it is the only criterion for later Lutheran orthodoxy. Calov lists a number of criteria for canonicity. To be canonical a book must be inspired by the Holy Spirit. It must be written by prophets or apostles. It must contain divine mysteries. It must be written in Hebrew or Greek. It must enjoy the recognition of the Hebrew or the Christian church, and it must have been in use in the ancient church.[149] Christocentricity is also a criterion mentioned by the orthodox Lutheran theologians.[150]

6. *The Authenticity of the Hebrew and Greek Texts of Scripture*

A second subordinate controversy that resulted from the antithesis between Lutheran and Roman Catholic theologians concerning the authority of Scripture centered in the authenticity of the texts of Scripture. The Roman Catholic theologians generally argued that our present Hebrew and Greek texts of the Scriptures contain many corruptions and perversions because of the carelessness and failings of copyists over the centuries. Such a skeptical position was no doubt motivated by the desire to enhance the value and authority of the Vulgate version, which had been pronounced authoritative by the Council of Trent.[151]

The Lutheran reply in defense of the authenticity of the apographal texts was most thorough indeed.[152] Certainly there can be no talk of corruptions in the Old Testament before Christ, for both He and the apostles showed confidence in the Scriptures of their day and commended them for use. After Christ there were indeed errors made by copyists out of ignorance or carelessness. But there was no general corruption of the Scriptures. A comparison of the extant manuscripts with all the variant readings bears out this fact. The variant readings are generally of a technical nature and of little importance, such as omissions, transpositions, spellings, and the like, and can be easily corrected. Moreover, the vigilance of both Jews and Christians after Christ and the reverence of both parties toward their Scriptures precludes the possibility of any general corruption taking place. Finally the church has every right to believe that God in

His goodness and providence will keep His Word in the church inviolate and unimpaired.

Having given lengthy and sound arguments for the authenticity and reliability of the apographal texts of Scripture, the Lutheran dogmaticians go on the offensive, attacking the Roman claim that the Latin Vulgate version should be regarded as authentic and normative. This was the real nub of the debate. It was the Lutheran view that only the original Hebrew and Greek Scriptures were authentic and possessed canonical authority in the church, for only the Hebrew and Greek Scriptures were inspired.[153] The extant apographa are today authentic because they contain not merely the content but the very words of the original Scriptures. A copy of any document is as valid and normative as the original. Translations, on the other hand, preserve at best only the divine meaning of Scripture, since the words are given in a different idiom. Produced as they are by fallible men, versions cannot be considered authentic but must be judged always according to the original text of Scripture. A version, such as the Vulgate, cannot command more authority than the text on which it is based. Thus in any controversy appeal must always be made to the apographal Hebrew and Greek Scriptures.

Underlying the debate concerning the authenticity of Scripture was the antithesis between Roman and Lutheran theology regarding the authority of Scripture and the authority of the church. The Lutheran position was very simple: just as the church cannot create the canon, it cannot decree a particular version of Scripture to be authentic. Authenticity, like canonicity, is due to God's act of inspiration.[154] The foundation of Scripture's authority is God, not the church.

7. *The Authenticity of the Hebrew Vowel Points*

A third dispute arising out of the controversy over authority between Lutherans and Jesuits had to do with the authenticity of the vowel points of the Hebrew Scriptures. In the 16th and 17th centuries most of the Lutheran and Reformed theologians believed that the vowel points were coeval with the autographic Hebrew Scriptures.[155] This may seem strange in the light of conclusions Hebrew scholars had come to almost a century earlier. Elias Levita (1468—1549), celebrated Hebrew scholar and grammarian and friend of Reuchlin, had convincingly shown in his *Massoreth Ha-Massoreth* that the Hebrew vowel pointing was not Mosaic or even from the time

of Ezra, but post-Talmudic. Levita did not question the validity of the vowel sounds, but only the vowel signs. The same view was advanced by Nicholas of Lyra, who however impugned also the authority of the vowel signs. Lyra was followed by Luther, Zwingli, Calvin, and Beza, as well as by most of the Roman Catholics of the day.

Why then did the later Lutheran and Reformed theologians argue for the concurrence of the Hebrew vowel points and the original Scriptures? It was not because a new theory of verbal inspiration had developed, as some scholars have uncritically suggested.[156] The reason for the Lutheran theologians, beginning with Flacius, changing their position was twofold. First, Roman Catholic controversialists, by championing the late origin of the vowel points, saw a way of exalting the authority of the Vulgate above that of the Masoretic text.[157] Furthermore, the late introduction of pointing showed, according to the Jesuits, that the Lutherans and the Reformed theologians were every bit as dependent on tradition (hundreds of years of oral tradition among the Jews) as the Roman Catholics. There is no question that such a polemic, which of course proved too much, goaded Flacius and Gerhard and the later dogmaticians into taking a strong opposing position without sufficiently weighing the arguments of Levita and, later, of the French Reformed scholar Louis Capellus, who purely for the sake of scholarship continued and elaborated Levita's position.

Second, the later Lutherans labored under a false linguistic principle that an adequate written representation of words required some sort of vowel symbol. They gave entirely too much credence to the specious argument of the Jesuits that an unpointed text could not present clear and unequivocal meaning. Like the Jesuits they assumed that vowels could not be implied but must be represented in writing. They believed it impossible that vowels could be supplied by the readers of Scripture; such a procedure, they concluded, would be too taxing on the memory of individual readers or of the Israelites as a whole; only confusion could result.[158] They did not realize that words, and thoughts as well, could be represented otherwise than by alphabetical symbols, so that the reader's memory was not overly strained. They did not understand that the Hebrew writing system, strictly speaking, was not an alphabet but a consonant syllabary, which did not represent or need to represent vowels with specific symbols.

That the doctrine of verbal inspiration had nothing to do with the

The Sufficiency of Scripture

Lutheran view regarding the antiquity of the Hebrew vowel points is obvious from the genesis and direction of the controversy concerning vowel points. It is obvious also from the fact that Leonard Hutter, for instance, who definitely taught the orthodox doctrine of inspiration, denied that the vowel points were contemporaneous with the original texts of the Old Testament Scriptures.[159] And among the later dogmaticians Dannhauer leaves the matter open, although he personally held to the popular opinion of his day.[160] He suggested, as Levita had done, that even if pointing itself was not coeval with the autographic Scriptures, the vowels were nevertheless understood and implied in the Hebrew script and thus inspired.

The controversy over the age of Hebrew vowel points is one of those sterile chapters in the history of Christian thought, a controversy in which both parties argued from prejudice and polemical interests and that brought no blessing to anyone.

THE SUFFICIENCY OF SCRIPTURE

In their conversations with Rome concerning the authority of Scripture all the Lutheran theologians from the time of the Reformation were led into a discussion of the sufficiency, or perfection, of Scripture. Indeed, the entire doctrine of Biblical authority in Lutheran theology stands or falls with Scripture's sufficiency.

By *sufficiency* Lutheran theology meant that Scripture contains everything that one must believe to be saved and everything one must do to live a God-pleasing life. Everything necessary for faith and life is stated in Scripture either expressly (αὐτολεξεί) or by implication with clear consequences being drawn from what is expressly written (*quoad verba κατὰ τὴν διάνοιαν*).[161] The sufficiency of Scripture is not absolute: Scripture does not contain all theological truth; God knows more theology (archetypal theology) than He has revealed in Scripture.[162] Rather the sufficiency of Scripture is restricted; Scripture is sufficient in reference to its end, which is faith in Christ and eternal salvation.[163] Neither is Scripture perfect in the sense that it offers us a complete system of doctrine, logical and valid for every age. There are paradoxes, logical and historical gaps *(lacunae)* in Scripture. Moreover, the perfection of Scripture resides in Scripture as a whole; not every book of Scripture contains every article

of faith.¹⁶⁴ But on the other hand the sufficiency of Scripture is a *sufficientia exclusiva:* nothing except Scripture can be allowed to determine doctrine and instruct us in what we are to believe and do as Christians, neither church councils nor tradition nor any other standard. We see from the foregoing that the sufficiency of Scripture and the principle of *sola Scriptura* are correlative. To affirm the authority of Scripture as the one *principium cognoscendi* infers the sufficiency of Scripture.

Much the same Biblical support is offered for the sufficiency as for the authority of Scripture. Actually such passages as Rom. 15:4 and John 20:31, which speak of the purpose of Scripture to bring the sinner to faith in Christ and eternal life, postulate the sufficiency of Scripture.¹⁶⁵ An imperfect or ambiguous Scripture would frustrate the very end to which Scripture was written. Also the prohibitions against adding to Scripture speak for the sufficiency of Scripture (Deut. 4:2; Prov. 30:5-6; Rev. 22: 18-19). Such prohibitions are not directed against the addition of canonical books from time to time, for God who creates the canon is not bound by such a decree; rather they forbid placing foreign doctrine beside the Scriptures. Paul is warning against much the same thing in Gal. 1:8 when he directs a curse against any who teach contrary to the Gospel. And to add to the Gospel is to teach contrary to it. Furthermore, the practice of Christ and the apostles in proving all doctrine from Scripture indicates that Scripture is sufficient.

The *sedes doctrinae* for the sufficiency of Scripture is 2 Tim. 3:15-16.¹⁶⁶ The inference drawn from this passage is that whatever is profitable for doctrine, reproof, and instruction to the end that one is made wise unto salvation is surely sufficient. That which renders the man of God fully equipped for every good work is surely perfect. Such sufficiency is the very purpose of the inspiration of Scripture that Paul speaks of in this passage. This perfection of Scripture does not, of course, pertain to every part of Scripture, but to Scripture as a whole. Such an interpretation of this passage leads to a difficulty. If the πᾶσα γραφή is to be taken distributively, as was the case when the passage was used to support the divine origin of Scripture, how can it be taken collectively as signifying the whole of Scripture now as the passage is used to support the perfection of Scripture? Calov attempts to explain this apparent discrepancy concerning the interpretation of πᾶσα in the following way. It is not impossible, he says, that the πᾶσα may be taken distributively in connection with

The Clarity of Scripture

the first predicate θεόπνευστος and collectively in connection with the second predicate ὠφέλιμος, as the immediate context and intent of the passage would seem to indicate. In other words, inspiration pertains to the whole of Scripture as well as to all its parts, and perfection pertains to the parts of Scripture as well as to the whole. For Scripture is a unit, and the parts cannot be dissociated from the whole. All passages of Scripture must be understood in their context and in the context of the general purpose of Scripture.[167] But whatever the difficulties connected with the interpretation of the πᾶσα, Paul's meaning is certainly clear in this passage. Calov concludes: "Inasmuch as Scripture is breathed by God to this end (that man might be made wise unto salvation) and inasmuch as its usefulness is directed to this same end, how can Scripture itself not be perfect and sufficient?"

It was almost invariably in a polemical tone that Lutheran theology dealt with the sufficiency of Scripture. The doctrine ran directly counter to the Roman claim concerning the authority of unwritten tradition. Roman theology claimed that Scripture was only a partial norm of faith. Only when supplemented by tradition could the Scriptures be considered a complete norm.[168] Thus tradition was placed beside Scripture as a basis for Christian doctrine, and teachings based on unwritten traditions were necessary to believe to be saved. The fourth session of the Council of Trent had articulated this principle, and the Jesuits became most adamant in upholding it. Here again, as in the debate concerning the *principium cognoscendi*, we observe how sharp the antithesis was and how hopeless was the possibility of rapprochement.

THE CLARITY OF SCRIPTURE

The Lutheran theologians of the 16th and 17th centuries all share Luther's confidence in the clarity of Scripture. The clarity of Scripture was not just a notion they casually inherited from the great Reformer but a principle of which they were fully persuaded. It was a principle that was closely bound to the sufficiency of Scripture. The sufficiency of Scripture could not possibly be maintained if Scripture was a dark and obscure book.

What did Lutheran theology mean by the clarity of Scripture?[169] First, the Lutheran position did not imply that everything in Scripture

(res Scripturae), the thoughts and the mysteries revealed therein, was clear. The thoughts of God and the mysteries contained in Scripture are often unclear to us and above our understanding. But it was maintained that these mysteries have been recorded in lucid and unambiguous language. It is enough, the Lutherans contend, that we accept the ὅτι of these deep mysteries without attempting to search out the διότι.

Second, the Lutheran position does not pertain to every verse of Scripture. In fact, many passages dealing with the articles of faith and divine precepts are obscure. However, all that is needful for faith and life is clearly revealed in Scripture. In the case of the difficult passages the hermeneutical rule that Scripture interprets Scripture ought to be applied; often obscure passages can be clarified by referring to lucid parallel verses and to the analogy of faith. More specifically, the perspicuity inhering in Scripture does not embrace onomastics, chronology, topography, allegory, or unfulfilled prophecy but rather matters pertaining to history, doctrine, and morals. Put briefly the Lutheran position, hedged as we have seen, might be stated as follows: In all matters pertaining to salvation and Christian life the Scriptures are clear enough to those who read them aright, prayerfully, and beseeching the guidance of the Holy Spirit.

It is important to understand that in Lutheran theology the clarity of Scripture pertains to the language and sense and words of Scripture, not to the teachings and mysteries of faith, which can never be understood but must be accepted on faith. Quenstedt puts the matter very succinctly:

> It is possible to write clearly of obscure things, to write in a humble fashion of sublime things, to write in a simple manner of difficult things, and to write openly of hidden things. The Incarnation is a great mystery (1 Tim. 3:16), and yet there are many passages pertaining to it that are clearer than the sun itself. The justification of a sinner before God and the Resurrection are numbered as mysteries. Could you wish for anything clearer than what the apostle writes of the former in his letter to the Romans and of the latter in 1 Corinthians 15? As touching mysteries we must distinguish between the *that* and the *how*. The former is clearly declared in Scripture; the latter, if not declared, is not necessary to know for salvation. For instance, I read in Scripture that clearly God is one and yet three persons, that the Son of God was conceived of the Holy Spirit and born of the Virgin Mary. Now if a person is not content with this but in an officious manner searches into the how and why of it, he has no

The Clarity of Scripture

reason to espouse the obscurity of Scripture but every reason to condemn his own effrontery. Faith does not rest on proofs from reason but on divine testimony.[170]

The clarity of Scripture is an intrinsic and objective clarity of its words and sense. If read according to its literal sense, i. e., its native and intended sense, Scripture is clear to anyone, also the unregenerate. An unbeliever is able to grasp the literal and historical sense of Scripture. A spiritual understanding that includes faith is, however, only given by the Spirit of God. And so it often happens that Scripture becomes exceedingly dark and difficult *per accidens,* because of the darkness and perversity of the unregenerate man (2 Cor. 4:3). But this tragic fact does not militate against the inherent clarity of Scripture. "The sun when it is absolutely clear is obscure to the man born blind."[171]

But the clarity of Scripture is more than a mere perspecuity inhering in the words and sense of the passages for the most part and in the message as a whole. It is a dynamic property that illumines our understanding and leads us to Christ; and when He is found we have everything necessary for salvation.[172] This fact is brought out with particular force as the Lutheran teachers attempt to support their position with Scripture. For the main part they substantiate their doctrine by those passages that speak of Scripture as a light and a lamp (Prov. 6:23; Ps. 19:8; 119:105). Particularly in the case of 2 Peter 1:19 the burden of the passage is that Scripture enlightens the minds of men. If this were not the case, then the Scriptures were written in vain. But if Scripture enlightens our minds, it must itself be a light. Therefore when Scripture is said to be clear and a light, we refer to the clarity of its words and sense and also its function to enlighten the mind and heart. "*Objectively,* the light and clarity of Scripture has to do with the sense of the words and to the content of the articles of faith necessary for salvation (if, as is proper, we are satisfied with the ὅτι of these articles). *Subjectively,* it pertains to the fact that Scripture kindles a light in our heart."[173] Furthermore, we are told that Scripture brings forth wisdom and understanding in children and unlearned people (Ps. 19:7; 2 Tim. 3:15). It reveals hidden mysteries (Rom. 16:25; 1 Cor. 2:9; Col. 1:26-27). Its purpose is to bring men to eternal life (John 20:31; Rom. 15:4). In all such cases Scripture functions as a light that is clear.

It is important to note that the clarity of Scripture is an article of

faith and is handled as such by Lutheran theology. It is not man's experience, i.e., the analytical study of Scripture, that determines the matter — such experience is not competent evidence — but the claims and assertions of Scripture itself. This does not imply that the Lutheran teachers wish to deny the obvious experience of countless Christians who have read and struggled with the Sacred Scriptures. Such Christians have found much that they cannot understand and seems unclear, even after the most exhaustive study. But there is a clarity Scripture claims for itself and we must hold as an article of faith, even though it is not always verifiable inductively through the sometimes arduous task of Biblical exegesis. For this reason the Lutherans earnestly desire to get at the intent of such passages as Deut. 30:11 and 2 Peter 1:19, and they insist on determining the state of the matter in this way only. At times Lutheran theology does attempt to show the clarity of Scripture deductively from the nature of God, but more often the Lutherans point to the claims of Christ, His mode of speaking and teaching, and the general tone and nature of His ministry.[174]

Roman theology maintained that Scripture was not clear and that the interpretation of the church was necessary for a correct understanding of Scripture. It argued its case more or less inductively from the many problems and obscure passages that have plagued the exegetes, the many heresies that have arisen because of a mistaken interpretation of Scripture, the disagreement among the exegetes, and the like.[175] Actually, the Lutheran theologians would hardly have questioned such arguments. Their commentaries on Scripture, which far outnumber those written by Roman Catholics, offer ample evidence of their awareness of the many difficulties connected with Biblical interpretation. Thus we see that in their debate over the clarity of Scripture Roman and Lutheran theologians were to some extent talking past one another. The real issue, however, as the Lutherans saw it, lay in the reasons for the Roman position and in the practical consequences of it. The Roman doctrine made tradition and the interpretation of the church essential for a true understanding of Scripture. Tradition consequently becomes more clear than Scripture, and the church more authoritative. But the most tragic result accruing from the Roman position is that Scripture is systematically and as a matter of principle kept from the laity. And why should the layman read the Scriptures if they are unnecessary, ambiguous, imperfect, and unclear? Bellarmine

The Interpretation of Scripture

and Stapleton even went so far as to insist that Scripture is the cause of heresies and is harmful to faith and morals if read uncritically by the laity.

The reason for the Lutheran insistence on the clarity of Scripture is totally practical. All people, without discrimination, are to read the Holy Scriptures in order to be edified by them. The power of Scripture and the comfort offered therein are what all people need. "Whatever writing witnesses to Christ in order that we might believe in Him and receive the forgiveness of sins and have eternal life ought to be denied no one." [176] In short, every aspect of the Lutheran doctrine of the Word calls for a Bible-reading church. The fact that there are obscure passages in Scripture should not cause the layman to deprive himself of the benefit of reading Scripture. It is his duty to judge all things on the basis of the Scriptures and thus to know the Scriptures firsthand; and it is his joy to draw water from these wells of salvation. It is this deep practical concern that Scripture be read and treasured in the church that prompts the Lutheran theologians to inveigh, sometimes with bitterness, against the practice of the Roman Church of the day in withholding Scripture from the laity. Such tyrannical conduct of the papists wrests from believers a precious gift of God and can only be inspired by the devil himself. Typical of the intense feeling on this matter is a statement found in one of Calov's exegetical works:

> What evil spirit has prompted the pope to place among the prohibited books the Holy Scripture, which has been committed to all men to read? Who gave him that power to grant one and not another the right to read the books of the Bible? How can he say that the divinely inspired Scripture, which is able to make us wise unto salvation, can bring damnation on anyone, without heaping shameful abuse upon Scripture, nay, blasphemy upon God, the author of Scripture? The good that God would have all enjoy without exception cannot by any ecclesiastical law be denied most people and reserved for only a certain number. He who does this sets himself above God and shows by this very action that he is the Antichrist.[177]

The Interpretation of Scripture

In the former discussions on prolegomena I have touched at times on the hermeneutical assumptions and rules that guide classical Lutheran orthodoxy in the interpretation of Scripture. It is necessary at the present juncture to pursue this matter in greater detail, for before we can appre-

ciate the position of the old Lutheran teachers on the various articles of faith, we must understand not only what they thought about Scripture as the source of theology — about its authority, clarity, sufficiency, etc. — but also how they approached Scripture. A doctrinal position may well seem like nonsense until we grasp the exegetical method and canons of hermeneutics that yield this position. Particularly in the case of the inerrancy of Scripture (treated in detail in the next major section), the doctrine of the orthodox Lutheran theologians will inevitably be misunderstood and caricatured unless one knows with what presuppositions Lutheran theology reads the Holy Scriptures. In what follows, these hermeneutical principles will be delineated so that we may understand the position of the old Lutheran theologians — not that the subject will or could be exhausted, for a thorough analytical study of all the more significant exegetical works of that era is an immense undertaking that is simply not feasible for this book.

The hermeneutics and exegetical procedure of the orthodox Lutherans can be gathered from four sources: their works in prolegomena, which we have considered briefly (e. g., the works of Hyperius, Chytraeus, Gerhard, and Calov); their dogmatic writings, which treat certain basic hermeneutical rules and problems that were under discussion in their day; their monographs dealing with the interpretation of Scripture;[178] and their exegetical works studied analytically. The conclusions sifted from these four sources will not always appear to be in agreement. The dogmatic works and monographs on Biblical interpretation often reflect the polemical situation of the day and lack balance for this reason. By drawing from all four sources I offer a brief but what I hope is a fair summary of their basic principles and chief concerns. It is quite impossible here to give any adequate treatment of the actual practice of Lutheran orthodoxy in interpreting Scripture, to say nothing of offering a complete presentation of all the contributions to Biblical hermeneutics that were produced in those days.

We must bear in mind that in our prior discussions we already found ourselves in the thick of hermeneutical concerns. All that has been said so far concerning Scripture — its divine origin, authority, and sufficiency; its Christological and doctrinal unity; its clarity and inerrancy; also its power and ability to authenticate itself — all constitutes a series of hermeneutical presuppositions of gigantic proportions that will and should

The Interpretation of Scripture 317

totally determine the interpreter's attitude and approach to the Sacred Scriptures. Anthropological and soteriological assumptions are also part of the baggage the theologian brings with him as he interprets Scripture. That the exegete is a poor sinner with an habitual inclination toward evil, that he is in constant need of the Spirit's enlightenment, that all his labors to be fruitful must be preceded by earnest prayer, that every thought even of the regenerate reason must be totally subjected to the words and revelation of God — these too are assumptions of sweeping consequence for the exegete as he goes about his task.

We now offer a series of observations relative to the more prevalent hermeneutical principles and the general exegetical procedure of Lutheran theologians during the period of orthodoxy.

1. *General Alertness of the Day*

It has sometimes been alleged that the later orthodox Lutheran teachers with their doctrine of the divine origin and inerrancy of Scripture became guilty of a "literalistic," wooden interpretation of Scripture.[179] Those who have charged them with such a mistake assume that the orthodox opinion on the nature and origin of Scripture will necessarily lead to such obtuse, atomistic exegesis. The critics do not bother, however, to support their charges with any concrete evidence. Do the Lutherans during the period of orthodoxy fail generally to recognize the various genres and bold imagery common to the Scriptures?

When we examine the manner in which these theologians actually use the Scriptures, we make some remarkable discoveries. We have already seen how, in contrast to the various enthusiasms of their day, the orthodox Lutheran teachers emphasize the stylistic traits and differences among the writers of the Scripture.[180] In fact, there were lengthy discussions on the subject of stylistics in Scripture [181] and painstaking analyses of the multifarious tropes and Hebraisms employed throughout the Scriptures.[182] The doctrine of inspiration did not lead to any sort of Aquila-like theory concerning the uniqueness of Biblical language. In every case the writers of Scripture employed the language and literary forms of their day (although not all of them, e. g., forms unworthy of the Spirit of truth), not some sort of divine metalanguage.[183] Therefore the orthodox Lutherans are open to any light that extra-Biblical linguistic analysis might shed on the understanding of Scripture, although their studies in this regard are

often primitive. In those days as today it was recognized that Scripture did not speak of God and divine things in the language of philosophic abstraction but in the concrete imagery of anthropomorphism. *Scriptura saepius se accommodat hominum captui:* e.g., Scripture speaks of eternity as successions of time and of the eternal God as though He was, is, and will be. (Rev. 1:4)[184]

The old Lutheran theologians are never bothered by loose New Testament citations or conflations from the Old Testament or by quotations from the Septuagint.[185] It is sufficient that the evangelist or apostle offer the sense of an Old Testament reference. Quoting from the Septuagint, inaccurate as it sometimes is, is the only option open to the New Testament writers if they are to accommodate themselves to the limitations *(imbecillitati)* of their readers. And such a practice is done with justification *(non immerito).* "At times we observe also parents speaking baby talk with their little ones." The orthodox Lutheran theologians were not troubled by the variant readings in the manuscripts of Scripture; but with the best scholarship available to them they sought to solve the textual problems by an appeal to the *probatissimi codices.*[186]

Neither were they troubled with the synoptic problem (and it was a problem for their day too, as we see from the grotesque attempt of Osiander to solve it).[187] Parallel and varying accounts of the same event seemed quite natural to them. They were not disturbed by the different wordings of the statements of Jesus. They made no frenzied effort to establish the *ipsissima verba* of Jesus. Their conviction concerning the integrity of Scripture and its unity convinced them that they possessed the *ipsissima res* of everything Jesus said; and in fact His *ipsissima verba* were identical with the words of His inspired evangelists. Walther[188] points out that the apostles preached and wrote the Word *(verbum)* that they received from their Lord. We have therefore in the apostolic writings the *ipsissimum verbum* of Jesus. Take, for instance, the diverse renderings of the institution of the Lord's Supper.[189] The later Lutherans, like Luther, grow impatient when this fact is thrown up against their exegesis of the words. The same truth can be expressed in any number of formulations. When Matthew and Mark have Jesus say, "This is My blood," and Paul and Luke have, "This is the New Testament in My blood," the four are saying precisely the same thing. Paul and Luke are merely employing hypallage, or metonymy; they are having Jesus speak of what is in the

The Interpretation of Scripture

cup. Again when Paul and Luke say "in My blood" rather than "of My blood," they are using a common Hebraism that often prefixed a genitive construction with ב. The point made by all the Lutherans in their discussions on the words of institution is that the meaning of all the formulations is the same; and this is all that matters.[190]

What I have attempted to show in these few prefatory remarks is that the orthodox Lutheran theologians, far from being exegetical obscurantists, were unhampered and alert exegetes who, laboring under the authority of the divine Word, desired to avail themselves of every help toward understanding and eliciting the meaning of that divine Word.

2. The Necessity of the Spirit's Guidance for the Interpretation of Scripture

The interpretation of Scripture is a gift of the Holy Spirit (1 Cor. 12:10). This was the most fundamental presupposition for all exegesis. The highest authority in interpreting Scripture is the Spirit of God Himself; He it is who enlightens the interpreter to find the mind and sense of Scripture, and this He accomplishes through Scripture itself.[191] Without the enlightenment of the Spirit no exegete can grasp with salutary results the content of Scripture. True, the meaning of words and syntax can be known without any special illumination, but not the saving message, the Gospel (Matt. 11:27; 16:17; Ps. 119:18; 1 Cor. 3:7; Eph. 1:17). On the basis of such Biblical evidence Calov concludes: "By his own powers without the gracious operation of God no man can understand the Scriptures with any benefit, neither can he render firm and trusting assent to them." [192] This point of departure for all profitable exegesis is supported by the fact that faith, with which the theologian must work in interpreting Scripture, is itself a gift of God and a result of divine grace (Eph. 1:19; Phil. 1:29). All that we know of God *salutariter* is wrought by God Himself. (2 Cor. 3:5; 2 Tim. 2:7; Deut. 29:4; 1 Cor. 12:3; Phil. 1:6)

This position, the converse of which was that the unregenerate man cannot grasp the meaning of Scripture but will only wrest it to his own destruction,[193] is not some minor consideration in the theology of classical Lutheranism. On the contrary, just as for Tertullian only the church was competent to interpret the Scriptures and possessed the right to do so, for Lutheran orthodoxy only the regenerate man could read and use Scripture

with any hope of fruitful results. Think only of the errors, for instance, in the understanding of the Pharisees and scribes in their interpretations of the Scriptures, and this in spite of their immense erudition. However, no need of any special revelation is necessary for the Christian to understand the Scriptures. There is nothing esoteric about the interpretation of Scripture; there are no secret meanings in Scripture. The meaning is clear for all who have ears to hear and understand; for Scripture is clear enough in itself and is its own interpreter.

The regenerate interpreter of Scripture requires the continual aid and enlightenment of the Spirit, because he is never free of his corrupt reason and sinful curiosity. What is this guidance and enlightenment the Holy Spirit provides the Christian interpreter? Essentially it consists in the Spirit guiding the interpreter not so much to understand the *sensus literae*, which is open even to an unbeliever, as to believe the intended sense of Scripture; it consists in His leading the believer to break with the dictates of reason and even with the apparent evidence of experience and to hold fast to the message of Scripture. The interpretation of Scripture, therefore, according to classical Lutheranism, often requires a virtual *sacrificium intellectus*. Faith is often in the impossible and the absurd — according to human reasoning. Whether the Word of Scripture agrees with our reason or not, we can only submit to it, believe it, and hold to it. Such submission (wrought in us by the Holy Spirit), such total commitment to the truthfulness of Sacred Writ, is an absolutely necessary hermeneutical presupposition. Typical of the Lutheran position is this statement by Calov:

> We ought to take captive every thought in obedience to Christ (2 Cor. 10:5). Now if our minds and thoughts are to be taken captive under the obedience of faith, it is incumbent upon us to accept the Word of God even if our mind cannot comprehend it at all, even if in our minds we are persuaded that it is false. With respect to the mysteries of faith the mode of thinking of God's Word is such "foolishness" to human judgment that "the carnal man cannot grasp or understand it all" (1 Cor. 2:14). It is exceedingly important for us therefore to believe the Word of God, however crassly foolish it may seem, and not to follow science and our erring conscience. Contrariwise, we must hold fast to the Word of God, whatever our erring conscience, which regards it all as absurd, may argue to the contrary. But we must add that the Word of God with its divinely instilled clarity and

efficacy has the power to free even the mistaken conscience from its errors and provide a knowledge of the truth.[194]

To the old Lutheran theologians Scripture was not just a dead book, as we shall see, but is God speaking, urging, pleading, striving to make His claim on us. This accounts for the fact that a man, dead spiritually and blind to the revelations of God, can be brought by the Spirit to sacrifice his intellect and understand and accept the Scriptures. For to understand the Scriptures is (by the guidance of the Holy Spirit) to accept the Scriptures.

3. *The Fundamental Hermeneutical Rule: Establishing the Literal Meaning of the Text*

Fundamentally the interpretation of Scripture is an analytical activity whereby the genuine sense of Biblical passages that are not immediately clear is accurately investigated, descriptively drawn out, and set forth.[195] According to Gerhard the public interpretation of the Sacred Scriptures in the church embraces two parts: interpretation, or explanation, of the text; and practical application. The interpretation in turn embraces an investigation of the true and genuine sense, and a plain and clear explanation *(enarratio)* of this sense.[196] Only the literal sense of Scripture is valid for establishing doctrine and teaching in the church.[197] This basic rule is directed against the use of the so-called mystical sense to establish doctrine and against the claim that all interpretation ultimately belongs to the pope.

The literal sense of Scripture is the meaning, or tenor *(proprietas)*, that the words directly and obviously convey.[198] For instance, in John 3:16 the literal sense is immediately clear. But there is also a literal sense to those passages that are tropical and figurative. Such passages we do not read superficially according to the surface tenor of the words *(prout verba ipsa secundum superficiem et proprietatem verborum)*, as when Herod is called a fox or when we are to cut off a hand that offends us — such an interpretation would be absurd. In figurative statements of this kind, not only the words according to their native sense but also the thing or point *(res)* that the words express according to their quondam imagery must be considered. The literal sense, then, is the sense intended by the writer, whatever trope or genre is used. Figures of speech, words *(vocabula)*, and even ideas all have their literal sense. And the literal

sense (meaning, intention) of a pericope is drawn from all these ingredients. Glassius makes it quite clear that the literal sense of a Scripture passage or pericope is not necessarily identical with the surface meaning of the words, but the genre of the text or the tropes therein must also be ascertained, when necessary, to determine the literal sense of a text. We quote him at length:

> The literal sense is that which is directly intended by the Holy Spirit or by Christ in the Sacred Scriptures. This literal sense is either *strict {proprius}* or *figurative*. For since the words of any writing or text must be taken in either a strict or loose sense, it is necessary that the literal sense of the words be of two kinds. The *strict literal sense* obtains when the words are taken according to their ordinary and native meaning. Thus, in the words of the Lord's Supper, "Take and eat; this is My body," the strict literal sense obtains, because in this case no word occurs in a modified sense or affected by a trope. "Take" is understood according to its common usage as meaning to take with the mouth or the hand. "Eat" denotes the usual eating done with the mouth. "This" in its normal sense denotes that which Christ gave the apostles to eat. "Is" normally connects the predicate with the subject and points to the substance of the Eucharistic sacrament. "Body" denotes properly the Lord's body itself, which subsists in the most glorious person of the Logos. "My," taken strictly, denotes the personal pronoun. A *figurative literal sense* obtains when the words are taken figuratively or in a modified sense, when very obviously in the writings and text of the Scripture to be explained there occurs some sort of trope. In this case we say that the appropriate and stylistic intention is sought, whereas in the text whose sense is strictly literal we say only that the words in their natural and ordinary meaning are taken into consideration. Thus when Christ in John 6 speaks of eating the bread of life, the literal sense is figurative. For "bread" is not to be understood as bread in the strict sense but means the life-giving flesh of Christ, which is called bread metaphorically. Neither is the eating to be understood in the ordinary sense as eating done with the mouth, but it is a spiritual eating done with the heart; that is to say, the eating is to be taken as faith in Christ. All this can be proved abundantly from the intention of Christ, from the connection of the context, and from analogy of Scripture.[199]

This statement by Glassius, which is typical of the position of all the Lutheran teachers of the era, again manifests the ardent concern of Lutheran exegesis to determine before all else the intention, the true meaning, of the Scripture texts under consideration. Any application of such

The Interpretation of Scripture 323

hermeneutical principles as the unity of Scripture or the *Scriptura Scripturam interpretat* is quite impossible without first determining the meaning of the individual texts in their broader and narrower contexts. And so the hermeneutical task is always first and foremost to establish the once-for-all meaning of the Scripture text. This meaning does not and cannot change. It remains the same for the Israelites of the Old Testament and for the Christians of the first century and of today. The intention (τὸ ῥητόν) of Scripture cannot be altered or vitiated *(deferendum)* according to the canons of human ingenuity *(argutiae)* or reason or according to cultural or intellectual advances.[200] Nothing can be brought to Scripture whereby the intention is altered in any pericope or passage or phrase. It was the contention of the Socinians that due to the degree of imagery in Scripture the interpreter was called on at times to render a meaning for a Scripture pericope that was foreign to the intention of the words themselves.[201] With a certain unexpected restraint Calov censures this view, which would undermine all normative and final exegesis:

> Now although we would not deny that on some occasions we can and ought to explain the words of Scripture in a figurative sense when the strict sense [of the passage] obviously opposes the manifest data of Scripture or is plainly foreign to the sweep and context [of the entire section], still the literal sense must not be immediately bypassed because of the critical investigation of human reasoning alone. Human judgment cannot follow or comprehend these things and with its own kind of subtle insights *{argutiis}* even opposes the intention of Scripture. No, we must stick with the intention and natural force of the words of the sacred writings, particularly in reference to those chief sections presenting the articles of faith and the classic utterances of Scripture, and we must do so no matter how absurd overweening reason may judge these words to be.[202]

In other words, there must be no receding from the literal sense of the words of Scripture unless there is some intimation by the author himself for our doing so.

This hermeneutical rule that we cannot depart from the natural, literal sense of Scripture unless Scripture itself suggests such a practice is predicated on a number of well-established facts. First, the high and lofty content of Scripture surpasses utterly the critical judgment of man's thoughts (1 Cor. 2:14). The message and assertions of Scripture cannot be investigated according to the canons of ordinary human insight, but

the words of Scripture can only be accepted in the simplicity of faith (Is. 55:8; Luke 1:36 ff.). Second, the clarity of Scripture is utterly vitiated when one twists its meaning according to his own preferences. Calov says: "If the words of Scripture were not to be accepted according to their intention *(prout sonant)* but only as they commend themselves to our way of thinking, then the thoughts that are taken from the Scriptures themselves cannot be considered to be clear and lucid." The failure to read Scripture according to its clear intention conflicts also with the perfection of Scripture, with the rule that the literal and native sense *(sensus proprius et literalis)* is one, and with the prohibition against bringing one's own private interpretation to Scripture. The interpretation of tropes and figurative language cannot change with the times. Otherwise no definite and consistent interpretation of any Scripture passage could obtain.

The Lutheran insistence on determining the *sensus literalis* of Scripture is clearly opposed to the theory of Origen, which filtered down to the Schoolmen, that every Scripture passage admitted of a *multiplex intelligentia* and a fourfold sense must be sought. But what about analogical meaning (allegory, type), which is at times assigned an Old Testament pericope by the New Testament? Strictly speaking, such a procedure is not interpretation but application. Such a practice in no way vitiates the historical and literal sense of the pericope or imposes a new meaning on the words; it is rather a case of drawing from the literal sense an analogy or application. In the case of type and antitype the historic literal sense of the passage remains unchanged; but from the words of the passage and the events the passage records, an analogy is drawn and a type is sought for purposes of illustration.[203]

Do figurative or parabolic utterances in Scripture present doctrine in such a clear fashion that they can be used as proof for doctrine? This question was considered in some detail by the later Lutheran teachers because of the categorical negative answer given by the Socinians. The Socinian Valentin Schmalz, for instance, as quoted by Calov, asserted dogmatically: "To attempt to construct a dogma of religion from figurative discourse is nothing else than to admit beforehand that the dogma is false."[204] For example, Schmalz would not allow Luke 16:19-31 to be used in support of any article of faith, because the pericope was a parable. Calov's rebuttal is definite but cautious. It is true, he admits, that the highly figurative genres of Scripture are not always capable of

any definite and certain interpretation and can therefore yield no dogmatic certainty. In some cases any interpretation is extremely dubious. However, there can be no reason for insisting a priori that figurative language, when its import is plain and clear, as it often is, cannot establish or support a dogma of faith. It is just such language that offers the definite sense of the Holy Spirit. An example of a dogma resting on figurative language is the doctrine of Christ's session at the right hand of the Father. Again the scope of some parables is quite dubious; and in general the aphorism holds true: *Theologia parabolica non est argumentativa.* But if the scope and intention *(scopus et intentio)* of a parable is clear — and there is no reason for assuming a priori that this may not be so — the parable may certainly be used to support doctrine, provided one does not venture beyond its scope. Thus, for instance, Luke 16:19-31 teaches clearly enough that the souls of men after this life are borne immediately and without delay either into the bosom of Abraham or into a place of torment. The problem created by the Socinian position becomes quite clear when we pause to consider how very little in Scripture is not figurative. Calov remarks: "If all those passages that contain figurative expressions are uncertain and cannot prove anything, what then, I ask, will be considered certain in Scripture, since well-nigh all things in Scripture are stated figuratively." It is a Biblical claim that all Scripture is profitable for doctrine (2 Tim. 3:16). Actually the very goal of figurative, symbolical, parabolic, and even typical language is to teach and establish doctrine, as Christ and the apostles make clear in their ministries. The brazen serpent, Jonah, the Old Testament priesthood, and purification ceremonies are types and images used in the New Testament to teach and clarify doctrine.

4. "Sensus literalis unus est"

Adjunct to the fundamental hermeneutical task of searching out the literal sense of Scripture was the principle that a given text or passage of Scripture offers only one genuine sense, the literal sense. This one meaning of individual words or passages in their given context is a constant and cannot be changed. Such a heremeneutical norm was directed against the medieval practice of allegorizing and attaching to Scripture a fourfold sense, a practice defended and followed by the Roman theologians of the 16th and 17th centuries.[205] It was also in opposition to the

Socinian opinion that the meaning of Scripture and its interpretation could change with the advances of history, science, and culture. The rule is stated concisely by Gerhard: "There is only one proper and legitimate sense to each Scripture passage, a sense intended by the Holy Spirit and derived from the natural meaning of the words; and only from this one literal sense can any valid argumentation be brought forth. Allegorical, tropological, and anagogical interpretations are not different meanings but different inferences drawn from the one meaning or different adaptations to the one meaning and sense that the writings express." [206] Another rule, correlative to the above, was that a definite meaning was intended by the Spirit of God in every individual pericope of Scripture.[207]

It is clear what motivated the Lutheran theologians in their insistence on the *unus sensus*. A multiplicity of meanings ascribed to a single Bible text turns Scripture into a waxen nose and makes a chaos of all Biblical exegesis. Furthermore, if a given text can possess many meanings, what then becomes of the clarity, the inerrancy, or even the authority of Scripture? All Christian doctrine becomes uncertain. Calov expresses the Lutheran concern: "Although there is much figurative speech and many tropical and parabolic utterances in Scripture, we must not suppose that Scripture offers uncertain doctrine or that the Holy Spirit spoke with a studied ambiguity concerning matters of faith. Neither must we think that He intended many meanings with the same words and at the same time; but one and the same words express only one sense." [208] One notes a certain sense of security and optimism among the Lutheran exegetes who operate with the principle *sensus literalis unus est*. True, there will be many times when an interpreter must content himself with a *possible* exegesis of a Biblical text. But the principle is still a source of constant encouragement to the interpreter. If careful investigation is made, the meaning of even difficult texts often becomes clear. Watching the context, the scope, and the intention of the text, as well as the analogy of faith, often aids the theologian in arriving at the true sense of passages that at first seem dark and obscure.[209]

But what about the allegorical application and typological interpretation that the New Testament often gives the Old? Do Jesus and the apostles by such a practice ascribe to passages of the Old Testament meanings different from the original intended sense? Such questions require a bit of answering, and the Lutherans are most thorough in their discussions

The Interpretation of Scripture

of the nature and validity of allegory and type. First, they insist against the Roman exegetes that typological and allegorical interpretation cannot be applied to every passage of Scripture but must be restricted to those cases where Scripture itself practices such a method.[210] Next, they carefully explain — and I am summarizing Glassius [211] at this point — what they mean by a *sensus duplex* that is both literal (historical) and mystical (spiritual). The sense of Scripture is the meaning that the Spirit of God intends to be known and understood by those who read it. But often the Spirit intends a higher *(sublimius)* meaning to be understood from the persons or events depicted in a text *(per rem ipsis verbis significatam)* than the reading of the text as a mere history immediately conveys. Thus, not only the history is the sense of the text, but through the history a certain mystery is introduced as the sense of the text. For instance, by causing the story of the fiery serpent to be recorded in Numbers 21:8-9, the Spirit intended more to be understood than what can be drawn from the text taken in its merely historical framework *(historice)*. Jesus makes it clear (John 3:14-15) that the story is more than a mere history; the story points to Him being lifted on a cross so that all men might live through Him. Granted that Jesus accommodates the text to Himself *(ad se fecit accommodationem)*, such an accommodation is however justified: this was the intention of the Spirit in the text from the Book of Numbers. The possibility that Jesus and the apostles by typological interpretation are imposing a meaning upon the Old Testament texts that is not there by intention is never entertained by the Lutheran theologians; in such a case Christ and the apostles would have twisted and perverted the sense of the Old Testament, a very immoral *(pejus)* practice that would have defeated their purpose of drawing their teaching from the Old Testament Scriptures.

What is the difference between allegory and type? Allegory as understood by Philo and the medieval scholastics was never employed in the Scriptures, according to the Lutheran exegetes. The one case in the New Testament where the apostle Paul "speaks through allegory" (Gal. 4:24) is taken by most of the classical Lutheran exegetes as a case of typology.[212] As used in the Scriptures, allegory, according to Flacius, is a heightened form of metaphor, employed for purposes of illustration.[213] An example of such a form is John the Baptist's preachment in Matt. 3:10, 12. Gerhard too sees allegory as a mere illustrative device.[214] Whereas type is an

instance of a concrete person or action in the Old Testament prefiguring or foreshadowing something in the New Testament, allegory gives a new meaning to something in the Old or New Testament for the sake of application only. For instance, we might say that David's victory over Goliath signifies the victory of our spirit over the flesh. This would be said to illustrate a point, not to prove it, and there is nothing in the story of David and Goliath that suggests the victory of our spirit over our flesh. The allegory is used merely for illustrative purposes. In this it differs from type.

With its emphasis on types in the Old Testament (Melchizedek, Adam, the stairs of Jacob, the sacrifices, the crossing of the Red Sea, the manna, the fiery serpent, etc.) and on direct predictive prophecy where the prophetic words themselves pointed directly to Christ, classical Lutheranism shows that in a sense it regarded the entire Old Testament as typological, as a foreshadowing and a blueprint, as it were, for the work of Christ and the coming of His kingdom. This would account for the fact that the New Testament so often and at times with apparent caprice finds allusions and types and prophecies of Christ throughout the Old Testament. The same Spirit of God is author of the Old Testament Scriptures, which point to the coming Christ and prepare for Him, and of the New Testament Scriptures, which testify of the Christ who has come according to the promises. Still, the old Lutherans were very cautious and generally did not find types lurking within every Old Testament figure; nor did they seek to discover or make anything of prophecy in the Old Testament where the New Testament did not find it.[215] They were careful, too, not to confuse type and prophecy, although to them type was a kind of prophecy.[216]

There were times, however, when agreement could not be reached over the classification of certain passages. For instance, Hos. 11:1, "Out of Egypt have I called My son," was taken by the majority of commentators — Calov, Quenstedt, A. Pfeiffer, et al. — as predictive prophecy. Their arguments were that "my son" in this context cannot refer to the backsliding Israel but only to the pure and holy Son, Christ. The term cannot be both collective and individual, and it is understood individually in Matt. 2:15. Furthermore, Matthew prefaces his citation of these words with ἵνα πληρωθῇ τὸ ῥηθὲν ὑπὸ κυρίου διὰ τοῦ προφήτου λέγοντος.[217] Michael Walther, on the other hand, takes the verse as an example of typology

The Interpretation of Scripture

where Israel's calling from Egypt foreshadows what took place in the life of our Lord.[218] He avers that *son* often refers to Israel in the Old Testament (Ex. 4:22; Jer. 31:9) and does in this case also. It is perfectly permissible, he says, to use the term collectively in reference to the type (Israel) and individually in reference to the antitype (Christ) as Matthew does. The term *seed*, for instance, is used collectively in Gen. 28:14 and at the same time refers to the individual, Christ. That Matthew speaks of Christ fulfilling the prophecy from Hosea fits in perfectly with a typical interpretation, for type is a mode of prophecy.

We might ask why Calov, Quenstedt, and others failed to follow Walther's more convincing exegesis of Hos. 11:1. The answer is clearly their fear — in this case unfounded — of violating the *unus sensus* principle. In all the long discussions of the Lutheran theologians on allegory (always as an extended metaphor) and typology we notice that the basic principle of *sensus literalis unus est* is never violated or weakened.

5. "Scriptura est suipsius interpres"

That Scripture interprets itself means for Lutheran theology merely that the true sense of Scripture must be derived from Scripture itself.[219] The Holy Spirit, who is the author of all Scripture, must be allowed to be His own interpreter. Any compromise of this principle turns Scripture into an inanimate skeleton or mute image that must be animated by the church. The Scriptures themselves offer sufficient light for us to read them correctly. One therefore cannot and must not interpret Scripture according to foreign thought forms or norms. The canons of Biblical interpretation *(media hermeneutica)* are found within Scripture itself.

Hollaz divides the hermeneutical aids suggested by Scripture itself into three classifications: *antecedent, formal,* and *consequent*. The *antecedent* aids for interpretation are prayer; a previous acquaintance with the articles of faith; a solid knowledge of the Biblical mode of speaking, which would enable one to recognize the genres, tropes, etc.; a love for the truth that desires only to find the genuine sense of a text and interpret it clearly; and finally, the continued and repeated reading of Scripture. The *formal* aids are a careful and analytical examination of the words and phrases of the Biblical text; a careful consideration of the scope and intention of the text (bearing in mind always that the aim of all Scripture is the glory of God and the instruction, comfort, and edification of be-

lievers); careful study of the context of every text and pericope; an exhaustive collation of parallel passages so as to gather all possible data on the great Biblical themes (remembering always that parallel passages must always deal with the same subject); and finally, continual reference to the analogy of faith. All this should provide the exegete with a mastery of the Biblical mode of speaking and theology so that he reads Scripture from the inside. The *consequent* aids for interpreting Scripture are the means necessary for serious application of the Biblical theology: we are to translate the literal sense of the divine words into teaching, reproof, correction, and instruction in righteousness.

As Hollaz has explained the *Scriptura per scripturam explicanda* principle, there is a good deal of overlap with other hermeneutical norms. But he is primarily concerned about what he calls the formal aids, and particularly the aid that one passage gives to the understanding of a parallel passage that is less clear. The clear passages of Scripture must shed light on the obscure passages dealing with the same subject matter. This is done by applying the so-called analogy of faith. The analogy of faith, according to all the old Lutheran theologians, was simply the articles of faith that could be summarized under the categories of Law and Gospel (2 Tim. 1:13).[220] No interpretation of any passage can conflict with these clear articles of faith. This does not mean that there are no theological *lacunae*, logical gaps, between the various articles of faith. It does mean that one passage of Scripture can often help us in finding the meaning of another passage that treats the same article of faith. Romans 3—4 can help us to understand James 2, since they both deal with the justification of a sinner before God.

But is it not reasoning in a circle to say that Scripture explains itself? By no means. The official document of a ruler is explained by that document itself. The meaning of a father's last will and testament is explained by that will. The sun is known by its own light. So it is with Scripture. The aid of theologians and doctors in Biblical interpretation is of course necessary, but not absolutely so; actually such aid is calculated merely to bring out the meaning of Scripture itself. The formal aids mentioned by Hollaz above are not human and probable but are implied by Scripture itself. To apply the principle that Scripture interprets itself will serve to lead the exegete deeper into Scripture; this was the optimistic conviction of all the Lutherans.

6. The Unity of Scripture

Following Luther, the theologians of Lutheran orthodoxy make Christ the central theme of all Scripture. Christ is the pearl, the scope, the center, the nucleus, the evangelical treasure of all Scripture, Old and New Testament alike.[221] All Scripture points to Him. Only in Him is Scripture read aright and understood. "The genuine scope and ultimate intention of the entire Scripture is that we might come to a knowledge of the person, the office, and the benefits of Christ. Without Christ the Scripture is not an instrument whereby the Spirit gives life, but a dead letter, a letter that kills. The goal of Scripture is not just that we might know something historically about Christ and then talk about that, but that we might come to Him, come to Him in faith and true repentance, and in Him and through Him find life. He who does not seek life in Christ but thinks that he can manage in some other way will never be a fit reader of Scripture."[222] The Christocentricity of Scripture is not therefore merely some worn cliché, but a principle established directly by Scripture and by Christ Himself (e.g., John 5:39; 2 Tim. 3:15) from the mass of prophecy and typology present throughout Scripture. The Christocentricity of Scripture becomes a hermeneutical norm. All Scripture must be read and expounded Christologically.

This conviction of all the orthodox Lutherans that the Christocentricity of Scripture is a hermeneutic principle dovetails perfectly with their belief that the theology of Scripture is one unified Christian theology, with their strong and consistent Christological exegesis of the Old Testament, with their emphasis on the analogy of faith as a hermeneutical norm, and with their understanding that all Scripture is Law or Gospel.[223] But what is of higher significance is that the Christocentricity of Scripture unites the formal *(sola Scriptura)* principle of theology with the material principle (justification through faith in Christ) in such a way that neither stands alone, but each complements the other perfectly. The Sacred Scriptures, which are the norm of doctrine, are the Scriptures that declare Christ throughout. Thus, Scripture is in no sense a mere authoritative history or book of rules. It is the norm for *Christian* doctrine. At the same time the Gospel is never and need never be divorced from Scripture as its source; for all Scripture is Christological, that is, evangelical.

The Christological unity in Scripture infers also a doctrinal unity in Scripture. If the same Gospel pervades all of Scripture, the doctrine in Scrip-

ture, which is really no more than the *doctrina evangelii,* will be the same throughout Scripture. The Gospel is not first proclaimed in the New Testament, neither does the New Testament teach a Gospel different essentially from the *Protevangelium.* Commenting on Romans 1, Calov says: "Now this Gospel [of St. Paul] is not something new, nor does he present anything new relative to the substance of his doctrine. Rather he teaches the same doctrine as the prophets taught. It is only that what they proclaimed would be performed, he now testifies has been completed and fulfilled in Jesus Christ."[224] To be sure, there is a vast difference between the Old and New Testament Scriptures in their presentation of doctrine; there is a definite unfolding and advance in clarity as well as phraseology and thought. The Old Testament Scriptures present the doctrine under different circumstances and different times; in the Old Testament Christ is prefigured under shadows and types as something to come.[225] But substantially the theology of Scripture is one, even as Christ is one. *Tempora variata sunt, non fides.*[226]

This means that Lutheran orthodoxy will, when tracing any theme or motif, quote indiscriminately from all over Scripture, not ignoring the differences in style and background and progression of thought in the different passages — the Lutheran theologians are careful to note these factors when they think it is important — but nevertheless recognizing that the theology (doctrine) of the different authors will not differ; and therefore their procedure is perfectly justified. Classical Lutheran orthodoxy holds that such a procedure, based on the conviction that all Biblical theology is one, is Scriptural; it is the practice of the New Testament Scriptures and of Christ as they explain the Old Testament Scriptures. The procedure will, of course, materially affect their use of Scripture. For instance, one might be surprised to find Quenstedt employing almost as much Old Testament evidence as New Testament evidence in developing the doctrine of the vicarious atonement. And Calov will at times employ almost exclusively New Testament evidence (e. g., John 5:39; Luke 16:29; Acts 10:43; 26:22; Rom. 4:6; 10:11; etc.) to show that justification by faith was taught in the Old Testament. And so a procedure that to many today might appear to be hopelessly unscholarly, aprioristic, and circular is really quite in order. Why not, if both the Old and the New Testament Scriptures are the Word of one God, pointing to one Christ, reflecting one theology (*theologia* ἔκτυπος), the theology of very

The Interpretation of Scripture 333

God? We must recall that for classical Lutheranism, Scripture, strictly speaking, is not man's word about God but God's Word to man about Himself; He, the one true God, is the author of all theology. *Autor Theologiae est Deus.*[227] That little aphorism was taken seriously by the old Lutherans and applied consistently. Today anyone who would dispute with their use of Scripture must attack them at this early and crucial point, not later. It goes without saying that the principle *Scriptura Scripturam interpretatur* cannot be applied unless there is doctrinal unity in Scripture, one *doctrina evangelii* proclaimed throughout.

7. New Testament Interpretation of the Old Testament Scriptures

The Old Testament Scriptures have a force, usefulness, and necessity equal to that of the New. Like the ancient church fathers, the Lutheran theologians believed that the Old Testament Scriptures belonged to the church.[228] This belief led them to the conviction that the Old Testament Scriptures were useful in convincing Jews concerning Christ and the Christian religion. This is particularly important in their day, they said, when the Jews, being far withdrawn from Christ's life and miracles and resurrection, had only His doctrine to examine in the light of the Old Testament. Repairing to the Old Testament Scriptures was the approach of both Christ and the apostles in dealing with the Jews; and this can and ought to be our approach today, wherever possible.

That the Old Testament Scriptures are Christian Scriptures and of equal force with the New Testament writings implies that the rule of St. Augustine be seriously practiced, *In veteri testamento novum latet, in novo vetus patet.* The New Testament explains and interprets the Old. And such exegesis of the Old Testament is final and unassailable. All Lutherans during the age of orthodoxy were content to read the Old Testament Scriptures trustingly and ingenuously in the light of their fulfillment in Christ, and this as interpreted in the New Testament. It never occurred to them to distrust or question the validity of any New Testament interpretation of the Old. The Socinians in those days advanced the theory similar to the view of many modern exegetes that the Old Testament prophecies had to be meaningful and have bearing on the people of the time when they were written.[229] The New Testament, however, in proclaiming Christ "accommodates" the Old Testament to the goal of bringing us to faith in Jesus Christ. (Examples of such accommo-

dation are Is. 49:8 with 2 Cor. 6:2; Is. 1:9 with Rom. 9:29; and Hos. 11:1 with Matt. 2:15.) "It is the very attribute of divine prophecies," Socinus said, "that they be obscure and cannot be perfectly understood until after the event has taken place." The Lutherans did not totally reject such a position. As we have seen, they were not averse to saying that the New Testament "accommodates" the Old Testament to Christ. But they were careful to point out that such a procedure does not impose a new or different meaning on the Old Testament prophecies. They were also concerned to maintain that the Old Testament prophecies, although not as clear as their fulfillment, were able to create a Messianic hope in the hearts of people of that day. And therefore there is no a priori reason for insisting that every Old Testament prophecy must somehow refer to the people who would first hear or read it. The Old Testament abounds in direct rectilinear prophecies that refer only to Christ; in such a way these prophecies are understood by the New Testament, and in the same way they were to be understood when first delivered in the Old Testament.

The New Testament, then, is the key to understanding these Old Testament prophecies; it is an inspired interpretation of these prophecies in the light of fulfillment. To take only one example, Hebrews 1 interprets many Old Testament prophecies as pointing directly to Christ and to no one else. To the writer of Hebrews, Ps. 102:25 in itself "demonstrates . . . that the Son is not some sort of creature but the very Creator Himself." [230] Psalm 8:5 refers directly and only to the humiliation and exaltation of Christ.[231] And Ps. 45:6 points to Christ's throne and in no sense to Solomon's, as the Jews contended.[232] Admittedly, according to such exegesis, the New Testament interpretation will settle the meaning of an Old Testament passage. This fact, however, does not imply that the Lutheran exegetes pay no consideration to the context of the Old Testament prophecies. On the contrary, they repeatedly attempt to show the Messianic character of such prophecies by the Old Testament context. For instance, Brochmand goes to great length in order to show from the Old Testament text alone that Ps. 45 can refer only to the coming King Christ. Some of his observations are that the throne of the King is the throne of God ("Thy throne, O God"); it is an eternal throne; it designates a rule of complete righteousness. No such description could possibly refer to Solomon's reign. That Solomon might have been a type of Christ does not occur to Brochmand in this instance. Of course, such

an interpretation of the Old Testament text must agree with the interpretation given it in the New Testament; and therefore the New Testament is often of invaluable help to the interpreter of the Old Testament. If the old Lutherans were charged, as they were at times by Socinians and Arminians, of not reading the Old Testament prophecies in their Old Testament context, they replied that the New Testament understands perfectly and takes into account the Old Testament context; and furthermore the fulfillment of prophecy in the New Testament belongs to the wider context of the prophecies themselves.

We must bear in mind as we attempt at this point to understand the classical Lutheran interpretation of Scripture that the theologians of that day saw the writing of Scripture in a *Sitz im Leben* quite different from that imagined by many scholars today. The conclusions of the so-called *Religionsgeschichtliche Schule* would have repelled them. They confidently assumed on the basis of internal Biblical evidence alone that the writers of Scripture were uninfected by Israel's neighbors, at least religiously; that, in spite of all her backsliding, God was directly leading Israel and revealing Himself to her through His prophets; and that Hebrew religion in the Old Testament was dominated by hope in a promised Savior. Modern theories on the development of theology, evolution of religion, and progressive revelation were foreign to their thinking, as such theories are foreign to the New Testament itself, and in fact were repudiated at great length when introduced by Socinians and certain Arminians. It is, of course, true, as Dorner says,[233] that justice was not done by the Lutherans of this era to the historical element of exegesis. History was barely a budding discipline in those days. But the reason for this is not due, I believe, to their doctrine of inspiration (that the writers of Scripture were instruments of the Holy Spirit), as Dorner alleges, but to the very rigid principle that the New Testament writings offer an absolutely authoritative interpretation of the Old Testament Scriptures. And we might ask, does the New Testament itself give any more weight to the historical context of the Old Testament Scriptures when it cites passages from them?

8. *The Legitimacy of Consequences Drawn from Scripture*

In their discussions concerning the sufficiency of Scripture Lutheran theologians maintained that it was proper to draw consequences from

Scripture, that these inferences, or conclusions, had the force of *doctrina divina,* and that they were even necessary for salvation at times. In other words, a legitimate consequence drawn from Scripture is as Scriptural as the Biblical passage from which it is drawn. It first became necessary to articulate this essential principle because of the precipitate suggestions of Bucer and other Calvinists that doctrinal controversies ought to be settled by an appeal to the *ipsissima verba* of Scripture, when in fact it was the interpretation of the *ipsissima verba* that was under debate. However, it was primarily against the Socinians that the principle was argued. Adopting a Sadducean-like exegesis, the Socinians held that doctrine could not be based on consequences drawn from Scripture. This rigid position lay behind their rejection of the Trinity and the deity of Christ: there was no passage in the Scriptures, they averred, that explicitly taught these dogmas. It was their boast that their theology was based on Scripture without any consequences.[234] The Lutherans on their part insisted that it was a legitimate exegetical procedure to draw consequences from Scripture and that these consequences had the force of doctrine.[235] Christ Himself appealed to consequences in demonstrating fundamental articles of faith. He proved the resurrection of the dead from a Scripture passage that did not explicitly teach the resurrection (Mark 12:26), and He predicted His own resurrection on the basis of Old Testament passages that did not explicitly teach this. That He was Messiah was based on an inference from the Old Testament Scriptures (John 5:39; Acts 10:43), and even today we cannot prove that Jesus is the Christ except through legitimate conclusions drawn from the Old Testament. Calov points out that even *fides specialis* is always built on an inference drawn from Scripture. To be certain of his salvation, a sinner must draw conclusions from Scripture passages that teach that God wishes to save all men.

Lutheran exegetes were most scrupulous not to carry too far the principle that consequences ought to be drawn from Scripture. They were generally anxious not to drag out long catenae of deductions from single Bible passages, although they were seldom averse to basing a single syllogism on a passage when this seemed called for. The Socinians sometimes argued around the import of certain passages by claiming that their application was limited to the times in which they were written. For instance, when Paul spoke of the necessity of sending preachers (Rom. 10:15), this applied only to his day. Although the Lutherans rejected

The Interpretation of Scripture 337

such narrow interpretations as this, they were careful not to make a doctrine or precept out of a mere Biblical precedent, for such a procedure could result in the worst kind of legalism and absurdity. They argued, for instance, against the Reformed who insisted on breaking the bread of the Sacrament of the Altar because Christ had first done so. Conclusions must be based on the general nature and intention of the Biblical statement and its obvious and unavoidable implications.[236]

As we conclude our résumé of the classical Lutheran hermeneutics, we must pause to make a few remarks relative to a rather general charge leveled against the exegesis of the Lutherans of the orthodox era. The charge is made that their exegesis was no longer free but bound to a rigid dogmatic consensus and that their interest in exegesis was confined to *dicta probantia,* as though Scripture were interested only in furnishing them.[237] This charge is not wholly unjustified. The scholastic methodology of at least the later orthodox Lutherans, their preoccupation with polemics, their deep concern with church dogma obviously affect their exegesis and give it at times an overly systematic, dogmatic, and deductive ring.[238] The exegetical works of Balduin, Giles Hunnius, Calov, Chytraeus, and even Gerhard are often replete with polemics concerning dogma. On the other hand, there is almost no polemics in the works of Brochmand and Sebastian Schmidt; their exegetical studies are analytical and inductive; their commentaries, like the *Harmonia Quatuor Evangelistarum* of Chemnitz, Gerhard and Leyser, are unmarred by unnecessary references to the fathers and other exegetes, and are most practical and even devotional in nature.

We must say, however, that the general charge that free inductive exegesis during the period of orthodoxy was obstructed by doctrinal exigencies and scruples is unfair, unless the criticism infers only that the pre-critical Lutheran exegesis paid very strict attention to the hermeneutical rules we have mentioned above. Luther's principle of Biblical Christocentricity, which implied also the doctrinal unity of all Scripture, was to the following generations of Lutherans not merely a vague, nebulous truism worthy of lip service but incapable of any application. It was rather a workable and necessary hermeneutical principle, drawn from Scripture. What might appear to be dogmatic exegesis was merely the application of Luther's Christological exegesis of Scripture, which necessarily involved employing the analogy of faith, the practice of drawing legitimate con-

sequences, and other Biblically founded hermeneutical principles. It is chiefly just these factors, these far-reaching assumptions, that give the exegesis of that day an apparent dogmatic tone to those who would follow the historicocritical method of interpretation introduced by Semler. But we must recognize that these principles according to which the orthodox Lutherans operate are not logical, historical, or dogmatic norms but in their considered opinion hermeneutical principles drawn from Scripture itself. Therefore the reason or basis for what has been called the dogmatic exegesis of Lutheran orthodoxy is due to their hermeneutics, not to their doctrine of inspiration, certainly not to their confessionalism. This statement is made in total opposition to the conjecture that the doctrine of verbal inspiration completely conditioned the old Lutheran exegesis. This allegation was first made by Semler, who because of his chronological proximity to the age of orthodoxy and his extreme prejudice against orthodox theology might understandably attribute everything he disliked in the orthodox Lutheran exegesis to the doctrine of inspiration that he repudiated. But the view is followed by a number of more dispassionate theologians such as Dorner, Farrar, and more recently Weber and Ebeling, theologians who unfortunately have not examined the hermeneutical and exegetical works of the orthodox Lutherans. In no case, however, do any of the critics offer any example of the so-called dogmatic exegesis in action. They all assume it to be the inevitable result of identifying Scripture with God's Word.

Now the several hermeneutical rules that govern Lutheran exegesis are certainly dependent on the divine origin of Scripture, its infallibility and clarity, and on the *sola Scriptura* principle; but it is nevertheless the hermeneutical rules that govern the exegesis. When Calov, for instance, finds Heb. 6:4-6 to be apparently at odds with the implications of other Biblical data relative to those who fall from grace and solicits the aid of other parallel passages that deal with the same subject in order to understand the Hebrews passage (an example of "dogmatic" exegesis), his procedure is not the direct result of any dogma of inspiration but is due to his application of the principle that Scripture interprets Scripture and all that is relative to this principle.[239] Examples illustrating this same point could be multiplied ad infinitum. Again when the old Lutherans find clear Christological references in the Old Testament, this has nothing whatever to do with an inspiration theory but is due to their

principle of Biblical Christocentricity and the principles that the New Testament interpretation of the Old Testament Scriptures is correct and final. Nor would they grant that such a procedure is tantamount to forcing exegesis into some sort of systematic schema; they rather insist that their exegetical method is inductive and Scriptural. And it is, if their hermeneutical rules are Scriptural. Everything depends on this.

It is quite clear from all that has been said in this chapter that the theology of Lutheran orthodoxy (and this would be true also of the theology of Luther or the Lutheran Symbols) will be acceptable only to the extent that we are able to approve the hermeneutics employed. This is the reason why principles of hermeneutics are spelled out in detail by the orthodox Lutherans even in works devoted to dogmatics. Doctrine must be the result of sound exegesis, and exegesis the result of the correct application of hermeneutical rules. Only when the hermeneutical principles are sound and Biblical will the doctrine be sound. Where the basic Biblical hermeneutical norms are abandoned, a radically different theology, unevangelical in nature, will result — as we see in the Roman theology of the day, which, we must recall, had no quarrel with the Lutheran teachers regarding the divine origin and infallibility of Scripture. Therefore to disparage today as precritical the hermeneutical principles employed by the theologians of the age of orthodoxy would on their terms be tantamount to a rejection of their theology. Of such importance is their hermeneutics.

THE TRUTHFULNESS OF SCRIPTURE [240]

In the course of history it sometimes happens that the clearest and most unequivocal affirmations of faith have become distorted and caricatured either out of bitterness or deliberate misunderstanding or simply because of changes in intellectual climate. Such has unfortunately been the case with the historic Lutheran doctrine of the truthfulness, or inerrancy, of Scripture. If we read the works of the 17th-century Lutherans, who first dwelt at length on the doctrine, with an eye also toward their hermeneutical principles and their theology as a whole, we shall find that they shared with Luther, Flacius, and all the Lutherans of the previous century a common pious conviction concerning the truthfulness and reliability of all of Scripture. Although their formulations are more elaborate and their arguments longer because of the antitheses of their

day, they have in this matter not advanced in doctrine one iota beyond the simple faith of Luther or Flacius or Selnecker or Chemnitz. What is more, their doctrine, when studied in the light of their hermeneutics and total theology, is so plain and uncomplicated as to defy misunderstanding. Viewed in its proper setting, the Lutheran doctrine of Scripture's truthfulness is couched in such careful terms and taken so clearly from Biblical evidence, without going beyond that evidence, that no development or discovery of the future could possibly assail it. Although orthodox Lutheranism could not have foreseen just how future attacks against the veracity of Scripture might be leveled, the doctrine had a built-in answer, as it were, to any possible attack. This meant in effect that every rational, empirical, or theological assault against the classic Lutheran doctrine had already been considered and refuted by the older Lutheran theologians as they spelled out their position and its implications. What I am attempting to say is that there is really only one possible doctrine of the veracity, or the inerrancy, to use a more modern term,[241] of Scripture: the doctrine advanced by orthodox Lutheranism. And today those who wish to teach and confess the truthfulness of Scripture cannot really add to what was said at that time.

1. *The Lutheran Position Stated*

In order to get at the precise position of orthodox Lutheranism relative to the inerrancy of Scripture, it is perhaps well to cite two typical statements of the old dogmaticians and then comment on the meaning and implications of these statements. The first is by Quenstedt:

> The prophets and apostles spoke and wrote not from the decision and impulse of their own free will, or as Scripture says, ἀφ' ἑαυτῶν, of themselves (John 11:51; 16:13), but ὑπὸ πνεύματος ἁγίου φερόμενοι, that is, led and moved by the Holy Spirit, or as θεοφόρητοι. This being true, it then follows that they could in no manner make mistakes in their writing, and no falsification, no error, no danger of error, no untruth obtained or could obtain in their preaching or writing, because the Holy Spirit, who is the Spirit of truth and the Fountain of all wisdom and who had as His hand and pen the holy writers, cannot deceive or be deceived, neither can He err or have a lapse of memory.[242]

Next a quotation from Calov:

> Because Scripture is God's Word, which is absolutely true, Scripture is itself truth (Ps. 119:43, 86, 142, 160; John 17:17, 19; cf. Ps. 33:4;

Gal. 3:1; Col. 1:5; 2 Tim. 2:18; 3:8; Titus 1:1; and James 1:18). Thus whatever the Sacred Scriptures contain is fully true and to be accepted with utmost certainty. Not only must we hold to be true what is set forth in Scripture concerning faith and morals, but we must hold to everything that happens to be included therein. Inasmuch as Scripture has been written by a direct and divine impulse and all the Scriptures recognize as their author Him who cannot err or be mistaken in any way (Heb. 6:18), no untruth or error or lapse can be ascribed to the God-breathed Scripture, lest God Himself be accused.[243]

If we examine these statements we shall find that they are very carefully worded and worthy of somewhat detailed analysis. I shall therefore make a number of comments on the basis of these statements and other evidence from the old Lutheran teachers relative to the claims of these statements.

2. *The Basis of Inerrancy*

According to the above cited passages the inerrancy of Scripture derives from its divine origin. Because Scripture comes to us from God it can contain no contradiction or error of fact, for it is impossible that God should lie or deceive or be deceived (Num. 23:19; Heb. 6:18). It is significant that the same Scripture passages used to support the inspiration and divine origin of Scripture are now marshalled to show that Scripture is in all points truthful (2 Tim. 3:16; 2 Peter 1:21; John 16:13; 1 Thess. 2:13; Gal. 1:12).[244] Commenting on such passages the Lutheran teachers in each case draw the necessary inference that the Scriptures as God's Word cannot err or mislead in any way. The statement of Quenstedt's above was a comment on 2 Peter 1:21. The same inference is drawn by Calov from 2 Tim. 3:16: "Whatever is inspired by God cannot be false, cannot be erroneous, unless you wish in a most impious manner to ascribe error to God. Now not merely certain portions of Scripture but πᾶσα γραφή in its entirety is said to be divinely inspired. And so nothing in Scripture can be false or erroneous."[245] Ultimately all arguments for inerrancy are reduced to this one claim that the Scriptures, which are the Word of very God, will not err or lead astray.

Admittedly this conclusion is an inference drawn from Scripture (like the inferences necessary if one is to possess a *fides specialis* or believe that God is triune), but it is a necessary and legitimate inference drawn also by Christ and the apostles, an inference that any child of God will make joyfully and unhesitatingly. We have already seen how, according to his-

toric Lutheran hermeneutics, a legitimate consequence, or inference, drawn from Scripture is as binding and authoritative as an express statement of Scripture. Inspiration and inerrancy are concomitants: the idea of an erring Scripture, an erring Word of God, is simple nonsense, a *contradictio in adjecto*. "Whatever is inspired by God," says Quenstedt, "is to be believed simply on account of itself and is quite above all criticism; it is true for all times and immutably so; it is free of all error and untruth. An inspired falsehood is an impossibility, since God cannot lie either directly or through others." To orthodox Lutheran theology, therefore, any charge against the truthfulness of Scripture is an attack on the truthfulness of God. And it is not only foolish but also wicked and blasphemous to charge the Holy Spirit with allowing any error to enter His book.[246] Quenstedt cannot refrain from pouring forth his indignation upon any who would allow that there could be errors or mistakes in Scripture:

> Whatever fault or untruth, whatever error or lapse of memory, is attributed to the prophets and apostles is not imputed to them without blaspheming the Holy Spirit, who spoke and wrote through them. By virtue of His infinite knowledge God the Holy Spirit cannot be ignorant of anything, cannot forget anything; by virtue of His infinite truthfulness and infallibility it is impossible for Him to err, deal falsely, or be mistaken, even in the smallest degree; and finally, by virtue of His infinite goodness He is unable to deceive anyone, nor is He capable of leading anyone into offence or error. Such an opinion [that there are errors in Scripture] vitiates the authenticity and authority of Scripture, and by such an opinion the certainty and assurance of our faith are destroyed. . . . Unless we are made infallibly certain of the source of our faith, how can there be any ὑπόστασις to our faith (Heb. 11:1), any assurance of salvation, or even any peace of conscience?[247]

It is most essential today, if we are to appreciate the historic Lutheran position concerning the truthfulness of Sripture, to understand how firmly it is based on the Lutheran conviction that Scripture is *vere et proprie* the Word of God. And we must understand too that the inerrancy of Scripture, like Scripture's inspiration, is a matter of faith, to be believed on the basis of the witness of Scripture itself, not to be demonstrated by any kind of extra-Biblical apologetics. Of course, here too the so-called external criteria for the authority of Scripture could be called forth as witnesses to support what is already believed on the basis of Scripture, but in fact such criteria are never mentioned by any dogmatician when

discussing the truthfulness of Scripture. It is always assumed that once the divine origin of Scripture is established exegetically, the truthfulness and reliability of Scripture follow.

3. *The Nature and Meaning of Biblical Inerrancy*

What is the nature of Biblical inerrancy? What precisely does classical Lutheranism mean when speaking of the truthfulness of Scripture? In reply to such questions we must make clear at the outset that the orthodox Lutherans when speaking of the truthfulness or infallibility of Scripture were not thinking of Scripture's soteriological purpose; they did not have in mind that Scripture infallibly achieves its purpose or that Scripture unerringly says what God wants said, although they would have agreed to all this without hesitation. Rather in speaking of the veracity of Scripture Lutheranism had in mind the form of Scripture as a cognitive, intelligible word or message; and is therefore referring to the truthfulness of its doctrine, its assertions, its statements. Scripture always speaks the truth and for this reason is always totally reliable. In every case and under all circumstances we can accept the utterances of Scripture without reservation. The truthfulness of Scripture, then, pertains to the statements of Scripture.

In working out and explaining their doctrine of inerrancy, the orthodox Lutherans derive their ideas neither from a philosophical definition of truth nor from a thorough Biblical study of the idea of truth, though in describing God or Scripture as true, they often speak of truth as Aristotle or Thomas had done — as the agreement or correspondence of our thoughts or words with a state of affairs *(adaequatio conceptuum cum ipsa re)*.[248] Understanding truth in this sense, they would insist that there are no degrees of truth, that any true statement, e. g., concerning history or nature, has the same formal character or quality as a statement from Scripture — they recognized no double-truth theory.[249] Such an understanding of truth as pertaining only to beliefs or statements is admittedly narrow and does not presume to represent the entire Biblical idea of truth. But such an understanding in this particular context is useful in that it places truth squarely in opposition to falsehood, as the Second and Eighth Commandments do. And this elementary idea of truth as it is understood by the plain man is often fundamental to an understanding of the deeper connotations given the concept of truth in Scripture.[250] Thus, when speak-

ing of the truthfulness or veracity of Scripture, Lutheran theology is not building on any esoteric or metaphysical theory of truth but has in mind only the straightforward correspondence idea of truth that is understood and accepted by the plain man. The Lutheran theologians are simply affirming that Scripture always speaks the truth, that Scripture is inerrant in the sense that its statements and assertions correspond to what obtains (e. g., theological affirmations or statements concerning fact) or to what has taken place (e. g., historical statements recorded throughout Scripture) or to what will take place (e. g., futuristic prophecy).

To sum up, the nature of this truthfulness of Scripture, taken negatively, is essentially two-sided as we may observe from the two lengthy citations from Calov and Quenstedt, above. First, the writers of Scripture do not lie or deceive (formal falsehood). Second, the writers of Scripture were not mistaken about anything as they wrote, nor were they deceived (material falsehood). In his discussion of the veracity of Scripture Dannhauer elaborates on these and other aspects of inerrancy as follows:[251] First, Scripture must be described as congruous and consistent *(plena)* in the sense that it is incapable of contradiction. God does not speak with a yes and a no, but with a yes or no (2 Cor. 1:17 ff.). "The Spirit by whose afflatus the Sacred Writings were imbued is not a spirit of confusion and disorder." Second, the truthfulness of Scripture is to be described as infallible. There is no guesswork (στοχασμοῦ *ignara*) in the Biblical writings. Third, the Scriptures are absolutely true in the sense that they are irrefragable, unassailable. They can neither be called into doubt nor set aside. Finally, the Scriptures are true in the sense that they are unchangeable and permanent. "The truth does not just spend the night in Scripture but dwells there." The truths of Scripture are not time-bound and relative, liable to modification and alteration with the changes of culture and times, and thus leaving us bewildered and without certainty.

From the foregoing it is clear that to classical Lutheran theology God in His Word conforms to the standards of honesty and integrity that He demands of His creatures.[252] As the source of all truth God hates all lying and dissimulation.[253] And God's written Word achieves its soteriological purpose by speaking the truth — for Law and Gospel are a cognitive and truthful message — and this is the only way to achieve such a purpose according to the economy of God. The Scriptures are therefore in every sense a reliable and trustworthy witness. Thus we see that it is not on

any Aristotelian or philosophical definition of truth that the Lutheran teachers base their doctrine of Scriptural inerrancy (although their doctrine does not conflict with the Aristotelian definition of truth). Such a definition was never consciously brought into the discussions of inerrancy. The Lutheran understanding of the meaning of inerrancy was rather derived from the idea, based on Scripture, of a true and honest witness in the sense of 2 Cor. 1:17, which was often cited in this connection. Scripture is thought of as a Word of witness, the witness of very God who will not deceive or prevaricate. In particular, the Lutheran fathers think of the evangelists and apostles as well as the writers of the historical portions of the Old Testament as witnesses, witnesses of a history *(historia)*. The term *"historia"* is by far the most common term used by the Lutheran teachers for the events that the writers of Scripture record, as well as for the record of those events. This history is a history of real events and concrete facts; and the writers are true witness of those events and facts. The Lutherans do not question the different styles, background, and purposes of the various evangelists, as we shall see, but neither do they question that the holy writers write concerning real history and present their *enarratio* unerringly. We cannot and must not measure Scripture's witness by what we may determine (e. g., empirically or historically) to be the truth. Rather, truth is measured by the Word of God; the Word determines what is true.[254] Again we notice how Scripture's truthfulness is accepted a priori, as a matter of faith, before any investigation or a posteriori verification, because God who witnesses in Scripture is wholly honest and will never deviate from the truth.

By limiting the idea of truth in their discussions on inerrancy to the simple meaning of the term as we have outlined above, the old Lutheran teachers do not ignore the more pregnant Biblical concept of truth with its breadth of connotations. They were fully aware that the Biblical idea of truth comprehends a great deal more than mere correspondence of words to reality or of promise to fulfillment, and they often comment at length on this matter. Flacius, for instance, in his *Clavis Scripturae,* has a very instructive article on the various meanings of *truth* as the term and concept occurs in Scripture.[255] He merely mentions that Scripture at times speaks of truth as the agreement of words or thoughts with the object of the words or thoughts (Deut. 17:4; 22:20; John 5:32; 8:14; 19:35) in the sense of a true witness. He then goes on to show that

truth is often linked in Scripture with God's faithfulness in keeping promises, with His goodness and mercy (Ps. 100:5; 86:15; 25:10; 57:10; 92:2), His power and protection (Ps. 91:4). Sometimes truth denotes God's righteousness (Judg. 9:19; Neh. 9:33; 2 Sam. 2:6), sometimes stability and firmness (2 Kings 20:19; Is. 39:8; Ps. 85:11), sometimes genuineness (John 1:9), sometimes right worship and knowledge (John 4:24), sometimes purity and soundness, which is once again close to the idea of correspondence (Gal. 2:5, 14; 3:1), etc. Flacius also considers the various ways in which God is called truth in Scripture and other usages of the term.

4. *Full Inerrancy*

The inerrancy of Scripture is plenary, or absolute, according to orthodox Lutheranism. Inerrancy pertains to everything written and asserted in Scripture. Not merely the substance of the doctrine and narratives in Scripture is truthful but also the statements or affirmations that appear to be nonessential, adjunct, or *obiter dicta*. Not merely the primary intent of the various verses and pericopes is wholly true and reliable but also any secondary intent that may be evident, such as a passing historical reference within the framework of a narrative. Not only the soteriological, religious, doctrinal intent and content of Scripture is inerrant but also all declarative statements touching history and the realm of nature. This unqualified position is clearly set forth by Quenstedt: "The holy canonical Scriptures in their original text are the infallible truth and are free from every error. That is to say, in the sacred canonical Scriptures there is no untruth, no deceit, no error, not even a minor one, either in content or words, but each and everything presented to us in Scripture is absolutely true, whether it pertains to doctrine, ethics, history, chronology, topography, or onomastics, and no ignorance, no lack of understanding, no forgetfulness or lapse of memory can or should be ascribed to the amanuenses of the Holy Spirit in their writing of the Holy Scriptures." [256]

The Lutheran conviction concerning the plenary inerrancy of Scripture was not formulated in a vacuum. The doctrine was worked out in the main as a response to the Socinians,[257] who maintained that Scripture, although generally reliable, happened to err at times in minor matters. Parables, for instance, might have been ill chosen; or there could be some error as the writers of Scripture record historical incidents. The Lutheran

teachers saw in such a liberal attitude a threat to the authority of Scripture also in matters of doctrine; and they were fully convinced that Socinianism at this point would ultimately lead to skepticism. First, they pointed out that it was arbitrary to grant that Scripture may err in details but not in important doctrinal concerns. What evidence is there for such a position? Second, can one successfully separate the essential doctrine of Scripture from that which is merely peripheral? Often Christian doctrine is dependent on the correctness of parabolic and historical utterances of Scripture. No, the fact is that all of Scripture pertains to doctrine either directly or indirectly (Rom. 15:4; 2 Tim. 3:16) and should be believed by Christians. There are no *levicula* in the Sacred Scriptures. Calov expresses the Lutheran concerns quite adequately as he attacks the Socinian position:

> If it is enough that we believe that to be true in Scripture which pertains to true doctrine, as Socinus would have it, then Holy Scripture contains errors in many places, such as historical portions, parables, and other matters that are contained in Scripture and that, according to Socinus, do not pertain to true doctrine. But if error, or even the intimation of error, is admitted in these matters, then not even that which pertains to true doctrine is above the suspicion of error, since both historical sections and parable contribute greatly to the truth of doctrine, nay, all things that are recorded in the sacred writings pertain to our doctrine and require our faith. We are to believe not merely some things or certain passages in Scripture but everything that is contained in the holy writings.[258]

Thus the notion that only the doctrinal sections of Holy Scripture are infallible casts suspicion on the whole Bible. That there are no *levicula* in Scripture, that everything in Scripture pertains somehow to Christian doctrine, makes the inerrancy of Scripture of real practical importance for Calov and the other orthodox Lutheran theologians.

5. The Background for the New Stress on Scripture's Infallibility

There is nothing new about the doctrine of the truthfulness of Scripture as taught by the Lutherans during the late period of orthodoxy. The same position was shared by Gerhard, Flacius, Luther, the Scholastics, and the early church fathers.[259] What is new is a rather marked preoccupation with the doctrine and a greater emphasis on it by Calov, Scherzer, Dannhauer, Quenstedt, and others at about the middle of the 17th century.[260]

What was the reason for this new emphasis? The reason is clearly that now for the first time in the history of the church a freer attitude toward the inerrancy of Scripture is being taken by theologians, notably Romanists, Socinians, and Arminians, who at the same time profess fidelity to the authority of Scripture. And as we know, a teaching or principle will often not be defended at length in the church until it has been overtly attacked.

It should not surprise us that many were thinking along more liberal lines. Empiricism and the scientific method were coming into their own in the 17th century and were gaining ascendancy over men's minds, especially the minds of men of letters, including theologians. It was a growing opinion among many scholars that Scripture must be read and understood in the light of empirical evidence. For instance, the Cartesians had long insisted that Scripture must be interpreted against the philosophy and science of the day, and if there is no agreement we must be content that the writers of Scripture wrote according to common contemporary opinions and therefore could not have spoken the truth in all matters. This position was firmly rejected by the Lutheran theologians.[261] By way of reply to the Cartesian position August Pfeiffer says: "We grant that when Scripture speaks of divine and profound matters it speaks to the understanding of its day, limited as it was *(loqui ad captum hominis, etiam plebii)*." But he will concede no more than that: "We deny," he says, "that Scripture speaks according to common errors in things of nature." The conflict between the apparent conclusions drawn from empirical data and the statements of Scripture was, of course, not so intense in the 17th century as today. Still the theologians of that day were quite aware of the conflict as it existed then, and they faced up to it squarely. And so, compelled by the circumstances of their time to deal more thoroughly with the inerrancy of Scripture than had been done before, they rise to the occasion admirably. They say what they felt must be said on the subject, not with haste and invective but with restraint and only after much struggle and intense study of the issues.

We must now enter in more detail into the background of the discussions on inerrancy so as to appreciate the Lutheran position better. There are two kinds of errors of which Scripture can be charged and that concerned the later orthodox Lutherans: First, cases in which one section of Scripture does not seem to agree or cannot be harmonized with an-

The Truthfulness of Scripture 349

other section so that Scripture appears to contradict itself; second, cases in which statements of Scripture do not seem to correspond to the data in the external world (astronomy, geography, topography, etc.) or to the accepted facts of history. It is perhaps with the first problem that the Lutheran theologians were more concerned; for this was nothing new in their day. However, as we shall see, they were also alive to the second problem. How they met each problem I shall now trace in some detail.

a. APPARENT CONTRADICTIONS. The first problem was faced by all the Lutheran theologians during the period of orthodoxy: Does Scripture contradict itself? This was an old question that plagued every serious theologian who read his Bible and found apparent discrepancies there. But now the problem was somewhat more acute because many exegetes and scholars, especially within the ranks of the Socinians, were maintaining that there were such contradictions in Scripture.

The tendency of many of the Lutheran teachers, at least in their systematic works, was at the outset to dismiss the problem by asserting a priori that contradictions in Scripture are only apparent, inasmuch as God, the author of Scripture, cannot lie or contradict Himself. Thus we find Gerhard saying: "All Scripture is inspired, and accordingly all the things in Scripture are in agreement and are not contrary or opposed to one another." [262] Such a procedure was quite in keeping with the conviction that the truthfulness of Scripture is an article of faith, like the divine origin of Scripture, and needs no proof by way of analysis or extra-Biblical evidence. It is really quite irrelevant that heretics or even serious exegetes seem to find errors or contradictions in Scripture.[263] Such "findings" do not constitute Scripture evidence, even though they may appear to be based on a careful reading of Scripture. For they fail to accept Scripture in terms of its own claims concerning itself. It is the claims of Scripture that settle the matter of its inerrancy, not what the reader of Scripture may think he finds in Scripture and deduce from that. In other words, when Scripture makes a clear assertion, even though logical analysis or the accepted canons of evidence might indicate otherwise, a Christian theologian must simply — and, we could add, blindly — cling to the divine claim of Scripture. Neither human experience nor human understanding can challenge the authority or truthfulness of Scripture. It is, in fact, one of the very objects of Scripture to enlighten the darkened mind and heart

of man *(mens hominis caligine obruta),* and this involves a complete conversion of man's understanding. (Is. 9:1; Luke 2:32; Eph. 4:18; 5:18)

It was, however, not enough for Lutherans to maintain in the almost perfunctory manner mentioned above that the Scriptures do not contradict themselves, however valid their argument was. Times were changing rapidly in the 16th and 17th centuries. Many exegetes and scholars, especially within the ranks of the Socinians,[264] were simply assuming in their writings that the writers of the Scriptures contradicted themselves at various points. It was argued that one writer came much closer to the truth at times than another and that there were sometimes out-and-out conflicts. The result was that in certain minor matters the writers of Scripture were able to err. This Socinian position had to be answered. The many apparent discrepancies found in Scripture had to be cleared up, if possible. It must be shown also inductively that the evangelists and other writers of Scripture do not disagree with one another.

The efforts to solve the difficulties and apparent discrepancies were carried out primarily in the exegetical works of the old Lutherans as well as in special studies devoted particularly to this purpose.[265] In his *Harmonia Biblica,* Michael Walther attempts to clear the air for a proper approach to the many apparent contradictions in Scripture by reminding the reader first of all what contradictions and contraries really are.[266] To be contradictory two statements must (1) speak of the same termini in number and order, (2) refer to the same part of the subject (3) at the same time and (4) in the same sense; and (5) the one statement must affirm, and the other deny. Walther first argues deductively that Scripture as the Word of God will not contradict itself, since God will not lie or deceive. But he points out that the predication of any contradiction to the Scriptures not only is an affront to the high majesty of God, who moved the penmen to write as they did, but also suggests laziness or lack of depth and scholarship in the interpreter of Scripture. It is the part of a pious and responsible exegete not to attack the Scriptures for contradicting themselves but to solve the problems he finds therein, if possible.[267] Walther then proceeds to list many reasons for the apparent discrepancies in Scripture and for the fact that no immediate solution can be found to these problems: (1) Ignorance of the original languages of Scripture, their peculiarities, figures of speech, stylistics, etc. (2) Equivocation and ambiguity of language (cf. Mark 12:43, where Christ uses the term *more* equivocally, in the sense that one gives "more" according to

The Truthfulness of Scripture

his ability). (3) Neglect of context. (4) Hasty consideration of attendant circumstances of the text, e. g., ignoring the person speaking or spoken to, or the time, place, mode, or scope of the statement or pericope. (5) Overhasty linking and relating of Bible passages. Statements that speak of diverse things cannot be contradictory. (6) Misuse of our reason, which does not understand the things of God. To attempt to understand and then to harmonize the things of God is Sadduceeism. (7) Failure to pray over our difficulties. It is clear that to Walther no exegete, with the limitations of perception and understanding that are his, is in a position to charge the Scriptures of containing contradictions or discrepancies.

This was precisely the position of Flacius, who in a briefer manner attempted to offer the same kind of aid for solving Bible difficulties as Walther. Flacius sums up his position as follows:

> There is absolutely no true contradiction anywhere in Scripture (just as Quintilian says about laws), but those things that seem to conflict with each other are so regarded because of our limitation {culpa} and extreme ignorance, inasmuch as we do not have an adequate understanding of the subject matter or the language of Scripture or do not consider sufficiently the attendant circumstances. Therefore those matters in Scripture that seem to be contrary to each other are so only to those who do not consider the background, persons, times, and relative circumstances of those matters. Meanwhile the matters themselves do not conflict with each other according to any tacit or expressed diversity of background, circumstances, places, times, or persons.[268]

Flacius and Walther then offer general rules of hermeneutics that sometimes help to solve our difficulties when we run across apparent discrepancies in Scripture. Walther finally takes up book by book, very meticulously, the specific discrepancies alleged to be found in Scripture. For it is the duty of the exegete to resolve as many of these problems as he can, just as it is his function to give help toward a solution of stylistic, grammatical, and other difficulties one may encounter in reading Scripture; all this is part of the exegetical task of bringing out the meaning of Scripture.

We cannot possibly offer here any extended coverage of specific answers that were proffered as solutions to the various alleged discrepancies in Scripture. However, a couple of general observations must be made, together with some necessary examples of how the old Lutherans went about their task of solving the problem of discrepancies.

In the first place, we observe that the Lutheran teachers were extremely cautious in offering explanations for apparent conflicts in Scripture. They will not dogmatically insist that their particular solution is the only one or the correct one. In fact they often suggest many possible solutions, as, for example, their treatment of Matt. 27:9-10, where the evangelist quotes apparently from Zech. 11:12-13, although he cites Jeremiah as his source. Replying to Erasmus, who believed that the evangelist simply suffered a loss of memory at this point, Gerhard comments as follows: "Since the evangelists when they constructed their sacred history were the Holy Spirit's penmen, who spoke and wrote as they were moved by the Holy Spirit (2 Peter 1:21), it would be a grave affront to the Holy Spirit Himself to attribute such an error to the evangelists."[269] Moreover there are more plausible explanations for the difficulty, and Gerhard lists no fewer than eight suggestions that had been made over the years. Some of these conjectures (e. g., that Zechariah was also called Jeremiah on occasion or that there was another apocryphal book of Jeremiah from which Jesus quoted) are indeed quite fanciful, but others are not unconvincing (e. g., that we have in this quotation a conflation that alludes to Jer. 32:7 ff.). To Gerhard neither the proper reverence toward the text nor cautious and responsible scholarship could possibly solve the apparent discrepancies of Scripture by charging an evangelist with error or forgetfulness. Michael Walther and Calov argue in the same vein; they too offer a number of possible explanations but seem to favor the theory that Christ's quotation is a conflation.[270]

In the second place, we observe that the orthodox Lutherans are very independent in offering their solutions to the apparent conflicts they find in Scripture. For instance, a number of explanations are advanced for the vexing problems connected with Christ's healing of the blind men at Jericho (Matt. 20:29-34; Mark 10:46-52; Luke 18:34-35). The old Lutherans find no difficulty with the fact that Mark and Luke mention only one of the men who were healed. Calov merely remarks that "one of the men was better known than the other; therefore Mark and Luke made mention of only the one to whom without doubt the main circumstances of this story pertain; Matthew tells his story more comprehensively."[271] It is the place where the miracle occurred that causes the most difficulty. Was it at Jesus' entrance into Jericho or at His departure? And here there is no unanimity among the Lutherans in the answers

they give. Leyser arrives at the conclusion that there were two miracles: Luke recounts the first when Jesus enters Jericho; after this occurs the incident with Zacchaeus and the telling of the parable of the nobleman and the ten pieces of money (Luke 19:1-27); and then Jesus leaves Jericho toward Jerusalem and heals Bartimaeus (as recounted in Matthew and Mark).[272] Calov maintains that there was only one miracle, which took place as Jesus departed Jericho. "And there is no problem," he says, "in the fact that Luke says ἐν τῷ ἐγγίζειν αὐτὸν εἰς 'Ιεριχώ. For ἐγγίζειν does not always mean motion toward a place but often merely signifies distance. Thus the sense of the passage is: when He was not far from the city. This is so in the case of Luke 19:29: ἤγγισεν εἰς Βηθφαγὴ καὶ Βηθανία; for He had already traveled through Bethany."[273] Michael Walther favors the conjecture of Cornelius a Lapide.[274] The theory was that Luke, as well as Matthew and Mark, speaks of Bartimaeus, who meets Jesus and cries to Him as He enters the city. But Jesus feigns not to hear because of the crowd, for He wants to test and strengthen the blind man's faith. Later the same Bartimaeus stands before Jesus as he leaves the city and is given His sight. Luke does not say that Jesus healed the blind man before He entered Jericho but merely that the blind man met him there. John Gerhard offers no final solution to the problem under consideration but in his cautious way simply compiles a list of all the reputable theories that have been suggested and lets the reader judge for himself.[275]

The independent spirit with which Lutheran exegetes go about solving the many problems that face them as they try to reconcile different pericopes and events recorded in Scripture is noticed again and again as one reads their commentaries, and this is the more remarkable when we consider that they were invariably conversant with the works of one another. We have noticed that often no final solution is suggested to some of the troublesome apparent discrepancies found in Scripture. The orthodox Lutherans would rather live with such difficulties than offer unfounded and unconvincing speculations as solutions. For although "God who speaks in Scripture does not reveal {proferre} things that are in opposition to Himself or contradictions (part of which are always false)," still "we grant that there are sometimes apparent contradictions [ἐναντιοφαντές] found in Scripture, sayings that appear on the face of it to be contrary and contradictory."[276]

b. APPARENT ERRORS OF FACT. The second problem facing all Lutheran theologians during the period of orthodoxy pertained to the possibility of errors of fact in Scripture. Are the Scriptures at times mistaken when they touch on matters relating to history, geography, and the world of nature? This problem was fully as troublesome at that time as the first, and the Lutheran theologians did not dodge it. We must recall that these scholars were not living in a prescientific age; and they were fully aware of the issues that faced them in this matter and of the implications of affirming a doctrine of Scripture's inerrancy. Their problem was, of course, not so great as ours today; for they were better equipped to meet the onslaught of empiricism and the scientific method than we are today — first, because they had fewer problems of this nature to cope with and, second, because they were more broadly educated than we are in our specialized age. The issue facing orthodox theology at this point is stated succinctly by Calov. The question is: "Whether faith should be extended to those matters in Scripture that do not pertain expressly to religion, such as refer to the physical sciences, mathematics, etc., or whether these things are spoken of only in a rough manner [παχυλῶς]?"[277] Calov answers the question: "In the whole Scripture there can be no error, not even in minor matters, no memory failures, no untruth."[278] Quenstedt offers an even more explicit answer to the question when he affirms: "Everything that is presented to us in Scripture is absolutely true *{verissima}*, whether it pertains to doctrine, ethics, history, chronology, topography, or onomastics, and no ignorance, no lack of understanding, no forgetfulness or lapse of memory can or should be ascribed to the amanuenses of the Holy Spirit in their writing of the Holy Scriptures."[279]

In affirming that there are no errors of fact in Scripture, orthodox Lutheranism is opposing two prevalent opinions of that day. First, it was commonly held among certain philosophers and theologians that Scripture spoke in a loose and careless fashion when alluding to matters not pertaining to the theological purpose of Scripture. Accordingly, no apodictic certainty can be derived from anything Scripture says on such matters (e. g., it would be improper to seek proofs from Scripture for a theory on the movement of the earth). Second, Socinians and certain Arminians[280] taught that Christ in His conversations accommodated Himself to errors and to the ordinary misconceptions of the day. The apostles did the same, and they did so purposely. It was therefore not necessary to accept the

The Truthfulness of Scripture

events recounted in Scripture as true or to believe the sermons offered therein, unless a chief article of faith was involved. Both of these common opinions amount to the same thing: there are errors in Scripture when it mentions matters that are not strictly doctrinal — e. g., allusions to science or history.

The orthodox Lutherans did not wholly reject either opinion. They recognized, as we shall see, that Scripture in describing the things of nature spoke according to the common uncritical opinions and nuances of the day and therefore ought not to be used as a textbook for natural science. They also taught a doctrine of condescension (συγκατάβασις) according to which the Spirit of God caused Scripture to be recorded not only in the accustomed speech and style of the holy writers but also in a manner that was clear and well suited to the hearers and readers.[281] Dannhauer, for instance, says: "Holy Scripture often adjusts its language not so much to the actual existence of a thing as to the common opinion of men, as when it calls Joseph the father of Christ because this was what was thought by the common people, or when it says that stars fall from heaven because uninformed people think comets are stars." [282] But with one voice the Lutherans insisted that the Scriptures did not accommodate themselves to error.

The main criticism of Lutheranism against the Socinian position is that it is arbitrary, has no foundation in Scripture, and is impossible to apply; and we have already outlined this above when describing the doctrine of plenary inerrancy. It should now be quite clear what is the fundamental issue separating Lutheranism from Socinianism on the question of the inerrancy of Scripture. Socinianism held that the empirical method as employed in the natural sciences and in historical studies could be used to judge the veracity and authenticity of Biblical affirmations. The Socinians were convinced that this procedure did no violence to the claims of Scripture concerning its own authority. For those things that are found wrong or contradictory in Scripture are always of a minor nature and do not affect doctrine. If such minor historical mistakes occur in Scripture, this only serves and bolsters the authority of Scripture and of faith. "In doctrine," says Socinus, "we can confidently affirm that nothing is found [in Scripture] that is manifestly recognized to be false." [283] However, in minor matters and on historical points there can be found divergencies and errors in Scripture.[284] How do we determine that there

are such historical errors in Scripture? By the use of the historical method, by subjecting the witness of Moses, Mark, or Matthew to the same critical historical analysis as the works of Livy or Plutarch or any careful writer or historian of the past. This is precisely the method used by Socinus as he defends the authenticity of the four Gospels. Their authenticity is based on the fact that they appear to be firsthand witness accounts of the life of Jesus; and Socinus had no reason in his day to doubt the traditional date and authorship of the Gospels. Thus, for Socinus, history is not only helpful for understanding Scripture; but the canons of the historical method of that day become normative for judging the truthfulness and authenticity of Biblical affirmations. Although the Socinians possessed far less historical judgment than Semler, the germs of the historicocritical method are clearly discernible in this approach to Scripture.

Is it any wonder that the Lutheran theologians of that day became excited? The Socinian approach spells the downfall of all faithful exegesis. It refuses to allow Scripture to be interpreted according to its literal sense and intention. If the obvious intention of a passage of Scripture seems to conflict with the evidence of science or of history, we must give a new meaning to the passage. Such a practice was an illicit usurpation of reason, according to Lutheran theology. Calov points out that in particular so-called empirical evidence *(demonstratio per causas vel effecta)* must not be used as a norm in interpreting or judging the message of Scripture.[285] Much that is recorded in Scripture is above the evidence of the investigations of nature or history, particularly such fundamental teachings as creation from nothing, a virgin birth, a conception by God's Spirit, resurrection of dead people, etc. Therefore the "evidence" or data from history or natural science cannot be used as norms in determining the truthfulness or authenticity of any Biblical account of things.

This is an immensely important principle for classical Lutheranism, which sets off its entire approach to Scripture from Socinianism and from most exegetes in our day. To Lutheranism the claims or intention of Biblical pericopes and statements must be accepted as they stand not only when they appear to conflict with analytic judgments (e. g., the doctrine of the Trinity or the Incarnation) but also when they run counter to the claims of the synthetic judgments of science or history. Such a posture was not the result of a naïve obscurantism but was the result of a position

taken reverently and deliberately with a full understanding of the consequences involved. The Lutherans were completely at odds with the view, increasingly popular since Leibniz, that truths of existences are only contingent. As a general rule they will not dispute with Leibniz' distinction between truths of reason and truths of experience, the former being based on the principle of conceivability, the latter on the principle of actuality (nature and history). But they will not countenance the practice of the Socinians and later of Lessing of bringing Leibniz' logical distinctions into the realm of God's revelation and theology. For then no event recorded in Scripture need be true. All Scripture becomes suspect and subject to Pyrrhonic doubt. And at best we can have only academic probability also in those matters that pertain to our salvation. No, Scripture, even though it has come to us under conditions of space and time, is by virtue of its divine origin infallible, and that in whatever area it may touch on. Calov sums up the Lutheran concern as follows:

> If the source of theology (divine revelation) is not entirely infallible, sure, and certain, but is only probable and limited to its day *{topicum}*, then no theological conclusions are infallible and sure, for a conclusion cannot be more certain than its own proper and legitimate basis. If this axiom, "Whatever God has spoken is infallibly true and to be believed with complete assurance," is not categorically binding but is made to be relative and doubtful, then some things have been spoken and promulgated by God that are only probable and not to be held with certainty as being absolutely necessary *{apodicticam}*. In that case who could make any definite affirmation or conclusion in theology about anything that is set forth in God's Word, and say that it is certainly true and worthy of all acceptation?[286]

It is clear that to orthodox Lutheranism the admission of any error in Scripture impugns the authority and integrity of all Scripture, makes man's experience and judgment (scientific or historical investigations) lord over the divine Word, and undermines all serious and reverent exegesis. As far as I have been able to determine, very little evidence from science or history (except the argument from the fulfillment of prophecy, which was called forth to show the divine nature of Scripture in a general way) is used by any orthodox Lutheran to support the truthfulness of any Scripture statement, although such evidence was often presented to clarify Biblical assertions. Such a procedure would have been considered unnecessary.

6. Adjuncts to the Doctrine of Scripture's Inerrancy: Inerrancy and Hermeneutics

The doctrine of inerrancy must be understood in the light of the actual hermeneutics of classical Lutheranism and can only be appreciated in this light. Too often historians have imputed to Lutheran orthodoxy a theory of inerrancy that could only have appeared grotesque and ludicrous to those old Lutheran theologians. The Lutheran theologians realize that Scripture will appear hopelessly obscure and filled with error not only to those who cannot divide Law and Gospel[287] but to those also who are uninformed and insensitive to the stylistics and hermeneutics of Scripture. For this reason several Lutherans list within their discussions on the truthfulness of Scripture a number of general rules of interpretation that might serve to reveal that what at first sight appears to be an error or contradiction in Scripture is in fact no such thing.[288] They realize, of course, that many problems will not be solved and many solutions can at best be only tentative and perhaps hazardous. The following are some of the helpful rules that Calov presents. His suggested helps apply to both apparent contradictions and apparent errors of fact in Scripture.

a. Statements that are simply repeated or portray a common opinion of the day are not to be taken as stating the truth expressly (*Locutiones Spiritus S.* κατὰ μίμησιν *non accipiendae, quasi* κατ' ἀλήθειαν *dicantur*).

b. That which is spoken to a relative situation must not be taken as though it were set forth as an absolute assertion.

c. Things are often described in Scripture as they appear to the senses, not as they really are (*In Scriptura nonnunquam res describitur, ut est* φαινομένως *et* κατὰ δόξαν, *non* κατὰ τὸ εἶναι). One can immediately perceive how helpful this principle might be when a statement in Scripture concerning the things of nature appears to conflict with the conclusions of science. And in fact this principle was often followed in the exegesis of the classical Lutherans. For instance, Bechmann in his comments on Gen. 1:14 points out that the moon is described as a great light only πρὸς ὀφθαλμόν, from our point of observation, "not because it is greater than the other stars in magnitude but because it is closer to us; and because of its nearness to our point of vision, it appears to be greater. And so Moses adds that God made a greater light (the sun) to rule by day and a lesser light (the moon) to rule by night. . . . Now the other stars are smaller bodies than the moon, not in truth but according to the

way they appear to us, for the size of the moon appears greater to us because of its proximity and because, brightened by the sun, it is able to dispel the darkness of night, which the other stars cannot do."[289] But Calov's principle above is not always followed, not even by Calov himself, who argues for the Ptolemaic theory of the universe on the basis of Joshua 10:13.[290] It is interesting, however, that Cort Aslakssen insisted that the Copernican theory of the universe was quite Biblical, and he defended this thesis by interpreting pertinent passages of Scripture phenomenally.[291]

d. The holy writers, inspired as they were, sometimes preach and urge things as spokesmen of God, sometimes as private individuals. I suppose Calov has such passages as 1 Cor. 7:6-7, 10, 25 in mind at this point.

e. When two authors do not offer the same arrangement of chronology in depicting the same events, this does not imply a contradiction. We must accord the Holy Spirit freedom in such matters.[292] What appear to be discrepancies of chronology, numbering, etc., must be ascribed to the diverse circumstances in which the various authors lived or to their different purposes in writing. And naturally we do not know these circumstances and purposes as well as they.

Chemnitz in the introduction to his *Harmonia Quatuor Evangelistarum* goes into this matter in minutest detail.[293] He points out the many, many diversities among the four evangelists in their arrangement of the chronology in the life of Christ. None of them, not even Luke, proposes to offer "an exact order" in the events he records. But each arranges the events as his particular purpose dictates, each has his own formulae for introducing certain events and tying events together. Again one evangelist may be more prone to anticipation or recapitulation in certain instances. Events are passed over or connected according to the plan of the author.

> For instance, Matthew links together the accounts of the call and the sending out of the apostles, although it is certain that these incidents happened at different times. Luke tells the story of the arrest of the Baptist (3:19) long before it happened. Mark in turn connects the arrest and the beheading of the Baptist, when obviously these events did not happen at the same time. . . . Luke also writes that when the parents of Christ had completed all things that had to be done according to the Law in regard to the circumcision and purification of the child, they returned to Nazareth, although it is certainly necessary to interpose between these events that which is written in Matt. 2:13 about the flight into Egypt.

And yet in keeping with the evangelical purpose of these narratives and with the authority of the inspired evangelists, it is always a true history and a sufficient history that is recorded (John 21:24; Rev. 22:18), and all "is directed truly and faithfully *{recte & fideliter}* for the edifying of our faith." [294] Obviously these four accounts of the life of Christ will present certain problems, and the interpreter may expect to labor in order to learn the proper order and agreement between the different accounts — this is the case also in the study of secular history — but it will be pleasant and rewarding work. For here the Spirit offers to us the "saving history *{salutarem historiam}* of the deeds and words of Christ." And the Spirit expects us to struggle with these precious writings not to find fault with them or errors in them, but He has vouchsafed them to us "according to a certain very concordant dissonance *{concordissima dissonantia}* (if one may speak in such a way) in order to exercise the minds of the faithful in humble and careful investigation of the truth, whereby we learn that the four evangelists did not write by mutual agreement but by divine inspiration."

f. Certain historical occurrences are spoken of in Scripture according to hysteron proteron.

g. Scripture sometimes spreads out time for the sake of symmetry and consistency.

h. Sometimes occurrences that have only begun are spoken of in Scripture as though they were already completed.

i. Future events are sometimes presented in Scripture as having already happened.

j. Specific statements in Scripture sometimes modify general statements.

k. Different names for the same object often make Scripture appear to contradict itself.

l. Scripture often speaks in round numbers *(Nonnulla dicuntur per rotundationem numerorum)*.

m. Law statements in Scripture cannot be placed in opposition to Gospel statements.

n. It must always be understood that divine threats in Scripture can always be averted through repentance.

o. Scripture employs the words of the world and of ordinary language to speak of things that concern God and eternity.

p. Sometimes precepts are set down in Scripture by example, not in so many words (*non κατὰ γράμμα, sed κατὰ πρᾶγμα*).

q. Often the so-called mystical sense must be preferred to the prima facie surface meaning of certain passages in Scripture.

7. The Concerns Behind the Lutheran Doctrine of Inerrancy

There are, I believe, two very important practical concerns that motivate the Lutherans as they express their belief in the truthfulness of the Sacred Scriptures. First, there is the deep conviction that everyone should repair to the Scriptures with complete confidence in all their promises and all their utterances, that everyone should be encouraged to accept all that Scripture says without hesitation or reservation or doubt of any kind. In other words, the Scriptures are wholly reliable, and every Christian can depend on the Scriptures at every point. This is all so important because the truth of Christianity and of the Gospel is bound up with the truth of Scripture.[295] It is therefore not merely the formal and material truthfulness of Scripture statements that is involved, or merely the correspondence between declarative statements of Scripture and a state of affairs, fundamental as this is to the entire discussion; but the truthfulness of Scripture involves the integrity and honesty of the prophets and apostles and of God Himself. There is a moral issue here. This is the reason why Calov and others so often call it blasphemous and an affront to the majesty and integrity of God to charge Scripture with error. God always speaks without prevarication or dissimulation of any kind. Because of their imperfection men err and dissemble, but God does not. The Polish Reformed theologian John Maccovius (Makowsky) had urged that not all deceit was evil. Calov, on the contrary, believes that all deceit is hypocrisy and sin. And this is particularly serious when we consider the importance of all that God speaks to us. He offers great promises to us, and these promises are according to truth.[296]

Second, we find the classical Lutheran thologians defending the inerrancy of Scripture so adamantly because they considered themselves to be serious exegetes who desired to face squarely the exegetical problems presented in Scripture. To Lutheran theology one who doubted the veracity of Scripture could be neither a faithful nor a scholarly exegete; for among other things, such a person would tend to offer facile or even superficial answers to difficult problems and thus never find sound, convincing ex-

planations. Such an approach would furthermore tend to overlook linguistic and hermeneutical helps that at times not only suggest solutions to many problems but yield as well a deeper insight into the message and meaning of Scripture. It is not the part of scholarship to solve the many difficulties in Scripture by suggesting error; such a procedure is not doing justice to the data or the serious intent of all Scripture. Today many might suppose that the orthodox Lutherans were quite naïve at this point, living as they did in a "precritical" era. But this would be a naïve supposition. Anyone reading Chemnitz' great harmony will see that the internal data relative to the synoptic problem as we approach it today were not only available also to Chemnitz but that he was thoroughly acquainted with them. Yet, unlike so many modern interpreters, he found no real contradictions or discrepancies in the synoptic gospels. To his own satisfaction and to that of his contemporaries he was able to solve the great preponderance of difficulties connected with the synoptic gospels. Why was this so? Very clearly because he, like all Lutherans of his day, approached the data with a childlike confidence in the reliability of the evangelists as God's witnesses, with a confidence that there could be no errors in God's holy Word. It will always remain true that whether one believes that errors can be found in Scripture or not depends not so much on one's analysis of the Scriptures as on the predilections one brings with one as one interprets the Scriptures. And so it is the mark both of piety and scholarship today to believe in the truthfulness of the Scriptures just as it was in Chemnitz' day.

THE EFFICACY OF SCRIPTURE

One of the most significant and rewarding features of the historic Lutheran doctrine of the Word is the strong emphasis (unique to Lutheranism) on the power of God's Word. The discussion of this subject is carried out at two points in the later Lutheran dogmatics: first, within the *locus* on Scripture in a section entitled "The Efficacy of Scripture"; and second, much later when Law and Gospel are considered. The earlier Lutherans through the time of Gerhard have no section on the efficacy of Scripture. This feature of the Lutheran doctrine of the Word is significant because the doctrine of Scripture or the Word of God is utterly incomplete if this aspect of it is not given its due prominence. The doctrine of the Word assumes its true significance only when viewed soteriologi-

cally, when considered as an operative factor in God's plan of salvation. And how often and how insistently do the Lutheran fathers repeat, as we have seen, that the purpose of God's self-disclosure and of His speaking to man is soteriological! Again this feature of the Lutheran doctrine of the Word is significant, because at this very point Lutheran orthodoxy proves itself to be faithful to the legacy of Luther, who viewed all Scripture as Law with its crushing power to condemn and Gospel with its power to give life and to rescue the lost sinner, and who constantly stressed the power and activity of the Word.

For classical Lutheran orthodoxy, as for Luther, the efficacy of Scripture is not an appendage that merely puts the finishing touches on the article *de Scriptura*. On the contrary, the power of the Word is fundamental to their doctrine of Scripture. Nor is the power of the Word to make men new creatures and bring them a new life in Christ ever subordinated to the authority of Scripture. No, only one who has been quickened by the Word of life will ever submit to the authority of the divine Word. The proper balance between the authority of the written Word (*auctoritas canonica seu normativa*) as the source of theology and the power of the Word to bring sinners to faith and to save them (*auctoritas causativa*) was always stressed by Lutheran theology. The Word of God must never be viewed only *ratione* γνώσεως, as a *principium cognoscendi*, but also *ratione* πράξεως, as a *principium operandi*, as a dynamic, effective means of converting men, regenerating, justifying, and saving them.[297]

1. *The Power and Work of the Gospel*

When the old Lutheran teachers speak of the power of the Word of God, they are not thinking of Scripture specifically but of the divine Word in general in whatever mode of expression it may assume. And when they refer directly to the efficacy of Scripture, they have in mind not Scripture considered as a book, consisting of letters and words and phrases (which are the vehicle of the divine content), but the message of Scripture.[298] At this point we must recall all that was said concerning the unity of the Word of God and concerning the so-called *forma* (the meaning, the inspired message), which strictly speaking was God's Word.[299] The written Word, the preached Word, the Word treasured in the believer's heart, is one Word of God, which carries with it by virtue of its divine *forma* (nature) the power of very God. There is something highly prac-

tical and comforting in the Lutheran doctrine of the unity of the Word in our present context. Here we are told that the Word taught or preached today is fully as effective and life-giving as the Word that issued from the mouth of God or the Word that is presented in the Sacred Scriptures.

Again when the orthodox Lutheran theologians speak of the power of the Word, they have in mind the Gospel Word. Strictly speaking, not the Scriptures as a whole but only the Gospel is a means of grace. Of course, "the entire history of Scripture ought by all means to be believed, but not the entire history offers the consolations that are available in the article of justification; for the thunderings of the Law, the threats, and the examples of those who are suffering [eternal] torment terrify consciences rather than cheer them up." [300] Only in a synechdochical sense, only by virtue of the fact that it contains the Gospel, is Scripture said to have the power to create faith and the spiritual life in a sinner. This does not imply that the Law of God has no power. On the contrary, its power is a consuming and inexorable power. But it has no power to produce faith in Christ or to justify; its power is only to threaten and to judge and to kill.[301] This is always the function of the Law and its chief function. "Whatever uncovers sin, whatever announces wrath and punishment, whatever incites terrors of conscience, whenever and wherever this may happen, carries out the function of the Law." [302] The Law does not lead the sinner to Christ — it knows nothing of Christ [303] — but away from Him. And yet, paradoxically, by showing the sinner his lost condition (Rom. 3:20), by working wrath (Rom. 4:15) and "only wrath," the Law compels the sinner to seek Christ.[304] And Hollaz can say: "Although the Law formally and directly knows nothing and teaches nothing about Christ, still by accusing, convicting, and terrifying, it indirectly constrains the sinner to seek comfort and help in Christ the Redeemer." [305] But strictly speaking, the Law, which pertains only to works, has nothing to do with the Gospel. "The Gospel is the Word of life; the Law cannot give life. The Gospel promises an inheritance; there is no inheritance from the Law. By the Gospel we are justified; but by the works of the Law no flesh shall be justified. Therefore the Law, or the doctrine of works, strictly speaking, does not pertain to the Gospel." [306] Not the Law, according to Lutheran theology, but the Word of Gospel is the seed by which we are born again, the food and drink by which we are nourished.[307]

The Efficacy of Scripture

And what is this efficacy of Scripture, this power of the Gospel Word? It is the intrinsic power to convert all men indiscriminately.[308] It is the power to enlighten, quicken, regenerate, and save the lost sinner. This is not a physical power or a power of moral suasion but a supernatural power to save. The Word accomplishes this saving work not alone and independently but as an instrument of the Spirit of God (ὀργανικῶς, *instrumentaliter*).[309] The Spirit does not ordinarily come to men and bestow His gifts of pardon and faith and eternal life without means, but works conversion and faith through the Word (Rom. 10:17; 1 Cor. 4:1, 5; Acts 11:21). The Spirit works and dwells in men through the ministry of the Word as through an instrument or organ (ὄχημα, *vehiculum*).[310] And Christ dwells in those who receive and keep His Word. (John 14:23; Eph. 3:16-17)

The Word of God as a means of grace is not a passive, inanimate instrument that, like a rock or stick, even when put in use has no power in itself. No, it is an *instrumentum activum & cooperativum*, like the eye or hand of a living man.[311] It is not a mere sign that points the way to eternal life, but it actually brings Christ and eternal life to the sinner and brings the sinner to faith in Christ. It is more than a mere invitation, offering us righteousness and salvation; it actually confers these blessings on us and makes us partakers of Christ's kingdom. Basing his remarks on 1 Peter 1:23, Gerhard says the following on this matter:

> [The Word] regenerates us not merely theoretically by enlightening the mind with a knowledge of the divine will and indicating to us what we must believe and do, but does so actually by really turning our will to accept the divine witness and by moving and transforming and awakening our heart to believe in it so that we cling to this grace that is offered in Christ and find happiness in it, and through this faith become children of God and heirs of eternal life. The Word quickens us not only in the sense that it invites us to enjoy God's favor towards us and encourages us with a living comfort, but it also makes us partakers of that spiritual life.[312]

The evidence offered by the old Lutheran teachers for the doctrine of the power of the Word is far too vast even to summarize adequately. Fully two thirds of Quenstedt's treatment of the subject in his *Systema* is devoted to lengthy exegeses of the pertinent Biblical evidence. We can only mention the line of thought that manifests itself in connection with the passages under consideration. According to John 6:63 the Word of God

is Spirit and life because it is animated with the Spirit of God and because it actually confers spiritual and eternal life on the believer. And from the great effects of this Word we perceive its great power. Again a comment of Gerhard's is pertinent: "To the Word of God is attributed not only an ἐνέργεια ζωοποιητική, an active power to make alive, but also a δύναμις, a power to save (Rom. 1:16). For this reason it is called a living Word of God, because as the Word of the living God it possesses an inner power to make alive, and this power it employs effectively in men who are to be quickened."[313] According to Rom. 1:16 there is a power and capacity inhering in the Gospel Word to enlighten, regenerate, and save those who believe. For this reason the Word is called the Gospel of salvation (Eph. 1:13). It is obvious in this verse that Paul as he speaks of power has in mind not the content or the object of the Gospel, which is Christ, or the mysteries of the Gospel, which are the articles of faith, but the preaching *(annunciatio, doctrina, concio, laetum nuncium)* of the Gospel (1 Cor. 1:18, 21).[314] And it must be noted that this Gospel Word is not merely powerful in some vague sense but it is the power of very God.[315]

The old dogmaticians bring up many other pertinent passages to support their doctrine of the power of the Word, specifically 1 Thess. 2:13, James 1:21, 1 Peter 1:23, and Heb. 4:12 (which is taken as including both Law and Gospel). They also point out how often Scripture ascribes to the Word of God the power and capacity to accomplish specific effects in people: to quicken (2 Cor. 3:6; Eph. 2:5; Phil. 2:16; Acts 5:20), to give life (Ps. 19:7-8; 2 Tim. 2:25; 1 Peter 1:23; James 1:18; 1 Cor. 4:15; Gal. 4:19), to bestow faith (John 17:20; Rom. 10:17; 1 Cor. 3:5; Col. 1:5; 2 Peter 1:19), to justify (Rom. 3:27-28), to purify (John 15:3), to sanctify (1 Peter 1:22), to preserve in faith and grace (1 Peter 5:10), to renew (Eph. 4:23), and to save (John 5:24, 39; 6:69; 1 Cor. 1:21; Acts 11:14). When the Word of God is said to grow and multiply and increase, this indicates the mighty spiritual impact it has on people (cf. Acts 6:7; 12:24; 19:20). Commenting on such passages, Brochmand says:

> If the Word of God, when it is read or promulgated by preaching, were not an efficacious medium through which souls are turned to God, why would the Scriptures say, "The Word grew, and the number of the disciples multiplied" (Acts 6:7)? Moreover, the Spirit of God addressed the Jews who did not accept the Gospel preachment

with these words: "It was necessary that the Word (which is the Word of salvation, v. 26) be preached to you, but because you reject it, you make yourselves unworthy of eternal life." (Acts 13:46) [316]

To the Law also are ascribed dynamic effects; it is said to harden, kill, and condemn. And so because of its great accomplishments the Word of God is likened to objects that have intrinsic power, such as medicine, rain and snow, a seed, wine, fire, etc.

Finally, Quenstedt and the other dogmaticians speak of the great impact the sword of the Spirit has had in the lives of specific people. Pharaoh was hardened and blinded by the Word to the point where he was compelled to plead for mercy. Felix was so overcome by the preachment of the captive Paul concerning righteousness and judgment that he trembled and became so frightened that he would listen to Paul no longer. At the preachment of Jonah the entire city of Nineveh repented in sackcloth and ashes and averted the judgment of God. And think of Peter's Pentecost sermon whereby 3,000 were pricked in their hearts and were converted. Small wonder that the Word is called living and powerful and sharper than any two-edged sword, piercing even to the dividing of the soul and spirit! It is indeed the Spirit's vehicle for crushing men and making them alive.

2. *The Inherent Power of the Word*

In 1621, Hermann Rathmann, Lutheran pastor at Danzig, published a book called *Vom Gnadenreich Christi,* which caused a great stir among the orthodox Lutherans.[317] To Rathmann Scripture was not a means of grace but in itself a dead letter, a mere sign *(Wegzeiger),* an index and witness *(Zeugnis)* to grace. It is the Holy Spirit alone who converts man; His testimony is an immediate, independent act. Strictly speaking, Scripture was not the Word of God; Christ was the Word. Scripture, the so-called outer word, merely testified to Christ; it was powerless to bring one to faith in Christ. Rathmann's views were immediately branded as Schwenckfeldian by the Lutherans and condemned as heretical; many of the Lutheran universities issued opinions against him, and a bitter controversy broke out. The controversy, however, served to unite all the Lutherans and forced them into a more elaborate formulation of their doctrine. Specifically, the orthodox Lutherans now speak more insistently of an inherent power of the Word. This is a power that constantly resides

in the Word, not a power that sporadically enters the Word from without, where and when it pleases God. The Word is never *otiosum* but always *operosum*. Although this power can be resisted, it can never be separated from God's Word.

In response to Rathmann the orthodox Lutherans even maintained Scripture possesses divine power *(vis, efficacia)* prior to and apart from its use *(ante et extra usum)*.[318] This teaching was a necessary correlate to the doctrine of the inherent power of the Word. Calov argues for the Lutheran position as follows: Scripture, by virtue of its divine origin, is invested with divine efficacy, and that *extra usum,* for Scripture is never uninspired, never a merely human word. True, divine power is only in God essentially (οὐσιωδῶς), but by communication this divine life-giving power inheres also in the Word and sacraments. But if the sacraments have no power *extra usum,* why should such efficacy be ascribed to the Scriptures? Because, says Calov, there is no sacrament *extra usum;* but there is a Word of God, whether in use or no, in the Sacred Scriptures. "The essence of the sacraments consists in their administration and cannot exist except in use. But the Word of God does not consist essentially in the act of meditation, reading, and preaching; these are accidental to the Word. When these have passed away, the Word will endure forever."[319] Of course, the power of Scripture is manifested always in its use — and one must never lose sight of this or the purpose of Scripture when speaking of its power — but if the Word is powerful in its saving action, it is powerful prior to that action. Calov is reasoning that if one can speak of Scripture as the Word of God *ante usum,* one must speak also of Scripture as possessing divine power *ante usum.* As the Word of God, Scripture carries with it God's power; otherwise it is not God's Word.

It is not surprising that this Lutheran doctrine was considered unsatisfactory by Rathmann, Caspar Movius, enthusiasts, and even many Calvinists of that day — in short, by all who felt that the Spirit worked independently of the Word in saving men. In every case these adversaries were impatient with the teaching of the Formula of Concord that there were two causes of the sinner's conversion, the Spirit and the Word. But in more recent times also, and even to Lutherans, this doctrine of high Lutheran orthodoxy has seemed both unacceptable and inconceivable.[320] What possible purpose can there be in speaking of Scripture or the Word of God *extra usum?* The very moment such a possibility has been con-

The Efficacy of Scripture

ceived, the Word has in fact been envisaged and is *in usu*. There is therefore some justification for Grützmacher's denunciation of Calov's doctrine as logical nonsense. But surely we can see what Calov, as a good Lutheran, was driving at in emphasizing his position as he did. He is concerned to maintain the doctrine that Scripture is in fact the Word of God and carries with it the power of very God, and this against every form of enthusiasm. How else could he and his contemporaries have expressed themselves in the light of Rathmann's and the Schwenckfeldian insistence that *extra usum* Scripture was neither powerful nor the Word of God? To claim for Scripture a power *ante et extra usum* was merely another way of expressing his conviction in the intrinsic power of Scripture as the Word of God. If this be true, then there is no real difference between the position of Calov, Quenstedt, and Hollaz and that of Dannhauer, who spoke only of Scripture's power in its appropriate use *(in suo debito usu)*, that is, when it is heard or read or preached.[321] Nor is there any real advance from the teaching of Luther and Chemnitz, who definitely affirm that the Word of God as such is powerful.[322]

But we must say a word about Dannhauer's treatment of the efficacy of Scripture at this point, for it is strange that his presentation should differ so markedly from the usual discussions of the day. On the face of it he appears to be at odds with much that Calov and others have taught. Is there any explanation for this? I shall cite Dannhauer's most pointed statement on the subject; and then perhaps we can discern whether there are real doctrinal differences or not. Dannhauer says the following:

> Finally, inasmuch as Scripture has been designated to be heard, read, thought upon, and preached, Scripture is effective in its appropriate use. Apart from its use, as it is deposited on parchment and paper, Scripture in itself does not have any kind of power, physical or inherent, that is capable of producing supernatural effects. Indeed, as often as Scripture speaks of its own efficacy, it always has reference to its use. Scripture is an organ of God (not a principal cause), and its entire power consists in its being put into use. Otherwise it would be the same kind of power as in the word that is used by magicians and witches in their incantations. Yes, just as the sacraments have no efficacy apart from that use to which they have been divinely instituted, just as the rod of Aaron had in itself no miraculous power apart from its use, just as the scepter of Ahasuerus as long as it was enclosed in its chest saved no one until it was stretched forth by the king, just as a musical instrument without a virtuoso cannot

make a sound, so also Holy Scripture enjoys power in its appointed use because of God's promises and because of the gracious presence of the Holy Spirit, who animates the λόγια θεοῦ so that they become ζῶντα and makes them heavenly oracles. By His afflatus He influences, moves, and transfigures ineffably the human mind from the inmost recesses of the divine mind.

On the basis of such a statement Grützmacher concludes that there is an irreconcilable difference between Dannhauer and the other later Lutheran teachers. I do not believe that this is necessarily the case. It is admittedly hard to get at Dannhauer's thought, because he says so little on the efficacy of Scripture and because there is so much that he does not say. He does not distinguish between the *forma* and the *materia* of the Word and of Scripture. He does not speak in the present context, as do the other dogmaticians, of Scripture in *actu primo* and in *actu secundo*, that is to say, he does not distinguish between the divine Word of Scripture prior to any effect on man and during its action on man. Nor does he make any reference to the continual union of the Spirit and the Word as this was emphasized by Luther and practically all the later Lutherans. There is no reason for supposing that Dannhauer would have rejected any of these emphases, which were common to the classical Lutheran position. His silence may merely indicate his desire to avoid the logical problems and pitfalls that sometimes accompanied these emphases. But one thing is certain: as Dannhauer writes, he has in mind an entirely different antithesis from Calov and the other Lutherans, and he is making an entirely different point. He gives neither Rathmann nor the enthusiasts a thought. Rather he seems to be bothered by a caricature of the Lutheran doctrine that would make of the Bible, considered as a book and apart from the working of the Holy Spirit, some sort of magical power that would coerce its victim into obedience. He clearly has in mind only the so-called *materia* of Scripture. Such a caricature, possibly advanced by Reformed theologians in close proximity to Strasbourg, he rejects. But so does Quenstedt, who denies that the *materia* of the written Word, the letters, syllables, and words, or of the spoken Word, the sounds and phonemes, have any power at all. "We deny," he says, "that any divine power to convert or regenerate or illuminate is present or inheres in the letters, characters, syllables, and vocables as such." And Quenstedt too rejects certain ancient superstitions that taught that holding or incanting Scriptures

in a certain way or simply wearing the Gospel of John about one's neck could produce healing and other effects.[323]

I have mentioned Dannhauer's different approach to the efficacy of Scripture to illustrate once again the marked independence of the representatives of classical Lutheran orthodoxy. To the undiscerning reader Dannhauer seems to say the very opposite of what Calov and others maintained and even to be disapproving the terms of Calov at times. And he surely knew exactly what the accepted position of his day on the efficacy of Scripture was. Yet he never expresses disagreement with his brethren. The very fact that he affirms the efficacy of Scripture (which was not affirmed by the non-Lutherans of the day) indicates his essential agreement. Yet he wishes to state the doctrine in his own way, expressing his own concerns, and omitting features of the usual presentation that he thought unfortunate or misleading. And who can deny that Dannhauer's treatment of the doctrine lends much-needed clarity and balance to the Lutheran teaching, especially in the light of the misunderstandings and misconceptions that had been drawn from the traditional position? We can only conclude that what Calov affirmed and what Dannhauer affirmed needed to be said.

3. *The Origin and Basis of the Word's Power*

Whence does the Word of God, written or preached, derive its power? The answer given by Lutheran orthodoxy to this highly important question is a trinitarian answer. By tracing this answer we should be able to clarify the Lutheran position on the efficacy of Scripture more fully and arrest any misgivings the reader may have in regard to that position.

a. GOD THE AUTHOR. First, the written Word of Scripture and the preached Word drawn from Scripture derive their power from God, who is the author of Scripture.[324] The power of the Word is due to its divine origin (it is inspired by God) and to its divine nature (it is the Word of very God). The Word, simply because it is God's Word, carries with it all the attributes of God. God cannot be separated from His Word. Any Word that proceeds from God brings God with it. Therefore, to deny that Scripture is efficacious is to deny that it is God's Word. It is significant that under the *locus* on the efficacy of Scripture Calov considers the question whether Scripture is *vere et proprie* the Word of God.[325] He sees that the divine nature of Scripture is not a matter of mere academic

interest; Scripture *is* God's Word, *is* God speaking. And the implications of this great fact in terms of efficacy are obvious. If the nature of Scripture is divine, then it is dynamic. And since it is the *forma,* the message and content of Scripture, that is dynamic and divine, the same mighty efficacy may be predicated of the preached Word. Speaking of the preached Word, Calov says: "It proceeds from the mouth of God, not in such a way that it is separated from God — for then it would not possess a divine power that *is* actually the same as the nature of God Himself — but in such a way that it goes forth externally not just by striking the ears of man but also by bringing forth that power with it, carrying it into our hearts and sowing the seed there." [326]

The reaction to the Lutheran doctrine at this point was rather violent. Movius and many Reformed theologians accused the Lutherans of deifying Scripture; and this has been the charge also in more recent times.[327] The reply of Hollaz and Calov and Quenstedt was that the Lutheran doctrine never attributed to the Scriptures a power different or independent from the power of God.[328] No, as God's Word Scripture's power is God's power. Hollaz says:

> If any persons should attribute divine power to a created thing in such a way that this power belonged to it originally and independent of anything else, such persons are idolaters. This I grant. But our evangelical teachers are of the opinion that the power to enlighten, regenerate, and renew a man belongs to the Sacred Scriptures dependently, by virtue of communication, and according to divine arrangement.

Furthermore, the Lutherans replied, it is not wrong to deify what is already divine, namely, the Sacred Scriptures. Viewed formally as the *mens et consilium Dei,* the Scriptures are not a created thing that one might deify. There is no necessity for saying that whatever is not the Creator Himself is a creature of God. The Word of God is indeed not *Creator;* it is *creatio;* but at the same time it is not *creatura.* The Word is what Paul speaks of in 1 Cor. 2:11, 14 when he refers to τὰ τοῦ θεοῦ. Therefore certain Lutheran theologians call the Word something of God *(aliquid Dei),* a sort of divine effluence (ἀπόρροια *quaedam divina).* What the old Lutherans are saying here is that the Word of God cannot be separated from God, just as my word cannot be separated from me. On this view the Christian can read Scripture or hear a Christian sermon

drawn from Scripture and say, "That is God's Word; that is God speaking to me." In this very practical and soteriological sense the Word of God is a part, an ἀπόρροια, of God. For what is God to me apart from His Word? Yes, Scripture, the divine Word, derives its power from its Author. As God's Word it carries out God's purpose in calling, justifying, making His claim on man.

b. CHRIST THE CONTENT. Second, the written and spoken Word derives its power from its content, Christ. We have already spoken of the Christocentricity of Scripture in the theology of Lutheran orthodoxy and of the fact that the Gospel alone can be considered a means of grace.[329] The Word of God, the Gospel, is powerful to save, then, because it proclaims a message, a cognitive message, concerning the saving work of Jesus Christ.[330] He is the essence, soul, and center of the Gospel. Only this message can restore hope to a lost sinner. This is the chief and central message of Scripture. Therefore, if one does not seek in the Word of the Bible the Word that was made flesh, it would be better to spend one's time reading adventure stories. For what is written in Scripture has to do totally with this Word. He is the Lord who lies in the crib and in the arms of Mary; and whoever does not believe in Him has no use for that Book which testifies concerning Him, but like Turks and papists will have his paradise and heaven with all the devils in hell.[331]

But the Gospel not merely preaches Christ in a meaningful and moving way — its power is more than moral suasion, as we have heard — it actually brings Christ to those who hear it. Calov says that the written and preached Word is dynamic and effective by virtue of its union with the hypostatic Word.[332] The saving power of the Word is the power of the risen and victorious Christ. To Calov the Word of Scripture and the Word of Christ, Old Testament as well as New Testament, are identical.[333] In fact, during Christ's ministry on earth it was necessary for Him to prove the power of His own Word from Scripture. When Scripture speaks, therefore, Christ speaks. When Scripture judges, Christ judges. When Scripture pledges forgiveness and salvation, Christ bestows forgiveness and salvation. And so for orthodox Lutheranism Christ is not merely the subject matter of the Scriptures, He is not in the Scriptures merely significatively as the one to whom the Scriptures point (σχετικῶς, *ut significatum in significante*); but Christ confronts us in the Word, the Word truly brings Christ to us. On this point the faculties of Jena and Wit-

tenberg wrote the following in response to Rathmann: "To the present time we have been taught in the churches and schools that Christ was the purpose for God recording Scripture (John 5:39), that He is the foundation (Eph. 2:20), the kernel and star, the treasure and holy place of Scripture, the one Man of whom Scripture testifies, to whom it directs us, whom it once proclaimed and promised, whom later it makes known and explains according to His person and work, and whom it bestows upon us."[334] The Lutheran theologians refuse to debate about how Christ is present in the Word of Scripture and how Scripture brings Christ to us. This is a mystery, and to try to probe such matters is not to theologize but to philosophize. Where the power of the Gospel is concerned, we must listen only to the Spirit of God as He speaks through the prophets and apostles.

c. THE HOLY SPIRIT UNITED WITH THE WORD. Third, the written and spoken Word of God derives its power from the Holy Spirit, who is united with the Word and operative through it. Orthodox Lutheranism, especially after the controversy with Rathmann, faithfully followed Luther in emphasizing the perpetual union of the Spirit with the Word of God. This is the reason for the Word always being efficacious. Quenstedt says: "The Word of God, insofar as it is the Word of God, is always and without any limitation efficacious, efficacious also in respect to its *actus primus*. For the union of the Word and the Holy Spirit is perpetual; as a result, wherever the Word is, the Holy Spirit is present also, as Luther said."[335] The power of the Word is never independent of the Spirit of God. It is rather dependent on the Spirit and subordinate to His working.[336] The work of the Word and the work of the Spirit are not two works, nor are they the union of two distinct operations, but they are one work, a unity of effect (*unitas* ἀποτελέσματος) and a unity of operation (*unitas* ἐνεργείας). John Adam Osiander says:

> When we affirm that the oral Word and the written Scripture have a power *in actu primo* to convert a person to salvation, we do not wish by this to imply that there is a twofold divine power that gives life, the one power of the Word, the other of the Holy Spirit, and the one power separate from the other; neither do we wish to imply that a certain part of this life-giving power is somehow severed from the Holy Spirit and infused, as it were, into Scripture and the oral Word. ... No, we hold that there is a single divine power that is appropriate and natural to the Holy Spirit, but actually united and communicated

The Efficacy of Scripture

to the divine Word, as to an instrument, according to the singular decision, decree, and good pleasure of God. Nor do we advocate a subordination of the Holy Spirit and the divine Word, as Rathmann jeers, since that divine life-giving power is attributed differently to the Holy Spirit and the divine Word: it belongs to the Spirit independently, from Himself and of Himself; but to the Word it belongs dependently, that is, according to divine will. The Word possesses this power in itself, but not from itself or of itself.[337]

From the above citation it should be clear that Lutheran theology never thought of the Spirit of God somehow abdicating His work of saving sinners to the Word, which then takes over God's soteriological purposes in some sort of automatic fashion.[338] How often do the theologians of the orthodox period stress in good Lutheran fashion that the Spirit alone works conversion and all spiritual effects in man! "The Sacred Scriptures ascribe to the Holy Spirit and to Him alone the entire work of our conversion." This is the constant refrain of Lutheran theology.[339] The power and work of the Word is never distinct from the Spirit's power and work but is His power and work. Quenstedt says:

> The Holy Spirit does not act and operate separately and independently without the Word, nor does the Word act separately and independently without God and the Holy Spirit in converting man. But the Holy Spirit acts simultaneously and in union with the Word, through the Word, and in the Word as His usual means; and the Word works with the Spirit from power that is divinely bestowed. And thus they accomplish by one and the same action one effect and activity, the conversion of man.[340]

If the Spirit were to be taken from the Word of God, it would no longer be the Word of God but a mere human word.[341] Later Lutheran orthodoxy is unable to conceive of the Word of God apart from the Spirit of God.

All this must be clearly understood when we consider the old Lutherans' doctrine of the power of God's Word *in se* and *extra usum*. They never mean that the Word is carrying out some activity apart from God or apart from its use. They mean to say, as Otto Ritschl has made abundantly clear,[342] that the Word is always actually capable of working marvelous results in poor sinners. And this had always been the concern of Lutheran theology. We see therefore that there is no real difference between this position, expressed especially by Osiander, Calov, Quenstedt,

and Hollaz, and the earlier teaching of Heerbrand, Hutter, Gerhard, and Brochmand, who preferred to speak of the Spirit being "efficacious" through the Word or of the Word as an "efficacious means" of the Spirit's working.[343] All Lutheran theologians from the time of the Reformation through the period of orthodoxy taught that the Spirit was the efficient cause of conversion and of all spiritual activity in man and that the Word (and sacraments) was His instrument. And all Lutheran theologians consistently taught that the Spirit did not work apart from His Word.

The difference in terminology and approach that developed prior to the middle of the 17th century is occasioned by the controversy with Rathmann and indicates no departure from the earlier position. It is a fact, of course, that the earlier Lutherans opposed the Schwenckfeldian abberations without an appeal to an inherent *efficacia Scripturae extra usum.* In fact, it seems highly improbable that a Hutter or a Brochmand would ever have happened upon such an expression, even after the advent of Rathmann. But this innovation of the later Lutheran teachers, as I have pointed out, merely illustrates their conviction that the Scriptures and preaching are the Word of God in its full compass, carrying with it the saving power of God, whatever its effect on the reader or hearer.

It remains to make two final, brief observations relative to the Lutheran doctrine of the power of the Word.

First, the Lutheran position was taken in pronounced antithesis to the notion of many Calvinists that the Spirit was not bound to the Word in His saving work but entered it only sporadically and that His call through the Word was not always serious, namely, in the case of the nonelect.[344] The Calvinistic teaching was clearly calculated to answer the *cur alii alii non* question, among other things: God was made wholly responsible for the conversion of the elect and for the nonconversion of the reprobate. In the latter case God was not serious when He called through the Gospel, and the Spirit did not enter the Word with His quickening power. Thus, the Spirit entering the Word accounts in part for the fact that some accept the Word and are converted while others are not. Lutheran theology refused to answer the *cur alii alii non* question. Any answer will result either in a denial of *gratia universalis,* as was the case with the Calvinistic teaching, or in a denial of *sola gratia,* as was the case with the synergists, who spoke of three causes in conversion — the Spirit, the Word, and man's will. No, if a man is converted and saved, the glory is due to

God alone, who works through the Word. If a man is lost, it is wholly because of his own stubborn resistance to the Gospel, and it is therefore his own fault. Hence, it is never because the Word has no power or because the Spirit chooses not to work through the Word that a sinner is lost. The efficacy of the Word extends to all men everywhere, just as God's grace covers all. "It is the intrinsic power and natural disposition of the divine Word to persuade people of its truth; and it is never nonpersuasive, except when its work is removed and impeded by a person's willful, self-determined stubbornness and natural resistance." [345] To deny the power of the Word or the perpetual union of the Spirit with the Word therefore tends to make the Spirit responsible if one fails to come to faith and to deny the universal grace of God.

Second, the Lutheran position was taken very consciously in antithesis to every form of enthusiasm and to every idea of an immediate illumination or conversion. It is through the Word and only through the Word that the Spirit comes to men and works faith in their hearts. All His blessings of forgiveness, peace, and salvation are brought through the Word.[346] Therefore the church lives by the Word of God, derives her strength from it; and where there is no Word there is no church. "Faith that clings to the Word of God is the heart pulse of the church. Therefore, just as a poison first of all goes to the heart and attacks it, Satan would lead man into perdition first of all by snatching the Word from him and in this way destroying his faith." [347] All Luther's strictures against enthusiasm are vehemently voiced by Lutheran orthodoxy. There can be no solid comfort, no objective certainty, in the mystical immediacy of enthusiasm with its depreciation of history (especially as it pertains to Christ's redemptive work), the Gospel, and all cognitive and meaningful discourse about God (theology). It is for this reason, no doubt, that the orthodox Lutheran theologians, particularly the later ones who had also Quakerism to contend with, considered it wise to speak of the efficacy of the Word so early in their dogmatics, as a part of prolegomena. For such an issue must be settled at the very outset of the dogmatic assignment.

To include a discussion of the efficacy of Scripture was, of course, also necessary at this point if a balanced doctrine of Scripture was to be offered. And it is to the credit of the later dogmaticians that they saw this necessity and included such a discussion. In this they were faithful to the legacy of Luther. If one were to study Luther's doctrine of the

Word as a whole, classifying and evaluating all his utterances concerning Scripture and the Word of God, one would discover, I believe, that two simple, evangelical concerns dominate all Luther's thinking on the subject. First, he wishes to uphold the *sola Scriptura* principle, the canonical authority of Scripture, against the encroachments of Dame Reason, experience, tradition, and any other human source of theological knowledge. Second, he wishes to emphasize what a great treasure the church has in the Sacred Scriptures by virtue of their power in the lives of Christians and to stress that the divine Word of Scripture brings Christ, forgiveness, the Spirit, and every divine blessing. These are, without doubt, the two chief concerns of Lutheran orthodoxy in its doctrine of Scripture.

NOTES TO CHAPTER THREE

1. Nikolaus Selnecker, *Notatio de Studio Sacrae Theologiae, et de Ratione Discendi Doctrinam Coelestem* (Leipzig, 1579), pp. 1 ff.
2. John Andrew Quenstedt, *Theologia Didactico-Polemica sive Systema Theologiae* (Leipzig, 1702), P. I, C. 1, S. 1, Th. 23 (I, 12). In the present discussion and all that ensues on the doctrine of Scripture I shall at times be following my book, *The Inspiration of Scripture* (Edinburgh: Oliver and Boyd, 1957), which offers a much more detailed and fully documented survey than can be given in the present volume.
3. John Conrad Dannhauer, *Christosophia seu Sapientiarum Sapientia, de Salvatore Christo, ejus Persona, Officio, Beneficiis, Explicita atque Variis Corruptelis Purgata* (Strasbourg, 1638), p. 2.
4. John Gerhard, *Loci Theologici*, ed. J. F. Cotta (Tübingen, 1762), II, 8.
5. *Systema*, P. I, C. 3, S. 1, Th. Nota 2 (I, 32).
6. This distinction was made much earlier by the Reformed theologian Bartholomew Keckermann, *Systema Sacrae Theologiae* (Hanover, 1602), p. 5.
7. John Adam Scherzer, *Systema Theologiae XXIX Definitionibus Absolutum* (Leipzig and Frankfort, 1698), p. 3; Abraham Calov, *Consensus Repetitus Fidei Vere Lutheranae* (Wittenberg, 1666), p. 12.
8. Balthasar Meisner, *Christologia Sacra* (Wittenberg, 1672), pp. 281—91.
9. Balthasar Meisner, *Philosophia Sobria* (Rinteln, 1626), II, 1 ff.; Abraham Calov, *Scripta Philosophica* (Lübeck, 1651), p. 465.
10. Leonard Hutter, *Loci Communes Theologici* (Wittenberg, 1619), pp. 77 ff.; Martin Chemnitz, *Examen Concilii Tridentini* (Berlin, 1861), pp. 69 ff.
11. Abraham Calov, *Systema Locorum Theologicorum* (Wittenberg, 1665), I, 367 ff. See also Balthasar Mentzer, *Apologia Primae ex Quatuor-decim Disputationis Anti-Pistorianae pro Divina Sacrae Scripturae Autoritate (Opera Latina.* Frankfort, 1669), II, 1817—2028.
12. *Systema*, P. I, C. 3, S. 1, Th. Nota 13 (I, 33).
13. Calov, *Systema*, I, 364 ff. See also Gerhard, *Loci Theologici*, II, 370 ff.

Jesper Rasmus Brochmand, *Universae Theologiae Systema* (Ulm, 1658), I, 35 ff.; Quenstedt, *Systema*, P. I, C. 3, S. 2, Q. 1, Porisma 2 (I, 38 ff.).
14. John Conrad Dannhauer, *Hodosophia Christiana sive Theologia Positiva* (Leipzig, 1695), p. 58.
15. Calov, *Systema*, I, 598.
16. *Loci Theologici*, II, 427.
17. Calov, *Systema*, I, 543. See also Gerhard, *Loci Theologici*, II, 17.
18. Matthias Hafenreffer, *Loci Theologici* (Wittenberg, 1622), p. 114. Gerhard, *Loci Theologici*, II, 426.
19. Giles Hunnius, *Thesaurus Apostolicus Complectens Commentarios in Omnes Novi Testamenti Epistolas et Apocalypsin Iohannis* (Wittenberg, 1705), p. 32.
20. *Loci Theologici*, II, 18. Jacob Andreae puts it just a little differently. He says that Scripture had many writers but only one author, the Spirit of God; for all the writers were governed by the Spirit of God and did not follow their own dreams. (See *Disputationes Theologicae, de Praecipuis Doctrinae Christianae Capitibus* [Montbeliard, 1593], p. 3.) The later Lutherans like to speak of God as the *auctor primarius* of Scripture, and the sacred writers as the *auctores secundarii*.
21. Abraham Calov, *Apodixis Articulorum Fidei* (Lüneburg, 1684), p. 29.
22. See Karl Barth, *Church Dogmatics*, trans. G. T. Thomson, et al., 4 vols. (Edinburgh: T. & T. Clark, 1936—69), I, 1, 123 ff.
23. Calov, *Systema*, p. 32; Giles Hunnius, *Thesaurus Apostolicus*, pp. 32 ff.
24. John Gerhard, *Disputationum Theologicarum . . . pars secunda* (Jena, 1625), p. 1116. See also Giles Hunnius, *Opera Latina* (Frankfort on the Main, 1608), II, 231: "Sed loquitur in illo [volumen Bibliorum] Deus ipse."
25. *Apodixis Articulorum Fidei*, p. 37.
26. Gerhard, *Loci Theologici*, II, 15: "Inter verbum Dei & scripturam sacram, materialiter acceptam non esse reale aliquod discrimen." John G. Dorsch, *Aphorismi Theologici* (Greifswald, no date), p. 1: "Inter verbum Dei de salute hominis prolatum & sacram scripturam non esse differentiam realem."
27. *Loci Theologici*, II, 360.
28. Jesper Rasmus Brochmand, *Commentarius in Epistolam ad Hebraeos* (Copenhagen, 1706), p. 13.
29. See Abraham Calov, *Commentarius in Genesin* (Wittenberg, 1671), p. 161. Calov cites in full and completely concurs with Luther's remarkable statement on Gen. 1:3: "God calls forth those things that are not, and they come into being. God does not speak grammatical words, but real and living events, so that what sounds as a voice among us is for God a deed. Thus sun, moon, heaven, earth, Peter, Paul, I, you, etc. — we are all words of God; rather, we are one syllable or letter in relation to the whole creation. We speak, but only grammatically; that is, we give terms to things that have already been created. But the divine grammar is something else again; when He says, Sun, shine, immediately the sun comes into being and shines. Thus the words of God are events, not mere vocables." (Martin Luther, *Opera Latina* [Frankfort and Erlangen: Heyder and Simmer, 1865—73], I, 29. Hereafter cited as Er. Lat.)
30. I, 528 ff.
31. Abraham Calov, *Theologia Positiva* (Wittenberg, 1682), p. 24; *Systema*, I, 454 ff., 707; Quenstedt, *Systema*, P. I, C. 4, S. 2, q. 16, Ekthesis 1 (1,169).
32. *Loci Theologici*, II, 14. Gerhard's ideas at this point were shared by some of

the Reformed theologians. See Keckermann, *Systema Sacrae Theologiae,* p. 193: "The Word of God without its *forma,* that is, without its true sense, is not the Word of God." The later Lutherans advance a bit beyond Gerhard's simple distinction by speaking of an outer and inner *forma.* See Quenstedt, *Systema,* P. I, C. 4, S. 1, Th. 5 (I, 56): "We must distinguish between the grammatical and outer meaning of the divine Word and the spiritual, inner, and divine meaning of the divine Word. The former is the *forma* of the Word of God insofar as it is a word, the latter is its *forma* insofar as it is a divine Word. The former can be grasped even by any unregenerate man; the latter, however, cannot be received except by a mind that has been enlightened."

33. *Hodosophia Christiana,* p. 29. See also Sebastian Schmidt, *Compendium Theologiae* (Strasbourg, 1697), p. 15.
34. *Systema,* P. I, C. 4, S. 1, Th. 1, Nota 2 (I, 54). See also Friedemann Bechmann, *Ad Institutiones Catecheticas Cunradi Dieterici . . . Annotationes Uberiores* (Frankfort and Leipzig, 1707), p. 5, who makes the Word of God any communication from God to man, whether in man's mind or in symbols.
35. Calov, *Systema,* I, 454. See also Calov, *Theologia Positiva,* p. 23.
36. George Dedekenn, *Thesauri Consiliorum et Decisionum* (Jena, 1671), Appendix nova, p. 160. Herein the Saxon Lutherans view the Word in five ways: in God, in the mind of an apostle, in the speech of an apostle, in the writings of an apostle, and in the believer's heart. See also Quenstedt, (*Systema,* P. I, C. 4, S. 2, Q. 16, Font. Sol. 17 [I, 186]), who views the Word also *dispensative,* in God's divine ordination and purpose.
37. Giles Hunnius, *Opera Latina,* I, 29; Gerhard, *Loci Theologici,* I, 10.
38. Abraham Calov, *Biblia Testamenti Veteris Illustrata* (Dresden and Leipzig, 1719), I, 223. See also Calov, *Systema,* I, 702; *Commentarius in Genesin,* 148. Calov no doubt has in mind many strong statements of Luther's on this vital point, e. g., Martin Luther, *Sämmtliche Schriften,* herausgegeben von Dr. Georg Walch, 2. Auflage (St. Louis: Concordia Publishing House, 1881 to 1930), XIII, 1556, hereafter cited as W^2: "All the works Christ performed are recorded in the Word, and in the Word and through the Word He will give us everything, and without the Word He will give us nothing."
39. Calov, *Systema,* I, 457.
40. *Christosophia seu Sapientiarum Sapientia,* p. 1. See also Quenstedt, *Systema,* P. IV, C. 7, S. 1, Th. 32 ff.; S. 2, q. 1 (IV, 267—78); Dedekenn, *Thesauri Consiliorum et Decisionum,* p. 332.
41. Dedekenn, *Thesauri Consiliorum et Decisionum,* Appendix nova, p. 327.
42. Calov, *Systema,* I, 131.
43. Nicholas Hunnius, *Epitome Credendorum* (Frankfort and Leipzig, 1702), p. 5; Calov, *Apodixis Articulorum Fidei,* p. 52; John Huelsemann, *Calvinismus Irreconciliabilis* (Wittenberg, 1667), p. 423.
44. Calov, *Systema,* I, 534 ff. Quenstedt, *Systema,* P. I, C. 4, S. 2, q. 1 (I, 62 ff.).
45. *Notatio de Studio Sacrae Theologiae,* pp. 12 ff.
46. *Loci Theologici,* II, 28.
47. Robert Bellarmine, *De Verbo Dei Scripto et non Scripto* (Sedan, 1618), IV, 4.
48. John Huelsemann, *Vindiciae S. Scripturae* (Leipzig, 1679), p. 208.
49. Leonard Hutter, *Libri Christianae Concordiae: Symboli Ecclesiarum, Novis-*

simo hoc Tempore, Longe Augustissimi; Explicatio Plana & Perspicua (Wittenberg, 1609), prol. p. 2.
50. Calov, *Consensus Repetitus Fidei Vere Lutheranae,* p. 7.
51. *Systema,* P. I, C. 4, S. 2, q. 3, Bebaiosis 1 & 2. (I, 69—70).
52. *Hodosophia Christiana,* pp. 18 ff.
53. John Gerhard, *Confessio Catholica* (Erfurt, 1679), II, 226; Calov, *Systema,* I, 543; Brochmand, *Universae Theologiae Systema,* I, 13; Quenstedt, *Systema,* P. I, C. 4, S. 2, q. 2 (I, 65 ff.).
54. Calov, *Systema,* I, 545.
55. Hutter, *Loci Communes Theologici,* p. 16.
56. Gerhard, *Loci Theologici,* II, 33. Quenstedt, *Systema,* P. I, C. 4, S. 2, q. 3 I, 65): "Quo non pervenit 'Αποστολή, eo ἐπιστολή, ad quos non penetravit sonus & pes Apostolorum, ad eos manus, vel Scriptura eorum pervenit."
57. Quenstedt, *Systema,* P. I, C. 4, S. 2, q. 3 (I, 65); Gerhard, *Loci Theologici,* II, 34.
58. Robert Bellarmine, *De Verbo Dei,* I, XV.
59. Calov, *Systema,* I, 551. Quenstedt, *Systema,* P. I, C. 4, S. 2, q. 3 (I, 67 ff.). David Hollaz, *Examen Theologicum Acroamaticum* (Rostoch and Leipzig, 1718), Prol. III, q. 16 (I, 92 ff.). Abraham Calov, *Biblia Novi Testamenti Illustrata,* II, 1037. Although plenary inspiration was the common belief of all the orthodox Lutherans, the matter was considered as a special question only after Calixt's time.
60. For the correct understanding of the word "amanuenses" (also *"mani," "calami"*), see p. 288. For the correct understanding of the terms *"dicto"* and *"suggero,"* see p. 290.
61. Calov, *Systema,* I, 552; Huelsemann, *Calvinismus Irreconciliabilis,* p. 415.
62. George Calixt, *De Autoritate Sacrae Scripturae* (Helmstedt, 1648), pp. 47 ff.; *Responsum Maledicis Theologorum Moguntinorum Vindiciis Oppositum* (Helmstedt, 1644), 72; Faustus Socinus, *De Auctoritate Scripturae,* ed. Conrad Vorst (Burgstemfurt, 1611), c. 1 (*Opera Omnia,* I, 266 ff.).
63. *Systema,* P. I, C. 4, S. 2, q. 4 (I, 72). See also Dannhauer, *Hodosophia Christiana,* p. 57; Hollaz, *Examen,* Prol. III, q. 27 (I, 94).
64. Calov, *Biblia Novi Testamenti Illustrata,* II, 1034. Calov's words are almost verbatim those of Leonard Hutter, *Loci Communes Theologici,* p. 32. See also John W. Baier, *Compendium Theologiae Positivae* (Jena, 1704), p. 126; Matthew Flacius, *Clavis Scripturae Sacrae* (Frankfort and Leipzig, 1719), II, 8, 142, 732.
65. Scherzer, *Systema Theologiae XXIX Definitionibus Absolutum,* p. 5.
66. *Systema,* I, 563. See also *Apodixis Articulorum Fidei,* pp. 29—30.
67. *Examen,* Prol. III, q. 27 (I, 95).
68. *Biblia Novi Testamenti Illustrata,* II, 1547.
69. John Gerhard, *Tractatus de Legitima Scripturae Sacrae Interpretatione* (Jena, 1663), p. 8.
70. Scherzer, *Systema,* p. 8.
71. Hollaz, *Examen,* I, 96 ff.
72. See also Dannhauer, *Hodosophia Christiana,* p. 58.
73. *Vindiciae S. Scripturae,* p. 215.
74. *Compendium Theologiae Positivae,* p. 83.

75. *Systema*, P. I, C. 4, S. 2, q. 19 (I, 206). Hollaz, *Examen*, Prol. III, q. 44 (I, 162).
76. Calov brings forth textual and manuscript evidence usually only when a dogmatic issue is at stake. He gives much more credence to the testimony of the fathers than we would today, but his concern to use only the *probatissimi codices* is always evident. See *Apodixis Articulorum Fidei*, pp. 124, 175, 179.
77. Dannhauer, *Hodosophia Christiana*, p. 51.
78. See the statements made by Oettingen and others in Adolph Hoenecke, *Evangelisch-Lutherische Dogmatik*, 4 vols. (Milwaukee: Northwestern Publishing House, 1909), I, 335.
79. For a more thorough presentation of the terminology used by the Lutheran dogmaticians on the relation of the Holy Spirit to the writers of Scripture, see my book, *The Inspiration of Scripture*, pp. 53 ff.
80. *Systema*, P. I, C. 4, S. 2, q. 15 (I, 157).
81. *Loci Communes Theologici*, p. 30. See also Gerhard, *Loci Theologici*, II, 26: "The instrumental causes of the Holy Scripture were holy men of God, men called and chosen by God in a unique and immediate manner to this end, that they might write divine revelations. Such men were the prophets in the Old Testament and the evangelists and apostles in the New Testament, men whom we therefore correctly call God's amanuenses, the hands of Christ, the secretaries and notaries of the Holy Spirit, since they did not speak or write according to their own human will but were φερόμενοι ὑπὸ τοῦ πνεύματος ἁγίου, prompted, moved, incited, inspired, and governed by the Holy Spirit. They wrote not as men but as men of God, that is, as servants of God and special organs of the Holy Spirit." See John Gerhard, *Commentarius super Posteriorem D. Petri Epistolam* (Jena, 1660), p. 137. Dannhauer, *Hodosophia Christiana*, p. 33, says that God took over the writing of the human authors as His own.
82. Abraham Calov, *Dissertationes Theologicae Rostochienses* (Rostock, 1637), p. 130.
83. *Systema*, P. I, C. 4, S. 1, (I, 57).
84. *Examen*, I, 87. See also Dedekenn, *Thesauri Consiliorum et Decisionum*, appendix nova, p. 181.
85. Baier, *Compendium Theologiae Positivae*, p. 73; Giles Hunnius, *Thesaurus Apostolicus*, p. 1056. But the writers themselves chose what they would write, just as one who is brought to faith in Christ himself chooses to believe in Christ. See John Gerhard, *Aphorismi Succincti & Selecti* (Jena, 1611), p. A7r.
86. Quenstedt, *Systema*, I, 57.
87. Quenstedt, *Systema*, P. I, C. 4, S. 2, q. 4 (I, 75). See also John Adam Osiander, *Systema Theologicum seu Theologia Positiva Acroamatica* (Tübingen, 1679), I, 238 ff. Osiander speaks of a singularity of style and language *(sermo)* in Scripture. But it is a uniformity in diversity *(in styli diversitate)*, a uniform majesty and unity that adorns all of Scripture. Osiander, like many of the old Lutherans, compares Scripture to a symphony where the same melody is played by the most different kinds of instruments. Thus, the diversity of style that one finds in the books of Scripture is completely compatible with the full inspiration of Scripture.
88. Salomon Glassius, *Philologia Sacra* (Leipzig, 1713), L. I., Trac. 3; Dannhauer, *Hodosophia Christiana*, p. 58; Baier, *Compendium Theologiae Positi-*

vae, p. 81; Hollaz, *Examen*, I, 95; Feustking (see Giles Hunnius, *Thesaurus Apostolicus*, p. 843); Flacius, *Clavis Scripturae Sacrae*, II, 459 ff.
89. *Systema*, I, 574—75. See Robert Preus, *The Inspiration of Scripture*, pp. 62—64.
90. *Systema*, P. I, C. 4, S. 2, q. 4, Ekthesis 6 (I, 73).
91. *Systema*, I, 565.
92. Quenstedt, *Systema*, P. I, C. 4, S. 2, q. 6 (I, 85). Quenstedt also says that a departure from the conventional mode of etymology is also not a solecism.
93. Desiderius Erasmus, *In Novum Testamentum Annotationes* (Basel, 1542), p. 317.
94. John Olearius, *De Stylo Novi Testamenti* (Schwabach, 1690), p. 98.
95. For a more thorough study of the meaning of the term *"dicto,"* see Robert Preus, *The Inspiration of Scripture*, pp. 71—73.
96. Dannhauer, *Hodosophia Christiana*, p. 58; Quenstedt, *Systema*, P. I, C. 4, S. 2, q. 4 (I, 75).
97. Quenstedt, *Systema*, P. I, C. 4, S. 1, Th. 7 (I, 57).
98. August Tholuck, *Der Geist der lutherischen Theologen Wittenbergs im Verlaufe des 17. Jahrhunderts* (Hamburg and Gotha: Friedrich und Andreas Parther, 1852), pp. 353—54; Richard Rothe, *Dogmatik* (Heidelberg: J. C. B. Mohr, 1870), I, 135.
99. Christoph Ernst Luthardt, *Compendium der Dogmatik*, neunte verbesserte Aufl. (Leipzig: Dörffling und Franke, 1893), p. 326. Variations of this criticism are offered by modern scholars. Paul Althaus (*Die Christliche Wahrheit* [Gütersloh: C. Bertelsmann, 1949], p. 218), commenting on Hollaz' statement that Luke in his use of human sources did not err or have a memory lapse (Hollaz, Prol. III, q. 16 [1750 ed.], p. 85), charges that the old doctrine of inspiration ignores the historic relation of a Luke to Jesus Himself. This judgment is echoed by Friedebert Hohmeier ("Zum dogmengeschichtlichen Ort der Inspirationslehre bei den alten lutherischen Dogmatikern" in *Evangelisch-Lutherische Kirchenzeitung*, 15, 22 [Nov. 15, 1961], pp. 1 ff.), who sees a motive for the doctrine in Hollaz' excessive psychologizing as he works out his *ordo salutis*. But what then could be the motive for Gerhard's doctrine of inspiration, for Gerhard never worked out an *ordo salutis?* Many modern scholars have not seen that the orthodox doctrine of inspiration is free of psychological explanations.
100. Isaac A. Dorner, *History of Protestant Theology*, trans. George Robson and Sophia Taylor, 2 vols. (Edinburgh: T. & T. Clark, 1871), II, 128.
101. *Realencyklopädie für protestantische Theologie und Kirche*, begründet von J. J. Herzog, in dritter verbesserter und vermehrter Auflage unter Mitwirkung vieler Theologen und anderer Gelehrten herausgegeben von Albert Hauck (Leipzig: J. C. Hinrichs'sche Buchhandlung, 1896—1913), 3d edition, VI, 755, hereafter cited as *RE*. Regin Prenter, *Skabelse og Genlösning* (Copenhagen: G. E. C. Gads Forlag, 1951), p. 84, offers the same shallow judgment.
102. Werner Elert, *Der Christliche Glaube*, 3d ed. (Hamburg: Furche Verlag, 1956), pp. 209 ff. How extensively these former conclusions have been accepted today may be seen from the fact that such competent Roman Catholic scholars as the Spanish Jesuits (*Sacrae Theologiae Summa* [Madrid: La Editorial Catolica, 1958], IV, 1065) and Cardinal A. Bea (*De Inspiratione et Inerrantia Sacrae Scripturae* [Rome: Pontificium Institutum Biblicum, 1954], p. 34) accuse Quenstedt and Calov of a mantic or mechanical theory

of inspiration, when in fact these Lutherans agree on this matter very closely with their critics. Bea portrays Calov, Quenstedt, and J. Buxtorf as teaching a mechanical dictation theory of inspiration. And this by one who defends rightly the use of the word *dictation* as it was used by the ancient church fathers and the Council of Trent; see p. 36. We must mention that many theologians (e. g., Wilhelm Rohnert, *Die Inspiration der heiligen Schrift und ihre Bestreiter* [Leipzig: Verlag von Georg Böhme, 1889]; Wilhelm Koelling, *Die Lehre von der Theopneustie* [Breslau: Verlag von Carl Dülfer, 1891]; Friedrich A. Philippi, *Kirchliche Glaubenslehre,* 5 vols. [Stuttgart: Verlag von Samuel Gottlieb Liesching, 1854]; Walther; Pieper; Hove; Hoenecke; et al.) have rightly understood the classical Lutheran doctrine of inspiration; but all these theologians agreed with it.

103. Emil Brunner, *Revelation and Reason,* trans. Olive Wyon (Philadelphia: The Westminster Press, 1946), p. 7; John K. S. Reid, *The Authority of Scripture* (New York: Harper and Brothers, 1957), p. 85.

104. Quenstedt, *Systema,* P. I, C. 7, S. 1, Th. 1, Nota 2 (I, 268).

105. Gerhard, *Loci Theologici,* II, 18; Dannhauer, *Hodosophia Christiana,* p. 44.

106. Gerhard, *Loci Theologici,* XIII, 2.

107. Gerhard, *Disputationum Theologicarum* . . . pars secunda, p. 245.

108. *Systema,* P. I, C. 4, S. 2, q. 3, Ekthesis 3 (I, 68).

109. Chemnitz, *Loci Theologici,* II, 210; Brochmand, *Commentarius in Epistolam ad Hebraeos,* p. 12.

110. Quenstedt, *Systema,* P. IV, C. 2, S. 1, Th. 9 (IV, 60).

111. Chemnitz, *Loci Theologici,* II, 204.

112. Ibid., II, 207. See Hans Poulsen Resen, *De Sancta Fide in verum Deum et quem Ille Misit, Jesum Christum* (Copenhagen, 1614), p. 8.

113. Ibid., II, 210.

114. Werner Elert, *The Structure of Lutheranism,* trans. Walter Hansen (St. Louis: Concordia Publishing House, 1962), p. 65. When Elert alludes to Calov's statement (*Systema,* I, 270) that defines revelation, he quotes *"informatio"* as the purpose of revelation but omits *"salutarem ejusdem,"* which modifies *"informationem."*

115. See above, pp. 186—88. See also Chemnitz, *Loci Theologici,* II, 212; Quenstedt, *Systema,* P. IV, C. 2, S. 1, Th 5 ff. (1701 ed., IV, 60).

116. Michael Reu, *In the Interest of Lutheran Unity* (Columbus: The Wartburg Press, 1940), p. 53.

117. Quenstedt, *Systema,* P. I, C. 4, S. 2, q. 7, Ekthesis 1 (I, 87). See also John G. Dorsch, *Synopsis Theologiae Zacharianae* (Frankfort, 1683), I, II, 11: "Auctoritas ejus est tanta, quanta Dei, qui in ea & per eam dominium suum gratiosum exhibet."

118. Dannhauer, *Hodosophia Christiana,* p. 39.

119. Abraham Calov, *Socinismus Profligatus, hoc est, Errorum Socinianorum Luculenta Confutatio,* editio secunda (Wittenberg, 1668), p. 78.

120. *Loci Theologici,* II, 36. See also *Confessio Catholica,* II, 279.

121. *Apodixis Articulorum Fidei,* p. 35.

122. See *Catechesis Racoviensis, seu Liber Socinianorum Primarius* (Frankfort and Leipzig, 1739), prol.; Socinus, *De Auctoritate Sacrae Scripturae (Opera Omnia,* I, 266—85). According to the Socinian position, *recta ratio* (and this included both deductive and inductive reasoning) was never at odds

with Scripture. But this *sana ratio* was often used against some of the most venerable and established articles of faith, such as the Trinity and the personal union. There is no doubt that such a principle and not just faulty exegesis led to the Socinian denial of the Trinity and the personal union. As time went on *ratio* became more and more overweening in the Socinian system until it saw fit by the middle of the 17th century to deny not only what seemed contradictory (e. g., that three persons could exist in one substance) but also what was deemed on critical grounds to be empirically or historically impossible (e. g., that the sun stood still, according to Joshua 10). See Klaus Scholder, *Ursprünge und Probleme der Bibelkritik im 17. Jahrhundert* (Munich: Chr. Kaiser Verlag, 1966), pp. 46—47. It was this later Socinianism that prompted the more refined arguments for the authority of Scripture in Calov's day.

123. Calov, *Systema*, I, 608.
124. Jacob Gretzer, *Opera Omnia* (Regensburg, 1736), VIII, 985. See also Bellarmine, *De Verbo Dei Scripto et non Scripto*, IV, IV, 317.
125. Gerhard, *Loci Theologici*, II, 36. See also Chemnitz, *Examen Concilii Tridentini*, p. 53.
126. Gerhard, *Confessio Catholica*, II, 279. Paul Althaus (*Die Christliche Wahrheit*, p. 200) faults orthodoxy for deriving the authority of the New Testament from its divine origin (inspiration) and not from the Gospel, and thereby confuses the distinction between the normative authority (*autoritas normativa*) of Scripture and the causative authority (*autoritas causativa*), or power, of the Gospel in the old Lutheran theology. This confusion leads Althaus next (p. 217) to charge orthodoxy with a departure from Luther's emphasis on the Christological message of Scripture as the criterion that authenticates Scripture *quoad nos* and with postulating Scripture as no more than a supernatural textbook. Thus Scripture is no longer a living Word of God expressing itself in Law and Gospel, but a sacred codex. The development of the inspiration doctrine in Lutheran orthodoxy was analogous to that of the papal system in Jesuit theology, according to Althaus. The falsity of Althaus' criticism will be brought out in some of the ensuing discussion (see above, pp. 263—71; and below, pp. 303, 363—67, and 371—72).
127. Abraham Calov, *Criticus Sacer vel Commentarii Apodictico-elenchtici super Augustanam Confessionem Evangelicarum Novissimi Temporis Symbolum vere Augustum Prothuron* (Leipzig, 1646), I, 275; *Systema*, I, 583.
128. Quenstedt, *Systema*, P. I, C. 4, S. 2, q. 7 (I, 88).
129. Calov, *Systema*, I, 583.
130. Hutter, *Loci Communes Theologici*, p. 25.
131. David Hollaz, *Examen Theologicum Acroamaticum* (Holm and Leipzig, 1750), Prol. III, q. 33. p. 121.
132. Calov, *Criticus Sacer*, I, 296.
133. See above, p. 100. Also Selnecker, *Notatio de Studio Sacrae Theologiae*, p. 25.
134. Hollaz, *Examen*, p. 125; John Adam Osiander, *Collegium Theologicum Systematicum* (Stuttgart and Frankfort, 1686), p. 108.
135. John Huelsemann, *Extensio Breviarii Theologici* (Leipzig, 1655), p. 6.
136. Jerome Kromayer, *Theologia Positiva-Polemica* (Frankfort and Leipzig), p. 21. Calov, *Systema*, I, 603.
137. Karl Heim, *Das Gewissheitsproblem in der systematischen Theologie bis zu Schleiermacher* (Leipzig: J. C. Hinrichs'sche Buchhandlung, 1911), p. 325.

386 CHAPTER THREE *The Doctrine of Scripture*

138. Typical is the following statement of Calov's (*Criticus Sacer*, p. 279): "We believe that the Word of God is the Word of God because of itself, not because of anything else. Just as every revelation is believed because of the divine Word that is contained in it, so it is with this revelation and Word of God; it is not believed because of any other word or revelation (which would give rise to an infinite regress) but on its own account."

139. Calov, *Systema*, I, 707; Hollaz, *Examen*, p. 125.

140. Quenstedt, *Systema*, P. I, C. 4, S. 2, q. 16 (1715 ed., I, 267).

141. Ibid., I, 251.

142. *Institutio Christianae Religionis*, I, 7, 1.

143. Dorner, *History of Protestant Theology*, II, 124.

144. *Examen*, p. 116.

145. Gerhard, *Confessio Catholica*, I, 85.

146. *Loci Theologici*, I, 11. See also Michael Walther, *Officina Biblica* (Wittenberg, 1703), p. 195; Quenstedt, *Systema*, P. I, C. 4, S. 2, q. 8 (1715 ed.), I, 135; Calov, *Criticus Sacer*, p. 237. For a thorough discussion of the problems of canonicity as they were treated in the 17th century by Lutheran theologians see Jacob Aall Ottesen Preus, "The New Testament Canon in the Lutheran Dogmaticians" in *The Springfielder*, XXV (Spring 1961), pp. 8—33.

147. Chemnitz, *Examen Concilii Tridentini*, pp. 51 ff.; Giles Hunnius, *Opera Latina*, V, 2; Hafenreffer, *Loci Theologici*, p. 140; Jacob Heerbrand, *Compendium Theologiae* (Wittenberg, 1573), pp. 3 ff.; Selnecker, *Notatio de Studio Sacrae Theologiae*, p. 35.

148. Some of the later dogmaticians, when speaking of canonicity, do not even mention the distinction between the antilegomena and homologoumena. See Gottfried Cundisius, *D. Leonhardi Hutteri Compendium Theologicum Notis Illustratum* (Jena, 1752), pp. 11 ff.; Scherzer, *Systema Theologiae*, p. 17. Hollaz (*Examen*, Pro. III, q. 39, p. 130) lists all the books of the New Testament as canonical without distinction. He admits to a distinction between protocanonical and deuterocanonical books but says that all evangelical teachers in his day accept the authority of the deuterocanonical books, and therefore the distinction is no longer of any moment.

149. *Apodixis Articulorum Fidei*, p. 29.

150. Calov, *Criticus Sacer*, p. 234; Kromayer, *Theologia Positiva-Polemica*, p. 29.

151. This was clearly the motivation of Cardinal Bellarmine. See *De Verbo Dei*, II, 2 (*Disputationes de Controversiis Christianae Fidei* [Paris, 1590], I, 71).

152. See Michael Walther, *Officina Biblica*, pp. 62—91; Salomon Glassius, *Philologia Sacra*, pp. 2—259; Brochmand, *Universae Theologiae Systema*, pp. 16 ff.; Calov, *Criticus Sacer*, I, 380—438; Quenstedt, *Systema*, P. I, C. 4, S. 2, q. 17—20 (1715 ed. I, 274—313); Gerhard, *Loci Theologici*, II, 258 ff. The Lutheran theologians also argued against the possibility of canonical books being lost.

153. The original idioms of Scripture were at times made too sacrosanct by the Lutherans. Calov believed that Hebrew was the original language God spoke in the Garden of Eden (*Criticus Sacer*, I, 311; *Commentarius in Genesin*, p. 16. See also Giles Hunnius, *Opera Latina*, I, 6). Thus the importance of repairing to the Hebrew text.

154. Quenstedt, *Systema*, P. I, C. 4, S. 2, q. 19 (I, 303): "θεοπνοή enim, sive, divina inspiratio est sola & unica causa αὐθεντίας."

155. Flacius, *Clavis Scripturae Sacrae,* II, 644 ff.; Gerhard, *Loci Theologici,* II, 265 ff.; Calov, *Biblia Illustrata Novi Testamenti,* I, 186 ff.; Calov, *Criticus Sacer,* I, 325 ff. Flacius seems to be the first Lutheran to endorse this position. Gerhard cites also Chemnitz, but he is by no means supported by Chemnitz' actual words (see Martin Chemnitz, Polycarp Leyser, John Gerhard, *Harmonia Quatuor Evangelistarum* [Hamburg, 1704], Cap. V, I, 439), which leave the matter open. Flacius is the only 16th-century Lutheran who presses his position. Giles Hunnius, for instance, does not even mention the problem in his large and thorough commentary on Matthew (see *Thesaurus Evangelico Apostolicus* [Zerbst, 1706]). The view was first pressed in Reformed circles by the elder Buxtorf, who was followed by the great preponderance of Reformed teachers. Gerhard must bear responsibility for bringing the view into general acceptance among Lutheran theologians. For a summary of the arguments advanced by Gerhard and the later dogmaticians, see Robert Preus, *The Inspiration of Scripture,* pp. 140—46. Some of these arguments were somewhat convincing in their day. Others were purely deductive, proceeding from the properties of Scripture.

156. Friedrich A. Nitzsch, *Lehrbuch der evangelischen Dogmatik,* 3d ed. (Tübingen: J. C. B. Mohr, 1912), p. 251; Cremer, *RE,* VI, 755; Otto Ritschl, *Dogmengeschichte des Protestantismus,* 4 vols. (Leipzig: J. C. Hinrichs'sche Buchhandlung, and Göttingen: Vandenhoeck & Ruprecht, 1908—27), I, 171; Bengt Hägglund, *Die Heilige Schrift und ihre Deutung in der Theologie Johann Gerhards* (Lund: CWK Gleerups Förlag, 1951), p. 86. Hägglund has, however, correctly understood that the issue for Gerhard and the other dogmaticians was not the inspiration of the vowel points but whether the points were present in the original texts of Scripture.

157. This was clearly the line taken by Bellarmine. See *De Verbo Dei,* II, 2 (*Disputationes de Controversiis Christianae Fidei,* I, 76).

158. This was the contention of Flacius (*Clavis Scripturae Sacrae,* II, 643) and of Gerhard (*Loci Theologici,* II, 271). But later Lutheran scholars granted that the rabbis, versed as they were in Scripture, read the Scriptures without a pointed text and did so accurately and with safety. See August Pfeiffer, *Critica Sacra de Sacri Codicis Partitione, Editionibus Variis, Linguis Originalibus et Illibata Puritate Fontium, Interpretatione Scripturae Legitima* (Dresden and Leipzig, 1721), p. 73; also Henry Hoepfner, *Loci Theologici* (Frankfort and Leipzig, 1673), p. 49. Calov (*Criticus Sacer,* I, 328) grants that Jerome may have used an unpointed Hebrew text as he translated Scripture. It is interesting, too, that the 17th-century Lutherans themselves in their own writings often do not bother to point Hebrew.

159. See *Triumph. de Regno Pontifico,* I, i, c. 6, quoted in August Pfeiffer, *Critica Sacra,* p. 71.

160. John Conrad Dannhauer, *Hermeneutica Sacra* (Strasbourg, 1669), p. 16.

161. Calov, *Systema,* I, 610.

162. John G. Dorsch, *Dissertationum Theologicarum . . .* (Strasbourg, 1638), p. Y i v.

163. John W. Baier, *Compendium Theologiae Positivae,* ed. C. F. W. Walther (St. Louis, Concordia Publishing House, 1879), Prol. C. II, par. 20. I, 123.

164. Quenstedt, *Systema,* P. I, C. 4, S. 2, q. 10, Ekthesis 10 and 12 (1715 ed. I, 149).

165. Calov, *Systema,* I, 616; Gerhard, *Confessio Catholica,* I, 30; John Schroeder,

388 CHAPTER THREE   *The Doctrine of Scripture*

Opusculum Theologicum de Principio Theologiae, et Naturali Notitia Dei (Schweinfurt, 1605), p. 54.

166. For the most thorough discussions of this passage as it pertains to the sufficiency of Scripture, see Calov, *Systema*, I, 618 ff.; Quenstedt, *Systema*, P. I, C. 4, S. 2, q. 10 (I, 156—57); Salomon Gesner, *Vera et Perspicua Explicatio Utilissimae Summaeque his Temporibus Necessariae Sententiae D. Pauli 2. Tim. 3* (Wittenberg, 1602), p. Dlr ff. 12r ff.

167. Calov, *Biblia Novi Testamenti Illustrata*, II, 1037 ff.

168. Bellarmine, *De Verbo Dei non Scripto*, IV, 4 (*Disputationes de Controversiis Christianae Fidei*, I, 174 ff.); Thomas Stapleton, *Principiorum Fidei Doctrinalium Relectio Scholastica & Compendiaria per Controversiae Quaestiones et Articulos Tradita* (Antwerp, 1596), pp. 442 ff.; Caesar Baronius, *Annales Ecclesiastici* (Rome, 1588), I, 400; Francis Suarez, *Defensio Fidei Catholicae et Apostolicae adversus Anglicanae Sectae Errores*, L. 6, C. 9 (*Opera Omnia* [Venice, 1760], XXI, 32).

169. See Gerhard, *Loci Theologici*, I, 26 ff.; II, 329 ff.; Quenstedt, *Systema*, P. I, C. 4, S. 2, q. 12 (I, 169 ff.); Friedemann Bechmann, *Theologia Polemica* (Jena, 1719), pp. 95 ff.; John Adam Scherzer, *Systema Theologiae* (Tübingen, 1679), pp. 23 ff.; Osiander, *Systema Theologicum*, p. 327 ff.; Walther, *Officina Biblica*, pp. 91—95.

170. *Systema*, P. I, C. 4, S. 2, q. 12. Fontes Solutionum 29 (I, 186). See also Giles Hunnius, *Opera Latina*, II, 209; Glassius, *Philologia Sacra*, L. I, T. 3, S. 2, p. 279.

171. Dannhauer, *Hermeneutica Sacra*, p. 51. See also Gerhard, *Loci Theologici*, I, 52.

172. Gerhard, *Loci Theologici*, I, 27. At this point we perceive that classical Lutheranism follows closely the approach of both Luther and the Confessions as they teach a double clarity of Scripture, "external clarity" and "internal clarity" (see *Martin Luthers Werke*, Kritische Gesammtausgabe [Weimar: H. Böhlau, 1883], XVIII, 607; hereafter cited as WA). For a lucid discussion of this matter, see Ralph Bohlmann, *Principles of Biblical Interpretation in the Lutheran Confessions* (St. Louis: Concordia Publishing House, 1968), pp. 57 f. See also Rudolf Hermann, *Von der Klarheit der Heiligen Schrift* (Berlin: Evangelische Verlagsanstalt, 1958); Holsten Fagerberg, *Die Theologie der lutherischen Bekenntnisschriften von 1529 bis 1537*, trans. Gerhard Klose (Göttingen: Vandenhoeck & Ruprecht, 1965), pp. 41 f.

173. Quenstedt, *Systema*, P. I, C. 4, S. 2, q. 12 (I, 175).

174. Calov, *Socinismus Profligatus*, p. 89.

175. See Bellarmine, *De Verbi Dei Interpretatione*, III, 1 (*Disputationes de Controversiis Christianae Fidei*, I, 135); Stapleton, *Principiorum Fidei*, pp. 442 ff. Bellarmine offers the following as proofs that Scripture is not plain *(aperta)* per se but requires the explanation of the church to settle its meaning in controversies: (1) There are many passages in Scripture that at first appear contrary to one another; (2) there are ambiguous words and statements in Scripture; (3) there are incomplete statements or thoughts in Scripture, e. g., anacolutha; (4) there are preposterous statements in Scripture, e. g., Gen. 10:32 speaks of the families of Noah according to nations, and chapter 11 speaks of the whole earth being one speech; (5) there are many different Hebraisms in Scripture; (6) there is much figurative speech in Scripture, e. g., metaphors, allegories, hyperboles, and numerous other tropes. Such facts, which were recognized by all the Lutherans and dealt with, simply do not disprove the clarity of Scripture in the sense meant by Lutheran theology.

176. Calov, *Apodixis Articulorum Fidei,* p. 47.
177. *Biblia Novi Testamenti Illustrata,* II, 1035. For a more dispassionate refutation of Bellarmine's arguments, see Gerhard, *Loci Theologici,* XII, 89 ff.
178. Among the more notable works dealing with Biblical interpretation are the following. The first formal effort by a Lutheran to deal extensively with the genres and figures of speech common to Scripture was by Andrew Hyperius (*De Theologo, seu de Ratione Studii Theologici Libri IIII* [Basel, 1556]), who exerted a profound influence in both Lutheran and Reformed circles. The most imposing and valuable contribution to the subject was the *Clavis Scripturae Sacrae* of Matthias Flacius, first published in 1567. The first volume of this large work resembles a Bible dictionary; it discusses the main themes of Scripture and seeks to explain troublesome terms and phrases. The second volume contains lengthy essays on basic hermeneutical principles. Flacius' work became a standard reference book through the period of orthodoxy and went through many editions. In the following century a number of less important studies appear. John Gerhard's *Tractatus de Legitima Scripturae Sacrae Interpretatione,* which was later incorporated into his *Loci Theologici,* deals mainly with the perfection of Scripture and related topics and has little to offer. The same might be said of Michael Walther's *Officina Biblica,* which deals more with the properties, texts, and translations of Scripture than with interpretation. A number of books like August Pfeiffer's *Dubia Vexata Scripturae Sacrae* (Dresden, 1679) and Wolfgang Franz's *Tractatus Theologicus Perspicuus de Interpretatione Sacrarum Scripturarum Maxime Legitima* (Wittenberg, 1693) also appeared; these works treated obscure and difficult passages of Scripture. One of the better contributions of the 17th century was the *Hermeneutica Sacra* of John Conrad Dannhauer. More useful still was John Olearius' *De Stylo Novi Testamenti* and his *Elementa Hermeneuticae Sacrae* (Leipzig, 1699). By far the most advanced and influential work of the orthodox period was Salomon Glassius' *Philologia Sacra,* which became immensely popular and went through a number of editions. This work presented a penetrating analysis of New and Old Testament stylistics and grammar, and it was the most thorough and scientific study yet to be undertaken. During the period of the decline of orthodoxy in the 18th century the names of two theologians stand out for their contributions to the study of hermeneutics: Gottfried Hoffmann (*Institutiones Theologicae Exegeticae* [Wittenberg, 1754]) and August Pfeiffer (*Thesaurus Hermeneuticus sive de Legitima Sacrae Scripturae Interpretione Tractatio Luculenta* [Leipzig and Frankfort, 1704]). The latter was highly respected by C. F. W. Walther (see *LuW,* I, 139 f.). Pfeiffer also wrote another work of some relevance, *Critica Sacra de Sacri Codicis Partitione, Editionibus Variis, Linguis Originalibus et Illibata Puritate Fontium, Interpretatione Scripturae Legitima.*
179. See Brunner, *Revelation and Reason,* pp. 274 ff.
180. See Quenstedt, *Systema,* P. I, C. 4, S. 2, q. 4. Fontes Solutionum 1 (I, 109 to 110); Baier, *Compendium Theologiae Positivae,* I, 110.
181. The most useful discussions are by Flacius, *Clavis Scripturae Sacrae,* II, V, pp. 459 ff.; and Glassius, *Philologia Sacra,* L. I, T. 3, pp. 262 ff. See also Gerhard, *Loci Theologici,* I, 87 ff.
182. Hyperius, *De Theologo,* pp. 118 ff.; Flacius, *Clavis Scripturae Sacrae,* II, IV, pp. 277 ff.
183. Baier, *Compendium Theologiae Positivae,* I, 110.
184. Friedemann Bechmann, *Annotationes Uberiores in Compendium Theologicum Leonhardi Hutteri* (Frankfort and Leipzig, 1703), p. 62.

185. Flacius, *Clavis Scripturae Sacrae,* II, I, 103—104. See also Pfeiffer, *Critica Sacra,* p. 95.
186. Textual criticism was still in a rudimentary stage in those days. But the Lutherans were as advanced in this science as any of their contemporaries. Calov in particular, whenever there is a serious problem, attempts to establish the best manuscript evidence and to appeal only to that; and this he does even in his dogmatic works (see *Apodixis Articulorum Fidei,* pp. 124, 175, 179, etc.). At times he gives too much credence to the early church fathers' use of a given passage.
187. The *Harmonia Quatuor Evangelistarum* of Chemnitz, Leyser, and Gerhard (Cap. V, I, 19) represents a complete break with Osiander and is not bothered by the same event being told in various ways.
188. *Officina Biblica,* p. 11.
189. Bechmann, *Annotationes Uberiores in Compendium Theologicum Leonhardi Hutteri,* 690 ff.; Calov, *Socinismus Profligatus,* p. 885.
190. This is consonant with the Lutheran position (see above, pp. 267—68) that, strictly speaking, only the *forma,* the meaning, of Scripture was the Word of God, and this *forma* could be brought out in different formulations or modes of expression *(materia).* It is of interest that Walther in this connection *(Officina Biblica,* p. 10) defined Scripture as *doctrina,* as *doctrina rerum divinarum.*
191. Hutter, *Loci Communes Theologici,* pp. 49 ff. This by no means precludes the fact that the Spirit uses the external persuasion of teachers of the church to enlighten the exegete. But the Spirit is not bound to the church as the only organ through which Scripture can be interpreted.
192. Calov, *Socinismus Profligatus,* pp. 89 ff.
193. Calov, *Socinismus Profligatus,* p. 87: "Now we readily grant that one can get the outward meaning of Scripture without any special gracious enlightenment of the Spirit. Even unbelievers can do this. However, we cannot grant that without the special illumination of the Spirit we can hear, read, and understand the Scriptures beneficially and fruitfully so that we give full assent to the Word and accept it with a saving faith."
194. *Consideratio Arminianismi* (Wittenberg, 1655), p. 49.
195. Hollaz, *Examen,* Prol. III, q. 48 (1718 ed.), p. 179. The position and practice of the later Lutheran exegetes in this regard does not differ from that of the Lutheran Confessions. See Ralph Bohlmann, *Principles of Biblical Interpretation in the Lutheran Confessions,* pp. 83 ff. One might compare this chapter with Bohlmann's entire book to see how closely the hermeneutics of the later Lutheran theologians resembled that manifested in the Lutheran Confessions.
196. *Loci Theologici,* II, 422.
197. Hutter, *Loci Communes Theologici,* p. 49.
198. Ibid.
199. *Philologia Sacra,* pp. 370—71. See also Quenstedt, *Systema,* P. I, C. 2, S. 2, q. 3 (1715 ed. I, 187).
200. Calov, *Socinismus Profligatus,* p. 96.
201. See Faustus Socinus, *Disputatio de Jesu Christo,* III, 11 (*Opera Omnia,* II, 213).
202. Calov, *Socinismus Profligatus,* p. 97.
203. Hutter, *Loci Communes Theologici,* pp. 49—50.

204. Calov, *Socinismus Profligatus*, p. 98.
205. See Bellarmine, *De Verbi Dei Interpretatione*, III, 3 (*De Controversiis Christianae*, I, 142); Jacob Gretzer, *Controversiarum Roberti Bellarmini S. R. E. Cardinalis Amplissimi Defensio* (Ingolstadt, 1607), I, 1175—1218. See also Gerhard, *Confessio Catholica*, pp. 421—29, for scores of statements of Roman Catholics both favoring and opposing the fourfold interpretation of Scripture.
206. *Loci Theologici*, I, 67. See also Glassius, *Philologia Sacra*, pp. 372 ff.; Selnecker, *Notatio de Studio Sacrae Theologiae*, p. 51; Meisner, *Philosophia Sobria*, S. I, C. 5, q. 6 (1655 ed. I, 106 ff.).
207. Calov, *Apodixis Articulorum Fidei*, p. 51.
208. Ibid., p. 48. The same concerns are expressed by the Calvinists, who insisted that the *unus sensus* of Scripture is bound up inseparably with the inerrancy of Scripture. There is an intention of a text or pericope, called the literal or grammatical sense, which if it were manifold (literal, allegorical, tropological, anagogical) would end in chaos. This means that the so-called literal or grammatical sense *(intentio dicentis)* may be allegorical or tropical or historical, but not all at once (Keckermann, *Systema Sacrae Theologiae*, p. 195; John Henry Alsted, *Lexicon Theologicum* [Hanover, 1620], pp. 6 to 11). Lutherans, however, accused the Calvinists of finding a double meaning in Scripture, for instance, in their interpretation of the eating and drinking in the Lord's Supper (Gerhard, *Loci Theologici*, I, 72—76).
209. Calov, *Socinismus Profligatus*, p. 101.
210. Quenstedt, *Systema*, P. I, C. 4, S. 2, q. 13, Ekthesis 10 (I, 188).
211. *Philologia Sacra*, pp. 348 ff.
212. Friedrich Balduin, *Commentarius in Omnes Epistolas Beati Apostoli Pauli*, editio altera priore longe emaculatior (Frankfort on the Main, 1710), p. 611; Giles Hunnius, *Thesaurus Apostolicus Complectens*, p. 417. Luther (WA 40, I, 656) understands the allegorizing of Paul as no more than the use of an extended metaphor for the sake of garnishing and illustrating a point already made. It is not an interpreting of the Genesis account as would be the case if the figures in Genesis were types.
213. *Clavis Scripturae*, II, 347.
214. *Loci Theologici*, I, 69.
215. There were of course some notable exceptions, as for instance the story of Abraham offering up his son Isaac. There is no explicit New Testament evidence for Isaac being a type of Christ in this story; but at this point the old Lutherans could not resist following the lead of Luther and the early church fathers in making a great deal out of the parallel. See Calov, *Biblia Testamenti Veteris Illustrata*, I, 290—92.
216. John Gerhard, *Annotationes Posthumae in Evangelium D. Matthaei* (Jena, 1663), p. 976.
217. Calov, *Biblia Testamenti Veteris Illustrata*, II, 740—48; Pfeiffer, *Dubia Vexata Scripturae Sacrae*, pp. 922—23; Quenstedt, *Systema*, P. I, C. 4, S. 2, q. 13; Fontes Solutionum 3 (I, 193).
218. Michael Walther, *Harmonia Biblica* (Nuremberg, 1696), pp. 425—31. This was also the conviction of Bechmann (*Institutiones Theologicae* [Jena, 1707], p. 86).
219. Hollaz, *Examen*, Pro. 3, q. 48 (1750 ed. 160 ff.).
220. Glassius, *Philologia Sacra*, p. 498; Gerhard, *Loci Theologici*, II, 424; Hutter,

Loci Communes Theologici, p. 50; Balthasar Mentzer, *Disputationes Theologicae et Scholasticae XIV (Opera Latina,* II, 1597 ff.); Flacius, *Clavis Scripturae,* I, 36; Calov, *Biblia Novi Testamenti Illustrata,* II, 207. Since there was an analogy of faith (Rom. 12:6), it would follow that obscure passages of Scripture could be explained through clear passages (2 Peter 1:20).

In fact, without an analogy of faith clearly and exegetically derived from the Scriptures, one of the most vexing problems for the exegete could never be solved, namely, the problem confronted when one passage seems to conflict with the *summa doctrinae* concerning Christ the Savior. And Scripture would descend to the level of an obscure hodgepodge of conflicting assertions. See Andreae, *Disputationes Theologicae,* p. 13. See also pp. 15, 21.

It was most important for Lutheran theology that possibly obscure passages of Scripture be clarified only by passages dealing with the same subject matter. The *sedes* for any article of faith must deal with that very article of faith. This would seem quite elementary. But Lutheran theologians would insist that at just this point much hermeneutical method breaks down. For instance, the Calvinists are accused of refusing to derive their doctrine of the Lord's Supper directly from the *sedes* for that article of faith, the very procedure of Paul himself in 1 Cor. 11:23 ff. See Martin Chemnitz, *Fundamenta Sanae Doctrinae de Vera et Substantiali Praesentia, Exhibitione, et Sumptione Corporis & Sanguinis Domini in Coena* (Frankfort and Wittenberg, 1653), pp. 3—4.

It is odd in this connection that Curtis E. Huber, commenting on the principle *Scriptura per scripturam explicanda,* should say: "There is no suggestion implied by that principle to the effect that one passage of a particular Biblical book will automatically [sic] throw the light of meaning on another passage which is in question" ("Meaning and the Word in Lutheran Orthodoxy," in *Concordia Theological Monthly* [hereafter cited as *CTM*], XXXVI [September 1965], 566). Hollaz (*Examen,* p. 160) specifically says that the subject of the statement *Scriptura per scripturam explicanda* is those prophetic and apostolic writings that are less clear, and the predicate *per scripturam* is to be understood as *eloquia prophetarum & apostolorum clariora.* As we might expect, he says, such passages can help explain those passages that at first seem to be more obscure. Huber also says that according to Lutheran orthodoxy "Biblical signs do not explain themselves" and "Verbal entities do not produce meaning. God gives meaning to men's words which makes them vehicles of God's own truth." But the old Lutherans never say that God gives meaning to the Scriptures, but rather understanding (and this means saving understanding) to those who read Scripture. The meaning *(sensus literalis)* of Scripture is already there in Scripture. Huber has apparently confused the subject matter *(res,* divine mysteries) of Scripture (see Hollaz, *Examen,* p. 149) with the meaning *(sensus literalis)* of passages and pericopes; but even this does not explain his strange conclusions.

221. Michael Walther, *Officina Biblica,* p. 15; Dannhauer, *Christosophia seu Sapientiarum Sapientia,* p. 1; Calov, *Systema,* I, 457; Dedekenn, *Thesauri Consiliorum et Decisionum,* p. 332. According to Luke 24:27 it was believed by the Lutherans that Moses, the psalms, and all the prophets agreed in proclaiming that Christ would suffer and die and rise again, and the church of the Old Testament placed its hope in this (see Wolfgang Franz, *Schola Sacrificiorum Patriarchalium Sacra* [Wittenberg, 1698], pp. 91 and 887). When the New Testament refers to the ἐπαγγελία of the Old Testa-

ment, this promise always has "reference first of all to the coming of Christ in the flesh" (Quenstedt, *Systema*, P. IV, C. 2, S. 2, q. 1, Ekthesis 2 [1615 ed., II, 1014]). In other words, all Old Testament prophecy in the broad sense is Christological.

222. Chemnitz, *Harmonia Quatuor Evangelistarum*, Cap. 46. I, 377. Chemnitz is voicing here a very common conviction that only the "chief locus of the Christian doctrine," namely, that we receive remission through faith in Christ, when rightly understood, enables us to understand the entire Scriptures and "alone opens the door to the entire Bible." See Apology of the Augsburg Confession, IV, 2 (German text). See also Edmund Schlink, *Theology of the Lutheran Confessions*, trans. Paul F. Koehneke and Herbert J. A. Bouman (Philadelphia: Muhlenberg Press, 1961), p. 27. See Bohlmann, *Principles of Biblical Interpretation in the Lutheran Confessions*, pp. 69 ff. See also Luther, WA 24, 549, 18; 42, 368, 35; 42, 377, 20.

223. Glassius, *Philologia Sacra*, p. 498; Chemnitz, *Loci Theologici*, II, 202 ff.; Osiander, *Systema Theologicum*, III, 90. See also Apology of the Augsburg Confession, IV, 5.

224. *Biblia Novi Testamenti Illustrata*, II, 21.

225. Quenstedt, *Systema*, P. IV, C. 2, S. 2, q. 1, Ekthesis 5—6 (IV, 1014). See ibid., C. 7, S. 2, q. 1 (IV, 1325); Hollaz, *Examen*, P. III, S. 2, C. 2, q. 22, p. 1052

226. Quenstedt is quoting from Augustine, *In Johannis Evangelium Tractatus*, 45, 9 (*Patrologia Cursus Completus* . . . Series Latina, ed. J.-P. Migne [Paris: Garnier, 1878—90], 35, 1722).

227. Hollaz, *Examen*, Pro. Q. 14 (1718 ed. p. 11).

228. Calov, *Socinismus Profligatus*, p. 80.

229. Socinus, *Opera Omnia*, I, 292 ff.

230. Brochmand, *Commentarius in Epistolam ad Hebraeos*, p. 53.

231. Ibid., p. 74.

232. Ibid., p. 47.

233. *History of Protestant Theology*, II, 137.

234. *Catechesis Racoviensis seu Liber Socinianorum Primarius* (Frankfort and Leipzig, 1739), praefatio.

235. John Adam Scherzer, *Collegii Anti-Sociniani* (Leipzig and Frankfort, 1702), pp. 25 ff.; Calov, *Socinismus Profligatus*, pp. 70 ff.; Calov, *Systema*, I, 653 ff.

236. Bechmann, *Annotationes Uberiores in Compendium Theologicum Leonhardi Hutteri*, p. 567.

237. This criticism was already brought against the classical Lutheran exegesis by John Semler, especially in his *Abhandlung von freier Untersuchung des Canon* (Halle, 1771—75), and the charge has been made with some regularity ever since. Among the older scholars are found Dorner (*History of Protestant Theology*, II, 136) and Frederic W. Farrar (*History of Interpretation* [New York: Macmillan and Co., 1886], pp. 260, 268), whose charges of dogmatic exegesis are not without vituperation. Those two scholars have for the most part been followed uncritically by modern historians and exegetes, some of whom have never looked into the exegetical or hermeneutical works of the orthodox Lutherans. (See Gerhard Ebeling, *Word and Faith*, trans. James W. Leitch [London: SCM Press, 1963], p. 308; Kurt Frör, *Biblische Hermeneutik* [Munich: Chr. Kaiser Verlag, 1964], p. 26; Edwin C. Blackman, *Biblical Interpretation* [Philadelphia: Westminster

Press, 1957], p. 128; Robert M. Grant, *The Bible in the Church* [New York: Macmillan Company, 1954], p. 128. Of the old Lutheran exegesis Grant's entire description, a masterpiece of superficiality, is the following: "It [Scripture] is used for the reconstruction of dogmatic systems. Protestant orthodoxy in the seventeenth century becomes as rigid as any Medieval theological construction.")

Similar criticisms are made by those who have studied somewhat more deeply the theology of Lutheran orthodoxy (see Hans Emil Weber, *Reformation, Orthodoxie und Rationalismus: Beiträge zur Förderung christlicher Theologie*, 2 vols. [Gütersloh: C. Bertelsmann, 1937—51], I, 1,309; Gottfried Hornig, *Die Anfänge der historisch-kritischen Theologie* [Göttingen: Vandenhoeck & Ruprecht, 1961], pp. 40—55). Hans-Joachim Kraus (*Geschichte der historisch-kritischen Erforschung des Alten Testaments von der Reformation bis zur Gegenwart* [Neukirchen: Verlag der Buchhandlung des Erziehungsvereins, 1956], pp. 28 ff.) makes the same charge and traces this alleged tendency in exegesis back to Melanchthon, who taught that all Biblical interpretation must be done in the service of pure doctrine (see *Corpus Reformatorum*, ed. Carl Gottlieb Bretschneider et al. [Halle: C. A. Schwetschke and Sons, 1834—], 21, 1099, hereafter cited as *CR*). Kraus' claim is that orthodoxy's concept of pure doctrine, based on a dogma of of inspiration, prevents sensitive exegesis or hermeneutics. The concept changed the Old Testament *dabar* which makes history into a timeless doctrine. *Heilsgeschichte* becomes mere *Menschheitsgeschichte* under the categories of an *ordo justificationis* or an *ordo regenerationis et renovationis*. Kraus believes that Calixt and the Reformed theologian Coccejus with his covenant theology were the first to break with the old *loci* method with its unhistorical concept of doctrine and were the first therefore to study Scripture historically. I fail to see how the analytic method or the federal theology comport necessarily with a more historical reading of Scripture rather than the older Law-Gospel motif of the earlier Lutheran and Reformed theologians. And I fail to see how the great concern for the purity of doctrine in itself should make an exegete less historically aware. It is not an uncommon implication among theologians today that verbal inspiration is somehow a denial of history (see Althaus, *Die Christliche Wahrheit*, p. 219).

Not all historians have charged the entire period of Lutheran orthodoxy with dogmatic exegesis. Henri Strohl, while believing that dogmatics reigned supreme at most Lutheran universities during this period, asserts that at Strasbourg, which was one of the most rigidly orthodox universities, exegesis was held in great honor. This was due to the deep exegetical interest of such professors as Johann Schmid, Dorsch, and Sebastian Schmidt. See Henri Strohl, *Le Protestantisme en Alsace* (Strasbourg: Editions Oberlin, 1950), p. 93.

238. For a good discussion of the influence of scholastic methodology on exegesis, see Hägglund, *Die heilige Schrift und ihre Deutung in der Theologie Johann Gerhards*, pp. 105—118.

239. *Biblia Novi Testamenti Illustrata*, II, 1233—37.

240. This section represents a thorough revision and expansion of an article appearing in *CTM*, XXXIII (August 1962), 469—83.

241. In speaking of Scripture the Lutheran teachers never use the word "inerrancy" *(inerrantia)*, which is of much later origin, but rather usually such adjective terms as *"infallibilis"* (e. g., Scherzer, *Systema Theologiae*, p. 18), *"erroris expers"* (e. g., Quenstedt, *Systema*, P. I, C. 4, S. 2, q. 5 [I, 112]),

"verissima" (e.g., Quenstedt, *Systema*), *"veracissima"* (e.g., Dannhauer, *Hodosophia Christiana*, p. 33), *"immunia ab omni errore"* (Bechmann, *Theologia Polemica*, p. 76). The Lutheran teachers also used noun terms such as *"veritas"* (Osiander, *Systema Theologicum*, p. 231) or *"veracitas"* (Hollaz, *Examen*, Prol. III, q. 25 [1750 ed., p. 104]) in the sense of truthfulness. Very often the Lutheran teachers express themselves by saying that the writers of Scripture did not suffer any lapse of memory *(Scriptores sacri nunquam memoria lapsi sunt)* or err *(errarunt)* in any matter (Bechmann, *Theologia Polemica*, p. 76; Quenstedt, *Systema*, P. I, C. 4, S. 2, q. 5, I, 112); or they say that the writers were unable to deceive or be deceived *(nec fallere, nec falli vult, aut potest)* in the sense that they could not be mistaken themselves or lead others into error (Hollaz, *Examen*, Prol. III, q. 25 [1750 ed., p. 104]; Baier, *Compendium Theologiae Positivae*, I, 119). Calov (*Socinismus Profligatus*, p. 60), entitles his discussion *"De Veritate Scripturae."* By no means do all the Lutheran dogmaticians offer a section dealing specifically with the inerrancy of Scripture. The earlier Lutherans (Giles Hunnius, Hutter, Gerhard) mention or assume the fact in their discussions on the authority of Scripture, and there is never the slightest doubt as to their convictions. This is also the case with Baier and Osiander. Those like Bechmann, Calov, Quenstedt, and Dannhauer who deal specifically with the doctrine are careful to discuss it between their treatment of the divine origin of Scripture and the authority of Scripture.

242. *Systema*, P. I, C. 4, S. 2, q. 5 (I, 112).
243. *Systema*, I, 462.
244. Calov, *Socinismus Profligatus*, pp. 60—61; Calov, *Theologia Positiva*, p. 19; Quenstedt, *Systema*, P. I, C. 4, S. 2, q. 5 (I, 115—17). It is also noteworthy that passages which have more recently been cited to support Scripture's infallibility (e.g., Matt. 5:18 and John 10:35) are not found among the orthodox Lutherans as support for their position.
245. *Socinismus Profligatus*, p. 61.
246. Gerhard, *Confessio Catholica*, II, 199.
247. *Systema*, P. I, C. 4, S. 2, q. 5 (I, 116); see also Calov, *Systema*, I, 552; Bechmann, *Theologia Polemica*, p. 76; Giles Hunnius, *Opera Latina*, I, 29.
248. Thomas Aquinas (*Summa contra Gentiles*, I, 59, ed. Parisiis, 1878, p. 147) defines truth, formally considered, as "adaequatio intellectus et rei, secundum quod intellectus dicit esse quod est, vel non esse quod non est." See also Francis Suarez (*Metaphysicae Disputationes* [*Opera Omnia* (Venice, 1760), 22, 146], P. I, Disp. VIII, S. 1), who says that truth is "conformitas intellectus ad rem, id est, conformitas conceptus objectivi intellectus enunciantis ad rem secundam esse reale ejus . . . ergo veritas solum est objective in intellectu. Atque ita nihil aliud erit, quam conformitas rei in esse objectivo ad se ipsam in esse reali." The Lutheran theologians follow this line of thought closely. For instance, Mentzer (*Opera Latina*, I, 375) defines truth in the following fashion: "Est enim veritas convenientia sive adaequatio conceptuum sive notionum cum ipsa re. Unde axioma verum definitur, quod dicit, uti res est." See also Calov, *Systema*, I, 69 ff.; Melanchthon, *CR* 16, 44. It is therefore generally this correspondence idea of truth that the old Lutherans operate with when they speak of the truthfulness of God and of Scripture (understood formally). But that God and Scripture are truthful means much more than conformity to such a category, as we shall see.
249. Quenstedt, *Systema*, P. I, C. 3, S. 2, q. 1, Porisma 2, Fontes Solutionum 22 (I, 63).

250. Lutheran theology assumed that the correspondence idea of truth was presupposed by the Eighth Commandment, which was quite unintelligible and incapable of application without a correspondence idea of truth as understood by the plain man. Thus, the Eighth Commandment makes speaking according to a correspondence understanding of truth a moral issue. Dannhauer in his celebrated work on the Decalog entitled *Deuteronomium Dannhawerianum* (Strasbourg, 1669, pp. 436 ff.), which incidentally ran to exactly 1,000 pages, discusses at length the question of moral truth. He first distinguishes moral truth from truth in the philosophical sense (ontological truth: *veritas rei ac transcendentalis, quae tota ad regionem metaphysicam pertinet*). Moral truth is especially a virtue of the Second Commandment, because, first, it is a species of doxology and, second, it is so often associated with oaths and vows. In the state of innocence truth was the agreement of the internal with the external, a complete harmony of the individual with everything about him (*harmonia* τοῦ ἔσω καὶ ἔξω), the opposite of pretense and dissimulation. Verbal truth (*veritas verbalis seu assertoria*) accordingly is simply to affirm something and consists formally in the agreement of the concept with the statement. In this connection Dannhauer speaks also of a *veritas promissoria* that involves sincerity and faithfulness, and consists formally of the agreement of statement or promise with the event or fact (*conformitas vocis & rei*), see Matt. 5:37. Thus, keeping a promise, like telling the truth, is a moral action. Anything that per se threatens or injures this idea of moral truth is called error or a lie (*fallacia, mendacium*). From discussions such as Dannhauer's it is clearly evident that when Lutheran theology speaks of God or Scripture as truthful, the moral imperatives of the Second and Eighth Commandments are clearly in the background, and it is evident that these imperatives are predicated on a correspondence idea of truth. We might observe that when truth is ascribed to God in Scripture, it has the character, according to Lutheran theologians, both of steadfastness (*constantia*) and of integrity and veracity (*veracitas, veritas*) in the sense explained above (see Resen, *De Sancta Fide in verum Deum*, p. 1). Quenstedt (*Systema*, P. I, C. 8, S. 1, Thesis 14 [I, 412—13]) in calling God truth distinguishes between metaphysical or transcendental truth — which is God's own divine and independent nature in contrast to every idol or false notion about Him — and ethical or moral truth, sometimes called veracity (*veracitas*) — which has to do with words, promises, or threats. Both are ascribed to God, but the former to His very essence. (Jer. 10:10; 1 Thess. 1:9; 1 John 5:20)

251. *Hodosophia Christiana*, p. 34.

252. Quenstedt, for instance, speaks of the truthfulness (*veracitas*) of God according to which He is absolutely truthful in all His words and promises (2 Sam. 7:28; John 17:17; Heb. 6:18) and also in all His activities and deeds (Deut. 32:4; Ps. 25:10). See *Systema*, P. I, C. 7, S. 1, Th. 37 (I, 422).

253. Mentzer, *Opera Latina*, I, 944.

254. Ibid., 776.

255. *Clavis Scripturae*, I, 1288—92. See also Dannhauer, *Deuteronomium Dannhawerianum*, p. 437 *passim*.

256. *Systema*, P. I, C. 4, S. 2, q. 5, Ekthesis (I, 112). See also Calov's statement (*Systema*, I, 462) cited above (pp. 340—41).

257. Socinus, *De Auctoritate Scripturae*, p. 13.

258. *Systema*, I, 552. See also *Socinismus Profligatus*, p. 62; *Consideratio Arminianismi*, p. 61; Quenstedt, *Systema*, P. I, C. 4, S. 2, q. 5, Fontes Solu-

tionum 1 (I, 116). The Socinians also taught that when Scripture touched on the realm of nature or morals, the affirmations were only relative *(topica)* and probable "because the divine revelations per se did not have as their purpose *(intendant)* a knowledge of natural things but rather information for our salvation" (Calov, *Systema,* I, 280). Calov replies that many knowable things in the realms of nature and morals are also revealed in Scripture, not as facts for their own sake but as facts and circumstances that attend the saving revelation and make it effective. Meanwhile we are simply to believe God as He gives His revelation, or all becomes merely academic. "If I will not believe God who reveals as such, but only as He reveals mysteries of faith to me, then it will not be legitimate for me with complete safety to believe even in these mysteries, but the certainty of the entire divine revelation will be jeopardized."

259. See Koelling, *Die Lehre von der Theopneustie,* for a discussion of the doctrine of inspiration and inerrancy throughout church history. We have already alluded to Gerhard's position and will have occasion to do so often in the course of this chapter. Flacius' view concerning Scripture's truthfulness and inerrancy is brought out in his *Norma seu Regula Coelestis Veritatis (Tractatus VII* in his *Clavis Scripturae,* II, 685 ff.). Among other things he says: "Now God alone is all-wise, true, and good. And all men, on the other hand, according to the testimony of Scripture, are liars, foolish, and evil — and cursed is he who trusts in man. So also only that doctrine or book which is in fact authored *{constat}* by the Holy Spirit, which was spoken through the mouth of the prophets and apostles and written through their hands, is a doctrine that is true and abundant in wisdom and saving" (694). See also *Clavis Scripturae,* II, 92: "As Paul writes the various churches in his own name, it is with good reason that he scrupulously makes a point of mentioning his calling and his office. For the entire authority of the books [of Scripture] depends on this. This is done that we might know who the author of these books really is: it is either God or (to say the same thing) persons through whom God Himself spoke, who are unable to err *{errare non possunt}* and whom God wants us simply to believe, such as the prophets and apostles; *or* it is men who are capable of misleading others and being mistaken themselves." Flacius was insistent that there were no contradictions (II, 39) or discrepancies (II, 165) in Scripture. For Luther's position on inerrancy, see Wilhelm Walther, *Das Erbe der Reformation* (Leipzig: A. Diechertsche Verlagsbuch-handlung 1917), pp. 99 ff.; Michael Reu, *Luther and the Scriptures* (Columbus: The Wartburg Press, 1944), pp. 65—102. On the position of the church fathers, see the Encyclical Letter, *Spiritus Paraclitus,* II, 3 (*Rome and the Study of Scriptures* [St. Meinrad: Grail Publications, 1958]), pp. 48—51 *et passim;* see also, e. g., James Franklin Bethune-Baker, *An Introduction to the Early History of Christian Doctrine* (London: Methuen and Company, 1954), p. 47 *et passim.* That the Scholastics held to the inerrancy of Scripture may be seen from Alexander of Hales, *Summa Theologica* (Florence, 1924), I, 5, and especially Thomas Aquinas, *Summa Theologica* (Rome: Marietti, 1948), I, 1, 8, and John Duns Scotus, *Opera Omnia* (Vatican City: Typis Polyglotis Vaticanis, 1950—), Prol. Para. II, who advances eight arguments for the *"veritas"* of Scripture. The doctrine of inerrancy, however, was stated more explicitly in the 17th century than ever before.

260. In the 18th century such theologians as Hollaz and Loescher offer little discussion on inerrancy, perhaps because the lines had now been clearly drawn and the Lutheran position made clear.

261. See Pfeiffer, *Thesaurus Hermeneuticus,* p. 26; Quenstedt, *Systema,* P. I, C. 3, S. 2, q. 1, Porisma 2, Antithesis 6 (I, 58). For the Cartesian position we might mention René Descartes, *The Principles of Philosophy,* par. 30 and 43 (See *A Discourse on Method* [London: J. M. Deut and Sons Ltd., 1949], pp. 177, 181), which emphasizes sense perception along with mathematics as normative for gaining the truth. It was no doubt the dogmatic optimism of this methodology, with no allusion to knowledge by revelation, that bothered the Lutherans more than anything else.
262. *Tractatus de Legitima Scripturae Sacrae Interpretatione,* p. 25.
263. Calov, *Apodixis Articulorum Fidei,* pp. 45 ff.
264. See Socinus, *De Auctoritate Scripturae,* p. 13 *passim.*
265. Two of the larger and more scholarly monographs of this sort were Michael Walther, *Harmonia Biblica, sive Brevis et Plana Conciliatio Locorum Veteris et Novi Testamenti Apparenter sibi Contradicentium* (Nuremberg, 1645); and August Pfeiffer, *Dubia Vexata Scripturae Sacrae, sive Loca Difficiliora Veteris Testamenti.*
266. *Harmonia Biblica,* pp. 1 ff. See also Gerhard, *Loci Theologici,* I, 81.
267. Flacius, *Clavis Scripturae,* II, 165.
268. Ibid., II, 39.
269. *Harmonia Quatuor Evangelistarum,* Cap. CXC (III, 1855).
270. Walther, *Harmonia Biblica,* pp. 539—41. Calov, *Biblia Illustrata Novi Testamenti,* I, 451. Hollaz (Prol. III, q. 16 [1750 ed.], p. 85) disposes of the problem with a kind of impatient flippancy: "Matthew's words are: 'Thus it was fulfilled which was spoken by the prophet saying.' Nothing is said in the text about Jeremiah's writing. And so what Jeremiah said his disciple Zechariah wrote."
271. *Biblia Illustrata Novi Testamenti,* I, 383. Both Gerhard (*Annotationes Posthumae in Evangelium D. Matthaei,* p. 900) and Calixt (*Quatuor Evangelicarum Concordia* [Helmstedt, 1663], p. 288) reason the same way as Calov at this point.
272. *Harmonia Quatuor Evangelistarum,* Cap. CXXXVI ff. (I, 1399 ff.). Giles Hunnius (*Thesaurus Evangelico Apostolicus,* pp. 243—44) agrees essentially with this interpretation. He says that Luke tells of one miracle as Jesus entered Jericho and Mark of another as He left town, and Matthew combines the two for the sake of brevity and because of the marked similarity of the two miracles *(propter congruentium circumstantiarum similitudinem & conformitatem).*
273. *Biblia Illustrata Novi Testamenti,* I, 383.
274. *Harmonia Biblica,* p. 527. Calixt also implies that there was only one miracle performed, and that when Jesus left the city. (*Quatuor Evangelicarum Scriptorum Concordia,* p. 288)
275. *Annotationes Posthumae in Evangelium D. Matthaei,* p. 899.
276. Quenstedt, *Systema,* P. I, C. 4, S. 2, q. 5, Fontes Solutionum 11 (I, 118).
277. *Systema,* I, 606 ff.
278. Ibid., I, 551.
279. *Systema,* P. I, C. 4, S. 2, q. 5, Thesis (I, 112).
280. Calov, *Consideratio Arminianismi,* p. 64.
281. Calov, *Systema,* I, 575; Flacius, *Clavis Scripturae,* II, 104; Pfeiffer, *Thesaurus Hermeneuticus,* p. 25.
282. *Hermeneutica Sacra,* p. 409.

283. *De Auctoritate S. Scripturae,* Cap. I (*Opera Omnia,* I, 267): "In doctrina, affirmari constanter potest, nihil inveniri, quod falsum esse aperta cognoscatur." Notice that Socinus does not say, "nihil inveniri posse."
284. Ibid: "Quamvis in quibusdam paucis rebus, quae nullius sunt ponderis, cum fieri possit, ut alius alio talium rerum veritatem melius tenuerit, fortasse aliquantum, aut etiam multum diverse alius ab alio scripserit."
285. *Socinismus Profligatus,* p. 79 *et passim.*
286. *Systema,* I, 608. Calov is not merely pressing an argument at this point. He is clearly concerned, deeply concerned, over the fact that the Socinian approach to Scripture in fact undermines the possibility of doctrinal certainty, a fact of prime importance to the church as it teaches and confesses the faith. Klaus Scholder (*Ursprünge und Probleme der Bibelkritik im 17. Jahrhundert* [Munich: Chr. Kaiser Verlag, 1966], pp. 15—55) has shown with ample evidence that the loss of doctrinal certainty, aided and abetted to a great extent by the Socinians even while advancing strong arguments for the basic reliability of Scripture, created a vacuum that the higher critical method could fill. Ironically, Calov and the Lutherans, as well as the Calvinists and Roman Catholics, saw this danger clearly and spoke out against it. But it was like seeing the beginning of an avalanche.
287. Flacius, *Clavis Scripturae,* II, 5, 556. See also II, 39: "To the papists the whole of Scripture seems to conflict with itself. . . . The reason is that they do not know the difference between the Law and the Gospel."
288. Calov, *Systema,* I, 464 ff.; Dannhauer, *Hodosophia Christiana,* pp. 34—36; Quenstedt, *Systema,* P. I, C. 4, S. 2, q. 5, Ekthesis 4, 6, 7, 8 (I, 113, 114).
289. *Annotationes Uberiores in Compendium Theologicum L. Hutteri,* p. 223.
290. *Systema,* III, 1036 ff. On the basis of such passages as Ps. 104:5; Eccl. 1:4; Ps. 19:6-7; 74:16; 104:19; and Jer. 31:35 Calov maintained that Scripture teaches that the earth does not move in an orbit but remains in a fixed position. Calov was fully aware of the theories of Copernicus and Kepler, which "appeared more probable to the reasonings in the physical sciences and mathematics," but on this particular issue he is convinced that Scripture has decided the issue. It does not occur to him that Scripture has used phenomenal or poetic language in this case. He obviously assumes in this case that the only alternative to his conclusion is that of Henry Nicolai and others that Scripture is not reliable when touching on astronomy and mathematics.
291. See above, note 2 to Chapter One, p. 66.
292. Pfeiffer, *Critica Sacra,* p. 94.
293. Chemnitz, *Harmonia Quatuor Evangelistarum,* Prol. Cap. V. I, 18—21. The details in chronology alluded to here are considered more carefully throughout the entire harmony.
294. Ibid., Cap. I. I, 3.4.
295. Nikolaus Selnecker, *Paedagogia Christiana* (Frankfort on the Main, 1577), p. 233.
296. Calov, *Apodixis Articulorum Fidei,* p. 74: "In hominibus ob imperfectionem nostram ita se habet [simulatio], in sanctissimo Deo non item, praesertim in iis hoc neutiquam concedendum ubi promissiones divinae exhibentur, sic enim fundamentum fidei nostrae deesset." Some of the other Lutherans appear to be somewhat less squeamish concerning the immorality of deception, although there is perhaps little essential difference between them and Calov on this point. Dannhauer, for instance, defines deceit in the following

way (*Deuteronomium Dannhawerianum,* p. 444): "Deceit can be defined in this way, as a pretense or dissimulation that in itself serves to introduce a false opinion and is harmful; in itself, I say, because it may happen that one gets steeped in a false idea from some source that is perceived by his sense perception and intellect in such a way that it is his understanding and judgment that is in error rather than the thing judged." For instance, a joke or comedy would not be a deception per se, in its own context. Dannhauer goes on: "Thus it is not deceit if one should sell you a blind horse that you believed to have its sight. You are the one who errs; he has not cheated you. You ought to learn to purchase things more carefully. However he does deceive, if, when questioned by the buyer concerning hidden defects in the horse, he denies that such is the case." On this principle, the truthfulness of Scripture could not be questioned if we are deceived when reading it. God's integrity cannot be called into question. Deception is always *injuriosa* per se. I do not believe that Calov would disagree with anything Dannhauer has said. It is a different matter when we approach something Selnecker (*Paedagogia Christiana,* p. 231) has written on the subject of deception. Following Peter Lombard (*Sententiarum Libri IIII* [Venice, 1620], Lib. III, Dist. 38, pp. 325 ff.), Selnecker speaks of three kinds of lies or deceptions: pernicious lies, helpful (*officiosa*) lies, and lies done in jest (jokes). The second classification obtains when one deceives for a just and honest cause (e.g., Rahab, the mothers who hid their children from Pharaoh, etc.). "Strictly speaking," Selnecker says, "a lie is the perversion *{depravatio}* of something that ought to be said." This means that Rahab did not lie. Calov does not like Lombard's distinction. To him there is no such thing as a *mendacium officiosum.* He says (*Biblia Testamenti Veteris Illustrata,* I, 657): "Since a lie is per se evil, it is certain that in no case can it become good or permissible. Neither can that which is formally and intrinsically wicked become lawful because of external circumstances such as time, place, and persons. For external circumstances cannot change the inner nature of a thing. Thus the apostle teaches (Rom. 3:5) that we 'ought not do evil in order that good may come of it'; for what is evil in itself cannot become allowable just because a good end is intended." Nor does Calov say that Rahab did not lie. But Rahab was commended not because of her lie but because of her faith (Heb. 11:31) and because she helped God's messengers (James 2:25). "It must be ascribed to her weakness that Rahab in her appointed perplexity, when she knew of no other way to provide escape for the spies, resorted to a helpful lie to deliver God's messengers from their very present danger."

297. Calov, *Systema,* IX, 2.

298. See Quenstedt, *Systema,* P. I, C. 4, S. 2, q. 16, Ekthesis I (I, 246).

299. See above, pp. 267—69.

300. Dannhauer, *Hodosophia Christiana,* p. 655.

301. Hutter, *Loci Communes Theologici,* p. 920; Quenstedt, *Systema,* P. I., C. 4, S. 2, q. 16, Ekthesis 2 (I, 247); Calov, *Apodixis Articulorum Fidei,* p. 341.

302. Gerhard, *Loci Theologici,* VI, 257.

303. Ibid., XIX, 219.

304. The passage usually cited in support of this idea is Gal. 3:22, where "Scripture" is taken to mean "Law" and "promise" to mean "Gospel." See Calov, *Systema,* V, 414: "(Legis) *Scriptura concluserit omnia sub peccatum, ut promissio* (in Evangelio facta, justitiae nempe, & vitae aeternae) *ex fide*

Jesu Christi (hoc est, in Jesum Christum) *detur credentibus."* See also Chemnitz, *Loci Theologici,* II, 206.

305. *Examen,* P. I, S. 2, C. 1, q. 39, p. 1021. See also Calov, *Systema,* V, 414: "The Law leads us to the Gospel of Christ, not directly, but only indirectly, not by teaching us anything about Christ, but by compelling us to seek Christ."

306. Gerhard, *Loci Theologici,* V, 107. This is a constant refrain of Gerhard and the other Lutheran theologians. See Quenstedt, *Systema,* P. IV, C. 2, S. 2, q. 4 (II, 1027). By this Gerhard means that Law and Gospel must be properly divided. Quenstedt points out that there is no hostile conflict between Law and Gospel, for both must be preached by the church and in the church (see Gerhard, *Loci Theologici,* V, 132 ff.); but there are tremendous differences, particularly in regard to its effects. "The Law accuses, terrifies, works wrath and damnation (Rom. 4:15). The Gospel comforts those who have been terrified. The Law announces death; the Gospel shows us the good Physician and cures our sickness. For it is the power of God unto salvation to all who believe (Rom. 1:16). The Law is a doctrine concerning what we are to do; the Gospel a doctrine concerning what we are to believe. The Law is the ministry of death, the Gospel the ministry of the Spirit." Both Law and Gospel have to do with sin, but in completely different ways. In this sense the Law has nothing to do with the Gospel, and the two must be strictly divided.

307. John Gerhard, *Commentarius super Priorem D. Petri Epistolam,* editio altera priori correctior (Jena, 1680), p. 163.

308. John Huelsemann, *Extensio Breviarii Theologici* (Heilbronn, 1667), p. 6.

309. Quenstedt, *Systema,* P. I, C. 4, S. 2, q. 16, Ekthesis 14 (I, 251).

310. Calov, *Systema,* I, 704.

311. Dedekenn, *Thesauri Consiliorum et Decisionum,* appendix nova, p. 272.

312. *Commentarius super Priorem D. Petri Epistolam,* p. 145.

313. Ibid., p. 140.

314. Balduin, *Commentarius in Omnes Epistolas Beati Apostoli Pauli,* p. 19.

315. Sebastian Schmidt, *Commentarii in Epistolas D. Pauli ad Romanos, Galatas & Colossenses* (Hamburg, 1704), p. 65.

316. *Systema Universae Theologiae,* I, 40.

317. Richard Heinrich Grützmacher, *Wort und Geist* (Leipzig: A. Deichert, 1902), pp. 220—61; Dedekenn, *Thesauri Consiliorum et Decisionum,* Vol. III, appendix nova, pp. 150—388, which produced the various faculty decisions against Rathmann; Christoph Hartknoch, *Preussische Kirchen-Historia* (Frankfort on the Main and Leipzig, 1684).

318. J. A. Osiander, *Systema Theologicum,* pp. 340 ff.; Hollaz, *Examen,* P. III, S. 2, C. 1, q. 4, pp. 992 ff.; Quenstedt, *Systema,* P. I, C. 4, S. 2, q. 16 (I, 246 ff.); Calov, *Systema,* I, 711 ff.

319. Calov, *Systema,* I, 718. See also Hollaz, *Examen,* P. III, S. 2, C. 1, q. 4, p. 994: "According to their very nature the sacraments consist in action. And so apart from their use they have no efficacy. But who would affirm that the Word of God is formally an action? Very obviously the act of preaching, the act of reading, and the act of meditating merely happen to the Word."

320. Grützmacher, *Wort und Geist,* p. 277.

321. *Hodosophia Christiana,* pp. 48—49.

322. See Chemnitz, *Harmonia Quatuor Evangelistarum,* I, 648: "The Word of

God has in itself *(in se)* the spiritual and life-giving power to regenerate man." See Martin Luther, *Sämmtliche Werke* (Erlangen: Carl Heyder, 1826 to 1857), 4, 307; 8, 288; 18, 215; 33:21; and especially 51, 377—88.

323. Quenstedt, *Systema*, P. I, C. 4, S. 2, q. 16, Ekthesis 1 (I, 246). See also Calov, *Biblia Novi Testamenti Illustrata*, II, 25. The caricature of the Lutheran position was apparently made long before Dannhauer arrived on the scene. Against the Schwenckfelders Brochmand says (*Universae Theologiae Systema*, I, 41): "We readily grant that Christians are not born again by ink and letters written on pages. This has nothing to do with our position. None of us ever ascribed the work of conversion to paper and ink, but to the sense and thought expressed by the words. It is through this divine meaning that the Spirit of God is efficacious. And as long as Sacred Scripture remains merely written on paper it is not suitable *(apta)* to enlighten man's mind and change his will for the better. No, if it is to be a suitable means of conversion, it must be inscribed on our heart by the power of the Spirit and must be made man's spirit and life, as it were, as James says (1:21)."

324. Calov, *Biblia Novi Testamenti Illustrata*, II, 25; Dedekenn, *Thesauri Consiliorum et Decisionum*, appendix nova, p. 271; Bechmann, *Institutiones Theologicae*, pp. 35—36.

325. When Elert complains (*Der Christliche Glaube*, p. 196) that the doctrine of inspiration by being brought to bear upon the efficacy of the Word tends to deny the efficacy of the Word, he reveals that he has failed to recognize what inspiration meant to later Luthern orthodoxy. Inspiration is not primarily a psychological theory about the relation between the writers of Scripture and the Holy Spirit but is a statement of the fact that Scripture is truly God's Word.

326. *Systema*, X, 3—4.

327. Dorner, *History of Protestant Theology*, II, 131. See also Karl Barth, *Church Dogmatics*, trans. G. T. Thomson, et. al., 4 vols. (Edinburgh: T. & T. Clark, 1936—69), I, 1, 124. Barth for some unexplained reason thinks that Hollaz and others substituted the concept *"vis hyperphysica"* for the concept "Word of God."

328. Hollaz, *Examen*, P. III, S. 2, C. 1, q. 4, pp. 992 ff.; Calov, *Systema*, I, 717; Quenstedt, *Systema*, P. I, C. 4, S. 2, q. 16, Fontes Solutionum 19 (I, 271).

329. See above, pp. 268—70 and 362—68.

330. Gerhard, *Loci Theologici*, VI, 106: "Propria evangelii doctrina, subjectum et materia (ut sic loquar) evangelii est Christus in officio redemptionis."

331. Dedekenn, *Thesauri Consiliorum et Decisionum*, appendix nova, p. 332.

332. *Systema*, IX, 2.

333. *Apodixis Articulorum Fidei*, p. 40.

334. Dedekenn, *Thesauri Consiliorum et Decisionum*, appendix nova, p. 332.

335. Quenstedt, *Systema*, P. I, C. 4, S. 2, q. 16, Ekthesis 8 (I, 249).

336. Hollaz, *Examen*, P. III, S. 2, C. 1, q. 4, p. 992; Dedekenn, *Thesauri Consiliorum et Decisionum*, appendix nova, p. 267.

337. *Systema Theologicum*, I, 341. See also Quenstedt, *Systema*, P. IV, C. 7, S. 1, Thesis 15, Nota (II, 704).

338. This is the conclusion of Grützmacher and of Dorner (*History of Protestant Theology*, II, 131), who charges that Calov with this doctrine of the power of the Word closed his eyes to the desire for direct fellowship with God, which characterized the Reformers. Barth follows this line of criticism when

he avers that the orthodox Lutheran theology by ascribing to the Word an innate power like that of a seed requiring no *nova elevatio* made of the Word something less than the Word of a personal God (see *Church Dogmatics*, I, 1, 124). Klaus Runia seems to be following Barth when he contends that the Lutheran doctrine of the power of the Word leaves no need for a special work of the Holy Spirit (*Karl Barth's Doctrine of Holy Scripture* [Grand Rapids: William B. Eerdmans Publishing Company, 1962], p. 142). Far more scholarly and fair are the observations of Otto Ritschl (*Dogmengeschichte des Protestantismus*, IV, 167—70), who maintains that the orthodox Lutheran position is faithful to the Scriptures and to the doctrine of Luther. It is without doubt an oversimplification for Ritschl to imply that the Lutheran doctrine on the efficacy of Scripture is drawn from the doctrine of inspiration, although the two teachings are closely related, as we have shown, and one of the reasons for the efficacy of Scripture is that it is God's Word. The Lutheran theologians did not hesitate at this very point to accuse Rathmann and the Schwenckfelders of denying that Scripture was God's Word (see Brochmand, *Universae Theologiae Systema*, I, 40). Ritschl further observes that most of the knowledgeable criticism of the old Lutheran position springs from a prejudice against the verbal inspiration of Scripture, a prejudice that colors historical perspective.

339. Calov, *Systema*, X, 30. See also X, 14, 19, 57, 79. See also Gerhard, *Loci Theologici*, VI, 230; Quenstedt, P. III, C. 7, S. 1, Thesis 10 (II, 702).
340. Quenstedt, *Systema*, P. IV, C. 7, S. 1, Thesis 16 (II, 705).
341. Calov, *Systema*, I, 713. Hollaz, *Examen*, P. III, S. 2, C. 1, q. 4, p. 993: "nam si a verbo Dei separetur Spiritus S. non esset id Dei verbum, vel verbum Spiritus, sed esset verbum humanum."
342. *Dogmengeschichte des Protestantismus*, IV, 172.
343. Jacob Heerbrand, *Compendium Theologiae*, p. 557; Brochmand, *Systema Universae Theologiae*, I, 40; Hutter, *Loci Communes Theologici*, p. 31; Gerhard, *Loci Theologici*, VI, 130. But Gerhard warns that we must not separate the efficacy of the Spirit from the Word of the Gospel as the enthusiasts do.
344. Ritschl, *Dogmengeschichte des Protestantismus*, IV, 171. For a summary of the Calvinistic position on this point see Heinrich Heppe, *Die Dogmatik der evangelisch-reformierten Kirche*, Neu durchgesehen und herausgegeben von Ernst Bizer (Neukirchen: Buchhandlung des Erziehungsvereins, 1935), pp. 411—15.
345. Quenstedt, *Systema*, P. I, C. 4, S. 2, q. 16, Ekthesis 10 (I, 249—50).
346. Dedekenn, *Thesauri Consiliorum et Decisionum*, appendix nova, pp. 194, 252.
347. John Gerhard, *Commentarius super Genesin*, editio novissima & emendatior (Jena, 1653), p. 82.

Summary Conclusion

"Soli Deo Gloria"
Certainty of Divine Origin
Correlation of Material and Formal Principles
  of Theology

Notes to Chapter Four: pages 411—413.

CHAPTER FOUR

So ends the long discussion of theological prolegomena in classical Lutheranism, prolegomena that are prolonged and tiresome at times, scholastic and perhaps picayunish, but still the testimony of unashamed allegiance to the spirit and principles of the Lutheran Reformation. Here is no equivocation, reservation, hesitation, but zealous commitment to the truth. The theologians we have studied believed in something, in the *solus Christus* and the *sola Scriptura,* and there they took their stand.[1] In such a theological posture there is power and life. And one is at a loss to find any foundation in the glib charge of "dead orthodoxy" often hurled against the theology of post-Reformation Lutheranism.[2]

There is no need of any prolonged conclusion to our summary and analysis of the theology of Lutheran orthodoxy as it pertained to theological prolegomena. I have tried to let the old Lutheran theologians speak for themselves as much as possible, and the reader will no doubt have formed his own conclusions concerning the value of what these theologians offered.

But a few points ought to be made in summing up the present study. After tracing the development of prolegomena from Melanchthon to Hollaz and Loescher, and after noting the emergence of new topics of discussion, new emphases, and new approaches to old questions, nevertheless one cannot fail to note the monolithic character of theological thought in this era. There is of course novelty and originality among the theologians in their treatment of issues. The concerns and approach of

a Hollaz to the issues of his day are sometimes radically different from those of a Chemnitz. But there is no doubt that the post-Reformation Lutheran theology, adhering consciously to the Scripture principle and orientated closely to the theology of Luther and the Lutheran Confessions, is of one piece. This has been generally recognized by historians and theologians, friends and foes alike.[3] As a consequence, either the theology and spirit of the orthodox Lutheran teachers from the Formula of Concord to the eclipse of orthodoxy is accepted by Lutherans with perhaps a few charitably spoken strictures, as in the case of Walther, Pieper, Philippi, Hoenecke, and others; or the entire spirit and theology of the age is summarily repudiated or discarded as prescientific, unevangelical, or what-have-you.

What is the rationale, what are the unifying features, the essential marks of this theology that distinguish it and give it its own individual character and vigor? We cannot answer this question fully until we have studied the theology of classical Lutheranism in its entirety. But on the basis of theological prolegomena alone a few words can be said by way of answer, for the basic motifs and dominant features of this theology are clearly discernible.

"SOLI DEO GLORIA"

The first characteristic that marks the discussions of theological prolegomena and all the theology during the period of Lutheran orthodoxy is a commitment, a devotion to the principle of *soli Deo gloria*. Belief in the divine monergism of grace, not only in man's conversion as that is discussed near the end of dogmatics but also as it applies to the theologian as he plies his task, becomes apparent at every step in the discussions of prolegomena. There was among the theologians of the orthodox period a deep awareness of man's — and this means also the theologian's — waywardness and sinfulness and congenital blindness, which pervaded also the realm of the intellect. This view of man's spiritual condition was not merely a dogma to which these theologians gave their assent, but it was also a principle that underlay and affected all their theological activity. Correlative to this view of man was a recognition among the theologians of that period that the theologian in particular was in constant need of God's grace and of the Spirit's enlightenment, that

the theologian to carry out his calling must depend in faith on Christ and His Word and must be a man of prayer. In other words, the personal experience of the Law and the Gospel in one's faith-life is the indispensable condition for all theologizing.

Applied specifically to the discussions of prolegomena, this principle meant that it is God, the subject, who has revealed Himself to man, the object. It is He who is the author and source *(principium essendi)* of all theology. Theology is not only language about God (λόγος περὶ τοῦ θεοῦ) but is God's language (λόγος τοῦ θεοῦ) about God. And the Scriptures, which are to be man's one cognitive source and norm of theology, are God's Word, breathed forth from Him. Therefore theology, when considered as a human aptitude, is θεόσδοτος, God's gift of inestimable grace. To know God as Creator, Redeemer, and Comforter, to have assurance of His past and present grace, a grace that is active in making its claim on a sinner, to have the assurance of eternal fellowship with Him and then to speak of all this, to talk about God and to Him — all this has its origin in God and His grace in Christ.

And so theology is not man's search for truth, man's quest, an imperfect tentative human enterprise, but a disposition and activity that is θεόσδοτος. That God alone makes one a theologian — just as He alone came forth from the hidden abode of His majesty and made Himself known to man, and just as He alone breathed forth a Word of revelation — this fact gives the theologian a very definite posture toward God and His Word. The theologian is never one who assesses the written Word of God or sits in judgment over it. He is rather one who owes his very being as a theologian to that divine Word.[4] And he carries out his work consciously, humbly, and prayerfully as a tool of the Holy Spirit.

This monergistic approach to theology was fundamental to Lutheranism, as it also was for orthodox Calvinism. It is just this approach that distinguishes the theology of classical Lutheranism from that of the more dispassionate, scientific, and, one might say, synergistic posture of Ernesti and Semler and the historicocritical approach to theology introduced by them. And the cleavage is very great at this point. Whereas Ernesti and Semler never tired of accusing the older orthodoxy of obfuscation, naïveté, and obscurantism,[5] the orthodox Lutherans continually brought charges of Pyrrhonism, impiety, and coarse synergism against the Socinians of their day, who were the precursors of Semler, and the historicocritical approach

to theology. This cleavage will still obtain today between a confessional Lutheran orthodoxy wherever it may be found and much of modern theology, and any rapprochement seems to me at least quite impossible.

Just here we may have a partial explanation for the unpopularity of the theology of the later Lutheran orthodoxy among more recent historians and theologians. The reason is to be found in orthodoxy's militant objections to Socinianism with its free approach to Scripture and to theology, an approach rather congenial to many theologians since the Enlightenment.

CERTAINTY OF DIVINE ORIGIN

The second characteristic that marks the theology of Lutheran orthodoxy is certainty, certainty of the divine origin of the Gospel and of all theology, certainty that true theology is attainable and certainty concerning one's own theological position and confession. This certitude is of course something highly subjective, but it is not therefore mere fancy or wishful thinking; it is rather a certitude and assurance wrought by the Spirit of God, a veritable *fides divina.* Just as I should not and need not doubt concerning my salvation, I should harbor no question or doubt concerning the doctrine of the Gospel, which I believe, teach, and confess. This doctrinal certainty was closely associated with the Lutheran doctrine of the divine origin and authority of Scripture, just as the doctrinal certainty that marked the Roman Catholic theology of the day was clearly dependent on Roman Catholic ecclesiology. There could be certainty of doctrine, the Lutheran teachers maintained, because the Christian doctrine was drawn from the Scriptures, which possessed an objective and absolutely irrefragable authority. This fact does not imply that the Lutheran idea of doctrinal certitude was dissociated from the Gospel and the work of the Spirit. Our long discussions concerning the internal criteria of Scripture and the power of the Word (the Gospel) make this point very clear. *Fides divina* was the very antithesis to a mere intellectual assent *(fides humana)* to the authority of Scripture or to the truth of any doctrinal position. It was the work of the Spirit through the power of the Gospel, a work wrought in the heart of the believer. (How often do the dogmaticians reject a theology of the unregenerate man!) And so personal faith in Jesus Christ and doctrinal certitude are in no way contrary to each other

Certainty of Divine Origin

but complement each other. Faith and orthodoxy are by no means the same — one is not justified by his orthodoxy — but they belong together. For the purpose of sound doctrine is to proclaim more effectively the Gospel, which sustains and nourishes faith in Christ.

Let me give an example of the importance placed on doctrinal certainty by the Lutheran teachers, an example that appears at first to be totally remote to the subject. I imagine that of all that has been discussed in this book, what might appear most sterile and unedifying to many of us in our day would be the intense discussions of archetypal theology as possessed by the incarnate Christ. What is the point of the Lutheran position? And what possible benefit can issue from it? Seen from the perspective of the Lutheran doctrine of certainty, the point of the discussion becomes really quite clear. The man Jesus Christ is God's revelation *par excellence,* and the Gospel revealed by Him and preached in the church is God's Gospel, His divine message to man. Furthermore, the theology represented in Scripture, guaranteed by Christ, and taught in the church is God's theology. And so the church possesses and proclaims the truth of very God.

It is because we today are no longer sensitive to the magnitude of the gift of *fides divina* that we fail to appreciate many of the debates so vital to historic Lutheranism. We can certainly criticize the old manner of presentation, which was couched in the prolixities of medieval scholasticism, but those of us who profess to be confessional today can hardly fault these theologians for what they were striving to maintain and thought they had every right to maintain: certainty of the truth, certainty of the divine origin of the Gospel and of all Christian theology, the gift of *fides divina*.

When one is convinced that purity of doctrine and doctrinal certainty are attainable, one will take doctrine seriously and will often be quite intolerant toward those who do not share one's convictions. This was very definitely the case with the orthodox Lutherans of the 16th and 17th centuries. And it is significant that the target for their polemics was as often the syncretism of George Calixt and his party as the outright heterodoxy of the Socinians. Why was this? It was because the Lutherans saw in the latitudinarianism of unionism a threat as dangerous as straight-out heresy.[6] For latitudinarianism and syncretism undermined doctrinal certainty, and here was a challenge to the Gospel itself.

Correlation of Material and Formal Principles of Theology

The third characteristic that marks the theology of Lutheran orthodoxy is the definite correlation of the material and formal principles of theology (the *sola fide* and the *sola Scriptura*). We have already brought attention to this fact when we discussed the Christological unity of Scripture.[7] It is the Christ of Scripture who is the object of saving faith, and it is the Scriptures guaranteed by Christ that must be the source of all theology. The formal and material principles of theology are never turned against each other in Lutheran theology, but they are made always to complement and support each other. A rather unimaginative statement by a rather unimpressive late representative of our period may serve to illustrate this point. J. P. Hebenstreit says:

> Thus the article concerning God's gracious will by which He from His own free disposition wishes to save all men is the fundamental and first of all articles; that is to say, the explicit knowledge of this article must be considered necessary for the begetting and sustaining of faith. Now saving faith rests on divine revelation; and nothing can or ought to be believed with a firm and fixed confidence unless it is seen to have been revealed by God, if not explicitly and in so many words, then at least implicitly so that it can be drawn from clear inferences.[8]

This statement is interesting and instructive because right in the middle of it Hebenstreit seems to change the subject. He first speaks of God's universal will of grace as *the* Gospel, *the* fundamental article of faith; but then immediately he proceeds to speak of God's revelation (in Scripture) as the foundation on which faith rests. He senses no contradiction here, no difficulty, and that simply because the *solus Christus* and *sola fide* imply the *sola Scriptura,* and vice versa.

It is curious that at just this point, the wedding of the organic and material principles of theology, the historic Lutheran theology has come in for some rather severe criticism. It has been said, for instance, that the *sola fide* was completely submerged by the strong emphasis on the *sola Scriptura* in Lutheran theology. This charge is completely without foundation.[9] Again and again Christ crucified is presented as the central theme of the Christian faith,[10] and the article of justification the *articulus stantis et cadentis ecclesiae.*

In recent times Paul Althaus has indulged in similar criticism, censur-

ing orthodoxy for deriving the authority of the New Testament from its divine origin (inspiration) and not from the Gospel.[11] This charge is correct in a sense. Lutheran orthodoxy teaches that the authority of Scripture is due to its divine origin; but what Althaus does not mention is that one's certainty of the authority of Scripture according to the old Lutheran theology is not due to one's accepting a doctrine of inspiration but to the inner testimony of the Spirit working through the internal criteria of Scripture (the Gospel). Althaus charges orthodoxy with a departure from Luther's emphasis on the Christian message of Scripture as the criterion that authenticates Scripture to us and with postulating Scripture as a supernatural textbook.[12] Scripture is no longer a living Word of God in Law and Gospel, he says, but has become for Lutheran orthodoxy a sacred codex. The doctrine of inspiration in Lutheran theology, he avers, had a development analogous to that of the Jesuistic papal system. This charge is unfair and contrary to the facts. Althaus seems to have ignored or perhaps confused the old well-known distinction in Lutheran theology between the normative authority of Scripture and the causative authority *(efficacia)* of Scripture, an authority that was a power residing in its Christological content. Lutheran theology, while insisting on the absolute normative authority of Scripture, never intimated that we are to accept this because of a doctrine of inspiration. Rather it was taught that we accept this authority as Christians, who have been touched by the power of the written Word of God, a power that resides in its message. Lutheran orthodoxy did not lose sight of the *solus Christus* and the *sola fide* by its faithful adherence to the verbal inspiration of Scripture. Nor did the *sola Scriptura* principle in any sense eclipse the Scriptures as the living and powerful Word of God. The great concern of the old orthodox Lutheran dogmatics was to employ all theology soteriologically and doxologically in the service of the living Christ. One of its great contributions was to present a doctrine of Scripture that accomplished just such an aim. Such a high view of Scripture did not shackle the theologian but freed him to become truly evangelical and to placard the Christ of Scripture before the eyes of poor sinners.

NOTES TO CHAPTER FOUR

1. A detailed study of the various *loci* (as planned in a sequel volume) demonstrates how the evangelical principle of *solus Christus* (the central emphasis

of Christ's person and work) dominates the theology of orthodox Lutheranism, at least in most cases. One might also consult a couple of articles relevant to the subject: see Robert Preus, "The Doctrine of Justification in the Theology of Classical Lutheran Orthodoxy," in *The Springfielder*, XXIX (Spring 1965), 24—39; Robert Preus, "The Justification of a Sinner Before God," in *Scottish Journal of Theology*, XIII (September 1960), 262—77. See also the massive evidence for this in John W. Baier, *Compendium Theologiae Positivae*, ed. C. F. W. Walther (St. Louis: Concordia Publishing House, 1879), III, 134 ff.

2. One can only echo the complaint of Hermann Sasse: "When will men stop this idle talk about 'dead orthodoxy,' a charge that is completely without historical foundation, resting only on a dogma of Pietism — for Pietism has also had its dogmas, and some very obvious ones at that." See his "Letters Addressed to Lutheran Pastors II, Concerning the Nature of Confession in the Churches," in *Quartalschrift*, XLVI (July 1949), 170.

3. There is an exception to this generalization. Many scholars have maintained that the inspiration and inerrancy of Scripture were not consciously held in 1580 but developed at some later time during the period of orthodoxy. In another book (*The Inspiration of Scripture* [Edinburgh: Oliver and Boyd, 1957], pp. 73—75) I have traced the various opinions on this matter and the almost complete lack of agreement among the scholars. I would however maintain that in this matter too the Lutheran theology before and after the Formula of Concord offers really only one doctrine.

The articles of verbal inspiration and inerrancy are not new in the 17th century. If John Gerhard in 1620 was defending the divine authority and origin of Scripture in his *Loci Theologici*, then so was Giles Hunnius (*Tractatus de Sacrosancta Maiestate, Autoritate, Fide, ac Certitudine Sacrae Scripturae Propheticae & Apostolicae Veteris & Novi Testamenti* [Frankfort, 1594]) and Jacob Andreae (*Disputationes Theologicae, de Praecipuis Doctrinae Christianae Capitibus* [Montbeliard, 1593], p. 15 *et passim*) and Jacob Heerbrand (*Compendium Theologiae* [Tübingen, 1575], 1582 ed., pp. 19 to 20) in the 16th century. And so was George Major much earlier in a special monograph on the subject (*De Origine et Autoritate Verbi Dei* [Wittenberg, 1556]). These theologians consistently call God the author of Scripture. Furthermore, if Calov and Quenstedt advance a clear doctrine of verbal inspiration, then so also does Flacius a century before, as G. Moldaenke (*Schriftverständnis und Schriftdeutung im Zeitalter der Reformation. I. Matthias Flacius Illyricus* [Stuttgart: W. Kohlhammer, 1936], p. 270 *et passim*) and Otto Ritschl (*Dogmengeschichte des Protestantismus*, 4 vols. [Leipzig: J. C. Hinrichs'sche Buchhandlung, and Göttingen: Vandenhoeck & Ruprecht, 1908 to 27], I, 142 ff.) have demonstrated with abundant evidence. Again, if the later Lutherans of the 17th century, Dannhauer and Calov, maintain the absolute truthfulness and trustworthiness of Scripture, then Major is surely doing the same when he says: "The calling of the prophets and apostles was done immediately by God as we have demonstrated above from Peter [2 Peter 1:21]. It was done in such a way that their doctrine was not introduced by any human initiative; but these men of God spoke being moved by the Holy Spirit. Therefore we are certain that they were not able to err." (*De Origine et Autoritate Verbi Dei*, p. 12)

At an even earlier date an entire book was devoted to the subject of the truthfulness and reliability of Scripture. I refer to the celebrated monograph of Andrew Althamer, *Diallage: hoc est Conciliatio Locorum Scripturae, Qui Prima Facie inter se Pugnare Videntur* (Nuremberg, 1527). Althamer's work

is very elementary, concerned mostly with the dogmatic statements in Scripture that appear to conflict with other such statements. For instance, the threats of God seem to undermine His promises. Or it seems that God does not always consistently carry out His Word in specific cases (e. g., He threatens to punish liars, but Abraham lies and is not punished). Althamer even considers the apparent conflict between James 1:13, which says that God tempts no one, and Gen. 22:1, which says that He tempted Abraham (p. D4r). Even the differences between Is. 56:7 ("Mine house shall be called an house of prayer for all people") and Matt. 6:6 ("Enter into thy closet . . ."), which appear to us to offer no real problem, are given attention (p. G3r). It is true that not all the problems encountered and discussed by Calov and Quenstedt are considered by Althamer; but there is no doubt nevertheless that his doctrine of Biblical inerrancy is the same as theirs.

That the bibliology of later Lutheran orthodoxy resembles at every point that of the Lutheran Confessions is made clear in a study by Ralph A. Bohlmann, *Principles of Biblical Interpretation in the Lutheran Confessions* (Saint Louis: Concordia Publishing House, 1968). See also Robert Preus, "Biblical Hermeneutics and the Lutheran Church Today," *Crisis in Lutheran Theology,* ed. John Warwick Montgomery (Grand Rapids: Baker Publishing House, 1967), pp. 82—86.

4. Abraham Calov, *Isagoges Theologicae. Liber II. Paedia Theologica, de Methodo Studii Theologici* (Wittenberg, 1652), p. 124.

5. For a thorough review of Semler's reaction to the orthodox bibliology, see Gottfried Hornig, *Die Anfänge der historisch-kritischen Theologie, Johann Salomo Semlers Schriftverständnis und seine Stellung zu Luther* (Göttingen: Vandenhoeck & Ruprecht, 1961), pp. 56 ff. It is interesting that Semler felt that he was not within the stream of catholic tradition and of Luther's thought as he adopted a method of exegesis that repudiated the principle that Scripture was the Word of God. See Amand Saintes, *Histoire Critique du Rationalisme en Allemagne.* deuxième édition (Paris: Librairie de Brockhaus et Avenarius, 1843), p. 135. See also pp. 132—59. See also Louis Perriraz, *Histoire de la Théologie Protestante aux XVIIIme XIXme Siècles surtout en Allemagne* (Neuchatel: Éditions Henri Messeiller, 1951), II, 56—64.

6. So intense was the feeling of the confessional Lutherans like Dannhauer and Calov and Dorsch that they did not hesitate to hurl such epithets as "veiled atheism" against the syncretists of their day. For the doctrinal indifference of syncretism led to atheism, they thought. For an excellent account of the approach of the Syncretists and of the confessional Lutheran reaction, see Heinrich Schmid, *Geschichte der synkretistischen Streitigkeiten in der Zeit Georg Calixts* (Erlangen: Verlag von Carl Heyder, 1846).

7. See above, pp. 331—33.

8. *Systema Theologicum* (Frankfort and Leipzig, 1718), p. 132.

9. I have discussed this point in my book *The Inspiration of Scripture* (pp. 208—211) and have demonstrated with ample evidence that the charge of Dorner and others is groundless.

10. See Friedrich Balduin, *Commentarius in Omnes Epistolas Beati Apostoli Pauli,* editio altera priore longe emaculatior (Frankfort on the Main, 1710), p. 300. See also Jesper Rasmus Brochmand, *Universae Theologiae Systema* (Ulm, 1658), I, 27.

11. Paul Althaus, *Die Christliche Wahrheit* (Gütersloh: C. Bertelsmann, 1949), p. 200.

12. Ibid., p. 217.

Preface to Melanchthon's *Loci Praecipui Theologici of 1559**

* CR 21, 603—607.

APPENDIX

God has formed men in such a way that they think in terms of numbers and arrangement, and in learning one thing or another they are frequently helped by numbers and orderly arrangement. Thus in transmitting the arts especial care is given the order of the divisions of the various arts; and the principles, the direction the arts take, and the limitations of the study are indicated. In philosophy this manner of making things clear is called method. But the method employed for demonstration in the arts is different from the method used in the teaching of the church. The demonstrative method proceeds from those things that are subject to the senses and from prime notions, called principles. In the teaching of the church only a proper order of arrangement is called for, not a method of demonstration. For the doctrine of the church is not obtained from demonstrations but from words that God has committed to our human race by means of sure and clear evidences, words through which out of His immense goodness He has disclosed Himself and His will.

Now in philosophy things that are certain are sought and are distinguished from uncertain things. The causes of certainty are to be found in general experience, in principles, and in demonstrations. In the teaching of the church however the cause of certitude is God's revelation, and we must therefore consider very seriously those thoughts that God has committed to us. Any sensible person is certain that twice four is eight, for this is a natural knowledge of principles. In like manner we are certain

and sure of the articles of faith, of the divine threats and promises, certain that if we repent our sins are remitted for the sake of the Son of God and we are numbered as and become heirs of eternal life. But the causes of such certainty are entirely different. The mind comes to a conviction about numbers by its own judgment. We become certain of the articles of faith by divine revelation, which God establishes with sure and clear testimonies, such as the resurrection of the dead and many other miracles. Now because these matters are outside the normal judgment of the human mind, the assent to them that takes place is less active because the mind is moved by those testimonies and miracles of God and aided by the Holy Spirit to assent.

Philosophy teaches that we should doubt those things that are not given to the senses, are not principles, and are not supported by demonstration. Thus we may doubt or suspend judgment whether the concavity of a cloud is the only reason for the rainbow being an arch. But the church doctrine that God has vouchsafed — this doctrine we know to be certain and immovable, even if we cannot discover it with our senses, even if it is not an innate principle with us, even if we cannot ascertain it by proofs. No, the cause of our certainty is God's revelation, which is simply true.

Let us therefore never allow this philosophical doubt, or ἐποχή, to touch the doctrine that has been delivered to us by God. An immense confusion of doubts concerning God always clings to our minds, sunk as they are in the corruption of human nature, doubts we must fight and oppose with the teachings God has entrusted to us. In this concern we must not feed our doubt or praise it, but our faith should become a certain assent, a conviction, a certainty, with which our mind, convinced of the divine testimonies, holds to the divine Word when it speaks of things that are not seen, as the Epistle to the Hebrews says.

It behooves me to begin with these remarks in order that we might know from the beginning that the things we teach in the church are sure and firm and immovable; as the Son of God said, "Heaven and earth shall pass away, but My words shall not pass away." Next we ought to be assured of this, that our faith is a firm assent that embraces the full doctrine of the Gospel; it is not (as in the school of Arcesilaus) a lot of vague exhibitions of opinions and arguments, as many clever smart alecks and proud men have thought, are thinking, and will think in the

future. God punishes their blasphemies with both present and eternal distress.

Now concerning the arrangement of the sections of doctrine, something ought to be said by way of introduction. The prophetic and apostolic books have been written according to a very fine order, and they offer us the articles of faith in a most splendid arrangement. Thus there is a historical sequence in the prophetic and apostolic books beginning with the first creation of things and with the founding of the church. Next there is in the prophetic books a succession of all the periods of time from the beginning of things to King Cyrus. In this sequence many things are told that repeat themselves in the church, and the teaching of Law and Gospel is scattered throughout these narratives. Next the apostles are witnesses of the self-disclosure of Christ, of His birth, His death and resurrection. These things are historical in nature. The articles of faith, the explanation of Law and Gospel, are contained in the sermons of Christ. The discourses of Paul also touch these matters; like an artist Paul speaks in his Letter to the Romans of the distinction between Law and Gospel, of sin, of grace or reconciliation; and by the knowledge of such things we are restored to eternal life.

It is true that one who is aware of this arrangement will not have much trouble with our commentaries and books and comparisons; nevertheless God wants the voice of teachers to sound forth clearly in His church (as we hear concerning ministers of the Gospel in Ephesians 4), and therefore it is not in vain that we enter upon the task of teaching in the church. We do not give birth to new opinions and subjects, like Hesiod who handed down a tradition different from the one that spoke of the fathers, Shem, and Japheth; and like the heretics who devise new ideas that have not been delivered by the apostles. No, pious interpreters simply recite in good faith those thoughts they have received from God in the prophetic and apostolic narrative. And because simple people do not everywhere understand the nature of theological discourse and do not immediately see the arrangement of the materials, the voice of interpreters must teach them about the nature of the language and the arrangement of the things discussed. Also because many corrupt opinions have been and are constantly being devised, pious pastors and teachers are witnesses of the pure teachings that have been accepted on certain authority, and they are the refuters of false interpretations. For these

reasons God preserves by His own hand and continuously reestablishes the ministry and study of the Gospel in churches and in schools, that we may be guardians of the prophetic and apostolic books and witnesses of their true interpretation and that we may refute all opinions that militate against the doctrine handed down by the prophets, Christ, and the apostles, lest the light of the Gospel be put out (as Ephesians 4 says), and lest the churches, being driven and scattered as by a wind, lose the truth and be involved in all sorts of errors, as happens so often.

The heathens who lost the light of the doctrine of the fathers were driven by many dreadful passions: they gloried in human sacrifices, worshiped fertility gods, violated wives and young women — and all that they might satisfy their idols. Think of the many kinds of madnesses that were present in the sects of Marcion and Manichaeus! What great blasphemy, wantonness, and strife! But today we have the ravings of the Anabaptists, who possess much of the taint of Manichaeanism. The ragings of the Mohammedans had their beginnings in Arius. And think of the madness involved in the invocation of the dead, in the worship of images, in the selling of masses, in defending the law of celibacy, and in many other things that are defended by Eck and Pighius and like-minded papistic parasites.

Let pious people take note of these examples of rash opinions of every age, let them heed the voice of those who teach correctly, let them embrace with both hands and with their whole heart the prophetic and apostolic books that have been committed to us by God, and let them attach themselves to the interpretations and testimonies of the pure church (such as the Apostles' Creed and Nicene Creed), that they might retain the light of the Gospel and not become involved in those raving opinions that, as I have said, follow when the light of the Gospel is extinguished. Those who read the prophetic and apostolic writings and the Symbols with pious devotion and who seek the opinion of the pure church will easily conclude afterwards that they are aided by these human interpretations, and they will know what usefulness is afforded by correct and skillful expositions of Scripture written by pious believers and by the preachments drawn from the fountains of Scripture. If we consecrate our wills in this undertaking, God by His holy Spirit will rule our wills in this study and in the practice of making decisions so that they will not be deceived by the

trickeries of the devil but will be bent toward recognizing, embracing, and retaining true teachings. Thus Paul says: "It is God which worketh in you both to will and to do of His good pleasure." When God sets aflame our will so that by sincere study it seeks the truth, He also helps it and rules over it, to the end that its labor is a blessing to us and to others.

BIBLIOGRAPHIES

PRIMARY SOURCES

Alexander of Hales. *Summa Theologica.* Florence, 1924.
Alsted, John Henry. *Lexicon Theologicum.* Hanover, 1620.
———. *Synopsis Theologiae.* Hanover, 1627.
———. *Theologia Scholastica Didactica Exhibens Locos Communes Theologicos.* Hanover, 1618.
Althamer, Andrew. *Diallage: hoc est Conciliatio Locorum Scripturae, Qui Prima Facie inter se Pugnare Videntur.* Nuremberg, 1527.
Ames, William. *Medulla Theologiae.* Amsterdam, 1623.
Andreae, Jacob. *Disputationes Theologicae, de Praecipuis Doctrinae Christianae Capitibus.* Montbeliard, 1593.
Aquinas, Thomas. *Summa Contra Gentiles.* Paris, 1878.
Aslakssen, Cort. *De Mundo.* Copenhagen, 1605—1607.
———. *De Natura Caeli Triplicis.* Sigena of Nassau, 1597.
Baier, John William. *Compendium Theologiae Positivae.* Jena, 1704.
Balduin, Friedrich. *Commentarius in Omnes Epistolas Beati Apostoli Pauli.* Frankfort on the Main, 1710.
Baronius, Caesar. *Annales Ecclesiastici.* Rome, 1588.
Bechmann, Friedemann. *Ad Institutiones Catecheticas Cunradi Dieterici . . . Annotationes Uberiores.* Frankfort and Leipzig, 1707.
———. *Annotationes Uberiores in Compendium Theologicum Leonhardi Hutteri.* Frankfort and Leipzig, 1703.
———. *Theologia Polemica.* Jena, 1719.
Bellarmine, Robert. *De Verbo Dei Scripto et non Scripto.* Sedan, 1618.

———. *Disputationes de Controversiis Christianae Fidei*. Milan, 1721.
Berg, John. *Analysis Controversiae de Persona Christi*. Frankfort, 1619.
———. *Decas Disputationum Theologicorum*. Frankfort, 1621.
Brochmand, Jesper Rasmus. *Commentarius in Epistolam ad Hebraeos*. Copenhagen, 1706.
———. *In Canonicam et Catholicam Jacobi Epistolam Commentarius*. Copenhagen, 1706.
———. *Universae Theologiae Systema*. Ulm, 1658.
Bucan, William. *Institutiones Theologicae*. Geneva, 1609.
Buddeus, Francis. *Institutiones Theologiae Dogmaticae*. Leipzig, 1724.
Calixt, George. *Apparatus Theologicus*. Helmstedt, 1628.
———. *Apparatus Theologici et Fragmenti Historiae Ecclesiae Occidentalis*. Helmstedt, 1661.
———. *Catholicae Ecclesiae et Oecumenicorum Conciliorum Symbola et Confessiones*. Helmstedt, 1651.
———. *De Autoritate Sacrae Scripturae*. Helmstedt, 1648.
———. *Desiderium et Studium Concordiae Ecclesiasticae*. Helmstedt, 1651.
———. *Epitome Theologiae*. Braunschweig, 1634.
———. *Epitome Theologiae Moralis*. Helmstedt, 1634.
———. *Responsum Maledicis Theologorum Moguntinorum Vindiciis Oppositum*. Helmstedt, 1644.
Calov, Abraham. *Apodixis Articulorum Fidei*. Lüneberg, 1684.
———. *Biblia Novi Testamenti Illustrata*. Dresden and Leipzig, 1719.
———. *Biblia Testamenti Veteris Illustrata*. Dresden and Leipzig, 1719.
———. *Commentarius in Genesin*. Wittenberg, 1671.
———. *Consensus Repetitus Fidei Vere Lutheranae*. Wittenberg, 1666.
———. *Criticus Sacer vel Commentarii Apodictico-Elenchtici super Augustanam Confessionem*. Leipzig, 1646.
———. *Dissertationes Theologiae Rostochienses*. Rostock, 1637.
———. *Isagoges Theologicae. Liber II. Paedia Theologica, de Methodo Studii Theologici*. Wittenberg, 1652.
———. *Scripta Philosophica*. Lübeck, 1651.
———. *Socinismus Profligatus, hoc est, Errorum Socinianorum Luculenta Confutatio*. 2d ed. Wittenberg, 1668.
———. *Syncretismus Calixtinus*. Wittenberg, 1653.
———. *Systema Locorum Theologicorum*. Wittenberg, 1655.
———. *Theologia Positiva*. Wittenberg, 1652.
Capreolus, John. *In Libros Sententiarum Amplissimae Quaestiones*. Venice, 1589.

Carpzov, John Benedict. *Isagoge in Libros Ecclesiarum Lutheranarum Symbolicos.* Leipzig, 1665.

Chemnitz, Martin. *De Duabus Naturis.* Frankfort and Wittenberg, 1653. (Available in English translation, *The Two Natures in Christ,* trans. J. A. O. Preus [St. Louis: Concordia Publishing House, 1970])

———. *Examen Concilii Tridentini.* Berlin, 1861.

———. *Fundamenta Sanae Doctrinae de Vera et Substantiali Praesentia, Exhibitione, et Sumptione Corporis & Sanguinis Domini in Coena.* Frankfort and Wittenberg, 1653.

———. *Loci Theologici.* Frankfort and Wittenberg, 1653.

Chemnitz, Martin, Polycarp Leyser, and John Gerhard. *Harmonia Quatuor Evangelistarum.* Hamburg, 1704.

Chytraeus, David. *Catechesis.* Wittenberg, 1555.

———. *De Studio Theologiae.* Wittenberg, 1562.

———. *Historia der Augsburgischen Confession.* Rostock, 1577.

———. *In Genesin Enarratio.* Wittenberg, 1568.

———. *Opera.* Leipzig, 1594.

Cundisius, Gottfried. *D. Leonhardi Hutteri Compendium Theologicum Notis Illustratum.* Jena, 1752.

Dannhauer, John Conrad. *Hermeneutica Sacra.* Strasbourg, 1669.

———. *Hodosophia Christiana sive Theologia Positiva.* Strasbourg, 1649.

———. *Mysterium Syncretismi Detecti, Proscripti, et Symphonismo Compensati.* Strasbourg, 1648.

Dedekenn, George. *Thesauri Consiliorum et Decisionum.* Jena, 1671.

Dorsch, John G. *Aphorismi Theologici.* Greifswald, n. d.

———. *Dissertationum Theologicarum* .... Strasbourg, 1638.

———. *Synopsis Theologiae Zacharianae.* Frankfort, 1683.

Erasmus, Desiderius. *In Novum Testamentum Annotationes.* Basel, 1542.

Fecht, John. *Compendium Universam Theologiam Theticam et Polemicam Complexum.* Zerbst, 1740.

———. *Dissertatio Theologica de Sensu Sacrarum Literarum Carnali.* Rostock, 1709.

———. *Philocalia Sacra.* Rostock, 1708.

Flacius, Matthias. *Clavis Scripturae Sacrae.* Copenhagen, 1695.

Foertsch, M. *Selectorum Theologicorum Breviarium, id est, Discussio Principalium Punctorum Theologicorum.* Jena, 1708.

Franz, Wolfgang. *Schola Sacrificiorum Patriarchalium Sacra.* Wittenberg, 1698.

———. *Tractatus Theologicus Perspicuus de Interpretatione Sacrarum Scripturarum Maxime Legitima.* Wittenberg, 1693.

Gerhard, John. *Annotationes Posthumae in Evangelium D. Matthaei.* Jena, 1663.

———. *Aphorismi Succincti & Selecti.* Jena, 1611.

———. *Catechesis Ecclesiarum Racoviae.* Cracow, 1609.

———. *Commentarius super Genesin.* Editio novissima & emendatior. Jena, 1653.

———. *Commentarius super Posteriorem D. Petri Epistolam.* Jena, 1660.

———. *Commentarius super Priorem D. Petri Epistolam.* Editio altera priori correctior. Jena, 1680.

———. *Confessio Catholica.* Erfurt, 1679.

———. *Loci Theologici.* Ed. Johann F. Cotta. Tübingen: John Georg Cotta, 1763.

———. *Methodus Studii Theologici.* Jena, 1654.

———. *Tractatus de Legitima Scripturae Sacrae Interpretatione.* Jena, 1663.

Gerson, John. *De Consolatione Theologiae.* Cologne, 1469.

Gesner, Salomon. *Vera et Perspicua Explicatio Utilissimae Summaeque his Temporibus Necessariae Sententiae D. Pauli 2. Tim. 3.* Wittenberg, 1602.

Glassius, Salomon. *Philologia Sacra.* Leipzig, 1713.

Gregory of Valencia. *Commentariorum Theologicorum Tomi Quatuor.* Ingolstadt, 1591.

Gretzer, Jacob. *Controversiarum Roberti Bellarmini S.R.E. Cardinalis Amplissimi Defensio.* Ingolstadt, 1607.

———. *Opera Omnia,* Regensburg, 1736.

Hafenreffer, Matthias. *Loci Theologici.* Wittenberg, 1622.

Hebenstreit, John Paul. *Systema Theologicum.* Frankfort and Leipzig, 1718.

Heerbrand, Jacob. *Compendium Theologiae.* Wittenberg, 1573.

Heidegger, John Henry. *Corpus Theologiae Christianae.* Zürich, 1700.

Hemmingsen, Niels. *Opuscula Theologica, Quae Conquiri Potuerunt Omnia in Unum Volumen Collecta.* Geneva, 1586.

Hoepfner, Henry. *Loci Theologici.* Frankfort and Leipzig, 1673.

Hoffmann, Daniel. *Disputatio pro Duplici Veritate Lutheri a Philosophis Impugnata et ad Pudendorum Locum Ablegata.* Magdeburg, 1600.

Hoffmann, Gottfried. *Institutiones Theologicae Exegeticae.* Wittenberg, 1754.

———. *Synopsis Theologiae Purioris Dogmaticae.* Tübingen, 1730.

Hollaz, David. *Examen Theologicum Acroamaticum.* Rostock and Leipzig, 1718.

Huelsemann, John. *Calvinismus Irreconciliabilis.* Wittenberg, 1667.

———. *Extensio Breviarii Theologici*. Leipzig, 1655.
———. *Manuale Confessionis Augustanae*. Wittenberg, 1624.
Hunnius, Giles. *Opera Latina*. Frankfort on the Main, 1608.
———. *Thesaurus Evangelico Apostolicus*. Zerbst, 1706.
———. *Theses de Augustana Confessione, Ecclesiarum Evangelicarum Symbolo Augustissimo*. Rostock, 1622.
Hunnius, Nicholas. *Diaskepsis Theologica*. Wittenberg, 1626.
———. *Epitome Credendorum*. Frankfort and Leipzig, 1702.
———. *Examen Errorum Photinianorum*. Wittenberg, 1618.
Hutter, Leonard. *Augustanae Confessionis Analysis Methodica*. Wittenberg, 1602.
———. *Concordia Concors, de Origine et Progressu Formulae Concordiae Ecclesiarum Confessionis Augustanae*. Wittenberg, 1614.
———. *Irenicum vere Christianum*. Wittenberg, 1641.
———. *Libri Christianae Concordiae: Symboli Ecclesiarum, Novissimo hoc Tempore, Longe Augustissimi; Explicatio Plana & Perspicua*. Wittenberg, 1609.
———. *Loci Communes Theologici*. Wittenberg, 1619.
———. *Quaestiones Duae de Fundamento Fidei Catholicae Apostolicae*. Wittenberg, 1616.
Hyperius, Andrew. *De Theologo, seu de Ratione Studii Theologici Libri IIII*. Basel, 1556.
Junius, Francis. *De Theologiae Verae; Ortu, Natura, Formis, Partibus, et Modo Illius*. Leyden, 1594.
———. *Opera Theologica*. Geneva, 1607.
Keckermann, Bartholomew. *Systema Sacrae Theologiae*. Hanover, 1602.
———. *Systema Theologicum*. Geneva, 1602.
Koenig, John Friedrich. *Nucleus Theologiae Positivae*. Leipzig, 1706.
Kromayer, Jerome. *Commentarius Didactico-Elenchticus in Augustanam Confessionem*. Frankfort and Leipzig, 1723.
———. *Theologia Positivo-Polemica*. Frankfort and Leipzig, 1711.
Lombard, Peter. *Sententiarum Libri IIII*. Venice, 1620.
Major, George. *De Origine et Autoritate Verbi Dei*. Wittenberg, 1556.
Martini, Cornelius. *Compendium Theologiae et Epitome Theologiae Naturalis*. Wolfenbüttel, 1650.
Meisner, Balthasar. *Christologia Sacra*. Wittenberg, 1672.
———. *Philosophia Sobria*. Rinteln, 1626.
Musaeus, John. *De Conversione Hominis Peccatoris ad Deum*. Jena, 1661.
———. *Introductio in Theologiam*. Jena, 1679.

Neumann, John George. *Theologia Aphoristica.* Wittenberg, 1718.
Olearius, John. *De Stylo Novi Testamenti.* Schwabach, 1690.
———. *Elementa Hermeneuticae Sacrae.* Leipzig, 1699.
Osiander, John Adam. *Collegium Theologicum Systematicum.* Stuttgart and Frankfort, 1686.
———. *Systema Theologicum seu Theologia Positiva Acroamatica.* Tübingen, 1679.
Pareus, David. *Collegiorum Theologicorum Decuria.* Heidelberg, 1621.
Pfeiffer, August. *Critica Sacra de Sacri Codicis Partitione, Editionibus Variis, Linguis Originalibus et Illibata Puritate Fontium, Interpretatione Scripturae Legitima.* Dresden and Leipzig, 1721.
———. *Dubia Vexata Scripturae Sacrae.* Dresden, 1679.
———. *Thesaurus Hermeneuticus sive de Legitima Sacrae Scripturae Interpretatione Tractatio Luculenta.* Leipzig and Frankfort, 1704.
Polanus, Amandus. *Systema Theologiae Christianae.* Geneva, 1612.
Quenstedt, John Andrew. *Theologia Didactico-Polemica sive Systema Theologiae.* Leipzig, 1702.
Ramus, Peter. *Commentarius de Religione Christiana.* Frankfort, 1577.
Resen, Hans Poulsen. *De Sancta Fide in verum Deum et quem Ille Misit, Jesum Christum.* Copenhagen, 1614.
Scherzer, John Adam. *Collegii Anti-Sociniani.* Leipzig and Frankfort, 1702.
———. *Systema Theologiae.* Tübingen, 1679.
———. *Systema Theologiae XXIX Definitionibus Absolutum.* Leipzig and Frankfort, 1698.
Schmidt, Sebastian. *Articulorum Formulae Concordiae Repetitio.* Strasbourg, 1696.
———. *Commentarii in Epistolas D. Pauli ad Romanos, Galatas & Colossenses.* Hamburg, 1704.
———. *Compendium Theologiae.* Strasbourg, 1697.
Schroeder, John. *Opusculum Theologicum de Principio Theologiae, et Naturali Notitia Dei.* Schweinfurt, 1605.
Scotus, John Duns. *Opera Omnia.* Vatican City, 1950—.
Selnecker, Nikolaus. *Erinnerung vom Concordienbuch.* Leipzig, 1581.
———. *Notatio de Studio Sacrae Theologiae, et de Ratione Discendi Doctrinam Coelestem.* Leipzig, 1579.
———. *Paedagogia Christiana.* Frankfort on the Main, 1577.
Socinus, Faustus. *De Auctoritate Scripturae.* Ed. Conrad Vorst. Burgstemfurt, 1611.
———. *Opera Omnia.* Amsterdam, 1656.
Sohn, George. *Opera.* Herborn, 1609.

Stapleton, Thomas. *Principiorum Fidei Doctrinalium Relectio Scholastica & Compendiaria per Controversiae, Quaestiones et Articulos Tradita.* Antwerp, 1596.

Suarez, Francis. *Defensio Fidei Catholicae et Apostolicae adversus Anglicanae Sectae Errores.* Venice, 1760.

———. *Opera Omnia.* Venice, 1740—60.

Sylvius, Francis. *Commentarius in Totam Primam Partem S. Tho. Aquinatis.* Douay, 1641.

Turrettin, Francis. *Institutio Theologiae Elencticae.* Geneva, 1688.

Ursinus, Zachariah. *Explicationum Catecheticarum D. Zachariae Ursini Silesii Absolutum Opus* . . . . Geneva, 1604.

Walaeus, Anthony. *Loci Communes S. Theologiae.* Leyden, 1640.

Walther, Michael. *Harmonia Biblica, sive Brevis et Plana Conciliatio Locorum Veteris et Novi Testamenti Apparenter sibi Contradicentium.* Nuremberg, 1645.

———. *Officina Biblica.* Wittenberg, 1703.

Wernsdorf, G. *Brevis et Nervosa de Indifferentismo Religionum Commentario.* Wittenberg, 1716.

Wigand, John, and Matthew Judex. *Syntagma seu Corpus Doctrinae Veri & Omnipotentis Dei.* Basel, 1560.

SECONDARY SOURCES

Adam, John. *Evangelische Kirchengeschichte der Stadt Strassburg bis zur französischen Revolution.* Strasbourg: Druck und Verlag von J. H. Ed. Heitz, 1922.

Adam, Melchior. *Vita Germanorum Theologorum.* Heidelberg: John George Geyder, 1720.

Adelung, Johann Christoph. *Fortsetzung und Ergaenzungen Christian Gottlieb Joechers allgemeinen Gelehrten-Lexikons.* Leipzig: Johann Friedrich Gleditschen, 1784.

Althaus, Paul. *Die Christliche Wahrheit.* Gütersloh: C. Bertelsmann, 1949.

Arnold, Gottfried. *Kirchen- und Ketzer-Historie.* Frankfort on the Main: Thomas Fritschens, 1729.

Baillie, John. *The Idea of Revelation in Recent Thought.* New York: Columbia University Press, 1956.

Bang, A. C. *Den Norske Kirkes Historie i Reformations-Aarhundredet.* Oslo: 1895.

Barnekow, Kjell. *Niels Hemmingsens teologiska Aaskaadning.* Lund: C. W. K. Gleerups Förlag, 1940.

Barth, Karl. *Church Dogmatics,* trans. G. T. Thomson, G. W. Bromily, et al. 4 vols. Edinburgh: T. & T. Clark, 1936—69.

Baur, Jörg. *Die Vernunft zwischen Ontologie und Evangelium: Eine Untersuchung zur Theologie Johann Andreas Quenstedts.* Gütersloh: Verlagshaus Gerd Mohn, 1962.

Bea, Augustinus. *De Inspiratione et Inerrantia Sacrae Scripturae.* Rome: Pontificium Institutum Biblicum, 1954.

Benzing, Josef. *Die Buchdrucker des 16. und 17. Jahrhunderts im deutschen Sprachgebiet.* Wiesbaden: Otto Harrassowitz, 1963.

Besodnerus, Peter. *Bibliotheca Theologia, hoc est, Index Bibliorum Praecipuorum.* Frankfort on the Oder: Johann Eichorn, 1608.

Besterman, Theodore. *A World Bibliography of Bibliographies.* 3 vols. Geneva: Societas Bibliographica, 1939—55.

Bethune-Baker, James Franklin. *An Introduction to the Early History of Christian Doctrine.* London: Methuen and Company, 1954.

Blackman, Edwin C. *Biblical Interpretation.* Philadelphia: Westminster Press, 1957.

Bohlmann, Ralph. *Principles of Biblical Interpretation in the Lutheran Confessions.* St. Louis: Concordia Publishing House, 1968.

Bring, Ragnar. *Förhaallandet mellan tro och gärningar inom Luthers teologi.* Abo: Abo Akademi, F. Tilgmanus Boktrykeri, 1934.

Brunner, Emil. *Revelation and Reason,* trans. Olive Wyon. Philadelphia: Westminster Press, 1946.

Bruun, Christian Walter. *Bibliotheca Danica. Systematisk fortegnelse over den danske Literatur 1482—1830.* Copenhagen: Gyldendalske Boghandel, 1877—1902.

Cragg, Gerald R. *The Church and the Age of Reason.* Baltimore: Penguin Books, 1960.

Descartes, René. *A Discourse on Method.* London: J. M. Deut and Sons, 1949.

Dorn, Johann Christoph. *Bibliotheca theologica critica quam secundum singulas divinioris scientiae partes disposuit atque instruxit.* Frankfort and Leipzig: E. C. Rauliar, 1721.

Dorner, Isaac A. *History of Protestant Theology,* trans. George Robson and Sophia Taylor. 2 vols. Edinburgh: T. & T. Clark, 1871.

Ebeling, Gerhard. *Word and Faith,* trans. James W. Leitch. London: SCM Press, 1963.

Elert, Werner. *Der Christliche Glaube.* 3d ed. Hamburg: Furche Verlag, 1956.

———. *The Structure of Lutheranism,* trans. Walter Hansen. St. Louis: Concordia Publishing House, 1962.

Fabricius, Johann Albert. *Centifolium Lutheranum sive notitia literaria scriptorum omnis generis de B. D. Luthero ejusque vita, scriptis, et reformatione ecclesiae, in lucem ab amicis et inimicis editorum digesta sub titulis C. C.* Hamburg: C. Koenig, 1728—30.

Fagerberg, Holsten. *Die Theologie der lutherischen Bekenntnisschriften von 1529 bis 1537,* trans. Gerhard Klose. Göttingen: Vandenhoeck & Ruprecht, 1965.

Farrar, Frederic W. *History of Interpretation.* New York: Macmillan and Co., 1886.

Feuerlin, Jacob Wilhelm, comp. *Bibliotheca Symbolica Evangelica Lutherana.* Göttingen: Jo. Wilh. Schmid, 1752.

Fischer, Erdmann R. *Vita Johannis Gerhardi.* Leipzig: 1723.

Frank, Gustav. *Geschichte der protestantischen Theologie.* 4 vols. Leipzig: Breitkopf und Härtel, 1862.

Friedensburg, Walter. *Geschichte der Universität Wittenberg.* Halle: M. Niemeyer, 1917.

Frör, Kurt. *Biblische Hermeneutik.* Munich: Chr. Kaiser Verlag, 1964.

Garstein, Oskar. *Cort Aslakssen.* Oslo: Lutherstiftelsen, 1953.

Gass, Friedrich Wilhelm J. H. *Geschichte der protestantischen Dogmatik.* 4 vols. Berlin: Georg Reimer, 1854—67.

Georg, Th. *Allgemeines europäisches Bücherlexicon.* Leipzig: Verlegung Gotthilfft Theoph. Georg, 1742—53.

Gerber, Johann. *Fortgesetzte theologische Berichte von neuen Büchern und Schriften.* Danzig and Leipzig: Daniel Ludwig Wedel, 1774.

———. *Theologische Berichte von neuen Büchern und Schriften von einer Gesellschaft zu Danzig.* Danzig: D. L. Wendel, 1772.

Gerrish, Brian Albert. *Grace and Reason.* Oxford: Oxford University Press, 1962.

Göransson, Sven. *Orthodoxi och Synkretism i Sverige 1647—1660.* Uppsala: Almgvist & Wiksells Boktryckeri, 1950.

Grant, Robert M. *The Bible in the Church.* New York: Macmillan Company, 1954.

Grützmacher, Richard Heinrich. *Wort und Geist.* Leipzig: A. Deichert, 1902.

Hägglund, Bengt. *Die Heilige Schrift und ihre Deutung in der Theologie Johann Gerhards.* Lund: CWK Gleerups Förlag, 1951.

———. *Theologie und Philosophie bei Luther und in der Occamistischen Tradition.* Lund CWK Gleerups Förlag, 1955.

———. *Theologins Historia.* Lund: CWK Gleerups Förlag, 1963. In English translation by Gene J. Lund, *History of Theology.* St. Louis: Concordia Publishing House, 1968.

Hartknoch, Christoph. *Preussische Kirchen-Historia.* Frankfort on the Main and Leipzig: Beckenstein, 1684.

Hase, Karl. *Hutterus Redivivus.* Leipzig: Breitkopf und Härtel, 1845.

Heim, Karl. *Das Gewissheitsproblem in der systematischen Theologie bis zu Schleiermacher.* Leipzig: J. C. Hinrichs'sche Buchhandlung, 1911.

Helwig, Ludwig N. *Den danske Kirkes Historie efter Reformationen.* Copenhagen: G. E. C. Gads Forlag, 1851.

Henke, Ernst Ludwig Th. *Georg Calixtus und seine Zeit.* Halle: Buchhandlung des Waisenhauses, 1853.

Heppe, Heinrich. *Die Dogmatik der evangelisch-reformierten Kirche,* newly rev. and ed. Ernst Bizer. Neukirchen: Buchhandlung des Erziehungsvereins, 1935.

———. *Dogmatik des deutschen Protestantismus.* Gotha: Verlag von Friedrich Andreas Perthes, 1857.

———. *Geschichte des deutschen Protestantismus in den Jahren 1555—1581.* Marburg: Elwert, 1852.

Hermann, Rudolf. *Von der Klarheit der heiligen Schrift.* Berlin: Evangelische Verlagsanstalt, 1958.

Hermelink, Heinrich. *Geschichte der evangelischen Kirche in Württemberg von der Reformation bis zur Gegenwart.* Stuttgart and Tübingen: Rainer Wunderlich Verlag, 1949.

Heussi, Karl. *Geschichte der theologischen Fakultät zu Jena.* Weimar: Hermann Boehlau, 1954.

Hirsch, Emanuel. *Hilfsbuch zum Studium der Dogmatik.* Berlin: Walter de Gruyter, 1937.

Hoenecke, Adolph. *Evangelisch-Lutherische Dogmatik.* 4 vols. Milwaukee: Northwestern Publishing House, 1909.

Hoffmann, Johann Wilhelm. *Bibliothecae Hoffmannianiae catalogus secundum materias distributus theologis iurisconsultis historicis philologis philosophis aliquatenus etiam medicis.* Wittenberg: E. G. Eichsfeld, 1740.

Hornig, Gottfried. *Die Anfänge der historisch-kritischen Theologie.* Göttingen: Vandenhoeck & Ruprecht, 1961.

Hornig, Wilhelm. *Dr. Johann Pappus von Lindau 1549 bis zu 1610.* Strasbourg: Druck und Verlag von J. H. Ed. Heitz, 1891.

Hove, Elling. *Christian Doctrine.* Minneapolis: Augsburg Publishing House, 1931.

Joecher, C. G. *Allgemeines Gelehrten-Lexikon.* Leipzig: Johann Friedrich Gleditschen, 1750.

Johnson, Gisle. *Den Systematiske Teologi.* Oslo: Dybwad, 1897.

Kirkehistoriske Samlinger. Udg. af Selskabet for Danmarks Kirkehistorie. Copenhagen: G. E. C. Gads Forlag, 1849.

Koelling, Wilhelm. *Die Lehre von der Theopneustie.* Breslau: Verlag von Carl Dülfer, 1891.

Koerner, Josef. *Bibliographisches Handbuch des Deutschen Schrifttums.* Bern: Francke, 1949.

Kornerup, Björn S. *Biskop Hans Poulsen Resen 1561—1615.* Copenhagen: G. E. C. Gads Forlag, 1928.

Krabbe, Otto. *David Chytraeus.* Rostock: Stiller'sche Hofbuchhandlung, 1870.

Kraft, Friedrich Wilhelm. *Theologische Bibliothek.* 14 vols. Leipzig: Bernhard Christoph Breitkopf, 1746—1759.

Kraus, Hans-Joachim. *Geschichte der historisch-kritischen Erforschung des Alten Testaments von der Reformation bis zur Gegenwart.* Neukirchen: Verlag der Buchhandlung des Erziehungsvereins, 1956.

Lawton, John Stewart. *Miracles and Revelation.* New York: Association Press, 1960.

Lessing, Gotthold E. *Lessing's Theological Writings,* trans. Henry Chadwick. Stanford: University Press, 1957.

Leube, Hans. *Die Reformideen in der deutschen lutherischen Kirche zur Zeit der Orthodoxie.* Leipzig: Verlag von Dörffling und Franke, 1924.

———. *Kalvinismus und Luthertum im Zeitalter der Orthodoxie.* Leipzig: Dörffling und Franke, 1928.

Lewalter, Ernst. *Spanisch-jesuitische und deutsch-lutherische Metaphysik des 17. Jahrhunderts.* Hamburg: Wissenschaftliche Buchgesellschaft, 1963.

Loescher, Valentin. *Catalogus Bibliothecae.* Dresden: Hermann, 1750—51.

Lohse, Bernhard. *Ratio und Fides: Eine Untersuchung über die Ratio in der Theologie Luthers.* Göttingen: Vandenhoeck & Ruprecht, 1958.

LeLong, J. *Bibliotheca Sacra seu syllabus omnium ferme sacrae scripturae editionum ac versionum.* Leipzig: Johann Ludwig Gleditsch, 1709.

Lewis, Conrad, ed. *Rome and the Study of Scripture.* St. Meinrad: Grail Publications, 1958.

Luthardt, Christoph Ernst. *Compendium der Dogmatik.* Leipzig: Dörffling und Franke, 1865.

Meyer, Hans. *The Philosophy of St. Thomas Aquinas.* St. Louis: B. Herder, 1944.

Moldaenke, Günter. *Schriftverständnis und Schriftdeutung im Zeitalter der Reformation.* I. *Matthias Flacius Illyricus.* Stuttgart: W. Kohlhammer, 1936.

Montgomery, John Warwick, ed. and trans. *Chytraeus on Sacrifice.* St. Louis: Concordia Publishing House, 1962.

———. *Crisis in Lutheran Theology.* 2 vols. Grand Rapids: Baker Book House, 1967.

Moser, Johann Jacob. *Beytrag zu einem lexico der jetzlebenden lutherisch- und reformirten theologen in und um Teutschland.* Zuellichau: Verlegung des Waysenhauses, 1740.

Nachrichten von einer Hallischen Bibliothek. Halle: J. J. Gebauer, 1748.

Neveux, J. B. *Vie Spirituelle et vie Sociale entre Rhin et Baltique en XVIIe Siècle.* Paris: Libraire C. Klincksieck, 1967.

Nicolau, Michaele, Ioachim Salaverri, et al. *Sacrae Theologiae Summa.* 4 vols. Madrid: Biblioteca de Autores Christianos, 1958.

Nitzsch, Friedrich A. *Lehrbuch der evangelischen Dogmatik,* 3d ed. Tübingen: J. C. B. Mohr, 1912.

Norvin, William. *Köbenhavns Universitet i Reformationens og Orthodoxiens Tidsalder.* Copenhagen: Gyldendalske Boghandel, 1937—40.

Ong, Walter J. *Ramus, Method, and the Decay of Dialogue.* Cambridge: Harvard University Press, 1958.

Osiander, Lucas. *Epitomes Historiae Ecclesiasticae Centuriae Decimae Sextae.* Tübingen: Philip Gruppenbach, 1608.

Perriraz, Louis. *Histoire de la Théologie Protestante aux XVIIIme et XIXme Siècles surtout en Allemagne.* Neuchatel: Éditions Henri Messieller, 1951.

Petersen, Peter. *Geschichte der Aristotelischen Philosophie im protestantischen Deutschland.* Leipzig: Felix Meiner, 1921.

Philippi, Friedrich A. *Kirchliche Glaubenslehre.* 5 vols. Stuttgart: Verlag von Samuel Gottlieb Liesching, 1854.

Pieper, Franz. *Christian Dogmatics,* trans. Theodore Engelder, John T. Mueller, and Walter W. F. Albrecht. 3 vols. St. Louis: Concordia Publishing House, 1951.

Planck, Gottlieb J. *Geschichte der protestantischen Theologie von der Konkordienformel an bis in die Mitte des achtzehnten Jahrhunderts.* 6 vols. Göttingen: Vandenhoeck & Ruprecht, 1831.

Prenter, Regin. *Skabelse og Genlösning.* Copenhagen: G. E. C. Gads Forlag, 1951.

Preus, Herman A., and Edmund Smits, eds. *The Doctrine of Man in Classical Lutheran Theology.* Minneapolis: Augsburg Publishing House, 1962.

Preus, Robert. *The Inspiration of Scripture.* Edinburg: Oliver and Boyd, 1957.

Ratschow, Carl. *Lutherische Dogmatik zwischen Reformation und Aufklärung.* Gütersloh: G. Mohn, 1964.

Reid, John K. S. *The Authority of Scripture.* New York: Harper and Brothers, 1957.

Reu, Michael. *In the Interest of Lutheran Unity.* Columbus: The Wartburg Press, 1940.

———. *Luther and the Scriptures.* Columbus: The Wartburg Press, 1944.

Richardson, Alan, and Wolfgang Schweitzer, eds. *Biblical Authority Today.* Philadelphia: Westminster Press, 1951.

Ritschl, Otto. *Dogmengeschichte des Protestantismus.* 4 vols. Leipzig: J C. Hinrichs'sche Buchhandlung; and Göttingen: Vandenhoeck & Ruprecht, 1908—27.

Rohnert, Wilhelm. *Die Inspiration der heiligen Schrift.* Leipzig: Verlag von Georg Böhme, 1889.

Rördam, Holger Frederik. *Kjöbenhavns Universitets Historie 1537—1621.* Copenhagen: Tryde, 1868—74.

Rothe, Richard. *Dogmatik.* Heidelberg: J. C. B. Mohr, 1870.

Runia, Klaus. *Karl Barth's Doctrine of Holy Scripture.* Grand Rapids: William B. Eerdmans Publishing Company, 1962.

Saintes, Amand. *Histoire Critique du Rationalisme en Allemangne.* 2d ed. Paris: Librairei de Brockhaus et Avenarius, 1843.

Schian, Martin. *Orthodoxie und Pietismus im Kampf um die Predigt.* Giessen: Verlag von Alfred Töpelmann, 1912.

Schlee, Ernst. *Der Streit des Daniel Hoffmann.* Marburg: Elwert, 1862.

Schlink, Edmund. *Theology of the Lutheran Confessions,* trans. Paul F. Koehneke and Herbert J. A. Bouman. Philadelphia: Muhlenberg Press, 1961.

Schlüsselburg, Conrad. *Haereticorum Catalogus.* 13 vols. Frankfort, 1597—1601.

Schmid, Heinrich. *Doctrinal Theology of the Evangelical Lutheran Church,* trans. Charles A. Hay and Henry E. Jacobs. Philadelphia: United Lutheran Publication House, 1899. Reissued 1961, Augsburg Publishing House, Minneapolis.

———. *Geschichte der synkretistischen Streitigkeiten in der Zeit Georg Calixts.* Erlangen: Carl Heyder, 1846.

Scholder, Klaus. *Ursprünge und Probleme der Bibelkritik im 17. Jahrhundert.* Munich: Chr. Kaiser Verlag, 1966.

Schüssler, Hermann. *Georg Calixtus: Theologie und Kirchenpolitik.* Wiesbaden: Franz Steiner Verlag, 1961.

Schütz, Ludwig. *Thomas-Lexikon.* New York: F. Unger Publishing Company, 1947.

Schweizer, Alexander. *Die Protestantischen Centraldogmen.* Zürich: Fuessli and Co., 1854.

Sincerus, Theoph. *Neue Sammlung von lauter alten und raren Büchern.* Frankfort: J. Stein, 1733.

Stengel, Johann. *Apparatus Liborum Theologicorum realis alphebeticus.* Ulm: D. Bartholomäi, 1724.

Stoeffler, F. Ernest. *The Rise of Evangelical Pietism.* Leiden: E. J. Brill, 1965.

Strohl, Henri. *Le Protestantisme en Alsace.* Strasbourg: Editions Oberlin, 1950.

Synave, Paul, and Pierre Benoit. *Prophecy and Inspiration,* trans. Avery R. Dulles and Thomas J. Sheridan. New York: Desclee Company, 1961.

Tholuck, August. *Der Geist der lutherischen Theologen Wittenbergs im Verlaufe des 17. Jahrhunderts.* Hamburg and Gotha: Friedrich und Andreas Parther, 1852.

——. *Geschichte des Rationalismus. Erste Abtheilung: Geschichte des Pietismus und des ersten Stadiums der Aufklärung.* Berlin: Wiegandt und Grieben, 1865.

——. *Lebenszeugen der lutherischen Kirche aus allen Ständen vor und während der Zeit des dreissigjährigen Krieges.* Berlin: Wiegandt und Grieben, 1859.

——. *Vorgeschichte des Rationalismus.* Berlin: Wiegandt und Grieben, 1861.

Thomasius, Gottfried. *Bibliothecae Thomasianae sive locupletissimi thesauri ex omni scientia librorum praestantissimorum rarissimorumque quos olim possedit vir illustris Gottfredus Thomasius,* ed. G. W. Panzer. Nuremberg: 1765.

Troeltsch, Ernst. *Vernunft und Offenbarung bei Johann Gerhard und Melanchthon.* Göttingen: Vandenhoeck & Ruprecht, 1891.

Uhlhorn, Friedrich. *Geschichte der deutschlutherischen Kirche.* Leipzig: Dörffling und Franke, 1911.

Walch, Johann Georg. *Bibliotheca Theologica Selecta.* Jena: Croeckeriane, 1757.

——. *Historische und Theologische Einleitung in die Religionsstreitigkeiten der Evangelisch-Lutherischen Kirchen von der Reformation an bis auf jetzige Zeiten.* Jena: Johann Meyer, 1730—39.

Wallmann, Johannes. *Der Theologiebegriff bei Johann Gerhard und Georg Calixt.* Tübingen: J. C. B. Mohr, 1961.

Walther, Wilhelm. *Das Erbe der Reformation.* Leipzig: A. Diechertsche Verlagsbuchhandlung, 1903—17.

Weber, Hans Emil. *Der Einfluss der protestantischen Schulphilosophie auf die orthodox-lutherische Dogmatik.* Leipzig, 1908.

——. *Die analytische Methode der lutherischen Orthodoxie.* Nuremberg: 1907.

——. *Die philosophische Scholastik des Deutschen Protestantismus im Zeitalter der Orthodoxie.* Leipzig: Quelle und Meyer, 1907.

———. *Reformation, Orthodoxie und Rationalismus: Beiträge zur Förderung christlicher Theologie.* 2 vols. Gütersloh: C. Bertelsmann, 1937—51.

Weismann, Christian E. *Introductio in Memorabilia Ecclesiastica Historiae Sacrae Novi Testamenti ad Juvandam Notitiam Regni Dei et Satanae Cordisque Humanae Salutem.* 2 vols. Halle: Magdeburg, 1745.

Wundt, Max. *Die deutsche Schulmetaphysik des 17. Jahrhunderts.* Tübingen: J. C. B. Mohr, 1939.

Zedler, Johann Heinrich. *Grosse Vollständiges Universal-Lexikon.* Graz: Akademische Druck — U. Verlagsanstalt, 1961. First published Halle and Leipzig, 1732.

Zeller, Winfred. *Der Protestantismus des 17. Jahrhunderts.* Bremen: Carl Schünemann, 1962.

INDEX

NAMES AND SUBJECTS

Aaron 293, 369
Abel 103
Aberrations in doctrine 74, 81, 141, 258, 261
Abraham 85, 261, 391, 413
Accident 78, 161
Accommodation 288-89, 291, 318, 333-34, 354
Adam, John 71, 427
Adam, Melchior 69-70, 427
Adam and Eve 91, 93, 98, 173
Adelung, Johann Christoph 427
Adiaphora 55
Adiumenta (human aids) 88
Affliction 106-7, 142, 221-22
Ahab 103
Ahasuerus 369
Albert the Great 171
Albrecht, Walter W. F. 25, 242, 432
Alexander 78
Alexander of Hales 249, 397, 421

Allegory 324-25, 327, 391
Alsace 58, 61
Alsted, John Henry 114, 159, 199, 238, 248-49, 391, 421
Altdorf 57, 64
Althamer, Andrew 412-13, 421
Althaus, Paul 383, 385, 394, 410-11, 413, 427
Amanuenses 263, 278, 283, 288, 346, 354, 381-82
Ambiguity 79, 326
America 65
Ames, William 163-64, 244, 421
Analogy of faith 97, 141, 223-24, 312, 326, 330-31, 337, 392
Analytic method 43, 46, 97, 143, 156, 198, 229, 243, 248
Anasceuastic function of philosophy 124-25
Ancient heresies 35, 67
Andradius 48
Andreae, Jacob 48, 66, 379, 392, 412, 421
Annotationes Uberiores in

Compendium Theologicum L. Hutteri (Bechmann) 63, 389 to 390, 393, 399, 421
Anthologies 17, 22
Anthropologia Sacra (Meisner) 55
Anthropology 79, 82, 236
Antichrist 55, 150, 315
Antilegomena 31, 305, 386
Antiquity 102, 210, 301
Antitheses 35, 45, 63, 65, 339
Apodixis Articulorum Fidei (Calov) 61, 244, 250-51, 379-82, 384, 386, 389-91, 398-400, 402, 422
Apographal Scriptures 285-86, 306-7
Apologetics 101, 124, 234 to 235
Application 45, 82, 164, 200, 204-5, 330
Approach 31, 35, 40, 44, 82, 316; *see also* New Approach
exegetico-historical 143
to theology 73-74, 76, 82-86, 408

Aptitude 30, 83, 112, 117, 155, 157, 162, 164-65, 194-96, 217-18, 232
 of intellect 229
Aptness to teach 221, 229
Aquila of Pontus 317
Aquila-like theory 317
Aquinas, Thomas 23, 32, 36, 75, 110, 114, 116, 125-26, 159, 170-71, 193, 195, 237-39, 241, 246-47, 249-50, 343, 395, 397, 421
Arcesilaus 416
Archetypal theology 112-14, 164, 167, 172, 309, 409
Argumentation 16-17, 20, 33, 101, 103, 235
Aristotelian anthropology 82, 236
Aristotelian terminology 45, 53, 63, 114-15, 133, 159
Aristotelianism 82, 129-32, 159
Aristotle 77-79, 85, 100, 109, 112, 115-16, 124, 130-32, 159-60, 163, 176, 195-96, 202-3, 206, 233, 236, 238-39, 244, 248, 250, 343
Arithmetic 78, 100
Arius 103, 171, 235, 418
Arminianism 21, 95, 178, 274, 335, 348, 354
Arndt, John 47, 52, 56
Arnold, Gottfried 65, 427
Arrangement 77, 81, 87, 89, 96-97, 115, 123, 141, 222, 415, 417
Article 145
 antecedent 148
 consequent 148-49
 constituent 148
 mixed 123, 152-54, 188
 pure 123, 152-54
Articles of faith 16, 19, 88, 123, 139, 145-46
 arrangement of 77, 81, 87, 96-97, 115, 123, 141, 222, 415, 417
 classification of 143-54, 242
 and didactic theology 224-25
 followed by *usus practicus* 30, 204
 gaps in 138-39
 and Gospel 146
 primary fundamental 148-49
 as *principia* 87, 94, 116, 237, 239
 as *principiata* 116
 searching out 105
 secondary fundamental 148-49
 source of 164
 summation of 90, 93-94, 96, 98, 104-5
 unity of 146-47
Aslakssen, Cort 32, 54, 66, 359, 421
Assent 78, 79, 101, 107, 201, 231-32, 408, 416
Assumptions 73
Astronomy 54, 66, 85, 132, 279, 349, 399
Athanasius 165
Atheism 175-76, 209
 and doctrinal indifference 413
Attacks on inspiration 291 to 292, 340
Attitude 30, 73-74, 121, 216, 317
Attributes
 of Scripture 116, 255-56, 296, 316
 of true religion 209-11
Augustine, St. 23, 35, 94, 106, 109-12, 126, 190, 225, 238, 245, 247, 333, 393
Augustus, Elector of Saxony 50
Authenticity 255
 of Hebrew and Greek texts 306
 of Hebrew vowel points 307-9
Authority 16
 in the church 43
 of the church 299-300
 of Symbols 38-39
Authority of Scripture 116, 257-58, 268, 296-309, 385, 411
 extent of 296-300
 and power of Gospel 411
Autopistia 262, 296-99, 301, 303
Autopistos 108, 116, 296-97, 300

Babel 151
Bacon, Francis 160
Baden 57
Baier, John William 18, 22, 25, 41, 64, 66, 71, 134, 147-49, 227, 242, 245, 251, 285, 381-82, 387, 389, 395, 412, 421
Baillie, John 247, 427
Balaam 231
Balance 43-44, 184
Balduin, Friedrich 55, 57, 66-67, 241, 337, 391, 401, 413, 421
Bang, A. C. 427
Baptism 48
Barclay, Robert 136
Barnekow, Kjell 68, 427
Baronius, Caesar 388, 421
Barth, Karl 19, 22, 25, 43, 241, 379, 402-3, 428
Bartimaeus 353
Basel 54-55, 61, 75, 82
Basis
 for doctrinal unity 144
 exegesis as 17
 of inerrancy 341-43
 of power of Word 371
 for teaching and preaching 257
Baur, Jörg 25, 68, 71, 240, 244, 428
Bea, Augustinus 383-84, 428
Beatific knowledge in Christ 169-71
Bechmann, Friedemann 32, 34, 63-64, 66, 134, 227, 232, 249-

INDEX

50, 252, 358, 380, 388-91, 393, 395, 402, 421
Behm, John 60
Bellarmine, Robert 33, 250, 278, 314, 380-81, 385-89, 391, 421
Benoit, Pierre 247, 434
Bente, Friedrich 69-70
Benzing, Josef 428
Bereans 223, 304
Berg, John 171, 199, 246-48, 422
Bergen 54
Berlin 51
Bernhard of Clairvaux 219
Bertelsmann, C. 394
Besodnerus, Peter 428
Best 16, 18
Besterman, Theodore 428
Bethune-Baker, James Franklin 397, 428
Beza, Theodorus 308
Bible
  as basis of theology 16-17
  as one book 49
  study of 222-25, 314-15
  translation into Danish 54
Biblia Illustrata (Calov) 49, 60, 381, 387-89, 391, 393-94, 398, 400, 402, 422
Biography of theologians 47-65, 66, 69
Bitter exchanges 19
Bizer, Ernst 403, 430
Blackman, Edwin C. 393, 428
Body of doctrine 15, 89-90, 96
Boettcher, Carl J. 70
Bohlmann, Arthur E. 24
Bohlmann, Ralph 388, 390, 393, 413, 428
Bonaventure 171, 194, 241, 248
Bondage of human will 41
Bonfrère, Jacques 278
Books 18, 50, 53, 57, 59, 63, 75
Bouman, Herbert J. A. 24, 68, 393, 433

Brahe, Tycho 54, 66
Brandenburg 47, 58, 60
Breithaupt, Joachim Justus 140
Bretschneider, Carl Gottlieb 236, 394
Breviarium Theologicum (Huelsemann) 57
Bring, Ragnar 68, 428
British Isles 21, 252
Brochmand, Jesper Rasmus 32, 44, 54-55, 67, 97, 157, 204, 228, 244, 249, 266, 305, 334, 337, 366, 376, 379, 384, 386, 393, 402-3, 413, 422
Bromily, G. W. 428
Brorson, Hans 29
Brunner, Emil 19, 384, 389, 428
Brutus 102
Bruun, Christian Walter 428
Bucan, William 246, 422
Bucer, Martin 336
Buddeus, Francis 66, 140, 252, 422
Bugenhagen, Johann 47
Buxtorf, Johann 384, 387

Caesar, Julius 268
Caiaphas 231
Cajetan, Thomas de Vio 247
Calixt, George 38-39, 43, 58-59, 68, 143, 154-57, 160-62, 242-44, 248, 250, 274, 278-81, 286, 381, 394, 398, 409, 422
Calov, Abraham 16, 18, 20, 22, 30, 32, 34-36, 39-40, 43-44, 47, 49, 51-52, 57-62, 64-68, 74, 93, 103, 113, 131-34, 147, 151-54, 156-229, 232, 241-51, 256, 259-60, 264 to 266, 269-70, 273, 282-83, 285, 289, 293, 296, 298, 302, 306, 310-11, 315-16, 319-20, 323-26, 328-29, 332, 336-38, 340 to 341, 344, 347, 352 to 354, 356-59, 361, 368-73, 375, 378-93, 395-403, 412-13, 422
Calov's impact and importance 226-28
Calvin, John 19, 292, 303, 308
Calvinism 45, 54, 58, 151, 376-78
Calvinists 29, 33, 37, 40, 46, 50, 51, 56, 58, 109, 113-14, 126, 141, 144, 159, 167-68, 170, 173, 227, 266, 336, 376, 391-92, 399
Cambridge theology 45
Canon (Biblical) 257, 304-6, 310, 386
  history of 305
Canon (norm) 90, 92-94, 116
Canon & certa regula 90
Canon Fidei 94
Canonicity 304-6, 386
  criteria for 306
Capellus, Louis 308
Capreolus, John 248, 422
Carpzov, John Benedict 64, 66-68, 423
Cartesianism 45, 53
Cartesians 348, 398
Caselius, John 155
Casuistry 16, 54, 64
Catalogus Testium Veritatis (Flacius) 36
Catasceuastic function of philosophy 123-24
Catechetical instruction 58
Catechetics 29
Categories 89, 96, 115, 133, 159
Catherine of Siena 36
Catholicity 35-39
Cato 102
Causal factors 114-20, 130
Cause 115, 117, 130, 161, 258
Certainty 78, 83-84, 100-103, 190, 303, 399, 408-9, 415
Chadwick, Henry 247, 431

Change 30, 31
 in prolegomena 107-43
Charitable disposition 23
Chemnitz, Martin 16-18, 20, 22-23, 25, 32, 35 to 36, 43-44, 46-49, 52-53, 62, 67-69, 76-77, 88-98, 141-43, 157, 159, 161, 184, 195, 205, 222, 235, 237, 245-46, 256, 295, 299, 305, 337, 340, 359, 362, 369, 378, 384-87, 390, 392-93, 399, 401, 406, 423
Chorales 29
Christ 77, 79-80, 83, 93, 99, 100, 113
 as central theme of Scripture 331-32
 as content of Word 373 to 374
 and doctrine about 146
 as foundation of faith 144
 as God's revelation *par excellence* 409
 as master theologian 215-16
 omniscience of 171-72, 246
 as personal Word 269-70, 271, 367
 practice of, to cite Scripture 258
 and practical nature of theology 205
 salvation without? 211 to 212
 as subject of theology 111, 373
 two natures of 168-69
Christian I, Elector of Saxony 50
Christian II, Elector of Saxony 51
Christian communions 27
Christocentricity of Scripture 270, 306, 331-33, 337, 339, 373, 410
Christologia Sacra (Meisner) 55, 378, 425

Christology 22, 32, 35, 43, 49-50, 54, 167-68, 171
Chrysostom 109, 112
Church
 authority in 43
 authority of 299-300
 and canonicity 304-6
 edification of 218-20
 and necessity of written Word 272-73
Church and the Age of Reason, The (Cragg) 19
Church councils 259-60, 310
Church fathers 23, 28, 35 to 37, 49, 63, 67 to 68, 92-94, 106, 108, 126, 141, 161, 347, 390, 397
Church history 82, 93, 98, 141, 225-26
Church union 59
Chytraeus, David 23, 61, 67, 98-108, 121, 140 to 142, 160, 210, 222, 238, 248, 255, 301, 316, 337, 423
Cicero 102
Citation theologian 22
Citations
 catenae of 36
 of dogmaticians 16, 18, 22, 49, 61
 of Scripture 17, 63
Clarity 42, 77, 311-15
 and causal terminology 115
 external and internal 251, 388
 objective and subjective 313
Classical Lutheran orthodoxy 15, 18-20
Classification of articles of faith 143-54, 242
Clavis Scripturae Sacrae (Flacius) 236-37, 243, 246, 345, 381, 383, 387, 389-92, 396-99, 423
Cleavage between Luther

and orthodoxy 41-42, 68-69
Clement of Alexandria 94
Clichés 16
Coccejus, Johannes 394
Colloquium Adiaphoristicum (Meisner) 55
Commentaries 32, 51, 55, 62, 87, 98-99, 106
Commission on Church Literature, Mo. Synod 24
Communication of attributes 49, 67, 126, 149, 168-69, 245
Communion of natures 49, 168-69
Compendium 76-77, 225
Compendium Doctrinae Coelestis (Hafenreffer) 51
Compendium Locorum Theologicorum (Hutter) 32, 37, 51
Compendium Theologiae (Heerbrand) 47, 237, 386, 403, 412, 424
Compendium Theologiae (Seb. Schmidt) 62, 380, 426
Compendium Theologiae Positivae (Baier) 18, 22, 64, 71, 242, 245, 381-82, 387, 389, 395, 412, 421
Conclusion 74, 83-84, 336, 405-11
Concordance study 43, 49
Concordia Concors (Hutter) 51, 67, 425
Concordia Seminary, Saint Louis 22, 24
Concordia Theological Seminary, Springfield, Ill. 23
Confessio Catholica (Gerhard) 36, 391, 395, 424
Confessional constant 30
Confessional loyalty 18, 31-32, 36
Confessional Lutherans 21 to 22, 44

INDEX

Confessionalism 35-39, 65, 338
Confessions 17-18, 21, 28, 37-38, 67
 inspiration of 38, 68
 and Scripture 37-39, 274
 as witness 38
Consensus 15-16, 302, 337
Consequence 137, 241, 309, 335-39
Conservative viewpoint 27 to 28, 35
Constantinople 47
Continuity of doctrine 36
Contradictions, apparent 349-53
Contribution 15, 47-65, 75
 of Calixt 154-57
 of Calov 157, 226-28
 of Chemnitz 88-98
 of Gerhard 107, 120, 130, 140, 142-43
 of heterodox 46
 of Hunnius 144-45
 of Hyperius 82-88
 of Melanchthon 77-82
Controversies (Bellarmine) 33, 250, 386-88, 422
Controversy 20, 31-32, 34, 61, 143, 272, 303-4
 Hoffmannian 129, 240
 Kenotic 32
Copenhagen 53, 54
Copernican theory 359
Copernicus 399
Cornelius a Lapide 353
Corpus doctrinae 88-90, 94, 96
 and Holy Spirit 88, 91
 as method of Scripture 89
Cotta, Johann Friedrich 70, 237-38, 378
Council of Trent 48, 92, 305-6, 311
Counter Reformation 47
Course of study 140-42
Cragg, Gerald R. 19, 24, 428
Creation in six days 154

Creeds 35, 49, 94, 105, 418
Cremer, Hermann 291, 387
Criteria 78, 86-88, 100-103, 156, 301, 303, 342
 for canonicity 306
 for judging revelation 186-87
 of Lutheran dogmatics 82, 86
 of Scripture 300-301, 303
Criticism 16, 18-19, 21
Crypto-Calvinists 19, 32, 50, 53
Cundisius, Gottfried 29, 32, 64, 386, 423
Cur alii alii non 376
Curiosity and faith 76
Cyprian 94
Cyril 35
Cyrus 417

Damascenus; *see* John of Damascus
Danish 54
Dannhauer, John Conrad 29, 31, 34, 44, 56-59, 64, 66, 68, 147, 150 to 151, 228, 232, 242, 251, 257, 262, 268, 270, 275-76, 296, 309, 344, 347, 355, 369-71, 378-79, 381-84, 387-89, 392, 395-96, 399-400, 402, 412-13, 423
Danzig 60, 206, 367
David 101-2, 150, 223, 328
De Auctoritate S. Scripturae (Socinus) 190, 247, 381, 384, 396, 398-99, 426
De Duabus Naturis (Chemnitz) 18, 35, 49, 67, 69, 237, 245 to 246, 250, 423
De Immanuele Nostro D. Jesu Christo (Aslakssen) 54

De Pontifice Romano (Brochmand) 55
De Republica (Plato) 109
De Sancta Fide (Resen) 54, 384, 396, 426
De Studio Theologiae (Chytraeus) 104-7, 238, 423
De Theologo, seu de Ratione Studii Theologici Libri IIII (Hyperius) 82-88, 236, 389, 425
De Votis Monasticis (Luther) 127
"Dead orthodoxy" 194, 405, 412
Deceit 361, 399-400
Decline of orthodoxy 46, 226-35
 18th-century thought 228-35
 Loescher and philosophers 233-35
 Neumann and pietists 228-32
Dedekenn, George 67, 380, 382, 392, 401-3, 423
Dedicatory letter 90, 93
Deerfield, Ill. 23
Definition 85, 106
 of religion 192, 208-9
 techniques of 78, 248
 of theology 109, 117-18, 159
Democritus, C. 234
Denmark 32, 53, 55
Derived theology 167
Descartes, René 160, 233, 398, 428
Deutschmann, Johannes 66
Development of prolegomena 19, 72-75, 81, 87-88, 98, 107-43, 158
Devotional literature 29, 50, 56
Devotional writers 29, 47, 50, 55
Dialectic theology 224-25
Dialectics 76-78, 80-81,

84-85, 105-6, 236, 244
Diaskepsis Theologica (N. Hunnius) 56, 144, 242, 251, 425
Dictation 278, 281, 283, 286, 290, 292, 384
Dicto 290, 381, 383
Didactic theology 34-35, 222, 224-25
Differences, seriousness of 58
Difficulties 85-86, 312, 352-53, 362, 389, 413
Discipline(s) 120, 181-82, 196
Discrepancies 349-53
Disputatio de Discrimine Evangelii et Philosophiae (Melanchthon) 80
Disputation on the Verse Verbum Caro Factum Est (Luther) 127, 130, 239
Distinctions
  in fundamental articles 148-49
  between pure and mixed articles 123, 152-53, 188
  scholastic 65, 79
  concerning theology 113-14
  in use of word *theology* 164-65
Divine command to write Scripture 277-78
Divine origin of Scripture 263-65, 273-77, 296, 385, 408-9
Divisive article 274
Doctrina evangelii 29, 145, 332-33
Doctrinal position 16, 19, 30, 45
Doctrinal statement 16, 17
Doctrinal Theology of the Evangelical Lutheran Church (H. Schmid) 16
Doctrinal unity 31-32, 59, 138-39

sufficient basis for 144
Doctrine 15-16, 78
  aberrations in 74, 81, 141, 258, 261
  continuity of 36
  as foundation of faith 147-48
  golden chain of 146
  indifference to 232, 413
  Scripture as 390
  in the singular 139, 146
  theology as 110-12, 163, 195-96, 248
Doctrine of Scripture 19, 21, 254-378
Dogmata 76
Dogmata Ecclesiastica 94
"Dogmatic" 35
"Dogmatic" exegesis 337-38, 393-94
Dogmatic works 18-20
Dogmatician(s) 16-17, 20, 22, 44, 47-66, 69, 73, 104, 145-46, 225
Dogmatics 15, 17, 19, 37, 45, 62, 73, 104
  changes in 107-143
  criteria for 82, 86
  of Dannhauer 59
  and exegesis 42-44, 222
  gaps in 43
  of Hoenecke, Philippi, or Pieper 17
  Melanchthon's preface to 80-81, 414-19
  of Pieper, Hoenecke, Hove 19
  purpose of 81-82
  of Quenstedt 62
  of Reformed 114
  subject matter of 74
  of Walther 22
  weakness in 43
Dogmatism 40
Dorn, Johann Christoph 428
Dorner, Isaac A. 20, 24, 114, 133, 238, 241, 291, 335, 338, 383, 386, 393, 402, 413, 428
Dorsch, John George 29, 36, 44, 56, 62, 66,

379, 384, 387, 394, 413, 423
Double-source theory 155 to 156
"Double truth" 135, 343
Dreier, Christian 38, 68
Dresden 50, 55
Dulles, Avery R. 247, 434
Durandus de Sancto Porciano 171
Dury, John 58, 144

East Prussia 59
Ebeling, Gerhard 338, 393, 428
Eck, Johann 418
Ectypal theology 112-14, 164, 167, 170-72
Ecumenicity 17
Edifying 18
Efficacy
  as mark of true religion 211
  of Scripture 42, 362-78, 411
Eilenburg 56
Elementa 94
Elementary questions of prolegomena 74
Elert, Werner 20, 22, 25, 40, 248, 251, 292, 295, 383-84, 402, 428
Empiricism 348, 354-55
Enchiridion (Augustine) 94
Engelder, Theodore 25, 242, 432
Enlightenment
  of Holy Spirit 121, 219 to 220, 229, 275, 319-20, 349, 390, 406, 408
  of intellect 230
  period of 20, 44, 130, 235
Enoch 93
Ensheim 62
Enthusiasm 271, 293, 317, 368, 377-78
Epicureanism 209
Epicurus 77
Epignosis 109, 111, 163
Epitome Credendorum

INDEX

(N. Hunnius) 56, 144-45, 241, 380, 425
Erasmus, Desiderius 75-77, 82, 290, 352, 383, 423
Ernesti, Johann August 407
Erotemata Dialectica (Melanchthon) 77-80, 236, 244
Erring brother 33
Error 81, 83, 148, 162, 166, 299, 340-41, 346-47
  apparent 354-57
  of pietists 232
  refutation of 126, 234
Ethics 75, 80-81, 85-86, 106, 122
Ethics (Aristotle) 112, 132, 236, 248, 250
Evangelical 23, 27-29, 331
Evangelical impact 28
Evangelical orthodoxy 18, 29
Examen Concilii Tridentini (Chemnitz) 48, 69, 141, 378, 385-86, 423
Examen Theologicum Acroamaticum (Hollaz) 45, 136, 241-42, 246, 249, 251-52, 381-83, 385-86, 390-93, 395, 401-3, 424
Exegesis 16-18, 42-45, 48-50, 55, 60, 63, 65, 87-88, 90, 98, 103-4, 161, 223-24, 315-19, 337, 350-51, 353, 361
  as Biblical basis of theology 17
  and dogmatics 42-44
  as part of Biblical study 222-24
Exegetico-historical approach 143
Existentialism 135
Experience 27, 101-2, 107, 134, 222, 301, 320,

preceded by faith 101, 107
Exposition 42
Expositiones Symboli (Cyprian) 94
Ezra 308

Fabricius, Johann Albert 429
Fagerberg, Holsten 388, 429
Faith 81, 408-9
  as assent 79
  and confidence in Scripture 303
  and curiosity 76
  foundation of 147-48
  as gift of God 319
  goal of 192
  as *habitus* 78-79, 155
  as *habitus intellectus* 78 to 79
  as *habitus voluntatis* 78-79
  imperfect 149
  and knowledge 199
  and life 203, 309, 312
  Melanchthon's definition of 78
  object of 146-47
  and orthodoxy 409
  and philosophy 131, 136
  practice of 194, 198-200, 250
  precedes experience 101, 107
  as response to God speaking 298
  and theology 231-32
  as trust 79
Faithfulness 17, 20, 31, 301
False doctrine 124, 235
False religion 209
False theology 165-66, 230
Farrar, Frederic W. 338, 393, 429
Fear of God 82-83
Fecht, John 151, 242, 251, 423
Feuerborn, Justus 57, 65
Feuerlin, Jacob Wilhelm 429

Feustking, Johann Heinrich 383
Fides 78
Fides activa 204
Fides divina 301, 408-9
Fides historica 231
Fides humana 231, 301, 303, 408
Fides qua creditur 145
Fides specialis 204, 336, 341
Fiducia misericordiae 79
Figurative sense 322-25
Fischer, Erdmann R. 70, 429
Fisher, Robert H. 69
Fiskaa, H. M. 24
Flacius (Illyricus), Matthias 36, 67, 81, 143, 176-77, 179, 225, 236-37, 243, 246, 308, 327, 339-40, 345-47, 351, 381, 383, 387, 389-90, 392, 397-99, 412, 423
Foelber, Elmer E. 23
Foertsch, M. 237, 251, 423
Followers of Luther 28, 66
Forerunners of Protestantism 36
Forma 117, 130, 195, 265, 267-68, 271, 282-83, 363, 370, 372, 390
Formal principle 20, 270-71, 331
Formation of theology 105
Formula of Concord 15, 45, 48, 50-51, 55, 257, 406, 412, et passim
Formulations 17
  change in 30-31
  scholastic 134
  theological 30-31, 34, 134
Foundation of faith 147-48
Frankfort 47, 50, 52
France 64
Frank, Gustav 70, 429
Franz, Wolfgang 66, 389, 392, 423
Frederick William 50

Friedensburg, Walter 429
Frör, Kurt 393, 429
Fundamental articles 143-44
  distinctions in 148-49
Fundamental and nonfundamental 56, 147-52
"Fundamental or primary points" 97
Fundamentalism 21
Future 22-23

Galileo 21
Gaps
  in articles of faith 138-39
  in dogmatics 43
  in Scripture 309, 330
Garstein, Oskar 67, 70, 429
Gass, Friedrich Wilhelm J. H. 20, 24, 429
Generalizations 20
Geneva 53-54
Genius 27
Genus 49, 78, 195-96, 248
Genus loquendi 288-89
Geography 76, 188-89, 299, 349, 354
Georg, Th. 429
Gerber, Johann 429
Gerhard, John 16-18, 20, 22-23, 29-30, 34-36, 40, 43-44, 46, 49, 52-55, 57, 60-63, 66, 68, 70, 74, 93, 97, 107-35, 137, 140-43, 145, 152-57, 159-61, 171, 174-75, 182, 184, 188, 194, 196, 202, 204, 207, 213, 222, 226, 228, 232, 234-35, 237-45, 251, 257, 263, 265-67, 296-97, 299, 304-5, 308, 316, 321, 326-27, 337, 347, 349, 352-53, 362, 365-66, 376, 378-91, 395, 397-98, 400-403, 412, 423-24
Gerhard, John Ernst 63, 66

Gerhardt, Paul 29
German 56
Germany 22, 31-32, 51, 54, 64-65, 129, 130
Gerrish, Brian Albert 69, 240, 429
Gerson, John 120, 175, 239, 424
Geschichte des Rationalismus 20
Gesner, Salomon 388, 424
Giessen 32, 52, 55, 65
Glassius, Salomon 322, 327, 382, 386, 388-89, 391, 393, 424
Glory of God 191, 218
Gnesio-Lutherans 47, 66
Gnosis 111-12, 163, 200
Goal
  of revealed theology 191-94
  of theology 30, 46, 74, 112, 117, 120, 191-94, 248
  of work of theologian 192, 216-17
God
  author of revelation 186-87
  author of Scripture 263-65, 287, 371-73, 412
  as *Autor theologiae* 333
  as *Deus pro me* 207
  fashions theologian 107, 183, 206, 407
  knowledge of 83
  natural knowledge of 86, 174-75, 179-80, 187
  as object of faith 145-46
  omnipotence of 125
  power of 125
  reliability of 190
  self-disclosure of 99
  as source of theology 182-83, 258
  as subject (content) of revelation 186-87
  as teacher 83
  as theology 172-73
  truthfulness of 83, 190, 344-46, 396
Golden age 45

Göransson, Sven 67, 429
Gospel
  and articles of faith 146
  as basis for understanding Scripture 187
  concern for 20
  as criterion for assessing revelation 187
  as heart of theology 74
  and heathen religions 100
  and natural theology 178
  not a philosophy 77, 80
  piety engendered by 29, 81
  piety in isolation from 29
  power and work of 363-67, 373
  same as *Protevangelium* 332
  and pure doctrine 30
  as revelation 294-95
Gospels 49, 51
Grant, Robert M. 394, 429
Greek 47, 76, 163, 165, 306-7
Gregory of Valencia 35, 247, 250, 424
Greifswald 63
Gretzer, Jacob 385, 391, 424
Grützmacher, Richard Heinrich 369-70, 401, 429

Habitus
  faith as 78-79, 155
  of intellect 232
  and mortal sin 230
  theology as 30, 112, 114, 162, 165, 195-96, 227
Habitus mixtus 198-201, 248-49
Habitus practicus 30, 112, 156, 195, 196-206, 226, 243, 249
  and application to life 204-5
  lack of Biblical basis in Calov 205-6

INDEX

445

not mixture of theoretical and practical 198-201
not "science" 202-4
not "wisdom" 201-2
proofs for 197-98
Hafenreffer, Matthias 32, 47, 66, 97, 108, 140, 305, 379, 386, 424
Hagar 85, 138
Hägglund, Bengt 19, 24-25, 69, 130, 133, 240-41, 387, 394, 429
Halle 64
Hanneken, Meno 70
Hansen, Walter A. 25, 68, 248, 384, 428
Harmonia Biblica (M. Walther) 350, 391, 398, 427
Harmonia Quatuor Evangelistarum (Chemnitz) 49, 337, 359, 387, 390, 393, 398, 399, 401, 423
Harmony 89, 97, 138-39, 224, 241, 362
Hartknoch, Christoph 71, 401, 430
Hase, Karl 25, 430
Hauck, Albert 70, 238, 383
Hay, Charles A. 24, 433
Heathen religion 100, 176, 418
Hebenstreit, John Paul 251, 410, 424
Hebraism 317, 319
Hebrew 52, 64, 76, 163, 306-9, 386
vowel points in 307-9
Heerbrand, Jacob 47, 50-51, 66, 97, 108, 237, 305, 376, 386, 403, 412, 424
Heermann, John 29
Hegelian 34
Heidegger, John Henry 247, 249, 424
Heidelberg 51, 54
Heilsegoismus 191-92
Heim, Karl 385, 430
Heldberg 53

Helmstedt 55, 129, 154
Helwig, Ludwig N. 67, 70, 430
Hemmingsen, Niels 32, 53, 244, 424
Henke, Ernst Ludwig Th. 68, 242, 430
Heppe, Heinrich 70, 403, 430
Heresy 34-35, 67, 148
and latitudinarianism of unionism 409
Heritage 15; *see also* Legacy
Hermann, Rudolf 388, 430
Hermas 94
Hermelink, Heinrich 430
Hermeneutics 21, 86, 312, 315-17, 351, 389, 413
fundamental rule of 321-25, 329
and inerrancy 358-61
and *media hermeneutica* 329-30
Herod the Great 103, 321
Herzog, J. J. 70, 238, 383
Hesiod 417
Hesse 50
Hessen Cassel 52
Heussi, Karl 70-71, 430
Heterodoxy 29
Hezekiah 304
High orthodoxy 45
Highest good 83, 110
Hilary 35
Hirsch, Emanuel 22, 25, 430
Historians 19-21, 23
Historical development 27
Historicocritical method 190-91, 297, 338, 356, 407
Historiography 21
History 15, 17, 20, 76, 98, 105-6, 108, 222, 279, 335, 354, 356
of canon 305
of Lutheranism 15, 19
in Scripture 189, 345-46, 356-57
study of 225-26
History of doctrine 93, 98
Hobbes, Thomas 233

Hodomoria Spiritus Calviniani (Dannhauer) 58
Hodosophia Christiana sive Theologia Positiva (Dannhauer) 59, 242, 251, 379-84, 395-96, 399-401, 423
Hoenecke, Adolph 17, 19, 22, 25, 61, 71, 109, 238, 382, 384, 406, 430
Hoepfner, Henry 57, 66, 387, 424
Hoffmann, Daniel 129-30, 132, 240, 424
Hoffmann, Gottfried 230, 248-49, 252, 389, 424
Hoffmann, Johann Wilhelm 430
Hohmeier, Friedebert 383
Holiness 210
Holaz, David 44-45, 52, 65, 134-39, 146-49, 151, 153-54, 158, 174, 227-29, 232, 238, 240-42, 246-47, 249, 251-52, 278-79, 282, 284-85, 288, 300-301, 303, 329-30, 364, 369, 372, 376, 381-83, 385-86, 390-93, 395, 397-98, 401-3, 405-6, 424
Holy Spirit
and authors of Scripture 286-92
and *corpus doctrinae* 88, 91
enlightenment of 121, 219-20, 229, 275, 319, 349, 390, 406, 408
freedom of, in arrangement of chronology 359
guidance and impulse of 82-84, 86
guidance of, for interpretation of Scripture 319-21

inner witness of 302-3, 411
inspiration as afflatus of 99, 275
and interpretation 224, 319-21
language of 95-96
sin against 150
and study of theology 105, 223-24
theologian made by 86
united with Word 302, 374-78
and writers 287-90
Homiletics 141
Horneius, Conrad 38
Hornig, Gottfried 394, 413, 430
Hornig, Wilhelm 71, 430
Hosius, Stanislaus 48
Hospinian, Rudolf 51
Hove, Elling 19, 22, 25, 384, 430
Huber, Curtis E. 392
Huelsemann, John 57, 59, 63, 66-67, 147, 149, 158, 226, 228, 274, 285, 302, 380-81, 385, 401, 424
Humanism 81-82, 129, 154
Humility 23
Hunnius, Giles (Aegidius) 34, 44, 50-51, 55-56, 66-67, 103, 238, 241 to 242, 263, 305, 337, 379-80, 382-83, 386-88, 391, 395, 398, 425
Hunnius, Nicholas 56, 143-52, 241-42, 251, 380, 412, 425
Hutter, Leonard 16, 18, 32, 37-38, 51-52, 56, 66-68, 109, 145, 242, 274, 287, 305, 309, 376, 378, 380-81, 385, 390-91, 395, 400, 403, 425
Hymns 29, 50
Hyperius, Andrew 61, 82-88, 92, 107, 121, 140-42, 222, 236, 255, 316, 389, 425

Hypocrisy 30
Hypostatic union 113
Hypostatic Word 269-70, 373
Hypotyposis 94, 105, 163

"Inadequacy of the Inspiration Doctrine, The" (Elert) 292
Indifference to doctrine 232, 413
Inductive method 46; see also Analytic method
Inerrancy 188-91, 256, 316, 394-95, 397, 412-13
 basis of 341-43
 concern behind doctrine of 361-62
 footnote on related terminology 394-95
 full 346-47, 355
 and hermeneutics (adjuncts) 358-61
 Lutheran position stand relative to 340-41
 nature and meaning of 343-46
 preoccupation with doctrine of 347-49
Infallibility of Scripture 189-90, 347
 apparent contradictions in Scripture 349-53
 apparent errors of fact 354-57
 background for new stress on 347-49
Inference 151-52, 260, 336, 341-42, 410
Infidelity 29
Innate ideas 175-78
Insight 27, 301
Inspiration 275, 412
 as adjunct to divine origin of Scripture 273-74
 as afflatus of Holy Spirit 99, 275
 attacks on 291-92, 340
 of Confessions 38, 68
 general definition of 275-76
 and inerrancy 342

as infused theology 180
 and insignificant matters 278-79, 347
 mechanical 292, 383-84
 monergistic doctrine of 287-88, 292
 objections to 284-86
 paradox of 290-91
 plenary 278-81, 381
 psychological theory of 286-87, 292, 383
 and revelation 191, 292 to 295
 as teaching of Scripture 282-84
 verbal 281-86
 of words and content 278-81, 284
Institutiones 94
Institutiones Christianae Religiones (Selnekker) 50
Intellect 79, 136
 active and passive 236
 aptitude of 229
 blindness of 406
 enlightenment of 230-31
 sacrifice of 298, 320-21
Intellectualism 20, 227
Interpretation 42, 82, 86, 103-4, 314-39, 389
 and alert exegetes 317-19
 and fundamental rule 321-25
 and hermeneutical aids 329-30
 and Holy Spirit's guidance 319-21
 and legitimacy of consequences 335-37
 and literal meaning 321-25
 of Old Testament by New 333-35
 "*Scriptura est suipsius interpres*" 329-30
 "*Sensus literalis unus est*" 325
 typological 326-29
 and unity of Scripture 331-33
Intolerance 40

INDEX

Invective 35
Invincibility 211
Irenaeus 94
Isagoge 94
Isagoges Theologicae (Calov) 61, 159, 184, 191, 204, 216, 246-47, 250-51, 413, 422
Isaiah 93
Issues 21-22, 27-28, 43, 234-35, 405-6

Jacobs, Henry E. 24, 433
Jena 50-53, 56-57, 59-60, 63-66
Jeremiah 352, 398
Jericho 352-53, 398
Jeroboam 103
Jerome 76, 106, 387
Jesuits 29, 47, 274, 278, 280-81, 298, 307-8, 311, 383, 411
Jews 306, 333-34, 366
Joecher, C. G. 69-71, 430
John the Baptist 91, 93, 327, 359
John of Damascus 35, 87, 94-95, 109
Johnson, Gisle 22, 25, 430
Jonah 325
Josiah 304
Judaism 208-9
Judex, Matthew 69, 88-89, 96, 237, 427
Judgments, negative 20
Julian 103
Juller, H. 47
Junius, Francis 114, 144, 166, 168-70, 238, 241, 245, 425
Justification 34, 95-98, 124, 149, 330, 410, 412

Kategesis 94
Keckermann, Bartholomew 114, 134, 159, 175, 206, 249-50, 378, 380, 391, 425
Kenotic Controversy 32
Kepler, Johannes 21, 399
Kierkegaard, Sören 35, 189, 191
Kingo, Thomas 29
Kirkehistoriske Samlinger 431
Klose, Gerhard 388, 429
Knowledge 83, 110-11, 202, 233-34
  and faith 199
  and practice 194
  threefold, in Christ 170
Koehneke, Paul F. 68, 393, 433
Koelling, Wilhelm 384, 397, 431
Koenig, John Friedrich 16, 57, 63, 134, 246, 425
Koerner, Josef 431
Königsberg 47, 60, 61
Kornerup, Björn S. 67, 70, 431
Krabbe, Otto 431
Kraft, Friedrich Wilhelm 431
Kramer, Fred 23
Kraus, Hans-Joachim 394, 431
Kriewaldt, E. 69
Kromayer, Jerome 59, 66-67, 147, 158, 241, 385-86, 425
Kunze, Johannes 61

Lactantius, L. Caecilius Firmianus 163
Lacunae
  in articles of faith 138-39, 291
  in Scripture 309, 330
Language 15, 59, 79, 84, 95-96, 106, 136, 317-18
  about God 74, 109, 162, 191, 407
  of God 109, 407
  of Holy Spirit 95-96
Languages 162
  oriental 61-62
  study of 76, 84, 122, 222
Lapsed 229
Later dogmaticians 145-46,
274, 302, 305, 317, 337, 376
Latermann, John 38
Latin 76
Law 79, 146, 176, 178-79, 294-95, 364
Law and Gospel 30, 42, 90, 95, 97-98, 100, 185-86, 205, 224, 226, 247, 261, 272, 294, 331, 358, 399, 407, 417
  dividing of 364-65, 400-401
Lawton, John Stewart 252, 431
Layman 143, 315
Leaders, theological 15, 18
Legacy 15, 27-28, 377
  of Calixt 154-55
Leibniz, Gottfried Wilhelm von 189, 233, 357
Leipzig 50-51, 56-57, 59, 64-66
Leitch, James W. 393, 428
LeLong, J. 431
Lessing, Gotthold E. 189, 235, 247, 357, 431
Leube, Hans 70-71, 242, 431
Levicula 279, 347
Levita, Elias 307-9
Lewalter, Ernst 431
Lewis, Conrad 431
Leyser, Polycarp 48-49, 63, 66, 90-93, 337, 353, 387, 390, 423
Liberal arts 29, 84, 133, 415
Liberal spirit 65, 348
Life 20, 27, 29, 46
  doctrine and 194
  faith and 203, 309, 312
  theology and 163-64, 200, 204-5, 216-17
Lindau 62
Linguistics 21
Literal sense 227, 321-25, 392
Literature 19-20, 22-23
Littell, Franklin H. 69
Livy 356

Loci communes 86, 94
Loci Communes (Melanchthon) 32, 45, 48, 75, 77-79, 87, 90, 92, 96, 142, 236-37
Loci Communes Theologici (Hutter) 32, 51, 378, 381-82, 385, 390, 392, 400, 403, 425
Loci method 43, 45, 75, 77, 86, 89-90, 93, 96-98, 248
Loci Praecipui Theologici (Melanchthon) 77, 81, 93, 174, 236-37, 414
Loci theologici 46, 53, 77, 90, 92, 96-98, 104-5, 107-8, 141, 221, 238
Loci Theologici (Chemnitz) 32, 43, 48-49, 62, 69-90, 92-98, 237, 248, 384, 393, 401, 423
Loci Theologici (Gerhard) 35, 43, 53-54, 70, 109, 126, 237-39, 242, 245, 250-51, 378-82, 384-91, 398, 400-403, 412, 424
Loci Theologici (Hafenreffer) 108, 379, 386, 424
Locke, John 45, 177, 233-34
Locus 34-35, 43, 45-46, 86, 96-97
Loesche, Georg 104
Loescher, Valentin 30, 44, 233-36, 397, 405, 431
Logic 85, 122-23, 125, 130, 132, 135, 162, 222
Lohse, Bernhard 69, 240, 431
Lombard, Peter 87, 170, 400, 425
Lord's Supper 48, 131, 262, 318-19, 322, 337, 391-92
Loyalty

to Christ and His Word 29
confessional 18, 31-32, 36
Luetkemann, Joachim 47
Luke 292, 383
Lund, Gene J. 24, 429
Luthardt, Christoph Ernst 25, 383, 431
Luther, Martin 17, 20-22, 27-28, 30-31, 34-35, 37, 40-42, 47, 49, 51-54, 58, 63, 66, 68-69, 73, 75, 80-83, 92, 95-96, 103-8, 112, 117, 121, 125, 127-31, 135-43, 154-55, 157, 174, 176-77, 194, 202, 204-5, 212, 214, 219, 222, 226, 235-36, 239-40, 243, 246-48, 251, 256, 261, 270, 302, 308, 311, 318, 331, 337, 339-40, 347, 363, 369-70, 374, 377-80, 385, 388, 391, 393, 397, 402-3, 406, 411, 413
Luther Seminary, St. Paul, Minn. 22
Lutheran Brotherhood Insurance Company of Minneapolis 23
Lutheranism 15, 18-19, 22, 27, 274
  and Christendom 214-15
  history of 15, 19
  theology of 15
  truncated 40
Lutherans 15, 21-22, 27, 29
Lyra; *see* Nicholas of Lyra

Maccovius (Makowsky), John 361
Magdeburg 47
Major, George 412, 425
Man 79, 261; *see also* Anthropology
  as object of theology 197

Mandatum scribendi 277-78
Manichaeus 418
Manuale Confessiones Augustanae (Huelsemann) 57, 67, 425
Marburg 50, 52, 56-57, 61
Marcion 418
Marks
  of theologian 121
  of true religion 209-11
Martini, Cornelius 55, 129, 152, 154-55, 425
Martini, Jacob 57, 63, 196, 240, 242
Mary 119, 312, 373
Massoreth Ha-Massoreth (Reuchlin) 307
Materia 117, 130, 267-68, 282, 370, 390
Material and formal principle 270-71
  correlation of 331, 410-11
Material principle 20, 270-71, 331
Mathematics 122, 131, 137, 222, 236, 354, 398
Mechanical inspiration 292, 383-84
Meditatio 221
Meisner, Balthasar 55, 57, 66, 130, 133-34, 166, 201, 245, 249-50, 378, 391, 425
Melanchthon 19, 32, 45, 47-48, 50, 68-69, 74-90, 92-93, 95-96, 100, 103-7, 118, 129, 142-43, 156-57, 160, 174-76, 179, 210, 236-37, 243-44, 246, 394-95, 405, 414
Melanchthonianism 48
Mentzer, Balthasar 51-52, 55, 57, 65, 67, 70, 251, 378, 392, 395-96
Metaphysics 85, 122, 129-30, 135, 161, 233, 236

INDEX 449

Metaphysics (Aristotle) 109, 112, 163, 236, 239, 247-48, 250
Method 32, 69, 77, 81, 89, 105, 160-62, 244, 415
  analytic 43, 46, 97, 143, 156, 198, 243, 248
  of Chemnitz 96-98
  of Gerhard 140-42
  in philosophy 415
  synthetic 45-46, 156, 198, 248
Methodology 15, 41, 69, 98, 244
  three tools for 161
Methodus Studii Theologici (Gerhard) 120-28, 140-42, 239, 424
Meyer, Hans 248, 431
Michelangelo 62
Middle Ages 75, 152
Migne, J.-P. 238, 393
Minneapolis, Minn. 23
Miracles 86, 99, 101, 186, 226, 295, 301
Mistakes 17
Mixed articles 123, 152-54, 188
Modern critical historicism 190-91, 297
Modern and novel dogmaticians 19
Modern Biblical theology 17
Modern concerns 21
Modern (dialectical) theology 18, 264, 408
Modern scholars 21
Moldaenke, Günter 412, 431
Monergistic doctrine of inspiration 287-88, 292
Monographs 23, 316, 398
Moon 358-59
Montgomery, John Warwick 23, 25, 70, 413, 431
Morality 102-3
Moritz of Hessen Cassel 52
Moser, Johann Jacob 432
Moses 91, 93, 99, 116, 220, 276, 278, 304, 356
Movius, Caspar 368, 372
Mueller, John Theodore 25, 69, 242, 432
Musaeus, John 64, 66, 74, 158, 227, 242, 250-51, 425
Myslenta, Cölestin 60
Mysteries of faith 120, 123-25, 127-28, 138, 219, 278, 295, 312, 397
Mysterium Syncretismi Detecti, Proscripti, et Symphonismo Compensati (Dannhauer) 59, 423
Mysticism 231-32
Mystics 136, 273

Naaman 261
Nachrichten von einer Hallischen Bibliothek 432
Nathan 101
Natural law 100
Natural phenomena 85, 106, 132, 134, 237
Natural theology 86, 113, 152-53, 156, 164-66, 173-80, 187, 257
  extent of 174
  and purpose of revelation 187
  value of, for Christian 179-80
Nature 84-85, 346, 348, 354, 397
Necessity 161, 210
  as mark of true religion 210
  for Scripture 272-73
  for theological study 216-17
Neo-Aristotelianism 130-31
Nero 103
Neumann, John George 228-33, 251-52, 426
Neumark, George 29
Neveux, J. B. 71, 432
New approach 28, 98, 107 to 143, 405
to Scripture 44, 89, 92, 129
New doctrines 28
New Testament 76
  and interpretation of Old Testament 333-35
Nicholas of Lyra 106, 308
Nicolai, Henry 399
Nicolai, Philipp 29
Nicolau, Michaele 432
Nitzsch, Friedrich A. 68, 387, 432
Noah 150
Nonfundamental articles 149-52
Norm 90, 92, 94, 105, 116-17, 245, 257, 303-4, 407
Norma 92
Norma normans 38
Norma normata 38
Normative authority 257-58, 268, 296, 303, 363, 385, 411
Norvin, William 432
Norway 24, 32, 53-54
Notatio de Studio Sacrae Theologiae (Selnekker) 241, 251, 255, 378, 380, 385-86, 391, 426
Notiones communes 233-34
Notitia 78, 110-11, 165, 201, 229, 231, 234, 252
Nuda scriptura 42

Objectivity 18
Obscurantism 21, 356, 407
Obscure authors 18
Obscure passages 312-13, 315, 389
Oettingen, Alexander von 382
Old Lutherans 21-22, 29-31, 34, 44, 263, 316, 405
Old Testament 257-58, 283, 306, 328, 332
  New Testament interpretation of 333-35

place of, in religion 212-14
Olearius, John 29, 383, 389, 426
Omniscience of Christ 171 to 172, 246
Omnipotence of God 125
Ong, Walter J. 244, 432
Opera (Chytraeus) 99-107, 238, 316, 337, 423
Opera Latina (Mentzer) 52, 67, 70, 395-96
Opinions 15, 19-21
Oratio, meditatio, tentatio 107-8, 121, 155, 198, 206, 219, 226
Order 45-46, 77, 81, 87, 89, 95, 224, 237, 415
Ordo salutis 56, 65
Organic function of philosophy 122, 124, 135
Oriental languages 61-62
Origen 94, 324
Origin of prolegomena 19, 75
Original theology 167-73
Orthodoxy 27, 29, 235, 406
  best side of 16, 18
  champions of 44-65
  characteristics of 31-44
  decline of 228-35
  evangelical 18, 29
  evil in 20
  faith and 409
  and fundamentalism 21
  influence of 15
  Luther and 40-42, 68-69
  periods of 45-47
  representatives of 18
  repudiation of 406
  seats of 65-66
  unpopularity of 408
Osiander, John Adam 41, 66, 134, 227, 246, 248-49, 301-2, 318, 374-75, 382, 385, 388, 390, 393, 395, 401, 426
Osiander, Andrew 271
Osiander, Lukas 56, 432

Oslo Universitetsbibliotek 24
Ostfriesland 57
Outline 19, 87, 122, 140, 156-57, 241, 243

Padua 53
Paedagogia Christiana (Selnecker) 50, 399-400, 426
Paedia 216
Panzer, G. W. 434
Papacy 55, 259, 315
Paradox of inspiration 290-91
Paraphrasing 17, 51, 224
Pareus, David 145, 248, 426
Parther, Andreas 70
Parther, Friedrich 70
Passive function of theology 76, 235
Pastoral concern 65
Patrology 23, 36, 82, 92
Peri Archon (Origen) 94
Periods of Lutheran orthodoxy 44-47
Perriraz, Louis 413, 432
Personal union 49, 67, 113, 167-69, 205
Petersen, Peter 236, 240, 432
Pfeiffer, August 328, 348, 387, 389-91, 398-99, 426
Pharaoh 367, 400
Pharisees 230-31, 320
Philippi, Friedrich A. 17, 22, 25, 384, 406, 432
Philippists 47, 51
Philo of Alexandria 292, 327
Philology 95-96
Philosophia sobria 134
Philosophia Sobria (Meisner) 55, 245, 249-50, 378, 391, 425
Philosophic terminology 45, 53-54, 95, 114-15, 122-23, 126, 128-29, 133, 159
Philosophy 41, 45, 55, 69, 72, 74-77, 79-81, 84 to 85, 88, 94-95, 106, 117-20, 128-34, 200, 235-36, 415
  in the abstract 128, 166
  abuses of 124-25
  catasceuastic function of 123-24
  in the concrete 128-29
  Calov's arguments for 131-34
  conflict over 129-30
  and faith 131, 136
  Gerhard's synthesis of 130-31
  Hollaz on 134-40
  Luther's views on 129
  organic function of 122, 124, 135
  outline of 122
  in polemics 126
  uses of 122-25
Physica et Ethica Mosaica (Aslakssen) 54
Physics 85, 106, 122-23, 130, 161, 233, 236, 279
Pia Desideria (Spener) 47
Pieper, Franz 17, 19, 22, 25, 196, 242, 248, 384, 406, 432
Piepkorn, Arthur C. 69
Pietism 44, 64-65, 140, 227, 232, 235, 252, 412
Pietists 64, 194, 228-32
Piety 29, 46, 53, 56, 81, 121, 200
  engendered by Gospel 81
  formed and incited by theology 29, 81
  in isolation from Gospel 29
Pighius, Albert 318
Planck, Gottlieb J. 20, 24, 432
Platform, doctrinal 30
Plato 77-79, 100, 109, 163, 174, 176, 233
Plenary inerrancy 346-47
Plenary inspiration 278-81
Plutarch 356

INDEX

Polanus, Amandus 114, 238, 246, 426
Polemics 16, 33-35, 45, 51-52, 57-58, 64, 337, 409
  art of 141
  from evangelical concern 52
  as kind of dialog 37
  as occasional blast 51
  use of philosophy in 126
Politics 86, 106, 122, 279
Polybius 105
Pomerania 65
Pope 258-60, 277, 321
Post-Reformation task 28
Posture of theologian 216 to 226
Power
  of God 125
  of Gospel 363-67, 408-9, 411
  as mark of true religion 211
  of Scripture 42, 362-78, 411
  of Word 266-71, 367-78
Practical and theoretical 198-201, 249
Practical application 54-55, 204-5
Practical nature of theology 196-206, 227, 229, 248
Practice of faith 194, 198 to 200, 250
Praecipui loci 90
Praenotiones Theologicae (Neumann) 233
Prayer 83, 86, 105, 121, 140, 219-21, 317, 407
Preknowledge needed by theologian 216-19
Prenter, Regin 25, 383, 432
Presupposition(s) 36, 73, 75, 81, 87, 158, 316
  Scripture as 116
Preus, Herman A. 25, 432
Preus, J. A. O. 23, 25, 67, 70, 237, 386, 423

Preus, Robert D. 68, 378, 382-83, 387, 412-13, 432
Preuschen, E. 52
Preuss, Edward 69
Primary fundamental articles 148-49
"Primary and fundamental points" 97
Primary sources 19, 23, 421
Principia 85, 87, 94, 116, 237, 239
Principiata 116
Principium 116, 123, 155
  Scripture as 116, 239, 258, 305
Principium cognoscendi 257-58, 310-11, 363
Principium essendi 258, 407
Principium operandi 363
Principles 73-75, 81, 415
Prolegomena 19, 73, 75, 84, 88, 107, 116, 255, 316, 405
  background to 73
  Calov's 158, 226
  changes in 107-43
  and Christology 167, 171
  discussions of 61
  18th-century thought on 228-35
  first 81
  first formal 142
  of Hoenecke 238
  origin and development of 19, 72-73, 75, 81, 87-88, 98, 107, 142, 158
  questions of 74
  among Reformed 114
  theological, of Chytraeus 98
Propaedeutics 122-28, 158
Prophecy and fulfillment 102, 328-29, 334
Prophets 93, 332
Propositiones 79
Propositions 79
Prudence 206
Psychology 21, 65, 227
Ptolemaic theory 359

Pure articles 123, 152-54
Purity of doctrine 29-30, 60, 97-98, 231, 272-73
  attainability of 409
Purpose
  of revelation 75, 186-88, 190
  of Scripture 75, 83, 192, 309-10, 331
  singleness of 29
  soteriological 186-88, 295
  of studying history 225 to 226
  of theologian's work 218-26

Quakers 136, 227, 273, 377
Qualification of theologian 216-226
Quasi-Lutherans 19
Quatenus 39
Quedlinburg 52
Quenstedt, John Andrew 18, 20, 22, 31-32, 35, 46, 52, 57, 62-63, 65-66, 74, 134, 146-50, 153, 158, 172, 174, 176, 200, 209, 212-13, 226-28, 238-42, 244-46, 248-51, 256, 258, 260, 268, 275-76, 278, 280-81, 283, 285, 287-89, 292-93, 312, 328-29, 332, 340-42, 346-47, 354, 365, 367, 369-70, 372, 374-75, 378-91, 393-96, 398-403, 412-13, 426
Questions in theology 123
Quia 39
Quistorp, Johann 60

Rahab 400
Ramus, Peter 248, 426
Rathmann, Hermann 271, 367-70, 374, 376, 403
Ratio magisterialis 261
Ratio recta 118, 384-85
*Ratio seu Methodus Com-

pendio Peruentendi ad Ueram Theologiam 75
Rationale 27, 406
Rationalism 20-21, 130, 140, 157, 234-35, 244, 303
Ratisbon 151
Ratschow, Carl Heinz 22, 24-25, 432
Reading 18, 20-22, 40, 46, 86-87
  of church fathers 92-93
  critically 36
  cursory 222-23
  of Scripture 82, 86, 105, 140-41, 221-23, 315, 351
Reason 41, 44, 72, 74-75, 80, 84, 95, 118-19, 125-28, 235-36, 239, 261-63, 298, 320, 378
  as gift of God 135
  Hollaz on theology and 134-40
  ignorance of 125
  and mixed articles 152-53
  as proof for doctrine 124
Reasoning 16, 79, 84, 124, 262, 298, 384-85
  a posteriori 126-27
Reformation 20, 27
  evangelical impact of 28
Reformed 21, 27, 52, 55-56, 58, 63, 114, 131, 144, 166, 172, 194, 199, 201-2, 247, 249, 307-8, 337, 361, 370, 372
Refutation of error 126, 234
Regula 90, 92-93, 94
Regula Fidei 94, 272
Rehtmeyer, Philipp Julius 69
Reid, John K. S. 384, 432
Relevance 16-19, 24, 35, 74
  of historical and geographical matters 188-89

Religion 74, 207-15
  definition of 192, 208-9
  false 209
  Lutheranism and Christendom 214-15
  marks of 209-11
  place of Old Testament in 212-14
  salvation without Christ? 211-12
Requisites for becoming a theologian 82, 84, 198, 218-22
  affliction 106-7, 142, 221-22
  prayer 83, 86, 105, 121, 140, 219-21, 317, 407
  study 221-26, 314-15
Resen, Hans Poulsen 53-54, 384, 396, 426
Reu, Michael 384, 397, 433
Reuchlin, Johannes 307
Revealed theology 180-91
  existence of 181-82
  goal of 191-94
Revelation 74-75, 110, 115-17, 152-54, 180, 416
  author of 186-87
  content of 83, 185, 188 to 191, 247
  by deed 295
  definition of 246
  and inerrancy 188, 190
  and inspiration 191, 292-95
  as *locus* 294
  and natural theology 187
  and nature of theology 196
  object of 185-86
  purpose of 75, 186-88, 190
  and saving faith 410
  and Scripture 115-17, 188-89, 191
  soteriological purpose of 186-89, 295
  as source of theology 182-83, 196, 245, 247, 257

  subject of 183-85
  criteria for judging of 186-87
Revival of interest 22
Richard of St. Victor 175
Richardson, Alan 25, 433
Ritschl, Otto 20, 25, 66, 70, 71, 236, 242-43, 375, 387, 403, 412, 433
Rhetoric 77, 105-6, 122-23, 130, 135
Rigid conservatism 27
Roman Catholics 21, 23, 27, 30, 32-33, 36-38, 40, 48, 55-58, 63-64, 159, 169, 173, 194, 199, 202, 204, 258-59, 266, 273, 277, 299-300, 304, 306-8, 311, 314-15, 325, 383, 399
Robson, George 24, 238, 383, 428
Roertschel, Wolfgang Gotlob 236
Rohnert, Wilhelm 384, 433
Romanism 21, 45, 349
Romanists 29, 37, 46
Rome 33, 305
Rördam, Holger Frederik 433
Rostock 53, 57, 63
Rothe, Richard 383, 433
Rule of faith 38, 94, 272
Rule(s)
  for interpreting Scripture 321-25, 337-39, 358-61
  for reading Scripture 86, 105, 140-41, 351
  for study of theology 104-7
Runia, Klaus 403, 433

Sagittarius, J. Christfried 240
Saint Louis, Mo. 22-24
Saint Paul, Minn. 22
Saintes, Amand 413, 433
Salaverri, Ioachim 432
Salvation of man 186-88, 191, 211-12

INDEX

Samson 150
Samuel 278
Sanctification 217
Sarah 85, 262
Sasse, Hermann 412
Satan 222, 377, 419
Scandinavian 54, 244
Schenke, Friedrich 70
Scherzer, John Adam 64, 66, 158, 226, 249, 347, 378, 381, 386, 388, 393-94, 426
Schian, Martin 252, 433
Schlee, Ernst 240, 433
Schlink, Edmund 42, 68-69, 393, 433
Schlüsselburg, Conrad 433
Schmalz, Valentin 324
Schmid, Heinrich 16-17, 22, 24-25, 242, 413, 433
Schmid, Johann 66, 394
Schmidt, Sebastian 44, 61, 66-67, 337, 380, 394, 401, 426
Scholarly prerequisites 222
Scholastic argumentation 16, 124
Scholastic formulations 134, 140
Scholastic theology 23, 36, 73, 75, 87, 94-95, 114, 142, 155, 194, 235, 237
Scholasticism 36, 41, 69, 140, 227, 237, 409
Scholastics 23, 36, 108, 124, 161, 170-72, 186, 201, 237, 347
Scholder, Klaus 385, 399, 433
Schroeder, John 248, 387, 426
Schüssler, Hermann 242-43, 433
Schütz, Ludwig 248, 433
Schweitzer, Wolfgang 25, 433
Schweizer, Alexander 433
Science 54, 66, 80, 110-12, 132, 161, 249, 348, 356-57
  and the arts 29, 133, 415

and faith 203-4
and *habitus practicus* 202-4, 250
Sciencia 78, 83, 110-11, 134, 181, 226
Scientific finds 85
"Scientific" theologian 44, 121
Scotus, John Duns 75, 114, 126, 159, 201, 249, 397, 426
Scriptura est suipsius interpres 323, 329-30
Scriptura per scripturam explicanda 330
Scripture
  attributes of 116, 255-56, 296
  authority of 116, 257-58, 268, 296-309, 385, 411
  causative authority of 257, 268, 301, 411
  clarity of 311-15
  and Confessions 37-39
  as dead letter 271, 331, 367
  as *Deus loquens* 265-66
  divine origin of 99, 263-65, 273-77, 296, 385, 408-9, 412
  as doctrine 390
  doctrine of 19, 21, 254 to 378
  efficacy of 42, 362-78, 411
  external criteria of 300-301
  as first *locus* 86
  gaps in 309, 330
  as God's voice today 263, 265-67
  as God's Word 99, 263 to 268, 287, 412
  infallibility of 189-90, 347-57
  and inner witness of Holy Spirit 302-3, 411
  internal criteria of 300-301
  as letter from God 263, 265-66
  necessity for 272-73

normative authority of 257-58, 268, 303, 385, 411
  as *principium* 116, 239, 258, 296, 305
  as prolegomenon 116, 255
  purpose and goal of 75, 83, 192, 309-10, 331
  and revelation 188-89, 191
  reverence for 83
  return to 95
  as sacred codex 411
  study of 161, 221-26, 314-15
  sufficiency of 309-11
  truthfulness of 339-62, 395, 412
  unity of Word of 268-72
  usefulness of 272-73, 311
  verbal inspiration taught by 282-84
  writing of, by divine command 277-78
Scripture passages 17, 42
Scriver, Christian 29
Seckendorf, Veit Ludwig von 225
Secondary fundamental articles 149
Secondary sources 22, 38, 427
Sedes doctrinae 35, 44, 46, 49
Seeland 54
Selectivity 18, 43-44, 96
Self-authenticating 38-39, 101-2, 155-56, 191, 301-2
Self-disclosure of God 99
Selnecker, Nikolaus 28-29, 48-50, 67, 141-42, 225-26, 241, 255-56, 272, 340, 378, 385-86, 391, 399-400, 426
Semi-Aristotelianism 132
Semler, Johann Salomon 244, 338, 356, 393, 407, 413
Sennacherib 103

Sense of sin 107
Sensus literalis unus est 325-26, 329
Septuagint 318
Sermon 29, 372
Sheridan, Thomas J. 247, 434
Silver age 45, 59, 64, 158, 207
Simplicity 149
Sin against Holy Spirit 150
Sincerus, Theoph. 433
Sitz im Leben 335
Skepticism 189, 299
Small Catechism 92, 225
Socinianism 21, 143-44, 158, 239, 297-99, 347, 355-56, 384-85, 408
Socinians 21, 37, 40, 55, 64, 140, 151, 177, 179, 189-90, 246, 274, 298-99, 323-26, 333, 335-36, 346-50, 354-55, 397, 407, 409
Sociology 21
Sola fide 410-11
Sola Scriptura 38, 116, 155, 161, 239, 256, 272, 310, 405
 and Biblical interpretation 260-61
 and inspiration 274
 meaning of 257
 principle of 256, 258-60, 262, 268, 271, 296, 304, 331, 338, 378, 410-11
"*Soli Deo gloria*" 406-8
Solomon 334
Solus Christus 405, 410-11
Son of God 78, 168, 193, 294-95
Sorbonne 127, 129-30
Soteriological purpose 186 to 188, 218, 295
Soteriology 43, 56
Source
 of articles of faith 164
 formal 19
 primary 19, 23, 421
 secondary 22, 38, 427

of theology 16-17, 19, 75, 99, 115-16, 120, 182-83, 196, 198, 245, 247, 256-61, 264, 407, 410
Smits, Edmund 25, 28, 432
Socinus, Faustus 190, 241, 246-47, 251, 281, 334, 347, 355-56, 381, 384, 390, 393, 396, 398-99, 426
Sohn, George 109, 238, 426
Speech 79, 84, 95-96
Spener, Philipp Jacob 47, 58, 61, 243
Spinoza, Baruch 44-45, 233
Spirit 17, 20, 27, 29-30, 40, 405-6
Spiritus Sancti sententia 223-24
Springfield, Ill. 23-24
Stapleton, Thomas 315, 388, 427
Statement of belief 30
Stengel, Johann 434
Stoeffler, F. Ernest 434
Strasbourg 31, 51, 55-58, 62, 65, 370, 394
Strohl, Henri 394, 434
Stub, Ivar 53
Student(s) 24, 121
Studium didacticum 222
Study
 of history 225-26
 of languages 76, 84, 122, 222
 of Scripture 161, 221-26, 314-15
 of theology 104-7, 140-42, 216-17
Stuttgart 50-51, 66
Stylistic differences 284, 288-89, 317
Suarez, Francis 388, 395, 427
Subjective faith 145
Substance 78, 161
Sufficiency of Scripture 309-11
Summa 75-77, 90, 93-94, 105, 237

new emphasis on 92
Summa Theologica (Thomas) 32, 237-39, 246-47, 249-50, 397
Summation 90, 93-94, 96, 98, 104-5
Summing up 405-11
Swabia 47
Swabians 50
Sweden 31-32, 51, 62
Syllogism 136-37, 151-52, 242
Sylvius, Francis 239, 249, 427
Symbolum 94
Symbol(s) 94, 105, 260; *see also* Confessions
 authority of 38-39
Sympathetic 15, 17-18, 20
Synave, Paul 247, 434
Syncretism 59, 64, 409, 413
Syncretistic Controversy 31, 60
Syncretists 38-39, 58, 64, 68, 154, 232, 413
 Lutheran 19, 38, 57-58
Synergism 64, 81-82, 227, 236, 407
Synergistic tendencies 64-65
Synopsis Theologiae Zacharianae (Dorsch) 57, 384, 423
Synoptic problem 318, 362
Syntagma seu Corpus Doctrinae Veri et Omnipotentis Dei (Wigand and Judex) 69, 88-90, 96, 237, 427
Synthesis of Gerhard 130-31
Synthetic method 45-46, 156, 198, 248
Systema 35, 46, 222
Systema Locorum Theologicorum (Calov) 61, 68, 179, 184, 191, 193, 204, 214, 241-42, 244-45, 247-48, 250-51, 266, 378-79, 381, 384-88,

INDEX

392, 393, 397, 399-403, 422
Systema Theologiae (Scherzer) 64, 249, 378, 381, 386, 388, 394, 426
Systema Theologicum (Hebenstreit) 251, 413, 424
Systema Theologicum seu Theologia Positiva Acroamatica (Osiander) 246, 248, 251, 382, 388, 393, 395, 401-2, 413, 426
Systematic theologians 23, 98
Systematic theology 87-88, 92, 229, 234
Systematization 62, 74, 87, 96, 98, 222, 237

Tanner, Adam 151
Taylor, Sophia 24, 238, 383, 428
Tentatio 106-8, 221-22
Terminology 15, 34, 37, 48-49, 94-96, 133, 237
  Aristotelian 45, 53, 114-15, 133, 159
  casual 115
  scholastic 133-34, 140
Tertullian 59, 94, 102, 319
Testimonium Spiritus Sancti internum 302 to 303
Testimony 33, 303
Textbook 37, 46-47, 51, 57, 59, 63, 236
Textualis 105, 235
Theodidaktos 76, 231
Theologia Aphoristica (Neumann) 228, 251, 426
Theologia Conscientiaria (Bechmann) 64
Theologia didactico-polemica 34
Theologia Didactico-Polemica sive Systema Theologiae (Quenstedt) 62-63, 65, 238 to 239, 241-42, 244-46, 248-51, 365, 378 to 391, 393-96, 398-403, 426
Theologia irregenitorum 229-32
Theologia impiorum 231
Theologia Polemica (Bechmann) 64, 249-50, 252, 388, 395, 421
Theologia Positiva Acroamatica (Koenig) 63
Theologia Positivo-Polemica (Krohmayer) 59, 241, 385-86, 425
Theologia unionis 113-14
Theologian(s) 15-18, 21, 23, 44-76, 107, 114, 216-26
  attitude of 30, 73-74, 121, 216
  biography of 47-66, 69
  fashioned by God 107, 183, 206, 407
  goal of 192, 216-17
  made by Holy Spirit 86
  marks of 121
  nature of goal of 216-17
  nature of work of 216-17
  noteworthy 47-66, 69
  preknowledge needed by 216-19
  purpose of work of 218-19
  qualifications and aptitudes of 217-18; *see also* Aptitude
  and *soli Deo gloria* 406-8
  training and posture of 216-26
Theological life 163-64
Theological method 160-62; *see also* Method
Theologins Historia (Hägglund) 19, 240 to 241, 429
Theologizing 40, 74, 82, 216, 407
Theology 15-20, 22, 27, 74, 107, 197-98

as aptitude; *see* Aptitude
definition of 109, 117-18, 159
as doctrine 110-12, 163, 195-96, 248
as faith and observance 164
as gift of God 206, 229, 407
goal of 30, 46, 74, 112, 117, 120, 191-94, 248
God as 172-73
Gospel heart of 74
as *habitus* 30, 112, 114, 162, 165, 195-96
healing nature of 193
language about God 74, 109, 162, 191, 407
language of God 109, 407
Luther's 20
meaning of term 162-67
nature of 74-75, 109, 120, 194-206, 248
object of 74
object (subject matter) of 74, 120, 207
objectives of 75-76
and other activity 120
practical nature of 196-206, 227, 229, 248
purpose of 75, 191, 197
in relation to philosophy 74-75, 77, 80, 85, 88, 90, 118-20, 128-40
rules for study of 104-7
separated from theologian 231-32
source of 75, 99, 115-17, 120, 182-83, 196, 198, 245, 247, 256 to 261, 407, 410
unpopularity of 408
of unregenerate 228-29
Theology of the church 173
Theology of paradise 173
Theophilus 94
Theopneustia 191

Theopneustos 108, 264, 276, 281-83, 297, 311
Theses 16, 20-21
Thirty Years' War 45, 56, 58, 60, 70
Tholuck, August 19-20, 24, 30, 56, 61, 67, 70-71, 383, 434
Thomas Aquinas; *see* Aquinas, Thomas
Th. Aquinas Confessor Veritatis (Dorsch) 36
Thomasius, Gottfried 240, 434
Thomson, G. T. 25, 379, 402, 428
Thumm, Theodor 66
Timothy 223, 282-83
Tools 84, 161, 216
Tractatus Historico-Politicus (Spinoza) 44
Tradition 28, 38, 154, 258-61, 274, 310-11, 314
Training of theologian 216-26
Translations 17, 22-23, 54, 76, 290, 302, 307
Trent 48, 292
Tres Libri Institutionum (Theophilus) 94
Trillhaas, W. 51
Trinity 48, 61, 125-28, 262
  analogies to 239
  and simple people 149
Trinity Evangelical Divinity School, Deerfield, Ill. 23
Troeltsch, Ernst 243, 434
Truisms 16, 337
Trust 78-79
Truth 132, 166, 190, 210, 340-41, 343-46, 395-96
  correspondence idea of 344, 396
  expressly stating of 358
  and God 83, 190
  as mark of true religion 210

objective and subjective 233-34
Truthfulness of Scripture 339-62, 395, 412; *see also* Inerrancy
Tübingen 32, 47, 50-51, 55-56, 65-66
Turrettin, Francis 247, 249, 427
Typological interpretation 326-29

Ubiquity 50
Uhlhorn, Friedrich 434
Una copulativa 138-39, 241
Understanding 79, 111, 202, 349-50
Union 58-59
Unionism 409
Unity
  doctrinal 31-32, 45, 59, 138-39, 144
  of God's Word 268-72, 363-64
  as mark of true religion 210
  of Scripture 268-69, 318, 323, 331-33, 410
  between Spirit and Word of God 302, 370, 374-78
Universae Theologiae Systema (Brochmand) 54, 157, 244, 249, 379, 381, 386, 401-3, 413, 422
Universities 65-66, 129-30
Unregenerate theology 111, 121, 227-31, 250
Ursinus, Zachariah 249, 427
Usefulness of Scripture 272-73, 311
Usus ministerialis 41
Usus practicus of article of faith 30, 204

Variant readings 285, 306, 318
Vasquez, Gabriel 250
Verbal inspiration 281-86

  as teaching of Scripture 282-84
Verbum endiatheton 269
Verbum prophorikon 269, 271
Virgin birth 119
Visitation 58
Vom Gnadenreich Christi (Rathman) 367
Vorgeschichte des Rationalismus 20
Vorst, Conrad 381
Vulgate 306-8

Walaeus, Anthony 169, 245-46, 427
Walch, Johann Georg 158, 235, 380, 434
Wallmann, Johannes 25, 155, 240, 243-44, 434
Walther, Carl F. W. 17-18, 22, 25, 61, 71, 242, 245, 248, 251, 318, 384, 387, 389, 406, 412
Walther, Michael 328-29, 350-53, 386, 388-92, 398, 427
Walther, Wilhelm 397, 434
Weakness in dogmatics 43
Weber, Hans Emil 71, 243, 338, 394, 434
Weigel, Valentin 136
Weismann, Christian E. 69-71, 435
Weller, Jacob 66
Wernsdorf, G. 251, 427
Wigand, John 69, 88-89, 96, 237, 427
Will
  of God 80, 185, 247, 294, 410
  human 41, 79, 236
Winkelmann, Johann 57
Wisdom 83, 109, 112, 167-68, 205, 249
  of Christ 170-71
  and *habitus practicus* 201-2, 249
  through prayer 220

INDEX 457

Witness 78, 100, 295
  Confessions as 38
Wittenberg 20, 31, 47, 50-53, 55-57, 59-63, 65-66, 228, 252
Wolfenbüttel 50
Wolff, Christian 235
Word 281-84; *see also* Word of God
  Christ the content of 373-74
  God author of 287, 371-73
  Holy Spirit united with 302, 370, 374-78
  inherent power of 300, 367-71
  internal and external 162
  origin and basis of power of 371-78
  unity of 268-72, 363-64

Word of God 99, 110, 115, 264, 271, 380
  as doctrine 196
  as event 264-65
  five ways of viewing 380
  as foundation of faith 147-48
  infallibility of 189-90, 347-57
  as inner Word 271
  as origin of Scripture 99, 263-68, 287, 371, 408-9, 412
  and revelation 180, 246
  Scripture as 263-73
  as source of theology 183, 247, 407
Word studies 48
Work of theologian 216-19
World picture, Biblical 54, 66

Wrath 364
Writers of Scripture 273-75, 277, 286-90, 395
Wunderlich, Lorenz 24
Wundt, Max 70-71, 243, 435
Württemberg 50-51
Wyon, Olive 384, 428

Zacchaeus 353
Zanchi, Hieronymus 170
Zeal 29-30, 60
Zechariah 352, 398
Zedler, Johann Heinrich 70-71, 435
Zeitgeist 21
Zeller, Winfred 435
Zoroaster 174
Zwingli, Huldreich 178, 308

SCRIPTURE PASSAGES

Genesis
  Book of — 238, 391
  1 — 102
  1—3 — 54
  1:3 — 379
  1:14 — 358
  3:1 — 269
  3:15 — 210
  10:32 — 388
  17:17 — 146
  18:14 — 125
  22:1 — 413
  28:14 — 329
  48:16 — 215

Exodus
  4:15 — 284
  4:22 — 329
  15:26 — 193
  23:4 — 33
  28:30 — 293
  40:31-32 — 218

Numbers
  21:8-9 — 327
  23:12 — 284

  23:19 — 341
  24:15-16 — 230

Deuteronomy
  1:5 — 93
  4:2 — 310
  6:6 — 136, 223
  17:4 — 345
  18:15 — 215
  18:18 — 291
  18:18-19 — 215
  22:20 — 345
  29:4 — 319
  30:11 — 314
  32:4 — 396

Joshua
  1:8 — 223
  10 — 385
  10:13 — 359

Judges
  9:19 — 346
  17:6 — 90
  21:25 — 90

1 Samuel
  2:21 — 229

2 Samuel
  2:6 — 346
  7:28 — 396
  23:2 — 271, 284

2 Kings
  17:32-33 — 209
  20:19 — 346

2 Chronicles
  5:12-13 — 132
  20:20 — 101

Nehemiah
  9:33 — 346

Job
  12:7 — 178
  28:28 — 109
  32:8 — 275
  38 — 132

Psalms
  1:1 — 221

1:2 — 221
5:2-3 — 220
8:5 — 334
13 — 251
14:3 — 176
18 — 102
19 — 132
19:1 — 132
19:2 ff — 178
19:6-7 — 399
19:7 — 399
19:7-8 — 300, 366
19:8 — 313
25:10 — 346, 396
32:1 — 210
33:4 — 340
40:7-8 — 270
45 — 334
45:6 — 334
57:10 — 346
74:16 — 399
85 — 219
85:11 — 346
86:15 — 346
91:4 — 346
92:2 — 346
100:5 — 346
102:25 — 334
103:22 — 178
104:5 — 399
104:19 — 399
119 — 121, 163, 223, 283
119:2 — 223
119:18 — 319
119:27 — 202
119:43 — 340
119:66 — 202
119:72 — 223
119:86 — 340
119:103 — 223
119:105 — 313
119:125 — 202
119:130 — 202, 217
119:142 — 340
119:160 — 340
148 — 132
150 — 132

Proverbs
1:2 — 202
2:3 — 220
2:4 — 221
3:5 — 128
3:14 — 223
6:23 — 313
8:33-34 — 215
9:10 — 202
30:5-6 — 310

Ecclesiastes
1:4 — 399
12:10 — 215

Isaiah
1:9 — 334
5:13 — 202
7:9 — 101, 111, 298
8:1 — 93
8:20 — 99
9:1 — 350
9:6 — 105
11:2 — 171
28:16 — 211
28:19 — 219, 222
39:8 — 346
40:26 — 132
45:24 — 210
49:8 — 334
51:16 — 99, 284, 289, 291
53:11 — 210
55:8 — 324
56:7 — 413
61:1 — 193
63:9 — 215

Jeremiah
Book of — 352
1:9 — 284, 291
10:10 — 396
23:6 — 178, 210
31:9 — 329
31:31 ff — 181
31:35 — 399
32:7 ff — 352

Hosea
11:1 — 328, 329, 334

Joel
2:28 — 181

Habakkuk
2:2 — 93

Zechariah
1:13 — 215
11:12-13 — 352

Malachi
4:4 — 91, 93

Matthew
Book of — 356, 359, 398
2:13 — 359
2:15 — 328, 334
3:9 — 162
3:10 — 327
3:12 — 327
4:4 — 304
5:17 — 213
5:18 — 395
5:37 — 396
6:6 — 413
6:22 — 121
6:22-23 — 218
7:15 — 211, 216
7:21 — 112
7:22 — 231
9:12 — 193
9:13 — 208
9:21 — 162
10:20 — 283, 291
11:21 — 210
11:25 — 219
11:27 — 115, 173, 178, 209, 319
15:9 — 99
16:17 — 111, 115, 178, 210, 219, 319
16:18 — 211
16:24 — 218
16:28 — 211
18:7 — 161
18:25 — 33
19:4 — 304
20:29-34 — 352
22:29 — 304
22:40 — 273
23:2-3 — 231
23:13 — 208
24:35 — 416
27:9-10 — 352
28:20 — 164

Mark
Book of — 356, 359, 398
9:12 — 304
9:23 — 217
10:46-52 — 352
12:26 — 152, 336

INDEX

12:43 — 350
13:11 — 284

Luke
  Book of — 398
  1:3 — 273, 279, 292
  1:36 ff — 324
  1:37 — 125
  1:70 — 284
  1:77 — 109, 111, 117, 163
  1:80 — 229
  2:28 — 213
  2:32 — 350
  2:52 — 170
  3:19 — 359
  4:18 — 193
  7:30 — 230
  10:26 — 304
  11:13 — 220
  16:19-31 — 324, 325
  16:29 — 259, 272, 332
  16:31 — 99
  18:1 — 220
  18:34-35 — 352
  19:1-27 — 353
  19:29 — 353
  21:15 — 221, 284
  24:27 — 259, 304, 392

John
  1:3 — 270
  1:9 — 346
  1:14 — 130, 239
  1:18 — 293, 295
  2:25 — 171
  3:3 — 211
  3:5 — 211
  3:14-15 — 327
  3:15-16 — 210
  3:16 — 178, 211, 321
  3:18 — 178
  3:32 — 169
  4:24 — 346
  5:20 — 169
  5:24 — 366
  5:32 — 345
  5:39 — 99, 117, 136, 152, 213, 216, 221, 223, 270, 273, 297, 331, 332, 336, 366, 374
  6 — 322
  6:29 — 200

6:45 — 112
6:63 — 230, 300, 303, 365
6:69 — 366
7:17 — 218
8:14 — 345
10:35 — 395
11:51 — 340
12:39 — 161
13:17 — 112, 219
14:6 — 210, 211
14:17 — 121
14:23 — 365
14:25 — 181
14:26 — 280
14:28 — 165
15:3 — 366
16:13 — 340, 341
16:17-27 — 171
16:24 — 220
16:30 — 171
17:3 — 178, 181, 216
17:17 — 217, 239, 340, 396
17:19 — 340
17:20 — 366
19:35 — 345
20:30-31 — 117
20:31 — 192, 198, 201, 223, 270, 310, 313
21:24 — 277, 360

Acts
  2:4 — 284
  3:19 — 270
  3:21 — 297
  3:22 — 304
  3:24 — 270, 297
  4:3 — 178
  4:12 — 211
  4:32 — 211
  5:20 — 366
  6:7 — 366
  6:26 — 367
  7:2 — 304
  8:14 — 298
  10:19 — 277
  10:26 — 277
  10:42 — 277
  10:43 — 210, 213, 270, 332, 336
  11:14 — 192, 366
  11:21 — 365
  12:24 — 366

13:33 — 304
13:46 — 366
14:15 — 176, 178
14:17 — 132
15:1 — 209
15:5 — 209
15:11 — 178, 214
15:27 — 269
16:16-18 — 187
17:11 — 223, 298, 304
17:16 — 275
17:21 ff — 178
17:24 — 176
17:27 — 132
18:25 — 163
19:20 — 366
24:8 — 230
24:14-15 — 164
24:14-16 — 213
26:5 — 208
26:22-26 — 213, 298, 304, 332

Romans
  Letter — 81, 87, 94, 300, 312, 417
  1 — 85, 332
  3—4 — 330
  1:16 — 178, 300, 303, 366, 401
  1:17 — 294, 295
  1:18 — 166
  1:18-19 — 176
  1:19 — 132, 293
  1:19-20 — 178
  1:20 — 113
  1:21 — 112, 127
  1:25 — 175
  2 — 234
  3:2 — 263, 271, 283
  3:5 — 400
  3:9 ff — 178
  3:20 — 364
  3:21-26 — 210
  3:24 — 178
  3:27-28 — 366
  4:3-8 — 210
  4:6 — 210, 332
  4:15 — 364, 401
  4:18 — 146
  4:23-24 — 214
  5:1 — 101
  6:17 — 91
  8:3 — 178

8:5 — 146
8:6 — 163
8:7 — 261, 298
9:29 — 334
10 — 99
10:4 — 270
10:11 — 332
10:14 — 179
10:15 — 336
10:17 — 178, 365, 366
12:6 — 97, 392
15:4 — 117, 188, 198, 223, 279, 310, 313, 347
15:8 — 294
16:17 — 91, 211, 216
16:25 — 178, 295, 313

1 Corinthians
1:5 — 117
1:16 — 292
1:17 — 146
1:18 — 300, 366
1:19 — 127
1:19-20 — 146
1:21 — 99, 132, 176, 366
1:24 — 294
1:30 — 210
2 — 267
2:2 — 205, 215
2:4 — 203, 265
2:6 — 223
2:7 — 109, 111, 125, 128, 163, 178
2:9 — 181, 313
2:10 — 115, 164
2:10-11 — 173
2:11 — 86, 209, 219, 230, 372
2:11-16 — 210
2:12-13 — 265, 283, 291
2:13 — 172, 218
2:14 — 127, 132, 135, 146, 176, 219, 232, 261, 297, 320, 323, 372
2:14-16 — 125
2:15 — 230
3:5 — 366
3:7 — 319
3:11 — 99, 144, 147
4:1 — 365

4:5 — 365
4:15 — 366
4:20 — 112
7:6-7 — 359
7:10 — 359
7:12 — 292
7:25 — 359
7:40 — 292
8:6 — 210
9:22 — 192
9:27 — 232
10:31 — 218
11:23 ff — 392
12:3 — 319
12:8 — 109, 163, 230, 250
12:10 — 319
13:1-2 — 232
13:8 — 250
13:12 — 113, 186
15 — 312

2 Corinthians
1:17 — 345
1:17 ff — 344
3:5 — 265, 319
3:5-6 — 229
3:6 — 366
4:3 — 313
4:6 — 109, 163
4:17 — 222
5:7 — 186
6:2 — 334
6:7 — 239
10:4-5 — 298
10:5 — 125, 128, 146, 320
12:7 — 222

Galatians
Letter — 34
1:8 — 211
1:12 — 295, 341
1:23 — 163
2:5 — 346
2:14 — 346
2:16 — 210
2:19-20 — 164
3:1 — 341, 346
3:8 — 214
3:21 — 178
3:22 — 400
3:26-27 — 211
4:9 — 135

4:9-10 — 209
4:19 — 366
4:24 — 327
5:4 — 209
5:6 — 208, 211
5:9 — 139
5:20 — 176

Ephesians
Letter — 94
1:7 — 210, 294
1:13 — 239, 366
1:17 — 220, 230, 319
1:19 — 319
2:1-2 — 183
2:5 — 366
2:12 — 165, 176
2:20 — 99, 147, 298, 374
3:8 — 128
3:8-9 — 125
3:10 — 163, 294
3:16 — 219, 220
3:16-17 — 365
3:20 — 128
4 — 417, 418
4:5 — 211, 214
4:11 — 229
4:14 — 90
4:17 — 127
4:18 — 350
4:23 — 366
5:14 — 121
5:18 — 350
5:26 — 178
6:11-18 — 222

Philippians
1:6 — 319
1:15 — 230
1:19 — 230
1:20 — 164
1:29 — 319
2 — 49
2:13 — 419
2:16 — 366
3:1 — 269, 272
4:6 — 219

Colossians
1 — 49
1:5 — 341, 366
1:9 — 109, 111, 163
1:10 — 109, 163

INDEX

1:14 — 210
1:26 — 178, 295
1:26-27 — 313
2:3 — 168, 171
2:8 — 135
2:9 — 168, 245
3:16 — 223
3:17 — 218

1 Thessalonians
  1:5-6 — 303
  1:9 — 396
  2:12 — 103
  2:13 — 229, 230, 271, 297, 300, 303, 341, 366
  4:5 — 176
  4:9 — 163, 229
  5:17 — 220
  5:21 — 89

2 Thessalonians
  2:3-5 — 230
  2:15 — 91
  3:1 — 220
  3:6 — 91

1 Timothy
  1 — 106
  1:5 — 112
  1:6 — 117
  1:18 ff — 121
  1:19 — 164
  2:6 — 210
  2:10 — 163
  3:2 — 221
  3:9 — 163
  3:16 — 109, 128, 163, 312
  4:1-3 — 211
  4:6 — 91
  4:7 — 218
  4:13 — 91, 221, 223, 273
  4:14-15 — 223
  4:16 — 91, 192, 218
  6:1-2 — 91
  6:4-5 — 218

2 Timothy
  1 — 106
  1:13 — 91, 163, 164, 330
  2:2 — 221
  2:7 — 219, 229, 319

2:15-17 — 198
2:17 — 211
2:18 — 341
2:24 — 106, 218
2:25 — 366
3:8 — 341
3:10 — 91
3:15 — 117, 192, 213, 216, 273, 300, 313, 331
3:15-16 — 310
3:15-17 — 83, 183, 272
3:16 — 117, 223, 264, 271, 273, 280, 281, 282, 285, 297, 325, 341, 347
3:16-17 — 188, 229
3:17 — 205, 213, 232
4:13 — 278

Titus
  1 — 106
  1:1 — 109, 163, 341
  1:9 — 91, 141
  1:12 — 209
  2:1 — 91
  2:10 — 91, 218
  3:8 — 164

Hebrews
  Letter — 55, 416
  1 — 334
  1:1 — 180, 264, 266
  4:12 — 366
  5 — 210
  5:14 — 195, 196, 229
  6:4-6 — 338
  6:18 — 190, 341, 396
  11:1 — 342
  11:3 — 154
  11:6 — 178
  11:26 — 214
  11:31 — 400
  13:7 — 32

James
  Letter — 55, 67
  1:5 — 219, 220
  1:13 — 413
  1:17 — 183
  1:18 — 239, 341, 366
  1:21 — 366, 402
  1:27 — 208
  2 — 330
  2:25 — 400

3:5 — 218
3:13 — 202
3:15 — 163

1 Peter
  1:7 — 219, 222
  1:10 — 215
  1:12 — 128
  1:22 — 366
  1:23 — 183, 271, 365, 366
  1:25 — 183
  2:6 — 211
  3:15 — 141, 224
  4:11 — 230
  5:2 — 218
  5:10 — 366

2 Peter
  1:4 — 217
  1:19 — 83, 103, 272, 273, 280, 313, 314, 366
  1:20 — 280, 392
  1:20-21 — 220
  1:21 — 271, 275, 277, 273, 280, 283, 341, 352, 412
  2:2 — 230
  2:15 — 230

1 John
  1:1 — 277
  2:2 — 178
  2:27 — 121
  3:2 — 113
  3:9 — 118
  4:1 — 216
  5:6 — 303
  5:10-12 — 211
  5:11-12 — 178
  5:20 — 396

2 John
  9 — 91
  10 — 211

Jude
  14 — 213

Revelation
  Book of — 163
  1:1 — 169
  1:4 — 318
  22:18 — 360
  22:18-19 — 310

The text of this edition of 1500 copies
was composed in Linotype Garamond, 11 on 13;
with display type in Linofilm Optima and Linotype Garamond.
The text is printed on 50 lb. Mountie Eggshell
supplied by *Beacon Paper Company* and reproduced by Letterpress.
The endsheets are Ticonderoga Text (Manderin)
supplied by *Shaughnessy-Kneip-Hawe Paper Company.*
The cloth front and back is Bradford Linen, the spine is Ontario Buckram
both supplied by *Columbia Mills Incorporated.*
The jacket is printed on Moss Point Label
supplied by *Shaughnessy-Kneip-Hawe Paper Company*
and reproduced by Offset Lithography

The design is by Edward Q. Luhmann